CENSUS OF THE PIMA, TOHONO O'ODHAM (PAPAGO), AND MARICOPA INDIANS OF THE GILA RIVER,

AK CHIN & GILA BEND RESERVATIONS 1932 WITH BIRTH & DEATH ROLLS 1924-1932

TRANSCRIBED BY
JEFF BOWEN

NATIVE STUDY
Gallipolis, Ohio
USA

Originally published:
Santa Maria, California
2019

Reprinted by:

Native Study LLC
Gallipolis, Ohio
www.nativestudy.com

Library of Congress Control Number: 2022906551

ISBN: 978-1-64968-160-7

Made in the United States of America.

Other Books and Series by Jeff Bowen

Compilation of History of the Cherokee Indians and Early History of the Cherokees by Emmet Starr with Combined Full Name Index (Hardbound & Softbound)

1901-1907 Native American Census Seneca, Eastern Shawnee, Miami, Modoc, Ottawa, Peoria, Quapaw, and Wyandotte Indians (Under Seneca School, Indian Territory)

1932 Census of The Standing Rock Sioux Reservation with Births And Deaths 1924-1932

Kiowa, Comanche, Apache, Fort Sill Apache, Wichita, Caddo and Delaware Indians Birth and Death Rolls 1924-1932

Census of The Blackfeet, Montana, 1897- 1901 Expanded Edition

Eastern Cherokee by Blood, 1906-1910, Volumes I thru XIII

Choctaw of Mississippi Indian Census 1929-1932 with Births and Deaths 1924-1931   Volume I
Choctaw of Mississippi Indian Census 1933, 1934 & 1937, Supplemental Rolls to 1934 & 1935 with Births and Deaths 1932-1938, and Marriages 1936-1938 Volume II

Eastern Cherokee Census Cherokee, North Carolina 1930-1939
Census 1930-1931 with Births And Deaths 1924-1931 Taken By Agent L. W. Page Volume I
Eastern Cherokee Census Cherokee, North Carolina 1930-1939
Census 1932-1933 with Births And Deaths 1930-1932 Taken By Agent R. L. Spalsbury   Volume II
Eastern Cherokee Census Cherokee, North Carolina 1930-1939
Census 1934-1937 with Births and Deaths 1925-1938 and Marriages 1936 & 1938 Taken by Agents R. L. Spalsbury And Harold W. Foght Volume III

Seminole of Florida Indian Census, 1930-1940 with Birth and Death Records, 1930-1938

Texas Cherokees 1820-1839 A Document For Litigation 1921

Starr Roll 1894 (Cherokee Payment Rolls) Districts: Canadian, Cooweescoowee, and Delaware Volume One
Starr Roll 1894 (Cherokee Payment Rolls) Districts: Flint, Going Snake, and Illinois   Volume Two
Starr Roll 1894 (Cherokee Payment Rolls) Districts: Saline, Sequoyah, and Tahlequah; Including Orphan Roll Volume Three

Cherokee Intruder Cases Dockets of Hearings 1901-1909 Volumes I & II

Other Books and Series by Jeff Bowen

Indian Wills, 1911-1921 Records of the Bureau of Indian Affairs
Books One thru Seven
Native American Wills & Probate Records 1911-1921

Turtle Mountain Reservation Chippewa Indians 1932 Census with Births & Deaths, 1924-1932

Chickasaw By Blood Enrollment Cards 1898-1914 Volume I thru V

Cherokee Descendants East An Index to the Guion Miller Applications Volume I
Cherokee Descendants West An Index to the Guion Miller Applications Volume II (A-M)
Cherokee Descendants West An Index to the Guion Miller Applications Volume III (N-Z)

Applications for Enrollment of Seminole Newborn Freedmen, Act of 1905

Eastern Cherokee Census, Cherokee, North Carolina, 1915-1922, Taken by Agent James E. Henderson   *Volume I (1915-1916)*
                                     Volume II (1917-1918)
                                     Volume III (1919-1920)
                                     Volume IV (1921-1922)

Complete Delaware Roll of 1898

Eastern Cherokee Census, Cherokee, North Carolina, 1923-1929, Taken by Agent James E. Henderson   *Volume I (1923-1924)*
                                     Volume II (1925-1926)
                                     Volume III (1927-1929)

Applications for Enrollment of Seminole Newborn Act of 1905 Volumes I & II

North Carolina Eastern Cherokee Indian Census 1898-1899, 1904, 1906, 1909-1912, 1914 Revised and Expanded Edition

1932 Hopi and Navajo Native American Census with Birth & Death Rolls (1925-1931) Volume 1 - Hopi
1932 Hopi and Navajo Native American Census with Birth & Death Rolls (1930-1932) Volume 2 - Navajo

Western Navajo Reservation Navajo, Hopi and Paiute 1933 Census with Birth & Death Rolls 1925-1933

Cherokee Citizenship Commission Dockets 1880-1884 and 1887-1889
Volumes I thru V

Applications for Enrollment of Chickasaw Newborn Act of 1905
Volumes I thru VII

Other Books and Series by Jeff Bowen

Cherokee Intermarried White 1906 Volume I thru *X*

Applications for Enrollment of Creek Newborn Act of 1905
Volumes I thru *XIV*

Applications for Enrollment of Choctaw Newborn Act of 1905 Volumes I thru *XX*

Choctaw By Blood Enrollment Cards 1898-1914 Volumes I thru *XX*

Oglala Sioux Indians Pine Ridge Reservation 1932 Census Book I
Oglala Sioux Indians Pine Ridge Reservation Birth and Death Rolls 1924-1932
Book II

Census of the Sioux and Cheyenne Indians of Pine Ridge Agency
1896 - 1897 Book I
Census of the Sioux and Cheyenne Indians of Pine Ridge Agency
1898 - 1899 Book II

Northern Cheyenne Tongue River, Montana 1904 - 1932 Census
1904-1916 Volume I
Northern Cheyenne Tongue River, Montana 1904 - 1932 Census
1917-1926 Volume II

Identified Mississippi Choctaw Enrollment Cards 1902-1909 Volumes I, II & III

Sac & Fox - Shawnee Estates 1885-1910 (Under Sac & Fox Agency)
Volumes I-VIII
Sac & Fox - Shawnee Estates 1920-1924 (Under The Sac & Fox Agency,
Oklahoma) & Wills 1889-1924 Volume IX
Sac & Fox - Shawnee Deaths, Cemetery, Births, & Marriage Cards (Under The Sac
& Fox Agency, Oklahoma) 1853-1933 Volume X
Sac & Fox - Shawnee Marriages, Divorces, Estates Log Books Volumes 1 & 2, Log
Book Births & Deaths (Under Sac & Fox Agency, Oklahoma)1846-1924 Volume XI
Sac & Fox - Shawnee Guardianships Part 1 (Under Sac & Fox Agency, Oklahoma)
1892-1909 Volume XII
Sac & Fox - Shawnee Guardianships, Part 2 (Under The Sac & Fox Agency,
Oklahoma) 1902-1910 Volume XIII
Sac & Fox - Shawnee Guardianships, Part 3 (Under The Sac & Fox Agency,
Oklahoma) 1906-1914 Volume XIV

Census of the Pima, Tohono O'odham (Papago), and Maricopa Indians of the Gila
River, Ak Chin & Gila Bend Reservations 1932 with Birth and Death Rolls 1924-
1932

Visit our website at **www.nativestudy.com** to learn more about these
and other books and series by Jeff Bowen

This book is dedicated to my brother
Dave Bowen
"The Stained Glass Artist"
and
The Tohono O'odham (Papago) Nation,
Pima and Maricopa Peoples

In Memory of
Eliu "Leo" and Tigger Crandall Ortega

Table of Contents

INTRODUCTION

Most everyone knows that there is a modern day struggle along the U.S.-Mexico border right now in 2019. People are coming across that southern line day and night, while many are never seen again. Both young and old succumb to an atmosphere that's deadly and treacherous. You are thinking what does this have to do with this census. This census was taken on the same ground, the same land space both in America and Mexico where the people in these pages lived and breathed. The people in these census' birth and death records are the ancestors of the very same Native People defending approximately a 76 mile stretch of land today. They are known as the, "Shadow Wolves". In contrast they are the children of those that proudly conquered and survived one of the harshest atmospheres ever, both yesterday and today. These very descendants are standing between those coming into the U.S. illegally (without permission), and are trackers of those who smuggle people that often become helpless victims and sometimes carry contraband with them. The Shadow Wolves main task is tracking those coming across the border of the Tohono O'odham Nation. Though having access to today's technology they use their ancestors' methods known as cutting sign. Tactically they have followed the Old One's techniques, honing these skills with the passing of each generation. Following the very same methods and traditions of their blood born family they read the intricate hidden clues nobody else can find. Their work has become so well known that now there is a huge demand for them to teach others these methods as far away and in places like Afghanistan, Pakistan, and Kazakhstan among others. There's no telling how many lives they have saved because of the teachings of their ancestors and a culture taught by the Pima, Papago, and Maricopa. They are their people of both past and present.

The **Papago** or known today as, "The Tohono O'odham, or Desert People, live in the dry Sonoran Desert region of southern Arizona and northern Mexico. Until 1986, the tribe was known as the Papago, a corruption of a Spanish phrase meaning "Bean Eaters." They are closely related to the Akimel O'odham tribes, or River People, sometimes known as the Pima. Both groups speak dialects of the same O'odham language, part of the Uto-Aztecan family, and claim descent from the Hohokam, an archaeological classification of the prehistoric farming peoples who lived in the same region of the Southwest prior to the disappearance of their civilization about 1400. The traditional Tohono O'odham life meant adapting to the harsh environment—where modern people might see a spiny, foreboding saguaro cactus, they saw food."[1]

In studying for these three respected tribes of the desert it has been enlightening while reading materials from as early as the 1940's by Ruth Underhill while trying to present a taste of their history from many years ago. It is only natural for the Tohono O'odham tribe to be mentioned first in this introduction being one of their own was the inspiration behind this study. Within these pages you'll find Ira Hayes and his family when he was approximately nine years old. His name within these pages long before being one of the Marines to raise the American flag on Iwo

---

[1] Indian Nations of North America, Tohono O'odham, Pg. 234, Para. 1

Jima in the Pacific after defeating the Japanese during World War II. This work consists of three separate reservations' census, Gila River, Gila Bend, and Ak Chin, along with Birth and Death Records 1924-1932. The very first death entry was of all things in the desert a snakebite. But along the way there were a few scorpion bites to the very young. But the most noticed and felt by the transcriber was the overwhelming amount of people of all ages that fell to the horrible disease tuberculosis. "The Papago and Pima have known the white men for almost two hundred and fifty years." [2]

"The Papago live in the hot, desert country of Arizona, on the border of Mexico. It is a land where the sky is bright blue for ten months of the year, with hardly a drop of rain. The thermometer (if you can find one) goes up to a hundred and twenty degrees in the summer. In winter the bright, cool days are about like spring in New England. You could drive over this country for miles without seeing a tree. You would see only gravel, sparkling in the sun, with low bushes spaced far apart, as if in a garden. Plants cannot grow close together here for they would not have water enough to live. On the hillsides, you might see tall cactus, like a forest of bare poles. This Giant Cactus, which grows in Arizona, has no leaves. It is nothing but a green stem, ten or fifteen feet high, covered with rows of thorns. After a while, you might see a few little crooked trees, growing by a place where the water flows in the summer rains. In the distance, you would see mountains, looking like piles of rock with nothing green on them. It does not look like good country for farming. Yet the Papago have been farming here for hundreds of years. They know how to find the low places where water sank into the ground after the summer rains. They knew a kind of beans which would grow in dry weather--weather so hot that even corn would die. In fact, they knew how to live where no white man could have lived at all, in former days. There were many tribes of Indians who could not have lived there either.

Many Americans, Indians and Whites too, know little about these Indians of southern Arizona. That is because their country belonged to Mexico until about eighty years ago. The Papago bought their knives and their horses from Mexico and, when they learned a White man's language, they learned Spanish. But about 1853 the United States bought some land from Mexico. With the land came some five thousand new citizens--the Papago Indians. They did not look like the Indians the White people were used to. They did not wear feather headdresses nor deerskin clothes nor moccasins. The did not hunt the buffalo. They did not spend their time in traveling, carrying all their possessions with them. Instead, they lived peacefully in villages, raising corn, beans, and squash. They wore clothes which were often made of cotton and they spun and wove the cotton cloth themselves. On their feet, they wore sandals which are flat soles tied to the feet with string. Indians from the north found this so strange that they called them Sandal People. That was not what they called themselves, however. Their own name was Aw-aw-tam, the people. That was the way with many Indian tribes who felt that outsiders, with different language and customs, were simply not people at all. The People were once a large nation, stretching over the border into what is now Old Mexico. Many of their groups are gone now, some driven out by Apaches, some intermarried with Mexicans. Two

---

[2] The Papago Indians of Arizona and Their Relatives the Pima, Pg. 5, Para. 1

groups remain on reservations, in the United States. One is the Papago group whom we have been telling about, and who live in the desert. They call themselves Tohono Aw-aw-tam, Desert People. The other group is very close to the Papago in language and customs. We call them Pima (pee-mah).

The **Pima** live north of the Papago, along the Gila River. (Gila is a Spanish word, pronounced Heela). You might not know it was a river if you crossed it now, for all its water has been drawn off into irrigation ditches. But, in old days, it was the one living stream in hundreds of miles of thirsty desert. No wonder those of 'The People' who lived along it had a special name, River People. We call them Pima (pee-mah). The real difference between Pima and Papago is that, in former days, the Pima had plenty of water and the Papago had almost none."[3] From Ms. Underhill's statement, "the country belonged to Mexico 80 years ago," would be approximately 159 years ago today in 2019.

"In 1870 a reservation was set aside for the Pima on the Gila River where they still are. But the Papago still were little known. They were given a small reservation at the San Xavier, where the Santa Cruz River gave them water in 1874. In 1883, they got another at Gila Bend, up near the Pima. It was only in 1917 that the government set aside the large reservation in the desert, where most of the Papago live. This is called the Sells Reservation."[4]

Not mentioned in Ms. Underwood's, *The Papago Indians of Arizona and Their Relatives the Pima*, or for that matter included in this census is the Salt River Reservation or its existence. Salt River's Census to be challenged later. But it was felt that it needed to be referenced because of the **Maricopa** communities deeply and traditionally among the Pima as a consolidation of two tribes for strength and security during early days against other tribes. "Salt River Pima-Maricopa Indian Community Current Location: New Mexico Total Area: 54,483 acres Tribal Enrollment: 8,217 The Salt River Pima-Maricopa Indian Community comprises two distinct tribes: the Pima--or Akimel Au Authm ('River People')--and the Maricopa--or Xalychidom Piipaash ('People Who Live Toward the Water'). Both groups have traditionally been river-basin desert farmers in the area, providing protection for one another against invasion by Yuman and Apache tribes; thus, their histories are intertwined. The Pima believe they descend from the ancient Hoo-hoogam, or Hohokam, who created an elaborate irrigation system to farm the arid desert land. Remnants of those ancient canals can still be found, although they are now modernized. The Maricopa, living in small bands along the lower Colorado and Gila Rivers, were less sedentary than the Pima. They were driven toward the Pima settlements by shortages of water and the pressure of warfare with other tribes. The earliest mention of the Pima was made by the Spaniard Marcos de Niza in 1589. Padre Eusebio Francisco Kino, a Jesuit made several trips into the Gila River area between 1694 and 1699. Agricultural production increased after the Pima received wheat from the Spanish, possibly from Father Kino. Increasing production and trading success led to more cooperation and to more economic specialization, with men concentrating on farming and women on producing

---

[3] The Papago Indians of Arizona and Their Relatives the Pima, Pg. 5-6, Para. 1-6
[4] The Papago Indians of Arizona and Their Relatives the Pima, Pg. 63, Para. 1

crafts for trade. Pima people are known for watertight, intricately woven basketry. Maricopa women specialized in pottery, typically made of red clay."[5]

In the author's search for Maricopa materials a few different sources were found leading to similar descriptions but different forms of vital information so it was felt those found needed to be provided for those interested in their Maricopa heritage. Please understand that if a few things have already been mentioned the actual text couldn't be changed while being quoted. "The Maricopa, Movers by Choice. From prehistoric times, various Yuma-speaking Indians moved up the Gila River and settled. About the beginning of the nineteenth century a group of Yuma-speaking Indians who called themselves *Pipatsje,* or 'The People', occupied an area along the Colorado River, south of present-day Parker, Arizona. The Anglos called these people 'Maricopas.' Apparently these disagreed with the other Yuma Indians with regard to selection of their leaders. As a consequence, they withdrew from the Colorado and moved eastward up the Gila River, where they made friends with the Pima Indians. There they were given land and protection from their hostile kinsmen. The Pima and Maricopa fought as allies in the battle of 1857 against Yuma and Mohave forces, whom they defeated severely. Although the Pima and Maricopa could not understand each other's mother tongue, this proved no barrier to a lasting relationship. The retreat of the Maricopa from the Colorado left a large area of river bottom land vacant, and it was into this territory that the Mohave expanded from the north, and the Ute-related Chemehuevi also, to become residents of what would be the Colorado River Reservation. Descendants of the Maricopa are found today among the Pima on the Gila River Reservation and on the Salt River Reservation, as previously discussed. Today, two Maricopa Indian settlements are recognized: one on the northwest corner of the Gila River Reservation and the other in the Lehi district of the Salt River Reservation. From their long association with the Pima, the Maricopa seem to have lost all knowledge of their ancestors having lived elsewhere. However, until recently they followed certain practices of the past, and it was said:

Their lives are dream directed as are the Mohaves; they cremate their dead; they have a clan-name system; and they speak the Yuman tongue. . . .In 1858, the U.S. Army census listed 518 Maricopas. Today, through intermarriage with Pimas they have lost most of their Yuman identity. They have adopted much of the Piman culture and are now almost one with them. (Johnston 1970:58.)"[6]

Vital Information About Land Bases Today

Here's a brief amount of information about the Papago, Pima and Maricopa reservations and the geography of today. "The **Tohono O'odham Nation** within the United States occupies a reservation that incorporates a portion of its people's original Sonoran desert lands. It is organized into eleven districts. The land lies in three counties of the present-day state of Arizona: Pima, Pinal, and Maricopa. The reservation's land area is 11,534.012 square kilometres (4,453.307 sq mi), the third-largest Indian reservation area in the United States (after the Navajo Nation and the Uintah and Ouray Indian Reservation). The 2000 census reported 10,787 people living

---

[5] Indian Nations of North America, Salt River Reservation, Pg. 227, Paras. 1-4
[6] American Indians of the Southwest, Bertha P. Dutton, Pgs. 222-223, Paras. 1-4.

on reservation land. The tribe's enrollment office tallies a population of 25,000, with 20,000 living on its Arizonan reservation lands."[7]

"The **Pima** /ˈpiːmə/ (or **Akimel O'odham**, also spelled **Akimel O'otham**, "River People", formerly known as *Pima*) are a group of Native Americans living in an area consisting of what is now central and southern Arizona. The majority population of the surviving two bands of the Akimel O'odham are based in two reservations: the *Keli Akimel O'otham* on the Gila River Indian Community (GRIC) and the *On'k Akimel O'odham* on the Salt River Pima-Maricopa Indian Community (SRPMIC). They are closely related to other river people, the Ak-Chin O'odham, now forming the Ak-Chin Indian Community. They are also related to the Sobaipuri, whose descendants reside on the San Xavier Indian Reservation or Waːk (together with the Tohono O'odham), and in the Salt River Indian Community. Together with the kindred Tohono O'odham ("Desert People", formerly known as the *Papago*) of Eastern Papagueria, and the Hia C-ed O'odham ("Sand Dune People", formerly known as *Sand Papago*) of the Western Papagueria, the *Akimel O'odham* form the Upper O'otham or Upper Pima (also known as *Pima Alto*). The short name, "Pima," is believed to have come from the phrase *pi 'añi mac* or *pi mac,* meaning "I don't know," which they used repeatedly in their initial meetings with Spanish colonists. The latter referred to them as the Pima. This term was adopted by later English speakers: traders, explorers and settlers. As of 2014, the majority of the population lives in the federally recognized Gila River Indian Community (GRIC). In historic times a large number of Akimel O'odham migrated north to occupy the banks of the Salt River, where they formed the Salt River Pima-Maricopa Indian Community (SRPMIC). Both tribes are confederations of two distinct ethnicities, which include the Maricopa. Within the O'odham people, four federally recognized tribes in the Southwest speak the same language: they are called the Gila River Indian Community (*Keli Akimel O'odham* – "Gila River People"); the Salt River Pima-Maricopa Indian Community (*Onk Akimel O'odham* – "Salt River People"); the Ak-Chin Indian Community (*Ak-Chin O'odham*); and the Tohono O'odham Nation (*Tohono O'odham* – "Desert People"). The remaining band, the Hia C-ed O'odham ("Sand Dune People"), are not federally recognized, but reside throughout southwestern Arizona. Today the GRIC is a sovereign tribe residing on more than 550,000 acres (2,200 km^2) of land in central Arizona. The community is divided into seven districts (similar to states) with a council representing individual subgovernments. It is self-governed by an elected Governor (currently Gregory Mendoza), Lieutenant Governor (currently Stephen Roe-Lewis) and 18-member Tribal Council. The council is elected by district with the number of electees determined by district population. There are more than 19,000 enrolled members overall."[8]

"The **Maricopa Reservation** was established by the federal government in 1912, under President William Howard Taft, at 47,600 acres (193 km^2) in size. Within months the administration gave in to opposition from European-American

---

[7] Tohono O'odham, Wikipedia
[8] Pima people, Wikipedia

farmers and other non-Natives and reduced the reservation to 22,000 acres (89 km²). The reservation is located in Pinal County within the Sonoran Desert, about 40 miles south of Phoenix and next to Maricopa. Averaging an elevation of 1,186 feet (361 m), the reservation is located 37 miles (60 km) south of Phoenix. Much of the land is good for farming, and 15,000 acres (6,100 ha) are under irrigation. As of the 2000 census, the population living in the community was 742, with a median age of 24.2, compared to a median age of 37.1 for all of Pinal County. According to the census, 89.4% of the population identified as American Indian, alone or in combination with other races. Most of the population lives in Ak-Chin Village, in the western part of the reservation. Part of the city of Maricopa also lies within reservation territory. As of January 2019, the current population of the Ak-Chin Indian Community is over 1100 members."[9]

"**Gila Bend** (/ˌhiːlə ˈbɛnd/; O'odham: **Hila Wiːn**), founded in 1872, is a town in Maricopa County, Arizona, United States. The town is named for an approximately 90-degree bend in the Gila River, which is near the community's current location. According to the 2010 census, the population of the town is 1,922."[10]

"The **Gila River** has its source in western New Mexico, in Sierra County on the western slopes of Continental Divide in the Black Range. It flows southwest through the Gila National Forest and the Gila Cliff Dwellings National Monument, then westward into Arizona, past the town of Safford. After flowing along the southern slope of the Gila Mountains in Graham County through a series of canyons, the Gila is impounded by Coolidge Dam in San Carlos Lake south of Peridot.

It emerges from the mountains into the valley southeast of Phoenix, Arizona, where it crosses the Gila River Indian Reservation as an intermittent stream due to large irrigation diversions. Well west of Phoenix, the river bends sharply southward along the Gila Bend Mountains, then it swings westward again near the town of Gila Bend. It flows southwestward between the Gila Mountains to the south and the Languna and Muggins ranges to the north in Yuma County, and finally it empties into the Colorado at Yuma, Arizona.

The Gila is joined by many tributaries, beginning with the East and West Forks of the river, which combine to form the main stem near Gila Hot Springs in New Mexico. Above Safford, it is joined by the San Francisco River and the intermittent San Simon River. Further downstream, it is joined by the San Carlos River from the north in San Carlos Lake. At Winkelman, Arizona, it picks up the San Pedro River and then is joined by the Santa Cruz River south of Casa Grande. The Salt River, its main tributary, joins in the Phoenix metropolitan area, and further west the Gila receives its last two major tributaries, the Agua Fria and Hassayampa Rivers, from the north.

---

[9] Ak-Chin Indian Community, Wikipedia
[10] Gila Bend, Arizona, Wikipedia

Although the Gila River flows entirely within the United States, the headwaters of two tributaries – the San Pedro and Santa Cruz Rivers – extend into Mexico. About 1,630 sq mi (4,200 km^2), or 2.8% of the Gila's 58,200-square-mile (151,000 km^2) watershed, is in Mexico. A further 3,300 sq mi (8,500 km^2) or 5.7% lies within New Mexico, while the remaining majority, 53,270 sq mi (138,000 km^2) or 91.5%, is in Arizona."[11]

"**Gila River Indian Reservation** was a reservation established in 1859 by the United States government in New Mexico Territory, to set aside the lands of the Akimel O'odham (Pima) and the Piipaash (Maricopa) people along the Gila River, in what is now Pinal County, Arizona. The self-government of the reservation as the Gila River Indian Community was established by Congress in 1939."[12]

"The **Salt River Pima–Maricopa Indian Community** comprises two distinct Native American tribes—the Pima (Akimel O'odham) and the Maricopa (Piipaash)—many of whom were originally of the Halchidhoma (Xalchidom) tribe. The community was officially created by an Executive Order of US President Rutherford B. Hayes on June 14, 1879. The community area includes 53,600 acres (217 km^2), of which 19,000 remain a natural preserve. The community is a federally recognized tribe located in Arizona."[13]

Sells (O'odham: **Komkc'eḍ 'e-Wa:'osidk**) is a census-designated place (CDP) in Pima County, Arizona, United States. The population was 2,799 at the 2000 census. It is the capital of the Tohono O'odham Nation and the home of several of their tribal businesses, such as Tohono O'Odham Ki:Ki Association. Originally named **Indian Oasis**, by cattle-ranchers/businessmen brothers, Joseph and Louis Ménager in 1912. The Ménager brothers also built and ran the Indian Oasis Mercantile Store. The settlement took its present English name in 1918 to honor Indian Commissioner Cato Sells. The O'odham name means "Tortoise Got Wedged."[14]

"The **San Xavier Indian Reservation** (O'odham: **Wa:k**) is an Indian reservation of the Tohono O'odham Nation located near Tucson, Arizona, in the Sonoran Desert. The San Xavier Reservation lies in the southwestern part of the Tucson metropolitan area and consists of 111.543 sq mi (288.895 km^2) of land area, about 2.5 percent of the Tohono O'odham Nation. It had a 2000 census resident population of 2,053 persons, or 19 percent of the Tohono O'odham population."[15]

This transcription took a great deal of time but it and the study of the people within was worth every moment. As always it is only hoped that the effort will be of great help for those searching for their heritage. It was felt that it couldn't hurt to search out information about the land bases of these tribes and some of their present

---

[11] Gila River, Wikipedia
[12] Gila River Indian Reservation, Wikipedia
[13] Salt River Pima–Maricopa Indian Community, Wikipedia
[14] Sells, Arizona, Wikipedia
[15] San Xavier Indian Reservation, Wikipedia

day statistics so descendants could understand how prevalent their tribes and people have become today. Also in case they have never been to these ancestral lands they could get a feel for not only the adventure of finding their heritage but also what they may miss if they don't travel to the place of the ancestor's birth. These records were transcribed from National Archives Film M-595 Roll 356.

Jeff Bowen
Gallipolis, Ohio
NativeStudy.com

Gila River Reservation

of the **Pima Agency**

as of **April 1**, 1932

[Papago-Pima-Maricopa]

Census of the **Gila River** reservation of the **Pima Agency** jurisdiction; as of **April 1** ; 1932; taken by **A. H. Kneale** ; Superintendent.

Key: Number; Surname; Given; Sex (M/F); Age at Last Birthday; Tribe; Degree of Blood (F=Full); Marital Status; Relationship to Head of Family & Last Census No; At Jurisdiction Where Enrolled (Yes/No); (If no - Where); Ward (Yes/No); Allotment Annuity and/or Identification Numbers

ACUNA
1; James; M; 34; Maricopa; F; M; Head; 1; Yes; Yes; AI./Id. 560
2; Louisa; F; 35; Maricopa; F; M; wife; 2; Yes; Yes; AI./Id. 561
3; Gilberto; M; 8; Maricopa; F; S; son; 3; Yes; Yes; AI./Id. 562
4; Florenze; M; 6; Maricopa; F; S; son; 4; Yes; Yes; AI./Id. 563
5; Aamoa[sic]; M; 5; Maricopa; F; S; son; 5; Yes; Yes; AI./Id. 564

ADAMS
6; Asperito; M; Unk.; Papago; F; M; Head; 6; Yes; Yes; AI./Id. 4166
7; Emily H. (Hendricks, Emily); F; 28; Papago; F; M; wife; 7; Yes; Yes;
AI. 1786/Id. 4167

ADAMS
8; Alice B. (Bending, Alice); F; 38; Pima; F; M; Head; 8; Yes; Yes; AI. 3612/Id. 4166

ADAMS
9; Henry; M; 92; Pima; F; M; 9; Yes; Yes; AI. 1004/Id. 6539
~~Martha; F; 86; Pima; F; M; wife; 10; (Died Dec. 3; 1931); Yes; AI. 1005/Id. 6540~~

ADAMS
10; Mark Eaton; M. 51; Pima; F; M; Head; 11; Yes; Yes; AI. 19/Id. 5567
11; Growing Flower; F; 50; Pima; F; M; wife; 12; Yes; Yes; AI. 20/Id. 5568

AHLIEL
12; Frank; M; 33; Pima; F; M; Head; 13; Yes; Yes; AI. 2396/Id. 4165

AHLEIL
13; Joseph; M; 52; Pima; F; M; Head; 14; Yes; Yes; AI. 1702/Id. 4291
14; Clara; F; 57; Pima; F; M; wife; 15; Yes; Yes; AI. 1703/Id. 4292
15; Monroe; M; 22; Pima; F; S; son; 16; Yes; Yes; AI. 2394/Id. 4294
16; Tillie; F; 13; Pima; F; S; Dau; 17; Yes; Yes; AI. 3810/Id. 4295

AHLIEL
17; Nathan T; M; 29; Pima; F; M; Head; 18; Yes; Yes; AI. 2395/Id. 4296
18; Dorothy H., (Stone, Dorothy); F; 32; Pima; F; M; wife; 19; Yes; Yes;
AI. 353/Id. 4897
19; Nathan Jr.; M; 11; Pima; F; S; son; 20; Yes; Yes; AI. 4842/Id. 4298
20; Lydia L.; F; 8; Pima; F; S; Dau. 21; Yes; Yes; AI./Id. 4219
21; Sarah Jane; F; 2; Pima; F; S; Dau.; 22; Yes; Yes; AI./Id. 4300
Marjorie; F; [?]; Pima; F; S; Dau.; -; Yes; Yes; Born 6-10-31; Died 9-10-31;
AI./Id. 3964

ALBERT
22; Davidson; M; 65; Maricopa; F; M; Head; 23; Yes; Yes; AI. 2765/Id. 200
23; Mary; F; 71; Maricopa; F; M; wife 24; Yes; Yes; AI. 2766/Id. 201

Key: Number; Surname; Given; Sex (M/F); Age at Last Birthday; Tribe; Degree of Blood (F=Full); Marital Status; Relationship to Head of Family & Last Census No; At Jurisdiction Where Enrolled (Yes/No); (If no – Where); Ward (Yes/No); Allotment Annuity and/or Identification Numbers

24; Paul; M; 29; Maricopa; F; S; son; 25; Yes; Yes; AI. 2771/Id. 202

[?] Bertha; F; 19; Maricopa; F; S; Dau.; 26; Yes; Yes; AI. 2865/Id. 203

ALBERT

[?] Sam; 40; M; 40; Maricopa; F; M; Head; 27; Yes; Yes; AI. 2767/Id. 204

[?] Maude ~~Eliza~~, (Maude Eliza); F; 32; Maricopa; F; M; wife; 28; Yes; Yes; AI. 583/Id. 205

[?] Enoch; M; 3; Maricopa; F; S; son; 29; Yes; Yes; AI./Id. 206

ALLEN

[?] John Ennis; M; 53; Pima; F; S; Head; 30; Yes; Yes; AI. 4273/Id. 4164

ALLEN

[?] Jose (Juan); M; 72; Pima; F; M; Head; 31; Yes; Yes; AI. 943/Id. 4927

[?] Felisia A., (Antione, Felisa); F; 53; Pima; F; M; wife 32; Yes; Yes; AI. 933/Id. 4928

ALLEN

[?] Jose Jr.; M; 29; Pima; F; S; Head; 33; Yes; Yes; AI. 945/Id. 1163

ALLEN

[?] Jose Marie; M; 47; Pima; F; M; Head; 34; Yes; Yes; AI. 944/Id. 4922

[?] Daisy, (Sampson, Daisy); F; 37; Pima; F; M; wife; 35; Yes; Yes; AI. 2557/Id. 4923

[?] Roy Clifford; M; 11; Pima; F; S; son; 36; Yes; Yes; AI./Id. 4924

[?] Walter; M; 8; Pima; F; S; son; 37; Yes; Yes; AI./Id. 4925

37; Rosalie; F; 4; Pima; F; S; Dau.; 38; Yes; Yes; AI./Id. 4296

ALLEN

38; Josiah; M; 47; Pima; F; S; Head; 39; Yes; Yes; AI. 1546/Id. 6831

ALLEN

39; Kisto J.; M; 45; Pima; F; M; Head; 40; Yes; Yes; AI. 1547/Id. 8833

40; Lucile; F; 45; Pima; F; M; Wife; 41; Yes; Yes; AI. 1548/Id. 8834

ALLEN

41; Lewis; M; 47; Pima; F; M; Head; 42; Yes; Yes; AI. 4067/Id. 1232

42; Mary; F; 44; Pima; F; M; Wife; 43; Yes; Yes; AI. 4068/Id. 1233

43; Gladys; F; 19; Pima; F; S; Dau.; 44; Yes; Yes; AI. 4069/Id. 1234

44; Louise; F; 17; Pima; F; S; Dau.; 45; Yes; Yes; AI. 4070/Id. 1235

45; Christine; F; 13; Pima; F; S; Dau.; 46; Yes; Yes; AI./Id. 1236

46; Lambert; M; 6; Pima; F; S; Son; 47; Yes; Yes; AI./Id. 1237

ALLEN

47; Manuel; M; Unk;; Papago; F; M; Head; 48; Yes; Yes; AI./Id. 6525

Census of the **Gila River** reservation of the **Pima Agency** jurisdiction; as of **April 1** ; 1932; taken by **A. H. Kneale** ; Superintendent.

Key: Number; Surname; Given; Sex (M/F); Age at Last Birthday; Tribe; Degree of Blood (F=Full); Marital Status; Relationship to Head of Family & Last Census No; At Jurisdiction Where Enrolled (Yes/No); (If no – Where); Ward (Yes/No); Allotment Annuity and/or Identification Numbers

48; Dorothy T., (Dorothy Thomas); F; 24; Papago; F; M; Wife; 49; Yes; Yes; AI. 2541 /Id. 6526

49; Ralston C.; M; 3; Papago; F; S; Son; 50; Yes; Yes; AI./Id. 6527

ALLIS

50; Mollie; F; 48; Pima; F; Wd.; Head; 51; No; Somewhere in California; Yes; AI. 2689/Id. 4162

ALLISON

51; May; F; 52; Pima; F; Wd.; Head; 52; Yes; Yes; AI. 233/Id. 5137

52; Blanche L.; F; 23; Pima; F; S; Dau.; 53; Yes; Yes; AI. 499/Id. 5138

53; Lloyd; M; 26; Pima; F; S; Son; 54; Yes; Yes; AI. 448/Id. 5142

54; Rema; F; 21; Pima; F; S; Dau;; 55; Yes; Yes; AI. 450/Id. 5139

55; Louis; M; 15; Pima; F; S; Son; 56; Yes; Yes; AI. 3638/Id. 5140

56; Ruth E; F; 10; Pima; F; S; Dau;; 57; Yes; Yes; AI. 732/Id. 5141

ALLISON

57; Charles; M; 67; Maricopa; F; M; Head; 58; Yes; Yes; AI. 2955/Id. 411

58; Sepie Wickey, (Sepie Wickey); F; 42; Pima; F; M; Wife; 59; Yes; Yes; AI. 2679/Id. 423

59; William; M; 31; Maricopa-Pima; F; S; Son; 60; Yes; Yes; AI. 2960/Id. 412

60; Edison; M; 21; Maricopa-Pima; F; S; Son; 61; Yes; Yes; AI. 2955/Id. 413

61; Lillian; F; 15; Maricopa-Pima; F; S; Dau.; 62; Yes; Yes; AI. 3722/Id. 415

ALLISON

62; Bertha; F; 30; Pima; F; S; Head; 63; Yes; Yes; AI. 447/Id. 5244

ALLISON

63; Harry; M; 23; Maricopa; F; M; Head; 64; Yes; Yes; AI. 2959/Id. 413

ALLISON

64; Herbert; M; 26; Pima; F; M; Head; 65; Yes; Yes; AI. 381/Id. 5250

65; Susie E, (Susie Ennis); F; 32; Pima; F; M; Wife; 66; Yes; Yes; AI. 63/Id. 5251

66; Lenora; F; 7; Pima; F; S; Dau.; 67; Yes; Yes; AI./Id. 5252

67; Geraldine; F; 6; Pima; F; S; Dau.; 68; Yes; Yes; AI./Id. 5253

68; Delbert; M; 2; Pima; F; S; Son; 69; Yes; Yes; AI./Id. 5780

ALLISON

69; James; M; 37; Pima; F; M; Head; 70; Yes; Yes; AI. 727/Id. 4860

70; Fannie; F; 36; Pima; F; M; Wife; 71; Yes; Yes; AI. 728/Id. 4861

71; Luther; M; 18; Pima; F; S; Son; 72; Yes; Yes; AI. 729/Id. 4862

72; Gilbert; M; 16; Pima; F; S; Son; 73; Yes; Yes; AI. 3164/Id. 4863

73; Dewey; M; 13; Pima; F; S; Son; 74; Yes; Yes; AI. 3871/Id. 4864

74; Ethel; F; 9; Pima; F; S; Dau.; 75; Yes; Yes; AI./Id. 4865

75; Thelma; F; 8; Pima; F; S; Dau.; 76; Yes; Yes; AI./Id. 4866

Key: Number; Surname; Given; Sex (M/F); Age at Last Birthday; Tribe; Degree of Blood (F=Full); Marital Status; Relationship to Head of Family & Last Census No; At Jurisdiction Where Enrolled (Yes/No); (If no – Where); Ward (Yes/No); Allotment Annuity and/or Identification Numbers

76; Beulah; F; 3; Pima; F; S; Dau.; 77; Yes; Yes; AI./Id. 4867
77; Rhoda; F; 2; Pima; F; S; Dau.; 78; Yes; Yes; AI./Id. 5788

ALLISON

78; Jessie; F; 32; Pima; F; S; Head; 79; Yes; Yes; AI. 1745/Id. 4262
79; Arnold; M; 12; Pima; F; S; Son; 80; Yes; Yes; AI. 4884/Id. 4263

ALLISON

80; John; M; 62; Pima; F; M; Head; 81; Yes; Yes; AI. 234/Id. 5242
81; Lucy; F; 69; Pima; F; M; Wife; 82; Yes; Yes; AI. 235/Id. 5243

ALLISON

82; Jose; M; 48; Pima; F; M; Head; 83; Yes; Yes; AI. 4272/Id. 1742
83; Lucy Ann, (Cheerles, Lucy Ann); F; 40; Pima; F; M; Wife; 84; Yes; Yes; AI. 34/Id. 4273

ALLISON

84; Joseph; M; 50; Pima; F; M; Head; 85; Yes; Yes; AI. 3343/Id. 5660
85; Ruth; F; 48; Pima; F; M; Wife; 86; Yes; Yes; AI. 3344/Id. 5661
~~Herman; M; 20; Pima; F; S; Son; 87; Died October 13; 1931; Yes; AI. 3347/Id. 5662~~
86; Harvey; M; 16; Pima; F; S; Son; 88; Yes; Yes; AI. 3813/Id. 5663

ALLISON

~~Damon; M; 46; Pima; F; M; Head; 89; Died October 23; 1931; Yes; AI. 373/Id. 5246~~
87; Annie; F; 45; Pima; F; M; Wd.; 90; Yes; Yes; AI. 374/Id. 5247
88; Tillie; F; 21; Pima; F; S; Dau.; 21[sic]; Yes; Yes; AI. 383/Id. 5248
~~Rachel; F; 19; Pima; F; S; Dau.; 92; Died October 2; 1931; Yes; AI. 384/Id. 5249~~

ALLISON

89; William; M; 31; Pima; F; M; Head; 93; Yes; Yes; AI. 2960/Id. 412
90; Cora Lewis, (Cora Lewis); F; 21; Pima; F; M; Head; 94; Yes; Yes; AI. 4097/Id. 1650

ALLISON

91; William S.; M; 31; Pima; F; M; Head; 95; Yes; Yes; AI. 3345/Id. 1822
92; Marguerite, (Marguerite Jose); F; 32; Papago; F; M; Wife; 96; Yes; Yes; AI./Id. 1823
93; Jane; F; 10; Papago-Pima; F; S; Dau.; 97; Yes; Yes; AI./Id. 1824
94; Lenora; F; 8; Papago-Pima; F; S; Dau.; 98; Yes; Yes; AI./Id. 1825
95; Warren; M; 7; Papago-Pima; F; S; Son; 99; Yes; Yes; AI./Id. 1826
96; Clifford; M; 5; Papago-Pima; F; S; Son; 100; Yes; Yes; AI./Id. 1827
97; Harold; M; 3; Papago-Pima; F; S; Son; 101; Yes; Yes; AI./Id. 1828
~~Colleen; F; 2; Papago-Pima; F; S; Dau.; 102; Died; May 21; 1931.; AI./Id. 1895~~
98; Louella Mary; F; 2/12; Papago-Pima; F; S; Dau.; --; Born. February 7; 1932.; AI./Id. 2055

Census of the **Gila River** reservation of the **Pima Agency** jurisdiction; as of **April 1** ; 1932; taken by **A. H. Kneale** ; Superintendent.

Key: Number; Surname; Given; Sex (M/F); Age at Last Birthday; Tribe; Degree of Blood (F=Full); Marital Status; Relationship to Head of Family & Last Census No; At Jurisdiction Where Enrolled (Yes/No); (If no - Where); Ward (Yes/No); Allotment Annuity and/or Identification Numbers

ALOYSA
99; Lucy; F; 76; Pima-Papago; F; Wd.; Head; 103; Yes; Yes; AI. 4273/Id. 4161

ANDREAS
100; Maria; F; 72; Pima; F; Wd.; Head; 104; Yes; Yes; AI. 4377/Id. 1784

ANDREW
101; John; M; 81; Pima; F; M.; Head; 105; Yes; Yes; AI. 3062/Id. 3261
102; Lucy H.; F; 81; Pima; F; M.; Wife; 106; Yes; Yes; AI. 3063/Id. 3202

ANDREW
103; Joseph; M; 72; Pima; F; S.; Head; 107; Yes; Yes; AI. 536/Id. 4852

ANGHILL
104; Juan; M; 42; Papago; F; Wd.; Head; 108; No; Rolls; Pima Ariz.; Yes; AI. 4138/Id. 1896
105; Rudolph; M; 17; Papago; F; S; Son; 109; Yes; Yes; AI. 4140/Id. 1897
106; Clinton; M; 15; Papago; F; S; Son; 110; Yes; Yes; AI. 4761/Id. 1898

ANTON
107; Albert; M; 65; Pima; F; Wd.; Head; 111; Yes; Yes; AI. 2990/Id. 3235

ANTON
108; Benjamin; M; 42; Pima; F; M; Head; 112; Yes; Yes; AI. 3409/Id. 7074
109; Lena; F; 18; Pima; F; S; Dau.; 113; Yes; Yes; AI. 3408/Id. 7076
110; Hayme; F; 16; Pima; F; S; Dau.; 114; Yes; Yes; AI./Id. 7077
111; Blaine; M; 13; Pima; F; S; Son; 115; Yes; Yes; AI./Id. 7078
112; Myrus; M; 10; Pima; F; S; Son; 116; Yes; Yes; AI./Id. 7079

ANTON
113; Ceveriano; M; 34; Pima; F; M; Head; 117; Yes; Yes; AI. 1870/Id. 3444
114; Elizabeth, (Elizabeth Jones); F; 33; Pima; F; M; Wife; 118; Yes; Yes; AI. 2028/Id. 3445
115; Edison; M; 13; Pima; F; S; Son; 119; Yes; Yes; AI. 4860/Id. 3446
116; Mary; F; 11; Pima; F; S; Dau; 120; Yes; Yes; AI./Id. 3447
117; Miles; M; 9; Pima; F; S; Son; 121; Yes; Yes; AI. Id. 3448
118; Clarence; M; 7; Pima; F; S; Son; 122; Yes; Yes; AI./Id. 3449
119; Annie; F; 5; Pima; F; S; Dau.; 123; Yes; Yes; AI./Id. 3450

ANTON
120; Charles; M; 45; Pima; F; M; Head; 124; Yes; Yes; AI. 4082/Id. 1579
121; Rosera S., (Santo, Rosera); F; 43; Pima; F; M; Wife; 125; Yes; Yes; AI. 4328/Id. 1580
122; Chester; M; 12; Pima; F; S; Son; 126; Yes; Yes; AI. Id. 1582
123; Lillian; F; 10; Pima; F; S; Dau.; 127; Yes; Yes; AI. Id. 1583

Census of the **Gila River** reservation of the **Pima Agency** jurisdiction; as of **April 1** ; 1932; taken by **A. H. Kneale** ; Superintendent.

Key: Number; Surname; Given; Sex (M/F); Age at Last Birthday; Tribe; Degree of Blood (F=Full); Marital Status; Relationship to Head of Family & Last Census No; At Jurisdiction Where Enrolled (Yes/No); (If no – Where); Ward (Yes/No); Allotment Annuity and/or Identification Numbers

124; Willsoot; M; 8; Pima; F; S; Son; 128; Yes; Yes; AI. Id. 1584
125; Nelle; F; 7/12; Pima; F; S; Dau.; --; Yes; Born; September 17; 1931; Yes; AI. Id. 3953

ANTON
126; Daniel; M; 32; Pima; F; M; Head; 129; Yes; Yes; AI. 501/Id. 5789
127; Esther A., (Allison, Esther); F; 26; Pima; F; M; Wife; 130; Yes; Yes; AI. 382/Id. 5790
128; Charles H.; M; 2; Pima; F; S; Son; 131; Yes; Yes; AI./Id. 5791

ANTON
129; David E.; M; 23; Pima; F; S; Head; 132; Yes; Yes; AI. 1609/Id. 7081

ANTON
130; David; M; 33; Pima; F; S; Head; 133; Yes; Yes; AI. 1726/Id. 4160

ANTON
131; Emma; F; 35; Pima; F; S; Head; 134; Yes; Yes; AI. 4325/Id. 1899

ANTON
132; George; M; 47; Pima; F; S; Head; 135; Yes; Yes; AI. 1230/Id. 6944

ANTON
133; Hale; M; 77; Pima; F; Wd.; Head; 136; Yes; Yes; AI. 1725/Id. 5576

ANTON
134; Hosea; M; 77; Pima; F; M; Head; 137; Yes; Yes; AI. 275/Id. 5350
135; Cevia; F; 52; Pima; F; M; Wife; 138; Yes; Yes; AI. 276/Id. 5351
136; Susanna; F; 29; Pima; F; S; Dau.; 139; Yes; Yes; AI. 715/Id. 5352

ANTON
137; Isaac; M; 38; Pima; F; M; Head; 140; Yes; Yes; AI. 810/Id. 5557
138; Dorothy E., (Enis, Dorothy); F; 36; Pima; F; M; Wife; 141; Yes; Yes; AI. 34/Id. 5558
139; Wesley; M; 14; Pima; F; S; Son; 142; Yes; Yes; AI. 4798/Id. 5559
140; Wesley; M; 13; Pima; F; S; Son; 143; Yes; Yes; AI. 4799/Id. 5560

ANTON
141; James W.; M; 38; Pima; F; Wd.; Head; 144; Yes; Yes; AI. 1265/Id. 6641
140; Carl W.; M; 22; Pima; F; S; Son; 145; Yes; Yes; AI. 4620/Id. 6642

ANTON
143; Jose; M; 72; Pima; F; Wd.; Head; 146; Yes; Yes; AI. 735/Id. 4417

Key: Number; Surname; Given; Sex (M/F); Age at Last Birthday; Tribe; Degree of Blood (F=Full); Marital Status; Relationship to Head of Family & Last Census No; At Jurisdiction Where Enrolled (Yes/No); (If no – Where); Ward (Yes/No); Allotment Annuity and/or Identification Numbers

ANTON
144; Jose; M; 47; Pima; F; Wd.; Head; 147; Yes; Yes; AI. 932/Id. 4159

ANTON
145; Jose; M; 62; Pima; F; Wd.; Head; 148; Yes; Yes; AI. 4427/Id. 1329

ANTON
146; Jose; M; 39; Pima; F; M; Head; 149; Yes; Yes; AI. 4334/Id. 1385
147; Antonia; F; 47; Pima; F; M; Wife; 150; Yes; Yes; AI. 4335/Id. 1386
148; Clara J.; F; 20; Pima; F; S; Dau.; 151; Yes; Yes; AI. 4280/Id. 1387
149; Steven; M; 15; Pima; F; S; Son; 152; Yes; Yes; AI. 4336/Id. 1388
150; Dorothy; F; 13; Pima; F; S; Dau.; 153; Yes; Yes; AI. 4338/Id. 1389
151; Vincent; M; 11; Pima; F; S; Son; 154; Yes; Yes; AI./Id. 1390
152; Joseph; M; 7; Pima; F; S; Son; 155; Yes; Yes; AI./Id. 1391
153; Isabel M.; F; 6; Pima; F; S; Dau.; 156; Yes; Yes; AI./Id. 1392

ANTON
154; Jose; M; 37; Pima; F; M; Head; 157; Yes; Yes; AI. 4058/Id. 1900

ANTON
155; Jose; M; 74; Pima; F; Wd.; Head; 158; Yes; Yes; AI. 4298/Id. 1329

ANTON
156; Jose; M; 56; Pima; F; S; Head; 159; Yes; Yes; AI./Id. 3134

ANTON
157; Jose; M; 67; Pima; F; M; Head; 160; Yes; Yes; AI. 4584/Id. 4685
158; Lizzie, (Antone, Lizzie); F; 66; Pima; F; M; Wife; 161; Yes; Yes; AI. 3292/Id. 4686

ANTON
159; Jose H.; M; 45; Pima; F; M; Head; 162; Yes; Yes; AI. 1703/Id. 6669
160; Jennie P., (Pablo, Jennie); F; 33; Pima; F; M; Wife; 163; Yes; Yes; AI. 1820/Id. 6670
161; Felix; M; 16; Pima; F; S; Son; 164; Yes; Yes; AI. 3387/Id. 4671
162; Ellen H.; M; 14; Pima; F; S; Dau.; 165; Yes; Yes; AI. 4463/Id. 4672
163; Richard; M; 12; Pima; F; S; Son; 166; Yes; Yes; AI. 4737/Id. 4673
164; Leonard; M; 11; Pima; F; S; Son; 167; Yes; Yes; AI./Id. 4674
165; Della; F; 7; Pima; F; S; Dau.; 168; Yes; Yes; AI./Id. 4675

ANTON
166; Jose M.; M; 33; Pima; F; M; Head; 169; Yes; Yes; AI. 1626/Id. 1847
167; Margaret B., (Boss, Margaret); F; 34; Pima; F; M; Wife; 170; Yes; Yes; AI. 1848/Id. 1514
168; Dorothy; F; 9; Pima; F; S; Dau.; 171; Yes; Yes; AI./Id. 1849

Census of the **Gila River** reservation of the **Pima Agency** jurisdiction; as of **April 1** ; 1932; taken by **A. H. Kneale** ; Superintendent.

Key: Number; Surname; Given; Sex (M/F); Age at Last Birthday; Tribe; Degree of Blood (F=Full); Marital Status; Relationship to Head of Family & Last Census No; At Jurisdiction Where Enrolled (Yes/No); (If no – Where); Ward (Yes/No); Allotment Annuity and/or Identification Numbers

169; Pauline; F; 5; Pima; F; S; Dau.; 172; Yes; Yes; AI./Id. 1851

ANTON
170; Jose; M; 69; Pima; F; M; Head; 173; Yes; Yes; AI. 1694/Id. 4375
171; Mollie J.; F; 72; Pima; F; M; Wife; 174; Yes; Yes; AI. 1695/Id. 4376

ANTON
172; Jose; M; 22; Pima; F; S; Head; 175; No; Ft. Leavenworth; Ft. Leavenworth; Ft. Leavenworth; Kans.; Yes; AI. 2004/Id. 4699

ANTON
173; Joseph; M; 68; Maricopa; F; M; Head; 176; Yes; Yes; AI. 3786/Id. 470
174; Lizzie; F; 62; Maricopa; F; M; Wife; 177; Yes; Yes; AI. 3787/Id. 476
175; Herman; M; 23; Maricopa; F; MS; Son; 178; Yes; Yes; AI. 3789/Id. 473

ANTON
176; Joseph; M; 23; Pima; F; M; Head; 179; Yes; Yes; AI. 339/Id. 5104
177; Albina J. (Snyder, Althahene); F; 22; Pima; F; M; Wife; 180; Yes; Yes; AI. 454/Id. 5105
178; Clayton; M; 3; Pima; F; MS; Son; 181; Yes; Yes; AI./Id. 5795

ANTON
179; Joshua; M; 63; Pima; F; M; Head; 182; Yes; Yes; AI./Id. 1588

ANTON
180; Juan; M; 46; Pima; F; M; Head; 183; Yes; Yes; AI./Id. 1330
181; Mattie, (Peters, Mattie); F; 61; Pima; F; M; Wife; 184; Yes; Yes; AI. 3637/Id. 1331

ANTON
182; Juan, (John); M; 47; Pima; F; Wd.; Head; 185; Yes; Yes; AI. 499/Id. 5170

ANTON
183; Juan S.; M; 38; Pima; F; M; Head; 186; Yes; Yes; AI. 160/Id. 5393
184; Mollie, (Anton, Mollie); F; 42; Pima; F; M; Wife; 187; Yes; Yes; AI. 3630/Id. 5394
185; Frances; F; 16; Pima; F; S; Dau.; 188; Yes; Yes; AI. [??]89/Id. 5395
186; Anthony; M; 10; Pima; F; S; Son; 189; Yes; Yes; AI./Id. 5396
187; Sims; M; 7; Pima; F; S; Son; 190; Yes; Yes; AI./Id. 5397

ANTON
188; Lancisco; M; 36; Pima; F; M; Head; 191; Yes; Yes; AI. 1453/Id. 6823
189; Virginia O., (Osife, Virginia); F; 35; Pima; F; M; Wife; 192; Yes; Yes; AI. 1868/Id. 6824
190; Briget; F; 18; Pima; F; S; Dau.; 193; Yes; Yes; AI. 3386/Id. 6825

Key: Number; Surname; Given; Sex (M/F); Age at Last Birthday; Tribe; Degree of Blood (F=Full); Marital Status; Relationship to Head of Family & Last Census No; At Jurisdiction Where Enrolled (Yes/No); (If no - Where); Ward (Yes/No); Allotment Annuity and/or Identification Numbers

191; Matilda; F; 16; Pima; F; S; Dau.; 194; Yes; Yes; AI. 4558/Id. 6826
192; Clarence; M; 4; Pima; F; S; Son; 195; Yes; Yes; AI./Id. 6827
193; Henry; M; 2; Pima; F; S; Son; 196; Yes; Yes; AI./Id. 7081

ANTON
194; Lopez; S.; M; 30; Pima; F; M; Head; 187; Yes; Yes; AI. 2599/Id. 7030
195; Loreta; S.; F; 30; Pima; F; M; Wife; 198; Yes; Yes; AI./Id. 7031
196; Edmund J.; M; 12; Pima; F; S; Son; 199; Yes; Yes; AI./Id. 7032
197; Stephen; M; 3; Pima; F; S; Son; 200; Yes; Yes; AI./Id. 7033

ANTON
198; Luke; M; 42; Pima; F; Wd.; Head; 201; Yes; Yes; AI. 813/Id. 3978
199; Anna D.; F; 3; Pima; F; S; Dau.; 202; Yes; Yes; AI./Id. 3977
200; Clara V.; F; 2; Pima; F; S; Dau.; 203; Yes; Yes; AI./Id. 3976

ANTON
201; Luther J.; M; 60; Pima; F; M; Head; 204; Yes; Yes; AI. 1450/Id. 6821
202; Maria; F; 59; Pima; F; M; Wife; 205; Yes; Yes; AI. 1451/Id. 6822

ANTON
203; Martha; F; 35; Pima; F; S; Head; 206; Yes; Yes; AI. 1266/Id. 6961
204; Mary A.; F; 10; Pima; F; S; Dau.; 207; Yes; Yes; AI./Id. 6962

ANTON
205; Martin; M; 32; Pima; F; M; Head; 208; Yes; Yes; AI. 4300/Id. 1901
206; Helen; F; 25; Papago; F; M; Wife; 209; Yes; Yes; AI./Id. 1902

ANTON
207; Mary; F; 73; Pima; F; Wd. Head; 210; Yes; Yes; AI. 2111/Id. 3006

ANTON
208; Mary; F; 42; Pima; F; Wd. Head; 211; Yes; Yes; AI. 3327/Id. 1903
209; Sarah; F; 18; Pima; F; S; Dau.; 212; Yes; Yes; AI./Id. 1904
210; Bernice; F; 10; Pima; F; S; Dau.; 213; Yes; Yes; AI./Id. 1905

ANTON
211; Isabel; F; 50; Pima; F; Wd. Head; 214; Yes; Yes; AI. 259/Id. 5038
212; Francisco; M; 18; Pima; F; S; Son; 215; Yes; Yes; AI. 262/Id. 5039
213; Jose; M; 14; Pima; F; S; Son; 216; Yes; Yes; AI. 4504/Id. 5040
214; Venancia N.; M; 16; Pima; F; S; Son; 217; Yes; Yes; AI. 4505/Id. 5041
215; Millie; F; 12; Pima; F; S; Dau.; 218; Yes; Yes; AI./Id. 5042

ANTON
216; Miguel; M; 57; Pima; F; Wd.; Head; 219; Yes; Yes; AI. 1602/Id. 1842
217; Juanita; F; 27; Pima; F; S; Dau.; 220; Yes; Yes; AI. 1605/Id. 1843

Key: Number; Surname; Given; Sex (M/F); Age at Last Birthday; Tribe; Degree of Blood (F=Full); Marital Status; Relationship to Head of Family & Last Census No; At Jurisdiction Where Enrolled (Yes/No); (If no – Where); Ward (Yes/No); Allotment Annuity and/or Identification Numbers

218; Matilda; F; 18; Pima; F; S; Dau.; 221; Yes; Yes; AI. 1604/Id. 1844

ANTON
219; Miguel; M; 51; Pima; F; M; Head; 222; Yes; Yes; AI. 1147/Id. 1735
220; Catherine, (Osife Giff, Catherine); F; 57; Pima; F; M; Wife; 223; Yes; Yes ; AI. 4743/Id. 1736

ANTON
221; Miguel; M; 43; Maricopa; F; Wd.; Head; 224; Yes; Yes; AI. 2763/Id. 250

ANTON
222; Miguel B.; M; 58; Pima; F; Wd.; Head; 225; Yes; Yes; AI. 1231/Id. 6942
223; Sarah; F; 57; Pima; F; S; Sister; 226; Yes; Yes; AI. 1252/Id. 6943

ANTON
224; Millie C.; F; 61; Pima; F; Wd.; Head; 227; Yes; Yes; AI. 4057/Id. 1807
225; Dominick; M; 38; Pima; F; S; Son; 228; Yes; Yes; AI. 4056/Id. 1808
226; Mary; F; 35; Pima; F; S; Dau.; 229; Yes; Yes; AI. 4059/Id. 1809

ANTON
227; Ruth H. (Ruth Hayes); F; 25; Pima; F; Wd.; Head; 230; Yes; Yes; AI. 1353/Id. 6717
228; Stanley; M; 4; Pima; F; S; Son; 231; Yes; Yes; AI./Id. 5795

ANTON
229; William; M; 28; Maricopa; F; M; Head; 232; Yes; Yes; AI. 3788/Id. 477
230; Edna W., (Whittaker, Edna); F; 22; Pima; F; M; Wife; 233; Yes; Yes; AI. 763/Id. 5215

ANTON
231; Vanice; M; 40; Pima; F; Wd.; Head; 234; Yes; Yes; AI. 161/Id. 5591

ANTON
232; William; M; 22; Pima; F; S; Head; 235; Yes; Yes; AI. 1610/Id. 7082

ANTONIO
233; Juan O.; M; 47; Pima; F; Wd.; Head; 236; Yes; Yes; AI. 3023/Id. 3231
234; Haskell; M; 23; Pima; F; S; Son; 237; Yes; Yes; AI. 3121/Id. 3232
235; Esther; F; 18; Pima; F; S; Dau.; 238; Yes; Yes; AI. 3270/Id. 3234
236; Warren G.; M; 22; Pima; F; S; Son; 239; Yes; Yes; AI. 3122/Id. 3233

ANTONIO
237; Kiato; M; 52; Pima; F; Wd.; Head; 240; Yes; Yes; AI. 1908/Id. 4687
238; Kiato; M; 24; Pima; F; S; Son; 241; Yes; Yes; AI. 2000/Id. 4688
239; Osife; Lucy K.; F; 26; Pima; F; Wd.; Dau.; 242; Yes; Yes; AI. 2001/Id. 4689

Census of the **Gila River** reservation of the **Pima Agency** jurisdiction; as of **April 1** ; 1932; taken by **A. H. Kneale** ; Superintendent.

Key: Number; Surname; Given; Sex (M/F); Age at Last Birthday; Tribe; Degree of Blood (F=Full); Marital Status; Relationship to Head of Family & Last Census No; At Jurisdiction Where Enrolled (Yes/No); (If no - Where); Ward (Yes/No); Allotment Annuity and/or Identification Numbers

240; Osife; Lawrence L.; M; 6; Pima; F; S; Gr.sn; 243; Yes; Yes; AI./Id. 4690

ANTONIO
241; Maria; F; 73; Pima; F; Wd.; Head; 244; Yes; Yes; AI. 3466/Id. 1767

APACHESE
242; Felix; M; 29; Pima; F; S; Head; 245; Yes; Yes; AI. 535/Id. 6973

APACHESE
243; Juan; M; 51; Pima; F; M; Head; 246; Yes; Yes; AI. 533/Id. 5012
244; Emma; F; 45; Pima; F; M; Wife; 247; Yes; Yes; AI. 534/Id. 5013

APKAW
245; Blue; M; 47; Pima; F; S; Head; 248; Yes; Yes; AI. 1704/Id. 4158

APKAW
246; Edith; F; 24; Pima; F; S; Head; 249; Yes; Yes; AI. 2349/Id. 3504

APKAW
247; Harvey; M; 32; Pima; F; M; Head; 250; Yes; Yes; AI. 2346/Id. 4306
248; Isabel E. (Enas, Isabella); F; 26; Pima; F; M; Wife; 251; Yes; Yes; AI. 1713/Id. 4301
249; Louisa M.; F; 7; Pima; F; S; Dau.; 252; Yes; Yes; AI./Id. 4302
250; Thelma V.; F; 5; Pima; F; S; Dau.; 253; Yes; Yes; AI./Id. 4303
251; Josephine; F; 2; Pima; F; S; Dau.; 254; Yes; Yes; AI./Id. 4157

APKAW
252; Henry; M; 23; Pima; F; S; Head; 255; Yes; Yes; AI. 1988/Id. 4158

ARMSTRONG
253; Frank; M; 65; Pima; F; M; Head; 256; Yes; Yes; AI. 176/Id. 4970
254; Martha; F; 62; Pima; F; M; Wife; 257; Yes; Yes; AI. 177/Id. 4971
255; Rufus; M; 24; Pima; F; S; Son; 258; Yes; Yes; AI. 178/Id. 4972
256; Richard; M; 23; Pima; F; S; Son; 259; Yes; Yes; AI. 180/Id. 4973
257; Carrie; F; 17; Pima; F; S; Dau.; 260; Yes; Yes; AI. 3161/Id. 4974

ARMSTRONG
Armstrong, Raymond, (See. Miles, Ramon)

ARTHUR
258; Ho-tah-ne-a-ba; F; 61; Pima; F; S; Head; 261; Yes; Yes; AI. 1596/Id. 7083

ARTHUR
259; Jose; M; 56; Pima; F; S; Head; 262; Yes; Yes; AI. 1594/Id. 7084

Key: Number; Surname; Given; Sex (M/F); Age at Last Birthday; Tribe; Degree of Blood (F=Full); Marital Status; Relationship to Head of Family & Last Census No; At Jurisdiction Where Enrolled (Yes/No); (If no – Where); Ward (Yes/No); Allotment Annuity and/or Identification Numbers

ARTHUR

260; Mary A.; F; 56; Pima; F; Wd.; Head; 263; Yes; Yes; AI. 1597/Id. 7085

ARTHUR

261; William; M; 42; Pima; F; S; Head; 264; Yes; Yes; AI. 1595/Id.

AVERY

262; John; M; 42; Pima; F; M; Head; 265; Yes; Yes; AI. 3868/Id. 1325
263; Luciana S. (Soos, Luciana S.); F; 37; Pima; F; M; Wife; 266; Yes; Yes; AI. 2610/Id. 1326
264; Soos, Velistina; F; 15; Pima; F; S; St.du.; 267; Yes; Yes; AI./Id. 1327
265; Avery, Nestor; M; 5; Pima; F; S; Son; 268; Yes; Yes; AI./Id. 1328
266; Avery, Antonetta; M; 3; Pima; F; S; Dau.; 269; Yes; Yes; AI./Id. 1907

AW-AW-KATCH

267; (Bones); M; 71; Pima; F; M; Head; 270; Yes; Yes; AI. 4643/Id. 5797
268; Guadaulupe, (Aw-aw-katch, Gualupa); F; 67; Pima; F; M; Wife; 271; Yes; Yes; AI. 4644/Id. 5798

AW-AW-KATCH

269; Lancisco; M; 27; Pima; F; S; Head; 272; Yes; Yes; AI. 4647/Id. 5799

AZULE

270; George; M; 57; Pima; F; M; Head; 273; Yes; Yes; AI. 1690/Id. 4248
271; Sarah; F; 55; Pima; F; M; wife; 274; Yes; Yes; AI. 1691/Id. 4249
272; Hugo, Daisy; F; 28; Pima; F; Wd.; St.du; 275; Yes; Yes; AI. 914/Id. 4251
273; Azule, Kenneth; M; 18; Pima; F; S; Son; 276; Yes; Yes; AI. 2389/Id. 4250

AZULE

274; Johnson; M; 43; Pima; F; M; Head; 277; Yes; Yes; AI. 1686/Id. 4366
275; George; F; 42; Pima; F; M; Wife; 278; Yes; Yes; AI. 1687/Id. 4367

AZULE

276; Opsie; F; 69; Pima; F; Wd.; Head; 279; Yes; Yes; AI. 1757/Id. 4381

AZULE

277; Paul; M; 37; Pima; F; M; Head; 280; Yes; Yes; AI. 64/Id. 5031
278; Anna Manuel, (Manuel, Anna); F; 28; Pima; F; M; Wife; 281; Yes; Yes; AI. 497/Id. 5032
279; Gilbert; M; 9; Pima; F; S; Son; 282; Yes; Yes; AI. 0/Id. 5033
280; Theodore; M; 5; Pima; F; S; Son; 283; Yes; Yes; AI./Id. 5034

AZULE

281; Roy; M; 47; Pima; F; S; Head; 284; Yes; Yes; AI. 3138/Id. 4382

Census of the **Gila River** reservation of the **Pima Agency** jurisdiction; as of **April 1** ; 1932; taken by **A. H. Kneale** ; Superintendent.

Key: Number; Surname; Given; Sex (M/F); Age at Last Birthday; Tribe; Degree of Blood (F=Full); Marital Status; Relationship to Head of Family & Last Census No; At Jurisdiction Where Enrolled (Yes/No); (If no – Where); Ward (Yes/No); Allotment Annuity and/or Identification Numbers

AZULE

282; William; M; 35; Pima; F; M; Head; 285; Yes; Yes; AI. 1961/Id. 5606
283; Edna W. (Wiston, Edna); F; 32; Pima; F; M; Wife; 286; Yes; Yes; AI. 1739/Id. 5607
284; Hazel L.; F; 10; Pima; F; S; Dau.; 287; Yes; Yes; AI./Id. 5608
285; Rudidaux[sic]; M; 9; Pima; F; S; Son; 288; Yes; Yes; AI./Id. 5609
286; Clyde E.; M; 7; Pima; F; S; Son; 289; Yes; Yes; AI./Id. 5610
287; John Clayton; M; 6; Pima; F; S; Son; 290; Yes; Yes; AI./Id. 5611

AZULE

Florence; (See Hall)
Kenneth; (See Hall)

BAPTISTO

288; Maria; F; 45; Pima; F; Wd.; Head; 291; Yes; Yes; AI. 3546/Id. 1746
289; Phillip; M; 22; Pima; F; S; Son; 292; Yes; Yes; AI. 3550/Id. 1747
290; Martha L.; F; 20; Pima; F; S; Dau.; 293; Yes; Yes; AI. 3548/Id. 1748
291; ----; F; 13; Pima; F; S; Gr.du; 294; Yes; Yes; AI./Id. 2036
292; Lucile.; F; 21; Pima; F; S; Dau.; 295; Yes; Yes; AI./Id. 1749

BAPTISTO

293; Isadore; M; 26; Pima; F; M; Head; 296; Yes; Yes; AI. 5547/Id. 7086
294; Minnie A.; (Anton, Minnie); F; 26; Pima; F; M; Wife; 297; Yes; Yes; AI. 1268/Id. 7087

BAREHAND

295; Brady; M; 30; Maricopa; F; M; Head; 298; Yes; Yes; AI. 3127/Id. 354
296; Olive P. (Peters, Olive); F; 28; Maricopa; F; M; Wife; 299; Yes; Yes; AI. 3677/Id. 335
297; Cymo; M; 6; Maricopa; F; M; Son; 300; Yes; Yes; AI./Id. 336
298; Carolina; F; 4; Maricopa; F; S; Dau.; 301; Yes; Yes; AI./Id. 337
299; -----; F; 2; Maricopa; F; S; Dau.; 302; Yes; Yes; AI./Id. 594

BAREHAND

300; Cleveland; M; 24; Pima; F; M; Head; 303; Yes; Yes; AI. 3130/Id. 1495
301; Kate L.; (Laws, Kate); F; 20; Pima; F; M; Wife; 304; Yes; Yes; AI. 3661/Id. 1496
302; Laws; Gladys; F; 17; Pima; F; S; Sister-in-law.; 305; No; Los Angeles; Los. Ang.; Cal.; Yes; AI. 3662/Id. 1497

BAREHAND

303; Cyrus; M; 53; Maricopa; F; M; Head; 306; Yes; Yes; AI. 3125/Id. 338
304; Emma; F; 53; Maricopa; F; M; Wife; 307; Yes; Yes; AI. 3126/Id. 339

Census of the **Gila River** reservation of the **Pima Agency** jurisdiction; as of **April 1** ; 1932; taken by **A. H. Kneale** ; Superintendent.

Key: Number; Surname; Given; Sex (M/F); Age at Last Birthday; Tribe; Degree of Blood (F=Full); Marital Status; Relationship to Head of Family & Last Census No; At Jurisdiction Where Enrolled (Yes/No); (If no – Where); Ward (Yes/No); Allotment Annuity and/or Identification Numbers

BAREHAND
305; Roy; M; 55; Pima; F; M; Head; 308; Yes; Yes; AI. 3690/Id. 1446
306; Eva; F; 49; Pima; F; M; Wife; 309; Yes; Yes; AI. 3691/Id. 1447

BARNAGO
307; Fernando; M; 24; Pima; F; S; Head; 310; Yes; Yes; AI. 3926/Id. 1421

BARNAGO
308; Laura; F; 65; Pima; F; Wd.; Head; 311; Yes; Yes; AI. 3923/Id. 1394

BASILIO
309; Essie; F; 40; Pima; F; Wife; Head; 312; No; San Zavier; ~~Tucson; Pima~~; Ariz.; Yes; AI./Id. 5353

~~BEGINNING~~
~~Chester; M; 57; Pima; F; Wd.; Head; 313; Died February 3; 1932; Yes; AI. 2164/Id. 3506~~

BENDING
310; Carl; M; 53; Pima; F; Wd.; Head; 314; Yes; Yes; AI. 3614/Id. 1451
311; Andrew; M; 25; Pima; F; S; Son; 315; Yes; Yes; AI. 3618/Id. 1453
312; Mildred; F; 20; Pima; F; S; Dau.; 316; Yes; Yes; AI. 3619/Id. 1454
313; Stella; F; 32; Pima; F; S; Dau.; 317; No; Los Angeles; Los Ang.; Cal.; Yes; AI. 3616/Id. 1452

BENDING
314; John; M; 83; Pima; F; M; Head; 318; Yes; Yes; AI. 3610/Id. 1448
315; Mary; F; 74; Pima; F; M; Wife; 319; Yes; Yes; AI. 3611/Id. 1449
316; Lulaine; F; 29; Pima; F; S; Dau.; 320; Yes; Yes; AI. 3613/Id. 1450

BENSON
317; Henry; M; 51; Maricopa; F; S; Head; 321; Yes; Yes; AI. 3990/Id. 361

BENSON
318; Carrie; F; 76; Maricopa; F; Wd.; Head; 322; Yes; Yes; AI. 3988/Id. 364
319; Maud; F; 28; Maricopa; F; S; Dau.; 323; Yes; Yes; AI. 3991/Id. 362
320; Maud; F; 42; Maricopa; F; S; Dau.; 324; Yes; Yes; AI. 3989/Id. 363

BIRD
321; Isaac; M; 66; Maricopa; F; Wd.; Head; 325; Yes; Yes; AI. 2752/Id. 165
322; Tella; F; 30; Maricopa; F; S; Dau.; 326; Yes; Yes; AI. 167/Id. 2755
~~Agnes; F; 27; Maricopa; F; S; Dau.; 327; Died October 22; 1931~~; Yes; AI. 2757/Id. 168

16

Census of the **Gila River** reservation of the **Pima Agency** jurisdiction; as of **April 1** ; 1932; taken by **A. H. Kneale** ; Superintendent.

Key: Number; Surname; Given; Sex (M/F); Age at Last Birthday; Tribe; Degree of Blood (F=Full); Marital Status; Relationship to Head of Family & Last Census No; At Jurisdiction Where Enrolled (Yes/No); (If no – Where); Ward (Yes/No); Allotment Annuity and/or Identification Numbers

BIRD

323; Albert; M; 26; Maricopa; F; S; Head; 328; Yes; Yes; AI. 2756/Id. 166

BIRD

324; Alice S., (Sanderson, Alice); F; 30; Maricopa; F; M; Wife; 329; Yes; Yes; AI. 4108/Id. 455

325; Eddie Jr.; M; 8; Maricopa; F; S; Son; 330; Yes; Yes; AI./Id. 456

BLACKWATER

326; Domingo; M; 45; Pima; F; Wd.; Head; 331; Yes; Yes; AI. 2080/Id. 4385

327; Raymond; M; 21; Pima; F; S; Son; 332; Yes; Yes; AI. 1656/Id. 4387

328; Grace; F; 12; Pima; F; S; Dau.; 333; Yes; Yes; AI. 4727/Id. 4388

329; Leo; M; 10; Pima; F; S; Son; 334; Yes; Yes; AI./Id. 4390

330; Maxwell; M; 9; Pima; F; S; Son; 335; Yes; Yes; AI./Id. 4389

331; Elmer; M; 7; Pima; F; S; Son; 336; Yes; Yes; AI./Id. 4391

332; Cora M.; F; 3; Pima; F; S; Dau.; 337; Yes; Yes; AI./Id. 4156

BLACKWATER

333; Emily; F; 72; Pima; F; Wd.; Head; 338; Yes; Yes; AI. 1696/Id. 4271

BLACKWATER

334; John; M; 31; Pima; F; M; Head; 339; Yes; Yes; AI. 2119/Id. 6623

335; Emma, (Harvier, Emma or Eunice); F; 33; Pima; F; M; Wife; Head; 340; Yes; Yes; AI. 1128/Id. 6624

336; Jackie; M; 6; Pima; F; S; Son; 341; Yes; Yes; AI./Id. 6625

337; Earling M.; M; 4; Pima; F; S; Son; 342; Yes; Yes; AI./Id. 6626

338; Marvin; M; 3/12; Pima; F; S; Son; --; Yes; Born January 25; 1932; Yes; AI./Id. 7291

BLACKWATER

339; Mary T.; F; 68; Pima; F; Wd.; Head; 343; Yes; Yes; AI. 2204/Id. 3029

BLACKWATER

340; Mark; M; 32; Pima; F; M; Head; 344; Yes; Yes; AI. 2118/Id. 4456

341; Julia, (Patton, Julia); M; 31; Pima; F; M; Wife; 345; Yes; Yes; AI. 1078/Id. 4457

BLACKWATER

342; Thomas A.; M; 54; Pima; F; M; Head; 346; Yes; Yes; AI. 2073/Id. 3031

343; Sue; F; 49; Pima; F; M; Wife; 347; Yes; Yes; AI. 2074/Id. 3032

344; Daniel; M; 26; Pima; F; S; Son; 348; Yes; Yes; AI. 2075/Id. 3033

345; Elihu A.; M; 24; Pima; F; S; Son; 349; Yes; Yes; AI. 2076/Id. 3034

346; Curtis; M; 21; Pima; F; S; Son; 350; Yes; Yes; AI. 2079/Id. 3035

347; Regina A.; F; 18; Pima; F; S; Dau.; 351; Yes; Yes; AI. 2077/Id. 3036

348; Norman A.; M; 15; Pima; F; S; Son; 352; Yes; Yes; AI. 3166/Id. 3037

349; Rollie; M; 14; Pima; F; S; Son; 353; Yes; Yes; AI. 4453/Id. 3038

Census of the **Gila River** reservation of the **Pima Agency** jurisdiction; as of **April 1** ; 1932; taken by **A. H. Kneale** ; Superintendent.

Key: Number; Surname; Given; Sex (M/F); Age at Last Birthday; Tribe; Degree of Blood (F=Full); Marital Status; Relationship to Head of Family & Last Census No; At Jurisdiction Where Enrolled (Yes/No); (If no – Where); Ward (Yes/No); Allotment Annuity and/or Identification Numbers

350; Lavina; F; 12; Pima; F; S; Dau.; 354; Yes; Yes; AI. 4850/Id. 3039

BLACKWATER
351; Vincent T.; M; 32; Pima; F; M; Head; 355; Yes; Yes; AI. 2205/Id. 3030
352; Josephine E., (Evans, Josephine); F; 30; Pima; F; M; Wife; 356; Yes; Yes; AI. 3067/Id. 3507
353; Orin; M. F; 2; Pima; F; S; Dau.; 357; Yes; Yes; AI./Id. 3503
354; Lewis T.; M; 1; Pima; F; S; Son; 358; Yes; Yes; AI./Id. 3603

BLACKWATER
355; William; M; 69; Pima; F; Wd.; Head; 359; Yes; Yes; AI. 2115/Id. 3028

BLAKE
356; Mollie J., (Jackson, Mollie); F; 36; Pima; F; M; Wife; 361; No.; Salt River Res. ~~Scottsdale~~; ~~Maricopa~~; ~~Ariz.~~; Yes; AI. 3956/Id.
357; Irene; F; 9; Pima; F; S; Dau.; 362; No.; Salt River Res. ~~Scottsdale~~; ~~Maricopa~~; ~~Ariz.~~; Yes; AI./Id. 5800
358; Joshua; M; 7; Pima; F; S; Son; 363; No.; Salt River Res. ~~Scottsdale~~; ~~Maricopa~~; ~~Ariz.~~; Yes; AI./Id. 5801

BOATMAN
359; Henry; M; 61; Maricopa; F; M; Head; 364; Yes; Yes; AI. 2883/Id. 176
360; Lucy A., (Allison, Lucy); F; 56; Maricopa; F; M; Wife; 365; Yes; Yes; AI. 3350/Id. 177

BOATMAN
361; Sallie; F; 33; Maricopa; F; M; Wife; 366; Yes; Yes; AI. 2885/Id. 565

BOSS
362; Joe; M; 59; Pima; F; Wd.; Head; 367; Yes; Yes; AI. 1509/Id. 5773
363; Arabella; F; 15; Pima; F; S; Dau.; 368; Yes; Yes; AI. 3801/Id. 5774
364; Helen; F; 11; Pima; F; S; Dau.; 369; Yes; Yes; AI./Id. 5775
365; Leonard; M; 10; Pima; F; S; Son; 370; Yes; Yes; AI./Id. 5776

BOSS
366; Juan P.; M; 30; Pima; F; S; Head; 371; Yes; Yes; AI. 1513/Id. 5802

BREAD
367; Albert; M; 59; Maricopa; F; M; Head; 372; Yes; Yes; AI. 2709/Id. 73
368; Mary; F; 59; Maricopa; F; M; Wife; 373; Yes; Yes; AI. 2710/Id. 74
369; Madie; F; 24; Maricopa; F; S; Dau.; 374; Yes; Yes; AI. 2708/Id. 77
370; Paul; M; 28; Maricopa; F; S; Son; 375; Yes; Yes; AI. 2706/Id. 75
371; David; M; 26; Maricopa; F; S; Son; 376; Yes; Yes; AI. 2707/Id. 76
372; Gladys; F; 18; Maricopa; F; S; Dau.; 378; Yes; Yes; AI. 2712/Id. 79
373; Laura; F; 14; Maricopa; F; S; Dau.; 379; Yes; Yes; AI. 4681/Id. 80

Census of the **Gila River** reservation of the **Pima Agency** jurisdiction; as of **April 1** ; 1932; taken by **A. H. Kneale** ; Superintendent.

Key: Number; Surname; Given; Sex (M/F); Age at Last Birthday; Tribe; Degree of Blood (F=Full); Marital Status; Relationship to Head of Family & Last Census No; At Jurisdiction Where Enrolled (Yes/No); (If no – Where); Ward (Yes/No); Allotment Annuity and/or Identification Numbers

BREAD
374; Hiram; M; 19; Maricopa; F; M; Head; 377; Yes; Yes; AI. 2711/Id. 78
~~Pauline George; F; Unk.; Unk.; Unk.; M; Wife; --~~; Yes; Yes; ---
~~---;F; Maricopa; F; S; Dau.; Dead 8-9-31~~; Yes; AI./Id. --

BREAD
375; Robert; M; 59; Maricopa; F; M; Head; 380; Yes; Yes; AI. 2860/Id. 36
376; Josephine; F; 59; Pima; F; M; Wife; 381; Yes; Yes; AI. 2877/Id. 37
377; George; M; 29; Pima-Maricopa; F; S; Son; 382; Yes; Yes; AI. 2879/Id. 38
378; Lizzie; F; 27; Pima-Maricopa; F; S; Dau.; 383; Yes; Yes; AI. 2880/Id. 39
379; Andrew C.; M; 19; Pima-Maricopa; F; S; Son; 384; Yes; Yes; AI. 2878/Id. 40
380; Janette H.; F; 12; Pima-Maricopa; F; S; Dau.; 385; Yes; Yes; AI. 4678/Id. 41

BRECKENRIDGE
381; John C.; M; 39; Maricopa; F; M; Head; 386; Yes; Yes; AI. 4127/Id. 345
382; William; M; 19; Maricopa; F; S; Son; 387; Yes; Yes; AI. 4128/Id. 347

BRECKENRIDGE
383; Tony; M; 44; Maricopa; F; M; Head; 388; Yes; Yes; AI. 4131/Id. 348
384; Elsie J. (Lewis, Elsie); F; 26; Maricopa; F; M; Wife; 389; Yes; Yes; AI. 2290/Id. 349
385; Hazel; F; 8; Maricopa; F; S; Dau.; 390; Yes; Yes; AI./Id. 350
386; Verna; F; 5; Maricopa; F; S; Dau.; 391; Yes; Yes; AI./Id. 351
387; Winifred; F; 4; Maricopa; F; S; Dau.; 392; Yes; Yes; AI./Id. 352
388; Harriet; F; 2; Maricopa; F; S; Dau.; 393; Yes; Yes; AI./Id. 556

BROOKS
389; Andrew; M; 81; Pima; F; Wd.; Head; 394; Yes; Yes; AI. 2583/Id. 6828

BROOKS
390; Lawrence; M; 82; Pima; F; S; Head; 395; Yes; Yes; AI. 1203/Id. 6632

BROWN
391; Barney; M; 75; Maricopa; F; Wd.; Head; 396; Yes; Yes; AI. 4368/Id. 328
392; Mabel; F; 24; Maricopa; F; S; Dau.; 397; Yes; Yes; AI. 4371/Id. 329
~~Ina; F; 22; Maricopa; F; M; Dau.; 398; (Married Bernard Williams—See Ina Brown Williams.);~~ Yes; AI. 4601/Id. 330
393; Louise; F; 16; Maricopa; F; S; Dau.; 399; Yes; Yes; AI. 4372/Id. 331

BROWN
394; Daniel; M; 31; Pima; F; S; Head; 400; Yes; Yes; AI. 3037/Id. 3152

BROWN
395; Fernando; M; 23; Pima; F; M; Head; 401; Yes; Yes; AI. 2497/Id. 6721

Key: Number; Surname; Given; Sex (M/F); Age at Last Birthday; Tribe; Degree of Blood (F=Full); Marital Status; Relationship to Head of Family & Last Census No; At Jurisdiction Where Enrolled (Yes/No); (If no – Where); Ward (Yes/No); Allotment Annuity and/or Identification Numbers

396; Irene D. James, (James, Irene); F; 20; Pima; F; M; Wife; 402; Yes; Yes; AI. 1382/Id. 4762

BROWN

397; Jennie; F; 67; Maricopa; F; Wd.; Head; 403; Yes; Yes; AI. 3999/Id. 526

BROWN

398; Jerry; M; 45; Maricopa; F; M; Head; 404; Yes; Yes; AI. 2798/Id. 109
399; Sarah; F; 45; Maricopa; F; M; Wife; 405; Yes; Yes; AI. 2799/Id. 110
400; Vesper; F; 7; Maricopa; F; S; Dau.; 406; Yes; Yes; AI./Id. 111

BROWN

401; John; M; 47; Pima; F; M; Head; 407; Yes; Yes; AI. 2493/Id. 6718
402; Isabelle; F; 44; Pima; F; M; Wife; 408; Yes; Yes; AI. 2494/Id. 6719
403; James; M; 20; Pima; F; S; Son; 409; Yes; Yes; AI. 2498/Id. 6720
404; Edna; F; 14; Pima; F; S; Dau.; 410; Yes; Yes; AI. 3389/Id. 6722
405; Agnes; F; 10; Pima; F; S; Dau.; 411; Yes; Yes; AI./Id. 6723
406; Lacita; F; 8; Pima; F; S; Dau.; 412; Yes; Yes; AI./Id. 6724

BROWN

407; John; M; 42; Maricopa; F; M; Head; 413; Yes; Yes; AI. 4000/Id. 524
408/; Etta C., (Cannon, Etta); F; 26; Maricopa; F; M; Wife; 414; Yes; Yes; AI. 3961/Id. 525

BROWN

409; Kisto; M; 73; Pima; F; M; Head; 415; Yes; Yes; AI. 4684/Id. 5705
410; Minnie; M; 63; Pima; F; S; Wife; 416; Yes; Yes; AI. 4685/Id. 5706

BROWN

411; Luke; M; 23; Pima; F; S; Head; 417; Yes; Yes; AI. 3040/Id. 3153

BROWN

412; Nathan; M; 25; Maricopa; F; M; Head; 418; Yes; Yes; AI. 4373/Id. 332
413; Minnie, (John, Minnie); F; 28; Maricopa; F; M; Wife; 419; Yes; Yes; AI. 2093/Id. 333
414; Irma Mae; F; 3; Maricopa; F; S; Dau.; 420; Yes; Yes; AI./Id. 566
415; Roderick; M; 6/12; Maricopa; F; S; Son; --; Yes; Born 10-22-31; Yes; AI./Id. 608

BROWN

416; Nathaniel; M; 38; Maricopa; F; M; Head; 421; Yes; Yes; AI. 3417/Id. 548
417; Lizzie; F; 39; Maricopa; F; M; Wife; 422; Yes; Yes; AI. 3418/Id. 549
418; Cato; M; 14; Maricopa; F; S; Son; 423; Yes; Yes; AI. 3419/Id. 550
419; Ernest; M; 5; Maricopa; F; S; Son; 424; Yes; Yes; AI./Id. 555

Census of the **Gila River** reservation of the **Pima Agency** jurisdiction; as of **April 1** ; 1932; taken by **A. H. Kneale** ; Superintendent.

Key: Number; Surname; Given; Sex (M/F); Age at Last Birthday; Tribe; Degree of Blood (F=Full); Marital Status; Relationship to Head of Family & Last Census No; At Jurisdiction Where Enrolled (Yes/No); (If no – Where); Ward (Yes/No); Allotment Annuity and/or Identification Numbers

BROWNING
420; J. Roe; M; 51; Pima; F; Wd.; Head; 425; Yes; Yes; AI. 239/Id.

421; Fern D.; F; 19; Pima; F; S; Dau.; 426; Yes; Yes; AI. 241/Id.

BURKE
422; Lydia H., (Howard, Lydia); F; 19; Pima; F; M; Wife; 427; No; Salt River Res; ~~Scottsdale; Maricopa; Arizon~~ Yes; AI. 2473/Id.

BURKE
423; Paul; M; 29; Pima; F; M; Head; 428; Yes; Yes; AI. 121/Id. 5571

424; Edna W., (Myers, Edna); F; 31; Pima; F; M; Wife; 429; Yes; Yes; AI. 27/Id. 5572

425; Wilson; Evelyn; F; 11; Pima; F; S; St.dau.; 430; Yes; Yes; AI./Id. 5573

426; Vasquez; Laurita; F; 7; Pima; F; S; St.dau.; 431; Yes; Yes; AI./Id. 5574

427; Eleanor; F; 3; Pima; F; S; Dau.; 432; Yes; Yes; AI./Id. 5575

BURNETTE
428; Pancho; M; 42; Pima; F; M; Head; 433; Yes; Yes; AI. 1890/Id. 5726

429; Lizzie; F; 44; Pima; F; M; Wife; 434; Yes; Yes; AI. 4702/Id. 5728

430; Mary B.; F; 20; Pima; F; S; Dau.; 435; Yes; Yes; AI. 4703/Id. 5729

431; Steven; M; 16; Pima; F; S; Son; 436; Yes; Yes; AI. 4704/Id. 5731

432; Enos; M; 13; Pima; F; S; Son; 437; Yes; Yes; AI./Id. 5732

433; Mildred; F; 9; Pima; F; S; Dau.; 438; Yes; Yes; AI./Id. 5733

434; Lynn A.; M; 6; Pima; F; S; Son; 439; Yes; Yes; AI./Id. 5734

435; Margarey; F; 4; Pima; F; S; Dau.; 440; Yes; Yes; AI./Id. 5735

CAMERON
436; May; F; 48; Maricopa; F; Wd.; Head; 441; Yes; Yes; AI. 259/Id. 2790

~~Hazel; F; 24; Maricopa; F; M; Dau.; 442; Yes; See Hazel Cameron Honwesina;~~ Yes; AI. 2791/Id. 260

437; Ralph; M; 16; Maricopa; F; S; Son; 443; Yes; Yes; AI. 4751/Id. 261

438; Lily; F; 7; Maricopa; F; S; Dau.; 444; Yes; Yes; AI./Id.

CAMERON
439; Onesemah; M; 61; Maricopa; F; Wd.; Head; 445; Yes; Yes; AI. 2792/Id. 258

CAMPBELL
440; Lucy W.; F; 37; Maricopa; F; Wd.; Head; 446; Yes; Yes; AI. 493/Id. 4953

441; Elizabeth; F; 4; Maricopa; F; S; Dau.; 447; Yes; Yes; AI./Id.4954

442; Delia; F; 3; Maricopa; F; S; Dau.; 448; Yes; Yes; AI./Id.6113

CAMPEN
443; Charles; M; 55; Pima; F; Wd.; Son; 449; No; Los Angeles; L.A. Cal.; Yes; AI. 3427/Id.

444; Roy; M; 20; Pima; F; S; Son; 450; No; Los Angeles; L.A. Cal.;Yes; AI. 3421/Id.

Census of the **Gila River** reservation of the **Pima Agency** jurisdiction; as of **April 1** ; 1932; taken by **A. H. Kneale** ; Superintendent.

Key: Number; Surname; Given; Sex (M/F); Age at Last Birthday; Tribe; Degree of Blood (F=Full); Marital Status; Relationship to Head of Family & Last Census No; At Jurisdiction Where Enrolled (Yes/No); (If no – Where); Ward (Yes/No); Allotment Annuity and/or Identification Numbers

CANNON
445; Alexander; M; 32; Pima; F; M; Head; 451; Yes; Yes; AI. 1192/Id. 6610
446; Cora R., (Rhodes, Cora); F; 32; Pima; F; M; Wife; 452; Yes; Yes; AI. 2837/Id. 6611
447; Constance; F; 5; Pima; F; S; Dau.; 453; Yes; Yes; AI./Id. 6612
448; Percy L.; M; 3; Pima; F4[sic]; S; Son; 454; Yes; Yes; AI./Id. 7089

CANNON
449; Elizabeth; F; Unk.; Pima; F; M; Wife; 455; No; Sells Ind.Agency; ~~Sells; Pima; Ariz.~~ Yes; AI. 1196/Id.

CANNON
450; Job; M; 52; Pima; F; M; Head; 456; Yes; Yes; AI. 1190/Id. 6651
451; Lydia; F; 52; Pima; F; M; Wife; 457; Yes; Yes; AI. 1191/Id. 6652
452; Isabel; F; 29; Pima; F; S; Dau.; 458; Yes; Yes; AI. 1194/Id. 6653
453; Ramon; M; 18; Pima; F4[sic]; S; Son; 459; Yes; Yes; AI. 1197/Id. 6654
454; Delmar; M; 15; Pima; F; S; Son; 460; Yes; Yes; AI. 3258/Id. 6655
455; Allen; M; 13; Pima; F; S; Son; 461; Yes; Yes; AI. 4560/Id. 6656

CANNON
456; Joe; M; 55; Pima; F; M; Head; 462; Yes; Yes; AI. 1186/Id. 6661
457; Sarah H., (Harvier, Sarah); F; 42; Pima; F; M; Wife; --; Yes; Yes; AI. 404/Id. 6662

CANNON
458; Mollie; F; 57; Pima; F; Wd.; Head; 463; Yes; Yes; AI. 4696/Id. 5654

CANNON
459; Severino; M; 32; Pima; F; M; Head; 464; Yes; Yes; AI. 4697/Id. 5665
460; Lucy Ann, (White, Lucy Ann); F; 32; Pima; F; M; Wife; 465; Yes; Yes; AI. 4410/Id. 5666
461; Mary Agnes; F; 12; Pima; F; S; Dau.; 466; Yes; Yes; AI./Id. 5667
462; Matilda; F; 11; Pima; F; S; Dau.; 467; Yes; Yes; AI./Id. 5668
463; Christina; F; 9; Pima; F; S; Dau.; 468; Yes; Yes; AI./Id. 5669
464; Benton; M; 6; Pima; F; S; Son; 469; Yes; Yes; AI./Id. 5670
465; Gabriel; M; 3; Pima; F; S; Son; 470; Yes; Yes; AI./Id. 5671
466; Harold G.; M; 2; Pima; F; S; Son; 471; Yes; Yes; AI./Id. 5782

CARD
467; Manuel; M; 53; Pima; F; M; Head; 472; Yes; Yes; AI. 2139/Id. 3120
468; Petra, (Smith, Petras[sic]); F; 44; Pima; F; M; Wife; 473; Yes; Yes; AI. 2147/Id. 3121
469; Russell; M; 15; Pima; F; S; Son; 474; Yes; Yes; AI. 3187/Id. 3122
470; Laverne; M; 10; Pima; F; S; Son; 475; Yes; Yes; AI./Id. 3123
471; Howard; M; 8; Pima; F; S; Son; 476; Yes; Yes; AI./Id. 3124

Census of the **Gila River** reservation of the **Pima Agency** jurisdiction; as of **April 1** ; 1932; taken by **A. H. Kneale** ; Superintendent.

Key: Number; Surname; Given; Sex (M/F); Age at Last Birthday; Tribe; Degree of Blood (F=Full); Marital Status; Relationship to Head of Family & Last Census No; At Jurisdiction Where Enrolled (Yes/No); (If no – Where); Ward (Yes/No); Allotment Annuity and/or Identification Numbers

CARLOS
472; Jose; M; Unk.; Papago; F; M; Head; 477; Yes; Yes; AI./Id. 6435
473; Edna S., (Scott, Edna); F; 29; Pima; F; M; Wife; 478; Yes; Yes; AI./Id. 6436

CARLOS
~~474; Rafael P.; M; 43; Papago; F; M; Head; 479; Yes; (~~Should have been omitted-N.C.); Yes; AI./Id. 4915
475; Mabel S., (Scott, Mabel); F; 33; Pima; F; M; Wife; 480; Yes; Yes; AI. 593/Id. 4916

CARLYLE
476; Anna L., (Lewis, Anna); F; 35; Pima; F; M; Wife; 481; Yes; Yes; AI. 3885/Id. 1597
477; Frances; F; 15; Pima; F; S; Dau.; 482; Yes; Yes; AI./Id. 1598
478; Lewis; Edgar R.; M; 11; Pima; F; S; St.son; 483; Yes; Yes; AI./Id. 1599
479; Christine; F; 8; Pima; F; S; Dau.; 484; Yes; Yes; AI./Id. 1600
480; Bennett; M; 7; Pima; F; S; Son; 485; Yes; Yes; AI./Id. 1601
481; Lillian; F; 4; Pima; F; S; Dau.; 486; Yes; Yes; AI./Id. 1602
482; Richard; M; 2; Pima; F; S; Son; 487; Yes; Yes; AI./Id. 2034

CARMAN
483; Jose; M; 31; Papago; F; M; Head; 488; Yes; Yes; AI./Id. 1878
484; Isabelle, (Webb, Isabelle); F; 29; Pima; F; M; Wife; 489; Yes; Yes; AI. 4090/Id. 1879
485; Edward; M; 7; Pima-Papago; F; S; Son; 490; Yes; Yes; AI./Id. 1880
486; Dorogene; F; 5; Pima-Papago; F; S; Dau.; 491; Yes; Yes; AI./Id. 1881
487; Raymond; M; 2; Pima-Papago; F; S; Son; 492; Yes; Yes; AI./Id. 1921

CASE
488; Annie; F; 62; Maricopa; F; S; Head; 493; Yes; Yes; AI. 3983/Id. 493

CASE
489; Jose; M; 56; Maricopa; F; M; Head; 494; Yes; Yes; AI. 3977/Id. 490
~~Agnes; M; F; 54; Maricopa; F; M; Wife; 495; Died 11-1-31~~; Yes; AI. 3978/Id. 491
490; Kenneth; M; 16; Maricopa; F; S; Son; 496; Yes; Yes; AI. 3982/Id. 494

CASE
491; Roy; M; 39; Maricopa; F; S; Head; 497; Yes; Yes; AI. 3979/Id. 492

CATHA
492; Jose M.; M; 32; Pima; F; Wd.; Head; 498; Yes; Yes; AI. 3596/Id. 1908
493; Alice; F; 30; Pima; F; S; Dau.[sic]; 499; Yes; Yes; AI./Id. 1909
494; Precida; F; 7; Pima; F; S; Dau.; 500; Yes; Yes; AI./Id. 1910

23

Census of the **Gila River** reservation of the **Pima Agency** jurisdiction; as of **April 1** ; 1932; taken by **A. H. Kneale** ; Superintendent.

Key: Number; Surname; Given; Sex (M/F); Age at Last Birthday; Tribe; Degree of Blood (F=Full); Marital Status; Relationship to Head of Family & Last Census No; At Jurisdiction Where Enrolled (Yes/No); (If no – Where); Ward (Yes/No); Allotment Annuity and/or Identification Numbers

CATHA
495; Lucille; F; 57; Pima; F; Wd.; Head; 501; Yes; Yes; AI. 3595/Id. 1435

CAVE
496; Jose; M; 87; Pima; F; M; Head; 502; Yes; Yes; AI. 3576/Id. 1282
497; Annily; F; 87; Pima; F; M; Wife; 503; Yes; Yes; AI. 3577/Id. 1283

CAWKER
498; Havier; M; 51; Pima; F; M; Head; 504; Yes; Yes; AI. 256/Id. 4801
499; Seipe; F; 51; Pima; F; M; Wife; 505; Yes; Yes; AI. 252/Id. 4802
500; Allen; M; 24; Pima; F; S; Son; 506; Yes; Yes; AI. 3945/Id. 4803
501; Herbert; M; 20; Pima; F; S; Son; 507; Yes; Yes; AI. 255/Id. 4804
502; Gertrude; F; 19; Pima; F; S; Dau.; 508; Yes; Yes; AI. 254/Id. 4805
503; Mary; F; 18; Pima; F; S; Dau.; 509; Yes; Yes; AI. 253/Id. 4806
504; Raymond; M; 17; Pima; F; S; Son; 510; Yes; Yes; AI. 3199/Id. 4807
505; Mabel G.; F; 16; Pima; F; S; Dau.; 511; Yes; Yes; AI. 3469/Id. 4808

CEPRIANO
506; Petra; F; 67; Pima; F; Wd.; Head; 512; Yes; Yes; AI. 285/Id. 5131

CHAPPO
507; -; M; 71; Maricopa; F; M; Head; 513; Yes; Yes; AI. 2817/Id. 193
508; Lucy; F; 71; Maricopa; F; M; Wife; 514; Yes; Yes; AI. 2855/Id. 194

CHAPPO
509; Juan; M; 57; Pima; F; Wd.; Head; 515; Yes; Yes; AI. 2105/Id. 3308

CHAPPO
510; Lottie; F; 55; Pima; F; S; Head; 516; Yes; Yes; AI. 2321/Id. 3509

CHARLES
511; Lewis; M; 38; Pima; F5[sic]; M; Head; 517; Yes; Yes; AI. 2564/Id. 5162
512; Clara Hall, (Marcus, Clara); F; 30; Pima; F; M; Wife; 518; Yes; Yes; AI. 767/Id. 5163
513; Hilda; F; 7; Pima; F; S; Dau.; 519; Yes; Yes; AI./Id. 5164

CHARLEY
514; John; M; 55; Pima; F; Wd.; Head; 520; Yes; Yes; AI. 4267/Id. 1619
515; Josiah; M; 32; Pima; F; S; Son; 521; Yes; Yes; AI. 4268/Id. 1620
516; Bessie; F; 22; Pima; F; S; Dau.; 522; Yes; Yes; AI. 4269/Id. 1621

CHEENO
517; -; M; 61; Pima; F; M; Head; 523; Yes; Yes; AI. 4364/Id. 1911
518; Cathrine; F; 53; Pima; F; M; Wife; 524; Yes; Yes; AI. 4365/Id. 1912

Census of the **Gila River** reservation of the **Pima Agency** jurisdiction; as of **April 1** ; 1932; taken by **A. H. Kneale** ; Superintendent.

Key: Number; Surname; Given; Sex (M/F); Age at Last Birthday; Tribe; Degree of Blood (F=Full); Marital Status; Relationship to Head of Family & Last Census No; At Jurisdiction Where Enrolled (Yes/No); (If no – Where); Ward (Yes/No); Allotment Annuity and/or Identification Numbers

CHEENO
519; Vincent; M; 39; Pima; F; S; Head; 525; Yes; Yes; AI. 4366/Id. 1913

CHEERLESS
520; Bernie; M; 22; Pima; F; S; Head; 526; Yes; Yes; AI. S.R.146/Id. 5805
521; Lola; F; 23; Pima; F; S; Sis.; 527; Yes; Yes; AI. S.R.145/Id. 5806

CHIAGO
522; Christopher; M; 52; Pima; F; Wd.; Head; 528; Yes; Yes; AI. 4143/Id. 1725

CHIAGO
523; Eloise; F; 40; Pima; F; Wd.; Head; 529; Yes; Yes; AI./Id. 1914
524; Eloise; F; 17; Pima; F; S; Dau.; 530; Yes; Yes; AI./Id. 1915
525; Johnnie; M; 15; Pima; F; S; Son; 531; Yes; Yes; AI./Id. 1916
526; Corinne; F; 11; Pima; F; S; Dau.; 532; Yes; Yes; AI./Id. 1917
527; Jackson; M; 7; Pima; F; S; Son; 533; Yes; Yes; AI./Id. 1918

CHIAGO
528; Henry; M; 57; Pima; F; M; Head; 534; Yes; Yes; AI. 3574/Id. 1268
529; Marie J., (Juanna, Maria); F; 47; Pima; F; M; Wife; 535; Yes; Yes; AI. 3575/Id. 1269

CHIAGO
530; Jacob; M; 57; Pima; F; M; Head; 536; Yes; Yes; AI. 4158/Id. 1230
531; Eva; F; 57; Pima; F; M; Wife; 537; Yes; Yes; AI. 4159/Id. 1231

CHIAGO
532; James; M; 59; Pima; F; M; Head; 538; Yes; Yes; AI. 3401/Id. 1919
533; Benito; M; 34; Pima; F; S; Son; 539; Yes; Yes; AI. 3403/Id. 1334

CHIAGO
534; Juan; M; 51; Pima; F; M; Head; 540; Yes; Yes; AI. 4274/Id. 1332
535; Rosa, (Rose); F; 51; Pima; F; M; Wife; 541; Yes; Yes; AI. 4275/Id. 1333

CHIAGO
536; Juan E.; M; 77; Pima; F; Wd.; Head; 542; Yes; Yes; AI. 3403/Id. 1424
537; Irene; F; 19; Pima; F; S; Dau.; 544; Yes; Yes; AI./Id. 1697
538; Justin; M; 15; Pima; F; S; Son; 545; Yes; Yes; AI./Id. 1698
539; Pauline; F; 13; Pima; F; S; Dau.; 546; Yes; Yes; AI./Id. 1699
540; Florence; F; 3; Pima; F; S; Dau.; 547; Yes; Yes; AI./Id. 1620

CHIAGO
541; Stanley; M; 23; Pima; F; M; Head; 543; Yes; Yes; AI./Id. 1696
~~Esther; F; 21; Unk.; F; M; Wife; --; Died 2-13-32.~~; Yes; AI. unk./Id.
542; Stanley, Jr.; M; 3/12; Pima; F; S; Son; --; Born 1-7-32.; Yes; AI./Id. 2048

Census of the **Gila River** reservation of the **Pima Agency** jurisdiction; as of **April 1** ; 1932; taken by **A. H. Kneale** ; Superintendent.

Key: Number; Surname; Given; Sex (M/F); Age at Last Birthday; Tribe; Degree of Blood (F=Full); Marital Status; Relationship to Head of Family & Last Census No; At Jurisdiction Where Enrolled (Yes/No); (If no – Where); Ward (Yes/No); Allotment Annuity and/or Identification Numbers

CHOPIN
543; Juan; M; 55; Pima; F; M; Head; 552; Yes; Yes; AI. 552/Id. 5462
544; Adelina T., (Thomas, Adelina); F; 51; Pima; F; M; Wife; 553; Yes; Yes; AI. 331/Id. 5463

CIGLAR
545; Peter; M; 57; Pima; F; Wd.; Head; 554; Yes; Yes; AI. 1843/Id. 5807
546; Henry; M; 23; Pima; F; S; Son; 555; Yes; Yes; AI. 2438/Id. 5808
547; Eugene; M; 21; Pima; F; S; Son; 556; Yes; Yes; AI. 2439/Id. 5809

CLARK
548; Catherine, (Emerson, Catherine); F; 38; Pima; F; M; Wife; 557; Yes; Yes; AI. 2165/Id.

COLLINS
549; Henry; M; 64; Maricopa; F; M; Head; 558; Yes; Yes; AI. 2945/Id. 48
550; Mary; F; 54; Maricopa; F; M; Wife; 559; Yes; Yes; AI. 2953/Id. 49
551; Howard; M; 35; Maricopa; F; S; Son; 560; Yes; Yes; AI. 2948/Id. 50
552; Benjamin; M; 21; Maricopa; F; S; Son; 561; Yes; Yes; AI. 2946/Id. 51
553; Nina; F; 18; Maricopa; F; S; Dau.; 562; Yes; Yes; AI. 2947/Id. 52

COLT
554; Lewis; M; 50; Maricopa; F; M; Head; 563; Yes; Yes; AI. 2724/Id. 117
555; Maggie; F; 42; Maricopa; F; M; Wife; 564; Yes; Yes; AI. 2725/Id. 118
556; Achsah; F; 24; Maricopa; F; S; Dau.; 565; Yes; Yes; AI. 2726/Id. 119
557; Polly A.; F; 20; Maricopa; F; S; Dau.; 566; Yes; Yes; AI. 2728/Id. 120
558; Zipporah; F; 16; Maricopa; F; S; Dau.; 567; Yes; Yes; AI. 4672/Id. 121
559; Naomi; F; 14; Maricopa; F; S; Dau.; 568; Yes; Yes; AI. 4673/Id. 122

COLT
560; Robert; M; 57; Maricopa; F; M; Head; 569; Yes; Yes; AI. 2692/Id. 112
561; Alice; F; 49; Maricopa; F; M; Wife; 570; Yes; Yes; AI. 2693/Id. 113
562; Robert L.; M; 20; Maricopa; F; S; Son; 571; Yes; Yes; AI. 2695/Id. 114
563; Irene; F; 19; Maricopa; F; S; Dau.; 572; Yes; Yes; AI. 2696/Id. 115
564; Nicodemus; M; 7; Maricopa; F; S; Son; 573; Yes; Yes; AI./Id. 116

CONSAILI
565; Consai; F; 54; Pima; F; Wd.; Head; 574; Yes; Yes; AI./Id. 5437

COOK
566; David; M; 42; Pima; F; M; Head; 575; Yes; Yes; AI. 794/Id. 4280
567; Emma W., (Whittaker, Emma); F; 38; Pima; F; M; Wife; 576; Yes; Yes; AI. 4281/Id. 2193
568; Wilbur M.; M; 12; Pima; F; S; Son; 577; Yes; Yes; AI. 2434/Id. 4282
569; Marwin F.; M; 9; Pima; F; S; Son; 578; Yes; Yes; AI./Id. 4283

Census of the **Gila River** reservation of the **Pima Agency** jurisdiction; as of **April 1** ; 1932; taken by **A. H. Kneale** ; Superintendent.

Key: Number; Surname; Given; Sex (M/F); Age at Last Birthday; Tribe; Degree of Blood (F=Full); Marital Status; Relationship to Head of Family & Last Census No; At Jurisdiction Where Enrolled (Yes/No); (If no – Where); Ward (Yes/No); Allotment Annuity and/or Identification Numbers

570; Delma H.; F; 4; Pima; F; S; Dau.; 579; Yes; Yes; AI./Id. 4284
571; Elinor; F; 3; Pima; F; S; Dau.; 580; Yes; Yes; AI./Id. 4285

COOK
572; Enos; M; 45; Pima; F; M; Head; 581; Yes; Yes; AI. 6545/Id. 1283
573; Emily; F; 43; Pima; F; M; Wife; 582; Yes; Yes; AI. 1284/Id. 6546
574; Frances; M; 18; Pima; F; S; Son; 583; Yes; Yes; AI. 1286/Id. 6547

COOK
575; Frank; M; 63; Pima; F; M; Head; 584; Yes; Yes; AI. 1277/Id. 6541
576; Alice; F; 57; Pima; F; M; Wife; 585; Yes; Yes; AI. 1278/Id. 6542

COOK
577; Luke; M; 37; Pima; F; M; Head; 586; Yes; Yes; AI. 1280/Id. 6543
578; Josephine; F; 16; Pima; F; S; Dau.; 587; Yes; Yes; AI. 2961/Id. 4657

COOK
579; Mollie; F; 84; Pima; F; Wd.; Head; 588; Yes; Yes; AI. 168/Id. 5461

COOK
580; Savie; F; 83; Pima; F; Wd.; Head; 589; Yes; Yes; AI. 1287/Id. 7090

COOLY
581; Walter; M; 23; Pima; F; S; Head; 590; Yes; Yes; AI. 3261/Id. 5814

COOPER
582; Harry; M; 35; Pima; F; M; Head; 591; Yes; Yes; AI. 186/Id. 5815
~~Mollie Leon; F; Unk.; Pima; F; M; Wife; --; Yes; (S.R.Allottee)~~ Yes; AI./Id.
583; Bernard; M; 16; Pima; F; S; Son; 592; Yes; Yes; AI./Id. 5817
584; Edwin; M; 14; Pima; F; S; Son; 593; Yes; Yes; AI./Id. 5818
585; Henry; M; 9; Pima; F; S; Son; 594; Yes; Yes; AI./Id. 5819
586; Melinda; F; 6; Pima; F; S; Dau.; 595; Yes; Yes; AI./Id. 5820
587; Arnold; M; 4; Pima; F; S; Son; 596; Yes; Yes; AI./Id. 5821
588; Margaret Mary; F; 4/12; Pima; F; S; Dau.; --; Born 11-26-31.; Yes; AI./Id. 6124

COOPER
589; Leonard R.; M; 26; Pima; F; S; Head; 597; Yes; Yes; AI. 189/Id. 4968
590; Sophia; F; 25; Pima; F; S; Sis.; --; Yes; Yes; AI. 190/Id. 4969

COOPER
591; Willie; M; 28; Pima; F; S; Head; 598; Yes; Yes; AI. 188/Id. 4967

COOPS
592; Sarah; F; 42; Pima; F; Wd.; Head; 599; Yes; Yes; AI. 572/Id. 5048
593; Santo, Felix; M; 21; Pima; F; S; Son; 600; Yes; Yes; AI. 574/Id. 5057

Census of the **Gila River** reservation of the **Pima Agency** jurisdiction; as of **April 1** ; 1932; taken by **A. H. Kneale** ; Superintendent.

Key: Number; Surname; Given; Sex (M/F); Age at Last Birthday; Tribe; Degree of Blood (F=Full); Marital Status; Relationship to Head of Family & Last Census No; At Jurisdiction Where Enrolled (Yes/No); (If no – Where); Ward (Yes/No); Allotment Annuity and/or Identification Numbers

COOPS

594; Vincent; M; 23; Pima; F; M; Head; 601; Yes; Yes; AI. 573/Id. 5034
595; Louise, (Wilson, Loise[sic]); F; 26; Pima; F; M; Wife; 602; Yes; Yes; AI. 3377/Id. 5055

COUGH

596; Grace S., (Stewart, Grace); F; 38; Maricopa; F; M; Wife; 603; No; Unk; Unk:; Unk; Unk; Yes; AI. 2908/Id. 182
597; Hollie M.; M; 5; Maricopa; Unk.; S; Son; 604; No; Unk; Unk; Yes; AI./Id. 183

CRAWFORD

598; Charles; M; 26; Pima; F; M; Head; 605; Yes; Yes; AI. 3135/Id. 3154
599; Nannie; F; 22; Pima; F; M; Wife; 606; Yes; Yes; AI./Id. 3156

CRAWFORD

600; Coe E.; M; 51; Pima; F; M; Head; 607; Yes; Yes; AI. 3133/Id. 3373
601; Emma; F; 51; Pima; F; M; Wife; 608; Yes; Yes; AI. 3134/Id. 3374

CROSS

602; William; M; 53; Pima; F; M; Head; 609; Yes; Yes; AI. 1105/Id. 6763
603; Irene; F; 23; Pima; F; S; Dau.; 610; Yes; Yes; AI. 1092/Id. 6765
604; Nelson; M; 18; Pima; F; S; Son; 611; Yes; Yes; AI. 1107/Id. 6766
605; Nellie; F; 16; Pima; F; S; Dau.; 612; Yes; Yes; AI. 3171/Id. 6767
606; Vana; F; 14; Pima; F; S; Dau.; 613; Yes; Yes; AI. 4363/Id. 6768
607; Carlile; F; 12; Pima; F; S; Dau.; 614; Yes; Yes; AI. 4395/Id. 6769
608; Nancy; F; 10; Pima; F; S; Dau.; 615; Yes; Yes; AI./Id. 6770
609; Myrtle; F; 5; Pima; F; S; Dau.; 616; Yes; Yes; AI./Id. 6771

CROSS

610; Alice; F; 37; Pima; F; M; Wife; 617; Yes; Yes; AI. 1106/Id. 6764

CROUSE

611; John; M; 63; Pima; F; M; Head; 618; Yes; Yes; AI. 1160/Id. 6940
612; Mary; F; 66; Pima; F; M; Wife; 619; Yes; Yes; AI. 1161/Id. 6941

CRUZ

613; Juan; M; 79; Pima; F; M; Head; 620; Yes; Yes; AI. 2108/Id. 3386
614; Maria; F; 79; Pima; F; M; Wife; 621; Yes; Yes; AI. 2109/Id. 3387

CRUZ

615; Juan; M; 57; Pima; F; Wd.; Head; 622; Yes; Yes; AI. 4548/Id. 7091

CUMHAYIA

616; Elizabeth; F; 27; Maricopa; F; S; Head; 623; No; Buckeye Maricopa Ariz.; Yes; AI. 2823/Id. 158

Census of the **Gila River** reservation of the **Pima Agency** jurisdiction; as of **April 1** ; 1932; taken by **A. H. Kneale** ; Superintendent.

Key: Number; Surname; Given; Sex (M/F); Age at Last Birthday; Tribe; Degree of Blood (F=Full); Marital Status; Relationship to Head of Family & Last Census No; At Jurisdiction Where Enrolled (Yes/No); (If no – Where); Ward (Yes/No); Allotment Annuity and/or Identification Numbers

CUMHAYIA

617; Elmer; M; 55; Maricopa; F; M; Head; 624; Yes; Yes; AI. 2818/Id. 156
618; Pahket; F; 57; Maricopa; F; M; Wife; 625; Yes; Yes; AI. 2819/Id. 157
619; Annie; F; 21; Maricopa; F; S; Dau.; 626; Yes; Yes; AI. 2824/Id. 160
620; Spangle; M; 12; Maricopa; F4[sic]; S; Son; 627; Yes; Yes; AI. 4745/Id. 161
621; John; M; 5/12; Maricopa; F; S; Gr.son; --; Born 11-23-31; Yes; AI./Id. 609

CUMHAYIA

622; Emily; F; 24; Maricopa; F; S; Head; 628; No; Buckeye Maricopa Ariz.; Yes; AI. 2822/Id. 159
623; Curran; Isabelle; F; 17; Pima; F; S; Dau.; 629; No; On Yuma Roll; ~~Yuma Imperial Cal.~~;Yes; AI. 1490/Id. 5288
624; Curran; Oliver; M; 14; Pima; F; S; Son; 630; No; On Yuma Roll; ~~Yuma Imperial Cal.~~;Yes; AI. 4546/Id. 5823
625; Curran; Luther; M; 12; Pima; F; S; Son; 631; No; On Yuma Roll; ~~Yuma Imperial Cal.~~;Yes; AI. 4801/Id. 5824

CYRUS

626; Henry; M; 52; Pima; F; M; Head; 632; Yes; Yes; AI. 1306/Id. 6491
627; Blanch; F; 50; Pima; F; M; Wife; 633; Yes; Yes; AI. 1307/Id. 6492
628; Stephen; M; 21; Pima; F; S; Son; 634; Yes; Yes; AI. 1309/Id. 6493

CYRUS

629; Nat.; M; 53; Pima; F; M; Head; 635; Yes; Yes; AI. 1206/Id. 6464
630; Velma; F; 10; Pima; F; S; Dau.; 636; Yes; Yes; AI./Id. 6466
631; Norma; F; 5; Pima; F; S; Dau.; 637; Yes; Yes; AI./Id. 6468
632; Dorothy; F; 8; Pima; F; S; Dau.; 638; Yes; Yes; AI./Id. 6467
633; Nelson; Antonio C.; M; 6; Pima; F; S; St.son; 639; Yes; Yes; AI./Id. 4991

DAVID

634; Gregory; M; 34; Maricopa; F; S; Head; 640; Yes; Yes; AI. 4169/Id. 567

DAVIS

635; Charley; M; 35; Pima; F; M; Head; 641; Yes; Yes; AI. 1117/Id. 4730
636; Lily; F; 32; Pima; F; M; Wife; 642; Yes; Yes; AI. 1944/Id. 4731

DAVIS

637; Jefferson; M; 26; Pima; F; S; Head; 643; Yes; Yes; AI. 1992/Id. 1203

DAVIS

638; John; M; 45; Pima; F; M; Head; 644; Yes; Yes; AI. 1989/Id. 1201
639; Lizzie; F; 46; Pima; F; M; Wife; 645; Yes; Yes; AI. 1990/Id. 1202
640; Myra; F; 13; Pima; F; S; Dau.; 646; Yes; Yes; AI. 4846/Id. 1206
641; Violet; F; 12; Pima; F; S; Dau.; 647; Yes; Yes; AI./Id. 1205
642; Sarah; F; 11; Pima; F; S; Dau.; 648; Yes; Yes; AI./Id. 1207

Key: Number; Surname; Given; Sex (M/F); Age at Last Birthday; Tribe; Degree of Blood (F=Full); Marital Status; Relationship to Head of Family & Last Census No; At Jurisdiction Where Enrolled (Yes/No); (If no – Where); Ward (Yes/No); Allotment Annuity and/or Identification Numbers

643; Jean; F; 8; Pima; F; S; Dau.; 649; Yes; Yes; AI./Id. 1208
644; Flora; F; 6; Pima; F; S; Dau.; 650; Yes; Yes; AI./Id. 1209
645; Marie; F; 3; Pima; F; S; Dau.; 651; Yes; Yes; AI./Id. 1210

DAVIS
646; Joseph; M; 62; Pima; F; M; Head; 652; Yes; Yes; AI. 1684/Id. 4344
647; Lily; F; 57; Pima; F; M; Wife; 653; Yes; Yes; AI. 1121/Id. 4441
648; Milda; F; 28; Pima; F; S; Dau.; 654; Yes; Yes; AI. 1121/Id. 4441
649; Leonora; F; 4; Pima; F; S; Gr.dau.; 655; Yes; Yes; AI./Id. 4442

DAVIS
650; Miles; M; 32; Pima; F; Wd.; Head; 656; Yes; Yes; AI. 1119/Id. 8941

DAVIS
651; Paul; M; 67; Pima; F; Wd.; Head; 657; Yes; Yes; AI. 198/Id. 5625

DAYMOND
652; Marie, (Jones, Marie); F; 25; Pima; F; M; Wife; 658; Yes; Yes; AI. 151/Id. 5410
653; Marie G.; F; 4; Pima; F; S; Dau.; 659; Yes; Yes; AI./Id. 5411
654; Lucille; F; 2; Pima; F; S; Dau.; 660; Yes; Yes; AI./Id. 6108

DELOW
655; Amos; M; 39; Pima; F; Wd.; Head; 661; Yes; Yes; AI. 4315/Id. 1922
656; Perry; M; 12; Pima; F; S; Son; 662; Yes; Yes; AI./Id. 1478
657; Viola; F; 9; Pima; F; S; Dau.; 663; Yes; Yes; AI./Id. 1479

DELOW
658; John; M; 42; Pima; F; M; Head; 664; Yes; Yes; AI. 4314/Id. 1477
659; ----; F; 2; Pima; F; S; Dau.; 665; Yes; Yes; AI./Id. 2039

DERREL
660; Charles; M; 46; Pima; F; M; Head; 666; Yes; Yes; AI. 225/Id. 5208
661; Susie; F; 42; Pima; F; M; Wife; 667; Yes; Yes; AI. 226/Id. 5209

DICKENS
662; Effie N., (Nelson, Effie); F; 24; Pima; F; M; Wife; 668; Yes; Yes; AI. 1258/Id. 6455

DIXON
663; Charles; M; 42; Pima; F; M; Head; 669; Yes; Yes; AI. 3305/Id. 1589
664; Narcia; F; 42; Pima; F; M; Wife; 670; Yes; Yes; AI. 3306/Id. 1590
665; Ralph; M; 14; Pima; F; S; Son; 671; Yes; Yes; AI. 3654/Id. 1591
666; Michael; M; 12; Pima; F; S; Son; 672; Yes; Yes; AI./Id. 1593
667; Jonah; M; 10; Pima; F; S; Son; 673; Yes; Yes; AI./Id. 1592
668; Roger; M; 16; Pima; F; S; Son; 674; Yes; Yes; AI./Id. 1594

669; Claudine; F; 5; Pima; F; S; Dau.; 675; Yes; Yes; AI./Id. 1595

DIXON
670; Elmer; M; 66; Pima; F; Wd.; Head; 676; Yes; Yes; AI. 3655/Id. 1545

DIXON
671; Eliza; F; 70; Pima; F; Wd.; Head; 677; Yes; Yes; AI. 2571/Id. 6836

DODGE
672; William; M; 68; Pima; F; Wd.; Head; 678; Yes; Yes; AI. 3903/Id. 1877

DOLORES
673; Mollie; F; 24; Papago; F; S; Head; 679; Yes; Yes; AI./Id. 7063
674; Lloyd; M; 3; Papago; F; S; Son; 680; Yes; Yes; AI./Id. 7064

DOMINGO
675; ----; M; 52; Pima; F; Wd.; Head; 681; Yes; Yes; AI./Id. 1738

DOMINGO
676; ----; M; 66; Pima; F; M; Head; 682; Yes; Yes; AI. 2999/Id. 3164
677; Josephine; F; 67; Pima; F; M; Wife; 683; Yes; Yes; AI. 3000/Id. 3165

DOMINGO
678; Leonard; M; 29; Pima; F; M; Head; 684; Yes; Yes; AI. 1711/Id. 4214
679; Mollie A., (Card, Mollianna); F; 28; Pima; F; M; Wife; 685; Yes; Yes; AI. 2140/Id. 1712
680; Mary C.; F; 6; Pima; F; S; Dau.; 686; Yes; Yes; AI./Id. 1713
681; Bernice L.; F; 4; Pima; F; S; Dau.; 687; Yes; Yes; AI./Id. 1714

DOMINGO
682; Michael; M; 57; Pima; F; M; Head; 688; Yes; Yes; AI. 4210/Id. 1715
683; Juana, (Juna); F; 50; Pima; F; M; Wife; 689; Yes; Yes; AI. 4211/Id. 1716
684; Margaretta; F; 13; Pima; F; S; Dau.; 690; Yes; Yes; AI. 4831/Id. 1717

DONOHUE
685; Jasper; M; 24; Pima; 1/4x; M; Head; 691; Yes; Yes; AI. 2740/Id. 234
686; (Elsie Lewis Smith); F; 18; Pima; F; M; Wife; 2188; Yes; Yes; AI. 3176/Id. 6887
687; Dorine; F; 6; Pima; 1/4x; S; Dau.; 692; Yes; Yes; AI./Id. 235
688; Byron; M; 3; Pima; 1/4x; S; Son; 693; Yes; Yes; AI./Id. 236
689; Bruce D.; M; 2; Pima; 1/4x; S; Son; 694; Yes; Yes; AI./Id. 593
690; Clarice Fidella; F; 1/12; Pima; 1/4x; S; Dau.; --; Born 2-21-32; Yes; AI./Id. 613

DONOHUE
691; Lillian; F; 46; Maricopa; F; Wd.; Head; 695; Yes; Yes; AI. 2739/Id. 237

Census of the **Gila River** reservation of the **Pima Agency** jurisdiction; as of **April 1** ; 1932; taken by **A. H. Kneale** ; Superintendent.

Key: Number; Surname; Given; Sex (M/F); Age at Last Birthday; Tribe; Degree of Blood (F=Full); Marital Status; Relationship to Head of Family & Last Census No; At Jurisdiction Where Enrolled (Yes/No); (If no – Where); Ward (Yes/No); Allotment Annuity and/or Identification Numbers

692; Beulah; F; 22; Maricopa; 1/4x; S; Dau.; --; Yes; Inadvertedly[sic] left off 1931 census.; Yes; AI. 2741/Id. 238

693; Gladys; F; 21; Maricopa; 1/4x; S; Dau.; 696; Yes; Yes; AI. 2742/Id. 239

694; George; M; 18; Maricopa; 1/4x; S; Son; 697; Yes; Yes; AI. 2743/Id. 240

695; Frank; M; 16; Maricopa; 1/4x; S; Son; 698; Yes; Yes; AI. 2744/Id. 241

696; Louise; F; 15; Maricopa; 1/4x; S; Dau.; 699; Yes; Yes; AI. 4652/Id. 242

697; Norma; F; 13; Maricopa; 1/4x; S; Dau.; 700; Yes; Yes; AI. 4653/Id. 243

698; Virginia; F; 12; Maricopa; 1/4x; S; Dau.; 701; Yes; Yes; AI./Id. 245

699; Helen; F; 11; Maricopa; 1/4x; S; Dau.; 702; Yes; Yes; AI./Id. 246

700; Lila; F; 3; Maricopa; 1/4x; S; Dau.; 703; Yes; Yes; AI./Id. 247

EARLE
701; Elizabeth, (Paul, Elizabeth); F; 23; Pima; F; M; Wife; 704; Yes; Yes; AI. 31/Id. 5825

EATON
~~Adam; M; 79; Pima; F; Wd.; Head; 705; Died~~ 1-6-32; Yes; AI. 277/Id. 5327

EATON
702; Elizabeth; F; 77; Pima; F; Wd.; Head; 706; Yes; Yes; AI. 379/Id. 5826

ELDRIDGE
703; Emily M., (Miles, Emily); F; 30; Pima; F; M; Wife; 707; Yes; Yes; AI. 584/Id. 5927

704; Mary F.; F; 9; Pima; F; S; Dau.; 708; Yes; Yes; AI./Id. 5828

ELIAS
705; Elsie T.; F; 46; Pima; F; Wd.; Head; 709; Yes; Yes; AI. 3571/Id. 1271

706; Edward; M; 20; Pima; F; S; Son; 710; Yes; Yes; AI. 3572/Id. 1272

707; Rebecca; F; 17; Pima; F; S; Dau.; 711; Yes; Yes; AI. 3573/Id. 1273

708; Lazzero; M; 14; Pima; F; S; Son; 712; Yes; Yes; AI. 3964/Id. 1274

709; Josephine; F; 10; Pima; F; S; Dau.; 713; Yes; Yes; AI./Id. 1275

710; Leo Paul; M; 9; Pima; F; S; Son; 714; Yes; Yes; AI./Id. 1276

ELLIS
711; Benjamin; M; 33; Pima; F; M; Head; 715; No; Unk.; Unk.; Unk.; Okla.; Yes; AI. 3075/Id. 3337

ELLIS
712; George; M; 56; Pima; F; S; Head; 716; Yes; Yes; AI. 3033/Id. 3288

ELLIS
~~713; Minnie; F; 88[?]; Pima; F; Wd.; Head; 717; Died 2-27-32 and inadvertedly[sic] left off 1931 Census~~; (N.E. Should have been Omitted); Yes; AI. 3034/Id. 3289

Census of the **Gila River** reservation of the **Pima Agency** jurisdiction; as of **April 1** ; 1932; taken by **A. H. Kneale** ; Superintendent.

Key: Number; Surname; Given; Sex (M/F); Age at Last Birthday; Tribe; Degree of Blood (F=Full); Marital Status; Relationship to Head of Family & Last Census No; At Jurisdiction Where Enrolled (Yes/No); (If no – Where); Ward (Yes/No); Allotment Annuity and/or Identification Numbers

ELLIS

714; James K.; M; 61; Pima; F; M; Head; 717; Yes; Yes; AI. 3052/Id. 3328
715; Carrie; F; 51; Pima; F; M; Wife; 718; Yes; Yes; AI. 3053/Id. 3329
716; Julian; M; 27; Pima; F; S; Son; 719; Yes; Yes; AI. 3076/Id. 3330
717; Olive; F; 25; Pima; F; S; Dau.; 720; Yes; Yes; AI. 3077/Id. 3331
718; Alice C.; F; 2; Pima; F; S; Dau.; 721; Yes; Yes; AI./Id. 3596
719; Bernice; F; 6; Pima; F; S; Gr.dau.; 722; Yes; Yes; AI./Id. 3335
720; Herman; M; 15; Pima; F; S; Son; 723; Yes; Yes; AI. 4873/Id. 3332
721; Fletcher; M; 12; Pima; F; S; Son; 724; Yes; Yes; AI./Id. 3333
722; Samuel; M; 9; Pima; F; S; Son; 725; Yes; Yes; AI./Id. 3334

ELLIS

723; Samuel; M; 87; Pima; F; Wd.; Head; 726; Yes; Yes; AI. 3034/Id. 3289

ELLIS

724; Reuben; M; 47; Pima; F; M; Head; 727; Yes; Yes; AI. 1956/Id. 4348
725; Emma; F; 47; Pima; F; M; Wife; 728; Yes; Yes; AI. 1957/Id. 4349
726; Herman; M; 21; Pima; F; S; Son; 729; Yes; Yes; AI. 1960/Id. 4350

ELSMERE

727; David; M; 35; Pima; F; M; Head; 730; Yes; Yes; AI. 2168/Id. 3101
728; Leta, (Barnago, Leta); F; 27; Pima; F; M; Wife; 731; Yes; Yes; AI. 3925/Id. 3102
729; Alphonso; M; 8; Pima; F; S; Son; 732; Yes; Yes; AI./Id. 3103

ELSMERE

730; Jennie; F; 51; Pima; F; S; Head; 733; Yes; Yes; AI. 2169/Id. 3104

EMERSON

731; Lucy N., (Nelson, Lucy); F; 47; Pima; F; S; Head; 734; Yes; Yes; AI. 2293/Id. 3359

EMERSON

732; Carl; M; 57; Pima; F; M; Head; 735; Yes; Yes; AI. 474/Id. 5107
733; Mollie; F; 42; Pima; F; M; Wife; 736; Yes; Yes; AI. 475/Id. 5108
734; Edith; F; 23; Pima; F; S; Dau.; 737; Yes; Yes; AI. 848/Id. 5109
735; Herbert; M; 20; Pima; F; S; Son; 738; Yes; Yes; AI. 849/Id. 5110
736; Elmer; M; 18; Pima; F; S; Son; 739; Yes; Yes; AI. 850/Id. 5111
737; Mildred; F; 16; Pima; F; S; Dau.; 740; Yes; Yes; AI. 3433/Id. 5112
738; Leo; M; 15; Pima; F; S; Son; 741; Yes; Yes; AI. 3434/Id. 5113
739; Adolph; M; 10; Pima; F; S; Son; 742; Yes; Yes; AI./Id. 5114
740; Levi; M; 9; Pima; F; S; Son; 743; Yes; Yes; AI./Id. 5115

EMERSON

Hazel W.; F; 28; Pima; F; Wd.; Head; 744; Died. 9-15-31.; Yes; AI. 1525/Id. 7092

741; Euretta; F; 6; Pima; F; S; Orp.; 745; Yes; Yes; AI./Id. 7093
742; Randall; M; 4; Pima; F; S; Orp.; 746; Yes; Yes; AI./Id. 7094

EMERSON
743; Juan T.; M; 32; Pima; F; S; Head; 747; Yes; Yes; AI. 473/Id. 5829

EMERSON
744; Sarah; F; 67; Pima; F; Wd.; Head; 748; Yes; Yes; AI. 2164/Id. 3015

EMERSON
745; William; M; 48; Pima; F; M; Head; 749; Yes; Yes; AI. 2343/Id. 1551
746; Lottie; F; 42; Pima; F; M; Wife; 750; Yes; Yes; AI. 4025/Id. 1552

ENARCIA
747; Johnson; M; 38; Pima; F; M; Head; 751; Yes; Yes; AI. 335/Id. 1238
748; Lottie; F; 42; Pima; F; M; Wife; 752; Yes; Yes; AI. 4025/Id. 1552
749; Ina; F; 19; Pima; F; S; Dau.; 753; Yes; Yes; AI. 4518/Id. 1240
750; Flora; F; 15; Pima; F; S; Dau.; 754; Yes; Yes; AI. 4519/Id. 1241
751; Bernice; F; 14; Pima; F; S; Dau.; 755; Yes; Yes; AI./Id. 1242
752; Theodore; M; 12; Pima; F; S; Son; 756; Yes; Yes; AI./Id. 1243
753; Harold; M; 9; Pima; F; S; Son; 757; Yes; Yes; AI./Id. 1244
754; Adeline; F; 8; Pima; F; S; Dau.; 758; Yes; Yes; AI./Id. 1245
755; Willard; M; 5; Pima; F; S; Son; 759; Yes; Yes; AI./Id. 1246

ENARCIA
756; Joseph; M; 32; Pima; F; S; Head; 760; Yes; Yes; AI. 341/Id. 5216

ENAS
757; Carroll; M; 30; Pima; F; Wd.; Head; 761; Yes; Yes; AI. 3050/Id. 1615

ENAS
758; Harvey; M; 61; Pima; F; Wd.; Head; 762; Yes; Yes; AI. 3694/Id. 1612

ENAS
759; Harvier; M; 77; Pima; F; M; Head; 763; Yes; Yes; AI./Id. 1397
760; Agnes; F; 73; Pima; F; M; Wife; 764; Yes; Yes; AI./Id. 1398

ENAS
761; Henry W.; M; 41; Pima; F; M; Head; 765; Yes; Yes; AI. 2998/Id. 3365
762; Norma; F; 7; Pima; F; S; Dau.; 766; Yes; Yes; AI./Id. 3367

ENAS
763; James; M; 52; Pima; F; M; Head; 767; Yes; Yes; AI. 3047/Id. 3375
764; Helen S., (Smith, Helen); F; 29; Maricopa; F; M; Wife; 768; Yes; Yes;
AI. 2928/Id. 3376

Census of the **Gila River** reservation of the **Pima Agency** jurisdiction; as of **April 1** ; 1932; taken by **A. H. Kneale** ; Superintendent.

Key: Number; Surname; Given; Sex (M/F); Age at Last Birthday; Tribe; Degree of Blood (F=Full); Marital Status; Relationship to Head of Family & Last Census No; At Jurisdiction Where Enrolled (Yes/No); (If no – Where); Ward (Yes/No); Allotment Annuity and/or Identification Numbers

765; Elsie; F; 10; Pima-Mar.; F; S; Dau.; 769; Yes; Yes; AI./Id. 3377
766; Hilda; F; 7; Pima-Mar.; F; S; Dau.; 770; Yes; Yes; AI./Id. 3378
767; Priscilla; F; 2; Pima-Mar.; F; S; Dau.; 771; Yes; Yes; AI./Id. 3501

ENAS
768; Lucy; F; 66; Pima; F; Wd.; Head; 772; Yes; Yes; AI. 1712/Id. 4304
769; Charles; M; 22; Pima-Mar.; F; S; Son; 773; Yes; Yes; AI. 1204/Id. 4305

ENAS
770; Marie O.; F; 75; Pima; F; Wd.; Head; 774; Yes; Yes; AI. 2343/Id. 3338

ENAS
771; Philip; M; 32; Pima; F; S; Head; 775; Yes; Yes; AI. 3402/Id. 1617

ENASIO
772; Harvier; M; 77; Pima; F; S; Head; 776; Yes; Yes; AI. 463/Id. 5839

ENGELOW
773; Jose; M; 47; Pima; F; S; Head; 777; Yes; Yes; AI. 1913/Id. 4154

ENIS
774; Abraham; M; 37; Pima; F; M; Head; 778; Yes; Yes; AI. 4451/Id. 1671
~~Helen Ambrose; F; 35; Navajo; F; M; Wife; --; (Luapp Agency allottee);~~ Yes; AI./Id.
775; Abraham; M; 9; Pima-Navijo[sic].; F; S; Son; 779; Yes; Yes; AI./Id. 1674
776; Catherine; F; 7; Pima-Navijo[sic].; F; S; Dau.; 780; Yes; Yes; AI./Id. 1675
777; Lester; M; 5; Pima-Navijo[sic].; F; S; Son; 781; Yes; Yes; AI./Id. 1676
778; Barbara; F; 4; Pima-Navijo[sic].; F; S; Dau.; 782; Yes; Yes; AI./Id. 1677
779; Lawrence; M; 3/12; Pima-Navijo[sic].; F; S; Son; --; Yes; Born 12-22-31.; Yes; AI./Id. 2049

ENIS
780; Francis; M; 26; Pima; F; S; Head; 783; Yes; Yes; AI. 922/Id. 4838

ENIS
781; Charles F.; M; 37; Pima; F; S; Head; 784; Yes; Yes; AI. 4435/Id. 1923

ENIS
782; Joseph; M; 78; Pima; F; M; Head; 785; Yes; Yes; AI. 1852/Id. 4683
783; Susie (Enis, Annie); F; 77; Pima; F; M; Wife; 786; Yes; Yes; AI. 2005/Id. 4684

ENIS
784; Harvier; M; 55; Pima; F; M; Head; 787; Yes; Yes; AI. 3537/Id. 1622
785; Ella; F; 42; Pima; F; M; Wife; 788; Yes; Yes; AI. 3538/Id. 1623
786; Bronson; M; 20; Pima; F; S; Son; 789; Yes; Yes; AI. 3541/Id. 1625

Key: Number; Surname; Given; Sex (M/F); Age at Last Birthday; Tribe; Degree of Blood (F=Full); Marital Status; Relationship to Head of Family & Last Census No; At Jurisdiction Where Enrolled (Yes/No); (If no – Where); Ward (Yes/No); Allotment Annuity and/or Identification Numbers

787; Regina; F; 17; Pima; F; S; Dau.; 790; Yes; Yes; AI. 3542/Id. 1626
788; Anne; F; 19; Pima; F; S; Dau.; 791; Yes; Yes; AI. 3540/Id. 1624
789; Felix; M; 15; Pima; F; S; Dau.[sic]; 792; Yes; Yes; AI. 3543/Id. 1627
790; Euphracia; F; 13; Pima; F; S; Dau.; 793; Yes; Yes; AI. 4542/Id. 1628
791; Eliza; F; 12; Pima; F; S; Dau.; 794; Yes; Yes; AI./Id. 1629
792; Marcus; M; 7; Pima; F; S; Son; 795; Yes; Yes; AI./Id. 1630
793; Hyacinth; F; 3; Pima; F; S; Dau.; 796; Yes; Yes; AI./Id. 1924

ENIS
794; Juan; M; 67; Pima; F; Wd.; Head; 797; Yes; Yes; AI. 4375/Id. 1683

ENIS
795; Juan; M; 83; Pima; F; S; Head; 798; Yes; Yes; AI. 4166/Id. 4153

ENIS
796; Juan; M; 57; Pima; F; M; Head; 799; Yes; Yes; AI. 4202/Id. 1708
797; Sevilla; F; 54; Pima; F; M; Wife; 800; Yes; Yes; AI. 4203/Id. 1709
798; Felix; M; 30; Pima; F; S; Son; 801; Yes; Yes; AI. 4204/Id. 1710

ENIS
799; Myrtle; F; 23; Pima; F; S; Head; 802; Yes; Yes; AI. 803/Id. 5635
800; Sophia; F; 20; Pima; F; S; Sis.; 803; Yes; Yes; AI. 804/Id. 5636
801; Herbert; M; 19; Pima; F; S; Bro.; 804; Yes; Yes; AI. 805/Id. 5637
802; Dorsia; F; 18; Pima; F; S; Sis.; 805; Yes; Yes; AI. 806/Id. 5638
803; Amelia; F; 13; Pima; F; S; Sis.; 806; Yes; Yes; AI. 4805/Id. 5639

ENIS
804; Ramon; M; 34; Pima; F; M; Head; 807; Yes; Yes; AI. 4239/Id. 1926
805; Juanita Y., (Yoken, Juanita); F; 20; Pima; F; M; Wife; 808; Yes; Yes; AI. 3569/Id. 1927

ENNIS
806; George; M; 45; Pima; F; Wd.; Head; 809; Yes; Yes; AI. 4235/Id. 1294
807; Germain; F; 15; Pima; F; S; Dau.; 810; Yes; Yes; AI. 4236/Id. 1995

ENNIS
808; Lela K.; F; 36; Maricopa; F; Wd.; Head; 811; Yes; Yes; AI. 2760/Id. 270
809; Daisy; F; 12; Maricopa; F; S; Dau.; 812; Yes; Yes; AI. 4752/Id. 271
810; Iva; F; 10; Maricopa; F; S; Dau.; 813; Yes; Yes; AI./Id. 272
811; Olin; M; 8; Maricopa; F; S; Son; 814; Yes; Yes; AI./Id. 273

ENNIS
812; John; M; 27; Pima; F; S; Head; 815; Yes; Yes; AI. 4424/Id. 1928

Census of the **Gila River** reservation of the **Pima Agency** jurisdiction; as of **April 1** ; 1932; taken by **A. H. Kneale** ; Superintendent.

Key: Number; Surname; Given; Sex (M/F); Age at Last Birthday; Tribe; Degree of Blood (F=Full); Marital Status; Relationship to Head of Family & Last Census No; At Jurisdiction Where Enrolled (Yes/No); (If no – Where); Ward (Yes/No); Allotment Annuity and/or Identification Numbers

ENNIS
813; Dora; F; 57; Pima; F; Wd.; Head; 816; Yes; Yes; AI. 442[?]/Id. 1929

ENNIS
814; Lapolia; F; 77; Pima; F; Wd.; Head; 817; Yes; Yes; AI. 4426/Id. 1930

ENNIS
815; Jose; M; 63; Pima; F; M; Head; 818; Yes; Yes; AI. 4340/Id. 1933
816; Susanna, (Susannah); F; 63; Pima; F; M; Wife; 819; Yes; Yes; AI. 4341/Id. 1934

ENOS
817; Adam G.; M; 57; Pima; F; M; Head; 820; Yes; Yes; AI. 791/Id. 5085
818; Sarah Snyder, (Snyder, Sarah); F; 42; Pima; F; M; Wife; 821; Yes; Yes; AI. 476/Id. 5086
819; Felicitas; F; 13; Pima; F; S; Dau.; 822; Yes; Yes; AI. 4779/Id. 5087
820; Anita F.; F; 12; Pima; F; S; Dau.; 823; Yes; Yes; AI./Id. 5088
821; Benedict; M; 5; Pima; F; S; Son; 824; Yes; Yes; AI./Id. 5089
822; Synder; Angelita; F; 19; Pima; F; S; St.dau.; 825; Yes; Yes; AI./Id. 3947
823; Synder; Milischia; M; 21; Pima; F; S; St.son; 826; Yes; Yes; AI./Id. 6058

ENOS
~~Alice; F; 40; Pima; F; S; M; Head; 827; Yes; Married to Ramon Miles "Alice; also known as; [?]lan Armstrong~~; Yes; AI. 2010/Id. 3070

ENOS
824; Andrew; M; 30; Maricopa; F; S; Head; 828; No; Ft. Sill; ~~Ft. Sill; Comache[sic]; Okla.~~; Yes; AI. 4065/Id. 343
825; Bertha E., (Evans, Bertha); F; 42; Pima; F; M; Wife; 829; Yes; Yes; AI. 3011/Id. 3510

ENOS
826; Daisy; F; 22; Pima; F; S; Head; 830; Yes; Yes; AI. 293/Id. 5026

ENOS
827; Daniel G.; M; 41; Pima; F; M; Head; 831; Yes; Yes; AI. 269/Id. 5014
828; Jane E., (Evans, Bertha); F; 33; Pima; F; M; Wife; 832; Yes; Yes; AI. 469/Id. 5015
829; Hazel; F; 10; Pima; F; S; Dau.; 833; Yes; Yes; AI./Id. 5016
830; Rachel; F; 9; Pima; F; S; Dau.; 834; Yes; Yes; AI./Id. 5017
831; Neal; M; 8; Pima; F; S; Son; 835; Yes; Yes; AI./Id. 5018
832; Daniel Jr.; M; 5; Pima; F; S; Son; 836; Yes; Yes; AI./Id. 5019
833; Gordon; M; 2; Pima; F; S; Son; 837; Yes; Yes; AI./Id. 5830
834; Dorothy; F; 15; Pima; F; S; Niece; 838; Yes; Yes; AI. 4598/Id. 3024

Census of the **Gila River** reservation of the **Pima Agency** jurisdiction; as of **April 1** ; 1932; taken by **A. H. Kneale** ; Superintendent.

Key: Number; Surname; Given; Sex (M/F); Age at Last Birthday; Tribe; Degree of Blood (F=Full); Marital Status; Relationship to Head of Family & Last Census No; At Jurisdiction Where Enrolled (Yes/No); (If no – Where); Ward (Yes/No); Allotment Annuity and/or Identification Numbers

ENOS
835; Frank; M; 32; Pima; F; M; Head; 839; Yes; Yes; AI. 290/Id. 5020
836; Josepha Ant, (Anton, Josepha); F; 22; Pima; F; M; Wife; 840; Yes; Yes; AI. 260/Id. 5021
837; Permelia; F; 2; Pima; F; S; Dau.; 841; Yes; Yes; AI./Id. 5831

ENOS
838; Frank W.; M; 36; Pima; F; M; Head; 842; Yes; Yes; AI. 322/Id. 5281
839; Grace J., (Juan, Grace); F; 24; Pima; F; M; Wife; 843; Yes; Yes; AI. 133/Id. 5282
840; Margaret; F; 9; Pima; F; S; Dau.; 844; Yes; Yes; AI./Id. 5283

ENOS
841; Tomassa L.; M; 63; Pima; F; Wd.; Head; 845; Yes; Yes; AI. 482/Id. 5091

ENOS
842; Mollie A.; F; 67; Pima; F; Wd.; Head; 846; Yes; Yes; AI. 441/Id. 5135

ENOS
843; Henry; M; 42; Pima; F; M; Head; 847; Yes; Yes; AI. 2044/Id. 3061
844; Lola Evans, (Lulu); F; 42; Pima; F; M; Wife; 848; Yes; Yes; AI. 2045/Id. 3062
845; Naomi H.; F; 16; Pima; F; S; Dau.; 849; Yes; Yes; AI. 3198/Id. 2063
846; Lois; F; 13; Pima; F; S; Dau.; 850; Yes; Yes; AI. 4576/Id. 3064
847; Rowland E.; M; 12; Pima; F; S; Son; 851; Yes; Yes; AI. 4594/Id. 3065
848; George P.; M; 10; Pima; F; S; Son; 852; Yes; Yes; AI./Id. 3066
849; Thelma M.; F; 8; Pima; F; S; Dau.; 853; Yes; Yes; AI./Id. 3067
850; Thoda; F; 6; Pima; F; S; Dau.; 854; Yes; Yes; AI./Id. 3068

ENOS
851; Lizzie A.; F; 68; Pima; F; Wd.; Head; 855; Yes; Yes; AI. 2014/Id. 3069

ENOS
852; Herbert; M; 55; Pima; F; M; Head; 856; Yes; Yes; AI. 2009/Id. 4408
853; Lucy J. (Johnson, Lucy); F; 32; Pima; F; M; Wife; 857; Yes; Yes; AI. 2248/Id. 4409
854; Norton; M; 11; Pima; F; S; Son; 858; Yes; Yes; AI./Id. 4410
855; Vernon; M; 9; Pima; F; S; Son; 859; Yes; Yes; AI./Id. 4411
856; Glena M.; F; 5; Pima; F; S; Dau.; 860; Yes; Yes; AI./Id. 4412
857; Marvin; M; 3; Pima; F; S; Son; 861; Yes; Yes; AI./Id. 4152

ENOS
858; Ida; F; 29; Pima; F; S; Head; 862; Yes; Yes; AI. 4327/Id. 1935
859; Edgar; M; 11; Pima; F; S; Son; 863; Yes; Yes; AI./Id. 1936

Census of the **Gila River** reservation of the **Pima Agency** jurisdiction; as of **April 1** ; 1932; taken by **A. H. Kneale** ; Superintendent.

Key: Number; Surname; Given; Sex (M/F); Age at Last Birthday; Tribe; Degree of Blood (F=Full); Marital Status; Relationship to Head of Family & Last Census No; At Jurisdiction Where Enrolled (Yes/No); (If no – Where); Ward (Yes/No); Allotment Annuity and/or Identification Numbers

ENOS

860; Jacob G.; M; 29; Pima; F; S; Head; 864; Yes; Yes; AI. 291/Id. 5022

ENOS

861; John; M; 63; Pima; F; Wd.; Head; 865; Yes; Yes; AI. 1646/Id.

ENOS

862; John; M; 52; Pima; F; Wd.; Head; 866; Yes; Yes; AI./Id. 1571

ENOS

863; John; M; 39; Maricopa; F; M; Head; 867; Yes; Yes; AI. 4344/Id. 315
864; Midam B., (Brown, Mida); F; 39; Maricopa; F; M; Wife; 868; Yes; Yes; AI. 4369/Id. 316
865; Eleanor; F; 12; Maricopa; F; S; Dau.; 869; Yes; Yes; AI. 4683/Id. 317
866; Esther L.; F; 11; Maricopa; F; S; Dau.; 870; Yes; Yes; AI./Id. 318
867; Viola; F; 9; Maricopa; F; S; Dau.; 871; Yes; Yes; AI./Id. 319
868; Walter; M; 3; Maricopa; F; S; Son; 872; Yes; Yes; AI./Id. 569
869; [No Name Entered]; F; 1; Maricopa; F; S; Dau.; 873; Yes; Yes; AI./Id. 602

ENOS

870; John; M; 47; Pima; F; S; Head; 874; Yes; Yes; AI. 3446/Id. 1441

ENOS

871; John W.; M; 69; Pima; F; M; Head; 875; Yes; Yes; AI. 602/Id. 5284
872; Sarah W., (Watson, Sarah); F; 69; Pima; F; M; M; 876; Yes; Yes; AI. 603/Id. 5258
873; Hubert; M; 19; Pima; F; S; Gr.son; 877; Yes; Yes; AI. 734/Id. 5286
874; Clyde; M; 18; Pima; F; S; Gr.son; 878; Yes; Yes; AI. 735/Id. 5287

ENOS

875; Jose; M; 57; Pima; F; Wd.; Head; 879; Yes; Yes; AI. 4231/Id. 570

ENOS

876; Jose; M; 57; Pima; F; M; Head; 880; Yes; Yes; AI. 2047/Id. 3269
877; Josie; F; 55; Pima; F; M; Wife; 881; Yes; Yes; AI. 2048/Id. 3270
878; Felix; M; 35; Pima; F; S; Son; 882; Yes; Yes; AI. 2052/Id. 3271
879; Jessie; F; 24; Pima; F; S; Dau.; 883; Yes; Yes; AI. 2051/Id. 3272
880; Oswald; M; 23; Pima; F; S; Son; 884; Yes; Yes; AI. 2049/Id. 3273
881; Mary Grace; F; 10; Pima; F; S; Gr.dau.; 885; Yes; Yes; AI./Id. 3274
882; Laurine; F; 5; Pima; F; S; Gr.dau.; 886; Yes; Yes; AI./Id. 3275

ENOS

883; Jose; M; 97; Pima; F; M; Head; 887; Yes; Yes; AI. 3235/Id. 4546
884; Juana (Juanna); F; 66; Pima; F; M; Wife; 888; Yes; Yes; AI. 3236/Id. 4547

Census of the **Gila River** reservation of the **Pima Agency** jurisdiction; as of **April 1** ; 1932; taken by **A. H. Kneale** ; Superintendent.

Key: Number; Surname; Given; Sex (M/F); Age at Last Birthday; Tribe; Degree of Blood (F=Full); Marital Status; Relationship to Head of Family & Last Census No; At Jurisdiction Where Enrolled (Yes/No); (If no – Where); Ward (Yes/No); Allotment Annuity and/or Identification Numbers

ENOS
885; Jose D.; M; 24; Pima; F; S; Head; 889; Yes; Yes; AI. 2015/Id. 4413

ENOS
886; Jose G.; M; 61; Maricopa; F; M; Head; 890; Yes; Yes; AI. 4342/Id. 320
887; Susanna; F; 60; Maricopa; F; M; Wife; 891; Yes; Yes; AI. 4343/Id. 321
888; Effie; F; 36; Maricopa; F; S; Dau.; 892; Yes; Yes; AI. 4345/Id. 322
889; Edwin; M; 26; Maricopa; F; S; Son; 893; Yes; Yes; AI. 4347/Id. 323
890; Jones; M; 22; Maricopa; F; S; Son; 894; Yes; Yes; AI. 4349/Id. 324
891; Mabel; F; 17; Maricopa; F; S; Dau.; 895; Yes; Yes; AI. 4350/Id. 325

ENOS
892; Jose P.; M; 55; Pima; F; M; Head; 896; Yes; Yes; AI. 328/Id. 5194
893; Laura R., (Ramone, Laura); F; 36; Pima; F; M; Wife; 897; Yes; Yes; AI. 407/Id. 5195
894; Mike R.; M; 18; Pima; F; S; St.son; 898; Yes; Yes; AI. 494/Id. 5196
895; Ella M.; F; 13; Pima; F; S; Dau.; 899; Yes; Yes; AI./Id. 5197
896; Jonathan; M; 10; Pima; F; S; Son; 900; Yes; Yes; AI./Id. 5198
897; Dorlie; F; 7; Pima; F; S; Dau.; 901; Yes; Yes; AI./Id. 5199
898; Euphrasia; F; 5; Pima; F; S; Dau.; 902; Yes; Yes; AI./Id. 5200

ENOS
899; Juan; M; 53; Pima; F; S; Head; 903; Yes; Yes; AI. 1945/Id. 6908

ENOS
900; Lena; F; 63; Pima; F; Wd.; Head; 904; Yes; Yes; AI. 1126/Id. 6939

ENOS
901; Josepha , (Cheewat, Sebie); F; 32; Pima; F; M; Wife; 905; Yes; Yes; AI. 1580/Id. 5764
902; Lester; M; 8; Pima; F; S; Son; 906; Yes; Yes; AI./Id. 5765
903; Daniel; M; 6; Pima; F; S; Son; 907; Yes; Yes; AI./Id. 5766
904; Matilda; F; 3; Pima; F; S; Dau.; 908; Yes; Yes; AI./Id. 5767

ENOS
905; Lewis; M; 36; Pima; F; Wd.; Head; 909; Yes; Yes; AI. 169/Id. 7095
906; Mildred; F; 16; Pima; F; S; Dau.; 910; Yes; Yes; AI. 171/Id. 7096
907; Richenda; F; 15; Pima; F; S; Dau.; 911; Yes; Yes; AI. 3155/Id. 7097

ENOS
908; Lassa; F; 97; Pima; F; Wd.; Head; 912; Yes; Yes; AI. 327/Id. 7098

ENOS
909; Reuben; M; 24; Pima; F; S; Head; 913; Yes; Yes; AI. 4326/Id. 1935

Census of the **Gila River** reservation of the **Pima Agency** jurisdiction; as of **April 1** ; 1932; taken by **A. H. Kneale** ; Superintendent.

Key: Number; Surname; Given; Sex (M/F); Age at Last Birthday; Tribe; Degree of Blood (F=Full); Marital Status; Relationship to Head of Family & Last Census No; At Jurisdiction Where Enrolled (Yes/No); (If no – Where); Ward (Yes/No); Allotment Annuity and/or Identification Numbers

ENOS
910; Savie; F; 91; Pima; F; Wd.; Head; 914; Yes; Yes; AI. 244/Id. 5102

ENOS
911; Susie; F; 57; Maricopa; F; Wd.; Head; 915; Yes; Yes; AI. 4063/Id. 342

912; Harrington; M; 24; Maricopa; F; S; Son; 916; Yes; Yes; AI. 4065/Id. 344

ENOS
913; William; M; 38; Maricopa; F; M; Head; 917; Yes; Yes; AI. 4064/Id. 417

914; Minnie P., (Patton, Minnie); F; 33; Maricopa; F; M; Wife; 918; Yes; Yes; AI. 1077/Id. 418

915; Esther P.; F; 10; Maricopa; F; S; Dau.; 919; Yes; Yes; AI./Id. 419

916; Lillian V.; F; 9; Maricopa; F; S; Dau.; 920; Yes; Yes; AI./Id. 420

917; Henry L.; M; 4; Maricopa; F; S; Son; 921; Yes; Yes; AI./Id. 421

918; Russell J.; M; 3; Maricopa; F; S; Son; 922; Yes; Yes; AI./Id. 571

ERASTUS
919; Olive; F; 68; Maricopa; F; Wd.; Head; 923; Yes; Yes; AI. 2705/Id. 199

ESCHIEF
920; Anna; F; 38; Maricopa; F; S; Head; 924; Yes; Yes; AI. 3643/Id. 1555

ESCHIEF
921; Benito; M; 26; Maricopa; F; M; Head; 925; Yes; Yes; AI. 689/Id. 5383

922; Joanna W., (Groanna White); F; 32; Maricopa; F; M; Wife; 926; Yes; Yes; AI. 2536/Id. 5384

923; Alexander; F[sic]; 5; Maricopa; F; S; Son; 927; Yes; Yes; AI./Id. 5385

ESCHIEF
924; Joe; M; 27; Maricopa; F; Wd.; Head; 928; Yes; Yes; AI. 687/Id. 5870

ESCHIEF
925; Josephine; F; 27; Maricopa; F; Wd.; Head; 929; Yes; Yes; AI./Id. 5600

926; George; M; 8; Maricopa; F; S; Son; 930; Yes; Yes; AI./Id. 5601

ESCHIEF
927; Juan; M; 59; Maricopa; F; M; Head; 931; Yes; Yes; AI. 2135/Id. 3224

928; Louisa; F; 59; Maricopa; F; M; Wife; 932; Yes; Yes; AI. 2136/Id. 3225

ESCHIEF
929; Juan; M; 97; Maricopa; F; M; Head; 933; Yes; Yes; AI. 1550/Id. 7101

930; Marianna (Mariana); F; 71; Maricopa; F; M; Wife; 934; Yes; Yes; AI. 1551/Id. 7102

Census of the **Gila River** reservation of the **Pima Agency** jurisdiction; as of **April 1** ; 1932; taken by **A. H. Kneale** ; Superintendent.

Key: Number; Surname; Given; Sex (M/F); Age at Last Birthday; Tribe; Degree of Blood (F=Full); Marital Status; Relationship to Head of Family & Last Census No; At Jurisdiction Where Enrolled (Yes/No); (If no – Where); Ward (Yes/No); Allotment Annuity and/or Identification Numbers

ESCHIEF

931; Lawrence; M; 37; Papago; F; M; Head; 935; Yes; Yes; AI. 2324/Id. 3156

932; Mabel, (Sankey, Mabel); F; 37; Papago; F; M; Wife; 936; Yes; Yes; AI. 2318/Id. 3157

933; Mamie; F; 14; Papago; F; S; Dau.; 937; Yes; Yes; AI. 4825/Id. 3158

934; Raymond; M; 13; Papago; F; S; Son; 938; Yes; Yes; AI. 3159/Id.

Lauren; M; 10; Papago; F; S; Son; 939; Died 12-21-31.; Yes; AI. 3160/Id.

935; Laurine; F; 5; Papago; F; S; Dau.; 940; Yes; Yes; AI. 4825/Id. 3161

936; Gerald; M; 3; Papago; F; S; Son; 941; Yes; Yes; AI./Id. 3162

937; Manuel, Gussie; F; 20; Papago; 1/4x; S; Niece; 942; Yes; Yes; AI. 2323/Id. 2129

938; Sankey; Gladys; F; 19; Papago; 1/4x; S; St.dau.; 943; Yes; Yes; AI. 2319/Id. 3583

ESCHIEF

939; Manuel; M; 61; Pima; F; M; Head; 944; Yes; Yes; AI. 3841/Id. 5866

940; Ida; F; 44; Pima; F; M; Wife; 945; Yes; Yes; AI. 3842/Id. 5867

941; Viola; F; 23; Pima; F; S; Dau.; 946; Yes; Yes; AI. 3843/Id. 5868

942; Helen; F; 20; Pima; F; S; Dau.; 947; Yes; AI. 3844/Id. 5869

ESCHIEF

943; Olham; M; 64; Pima; F; M; Head; 948; Yes; Yes; AI. 3641/Id. 1553

944; Lola; F; 62; Pima; F; M; Wife; 949; Yes; Yes; AI. 3642/Id. 1554

945; Julia; F; 21; Pima; F; S; Dau.; 950; Yes; Yes; AI. 3647/Id. 1556

ESCHIEF

946; Ollie; M; 32; Pima; F; M; Head; 951; Yes; Yes; AI. 6440/Id. 3645

947; (Jones, Dorothy); F; 25; Pima; F; M; Wife; 952; Yes; Yes; AI. 1330/Id. 6441

948; Ruth Ann; F; 3; Pima; F; S; Dau.; 953; Yes; Yes; AI./Id. 7072

ESCHIEF

949; Walter; M; 37; Pima; F; S; Head; 954; Yes; Yes; AI. 2138/Id. 3228

ESTRELLA

950; Avalon; M; 22; Pima; F; S; Head; 955; Yes; Yes; AI. 4380/Id. 1938

EVANS

951; Alice; F; 71; Pima; F; Wd.; Head; 956; Yes; Yes; AI. 2987/Id. 3268

952; Felix; M; 40; Pima; F; S; Son; 957; Yes; Yes; AI. 2988/Id. 3267

953; John; M; 32; Pima; F; S; Son; 958; Yes; Yes; AI. 2989/Id. 3268

EVANS

954; Charles; M; 58; Pima; F; Wd.; Head; 959; Yes; Yes; AI. 1763/Id. 4243

EVANS

955; Edison; M; 25; Pima; F; S; Head; 960; Yes; Yes; AI. 857/Id. 5062

Census of the **Gila River** reservation of the **Pima Agency** jurisdiction; as of **April 1** ; 1932; taken by **A. H. Kneale** ; Superintendent.

Key: Number; Surname; Given; Sex (M/F); Age at Last Birthday; Tribe; Degree of Blood (F=Full); Marital Status; Relationship to Head of Family & Last Census No; At Jurisdiction Where Enrolled (Yes/No); (If no - Where); Ward (Yes/No); Allotment Annuity and/or Identification Numbers

EVANS
~~Emily; F; 61; Pima; F; Wd.; Head; 961; Died 10-9-31.~~; Yes; AI. 15/Id. 5063

EVANS
956; John; M; 27; Pima; F; M; Head; 962; Yes; Yes; AI. 3014/Id. 3297
957; Edith, (Azule, Edith); F; 25; Pima; F; M; Wife; 963; Yes; Yes; AI. 1972/Id. 3298
958; George; M; 3; Pima; F; S; Son; 964; Yes; Yes; AI./Id. 3511
959; Erma; F; 1; Pima; F; S; Dau.; 965; Yes; Yes; AI./Id. 3602

EVANS
960; John; M; 42; Pima; F; M; Head; 966; Yes; Yes; AI. 4309/Id. 1504
961; Winnie D., (Davis, Winnie); F; 38; Pima; F; M; Wife; 967; Yes; Yes; AI. 1991/Id. 1505
962; Bernice; F; 20; Pima; F; S; Dau.; 968; Yes; AI. 4311/Id. 1506
963; Harriet; F; 12; Pima; F; S; Dau.; 969; Yes; Yes; AI./Id. 1507
964; Margarita; F; 10; Pima; F; S; Dau.; 970; Yes; Yes; AI./Id. 1508
965; Clayton A.; M; 8; Pima; F; S; Son; 971; Yes; Yes; AI./Id. 1509
966; Frances; F; 6; Pima; F; S; Dau.; 972; Yes; Yes; AI./Id. 1510
967; Clayton A.; M; 4; Pima; F; S; Son; 973; Yes; Yes; AI./Id. 1511
968; John; M; 5/12; Pima; F; S; Son; --; Yes; Born; 11-16-31 Yes; AI./Id. 2050

EVANS
969; Lloyd; M; 67; Pima; F; M; Head; 974; Yes; Yes; AI. 4039/Id. 1474
970; Minnie; F; 57; Pima; F; M; Wife; 975; Yes; Yes; AI. 4040/Id. 1475
971; Carl; M; 43; Pima; F; S; Son; 976; Yes; Yes; AI. 4041/Id. 1476

EVANS
972; Fannie; F; 66; Pima; F; Wd.; Head; 977; Yes; Yes; AI. 3010/Id. 3410

EVANS
973; Luther; M; 61; Pima; F; M; Head; 978; Yes; Yes; AI. 4287/Id. 1498
974; Nellie; F; 56; Pima; F; M; Wife; 979; Yes; Yes; AI. 4288/Id. 1499
975; Irene; F; 33; Pima; F; S; Dau.; 980; Yes; Yes; AI. 4316/Id. 1500
976; Eugene; M; 22; Pima; F; S; Son; 981; Yes; Yes; AI. 4317/Id. 1501

EVANS
977; Minnie; F; 39; Pima; F; M; Wife; 982; Yes; Yes; AI. 4310/Id.

EVANS
978; Otto; M; 29; Pima; F; S; Son; 983; Yes; Yes; AI. 3013/Id. 3411

EVANS
979; Thomas; M; 34; Pima; F; M; Head; 984; Yes; Yes; AI. 3012/Id. 3401
980; Ida M., (Jackson, Ida); F; 32; Pima; F; M; Wife; 985; Yes; Yes; AI. 2061/Id. 3402

Census of the **Gila River** reservation of the **Pima Agency** jurisdiction; as of **April 1** ; 1932; taken by **A. H. Kneale** ; Superintendent.

Key: Number; Surname; Given; Sex (M/F); Age at Last Birthday; Tribe; Degree of Blood (F=Full); Marital Status; Relationship to Head of Family & Last Census No; At Jurisdiction Where Enrolled (Yes/No); (If no – Where); Ward (Yes/No); Allotment Annuity and/or Identification Numbers

981; Delbert; M; 8; Pima; F; S; Son; 986; Yes; Yes; AI./Id. 3403
982; Mardella; F; 6; Pima; F; S; Dau.; 987; Yes; Yes; AI./Id. 3404
983; Rachel; F; 4; Pima; F; S; Dau.; 988; Yes; Yes; AI./Id. 3405

FOHRENKEMP

984; Alice Mc., (McArthur, Alice); F; 27; Maricopa; F; M; Wife; 989; Yes; Yes; AI. 645/Id. 401
985; Richard; M; 4; Maricopa; F; 1/2x; Son; 990; Yes; Yes; AI./Id. 402
986; Milton H.; M; 1; Maricopa; F; 1/2x; Son; 991; Yes; Yes; AI./Id. 597

FRANCISCO

987; Anton; M; 61; Pima; F; M; Head; 992; Yes; Yes; AI. 44/Id. 5589
988; Mathias; M; 27; Pima; F; S; Son; 993; Yes; Yes; AI. 221/Id. 5592
989; Pancho; M; 23; Pima; F; S; Son; 994; Yes; Yes; AI. 698/Id. 5593
990; May; F; 22; Pima; F; S; Dau.; 995; Yes; Yes; AI. 224/Id. 5594
991; Cecilie; F; 19; Pima; F; S; Dau.; 996; Yes; Yes; AI. 4783/Id. 5095
992; Jacob; M; 17; Pima; F; S; Son; 997; Yes; Yes; AI. 3683/Id. 5596
993; Cecilie; F; 16; Pima; F; S; Dau.; 998; Yes; Yes; AI. 3633/Id. 5597
994; Mildred; F; 3; Pima; F; S; Gr.dau.; 999; Yes; Yes; AI./Id. 5871
995; Phillipson; Felicitas; F; 13; Pima; F; S; Sis-in-law.; 1000; Yes; Yes; AI. 4621/Id. 5768

FRANCISCO

996; Juan; M; 30; Pima; F; M; Head; 1001; Yes; Yes; AI. 3399/Id. 5760
997; Petra, (Cheewat, Petra); F; 23; Pima; F; M; Wife; 1002; Yes; Yes; AI. 1583/Id. 5761
998; Gladys; F; 8; Pima; F; S; Dau.; 1003; Yes; Yes; AI./Id. 5762

FRANK

999; Frank; M; 37; Pima; F; Wd.; Head; 1004; Yes; Yes; AI. 4232/Id. 1741
1000; Ida; F; 14; Pima; F; S; Dau.; 1005; Yes; Yes; AI. 4234/Id. 1742
1001; Marcella; F; 13; Pima; F; S; Dau.; 1006; Yes; Yes; AI./Id. 1743
1002; Marguerita; F; 12; Pima; F; S; Dau.; 1007; Yes; Yes; AI./Id. 1744
1003; Bernard; M; 11; Pima; F; S; Son; 1008; Yes; Yes; AI./Id. 1745

FRENCH

1004; Ada Q., (Quoroh, Ada); F; 55; Maricopa; F; M; Wife; 1009; Yes; Yes; AI. 2848/Id. 82
1005; Daniel; M; 13; Maricopa; F; S; Son; 1010; Yes; Yes; AI. 4764/Id. 83
1006; Mary; F; 12; Maricopa; F; S; Dau.; 1011; Yes; Yes; AI. 4879/Id. 84
1007; Albert; M; 8; Maricopa; F; S; Son; 1012; Yes; Yes; AI./Id. 85
1008; Eddie; M; 6; Maricopa; F; S; Son; 1013; Yes; Yes; AI./Id. 86

Census of the **Gila River** reservation of the **Pima Agency** jurisdiction; as of **April 1** ; 1932; taken by **A. H. Kneale** ; Superintendent.

Key: Number; Surname; Given; Sex (M/F); Age at Last Birthday; Tribe; Degree of Blood (F=Full); Marital Status; Relationship to Head of Family & Last Census No; At Jurisdiction Where Enrolled (Yes/No); (If no – Where); Ward (Yes/No); Allotment Annuity and/or Identification Numbers

FROM

1009; Peter; M; 48; Maricopa; F; M; Head; 1014; Yes; Yes; AI. 3773/Id. 522

1010; May L., (Liston, May); F; 57; Maricopa; F; M; Wife; 1015; Yes; Yes; AI. 4307/Id. 523

FULTON

1011; James; M; 55; Pima; F; Wd.; Head; 1016; Yes; Yes; AI. 2291/Id. 3512

FULTON

1012; Philip; M; 47; Pima; F; M; Head; 1017; Yes; Yes; AI. 3003/Id. 3513

1013; Sarah; F; 42; Pima; F; M; Wife; 1018; Yes; Yes; AI. 3004/Id. 3514

1014; Nora; F; 21; Pima; F; S; Dau.; 1019; Yes; Yes; AI. 3005/Id. 3515

Nina; F; 16; Pima; F; S; Dau.; 1020; Died 3-11-32.; Yes; AI. 3006/Id. 3516

1015; Amanda; F; 13; Pima; F; S; Dau.; 1021; Yes; Yes; AI./Id. 3517

GAGE

1016; Gee; M; 34; Pima; F; M; Head; 1022; Yes; Yes; AI. 3441/Id. 1481

1017; Eliza C., (Case, Eliza); F; 28; Pima; F; M; Wife; 1023; Yes; Yes; AI. 3981/Id. 1482

1018; Lorena; F; 2; Pima; F; S; Dau.; 1024; Yes; Yes; AI./Id. 1894

GAGE

1019; Lula; F; 63; Pima; F; Wd.; Head; 1025; Yes; Yes; AI. 3443/Id. 1484

GAGE

1020; Lee; M; 34; Pima; F; M; Head; 1026; Yes; Yes; AI. 3442/Id. 1485

1021; Eunice Lewis, (Lewis, Eunice); F; 18; Pima; F; M; Wife; 1027; Yes; Yes; AI./Id.

1022; Maurine; F; 1; Pima; F; S; Dau.; 1028; Yes; Yes; AI./Id. 2040

GARCIA

1023; Jose; M; 72; Pima; F; M; Head; 1029; Yes; Yes; AI. 3832/Id. 1467

1024; Susie; F; 71; Pima; F; M; Wife; 1030; Yes; Yes; AI. 3833/Id. 1468

GARCIA

1025; Jose; M; 45; Pima; F; Wd.; Head; 1031; Yes; Yes; AI. 998/Id. 6974

GARCIA

1026; Roselie V.; F; 67; Pima; F; Wd.; Head; 1032; Yes; Yes; AI. 4495/Id. 5872

GARCIA

1027; Peter; M; 44; Pima; F; M; Head; 1033; Yes; Yes; AI. 1948/Id. 5873

1028; Carmilita; F; 39; Pima; F; M; Wife; 1034; Yes; Yes; AI. 1949/Id. 5874

Census of the **Gila River** reservation of the **Pima Agency** jurisdiction; as of **April 1** ; 1932; taken by **A. H. Kneale** ; Superintendent.

Key: Number; Surname; Given; Sex (M/F); Age at Last Birthday; Tribe; Degree of Blood (F=Full); Marital Status; Relationship to Head of Family & Last Census No; At Jurisdiction Where Enrolled (Yes/No); (If no – Where); Ward (Yes/No); Allotment Annuity and/or Identification Numbers

GARCIA
1029; Robert; M; 37; Pima; F; M; Head; 1035; Yes; Yes; AI. 1288/Id. 6674
1030; Louisa; F; 6; Pima; F; S; Dau.; 1036; Yes; Yes; AI./Id. 6676

GATAI
James P.; M; 47; Pima; F; M; Head; 1037; Yes; Died 5-6-31.; Yes; AI. 1555/Id. 7103
1031; Susanna P., (Paloma, Susanna); F; 45; Pima; F; Wd.; Head; 1038; Yes; Yes; AI. 2636/Id. 7104
1032; Bernard J.; M; 16; Pima; F; S; Son; 1039; Yes; Yes; AI. 4322/Id. 7105
1033; Paul; M; 7; Pima; F; S; Son; 1040; Yes; Yes; AI./Id. 7106
1034; Victoria; F; 3; Pima; F; S; Dau.; 1041; Yes; Yes; AI./Id. 7107

GATAI
1035; Sythia; F; 65; Pima; F; Wd.; Head; 1042; Yes; Yes; AI. 1556/Id. 7108

GATSIN
1036; Bilcham; M; 77; Pima; F; Wd.; Head; 1043; Yes; Yes; AI. 1115/Id. 5727

GAZULA
1037; Andrew; M; 53; Pima; F; M; Head; 1044; Yes; Yes; AI. 700/Id. 4945

GAZULA
1038; Millsing, (Parsons, Milsing); F; 35; Pima; F; M; Head; 1045; Yes; Yes; AI. 247/Id. 4946
1039; Ivan; M; 13; Pima; F; S; Son; 1046; Yes; Yes; AI. 1915/Id. 4947
1040; Eddy; M; 12; Pima; F; S; Son; 1047; Yes; Yes; AI./Id. 4948
1041; Ethel; F; 10; Pima; F; S; Dau.; 1048; Yes; Yes; AI./Id. 4949
1042; Cora; F; 7; Pima; F; S; Dau.; 1049; Yes; Yes; AI./Id. 4950
1043; Iva; F; 2; Pima; F; S; Dau.; 1050; Yes; Yes; AI./Id. 5777

GAZULA
1044; Daniel; M; 62; Pima; F; M; Head; 1051; Yes; Yes; AI. 4457/Id. 1810
1045; Grace; F; 37; Pima; F; M; Wife; 1052; Yes; Yes; AI. 4456/Id. 1811

GAZULA
1046; Leta E.; F; 49; Pima; F; Wd.; Head; 1053; Yes; Yes; AI. 380/Id. 4951

GEORGE
1047; Daniel; M; 34; Maricopa; F; M4[sic]; Head; 1054; Yes; Yes; AI./Id. 169
1048; May Loring, (Loring, May); F; 27; Maricopa; F; M; Wife; 1055; Yes; Yes; AI. 2251/Id. 170
1049; Neva M.; F; 4; Maricopa; F; S; Dau.; 1056; Yes; Yes; AI./Id. 171

GEORGE
1050; Henry; M; 49; Pima; F; M; Head; 1057; Yes; Yes; AI. 4715/Id. 7109

Key: Number; Surname; Given; Sex (M/F); Age at Last Birthday; Tribe; Degree of Blood (F=Full); Marital Status; Relationship to Head of Family & Last Census No; At Jurisdiction Where Enrolled (Yes/No); (If no – Where); Ward (Yes/No); Allotment Annuity and/or Identification Numbers

GEORGE
1051; Luciana, (Sucianna); F; 71; Pima; F; Wd.; Head; 1058; Yes; Yes; AI. 4716/Id. 7110

1052; Jose; M; 20; Pima; F; S; Son; 1059; Yes; Yes; AI. 4717/Id. 7111

1053; Lena; F; 16; Pima; F; S; Dau.; 1060; Yes; Yes; AI. 4718/Id. 7112

GIBSON
1054; Alice; F; 77; Pima; F; Wd.; Head; 1061; Yes; Yes; AI. 1152/Id. 7115

GIBSON
1055; John; M; 40; Pima; F; M; Head; 1062; No. (Somewhere in Penna.; Yes; AI. 1339/Id. 6429

1056; John Jr.; M; 14; Pima; 1/4x; S; Son; 1063; No. (Somewhere in Penna.; Yes; AI./Id. 6431

1057; Jane E.; F; 9; Pima; 1/4x; S; Dau.; 1064; No. (Somewhere in Penna.; Yes; AI./Id. 6432

GIBSON
1058; Joseph S.; M; 56; Pima; F; S; Head; 1065; Yes; Yes; AI. 1340/Id. 6425

GIBSON
1059; Lizzie; F; 66; Pima; F; Wd.; Head; 1066; Yes; Yes; AI. 1332/Id. 6426

1060; Ida; F; 28; Pima; F; S; Dau.; 1067; Yes; Yes; AI. 1336/Id. 6427

1061; Mathew; M; 22; Pima; F; S; Son; 1068; Yes; Yes; AI. 1334/Id. 6428

GIFF
1062; Frank; M; 65; Pima; F; M; Head; 1069; Yes; Yes; AI. 4721/Id. 1730

1063; Eliza; F; 67; Pima; F; M; Wife; 1070; Yes; Yes; AI. 4222/Id. 1731

GIFF
1064; Joseph; M; 25; Pima; F; M; Head; 1071; Yes; Yes; AI. 4223/Id. 1732

1065; Ruth, (Juan, Ruth); F; 21; Pima; F; M; Wife; 1811; Yes; Yes; AI. 4246/Id. 1299

1066; Joseph Jr.; M; 2/12; Pima; F; S; Son; --; Yes; Born 1-28-32.; Yes; AI./Id. 2051

GIFF
1067; James; M; 29; Pima; F; M; Head; 1072; Yes; Yes; AI. 4224/Id. 1736

1068; Ida N., (Nolan, Ida Jose); F; 35; Pima; F; M; Wife; 1073; Yes; Yes; AI. 4029/Id. 1937

GIVENS
1069; Sepie; F; 65; Pima; F; Wd.; Head; 1074; Yes; Yes; AI. 1211/Id. 6712

GLEICK
1070; Francis; M; 47; Pima; F; M; Head; 1075; Yes; Yes; AI. 172/Id. 4995

1071; Chona; F; 43; Pima; F; M; Wife; 1076; Yes; Yes; AI. 173/Id. 4996

Census of the **Gila River** reservation of the **Pima Agency** jurisdiction; as of **April 1** ; 1932; taken by **A. H. Kneale** ; Superintendent.

Key: Number; Surname; Given; Sex (M/F); Age at Last Birthday; Tribe; Degree of Blood (F=Full); Marital Status; Relationship to Head of Family & Last Census No; At Jurisdiction Where Enrolled (Yes/No); (If no – Where); Ward (Yes/No); Allotment Annuity and/or Identification Numbers

1072; Cecilia; F; 21; Pima; F; S; Dau.; 1077; Yes; Yes; AI. 175/Id. 4997

GLEICK
1073; Sepie; F; 67; Pima; F; Wd.; Head; 1078; Yes; Yes; AI. 91/Id. 7992

GOODWIN
1074; Mattie S. (Stewart, Mattie); F; 27; Pima; F; M; Wife; 1079; Yes; Yes; AI. 1150/Id. 7113
1075; Elmer F.; M; 3; Pima; F; S; Son; 1080; Yes; Yes; AI./Id. 7114

GORE
1076; Manuel; M; 76; Pima; F; Wd.; Head; 1081; Yes; Yes; AI. 396/Id. 5150

GRANT
1077; Herbert; M; 44; Maricopa; F; M; Head; 1082; Yes; Yes; AI. 4021/Id. 505
1078; Anna B.; F; 40; Maricopa; F; M; Wife; 1083; Yes; Yes; AI. 4022/Id. 506
1079; James; M; 22; Maricopa; F; S; Son; 1084; Yes; Yes; AI. 4020/Id. 507
1080; Wallace; M; 20; Maricopa; F; S; Son; 1085; Yes; Yes; AI. 4023/Id. 508
1081; Chanaford; M; 16; Maricopa; F; S; Son; 1086; Yes; Yes; AI. 4024/Id. 509
1082; Eugenia M.; F; 14; Maricopa; F; S; Dau.; 1087; Yes; Yes; AI. 4025/Id. 510
1083; Charlotte; F; 12; Maricopa; F; S; Dau.; 1088; Yes; Yes; AI./Id. 511

GRANT
1084; Richard; M; 39; Maricopa; F; M; Head; 1089; Yes; Yes; AI. 4708/Id. 5683
1085; Emily; F; 41; Maricopa; F; M; Wife; 1090; Yes; Yes; AI. 4707/Id. 5664

GRANT
1086; Vera M.; F; 77; Maricopa; F; Wd.; Head; 1091; Yes; Yes; AI. 4016/Id. 517
1087; Edwards, Charles; M; 10; Maricopa; 1/4x; S; Gr.son; 1092; Yes; Yes; AI./Id. 518

GUADALUPA
1088; --; M; 92; Pima; F; Wd.; Head; 1093; Yes; Yes; AI. 2483/Id. 7116

GUADALUPA
1089; --; M; Unk.; Pima; F; Wd.; Head; 1094; Yes; Yes; AI. 4674/Id. 2041

HAH-HAH-TO-VEN
1090; Carlmi; M; 72; Pima; F; Wd.; Head; 1095; Yes; Yes; AI. 2474/Id. 6909

HALL
1091; Clara M., (Marcus, Clara); F; 30; Pima; F; M; Wife; 1096; Yes; Yes; AI. 767/Id. 5163
1092; Hilda; F; 7; Pima; F; S; Dau.; 1097; Yes; Yes; AI./Id. 5164

Census of the **Gila River** reservation of the **Pima Agency** jurisdiction; as of **April 1** ; 1932; taken by **A. H. Kneale** ; Superintendent.

Key: Number; Surname; Given; Sex (M/F); Age at Last Birthday; Tribe; Degree of Blood (F=Full); Marital Status; Relationship to Head of Family & Last Census No; At Jurisdiction Where Enrolled (Yes/No); (If no – Where); Ward (Yes/No); Allotment Annuity and/or Identification Numbers

HALL
1093; Hiram; M; 42; Pima; F; S; Head; 1098; Yes; Yes; AI. 526/Id. 4898

HALL
1094; James; M; 40; Pima; F; S; Head; 1099; Yes; Yes; AI. 538/Id. 4899

HALL
1095; Joseph; M; 40; Pima; F; M; Head; 1100; Yes; Yes; AI. 21/Id. 4437
1096; Sarah A., (Azule, Sarah); F; 43; Pima; F; M; Wife; 1101; Yes; Yes; AI. 1668/Id. 4438
1097; Florence Azule; F; 22; Pima; F; S; St.dau.; 1102; Yes; Yes; AI. 1697/Id. 4439
1098; Harold Azule; M; 18; Pima; F; S; St.son; 1103; Yes; Yes; AI. 3182/Id. 4440

HALL
1099; Lewis M.; M; 46; Pima; F; S; Head; 1104; Yes; Yes; AI. 4055/Id. 1939

HALL
1100; Manuel; M; 84; Pima; F; Wd.; Head; 1105; Yes; Yes; AI. 4054/Id. 1940

HALL
1101; Philip; M; 30; Pima; F; M; Head; 1106; Yes; Yes; AI. 828/Id. 5442
1102; Elsie, (Matthews, Elsie); F; 23; Pima; F; M; Wife; 1107; Yes; Yes; AI. 907/Id. 1944

HALL
1103; Stephen; M; 34; Pima; F; M; Head; 1108; Yes; Yes; AI. 827/Id. 4553
1104; Margaret J., (Jackson, Margaret); F; 32; Pima; F; M; Wife; 1109; Yes; Yes; AI. 822/Id. 4554
1105; Roger H.; M; 10; Pima; F; S; Son; 1110; Yes; Yes; AI./Id. 4555
1106; Norma B.; F; 4; Pima; F; S; Dau.; 1111; Yes; Yes; AI./Id. 4556

HALLIAN
1107; Martha M., (Mack, Martha); F; 32; Pima; F; M; Wife; 1112; Yes; Yes; AI. 864/Id. 7117
1108; Leona P.; F; 11; Pima; F; S; Dau.; 1113; Yes; Yes; AI./Id. 7118

HAR-JONICK
1109; --; M; 70; Pima; F; M; Head; 1114; Yes; Yes; AI. 1519/Id. 6849
1110; Louisa; F; 70; Pima; F; M; Wife; 1115; Yes; Yes; AI. 1520/Id. 6850

HARRIS
1111; May Ellis, (May M. Ellis); F; 43; Pima; F; M; Wife; 1116; No; Clarkdale Yavapai Ariz.; Yes; AI. 2658/Id. 7119
1112; Georgia Thurza; F; 19; Pima; F; S; st.dau.; 1117; No; Clarkdale Yavapai Ariz.; Yes; AI. 2659/Id. 7120

49

Census of the **Gila River** reservation of the **Pima Agency** jurisdiction; as of **April 1** ; 1932; taken by **A. H. Kneale** ; Superintendent.

Key: Number; Surname; Given; Sex (M/F); Age at Last Birthday; Tribe; Degree of Blood (F=Full); Marital Status; Relationship to Head of Family & Last Census No; At Jurisdiction Where Enrolled (Yes/No); (If no – Where); Ward (Yes/No); Allotment Annuity and/or Identification Numbers

1113; Leonard; M; 13; Pima; F; S; Son; 1118; No; Clarkdale Yavapai Ariz.; Yes; AI./Id. 7121

1114; Frederick; M; 11; Pima; F; S; Son; 1119; No; Clarkdale Yavapai Ariz.; Yes; AI./Id. 7122

HARRIS

1115; James; M; 46; Pima; F; M; Head; 1120; Yes; Yes; AI. 585/Id. 5004

1116; Anna C., (Cepriano, Anna); F; 31; Pima; F; M; Wife; 1121; Yes; Yes; AI. 286/Id. 5005

~~Sybil; F; 22; Pima; F; M; --; 1122; (See Sybil Harris Jack)~~; Yes; AI. 500/Id. 5006

1117; Melissa; F; 12; Pima; F; S; Dau.; 1123; Yes; Yes; AI. 4516/Id. 5008

1118; Mary M.; F; 11; Pima; F; S; Dau.; 1124; Yes; Yes; AI. 4824/Id. 5007

1119; Dorothy; F; 8; Pima; F; S; Dau.; 1125; Yes; Yes; AI./Id. 5009

1120; Adeline; F; 7; Pima; F; S; Dau.; 1126; Yes; Yes; AI./Id. 1925

1121; Frederick; M; 4; Pima; F; S; Son; 1127; Yes; Yes; AI./Id. 5011

HARRISON

1122; Cepriano; M; 24; Pima; F; M; Head; 1128; Yes; Yes; AI. 928/Id. 4857

1123; Anna Isk, (Isk, Anna); F; 24; Pima; F; M; Wife; 1129; Yes; Yes; AI. 43/Id. 4858

1124; Bennett; M; 4; Pima; F; S; Son; 1130; Yes; Yes; AI./Id. 4859

HARRISON

1125; James J.; M; 29; Pima; F; M; Head; 1131; Yes; Yes; AI. 926/Id. 5045

1126; Ina T., (Thomas, Ina); F; 24; Pima; F; M; Wife; 1132; Yes; Yes; AI. 333/Id. 5044

1127; Cora; F; 6; Pima; F; S; Dau.; 1133; Yes; Yes; AI./Id. 5045

1128; Clayton; M; 4; Pima; F; S; Son; 1134; Yes; Yes; AI./Id. 5046

HARRISON

1129; Narcho; M; 26; Pima; F; M; Head; 1135; Yes; Yes; AI. 927/Id. 5047

1130; Clinton A.; M; 18; Pima; F; S; Bro.; 1136; Yes; Yes; AI. 956/Id. 7123

HARVEY

1131; Jose Juan; M; 40; Pima; F; M; Head; 1137; Yes; Yes; AI. 2603/Id. 7005

1132; Barbara T.; F; 32; Pima; F; M; Wife; 1138; Yes; Yes; AI. 0/Id. 7006

1133; Veronica; F; 10; Pima; F; S; Dau.; 1139; Yes; Yes; AI./Id. 7007

1134; Carmelita; F; 9; Pima; F; S; Dau.; 1140; Yes; Yes; AI./Id. 7008

HARVEY

1135; Joseph; M; 42; Pima; F; M; Head; 1141; Yes; Yes; AI. 2602/Id. 7009

1136; Margaret; F; 34; Pima; F; M; Wife; 1142; Yes; Yes; AI. 4528/Id. 7010

HARVEY

1137; Juan; M; 62; Pima; F; M; Head; 1143; Yes; Yes; AI. 2600/Id. 7011

Census of the **Gila River** reservation of the **Pima Agency** jurisdiction; as of **April 1** ; 1932; taken by **A. H. Kneale** ; Superintendent.

Key: Number; Surname; Given; Sex (M/F); Age at Last Birthday; Tribe; Degree of Blood (F=Full); Marital Status; Relationship to Head of Family & Last Census No; At Jurisdiction Where Enrolled (Yes/No); (If no – Where); Ward (Yes/No); Allotment Annuity and/or Identification Numbers

1138; Narcia; F; 60; Pima; F; M; Wife; 1144; Yes; Yes; AI. 2601/Id. 7012
1139; Lewis M.; M; 37; Pima; F; S; Son; 1145; Yes; Yes; AI. 2604/Id. 7013

HARVEY
1140; Juana; F; 82; Pima; F; Wd.; Head; 1146; Yes; Yes; AI. 2621/Id. 7124

HARVEY
1141; Paul; M; 57; Pima; F; M; Head; 1147; Yes; Yes; AI. 2220/Id. 3075
1142; Alice; F; 43; Pima; F; M; Wife; 1148; Yes; Yes; AI. 2231/Id. 3076
1143; Melinda; F; 19; Pima; F; S; Dau.; 1149; Yes; Yes; AI. 2419/Id. 3077
1144; Howard; M; 15; Pima; F; S; Son; 1150; Yes; Yes; AI. 3257/Id. 3078
1145; Frederick; M; 8; Pima; F; S; Gr.son; 1151; Yes; Yes; AI./Id. 3079

HARVEY
1146; Paul; M; 62; Pima; F; M; Head; 1152; Yes; Yes; AI. 70/Id. 5509
1147; Juanna M. (Miguel, Juanna); F; 67; Pima; F; M; Wife; 1153; Yes; Yes; AI. 480/Id. 5510
1148; Alexander; M; 26; Pima; F; S; Son; 1154; Yes; Yes; AI. 747/Id. 5511

HARVIER
1149; Francis; M; 48; Pima; F; M; Head; 1155; Yes; Yes; AI. 1751/Id. 4610
1150; Patrae; F; 52; Pima; F; M; Wife; 1156; Yes; Yes; AI. 1732/Id. 4611
1151; Lalyah; F; 25; Pima; F; S; Dau.; 1157; Yes; Yes; AI. 1735/Id. 4612
1152; Cora; F; 18; Pima; F; S; Dau.; 1158; Yes; Yes; AI. 3191/Id. 4614

HARVIER
1153; Gilman; M; 24; Pima; F; M; Head; 1159; Yes; Yes; AI. 1736/Id. 4613
1154; Eileen G.; F; 1; Pima; F; S; Dau.; 1160; Yes; Yes; AI./Id. 3974

HARVIER
1155; Jose; M; 63; Pima; F; Wd.; Head; 1161; Yes; Yes; AI./Id. 1739

HARVIER
1156; Frank; M; 29; Pima; F; M; Head; 1162; Yes; Yes; AI. 1734/Id. 4615
1157; Rachel D., (Losell Rachel Davis); F; 24; Pima; F; M; Wife; 1163; Yes; Yes; AI. 1122/Id. 4346
1158; Harold; M; 3; Pima; F; S; Son; 1164; Yes; Yes; AI./Id. 4347

HARVIER
1159; Joe Kisto; M; 36; Pima; F; M; Head; 1165; Yes; Yes; AI./Id. 1750
1160; Martina; F; 37; Pima; F; M; Wife; 1166; Yes; Yes; AI./Id. 1751
1161; Salome; F; 14; Pima; F; S; Dau.; 1167; Yes; Yes; AI./Id. 1752
1162; Helen; F; 10; Pima; F; S; Dau.; 1168; Yes; Yes; AI./Id. 1753
1163; Burnett; M; 7; Pima; F; S; Son; 1169; Yes; Yes; AI./Id. 1754
1164; Agatha; F; 4; Pima; F; S; Dau.; 1170; Yes; Yes; AI./Id. 1755

Census of the **Gila River** reservation of the **Pima Agency** jurisdiction; as of **April 1** ; 1932; taken by **A. H. Kneale** ; Superintendent.

Key: Number; Surname; Given; Sex (M/F); Age at Last Birthday; Tribe; Degree of Blood (F=Full); Marital Status; Relationship to Head of Family & Last Census No; At Jurisdiction Where Enrolled (Yes/No); (If no – Where); Ward (Yes/No); Allotment Annuity and/or Identification Numbers

HARVIER

1165; Louis; M; 44; Pima; F; M; Head; 1171; Yes; Yes; AI. 1125/Id. 6937

1166; Josie; F; 41; Pima; F; M; Wife; 1172; Yes; Yes; AI. 1124/Id. 6938

HARVIER

1167; Mark; M; 43; Pima; F; M; Head; 1173; Yes; Yes; AI. 227/Id. 5612

1168; Nancy P., (Paddis, Nancy); F; 41; Pima; F; M; Wife; 1174; Yes; Yes; AI. 192/Id. 5613

1169; N.J. Riley; M; 18; Pima; F; S; Son; 1175; Yes; Yes; AI. 3475/Id. 5615

1170; Lydia; F; 10; Pima; F; S; Dau.; 1176; Yes; Yes; AI./Id. 5616

HAVALINA

1171; Bryant; M; 62; Pima; F; M; Head; 1177; Yes; Yes; AI. 2978/Id. 3355

1172; Nina, (Havalina, Nina); F; 62; Pima; F; M; Wife; 1178; Yes; Yes; AI. 2979/Id. 3354

1173; Scott; M; 30; Pima; F; S; Son; 1179; Yes; Yes; AI. 3106/Id. 3355

1174; Edward; M; 10; Pima; F; S; Son; 1180; Yes; Yes; AI. 3186/Id. 3357

HAWTHORNE

1175; Nellis; F; 60; Pima; F; Wd.; Head; 1181; Yes; Yes; AI. 1311/Id. 6447

HAYES

1176; Andrew; M; 44; Pima; F; M; Head; 1182; Yes; Yes; AI. 974/Id. 6811

1177; Catherine; F; 38; Pima; F; M; Wife; 1183; Yes; Yes; AI. 975/Id. 6812

1178; Hiram; M; 25; Pima; F; S; Son; 1184; Yes; Yes; AI. 1395/Id. 6817

1179; Edward; M; 19; Pima; F; S; Son; 1185; Yes; Yes; AI. 977/Id. 6813

1180; Minnie; F; 12; Pima; F; S; Dau.; 1186; Yes; Yes; AI./Id. 6814

1181; Willard; M; 9; Pima; F; S; Son; 1187; Yes; Yes; AI. 977/Id. 6815

1182; Julia; F; 8; Pima; F; S; Dau.; 1188; Yes; Yes; AI./Id. 6816

HAYES

~~Eugene; M; 57; Maricopa; F; M; Head; 1189; Died 9-27-31~~.; Yes; AI. 1390/Id. 340

1183; Mary; F; 53; Mar.; F; Wd.; Head; 1190; Yes; Yes; AI. 1391/Id. 341

HAYES

1184; Joe; M; 30; Pima; F; M; Head; 1191; Yes; Yes; AI. 1354/Id. 6713

1185; Nancy W., (Whittaker, Nancy); F; 28; Pima; F; M; Wife; 1192; Yes; Yes; AI. 2190/Id. 6714

1186; Ira; M; 9; Pima; F; S; Son; 1193; Yes; Yes; AI./Id. 6715

1187; Leonard; M; 6; Pima; F; S; Son; 1194; Yes; Yes; AI./Id. 7125

HAYES

1188; Joseph; M; 39; Pima; F; M; Head; 1195; Yes; Yes; AI. 1746/Id. 4151

1189; Dollie; F; 36; Pima; F; M; Wife; 1196; Yes; Yes; AI. 1747/Id. 4150

1190; Sybil; F; 9; Pima; F; S; Dau.; 1197; Yes; Yes; AI./Id. 4149

Census of the **Gila River** reservation of the **Pima Agency** jurisdiction; as of **April 1** ; 1932; taken by **A. H. Kneale** ; Superintendent.

Key: Number; Surname; Given; Sex (M/F); Age at Last Birthday; Tribe; Degree of Blood (F=Full); Marital Status; Relationship to Head of Family & Last Census No; At Jurisdiction Where Enrolled (Yes/No); (If no – Where); Ward (Yes/No); Allotment Annuity and/or Identification Numbers

1191; Logan; M; 5; Pima; F; S; Son; 1198; Yes; Yes; AI./Id. 4148
1192; Lillian; F; 2; Pima; F; S; Dau.; 1199; Yes; Yes; AI./Id. 3982

HAYES

1193; Mathew L.; M; 67; Pima; F; M; Head; 1200; Yes; Yes; AI. 1319/Id. 6507
1194; Ellen; F; 53; Pima; F; M; Wife; 1201; Yes; Yes; AI. 1320/Id. 6508
1195; John L.; M; 32; Pima; F; S; Son; 1202; Yes; Yes; AI. 1323/Id. 6509

HAYES

1196; Ralph; M; 57; Pima; F; S; Head; 1203; Yes; Yes; AI. 1352/Id. 7126

HAYES

1197; Simon; M; 42; Pima; F; M; Head; 1204; No 3612 Baldwin St. Los Angeles; Los Angeles Cal.; Yes; AI. 1321/Id. 6494
1198; Anna E., (Enis, Anna Hayes); F; 32; Pima; F; M; Wife; 1205; No 3612 Baldwin St. Los Angeles; Los Angeles Cal.; Yes; AI. 1669/Id. 6495
1199; Vivian L.; F; 16; Pima; F; S; Dau.; 1206; No 3612 Baldwin St. Los Angeles; Los Angeles Cal.; Yes; AI. 3392/Id. 6496
1200; Leslie; M; 9; Pima; F; S; Son; 1207; No 3612 Baldwin St. Los Angeles; Los Angeles Cal.; Yes; AI./Id. 6497

HAYES

1201; Stewart Lewis; M; 29; Pima; F; M; Head; 1208; No Phoenix Maricopa Ariz.; Yes; AI. 1324/Id. 6498
1202; Minnie S., (Soatikee, Minnie); F; 31; Pima; F; M; Wife; 1209; No Phoenix Maricopa Ariz.; Yes; AI. 3729/Id. 6499
1203; Victor; M; 8; Pima; F; S; Son; 1210; No Phoenix Maricopa Ariz.; Yes; AI./Id. 6500
1204; -----; F; 5; Pima; F; S; Dau.; 1211; No Phoenix Maricopa Ariz.; Yes; AI./Id. 6501

HAYES

1205; Victor M.; M; 45; Pima; F; M; Head; 1212; Yes; Yes; AI. 1322/Id. 6502
1206; Hilda; F; 17; Pima; F; S; Dau.; 1213; Yes; Yes; AI. 3390/Id. 6504
1207; Josephine; F; 16; Pima; F; S; Dau.; 1214; Yes; Yes; AI. 3206/Id. 6505
1208; Mildred R.; F; 12; Pima; F; S; Dau.; 1215; Yes; Yes; AI./Id. 6506

HEAD

1209; Eunice; F; 68; Maricopa; F; Wd.; Head; 1216; Yes; Yes; AI. 3754/Id. 468

HEAD

1210; Paul; M; 33; Maricopa; F; M; Head; 1217; Yes; Yes; AI. 3755/Id. 464
1211; Lena E., (Evans, Lena); F; 32; Maricopa; F; M; Wife; 1218; Yes; Yes; AI. 4042/Id. 466
1212; Colleen; F; 9; Maricopa; F; S; Dau.; 1219; Yes; Yes; AI./Id. 467

Census of the **Gila River** reservation of the **Pima Agency** jurisdiction; as of **April 1** ; 1932; taken by **A. H. Kneale** ; Superintendent.

Key: Number; Surname; Given; Sex (M/F); Age at Last Birthday; Tribe; Degree of Blood (F=Full); Marital Status; Relationship to Head of Family & Last Census No; At Jurisdiction Where Enrolled (Yes/No); (If no – Where); Ward (Yes/No); Allotment Annuity and/or Identification Numbers

HENDRICKS

~~Tony; M; Unk.; Papago; F; M; Head; --; Sells Agency allottee; Yes; AI./Id.~~
1213; Emma, (Vavages, Emma); F; 24; Pima; F; M; Wife; 4212; Yes; Yes; AI. 1530/Id. 6907

HENDRICKS

1214; Lewis; M; 32; Pima; F; Wd.; Head; 1220; Yes; Yes; AI. 1785/Id. 4478
~~Angelita, (Miguel, Angelita); F; 27; Pima; F; M; Wife; 1221; Died 3-20-32.~~; Yes; AI. 1275/Id. 4479
1215; Elmer J.; M; 8; Pima; F; S; Son; 1222; Yes; Yes; AI./Id. 4480

HENDRICKS

1216; Meecham; M; 52; Papago; F; M; Head; 1223; Yes; Yes; AI. 3485/Id. 4402
1217; Sarah; F; 52; Papago; F; M; Wife; 1224; Yes; Yes; AI. 3486/Id. 4403
1218; Rose; F; 19; Papago; F; S; Dau.; 1225; Yes; Yes; AI. 3179/Id. 4404
1219; Laura; F; 18; Papago; F; S; Dau.; 1226; Yes; Yes; AI. 3180/Id. 4405
1220; Gerard; M; 14; Papago; F; S; Son; 1227; Yes; Yes; AI. 4471/Id. 4406

HER VAL THOP VAIN

1221; --; M; 65; Pima; F; M; Head; 1228; Yes; Yes; AI. 3364/Id. 5685
1222; Lupa; F; 63; Pima; F; M; Wife; 1229; Yes; Yes; AI. 3365/Id. 5686

HICE

1223; Susie; F; 57; Pima; F; Wd.; Head; 1230; Yes; Yes; AI. 1349/Id. 6852

HICKS

1224; May Lyons, (Lyons, May); F; 33; Pima; F; M; Wife; 1231; Yes; Yes; AI. 795/Id. 5530
1225; Hazel; F; 7; Pima; F; S; Dau.; 1232; Yes; Yes; AI./Id. 5531

HILL

1226; James; M; 27; Pima; F; S; Head; 1233; Yes; Yes; AI. 4121/Id. 4743

HILL

1227; John; M; 44; Pima; F; Wd.; Head; 1234; Yes; Yes; AI. 3110/Id. 7127
1228; Telerovito; M; 18; Pima; F; S; Son; 1235; Yes; Yes; AI. 3111/Id. 7128

HILL

1229; Lancisco; M; 59; Maricopa; F; S; Head; 1236; Yes; Yes; AI. 1976/Id. 572

HILL

1230; Lewis; M; 33; Pima; F; M; Head; 1237; Yes; Yes; AI. 2360/Id. 4798
1231; Petra; F; 23; Papago; F; M; Wife; 1238; Yes; Yes; AI./Id. 3969
1232; Stephen; M; 5; Pima-Papago; F; S; Son; 1239; Yes; Yes; AI./Id. 3968
1233; Lena; F; 3; Pima-Papago; F; S; Dau.; 1240; Yes; Yes; AI./Id. 3967

Census of the **Gila River** reservation of the **Pima Agency** jurisdiction; as of **April 1** ; 1932; taken by **A. H. Kneale** ; Superintendent.

Key: Number; Surname; Given; Sex (M/F); Age at Last Birthday; Tribe; Degree of Blood (F=Full); Marital Status; Relationship to Head of Family & Last Census No; At Jurisdiction Where Enrolled (Yes/No); (If no – Where); Ward (Yes/No); Allotment Annuity and/or Identification Numbers

1234; Mary; F; 2/12; Pima-Papago; F; S; Dau.; --; Yes; Born 1-30-32.; Yes; AI./Id. 3935

HILL

1235; Roy B.; M; 52; Pima; F; M; Head; 1241; Yes; Yes; AI. 1815/Id. 4710
1236; Maria R., (Roveles, Maria); F; 52; Pima; F; M4[sic]; Wife; 1242; Yes; Yes; AI. 1827/Id. 4711
1237; Rovales[sic], Reuben P.; M; 22; Pima; F; S; St.son; 1243; Yes; Yes; AI./Id. 4712

HISCO

1238; Thomas; M; 42; Pima; F; M; Head; 1244; Yes; Yes; AI. 1566/Id. 7129
1239; Emily; F; 50; Pima; F; M; Wife; 1245; Yes; Yes; AI. 1567/Id. 7130
1240; Licensia; M; 22; Pima; F; S; Son; 1246; Yes; Yes; AI. 1568/Id. 7131
1241; Legis; M; 19; Pima; F; S; Son; 1247; Yes; Yes; AI. 1569/Id. 7132
1242; Regina; F; 18; Pima; F; S; Dau.; 1248; Yes; Yes; AI. 1570/Id. 7133

HOMA

1243; Anton; M; 43; Pima; F; S; Head; 1249; Yes; Yes; AI./Id. 1652

HOMA

1244; Juan C.; M; 58; Pima; F; M; Head; 1250; Yes; Yes; AI. 4150/Id. 1694
1245; Annie; F; 42; Pima; F; M; Wife; 1251; Yes; Yes; AI. 4151/Id. 1695
1246; Pauline; F; 14; Pima; F; S; Dau.; 1252; Yes; Yes; AI. 4712/Id. 1941
1247; Katherine; F; 9; Pima; F; S; Dau.; 1253; Yes; Yes; AI./Id. 1942
1248; Margaret; F; 20; Pima; F; S; Dau.; 1254; Yes; Yes; AI. 4153/Id. 1943
1249; Patricia; F; 12; Pima; F; S; Gr.dau.; 1255; Yes; Yes; AI./Id. 2037

HONWESIMA

~~Randall; M; unk.; Hopi; F; M; Head; --; Hopi Indian from Michongnovi~~[sic]; AI./Id.
1250; Hazel Cameron; F; 23; Maricopa; F; M; Wife; 442; No; Ariz.; Yes; AI. 2791/Id. 1260
1251; Barbara L.; F; 5; Maricopa-Hopi; F; S; Dau.; 1256; No; Ariz.; Yes; AI./Id. 5217
1252; Nadine; F; 4/12; Maricopa-Hopi; F; S; Dau.; --; No; Born 12-9-31.; Ariz.; Yes; AI./Id. 610

HOOVER

1253; Job; M; 65; Pima; F; M; Head; 1257; Yes; Yes; AI. 2628/Id. 1573
1254; Emma; F; 60; Pima; F; M; Wife; 1258; Yes; Yes; AI. 2629/Id. 1574
1255; Elizabeth; F; 26; Pima; F; S; Dau.; 1259; Yes; Yes; AI. 2631 /Id. 1575
1256; Irene; F; 4; Pima; F; S; Dau.; 1260; Yes; Yes; AI. /Id. 1576

HOOVER

1257; Stephen; M; 32; Pima; F; Wd.; Head; 1261; Yes; Yes; AI. 2666/Id. 1577
1258; Virginia; F; 12; Pima; F; S; Dau.; 1262; Yes; Yes; AI./Id. 1578

HOUSTON
1259; Arthur; M; 47; Pima; F; M; Head; 1263; Yes; Yes; AI. 1051/Id. 6580
1260; Martha; F; 47; Pima; F; M; Wife; 1264; Yes; Yes; AI. 1052/Id. 6581
1261; Leonard; M; 18; Pima; F; S; Son; 1265; Yes; Yes; AI. 921/Id. 6582
1262; Margery; F; 16; Pima; F; S; Dau.; 1266; Yes; Yes; AI. 3320/Id. 6583
1263; Hiram; M; 14; Pima; F; S; Son; 1267; Yes; Yes; AI. 4617/Id. 6584
1264; Bernice; F; 9; Pima; F; S; Dau.; 1268; Yes; Yes; AI./Id. 6585
1265; Irene; F; 7; Pima; F; S; Dau.; 1269; Yes; Yes; AI./Id. 6586
1266; Ola May; F; 3; Pima; F; S; Dau.; 1270; Yes; Yes; AI./Id. 7100

HOUSTON
1267; Ellie; F; 72; Pima; F; Wd.; Head; 1271; Yes; Yes; AI. 1050/Id. 6587

HOWARD
1268; Anna; F; 62; Pima; F; Wd.; Head; 1272; Yes; Yes; AI. 740/Id. 3517

HOWARD
1269; Antonio; M; 77; Maricopa; F; M; Head; 1273; Yes; Yes; AI. 3869/Id. 416
1270; Alice; F; 81; Maricopa; F; M; Wife; 1274; Yes; Yes; AI. 3870/Id. 417

HOWARD
1271; Barney; M; 43; Maricopa; F; M; Head; 1275; Yes; Yes; AI. 212/Id. 101
1272; Lulu; F; 42; Maricopa; F; M; Wife; 1276; Yes; Yes; AI. 213/Id. 100
1273; Burnham; M; 23; Maricopa; F; S; Son; 1277; Yes; Yes; AI. 215/Id. 99
1274; Lydia; F; 13; Maricopa; F; S; Dau.; 1278; Yes; Yes; AI. 4578/Id. 98
1275; Raymond; M; 10; Maricopa; F; S; Son; 1279; Yes; Yes; AI./Id. 97

HOWARD
1276; Daniel; M; 87; Pima; F; M; Head; 1280; Yes; Yes; AI. 297/Id. 5341
~~Agnes; F; 47; Pima; F; M; Wife; 1281; Died 4-21-31.~~; Yes; AI. 298/Id. 5341
1277; Johnson, Ella; F; 6; Pima; F; S; Gr.dau.; 1282; Yes; Yes; AI./Id. 5343

HOWARD
1278; Daniel; M; 35; Pima; F; Wd.; Head; 1283; Yes; Yes; AI. 502/Id. 3518

HOWARD
1279; Ernest; M; 30; Pima; F; Wd.; Head; 1285; Yes; Yes; AI. 312/Id. 5342
1280; Winnie; F; 7; Pima; F; S; Dau.; 1286; Yes; Yes; AI./Id. 5786

HOWARD
1281; Frank; M; 69; Pima; F; Wd.; Head; 1287; Yes; Yes; AI. 4407/Id. 353

HOWARD
1282; Eugene B.; M; 24; Pima; F; M; Head; 1288; Yes; Yes; AI. 657/Id. 4147

Census of the **Gila River** reservation of the **Pima Agency** jurisdiction; as of **April 1** ; 1932; taken by **A. H. Kneale** ; Superintendent.

Key: Number; Surname; Given; Sex (M/F); Age at Last Birthday; Tribe; Degree of Blood (F=Full); Marital Status; Relationship to Head of Family & Last Census No; At Jurisdiction Where Enrolled (Yes/No); (If no – Where); Ward (Yes/No); Allotment Annuity and/or Identification Numbers

HOWARD

1283; Frank; M; 44; Pima; F; M; Head; 1289; Yes; Yes; AI. 724/Id. 4145
1284; Albert; M; 14; Pima; F; S; Son; 1290; Yes; Yes; AI. 4469/Id. 4144
1285; Gerald; M; 5; Pima; F; S; Son; 1291; Yes; Yes; AI./Id. 4143

HOWARD

1286; George; M; 36; Pima; F; M; Head; 1292/1295; Yes; Yes; AI. 2626/Id. 6984
1287; Clara O., (Osife, Clara); F; 32; Pima; F; M; Wife; 1293/1296; Yes; Yes; AI. 1563/Id. 6985
1288; Mildred; F; 9; Pima; F; S; Dau.; 1294/1297; Yes; Yes; AI./Id. 6986

HOWARD

1289; Glenn; M; 23; Pima; F; S; Head; 1298; Yes; Yes; AI. 656/Id. 7137

HOWARD

1290; Isaac; M; 32; Pima; F; M; Head; 1299; Yes; Yes; AI. 369/Id. 6565
1291; Margaret M., (Miller, Margaret); F; 19; Pima; F; M; Wife; 1300; Yes; Yes; AI. 296/Id. 6566

HOWARD

1292; Isaac; M; 38; Pima; F; Wd.; Head; 1301; Yes; Yes; AI. 2627/Id. 6987
1293; Adolph; M; 7; Pima; F; S; Son; 1302; Yes; Yes; AI./Id. 6990
1294; Elinora; F; 5; Pima; F; S; Dau.; 1303; Yes; Yes; AI./Id. 7138

HOWARD

1295; James; M; 75; Pima; F; M; Head; 1304; Yes; Yes; AI. 2623/Id. 6991
1296; Lucy; F; 75; Pima; F; M; Wife; 1305; Yes; Yes; AI. 2624/Id. 6992

HOWARD

1297; John; M; 63; Maricopa; F; M; Head; 1306; Yes; Yes; AI. 2675/Id. 512
1298; Emma Grant, (Grant, Emma); F; 40; Maricopa; F; M; Wife; 1307; Yes; Yes; AI. 4017/Id. 513
1299; Catherine L.; F; 8; Maricopa; F; S; Dau.; 1308; Yes; Yes; AI./Id. 514
1300; Marie M.; F; 6; Maricopa; F; S; Dau.; 1309; Yes; Yes; AI./Id. 515
1301; Frances; F; 4; Maricopa; F; S; Dau.; 1310; Yes; Yes; AI./Id. 516
1302; Havier G.; M; 2; Maricopa; F; S; Son; 1311; Yes; Yes; AI./Id. 573
1303; Caroline Doris; F; 1/12; Maricopa; F; S; Dau.; --; Yes Born 3-18-32.; Yes; AI./Id. 611

HOWARD

1304; John; M; 41; Pima; F; M; Head; 1312; Yes; Yes; AI. 217/Id. 3519
1305; Emily; F; 39; Pima; F; M; Wife; 1313; Yes; Yes; AI. 218/Id. 3520
1306; Jasper; M; 18; Pima; F; S; Son; 1314; Yes; Yes; AI. 3726/Id. 3521
1307; Allen; M; 16; Pima; F; S; Son; 1315; Yes; Yes; AI. 3723/Id. 3522
1308; Esther E.; F; 13; Pima; F; S; Dau.; 1316; Yes; Yes; AI. 4658/Id. 3523

1309; Luther; M; 11; Pima; F; S; Son; 1317; Yes; Yes; AI./Id. 3524
1310; Gertrude; F; 7; Pima; F; S; Dau.; 1318; Yes; Yes; AI./Id. 3525
1311; Vivian; F; 5; Pima; F; S; Dau.; 1319; Yes; Yes; AI./Id. 3526

HOWARD
1312; Joshua; M; 42; Pima; F; M; Head; 1320; Yes; Yes; AI. 1260/Id. 7134
1313; Josephine; F; 51; Pima; F; M; Wife; 1321; Yes; Yes; AI. 1261/Id. 7135

HOWARD
1314; Mathew; M; 40; Pima; F; M; Head; 1322; Yes; Yes; AI. 1545/Id. 6993
1315; Josephine, (Osife, Josephine); F; 33; Pima; F; M; Wife; 1323; Yes; Yes; AI. 1564/Id. 6994
1316; Anthony; M; 14; Pima; F; S; Son; 1324; Yes; Yes; AI./Id. 6996
1317; Wallace; M; 13; Pima; F; S; Son; 1325; Yes; Yes; AI. 4638/Id. 6995

HUBERD
1318; Jacob; M; 82; Maricopa; F; M; Head; 1326; Yes; Yes; AI. 2676/Id. 520
1319; Emma L. (Logan, Emma); F; 82; Maricopa; F; M; Wife; 1327; Yes; Yes; AI. 4013/Id. 521

HUGHES
1320; Andrew; M; 31; Pima; F; S; Head; 1328; Yes; Yes; AI. 4417/Id. 1357

HUGHES
1321; Sibley L.; M; 40; Pima; F; M; Head; 1329; Yes; Yes; AI. 4418/Id. 1356

HUGO
1322; Burns; M; 40; Pima; F; M; Head; 1330; Yes; Yes; AI. 1749/Id. 4264
1323; Emily; F; 39; Pima; F; M; Wife; 1331; Yes; Yes; AI. 1750/Id. 4265
1324; Catherine; F; 20; Pima; F; S; Dau.; 1332; Yes; Yes; AI. 1751/Id. 4266
1325; Margery; F; 18; Pima; F; S; Dau.; 1333; Yes; Yes; AI. 1752/Id. 4267
1326; Clarence; M; 14; Pima; F; S; Son; 1334; Yes; Yes; AI. 3212/Id. 4268
1327; Blanche L.; F; 11; Pima; F; S; Dau.; 1335; Yes; Yes; AI. 4882/Id. 4269
1328; Melinda H.; F; 7; Pima; F; S; Dau.; 1336; Yes; Yes; AI./Id. 4270

ICKS
1329; Anton; M; 47; Maricopa; F; S; Head; 1338; Yes; Yes; AI. 4284/Id. 574

INNIS
1330; John; M; 52; Maricopa; F; Wd.; Head; 1339; Yes; Yes; AI. 2684/Id. 254
1331; Ione; F; 21; Maricopa; F; S; Dau.; 1340; Yes; Yes; AI. 2686/Id. 255
1332; Blanche; F; 19; Maricopa; F; S; Dau.; 1341; Yes; Yes; AI. 2687/Id. 256
1333; John Jr.; M; 12; Maricopa; F; S; Son; 1342; Yes; Yes; AI. 4744/Id. 257

Census of the **Gila River** reservation of the **Pima Agency** jurisdiction; as of **April 1** ; 1932; taken by **A. H. Kneale** ; Superintendent.

Key: Number; Surname; Given; Sex (M/F); Age at Last Birthday; Tribe; Degree of Blood (F=Full); Marital Status; Relationship to Head of Family & Last Census No; At Jurisdiction Where Enrolled (Yes/No); (If no – Where); Ward (Yes/No); Allotment Annuity and/or Identification Numbers

ISK

1334; Henry; M; 45; Pima; F; M; Head; 1343; Yes; Yes; AI. 512/Id. 4853
1335; Frances; M; 18; Pima; F; S; Son; 1344; Yes; Yes; AI. 3962/Id. 4855
1336; Irene; F; 10; Pima; F; S; Dau.; 1345; Yes; Yes; AI./Id. 4856

ISK

1337; Jose M.; M; 57; Pima; F; Wd.; Head; 1346; Yes; Yes; AI. 40/Id. 5534

IST[sic]

~~Maud; F; 61; Pima; F; Wd.; Head; 1347; Died 9-13-31.~~; Yes; AI. 2750/Id. 5872
1338; Velma J.; F; 9; Pima; F; S; Orp.; 1348; Yes; Yes; AI./Id. 5878

JACK

~~Mitchell; M; Unk.; Mission; F; M; Head; --; Mission allottee;~~ Yes; AI./Id.
1339; Sybil, (Harris, Sybil); F; 21; Pima; F; M; Wife; 1122; Yes; Yes; AI. 600/Id. 5006
1340; Mitchell Harris; M; 5/12; Pima-Mission; F; S; Son; --; Born; 10-24-31.; Yes; AI./Id. 6126

JACKSON

1341; Henry; M; 34; Pima; F; M; Head; 1349; Yes; Yes; AI. 104/Id. 4210
~~Florence; F; 39; Oneida; F; M; Wife; 1122; Yes~~; AI./Id.
1342; Albert, Jr.; M; 10; Pima-Oneida; F; S; Son; 1350; Yes; Yes; AI./Id. 4212
1343; Ione; F; 9; Pima-Oneida; F; S; Dau.; 1351; Yes; Yes; AI./Id. 4213
1344; Milton; M; 4; Pima-Oneida; F; S; Son; 1352; Yes; Yes; AI./Id. 4214

JACKSON

1345; Alford; M; 37; Pima; F; M; Head; 1353; Yes; Yes; AI. 858/Id. 4256
1346; Elizabeth, (Enos, Lizzie); F; 32; Pima; F; M; Wife; 1354; Yes; Yes; AI. 1905/Id. 4257
1347; Ruth; F; 12; Pima; F; S; Dau.; 1355; Yes; Yes; AI. 2423/Id.
1348; Violet; F; 10; Pima; F; S; Dau.; 1356; Yes; Yes; AI./Id. 4258
1349; Alford Jr.; M; 9; Pima; F; S; Son; 1357; Yes; Yes; AI./Id. 4261
1350; Walter; M; 8; Pima; F; S; Son; 1358; Yes; Yes; AI./Id.
1351; Julia; F; 5; Pima; F; S; Dau.; 1359; Yes; Yes; AI./Id. 4260

JACKSON

1352; Ambrose; M; 37; Pima; F; Wd.; Head; 1360; Yes; Yes; AI./Id. 4122

JACKSON

1353; Antonio; M; 33; Pima; F; M; Head; 1361; Yes; Yes; AI. 2161/Id. 3324
1354; Peedlah L., (Lahpai, Peedlah); F; 27; Pima; F; M; Wife; 1362; Yes; Yes; AI. 3099/Id. 3327
1355; Vincent; M; 11; Pima; F; S; Son; 1363; Yes; Yes; AI./Id. 3324
1356; Alice; F; 7; Pima; F; S; Dau.; 1364; Yes; Yes; AI./Id. 3325

Census of the **Gila River** reservation of the **Pima Agency** jurisdiction; as of **April 1** ; 1932; taken by **A. H. Kneale** ; Superintendent.

Key: Number; Surname; Given; Sex (M/F); Age at Last Birthday; Tribe; Degree of Blood (F=Full); Marital Status; Relationship to Head of Family & Last Census No; At Jurisdiction Where Enrolled (Yes/No); (If no – Where); Ward (Yes/No); Allotment Annuity and/or Identification Numbers

1357; Bernard; M; 5; Pima; F; S; Son; 1365; Yes; Yes; AI./Id. 3251

JACKSON

1358; Daniel O.; M; 29; Pima; F; M; Head; 1366; Yes; Yes; AI. 2963/Id. 3179
1359; Isabelle, (McArthur, Isabelle); F; 29; Pima; F; M; Wife; 1367; Yes; Yes; AI. 646/Id. 3180
1360; Daniel; M; 6; Pima; F; S; Son; 1368; Yes; Yes; AI./Id. 3182
1361; Klannath; M; 5; Pima; F; S; Son; 1369; Yes; Yes; AI./Id. 3181

JACKSON

1362; Edward; M; 57; Pima; F; M; Head; 1370; Yes; Yes; AI. 136/Id. 4505
1363; Elliott; M; 21; Pima; F; S; Son; 1371; Yes; Yes; AI. 825/Id. 4507
1364; Adeline G.; F; 12; Pima; F; S; St.dau.; 1372; Yes; Yes; AI./Id. 4509
1365; Felix; M; 16; Pima; F; S; St.son; 1373; Yes; Yes; AI. 825/Id. 4508
1366; Ellena; F; 11; Pima; F; S; Gr.dau.; 1374; Yes; Yes; AI./Id. 3457
1367; Willard; M; 9; Pima; F; S; Gr.son; 1375; Yes; Yes; AI./Id. 3218

JACKSON

1368; Frances; M; 27; Pima; F; M; Head; 1376; Yes; Yes; AI. 824/Id. 4181
1369; Marie F., (Francisco, Marie); F; 25; Pima; F; M; Wife; 1377; Yes; Yes; AI. 697/Id. 4180
1370; Elmer; M; 5; Pima; F; S; Son; 1378; Yes; Yes; AI./Id. 4170
1371; -----; F; 2; Pima; F; S; Dau.; 1379; Yes; Yes; AI./Id. 4140

JACKSON

1372; Frank; M; 46; Pima; F; M; Head; 1380; Yes; Yes; AI. 2449/Id. 3194
1373; Bertha; F; 47; Pima; F; M; Wife; 1381; Yes; AI. 2450/Id. 3195
1374; Mabel; F; 21; Pima; F; S; Dau.4[sic]; 1382; Yes; Yes; AI. 2452/Id. 3197
1375; Richard; M; 20; Pima; F; S; Son; 1383; Yes; Yes; AI. 2453/Id. 3198
1376; Hazel; F; 19; Pima; F; S; Dau.; 1384; Yes; Yes; AI. 2454/Id. 3199
1377; Audrey Geraldine; F; 8/12; Pima; F; S; Gr.dau.; --; Yes Born 8-2-31; Yes; AI./Id. 3614

JACKSON

1378; Fred; M; 33; Pima; F; Wd.; Head; 1385; Yes; Yes; AI./Id. 6469
1379; Bertha; F; 7; Pima; F; S; Dau.; 1386; Yes; Yes; AI. 2450/Id. 6471
1380; Ernest; M; 4; Pima; F; S; Son; 1387; Yes; Yes; AI. 2453/Id. 6472

JACKSON

1381; Hanna; F; 29; Pima; F; S; Dau.; 1388; Yes; Yes; AI. 2451/Id. 3195
1382; Marion S.; F; 6; Pima; 1/4x; S; Sau.[sic]; 1389; Yes; Yes; AI./Id. 3200

JACKSON

1383; Harvier; M; 67; Pima; F; M; Head; 1390; Yes; Yes; AI. 3946/Id. 5707
1384; Mary; F; 64; Pima; F; M; Wife; 1391; Yes; Yes; AI. 3947/Id. 5708

60

Census of the **Gila River** reservation of the **Pima Agency** jurisdiction; as of **April 1** ; 1932; taken by **A. H. Kneale** ; Superintendent.

Key: Number; Surname; Given; Sex (M/F); Age at Last Birthday; Tribe; Degree of Blood (F=Full); Marital Status; Relationship to Head of Family & Last Census No; At Jurisdiction Where Enrolled (Yes/No); (If no – Where); Ward (Yes/No); Allotment Annuity and/or Identification Numbers

1385; Bessie; F; 13; Pima; F; S; Dau.; 1392; Yes; Yes; AI. 3958/Id. 5709
1386; Abraham; M; 22; Pima; F; S; Son; 1393; Yes; Yes; AI. 3951/Id. 5710
1387; May; F; 21; Pima; F; S; Dau.; 1394; Yes; Yes; AI. 3952/Id. 5711
1388; Verton; M; 2; Pima; F; S; Gr.son; 1395; Yes; Yes; AI./Id. 5787

JACKSON

1389; Herbert; M; 36; Pima; F; M; Head; 1396; Yes; Yes; AI. 3021/Id. 3183
1390; Dora, (Davis, Dora); F; 22; Pima; F; M; Wife; 1397; Yes; Yes;
AI. 1994/Id. 1204
1391; Bettie; F; 5; Pima; F; S; Dau.; 1398; Yes; Yes; AI./Id. 3184
~~Calvin; M; 2; Pima; F; S; Son; --; Died 11-22-31.~~; Not reported before.; AI./Id.

JACKSON

1392; James; M; 50; Pima; F; M; Head; 1399; Yes; Yes; AI. 1571/Id. 1799
1393; Tomassie; F; 45; Pima; F; M; Wife; 1400; Yes; Yes; AI. 1572/Id. 1801
1394; Vincent; M; 21; Pima; F; S; Son; 1401; Yes; Yes; AI. 1574/Id. 1805
1395; Andreas; M; 16; Pima; F; S; Son; 1403; Yes; Yes; AI. 3512/Id. 1800
1396; Thomas; M; 14; Pima; F; S; Son; 1404; Yes; Yes; AI. 3847/Id. 1802
1397; Steven; M; 12; Pima; F; S; Son; 1405; Yes; Yes; AI./Id. 1803

JACKSON

1398; Aloysius; M; 18; Pima; F; M; Head; 1402; Yes; Yes; AI. 1573/Id. 1806
~~Rosilda, (Pratt, Rosilda); F; 19; Unk.; F; M; Wife; --; Yes~~; AI./Id.
1399; Leonard; M; 1/12; Pima; F; S; Son; --; Born 3-4-32.; Yes; AI./Id. 2052

JACKSON

1400; James; M; 42; Pima; F; M; Head; 1406; Yes; Yes; AI. 3059/Id. 3299
1401; Josephine; F; 41; Pima; F; M; Wife; 1407; Yes; Yes; AI. 3060/Id. 3300
1402; Clyde; M; 18; Pima; F; S; Son; 1408; Yes; Yes; AI. 3061/Id. 3301
1403; Ernie M.; F; 14; Pima; F; S; Dau.; 1409; Yes; Yes; AI. 4634/Id. 3302
1404; Nadine R.; F; 14; Pima; F; S; Dau.; 1410; Yes; Yes; AI./Id. 3303
1405; Clifton; M; 12; Pima; F; S; Son; 1411; Yes; Yes; AI./Id. 3304
1406; Edna; F; 7; Pima; F; S; Dau.; 1412; Yes; Yes; AI./Id. 3305
1407; Standford; M; 6; Pima; F; S; Son; 1413; Yes; Yes; AI./Id. 3306
1408; Gilbert; M; 3; Pima; F; S; Son; 1414; Yes; Yes; AI./Id. 3307

JACKSON

1409; Jessie; M; 62; Pima; F; Wd.; Head; 1415; Yes; Yes; AI. 2160/Id. 3327

JACKSON

1410; Cecilia T.; F; 27; Maricopa; F; Wd.; Wife; 1416; Yes; Yes; AI./Id. 530

JACKSON

1411; John; M; 36; Pima; F; S; Head; 1417; Yes; Yes; AI. 1362/Id. 7280

Key: Number; Surname; Given; Sex (M/F); Age at Last Birthday; Tribe; Degree of Blood (F=Full); Marital Status; Relationship to Head of Family & Last Census No; At Jurisdiction Where Enrolled (Yes/No); (If no – Where); Ward (Yes/No); Allotment Annuity and/or Identification Numbers

JACKSON

1412; John; M; 40; Pima; F; M; Head; 1418; Yes; Yes; AI. 3948/Id. 6741
1413; Maggie, (Thomas, Maggie); F; 52; Pima; F; M; Wife; 1419; Yes; Yes; AI. 1035/Id. 6742
1414; Raymond; M; 10; Pima; F; S; Son; 1420; Yes; Yes; AI./Id. 6743
1415; Matilda E.; F; 8; Pima; F; S; Dau.; 1421; Yes; Yes; AI./Id. 6744
1416; John Jr.; M; 5; Pima; F; S; Son; 1422; Yes; Yes; AI./Id. 6745
1417; Elmira E.; F; 2; Pima; F; S; Dau.; 1423; Yes; Yes; AI./Id. 7131

JACKSON

1418; Johnson; M; 35; Pima; F; M; Head; 1424; Yes; Yes; AI. 859/Id. 4201
1419; Anna E., (Evans, Anna); F; 29; Pima; F; M; Wife; 1425; Yes; Yes; AI. 1766/Id. 4202

JACKSON

1420; Joseph; M; 44; Pima; F; M; Head; 1426; Yes; Yes; AI. 99/Id. 5453
1421; Angelita; F; 42; Pima; F; M; Wife; 1427; Yes; Yes; AI. 100/Id. 5454
1422; Catherine; F; 18; Pima; F; S; Dau.; 1428; Yes; Yes; AI. 101/Id. 5455
1423; Fred R.; M; 15; Pima; F; S; Son; 1429; Yes; Yes; AI. 4660/Id. 5456
1424; Hilda N.; F; 12; Pima; F; S; Dau.; 1430; Yes; Yes; AI. 14795/Id. 5457
1425; Leonora; F; 10; Pima; F; S; Dau.; 1431; Yes; Yes; AI./Id. 5458
1426; Patrick; M; 6; Pima; F; S; Son; 1432; Yes; Yes; AI./Id. 5459
1427; Ross; M; 2; Pima; F; S; Son; 1433; Yes; Yes; AI./Id. 5460

JACKSON

1428; Juan L.; M; 38; Pima; F; M; Head; 1434; Yes; Yes; AI. 2417/Id. 3248
1429; Rosetta S., (Senero, Carman); F; 24; Pima; F; M; Wife; 1435; Yes; Yes; AI. 3184/Id. 3249

JACKSON

1430; Juan O.; M; 71; Pima; F; Wd.; Head; 1436; Yes; Yes; AI. 3064/Id. 3185
~~Annie; F; 70; Pima; F; M; Wife; 1437; Died 2-25-32.~~; Yes; AI. 3065/Id. 3186
1431; Lily; F; 23; Pima; F; S; Dau.; 1438; Yes; Yes; AI. 2964/Id. 3187

JACKSON

1432; Juanna A.; F; 87; Pima; F; Wd.; Head; 1439; Yes; Yes; AI. 2308/Id. 3009

JACKSON

1433; Kisto; M; 65; Pima; F; Wd.; Head; 1441; Yes; Yes; AI. 2577/Id. 6884

JACKSON

1434; Leonard; M; 29; Pima; F; M; Head; 1442; Yes; Yes; AI. 3950/Id. 5715
1435; Susie; F; 32; Pima; F; M; Wife; 1443; Yes; Yes; AI./Id. 5716
1436; Blanche; F; 3; Pima; F; S; Dau.; 1444; Yes; Yes; AI./Id. 5717
1437; Bernice; F; 11; Pima; F; S; St.dau.; 1445; Yes; Yes; AI. 2459/Id. 5712

Key: Number; Surname; Given; Sex (M/F); Age at Last Birthday; Tribe; Degree of Blood (F=Full); Marital Status; Relationship to Head of Family & Last Census No; At Jurisdiction Where Enrolled (Yes/No); (If no – Where); Ward (Yes/No); Allotment Annuity and/or Identification Numbers

1438; Adeline; F; 11; Pima; F; S; St.dau.; 1446; Yes; Yes; AI./Id. 5713
1439; Clayton; M; 6; Pima; F; S; St.son; 1447; Yes; Yes; AI./Id. 5714

JACKSON
1440; Nathan; M; 26; Pima; F; S; Head; 1448; Yes; Yes; AI. 2186/Id. 3528

JACKSON
1441; Orley; M; 60; Pima; F; M; Head; 1449; Yes; Yes; AI. 2275/Id. 3254
1442; Fannie; F; 54; Pima; F; M; Wife; 1450; Yes; Yes; AI. 2276/Id. 3255
1443; Thackery; M; 17; Pima; F; S; Son; 1451; Yes; Yes; AI. 2066/Id. 3259

JACKSON
1444; Homer; M; 20; Pima; F; M; Head; 1452; Yes; Yes; AI. 2065/Id. 3258
1445; Grace P., (Pablo, Grace); F; 19; Pima; F; M; Wife; 1453; Yes; Yes; AI. 2279/Id. 3086
1446; Loraine; F; 1; Pima; F; S; Dau.; 1454; Yes; Yes; AI./Id. 3601

JACKSON
1447; Ramon; M; 60; Pima; F; M; Head; 1455; Yes; Yes; AI. 2553/Id. 6838
1448; Susanna; F; 60; Pima; F; M; Wife; 1456; Yes; Yes; AI. 2554/Id. 6839
1449; Robert A.; M; 11; Pima; F; S; Gr.son; 1457; Yes; Yes; AI./Id. 7139

JACKSON
1450; Richard; M; 27; Pima; F; S; Head; 1458; Yes; Yes; AI. 2063/Id. 3257

JACKSON
1451; Simon; M; 26; Pima; F; S; Head; 1459; Yes; Yes; AI. 2018/Id. 4205

JACKSON
1452; Tawmego; M; 55; Pima; F; M; Head; 1460; Yes; Yes; AI. 2410/Id. 3239
1453; Lupi; F; 57; Pima; F; M; Wife; 1461; Yes; Yes; AI. 2411/Id. 3240
1454; Matilena; F; 27; Pima; F; S; Dau.; 1462; Yes; Yes; AI. 2413/Id. 3242
1455; Mathis; M; 21; Pima; F; S; Son; 1463; Yes; Yes; AI. 2412/Id. 3243
1456; Ambrose; M; 17; Pima; F; S; Son; 1464; Yes; Yes; AI. 3245/Id. 4631
1457; Cora; F; 15; Pima; F; S; Dau.; 1465; Yes; Yes; AI./Id. 3346
1458; Fernando; M; 5; Pima; F; S; Gr.son; 1466; Yes; Yes; AI./Id. 3347

JACKSON
1459; Thomas; M; 30; Pima; F; M; Head; 1467; Yes; Yes; AI. 2016/Id. 4204
1460; Lucy P., (Pedro, Josephine); F; 25; Pima; F; M; Wife; 1468; Yes; Yes; AI. 2357/Id. 4290
1461; Fern; F; 3; Pima; F; S; Dau.; 1469; Yes; Yes; AI./Id. 4141
1462; Corrine Doris; F; 3/12; Pima; F; S; Dau.; 1--; Yes; Born 1-8-32.; Yes; AI./Id. 3952

Key: Number; Surname; Given; Sex (M/F); Age at Last Birthday; Tribe; Degree of Blood (F=Full); Marital Status; Relationship to Head of Family & Last Census No; At Jurisdiction Where Enrolled (Yes/No); (If no – Where); Ward (Yes/No); Allotment Annuity and/or Identification Numbers

JACKSON
1463; Veelinaro; M; 26; Pima; F; S; Head; 1470; Yes; Yes; AI. 2414/Id. 3241

JACKSON
1464; Viola; F; 59; Pima; F; Wd.; Wife; 1471; Yes; Yes; AI. 1708/Id. 4203
1465; Davis; M; 19; Pima; F; S; Son; 1472; Yes; Yes; AI. 1559/Id. 4207
1466; Ernest; M; 16; Pima; F; S; Son; 1473; Yes; Yes; AI. 3289/Id. 4208

JACKSON
1467; Wilson; M; 62; Pima; F; S; Head; 1474; Yes; Yes; AI. 872/Id. 6926
1468; Helen N., (Nathan, Helen); F; 39; Pima; F; M; Wife; 1475; Yes; Yes; AI. 881/Id. 6927
1469; Nathan; Donald; M; 20; Pima; F; S; St.son; 1476; Yes; Yes; AI. 882/Id. 6928
1470; Nathan; Bernice; F; 17; Pima; F; S; St.dau.; 1477; Yes; Yes; AI. 3157/Id. 6929
1471; Nathan; Anthony; M; 12; Pima; F; S; St.son; 1478; Yes; Yes; AI./Id. 6930

JAMES
1472; Addie; F; 57; Pima; F; Wd.; Head; 1479; Yes; Yes; AI. 1672/Id. 4383

JAMES
1473; Albert; M; 63; Pima; F; Wd.; Head; 1480; Yes; Yes; AI. 606/Id. 4993

JAMES
1474; George; M; 67; Pima; F; M; Head; 1481; Yes; Yes; AI. 631/Id. 5118
1475; Emma; F; 67; Pima; F; M; Wife; 1482; Yes; Yes; AI. 632/Id. 5119
1476; William; M; 28; Pima; F; S; Son; 1483; Yes; Yes; AI. 958/Id. 5126

JAMES
1477; Herbert; M; 36; Pima; F; S; Head; 1484; Yes; Yes; AI. 609/Id. 5834

JAMES
1478; Herbert; M; 42; Pima; F; M; Head; 1485; Yes; Yes; AI. 957/Id. 5120
1479; Emily A., (Lewis, Amily[sic] Amelia); F; 30; Pima; F; M; Wife; 1486; Yes; Yes; AI. 1479/Id. 5121
1480; Priscilla; F; 10; Pima; F; S; Dau.; 1487; Yes; Yes; AI./Id. 5122
1481; -----; F; 2; Pima; F; S; Dau.; 1488; Yes; Yes; AI./Id. 5855

JAMES
1482; John; M; 47; Pima; F; M; Head; 1489; Yes; Yes; AI. 1379/Id. 4759
1483; Dorothy P., (Pablo, Dorothy); F; 31; Pima; F; M; Wife; 1490; Yes; Yes; AI. 1782/Id. 4760
1484; Leonard; M; 22; Pima; F; S; Son; 1491; Yes; Yes; AI. 1383/Id. 4761
1485; Listine; F; 19; Pima; F; S; Dau.; 1492; Yes; Yes; AI. 1381/Id. 4763
1486; Edmund; M; 14; Pima; F; S; Son; 1493; Yes; Yes; AI. 4574/Id. 4764
1487; Bernard J.; M; 6; Pima; F; S; Son; 1494; Yes; Yes; AI./Id. 4765

Census of the **Gila River** reservation of the **Pima Agency** jurisdiction; as of **April 1** ; 1932; taken by **A. H. Kneale** ; Superintendent.

Key: Number; Surname; Given; Sex (M/F); Age at Last Birthday; Tribe; Degree of Blood (F=Full); Marital Status; Relationship to Head of Family & Last Census No; At Jurisdiction Where Enrolled (Yes/No); (If no – Where); Ward (Yes/No); Allotment Annuity and/or Identification Numbers

JAMES
1488; Joseph; M; 39; Pima; F; S; Head; 1495; Yes; Yes; AI. 2055/Id. 3017

JAMES
1489; Luke; M; 49; Pima; F; M; Head; 1496; Yes; Yes; AI. 1482/Id. 4603
1490; Mabel; F; 45; Pima; F; M; Wife; 1497; Yes; Yes; AI. 1483/Id. 4604
1491; Fred; M; 18; Pima; F; S; Son; 1498; No; Unk; Unk; Unk; Yes; AI. 1484/Id. 4605
1492; Albert; M; 14; Pima; F; S; Son; 1499; Yes; Yes; AI. 3484/Id. 4606
1493; Matilda; F; 12; Pima; F; S; Dau.; 1500; Yes; Yes; AI. 4810/Id. 4607
1494; Edison; M; 10; Pima; F; S; Son; 1501; Yes; Yes; AI./Id. 4608
1495; Roger; M; 2; Pima; F; S; Son; 1502; Yes; Yes; AI./Id. 4117

JAMES
1496; Moffitt; M; 25; Pima; F; M; Head; 1503; Yes; Yes; AI. 633/Id. 5123
1497; Elizabeth K., (Kisto, Elizabeth); F; 24; Pima; F; M; Wife; 1504; Yes; Yes; AI. 2312/Id. 5124
1498; Leroy; M; 4; Pima; F; S; Son; 1505; Yes; Yes; AI./Id. 5125
1499; Mary Ann; F; 1; Pima; F; S; Dau.; 1506; Yes; Yes; AI./Id. 6104

JAMES
~~Peter; M; 58; Pima; F; Wd.; Head; 1507; Died; 1-31-32~~; Yes; AI. 1234/Id. 6959
1500; Domigo; M; 33; Pima; F; S; Head; 1508; Yes; Yes; AI. 1236/Id. 6960

JAMES
1501; Preston; M; 40; Pima; F; M; Head; 1509; Yes; Yes; AI. 610/Id. 5070
1502; Ruth O., (Osife, Ruth); F; 32; Pima; F; M; Wife; 1510; Yes; Yes; AI. 629/Id. 5071

JAMES
1503; Simon; M; 40; Pima; F; M; Head; 1511; Yes; Yes; AI. 968/Id. 6917
1504; Lena; F; 40; Pima; F; M; Wife; 1512; Yes; Yes; AI. 969/Id. 6618
1505; Hattie; F; 19; Pima; F; S; Dau.; 1513; Yes; Yes; AI. 970/Id. 6919
~~Inez; F; 18; Pima; F; S; Dau.; 1514; Died; 10-25-31~~; Yes; AI. 971/Id. 6920
1506; Clarence N.; M; 17; Pima; F; S; Son; 1515; Yes; Yes; AI. 3187/Id. 6921
1507; Helen; F; 12; Pima; F; S; Dau.; 1516; Yes; Yes; AI. 4833/Id. 6922
1508; Lloyd; M; 6; Pima; F; S; Son; 1517; Yes; Yes; AI./Id. 6923

JAY
1509; John; M; 52; Pima; F; M; Head; 1518; Yes; Yes; AI. 1723/Id. 4324
1510; (Eliza) Malassa; F; 50; Pima; F; M; Wife; 1519; Yes; Yes; AI. 1724/Id. 4325
1511; John Jr.; M; 25; Pima; F; S; Son; 1520; Yes; Yes; AI. 1977/Id. 4326
1512; Jose Juan; M; 27; Pima; F; S; Son; 1521; Yes; Yes; AI. 1978/Id. 4327
1513; Andrew; M; 26; Pima; F; S; Son; 1522; Yes; Yes; AI. 1980/Id. 4328
1514; Isabella; F; 23; Pima; F; S; Dau.; 1523; Yes; Yes; AI. 1981/Id. 4329

65

Key: Number; Surname; Given; Sex (M/F); Age at Last Birthday; Tribe; Degree of Blood (F=Full); Marital Status; Relationship to Head of Family & Last Census No; At Jurisdiction Where Enrolled (Yes/No); (If no – Where); Ward (Yes/No); Allotment Annuity and/or Identification Numbers

1515; Daisy; F; 18; Pima; F; S; Dau.; 1524; Yes; Yes; AI. 3280/Id. 4330

JOHN
1516; Anna; F; 28; Pima; F; S; Head; 1525; Yes; Yes; AI. 230/Id. 3529

JOHN
1517; Ben; M; 59; Pima; F; M; Head; 1526; Yes; Yes; AI. 3031/Id. 3209
1518; Alice J., (Jackson, Alice); F; 32; Pima; F; M; Wife; 1527; Yes; Yes; AI. 3022/Id. 3210
1519; Harry; M; 24; Pima; F; S; Son; 1528; Yes; Yes; AI. 3026/Id. 3211
1520; Edison; M; 21; Pima; F; S; Son; 1529; Yes; Yes; AI. 3029/Id. 3214
1521; Elliott; M; 19; Pima; F; S; Son; 1530; Yes; Yes; AI. 3030/Id. 3215
1522; Boyd; M; 17; Pima; F; S; Son; 1531; Yes; Yes; AI. 3794/Id. 3216
1523; Jackson; Wilford; M; 9; Pima; F; S; St.son; 1532; Yes; Yes; AI./Id. 3218

JOHN
1524; Dennis; M; 38; Pima; F; Wd.; Head; 1533; Yes; Yes; AI. 2092/Id. 4115
1525; Byron; M; 14; Pima; F; S; Son; 1534; Yes; Yes; AI. 4813/Id. 5971
1526; Gwendolyn; F; 13; Pima; F; S; Dau.; 1535; Yes; Yes; AI. 4812/Id. 5972
1527; Patrick S.; M; 12; Pima; F; S; Son; 1536; Yes; Yes; AI./Id. 4919
1528; Geraldine; F; 7; Pima; F; S; Dau.; 1537; Yes; Yes; AI./Id. 4920
1529; Muriel P.; M; 4; Pima; F; S; St.son; 1538; Yes; Yes; AI./Id. 5977

JOHN
1530; James L.; M; 48; Pima; F; M; Head; 1539; Yes; Yes; AI. 2088/Id. 3080
1531; Nellie; F; 32; Pima; F; M; Wife; 1540; Yes; Yes; AI./Id. 3081
1532; Albert L.; M; 18; Pima; F; S; Son; 1541; Yes; Yes; AI. 2090/Id. 3057
1533; Inez; F; 17; Pima; F; S; Dau.; 1542; Yes; Yes; AI. 4595/Id. 3058
1534; Edward; M; 11; Pima; F; S; Son; 1543; Yes; Yes; AI. 4866/Id. 3059
1535; Delsie I.; F; 4; Pima; F; S; Dau.; 1544; Yes; Yes; AI./Id. 3082

JOHN
1536; Joseph; M; 58; Pima; F; M; Head; 1545; Yes; Yes; AI. 2094/Id. 3055
1537; Flora; F; 57; Pima; F; M; Wife; 1546; Yes; Yes; AI. 2095/Id. 3056

JOHNS
1538; Catherine; F; 57; Pima; F; Wd.; Head; 1547; Yes; Yes; AI. 556/Id. 5052

JOHNS
1539; Jacob; M; 29; Pima; F; Wd.; Head; 1548; Yes; Yes; AI. 553/Id. 5879
~~Clara T., (Chopin, Clara Terry); F; 25; Pima; F; M; Wife; 548; Died 2-15-32.~~; Yes; AI. 756/Id. 5330
1540; Robert; M; 5/12; Pima; F; S; Son; --; ~~Born 11-21-31.~~; Yes; AI./Id. 6128
1541; Chopin, Gladys J.; F; 8; Pima; F; S; St.dau.; 549; Yes; Yes; AI./Id. 5331
1542; Chopin, Esther; F; 5; Pima; F; S; St.dau.; 550; Yes; Yes; AI./Id. 5332

66

Census of the **Gila River** reservation of the **Pima Agency** jurisdiction; as of **April 1** ; 1932; taken by **A. H. Kneale** ; Superintendent.

Key: Number; Surname; Given; Sex (M/F); Age at Last Birthday; Tribe; Degree of Blood (F=Full); Marital Status; Relationship to Head of Family & Last Census No; At Jurisdiction Where Enrolled (Yes/No); (If no – Where); Ward (Yes/No); Allotment Annuity and/or Identification Numbers

1543; Chopin, Lester; M; 3; Pima; F; S; St.son; 551; Yes; Yes; AI./Id. 5333

JOHNS

1544; Jonna; F; 57; Pima; F; Wd.; Head; 1549; Yes; Yes; AI. 2087/Id. 3060

JOHNS

1545; Mekales; M; 53; Pima; F; M; Head; 1550; Yes; Yes; AI. 876/Id. 6931
1546; Mary C., (Caroline Johns); F; 47; Pima; F; M; Wife; 1551; Yes; Yes; AI. 877/Id. 6932
1547; Carolina; F; 19; Pima; F; S; Dau.; 1552; Yes; Yes; AI. 2499/Id. 7140

JOHNS

1548; Helen E., (Randell, Helen Elena); 28; Pima; F; M; Wife; 1553; Yes; Yes; AI. 305/Id. 4986

JOHNS

1549; Magill; M; 29; Pima; F; M; Head; 1554; Yes; Yes; AI. 879/Id. 6933
1550; Anna P., (Peterson, Annie); F; 47; Pima; F; M; Wife; 1555; Yes; Yes; AI. 122/Id. 5129

JOHNS

1551; Miguel; M; 29; Pima; F; M; Head; 1556; Yes; Yes; AI. 1890/Id. 4307
1552; Mary M., (Marago, Mary); F; 25; Pima; F; M; Wife; 1557; Yes; Yes; AI. 2455/Id. 4308
1553; Georgiana; F; 7; Pima; F; S; Dau.; 1558; Yes; Yes; AI./Id. 4309
1554; Mary; F; 5; Pima; F; S; Dau.; 1559; Yes; Yes; AI./Id. 4310
1555; Miguel Jr.; M; 2; Pima; F; S; Son; 1560; Yes; Yes; AI./Id. 4114

JOHNS

1556; Peter; M; 19; Pima; F; M; Head; 1561; Yes; Yes; AI. 886/Id. 6934
1557; Belle N., (Norris, Bell[sic]); F; 21; Pima; F; M; Wife; 1562; Yes; Yes; AI. 890/Id. 7053

JOHNS

1558; Philip; M; 36; Pima; F; M; Head; 1563; Yes; Yes; AI. 902/Id. 5049
~~Fannie C., (Cook, Fannie); 33; Pima; F; M; Wife; 1564; Died 1-23-32.~~; Yes; AI. 1279/Id. 5050
1559; Jannette; F; 14; Pima; F; S; Dau.; 1565; Yes; Yes; AI. 3322/Id. 5051

JOHNS

1560; San Jose; M; 67; Pima; F; M; Head; 1566; Yes; Yes; AI. 896/Id. 6343
1561; Mary Anna; 57; Pima; F; M; Wife; 1567; Yes; Yes; AI. 897/Id. 6644

Census of the **Gila River** reservation of the **Pima Agency** jurisdiction; as of **April 1** ; 1932; taken by **A. H. Kneale** ; Superintendent.

Key: Number; Surname; Given; Sex (M/F); Age at Last Birthday; Tribe; Degree of Blood (F=Full); Marital Status; Relationship to Head of Family & Last Census No; At Jurisdiction Where Enrolled (Yes/No); (If no – Where); Ward (Yes/No); Allotment Annuity and/or Identification Numbers

JOHNS

1562; Thomas C.; M; 47; Pima; F; M; Head; 1568; Yes; Yes; AI. 891/Id. 4244
1563; Sarah M., (Martiniz, Sarah); F; 43; Pima; F; M; Wife; 1569; Yes; Yes; AI. 2025/Id. 4245
 1564; Irene C.; F; 24; Pima; F; S; Dau.; 1570; Yes; Yes; AI. 894/Id. 6647
1565; Bertha C.; F; 22; Pima; F; S; Dau.; 1571; Yes; Yes; AI. 895/Id. 6648
1566; Pearl E.; F; 1; Pima; F; S; Gr.dau.; 1572; Yes; Yes; AI./Id. 7273

JOHNSON

1567; Ambrose; M; 43; Pima; F; M; Head; 1573; Yes; Yes; AI. 749/Id. 5485
1568; Victor; M; 21; Pima; F; S; Son; 1574; Yes; Yes; AI. 752/Id. 5488
1569; Edith; F; 19; Pima; F; S; Dau.; 1575; Yes; Yes; AI. 751/Id. 5489
1570; Nellie; F; 16; Pima; F; S; Dau.; 1576; Yes; Yes; AI. 495/Id. 5490

JOHNSON

1571; Annie; F; 72; Pima; F; Wd.; Head; 1577; Yes; Yes; AI. 158/Id. 4255

JOHNSON

1572; Arthur; M; 48; Maricopa; F; Wd.; Head; 1578; Yes; Yes; AI. 2849/Id. 162
1573; Fannie; 22; Maricopa; F; S; Dau; 1579; Yes; Yes; AI. 2858/Id. 163

JOHNSON

1574; David; M; 37; Pima; F; M; Head; 1580; No; Wewoka; Seminole; Okla.; Yes; AI. 2024/Id. 4139
1575; Wilbert; M; 16; Pima; F; S; Son; 1581; No; Wewoka; Seminole; Okla.; Yes; AI. 4789/Id. 4138
1576; Pauline; F; 13; Pima; F; S; Dau.; 1582; No; Wewoka; Seminole; Okla.; Yes; AI. 4710/Id. 4137

JOHNSON

1577; Frank; M; 30; Pima; F; M; Head; 1583; Yes; Yes; AI. 1987/Id. 4252
1578; Isabelle, (Davis, Isabelle); F; 24; Pima; F; M; Wife; 1584; Yes; Yes; AI. 1993/Id. 4253
 1579; Evelyn C.; F; 2; Pima; F; S; Dau.; 1585; Yes; Yes; AI./Id. 4170

JOHNSON

1580; Frank; M; 46; Pima; F; M; Head; 1586; Yes; Yes; AI. 3278/Id. 6649
1581; Helen J., (James, Helen); F; 42; Pima; F; M; Wife; 1587; Yes; Yes; AI. 959/Id. 6650

JOHNSON

1582; George; M; 43; Pima; F; Wd.; Head; 1588; Yes; Yes; AI. 2068/Id. 3553

JOHNSON

1583; George; M; 43; Maricopa; F; M; Head; 1589; Yes; Yes; AI. 2780/Id. 172

Key: Number; Surname; Given; Sex (M/F); Age at Last Birthday; Tribe; Degree of Blood (F=Full); Marital Status; Relationship to Head of Family & Last Census No; At Jurisdiction Where Enrolled (Yes/No); (If no – Where); Ward (Yes/No); Allotment Annuity and/or Identification Numbers

1584; Lou A., (Albert, Lou); 34; Maricopa; F; M; Wife; 1590; Yes; Yes; AI. 2769/Id. 173
1585; Josephine; 14; Maricopa; F; S; Dau; 1591; Yes; Yes; AI. 4675/Id. 174
1586; Leo; M; 7; Maricopa; F; S; Son; 1592; Yes; Yes; AI./Id. 175
1587; Ethel; 3; Maricopa; F; S; Dau; 1593; Yes; Yes; AI./Id. 578

JOHNSON
1588; George; M; 53; Pima; F; Wd.; Head; 1594; Yes; Yes; AI. 59/Id. 5652
1589; Cyrus; M; 20; Pima; F; S; Son; 1595; Yes; Yes; AI. 61/Id. 5653

JOHNSON
1590; Henry; M; 41; Pima; F; M; Head; 1596; Yes; Yes; AI. 154/Id. 5386
1591; Jessie; F; 37; Pima; F; M; Wife; 1597; Yes; Yes; AI. 155/Id. 5387
1592; Margaret; F; 20; Pima; F; S; Dau.; 1598; Yes; Yes; AI. 2386/Id. 5388
1593; Mildred; F; 18; Pima; F; S; Dau.; 1599; Yes; Yes; AI. 2387/Id. 5389
1594; Daniel; M; 9; Pima; F; S; Son; 1600; Yes; Yes; AI./Id. 5390
1595; Simon; M; 6; Pima; F; S; Son; 1601; Yes; Yes; AI./Id. 5391
1596; May; F; 4; Pima; F; S; Dau.; 1602; Yes; Yes; AI./Id. 5392

JOHNSON
1597; Isaac; M; 62; Pima; F; Wd.; Head; 1603; Yes; Yes; AI. 2228/Id. 3141
1598; Eugene; M; 26; Pima; F; S; Son; 1604; Yes; Yes; AI. 2273/Id. 3142
1599; Esther; F; 18; Pima; F; S; Dau.; 1605; Yes; Yes; AI. 2254/Id. 3146
1600; Catherine; F; 22; Pima; F; S; Dau.; 1606; Yes; Yes; AI. 2252/Id. 3144

JOHNSON
1601; E. Howard; M; 37; Pima; F; Wd.; Head; 1607; Yes; Yes; AI. 2385/Id. 3554

JOHNSON
1602; James; M; 36; Pima; F; Wd.; Head; 1608; Yes; Yes; AI. 2305/Id. 3236
1603; Clarence; M; 18; Pima; F; S; Son; 1609; Yes; Yes; AI. 2306/Id. 3237
1604; Harold L.; M; 15; Pima; F; S; Son; 1610; Yes; Yes; AI. 4615/Id. 3238
1605; Mertie M.; F; 13; Pima; F; S; Dau.; 1611; Yes; Yes; AI. 4616/Id. 3555
1606; Ella; F; 6; Pima; F; S; Dau.; 1612; Yes; Yes; AI. 4616/Id. 3556

JOHNSON
1607; Job; M; 59; Pima; F; Wd.; Head; 1613; Yes; Yes; AI. 1571/Id. 4279

JOHNSON
1608; John A.E.; M; 44; Pima; F; M; Head; 1614; Yes; Yes; AI. 3087/Id. 3188
1609; Jessie; F; 37; Pima; F; M; Wife; 1615; Yes; Yes; AI. 3088/Id. 3189
1610; Eben; M; 18; Pima; F; S; Son; 1616; Yes; Yes; AI. 3089/Id. 3190
1611; Enoch; M; 16; Pima; F; S; Son; 1617; Yes; Yes; AI. 3271/Id. 3191
1612; Otis; M; 13; Pima; F; S; Son; 1618; Yes; Yes; AI. 4629/Id. 3192
1613; Allen; M; 5; Pima; F; S; Son; 1619; Yes; Yes; AI. 0/Id. 3193

69

Census of the **Gila River** reservation of the **Pima Agency** jurisdiction; as of **April 1** ; 1932; taken by **A. H. Kneale** ; Superintendent.

Key: Number; Surname; Given; Sex (M/F); Age at Last Birthday; Tribe; Degree of Blood (F=Full); Marital Status; Relationship to Head of Family & Last Census No; At Jurisdiction Where Enrolled (Yes/No); (If no – Where); Ward (Yes/No); Allotment Annuity and/or Identification Numbers

JOHNSON

1614; Joseph; M; 38; Pima; F; M; Head; 1620; Yes; Yes; AI. 2328/Id. 3395
1615; Cheerless; F; 38; Pima; F; M; Wife; 1621; Yes; Yes; AI. 2329/Id. 3396
1616; Ernest W.; M; 18; Pima; F; S; Son; 1622; Yes; Yes; AI./Id. 3397
1617; Eddy; F; 13; Pima; F; S; Dau.; 1623; Yes; Yes; AI. 4624/Id. 3398
1618; Leta; F; 11; Pima; F; S; Dau.; 1624; Yes; Yes; AI./Id. 3399
1619; Elsie; F; 5; Pima; F; S; Dau.; 1625; Yes; Yes; AI./Id. 3400

JOHNSON

1620; Lottie; F; 25; Pima; F; S; Head; 1626; Yes; Yes; AI. 2251/Id. 3143
1621; Eugene; M; 3; Pima; F; S; Son; 1627; Yes; Yes; AI./Id. 3557

JOHNSON

1622; Luke; M; 41; Pima; F; M; Head; 1628; Yes; Yes; AI. 249/Id. 4941
1623; Helen L., (Lewis, Helen); F; 36; Pima; F; M; Wife; 1629; Yes; Yes; AI. 1208/Id. 4942
1624; Luke H.; M; 7; Pima; F; S; Son; 1630; Yes; Yes; AI./Id. 4943

JOHNSON

1625; Martie; F; 71; Pima; F; Wd.; Head; 1631; Yes; Yes; AI. 2778/Id. 5880

JOHNSON

1626; Philip; M; 34; Pima; F; M; Head; 1632; Yes; Yes; AI. 915/Id. 7142
1627; May E., (Enos, May); F; 33; Pima; F; M; Wife; 1633; Yes; Yes; AI. 2011/Id. 7143
1628; Ruth; F; 12; Pima; F; S; Dau.; 1634; Yes; Yes; AI./Id. 7144
1629; Viola; F; 8; Pima; F; S; Dau.; 1635; Yes; Yes; AI./Id. 7145
1630; Len; M; 5; Pima; F; S; Son; 1636; Yes; Yes; AI./Id. 7146
1631; Wayne; M; 3; Pima; F; S; Son; 1637; Yes; Yes; AI./Id. 7147
1632; Marcella; F; 4/12; Pima; F; S; Dau.; --; Yes Born 12-05-31.; Yes; AI./Id. 7292

JOHNSON

1633; Rudolph; M; 46; Pima; F; M; Head; 1638; Yes; Yes; AI. 790/Id. 4461
1634; Jessie; F; 45; Pima; F; M; Wife; 1639; Yes; Yes; AI. 761/Id. 4462
1635; Grace V.; F; 3; Pima; F; S; Gr.dau.; 1640; Yes; Yes; AI./Id. 7113
1636; Hall; Nora.; F; 27; Pima; F; S; St.dau.; 1641; Yes; Yes; AI./Id. 4464

JOHNSON

1637; Thomas; M; 39; Pima; F; M; Head; 1642; Yes; Yes; AI. 964/Id. 1845
1638; Agnes; F; 39; Pima; F; M; Wife; 1643; Yes; Yes; AI. 965/Id. 1846
1639; Mary C.; F; 3; Pima; F; S; Dau.; 1644; Yes; Yes; AI./Id. 1978

JOHNSON

William; M; 67; Pima; F; M; Head; 1645; Died 10-21-31.; Yes; AI. 103/Id. 5491
1640; Louise; F; 65; Pima; F; M; Wd.; 1646; Yes; Yes; AI. 105/Id. 5492

Census of the **Gila River** reservation of the **Pima Agency** jurisdiction; as of **April 1** ; 1932; taken by **A. H. Kneale** ; Superintendent.

Key: Number; Surname; Given; Sex (M/F); Age at Last Birthday; Tribe; Degree of Blood (F=Full); Marital Status; Relationship to Head of Family & Last Census No; At Jurisdiction Where Enrolled (Yes/No); (If no – Where); Ward (Yes/No); Allotment Annuity and/or Identification Numbers

JOHNSON

1641; Yulick; M; 72; Pima; F; M; Head; 1647; Yes; Yes; AI. 2560/Id. 6843
1642; Catherine; F; 70; Pima; F; M; Wife; 1648; Yes; Yes; AI. 2561/Id. 6844
1643; Herbert; M; 24; Pima; F; S; Son; 1649; Yes; Yes; AI. 2563/Id. 6845

JOHNSON

1644; Wilbur; M; 22; Pima; F; M; Head; 1650; Yes; Yes; AI. 753/Id. 5487
1645; Marie R., (Howard, Lydia); F; 20; Pima; F; M; Wife; 1651; Yes; Yes; AI. 2473/Id. 5626
1646; Delbert R.; M; 2; Pima; F; S; Son; 1652; Yes; Yes; AI./Id. 5778
1647; Ramires, Delphine; F; 14; Pima; F; S; Sis-in-law; 1653; Yes; Yes; AI. 3623/Id. 4102
1648; Ramires, Ramon; M; 10; Pima; F; S; Bro-in-law; 1654; Yes; Yes; AI./Id. 4000

JONES

~~Alberta; F; 11; Pima; F; S; See Donald Ramon Family~~; AI./Id. 5881
~~Edison; M; 15; Pima; F; S; See Donald Ramon Family~~; AI. 3267/Id. 3129

JONES

1649; Andrew; M; 33; Pima; F; S; Head; 1657; Yes; Yes; AI. 2272/Id. 3127

JONES

1650; Carrie V.; F; 53; Pima; F; Wd.; Head; 1658; Yes; Yes; AI. 1326/Id. 6445

JONES

1651; Frank M.; M; 43; Pima; F; M; Head; 1659; Yes; Yes; AI. 2509/Id. 5569
1652; Mabel M., (Myers, Mabel); F; 29; Pima; F; M; Wife; 1660; Yes; Yes; AI. 28/Id. 5570

JONES

1653; Harry; M; 59; Pima; F; M; Head; 1661; Yes; Yes; AI. 2026/Id. 3442
1654; Martha; F; 55; Pima; F; M; Wife; 1662; Yes; Yes; AI. 2027/Id. 3443
1655; Hiram; M; 18; Pima; F; S; Neph.; 1663; Yes; Yes; AI. 2196/Id. 3128

JONES

1656; Charles; M; 21; Pima; F; M; Head; 1664; Yes; Yes; AI. 152/Id. 5419
1657; Olive S., (Stewart, Olive); F; 22; Pima; F; M; Wife; 1665; Yes; Yes; AI. 1099/Id. 5420
~~Isadora; F; 1; Pima; F; S; Dau.; 1666; Died 9-19-31.~~; Yes; AI./Id. 6102
1658; Marie; F; 3/12; Pima; F; S; Dau.; --; Yes; Born 1-10-32;; Yes; AI./Id. 6127

JONES

1659; John; M; 44; Pima; F; M; Head; 1667; Yes; Yes; AI. 142/Id. 5398
1660; Edna; F; 46; Pima; F; M; Wife; 1668; Yes; Yes; AI. 143/Id. 5390
1661; Cora; F; 26; Pima; F; S; Dau.; 1669; Yes; Yes; AI. 146/Id. 5408

Key: Number; Surname; Given; Sex (M/F); Age at Last Birthday; Tribe; Degree of Blood (F=Full); Marital Status; Relationship to Head of Family & Last Census No; At Jurisdiction Where Enrolled (Yes/No); (If no – Where); Ward (Yes/No); Allotment Annuity and/or Identification Numbers

1662; O'Brien; M; 24; Pima; F; S; Son; 1670; Yes; Yes; AI. 145/Id. 5400
1663; J. Roe; M; 22; Pima; F; S; Son; 1671; Yes; Yes; AI. 147/Id. 5401
1664; Sarah M.; F; 20; Pima; F; S; Dau.; 1672; Yes; Yes; AI. 148/Id. 5402
1665; Lester; M; 18; Pima; F; S; Son; 1673; Yes; Yes; AI. 1662/Id. 5403
1666; John, Jr.; M; 16; Pima; F; S; Son; 1674; Yes; Yes; AI. 3272/Id. 5404
1667; Agnes; F; 13; Pima; F; S; Dau.; 1675; Yes; Yes; AI. 4462/Id. 5405
1668; Willard; M; 9; Pima; F; S; Son; 1676; Yes; Yes; AI./Id. 5406
1669; Pamela; F; 6; Pima; F; S; Dau.; 1677; Yes; Yes; AI./Id. 5407

JONES

1670; Jose; M; 47; Pima; F; M; Head; 1678; Yes; Yes; AI. 115/Id. 5414
1671; Hattie; F; 45; Pima; F; M; Wife; 1679; Yes; Yes; AI. 116/Id. 5415
1672; Josephine; F; 15; Pima; F; S; Dau.; 1680; Yes; Yes; AI. 3809/Id. 5416
1673; Bessie; F; 10; Pima; F; S; Dau.; 1681; Yes; Yes; AI./Id. 5417
1674; Thomas; M; 9; Pima; F; S; Son; 1682; Yes; Yes; AI./Id. 5418

JONES

1675; Lena; F; 72; Pima; F; Wd.; Head; 1683; Yes; Yes; AI. 2224/Id. 3100

JONES

1676; Minnie; F; 67; Pima; F; Wd.; Head; 1684; Yes; Yes; AI. 18/Id. 5513

JONES

1677; Melissa; F; 67; Pima; F; Wd.; Head; 1685; Yes; Yes; AI. 2431/Id. 4397
1678; Lillian; F; 36; Pima; F; S; Dau.; 1686; Yes; Yes; AI. 1688/Id. 4398
1679; Truman; M; 27; Pima; F; S; Son; 1687; Yes; Yes; AI. 2433/Id. 4399
~~Anna L.; F; 24; Pima; F; M; Dau.; 1688; Yes; (Married to Henry ???ton~~ Yes; AI. 4232/Id. 4400
1680; Joseph A.; M; 10; Pima; F; S; Gr.son; 1689; Yes; Yes; AI./Id. 4401

JONES

1681; Nora; F; 23; Pima; F; S; Head; 1690; Yes; Yes; AI. 2199/Id. 3558

JONES

1682; Peter; M; 46; Pima; F; M; Head; 1691; Yes; Yes; AI. 3043/Id. 3135
1683; Sarah; F; 43; Pima; F; M; Wife; 1692; Yes; Yes; AI. 3044/Id. 3136
1684; Herman; M; 19; Pima; F; S; Son; 1693; Yes; Yes; AI. 3046/Id. 3138
1685; Luther; M; 16; Pima; F; S; Son; 1694; Yes; Yes; AI. 4628/Id. 3139
1686; Ruth; F; 11; Pima; F; S; Dau.; 1695; Yes; Yes; AI./Id. 3140

JONES

1687; Robert; M; 31; Pima; F; M; Head; 1696; Yes; Yes; AI. 1328/Id. 6442
1688; Mildred, (Knox, Mildred); F; 26; Pima; F; M; Wife; 1697; Yes; Yes; AI. 1008/Id. 6443
1689; Virginia; F; 9; Pima; F; S; Dau.; 1698; Yes; Yes; AI./Id. 6444

Key: Number; Surname; Given; Sex (M/F); Age at Last Birthday; Tribe; Degree of Blood (F=Full); Marital Status; Relationship to Head of Family & Last Census No; At Jurisdiction Where Enrolled (Yes/No); (If no – Where); Ward (Yes/No); Allotment Annuity and/or Identification Numbers

JONES

~~N.E.; Robert; M; Unk.; Unk.; F; M; Head;~~
1690; Julia, (Gibson, Julia); F; 36; Pima; F; M; Wife; 1699; Yes; Yes; AI. 1338/Id. 6420
1691; Myrtle; F; 10; Pima; F; S; Dau.; 1700; Yes; Yes; AI./Id. 6421
1692; Marvin L.; M; 8; Pima; F; S; Son; 1701; Yes; Yes; AI./Id. 6422
1693; May Fern; F; 6; Pima; F; S; Dau.; 1702; Yes; Yes; AI./Id. 6423
1694; Sylvester; M; 4; Pima; F; S; Son; 1703; Yes; Yes; AI./Id. 6424

JONES

1695; Zacha; M; 77; Pima; F; M; Head; 1704; Yes; Yes; AI. 113/Id. 5412
1696; Sarah; F; 72; Pima; F; M; Wife; 1705; Yes; Yes; AI. 114/Id. 5413

JOSE

1697; Anton; M; 41; Pima; F; S; Head; 1706; Yes; Yes; AI. 4544/Id. 3530

JOSE

1698; Elizabeth, (Jackson, Elizabeth); F; 32; Pima; F; M; Wife; 1707; Yes; Yes; AI. 1576/Id. 4770

JOSE

1699; George; M; 33; Pima; F; M; Head; 1708; Yes; Yes; AI. 3353/Id. 4136
1700; Catherine, (Nelson, Catherine); F; 27; Pima; F; M; Wife; 1709; Yes; Yes; AI. 1228/Id. 4135
1701; Eddie; M; 2; Pima; F; S; Son; 1710; Yes; Yes; AI./Id. 4134

JOSE

1702; Marie; F; 52; Pima; F; Wd.; Head; 1711; Yes; Yes; AI. 4277/Id. 1423
1703; Lila; F; 24; Pima; F; S; Niece; 1712; Yes; Yes; AI. 4280/Id. 1945

JOSE

1704; Hill; M; 37; Pima; F; M; Head; 1713; Yes; Yes; AI. 4545/Id. 1946
1705; Amelia H.; F; 34; Pima; F; M; Wife; 1714; Yes; Yes; AI./Id. 1947

JOSE

1706; John; M; 54; Pima; F; M; Head; 1715; Yes; Yes; AI. 3858/Id. 1526
1707; Mattie; F; 67; Pima; F; M; Wife; 1716; Yes; Yes; AI. 3859/Id. 1527

JOSE

1708; Jose C.; M; 27; Pima; F; M; Head; 1717; Yes; Yes; AI. 3361/Id. 5723
1709; Hazel Thomas, (Thomas, Hazel); F; 21; Pima; F; M; Wife; 1718; Yes; Yes; AI. 1345/Id. 5724
1710; Byron; M; 3; Pima; F; S; Son; 1719; Yes; Yes; AI./Id. 5725
1711; Doris; F; 1; Pima; F; S; Dau.; 1720; Yes; Yes; AI./Id. 6109

Census of the **Gila River** reservation of the **Pima Agency** jurisdiction; as of **April 1** ; 1932; taken by **A. H. Kneale** ; Superintendent.

Key: Number; Surname; Given; Sex (M/F); Age at Last Birthday; Tribe; Degree of Blood (F=Full); Marital Status; Relationship to Head of Family & Last Census No; At Jurisdiction Where Enrolled (Yes/No); (If no – Where); Ward (Yes/No); Allotment Annuity and/or Identification Numbers

JOSE

1712; Hose K.; M; 57; Pima; F; M; Head; 1721; Yes; Yes; AI. 4254/Id. 1381
1713; Carrie; F; 49; Pima; F; M; Wife; 1722; Yes; Yes; AI. 4255/Id. 1382
1714; Viola; F; 21; Pima; F; S; Dau.; 1723; Yes; Yes; AI. 4258/Id. 1383
1715; Rosita; F; 9; Pima; F; S; Dau.; 1724; Yes; Yes; AI. 4258/Id. 1384

JOSE

~~Juan; M; 70; Pima; F; M; Head; 1725; Died; 1-19-32.~~; Yes; AI. 3578/Id. 1284
1716; Maggie; F; 58; Pima; F; M; Wife; 1726; Yes; Yes; AI. 3579/Id. 1285
1717; Eugene; M; 21; Pima; F; S; Son; 1727; Yes; Yes; AI. 3580/Id. 1286
1718; Celestine; F; 18; Pima; F; S; Dau.; 1728; Yes; Yes; AI. 3584/Id. 1287
1719; Anthony; M; 12; Pima; F; S; Son; 1729; Yes; Yes; AI. 4839/Id. 1288

JOSE

1720; Juan; M; 62; Pima; F; Wd.; Head; 1730; Yes; Yes; AI. 3351/Id. 5717
1721; Elene H.; F; 21; Pima; F; S; Dau.; 1731; Yes; Yes; AI. 3356/Id. 5719
1722; Angelo; F; 20; Pima; F; S; Dau.; 1732; Yes; Yes; AI. 3357/Id. 5720
1723; Isaiah; M; 18; Pima; F; S; Son; 1733; Yes; Yes; AI. 3358/Id. 5721
1724; Alacoque; F; 12; Pima; F; S; Dau.; 1734; Yes; Yes; AI./Id. 5722

JOSE

1725; Juan; M; 52; Pima; F; S; Head; 1735; Yes; Yes; AI. 4219/Id. 5882

JOSE

1726; Juan; M; 42; Pima; F; M; Head; 1736; Yes; Yes; AI. 3984/Id. 1568
1727; Mary J., (Jackson, Mary); F; 34; Pima; F; M; Wife; 1737; Yes; Yes; AI. 2189/Id. 1569
1728; Elinore; F; 12; Pima; F; S; Dau.; 1738; Yes; Yes; AI. 4775/Id. 1570
1729; Ida May; F; 10; Pima; F; S; Dau.; 1739; Yes; Yes; AI./Id. 1571
1730; Ernestine; F; 8; Pima; F; S; Dau.; 1740; Yes; Yes; AI./Id. 1572
1731; Gladys; F; 7; Pima; F; S; Dau.; 1741; Yes; Yes; AI./Id. 1948

JOSE

1732; Logan; M; 75; Pima; F; S; Head; 1742; Yes; Yes; AI./Id. 1289

JOSE

1733; Pedro; M; 40; Pima; F; M; Head; 1743; Yes; Yes; AI. 281/Id. 5434
1734; Carmi; F; 32; Pima; F; M; Wife; 1744; Yes; Yes; AI./Id. 5435
1735; Francisco; M; 20; Pima; F; S; Son; 1745; Yes; Yes; AI. 720/Id. 5436

JOSE

1736; Pablo; M; 49; Papago; F; M; Head; 1746; Yes; Yes; AI. 4510/Id. 4890
1737; Petro; F; 47; Papago; F; M; Wife; 1747; Yes; Yes; AI. 4511/Id. 4891
1738; Lucille; F; 23; Papago; F; S; Dau.; 1748; Yes; Yes; AI. 4512/Id. 4892
1739; Albert; M; 22; Papago; F; S; Son; 1749; Yes; Yes; AI. 4513/Id. 4897

Census of the **Gila River** reservation of the **Pima Agency** jurisdiction; as of **April 1** ; 1932; taken by **A. H. Kneale** ; Superintendent.

Key: Number; Surname; Given; Sex (M/F); Age at Last Birthday; Tribe; Degree of Blood (F=Full); Marital Status; Relationship to Head of Family & Last Census No; At Jurisdiction Where Enrolled (Yes/No); (If no – Where); Ward (Yes/No); Allotment Annuity and/or Identification Numbers

1740; Delecia; F; 19; Papago; F; S; Dau.; 1750; Yes; Yes; AI. 4514/Id. 4893
1741; Anita; F; 12; Papago; F; S; Dau.; 1751; Yes; Yes; AI./Id. 4894
1742; Thomas; M; 10; Papago; F; S; Son; 1752; Yes; Yes; AI./Id. 4895
1743; Samuel; M; 7; Papago; F; S; Son; 1753; Yes; Yes; AI./Id. 4896
1744; Elizabeth; F; 2; Papago; F; S; Gr.dau.; 1754; Yes; Yes; AI./Id. 5783

JOSE
1745; Meguilla A., (Anton, Meguilla); F; 29; Pima; F; M; Wife; 1755; Yes; Yes; AI. 2511/Id. 7148
1746; John Jose; M; 7; Pima; F; S; Son; 1756; Yes; Yes; AI./Id. 4179

JOSPEH[sic]
1747; Christopher; M; 41; Pima; F; Wd.; Head; 1757; Yes; Yes; AI. 2476/Id. 1950
1748; Jose, Vincent; M; 18; Pima; F; S; Son; 1758; Yes; Yes; AI. 1399/Id. 2478
1749; Jose, Linue; M; 17; Pima; F; S; Son; 1759; Yes; Yes; AI. 3156/Id. 1400

JOSEPH
1750; Enos Jose; M; 40; Pima; F; S; Head; 1760; Yes; Yes; AI. 1368/Id. 7150

JOSEPH
1751; Esau; M; 30; Pima; F; M; Head; 1761; Yes; Yes; AI. 1068/Id. 7151
1752; Alice N., (Newman, Alice); F; 31; Pima; F; M; Wife; 1762; Yes; Yes; AI. 4303/Id. 7152
1753; Eddie; M; 5; Pima; F; S; Son; 1763; Yes; Yes; AI./Id. 7153

JOSEPH
1754; Frank; M; 50; Pima; F; M; Head; 1764; Yes; Yes; AI. 1366/Id. 7154
1755; Juanna D., (Juanna Dora); F; 65; Pima; F; M; Wife; 1765; Yes; Yes; AI. 1367/Id. 7155

JOSEPH
1756; Fred; M; 26; Pima; F; M; Head; 1766; Yes; Yes; AI. 1069/Id. 6462
1757; Margaret; F; 25; Papago; F; M; Wife; --; Yes; Yes; AI./Id. 6463
1758; Theoro; F; 1; Pima-Papago; F; S; Dau.; 1767; Yes; Yes; AI./Id. 7273

JOSEPH
1759; John; M; 53; Pima; F; Wd.; Head; 1768; Yes; Yes; AI. 4200/Id. 1688
1760; Joseph; M; 22; Pima; F; S; Son; 1769; Yes; Yes; AI. 4201/Id. 1951

JOSEPH
1761; Leonard; M; 40; Pima; F; M; Head; 1770; Yes; Yes; AI. 2397/Id. 3203
1762; Ramona; F; 39; Pima; F; M; Wife; 1771; Yes; Yes; AI. 2398/Id. 3204
1763; Enos4[sic]; M; 18; Pima; F; S; Son; 1772; Yes; Yes; AI. 2399/Id. 3205
1764; William; M; 15; Pima; F; S; Son; 1773; Yes; Yes; AI. 3020/Id. 3206
1765; Ronica; F; 13; Pima; F; S; Dau.; 1774; Yes; Yes; AI. 3132/Id. 3207

Census of the **Gila River** reservation of the **Pima Agency** jurisdiction; as of **April 1** ; 1932; taken by **A. H. Kneale** ; Superintendent.

Key: Number; Surname; Given; Sex (M/F); Age at Last Birthday; Tribe; Degree of Blood (F=Full); Marital Status; Relationship to Head of Family & Last Census No; At Jurisdiction Where Enrolled (Yes/No); (If no – Where); Ward (Yes/No); Allotment Annuity and/or Identification Numbers

JOSEPH
1766; Maggie; F; 37; Pima; F; Wd.; Head; 1775; Yes; Yes; AI. 1067/Id. 3531
1767; James; M; 20; Pima; F; S; Son; 1776; Yes; Yes; AI. 1071/Id. 3532

JOSEPH
1768; Malya; M; 87; Pima; F; Wd.; Head; 1777; Yes; Yes; AI. 424/Id. 5627

JOSEPH
1769; Perfalo; M; 71; Pima; F; Wd.; Head; 1778; Yes; Yes; AI. 2645/Id. 6869

JUAN
1770; Adam; M; 47; Pima; F; M; Head; 1779; Yes; Yes; AI. 236/Id. 5481
1771; Mary M., (Mark, Mary); F; 52; Pima; F; M; Wife; 1780; Yes; Yes; AI. 3741/Id. 5482
1772; Nathaniel; M; 12; Pima; F; S; Son; 1781; Yes; Yes; AI. 4581/Id. 5483
1773; Germaine; F; 4; Pima; F; S; Dau.; 1782; Yes; Yes; AI. 3132/Id. 5484

JUAN
1774; Adolph; M; 48; Pima; F; M; Head; 1783; Yes; Yes; AI. 3854/Id. 1633
1775; Susie A., (Lewis, Susie Anna); F; 34; Pima; F; M; Wife; 1784; Yes; Yes; AI. 4250/Id. 1634
1776; Felix; M; 16; Pima; F; S; Son; 1785; Yes; Yes; AI. 4856/Id. 1635

JUAN
1777; Annie; F; 53; Pima; F; Wd.; Head; 1786; Yes; Yes; AI. 4387/Id. 3166
1778; Gerald; M; 24; Pima; F; S; Son; 1787; Yes; Yes; AI. 4388/Id. 3168
1779; Ina; F; 16; Pima; F; S; Dau.; 1788; Yes; Yes; AI. 4630/Id. 3169

JUAN
1780; Antonio; M; 58; Pima; F; M; Head; 1789; Yes; Yes; AI. 1/Id. 5538
1781; Jennie K.; F; 55; Pima; F; M; Wife; 1790; Yes; Yes; AI. 2/Id. 5539
1782; Effie; F; 24; Pima; F; S; Dau.; 1791; Yes; Yes; AI. 3/Id. 5540
~~Isabella; F; 20; Pima; F; S; Dau.; 1792; Died; 1-4-32.;~~ Yes; AI. 4/Id. 5541
1783; Joseph; M; 12; Pima; F; S; Son; 1793; Yes; Yes; AI. 4793/Id. 5542

JUAN
1784; Chilita; F; 30; Pima; F; S; Head; 1794; Yes; Yes; AI. 1432/Id. 6782
1785; Hazel F.; F; 4; Pima; F; S; Dau.; 1795; Yes; Yes; AI./Id. 6784

JUAN
1786; Juanna; F; 67; Pima; F; Wd.; Head; 1796; Yes; Yes; AI. 4383/Id. 5978

JUAN
1787; Sepia; F; 44; Pima; F; Wd.; Head; 1797; Yes; Yes; AI. 1804/Id. 4746
1788; Christo; M; 19; Pima; F; S; Son; 1798; Yes; Yes; AI. 1912/Id. 4747

Census of the **Gila River** reservation of the **Pima Agency** jurisdiction; as of **April 1** ; 1932; taken by **A. H. Kneale** ; Superintendent.

Key: Number; Surname; Given; Sex (M/F); Age at Last Birthday; Tribe; Degree of Blood (F=Full); Marital Status; Relationship to Head of Family & Last Census No; At Jurisdiction Where Enrolled (Yes/No); (If no – Where); Ward (Yes/No); Allotment Annuity and/or Identification Numbers

JUAN

1789; Jose; M; 52; Pima; F; M; Head; 1799; Yes; Yes; AI. 990/Id. 6706
1790; Emma; F; 50; Pima; F; M; Wife; 1800; Yes; Yes; AI. 991/Id. 6707
1791; Viola; F; 19; Pima; F; S; Dau.; 1801; Yes; Yes; AI. 992/Id. 6708
1792; Eugene; M; 9; Pima; F; S; Son; 1802; Yes; Yes; AI./Id. 6710
1793; Leonora; F; 11; Pima; F; S; Dau.; 1803; Yes; Yes; AI./Id. 6709
1794; Grace; F; 5; Pima; F; S; Dau; 1804; Yes; Yes; AI./Id. 6711

JUAN

1795; Jose N.; M; 36; Pima; F; Wd.; Head; 1805; Yes; Yes; AI. 1433/Id. 6780

JUAN

1796; Jose P.; M; 65; Pima; F; M; Head; 1806; Yes; Yes; AI. 1462/Id. 4133
1797; Lancina, (Lancina Lancisco); F; 60; Pima; F; M; Wife; 1807; Yes; Yes; AI. 1463/Id. 4432

JUAN

1798; Jose; M; 48; Pima; F; M; Head; 1808; Yes; Yes; AI. 4243/Id. 1296
1799; Fannie; F; 33; Pima; F; M; Wife; 1809; Yes; Yes; AI. 4244/Id. 1297
1800; Samuel; M; 23; Pima; F; S; Son; 1810; Yes; Yes; AI. 4245/Id. 1298
~~Ruth; F; 22; Pima; F; S; Dau.; 1811; Yes; (Married to Joseph Giff)~~; Yes; AI. 4246/Id. 1299
1801; Josie; F; 19; Pima; F; S; Dau.; 1812; Yes; Yes; AI./Id. 1300
1802; Ambrose; M; 14; Pima; F; S; Son; 1813; Yes; Yes; AI./Id. 1301
1803; Helen; F; 13; Pima; F; S; Dau.; 1814; Yes; Yes; AI./Id. 1302

JUAN

1804; Josepha; F; 71; Maricopa; F; Wd.; Head; 1815; Yes; Yes; AI. 2905/Id. 155

JUAN

1805; Juanita D.; F; 40; Pima; F; Wd.; Head; 1816; Yes; Yes; AI. 1452/Id. 7152

JUAN

~~Luhena; F; 67; Pima; F; S; Head; 1817; Died 2-15-32.~~; Yes; AI. 77/Id. 5883

JUAN

1806; Martin A.; M; 37; Pima; F; S; Head; 1818; Yes; Yes; AI./Id. 7157

JUAN

1807; Mary; F; 40; Maricopa; F; Wd.; Head; 1819; Yes; Yes; AI. 2906/Id. 154

JUAN

1808; Mildred; F; 28; Maricopa; F; Wd.; Head; 1820; Yes; Yes; AI. 2918/Id. 285
1809; ---; F; 5; Maricopa; F; S; Dau.; 1821; Yes; Yes; AI./Id. 286

Census of the **Gila River** reservation of the **Pima Agency** jurisdiction; as of **April 1** ; 1932; taken by **A. H. Kneale** ; Superintendent.

Key: Number; Surname; Given; Sex (M/F); Age at Last Birthday; Tribe; Degree of Blood (F=Full); Marital Status; Relationship to Head of Family & Last Census No; At Jurisdiction Where Enrolled (Yes/No); (If no – Where); Ward (Yes/No); Allotment Annuity and/or Identification Numbers

JUAN
1810; Mollie; F; 67; Pima; F; Wd.; Head; 1822; Yes; Yes; AI. 3008/Id. 3533

JUAN
1811; Mose; M; 28; Papago; F; M; Head; 1823; Yes; Yes; AI./Id. 1835
1812; Lucy H., (Homa, Lucy); F; 33; Pima; F; M; Wife; 1824; Yes; Yes; AI. 4152/Id. 1836
1813; Patrick; M; 3; Pima-Papago; F; S; Son; 1825; Yes; Yes; AI./Id. 1952

JUAN
1814; Nacho; M; 45; Pima; F; M; Head; 1826; Yes; Yes; AI. 279/Id. 5320
1815; Anna; F; 45; Pima; F; M; Wife; 1827; Yes; Yes; AI. 280/Id. 5321
1816; Mildred; F; 17; Pima; F; S; Dau.; 1828; Yes; Yes; AI. 4506/Id. 5322
1817; Nellie; F; 15; Pima; F; S; Dau.; 1829; Yes; Yes; AI. 4507/Id. 5323
1818; Melinda; F; 13; Pima; F; S; Dau.; 1830; Yes; Yes; AI. 4780/Id. 5324
1819; Ellsworth; M; 7; Pima; F; S; Son; 1831; Yes; Yes; AI./Id. 5325
1820; Lauretta; F; 4; Pima; F; S; Dau.; 1832; Yes; Yes; AI./Id. 5326

JUAN
1821; Nelson; M; 46; Pima; F; M; Head; 1833; Yes; Yes; AI. 76/Id. 5496
1822; Rita F., (Francisco, Reta[sic]); F; 33; Pima; F; M; Wife; 1834; Yes; Yes; AI. 223/Id. 5497
1823; Grace; F; 11; Pima; F; S; Dau.; 1835; Yes; Yes; AI./Id. 5498
1824; Matilda; F; 5; Pima; F; S; Dau.; 1836; Yes; Yes; AI./Id. 5499
1825; ---; M; 2; Pima; F; S; Son; 1837; Yes; Yes; AI./Id. 5979

JUAN
1826; Norris; M; 69; Pima; F; M; Head; 1838; Yes; Yes; AI. 1428/Id. 6778
1827; Mary; F; 67; Pima; F; M; Wife; 1839; Yes; Yes; AI. 1429/Id. 6779
1828; Arnold; M; 8; Pima; F; S; Son; 1840; Yes; Yes; AI./Id. 6783

JUAN
1829; Vincent; M; 53; Pima; F; Wd.; Head; 1841; Yes; Yes; AI. 279/Id. 5300

JUSTINE
1830; Harvey; M; 52; Pima; F; M; Head; 1842; Yes; Yes; AI. 4146/Id. 1837
1831; Mollie; F; 52; Pima; F; M; Wife; 1843; Yes; Yes; AI. 4147/Id. 1838
1832; John; M; 32; Pima; F; S; Son; 1844; Yes; Yes; AI. 4148/Id. 1839

JUSTIN[sic]
1833; Juan; M; 51; Pima; F; M; Head; 1845; Yes; Yes; AI. 3892/Id. 1221
1834; Eva; F; 49; Pima; F; M; Wife; 1846; Yes; Yes; AI. 3893/Id. 1222

Census of the **Gila River** reservation of the **Pima Agency** jurisdiction; as of **April 1** ; 1932; taken by **A. H. Kneale** ; Superintendent.

Key: Number; Surname; Given; Sex (M/F); Age at Last Birthday; Tribe; Degree of Blood (F=Full); Marital Status; Relationship to Head of Family & Last Census No; At Jurisdiction Where Enrolled (Yes/No); (If no – Where); Ward (Yes/No); Allotment Annuity and/or Identification Numbers

JUSTINE

1835; Miles; M; 52; Pima; F; M; Head; 1847; Yes; Yes; AI. 3500/Id. 1455
1836; Mollie; F; 43; Pima; F; M; Wife; 1848; Yes; Yes; AI. 3501/Id. 1456
1837; Sampson; M; 23; Pima; F; S; Son; 1849; Yes; Yes; AI. 3503/Id. 1457
1838; Eliza; F; 17; Pima; F; S; Dau.; 1850; Yes; Yes; AI. 3522/Id. 1458
1839; Elsie; F; 4; Pima; F; S; Dau.; 1851; Yes; Yes; AI./Id. 1459

JUSTINE

~~Nathan; M; 71; Maricopa; F; Wd.; Head; 1852; Died; 5-9-31.~~; Yes; AI. 2758/Id. 579

JUSTIN[sic]

1840; Paul; M; 45; Maricopa; F; M; Head; 1853; Yes; Yes; AI. 2528/Id. 457
1841; Ruth; F; 37; Maricopa; F; M; Wife; 1854; Yes; Yes; AI. 2529/Id. 458
1842; Myra; F; 21; Maricopa; F; S; Dau.; 1855; Yes; Yes; AI. 2532/Id. 459
1843; Boyle; M; 19; Maricopa; F; S; Son; 1856; Yes; Yes; AI. 2531/Id. 460
1844; Willis; M; 18; Maricopa; F; S; Son; 1857; Yes; Yes; AI. 2530/Id. 461
1845; Leonard; M; 11; Maricopa; F; S; Son; 1858; Yes; Yes; AI./Id. 462
1846; Roland; M; 9; Maricopa; F; S; Son; 1859; Yes; Yes; AI./Id. 463
1847; Paul Jr.; M; 3; Maricopa; F; S; Son; 1860; Yes; Yes; AI./Id. 465

JUSTIN

1848; Thomas; M; 58; Pima; F; Wd.; Head; 1861; Yes; Yes; AI./Id. 1953

KALKA

1849; Eschief; M; 52; Pima; F; M; Head; 1862; Yes; Yes; AI. 2607/Id. 5771
1850; Emily B., (Boss, Emily); F; 26; Pima; F; M; Wife; 1863; Yes; Yes; AI. 1512/Id. 5772

KALKA

1851; Jose; M; 47; Pima; F; M; Head; 1864; Yes; Yes; AI. 119/Id. 5443
1852; Martini; F; 42; Pima; F; M; Wife; 1865; Yes; Yes; AI. 118/Id. 5444
1853; Walter; M; 15; Pima; F; S; Son; 1866; Yes; Yes; AI. 4592/Id. 5445
1854; Mary; F; 8; Pima; F; S; Dau.; 1867; Yes; Yes; AI./Id. 5446

KALKA

1855; Mark; M; 42; Pima; F; M; Head; 1868; Yes; Yes; AI. 814/Id. 5856
1856; Lena; F; 41; Pima; F; M; Wife; 1869; Yes; Yes; AI. 815/Id. 5857
1857; Mark Jr.; M; 18; Pima; F; S; Son; 1870; Yes; Yes; AI. 2682/Id. 5858
1858; Pearl; F; 17; Pima; F; S; Dau.; 1871; Yes; Yes; AI. 3797/Id. 5859
1859; Rowland J.; M; 12; Pima; F; S; Son; 1872; Yes; Yes; AI. 4790/Id. 5860
1860; William; M; 9; Pima; F; S; Son; 1873; Yes; Yes; AI./Id. 5861
1861; Clinton; M; 6; Pima; F; S; Son; 1874; Yes; Yes; AI./Id. 5862
1862; Dirk L.; M; 4; Pima; F; S; Son; 1875; Yes; Yes; AI./Id. 5863
1863; Marjorie Dorothy; F; 2/12; Pima; F; S; Dau.; --; Yes; ~~Born; 2-21-32.~~ Yes; AI./Id. 6129

Census of the **Gila River** reservation of the **Pima Agency** jurisdiction; as of **April 1** ; 1932; taken by **A. H. Kneale** ; Superintendent.

Key: Number; Surname; Given; Sex (M/F); Age at Last Birthday; Tribe; Degree of Blood (F=Full); Marital Status; Relationship to Head of Family & Last Census No; At Jurisdiction Where Enrolled (Yes/No); (If no – Where); Ward (Yes/No); Allotment Annuity and/or Identification Numbers

KANDALAYA
1864; ---; M; 61; Pima; F; S; Head; 1876; Yes; Yes; AI./Id. 5884

KAVACO
1865; Henry; M; 52; Pima; F; Wd.; Head; 1877; Yes; Yes; AI. 2901/Id. 7158

KELLY
1866; John; M; 49; Pima; F; M; Head; 1878; Yes; Yes; AI. 843/Id. 4234
1867; Mary J.; F; 45; Pima; F; M; Wife; 1879; Yes; Yes; AI. 844/Id. 4235
1868; Lucy; F; 24; Pima; F; S; Dau.; 1880; Yes; Yes; AI. 845/Id. 4236
1869; Briget; F; 5; Pima; F; S; Gr.dau.; 1881; Yes; Yes; AI./Id. 4242
1870; Gertrude; F; 22; Pima; F; S; Dau.; 1882; Yes; Yes; AI. 846/Id. 4237
1871; Clement; M; 13; Pima; F; S; Son; 1884; Yes; Yes; AI. 4735/Id. 4239
1872; Patrick; M; 11; Pima; F; S; Son; 1885; Yes; Yes; AI./Id. 4240
1873; Bertha; F; 9; Pima; F; S; Dau.; 1886; Yes; Yes; AI./Id. 4241

KELLY
1874; Paul H.; M; 19; Pima; F; M; Head; 1883; Yes; Yes; AI. 847/Id.
4238; ~~Hyasintha Enos; F; 19; Pima; F; M; Wife; ---; Yes; (S.R. Allottee)~~; Yes; AI./Id.

KELLY
1875; Joseph; M; 47; Pima; F; S; Head; 1887; Yes; Yes; AI. 4101/Id. 1954

KIND
1876; Juanna K., (Howard, Juanna); F; 43; Pima; F; M; Wife; 1888; Yes; Yes; AI. 98/Id. 5885

KING
1877; Preston; M; 51; Pima; F; S; Head; 1889; Yes; Yes; AI. 3084/Id. 3208

KING
1878; Samuel; M; 72; Pima; F; M; Head; 1890; Yes; Yes; AI. 2736/Id. 232

KING
1879; Sallie; F; 64; Pima; F; M; Wife; 1891; Yes; Yes; AI. 2737/Id. 233

KIP[sic]
1880; Emily; F; 78; Pima; F; Wd.; Head; 1892; Yes; Yes; AI. 3720/Id. 1567
1881; Sadie; F; 21; Pima; F; S; gr.dau.; 1893; Yes; Yes; AI. 3718/Id. 1888

KIPP
~~John; M; 70; Pima; F; Wd.; Head; 1894; Died; 12-19-31~~; Yes; AI. 3721/Id. 1611

80

Key: Number; Surname; Given; Sex (M/F); Age at Last Birthday; Tribe; Degree of Blood (F=Full); Marital Status; Relationship to Head of Family & Last Census No; At Jurisdiction Where Enrolled (Yes/No); (If no – Where); Ward (Yes/No); Allotment Annuity and/or Identification Numbers

KIRK

1882; Lewis; M; 57; Pima; F; M; Head; 1895; Yes; Yes; AI. 4160/Id. 1678
1883; Mary Rose; F; 53; Pima; F; M; Wife; 1896; Yes; Yes; AI. 4161/Id. 1679
1884; Lottie; F; 22; Pima; F; S; Dau.; 1897; Yes; Yes; AI. 4164/Id. 1680
1885; Angelita; F; 17; Pima; F; S; Dau.; 1898; Yes; Yes; AI. 4165/Id. 1681
1886; Mildred; F; 6; Pima; F; S; Dau.; 1899; Yes; Yes; AI./Id. 1682

KISTO

1887; Ambrose; M; 38; Pima; F; S; Head; 1900; Yes; Yes; AI. 2506/Id. 6852

KISTO

1888; Andrew Williams; M; 47; Pima; F; M; Head; 1901; Yes; Yes; AI. 2985/Id. 3114
1889; Effie Perkins, (Perkins, Effie); F; 30; Pima; F; M; Wife; 1902; Yes; Yes; AI. 2338/Id. 3115
1890; Myrtle D.; F; 11; Pima; F; S; Dau.; 1903; Yes; Yes; AI./Id. 3116
1891; Bernard; M; 7; Pima; F; S; Son; 1904; Yes; Yes; AI./Id. 3117
1892; Robert; M; 4; Pima; F; S; Son; 1905; Yes; Yes; AI./Id. 3118

KISTO

1893; Anton; M; 69; Pima; F; M; Head; 1906; Yes; Yes; AI. 1774/Id. 4748
1894; Manuella; F; 67; Pima; F; M; Wife; 1907; Yes; Yes; AI. 1775/Id. 4749

KISTO

1895; Carlos O.; M; 63; Pima; F; M; Head; 1908; Yes; Yes; AI. 3435/Id. 1351
1896; Annie; F; 41; Pima; F; M; Wife; 1909; Yes; Yes; AI. 3436/Id. 1352
1897; Harry; M; 19; Pima; F; S; Son; 1910; Yes; Yes; AI. 3438/Id. 1353
1898; Mattie; F; 15; Pima; F; S; Dau.; 1911; Yes; Yes; AI. 3440/Id. 1354
1899; Ada; F; 12; Pima; F; S; Dau.; 1912; Yes; Yes; AI. 4451/Id. 1355

KISTO

1900; Frank; M; 25; Pima; F; M; Head; 1913; Yes; Yes; AI. 1879/Id. 4664
1901; Agnes, (Thomas, Angelita); F; 22; Pima; F; M; Wife; 1914; Yes; Yes; AI. 2372/Id. 4665
1902; Everett; M; 2; Pima; F; S; Son; 1915; Yes; Yes; AI./Id. 4131
1903; Sylvester; M; 1/12; Pima; F; S; Son; ---; Yes; ~~Born 3-17-32.~~; Yes; AI./Id. 3951

KISTO

1904; Henry A.; M; 41; Pima; F; M; Head; 1916; Yes; Yes; AI. 1776/Id. 4540
1905; Maggie J., (James, Maggie); F; 47; Pima; F; M; Wife; 1917; Yes; Yes; AI. 788/Id. 4541
1906; Jackson; Bernice; F; 18; Pima; F; S; St.dau.; 1918; Yes; Yes; AI. 790/Id. 4542
1907; Jackson; Selma; F; 16; Pima; F; S; St.dau.; 1919; Yes; Yes; AI. 3483/Id. 4543
1908; Jackson; Marian; F; 13; Pima; F; S; St.dau.; 1920; Yes; Yes; AI. 4553/Id. 4544
1909; Jackson; Leonard; M; 10; Pima; F; S; St.son; 1921; Yes; Yes; AI./Id. 4545

Census of the **Gila River** reservation of the **Pima Agency** jurisdiction; as of **April 1** ; 1932; taken by **A. H. Kneale** ; Superintendent.

Key: Number; Surname; Given; Sex (M/F); Age at Last Birthday; Tribe; Degree of Blood (F=Full); Marital Status; Relationship to Head of Family & Last Census No; At Jurisdiction Where Enrolled (Yes/No); (If no – Where); Ward (Yes/No); Allotment Annuity and/or Identification Numbers

KISTO

1910; Isaac; M; 29; Pima; F; S; Head; 1922; Yes; Yes; AI. 2301/Id. 3352

KISTO

1911; Isabelle; F; 35; Pima; F; S; Head; 1923; Yes; Yes; AI. 2547/Id. 7159

KISTO

1912; James; M; 52; Pima; F; S; Head; 1924; Yes; Yes; AI. 1878/Id. 4786

KISTO

1913; Jose; M; 49; Pima; F; M; Head; 1925; Yes; Yes; AI. 1778/Id. 4658
1914; Lupa; F; 44; Pima; F; M; Wife; 1926; Yes; Yes; AI. 1779/Id. 4659
1915; Ahlelai; F; 18; Pima; F; S; Dau.; 1927; Yes; Yes; AI. 1882/Id. 4661
1916; Stanislaus; M; 12; Pima; F; S; Son; 1928; Yes; Yes; AI./Id. 4662
1917; Gerard; M; 5; Pima; F; S; Son; 1929; Yes; Yes; AI./Id. 4663

KISTO

1918; Cyrus; M; 22; Pima; F; M; Head; 1930; Yes; Yes; AI. 1881/Id. 4660
1919; Mertie, (Anton, Mertie); F; 34; Pima; F; M; Wife; 1931; Yes; Yes; AI. 1936/Id. 4584
1920; Anton, Aleen A.; F; 14; Pima; F; S; St.dau.; 1932; Yes; Yes; AI. 3943/Id. 4586
1921; Anton; Cornelius; M; 10; Pima; F; S; St.son; 1933; Yes; Yes; AI./Id. 4587
1922; Anton; Simon; M; 8; Pima; F; S; St.son; 1934; Yes; Yes; AI./Id. 4588

KISTO

1923; Jose A.; M; 55; Pima; F; Wd.; Head; 1935; Yes; Yes; AI. 2503/Id. 6830

KISTO

~~Jose; M; 29; Pima; F; M; Head; 1936; Died; 5-7-31.~~; Yes; AI. 1496/Id. 6619
1924; Susie B., (Brown, Susie); F; 27; Pima; F; M; Wife; 1937; Yes; Yes; AI. 3039/Id. 6620
1925; Leonard J.; M; 5; Pima; F; S; Son; 1938; Yes; Yes; AI./Id. 6621
1926; Helen; F; 2/12; Pima; F; S; Dau.; ---; Yes; Yes; AI./Id. 7293

KISTO

1927; Juan A.; M; 77; Pima; F; Wd.; Head; 1939; Yes; Yes; AI. 2504/Id. 6829

KISTO

1928; Juan B.; M; 66; Pima; F; M; Head; 1940; Yes; Yes; AI. 2309/Id. 3346
1929; Ella; F; 63; Pima; F; M; Wife; 1941; Yes; Yes; AI. 2310/Id. 3347
1930; Henry; M; 22; Pima; F; S; Son; 1942; Yes; Yes; AI. 2313/Id. 3349
1931; Jennie; F; 21; Pima; F; S; Dau.; 1943; Yes; Yes; AI. 2314/Id. 3350
1932; Mathew; M; 20; Pima; F; S; Son; 1944; Yes; Yes; AI. 2315/Id. 3351

Census of the **Gila River** reservation of the **Pima Agency** jurisdiction; as of **April 1** ; 1932; taken by **A. H. Kneale** ; Superintendent.

Key: Number; Surname; Given; Sex (M/F); Age at Last Birthday; Tribe; Degree of Blood (F=Full); Marital Status; Relationship to Head of Family & Last Census No; At Jurisdiction Where Enrolled (Yes/No); (If no – Where); Ward (Yes/No); Allotment Annuity and/or Identification Numbers

KISTO
1933; Katie C.; F; 37; Pima; F; Wd.; Head; 1945; Yes; Yes; AI. 2022/Id. 3534

KISTO
1934; James; M; 39; Pima; F; S; Head; 1946; Yes; Yes; AI. 2311/Id. 3348

KNOX
1935; Frances; F; 43; Pima; F; Wd.; Head; 1947; Yes; Yes; AI. 1456/Id. 6860
1936; Josephine; F; 19; Pima; F; S; Dau.; 1948; Yes; Yes; AI. 1457/Id. 6861
1937; Lewis; M; 18; Pima; F; S; Son; 1949; Yes; Yes; AI. 1459/Id. 6862

KNOX
1938; Hanna L.; F; 70; Pima; F; Wd.; Head; 1950; Yes; Yes; AI. 1460/Id. 5452

KNOX
1939; Jennie; F; 43; Pima; F; Wd.; Head; 1951; Yes; Yes; AI. 1007/Id. 5887

KNOX
1940; Clattus; M; 46; Pima; F; Wd.; Head; 1952; Yes; Yes; AI. 4361/Id. 5887

KNOX
1941; Philip; M; 35; Pima; F; M; Head; 1953; No; Tacoma; Wash.; ~~Phoenix~~; ~~Maricopa; Ariz.~~; Yes; AI. 1461/Id. 6774

KNOX
1942; Stephen; M; 45; Pima; F; M; Head; 1954; Yes; Yes; AI. 1455/Id. 6855
1943; Lucy M., (Miller, Lucy); F; 33; Pima; F; M; Wife; 1955; Yes; Yes; AI. 2795/Id. 6856
1944; Stephen Jr.; M; 12; Pima; F; S; Son; 1956; Yes; Yes; AI. 4817/Id. 6857
1945; Thelman; F; 10; Pima; F; S; Dau.; 1957; Yes; Yes; AI./Id. 6858
1946; George L.; M; 7; Pima; F; S; Son; 1958; Yes; Yes; AI. 4817/Id. 6859
1947; Adeline; F; 4; Pima; F; S; Dau.; 1959; Yes; Yes; AI./Id. 6860

KOMCESS
1948; O-see-taf-ee; F; 60; Maricopa; F; Wd.; Head; 1960; Yes; Yes; AI. 2936/Id. 134

KOMCESS
1949; Mary S.; F; 101; Pima; F; Wd.; Head; 1961; Yes; Yes; AI. 4753/Id. 7160

KOO-SIL-CHIN-I-KIN
1950; ---; M; 92; Pima; F; M; Head; 1962; Yes; Yes; AI. 1623/Id. 5888
1951; Lucy; F; 92; Pima; F; M; Wife; 1963; Yes; Yes; AI. 1624/Id. 5889

KOTAH
1952; ---; M; 58; Pima; F; Wd.; Head; 1964; Yes; Yes; AI. 2894/Id. 148

Census of the **Gila River** reservation of the **Pima Agency** jurisdiction; as of **April 1** ; 1932; taken by **A. H. Kneale** ; Superintendent.

Key: Number; Surname; Given; Sex (M/F); Age at Last Birthday; Tribe; Degree of Blood (F=Full); Marital Status; Relationship to Head of Family & Last Census No; At Jurisdiction Where Enrolled (Yes/No); (If no – Where); Ward (Yes/No); Allotment Annuity and/or Identification Numbers

KYYITAN

1953; Miguel; M; 55; Pima; F; M; Head; 1965; Yes; Yes; AI. 1400/Id. 6797
1954; Adeloya; F; 49; Pima; F; M; Wife; 1966; Yes; Yes; AI. 1401/Id. 6798
1955; Jose S.; M; 25; Pima; F; S; Son; 1967; Yes; Yes; AI. 1475/Id. 6799
1956; George; M; 19; Pima; F; S; Son; 1968; Yes; Yes; AI. 1402/Id. 6800

KYYITAN

1957; Syblian; M; 34; Pima; F; M; Head; 1969; Yes; Yes; AI. 1473/Id. 6863
1958; Lucy L., (Jose, Lucy); F; 35; Pima; F; M; Wife; 1970; Yes; Yes; AI. 1441/Id. 6864
1959; Felix; M; 12; Pima; F; S; Son; 1971; Yes; Yes; AI. 4740/Id. 6865
1960; Marcus; M; 11; Pima; F; S; Son; 1972; Yes; Yes; AI./Id. 6866
1961; Gertrude; F; 6; Pima; F; S; Dau.; 1973; Yes; Yes; AI./Id. 6867
1962; Carmelia; F; 4; Pima; F; S; Dau.; 1974; Yes; Yes; AI./Id. 6868

LAHPAI

1963; ---; M; 62; Pima; F; Wd.; Head; 1975; Yes; Yes; AI. 3095/Id. 3252

LAMORE

N.E.; Arthur; M; 30; Mexican; F; M; Head; ---; No; Los Angeles L.A.; Cal.; --; --
1964; Marianna, (Rhodes, Marianna); F; 34; Maricopa; F; M; Wife; 1976; No; Los Angeles L.A.; Cal.; Yes; AI. 2836/Id. 88
1965; Frank; M; 11; Maricopa; F; S; Son; 1977; No; Ft. Grant Graham; Ariz.; Yes; AI./Id. 89
1966; Arthur, Jr.; M; 9; Maricopa; F; S; Son; 1978; No; Los Angeles L.A.; Cal.; Yes; AI./Id. 90
1967; Mary M.; F; 7; Maricopa; F; S; Dau.; 1979; No; Los Angeles L.A.; Cal.; Yes; AI./Id. 91
1968; Jewell; F; 5; Maricopa; F; S; Dau.; 1980; No; Los Angeles L.A.; Cal.; Yes; AI./Id. 92
1969; Gladys; F; 3; Maricopa; F; S; Dau.; 1981; No; Los Angeles L.A.; Cal.; Yes; AI./Id. 579
1970; Jones; M; 5/12; Maricopa; F; S; Son; --; No; Born; 11-4-31.; Los Angeles L.A.; Cal.; Yes; AI./Id. 612

LAPPIE

1971; Henry; M; 30; Pima; F; M; Head; 1982; Yes; Yes; AI. 4432/Id. 1223
1972; Lulu J., (Justin, Lulu); F; 30; Pima; F; M; Wife; 1983; Yes; Yes; AI. 3894/Id. 1224
1973; Hudson; M; 8; Pima; F; S; Son; 1984; Yes; Yes; AI./Id. 1225
1974; Margaret; F; 6; Pima; F; S; Dau.; 1985; Yes; Yes; AI./Id. 1226
1975; Katherine; F; 5; Pima; F; S; Dau.; 1986; Yes; Yes; AI./Id. 1227
1976; Henry Jr.; M; 1; Pima; F; S; Son; 1987; Yes; Yes; AI./Id. 2033

Census of the **Gila River** reservation of the **Pima Agency** jurisdiction; as of **April 1** ; 1932; taken by **A. H. Kneale** ; Superintendent.

Key: Number; Surname; Given; Sex (M/F); Age at Last Birthday; Tribe; Degree of Blood (F=Full); Marital Status; Relationship to Head of Family & Last Census No; At Jurisdiction Where Enrolled (Yes/No); (If no – Where); Ward (Yes/No); Allotment Annuity and/or Identification Numbers

LAPPIE
1977; Luke; M; 53; Pima; F; M; Head; 1988; Yes; Yes; AI. 4430/Id. 1317
1978; Sarah; F; 52; Pima; F; M; Wife; 1989; Yes; Yes; AI. 4431/Id. 1318

LASH
1979; Nelson; M; 38; Maricopa; F; S; Head; 1990; Yes; Yes; AI. 3998/Id. 292

LASH
1980; Thomas; M; 66; Maricopa; F; M; Head; 1991; Yes; Yes; AI. 3995/Id. 289
1981; Mary; F; 38; Maricopa; F; M; Wife; 1992; Yes; Yes; AI. 3996/Id. 290
1982; Paul; M; 23; Maricopa; F; S; Son; 1993; Yes; Yes; AI. 3997/Id. 291

LAWS
1983; Charles; M; 36; Pima; F; M; Head; 1994; No; (Not in Indian Recs.) Phoenix Maricopa Ariz.; Yes; AI. 3663/Id. 5890
1984; Sarah N., (Nelson, Sarah); F; 25; Pima; F; M; Wife; 1995; No; Phoenix Maricopa Ariz.; Yes; AI. 2031/Id. 5891
1985; Charles Jr.; M; 11; Pima; F; S; Son; 1996; No; Phoenix Maricopa Ariz.; Yes; AI. 4867/Id. 5892
1986; Rose D.; F; 9; Pima; F; S; Dau.; 1997; No; Phoenix Maricopa Ariz.; Yes; AI./Id. 5893
1987; Evan J.; M; 7; Pima; F; S; Son; 1998; No; Phoenix Maricopa Ariz.; Yes; AI./Id. 5894
1988; Joan C.; F; 2; Pima; F; S; Dau.; 1999; No; Phoenix Maricopa Ariz.; Yes; AI./Id. 5895

LAWS
1989; Thomas; M; 44; Pima; F; M; Head; 2000; Yes; Yes; AI. 3697/Id. 1488
1990; Olive; F; 43; Pima; F; M; Wife; 2001; Yes; Yes; AI. 3698/Id. 1489
1991; Irene; F; 22; Pima; F; S; Dau.; 2002; Yes; Yes; AI. 3699/Id. 1490
1992; Nettie; F; 21; Pima; F; S; Dau.; 2003; Yes; Yes; AI. 3700/Id. 1491
1993; Ina; F; 20; Pima; F; S; Dau.; 2004; Yes; Yes; AI. 3701/Id. 1492
1994; Willard; M; 11; Pima; F; S; Son; 2005; Yes; Yes; AI./Id. 1493
1995; Fred; M; 6; Pima; F; S; Son; 2006; Yes; Yes; AI./Id. 1494

LEIDIG
1996; Annily L., (Lewis, Annily); F; 31; Pima; F; M; Wife; 2007; Yes; Yes; AI. 3965/Id. 5896

LEONARD
1997; Minnie M., (Mack, Minnie); F; 36; Pima; F; M; Wife; 2008; Yes; Yes; AI. 863/Id. 7161
1998; Fred; M; 13; Pima; F; S; Son; 2009; Yes; Yes; AI./Id. 7162
1999; Anita; F; 11; Pima; F; S; Dau.; 2010; Yes; Yes; AI./Id. 7163
2000; Luella; F; 7; Pima; F; S; Dau.; 2011; Yes; Yes; AI./Id. 7164

Census of the **Gila River** reservation of the **Pima Agency** jurisdiction; as of **April 1** ; 1932; taken by **A. H. Kneale** ; Superintendent.

Key: Number; Surname; Given; Sex (M/F); Age at Last Birthday; Tribe; Degree of Blood (F=Full); Marital Status; Relationship to Head of Family & Last Census No; At Jurisdiction Where Enrolled (Yes/No); (If no – Where); Ward (Yes/No); Allotment Annuity and/or Identification Numbers

LESSO

2001; Ida R., (Russell, Ida); F; 29; Pima; F; M; Wife; 2012; Yes; Yes; AI. 394/Id. 5896

2002; Luella M.; F; 8; Pima; F; S; Dau.; 2013; Yes; Yes; AI./Id. 5897

2003; Eloise M.; F; 6; Pima; F; S; Dau.; 2014; Yes; Yes; AI./Id. 5898

LEWIS

2004; Albert; M; 44; Pima; F; M; Head; 2015; Yes; Yes; AI. 4095/Id. 1656

2005; Susie; F; 42; Pima; F; M; Wife; 2016; Yes; Yes; AI. 4096/Id. 1657

2006; Martin; M; 20; Pima; F; S; Son; 2017; Yes; Yes; AI. 4098/Id. 1659

2007; Austin; M; 15; Pima; F; S; Son; 2018; Yes; Yes; AI. 4099/Id. 1660

2008; Anson; M; 14; Pima; F; S; Son; 2019; Yes; Yes; AI. 4099/Id. 1661

2009; Aaron D.; M; 12; Pima; F; S; Son; 2020; Yes; Yes; AI. 4773/Id. 1662

2010; Marion F.; F; 8; Pima; F; S; Dau.; 2021; Yes; Yes; AI./Id. 1663

2011; Idella; F; 2; Pima; F; S; Dau.; 2022; Yes; Yes; AI./Id. 1893

LEWIS

2012; Ada M.; F; 33; Pima; F; Wd.; Head; 2023; Yes; Yes; AI. 1064/Id. 4526

2013; Eleanor B.; F; 10; Pima; F; S; Dau.; 2024; Yes; Yes; AI./Id. 4527

LEWIS

2014; Anton J.; M; 38; Pima; F; M; Head; 2025; Yes; Yes; AI. 2520/Id. 6840

2015; Pabloa J., (Jones, Pabloa); F; 30; Pima; F; M; Wife; 2026; Yes; Yes; AI. 2508/Id. 6841

LEWIS

2016; Benjamin; M; 77; Pima; F; M; Head; 2027; Yes; Yes; AI. 3888/Id. 5769

2017; Maria C., (Cruz, Maria); F; 57; Pima; F; M; Wife; 2028; Yes; Yes; AI. 4549/Id. 5770

2018; Lizzie; F; 20; Pima; F; S; St.dau.; 2029; Yes; Yes; AI. 3977/Id. 5980

LEWIS

2019; Candalay; F; 29; Maricopa; F; S; Head; 2030; Yes; Yes; AI. 3302/Id. 535

LEWIS

2020; Casper; M; 30; Pima; F; M; Head; 2031; Yes; Yes; AI. 3328/Id. 5621

2021; Mabel J., (Joseph, Mabel); F; 30; Pima; F; M; Wife; 2032; Yes; Yes; AI. 425/Id. 5622

2022; Elinora M.; F; 9; Pima; F; S; Dau.; 2033; Yes; Yes; AI./Id. 5625

2023; Theodore; M; 5; Pima; F; S; Son; 2034; Yes; Yes; AI./Id. 5624

LEWIS

2024; Charles; M; 43; Pima; F; M; Head; 2035; Yes; Yes; AI. 1517/Id. 6846

2025; Katie H., (Hall, Katie); F; 37; Pima; F; M; Wife; 2036; Yes; Yes; AI. 539/Id. 6847

Census of the **Gila River** reservation of the **Pima Agency** jurisdiction; as of **April 1** ; 1932; taken by **A. H. Kneale** ; Superintendent.

Key: Number; Surname; Given; Sex (M/F); Age at Last Birthday; Tribe; Degree of Blood (F=Full); Marital Status; Relationship to Head of Family & Last Census No; At Jurisdiction Where Enrolled (Yes/No); (If no – Where); Ward (Yes/No); Allotment Annuity and/or Identification Numbers

LEWIS

2026; Cyrus; M; 32; Pima; F; M; Head; 2037; Yes; Yes; AI. 3886/Id. 1522
2027; Lily; F; 29; Pima; F; M; Wife; 2038; Yes; Yes; AI. 4081/Id. 1523
2028; Norman H.; M; 6; Pima; F; S; Son; 2039; Yes; Yes; AI./Id. 1524
2029; Edmund R.; M; 4; Pima; F; S; Son; 2040; Yes; Yes; AI./Id. 1525

LEWIS

2030; Cyrus S.; M; 62; Pima; F; M; Head; 2041; Yes; Yes; AI. 1212/Id. 4936
2031; Emma, (Stone, Emma); F; 62; Pima; F; M; Wife; 2042; Yes; Yes; AI. 1213/Id. 4937
2032; Vasele; F; 22; Pima; F; S; Dau.; 2043; Yes; Yes; AI. 1217/Id. 4938
2033; Clayton; M; 19; Pima; F; S; Son; 2044; Yes; Yes; AI. 1218/Id. 4939
2034; Mildred; F; 28; Pima; F; S; Dau.; 2045; Yes; Yes; AI. 1215/Id. 4940

LEWIS

2035; Davis; M; 22; Pima; F; M; Head; 2046; Yes; Yes; AI. 3334/Id. 5903
2036; Agnes, (Miguel, Agnes); F; 16; Pima; F; M; Wife; 2047; Yes; Yes; AI. 3173/Id. 5959

LEWIS

2037; David; M; 20; Pima; F; S; Head; 2048; Yes; Yes; AI. 707/Id. 5900

LEWIS

2038; Edith; F; 34; Pima; F; Wd.; Head; 2049; Yes; Yes; AI. 3944/Id. 5901
2039; David Jr.; M; 7; Pima; F; S; Son; 2050; Yes; Yes; AI./Id. 5902

LEWIS

2040; Elemaine; F; 41; Pima; F; S; Head; 2051; Yes; Yes; AI. 1997/Id. 4750

LEWIS

2041; Enoch; M; 28; Pima; F; M; Head; 2052; Yes; Yes; AI. 2442/Id. 3452
~~Josephine Smith; F; Unk.; Papago; F; M; Wife; --; Yes; (Sells allottee)~~ Yes; AI./Id.
2042; Enoch Jr.; M; 6; Pima-Papago; F; S; Son; 2053; Yes; Yes; AI./Id. 3453
2043; Glenn; M; 5; Pima-Papago; F; S; Son; 2054; Yes; Yes; AI./Id. 3454
2044; Lena; F; 3; Pima-Papago; F; S; Dau.; 2055; Yes; Yes; AI./Id. 3535

LEWIS

2045; Frank; M; 34; Pima; F; M; Head; 2056; Yes; Yes; AI. 3339/Id. 5680
~~Anna Osife; F; 28; Pima; F; M; Wife; --; Yes; (S.R. Allottee)~~ Yes; AI./Id.
2046; Carolina F.; F; Unk.; Pima; F; S; Dau.; 2057; Yes; Yes; AI./Id. 5981
2047; Isadore; F; 4; Pima; F; S; Dau.; 2058; Yes; Yes; AI./Id. 5682

LEWIS

2048; Frank; M; 41; Pima; F; M; Head; 2059; Yes; Yes; AI. 267/Id. 5317

Census of the **Gila River** reservation of the **Pima Agency** jurisdiction; as of **April 1** ; 1932; taken by **A. H. Kneale** ; Superintendent.

Key: Number; Surname; Given; Sex (M/F); Age at Last Birthday; Tribe; Degree of Blood (F=Full); Marital Status; Relationship to Head of Family & Last Census No; At Jurisdiction Where Enrolled (Yes/No); (If no – Where); Ward (Yes/No); Allotment Annuity and/or Identification Numbers

2049; Elizabeth, (Anton, Elizabeth); F; 40; Pima; F; M; Wife; 2060; Yes; Yes; AI. 2510/Id. 5318

2050; Frances; F; 18; Pima; F; S; Dau.; 2061; Yes; Yes; AI. 3472/Id. 5319

LEWIS

2051; Henry; M; 72; Pima; F; M; Head; 2062; Yes; Yes; AI. 3910/Id. 1419

2052; Lassa; F; 62; Pima; F; M; Wife; 2063; Yes; Yes; AI. 3911/Id. 1420

LEWIS

2053; Howard M.; M; 25; Pima; F; S; Head; 2064; Yes; Yes; AI. 655/Id. 4889

LEWIS

2054; Jacob; M; 39; Pima; F; M; Head; 2065; Yes; Yes; AI. 1899/Id. 4643

2055; Emma, (Pasquale, Emma); F; 42; Pima; F; M; Wife; 2066; Yes; Yes; AI. 1900/Id. 4644

LEWIS

2056; James T.; M; 72; Pima; F; Wd.; Head; 2067; Yes; Yes; AI. 1142/Id. 6686

LEWIS

2057; Joe; M; 42; Pima; F; M; Head; 2068; Yes; Yes; AI. 1207/Id. 6679

2058; Mamie, (Howard, Mamie); F; 35; Pima; F; M; Wife; 2069; Yes; Yes; AI. 1262/Id. 6680

2059; Christine; F; 16; Pima; F; S; Dau.; 2070; Yes; Yes; AI. 3931/Id. 6681

2060; Oscar; M; 12; Pima; F; S; Son; 2071; Yes; Yes; AI. 4738/Id. 6682

2061; Tilliman; M; 10; Pima; F; S; Son; 2072; Yes; Yes; AI./Id. 6683

2062; Evelyn; F; 8; Pima; F; S; Dau.; 2073; Yes; Yes; AI./Id. 6684

2063; Raymond; M; 6; Pima; F; S; Son; 2074; Yes; Yes; AI./Id. 6685

2064; Dan; M; 2; Pima; F; S; Son; 2075; Yes; Yes; AI./Id. 7212

LEWIS

2065; John; M; 77; Pima; F; Wd.; Head; 2076; Yes; Yes; AI. 658/Id. 5642

LEWIS

2066; John; M; 46; Pima; F; M; Head; 2077; Yes; Yes; AI. 4367/Id. 1631

2067; Vivian; F; 45; Pima; F; M; Wife; --; Yes; Yes; AI./Id. 1632

LEWIS

2068; Jose T.; M; 41; Pima; F; M; Head; 2078; No; Ajo Pima Ariz.; Yes; AI. 194/Id. 5561

2069; Lucy G.; F; 42; Pima; F; M; Wife; 2079; No; Ajo Pima Ariz.; Yes; AI. 195/Id. 5562

2070; Amanda; F; 16; Pima; F; S; Dau.; 2080; No; Ajo Pima Ariz.;; Yes; AI. 4536/Id. 5563

Census of the **Gila River** reservation of the **Pima Agency** jurisdiction; as of **April 1** ; 1932; taken by **A. H. Kneale** ; Superintendent.

Key: Number; Surname; Given; Sex (M/F); Age at Last Birthday; Tribe; Degree of Blood (F=Full); Marital Status; Relationship to Head of Family & Last Census No; At Jurisdiction Where Enrolled (Yes/No); (If no – Where); Ward (Yes/No); Allotment Annuity and/or Identification Numbers

2071; Reuben T.; M; 17; Pima; F; S; Son; 2081; No; Ajo Pima Ariz.;; Yes; AI. 3118/Id. 5564

LEWIS

2072; John; M; 67; Pima; F; M; Head; 2082; Yes; Yes; AI. 3254/Id. 3286
2073; Mary; F; 57; Pima; F; M; Wife; 2083; Yes; Yes; AI. 3255/Id. 3287

LEWIS

2074; Joseph; M; 33; Pima; F; M; Head; 2084; Yes; Yes; AI. 708/Id. 4887
2075; Lupa M. (Miguel, Lupta[sic]); F; 33; Pima; F; M; Wife; 2085; Yes; Yes; AI. 532/Id. 4888

LEWIS

2076; J. Roe; M; 46; Pima; F; Wd.; Head; 2086; Yes; Yes; AI. 1219/Id. 6696
2077; Amy; F; 18; Pima; F; S; Dau.; 2087; Yes; Yes; AI. 1221/Id. 6697

LEWIS

2078; Juan; M; 52; Pima; F; S; Head; 2088; Yes; Yes; AI. 3359/Id. 6848

LEWIS

2079; Juan; M; 38; Papago; F; M; Head; 2089; Yes; Yes; AI./Id. 4432
2080; Margaret; F; 33; Papago; F; M; Wife; 2090; Yes; Yes; AI./Id. 4433
2081; Dolores; F; 11; Papago; F; S; Dau.; 2091; Yes; Yes; AI./Id. 4434
2082; Marinia; F; 6; Papago; F; S; Dau.; 2092; Yes; Yes; AI./Id. 4435
2083; Clemencia; F; 4; Papago; F; S; Dau.; 2093; Yes; Yes; AI./Id. 4436

LEWIS

2084; Juan; M; 52; Pima; F; S; Head; 2094; Yes; Yes; AI. 4614/Id. 3604

LEWIS

2085; Juan; M; 70; Pima; F; M; Head; 2095; Yes; Yes; AI. 1476/Id. 6785
2086; Narsia; F; 70; Pima; F; M; Wife; 2096; Yes; Yes; AI. 1477/Id. 6786

LEWIS

2087; Juan; M; 51; Pima; F; S; Head; 2097; Yes; Yes; AI. 616/Id. 6114

LEWIS

2088; Juan; M; 55; Pima; F; Wd.; Head; 2098; Yes; Yes; AI. 1533/Id. 6911

LEWIS

2089; Juan; M; 59; Pima; F; M; Head; 2099; Yes; Yes; AI. 2513/Id. 7165
2090; Maria; F; 60; Pima; F; M; Wife; 2100; Yes; Yes; AI. 2514/Id. 7166

LEWIS

2091; Juan Enos; M; 55; Pima; F; M; Head; 2101; Yes; Yes; AI. 162/Id. 5358

Census of the **Gila River** reservation of the **Pima Agency** jurisdiction; as of **April 1** ; 1932; taken by **A. H. Kneale** ; Superintendent.

Key: Number; Surname; Given; Sex (M/F); Age at Last Birthday; Tribe; Degree of Blood (F=Full); Marital Status; Relationship to Head of Family & Last Census No; At Jurisdiction Where Enrolled (Yes/No); (If no – Where); Ward (Yes/No); Allotment Annuity and/or Identification Numbers

2092; Hattie; F; 47; Pima; F; M; Wife; 2102; Yes; Yes; AI. 163/Id. 5359
2093; Nellie; F; 29; Pima; F; S; Dau.; 2103; Yes; Yes; AI. 4520/Id. 5366
2094; Lavender; M; 23; Pima; F; S; Son; 2104; Yes; Yes; AI. 4521/Id. 5360
2095; McCurry; M; 17; Pima; F; S; Son; 2105; Yes; Yes; AI. 4523/Id. 5361
2096; Clanton; M; 11; Pima; F; S; Son; 2106; Yes; Yes; AI./Id. 5362
2097; Edward T.; M; 9; Pima; F; S; Son; 2107; Yes; Yes; AI./Id. 5363
~~Robert O.; M; 5; Pima; F; S; Son; 2108; Died; 1-3-32.;~~ Yes; AI./Id. 5364
2098; Dennis O.; M; 4; Pima; F; S; Son; 2109; Yes; Yes; AI./Id. 5365

LEWIS

2099; Juan N.; M; 41; Pima; F; M; Head; 2110; Yes; Yes; AI. 1481/Id. 6787
2100; Lizzie E., (Eddy, Lizzie); F; 60; Pima; F; M; Wife; 2111; Yes; Yes; AI. 1493/Id. 6788
2101; Mathew E.; M; 20; Pima; F; S; Son; 2112; Yes; Yes; AI. 1494/Id. 6791
2102; Margery; F; 18; Pima; F; S; Dau.; 2113; Yes; Yes; AI. 3387/Id. 6789
2103; Melissa; F; 7; Pima; F; S; Dau.; 2114; Yes; Yes; AI./Id. 6790
2104; Juan N.; M; 5; Pima; F; S; Son; 2115; Yes; Yes; AI./Id. 7167

LEWIS

2105; Juan T.; M; 47; Pima; F; M; Head; 2116; Yes; Yes; AI. 2128/Id. 3105
2106; Petro; F; 46; Pima; F; M; Wife; 2117; Yes; Yes; AI. 2129/Id. 3106
2107; Daniel; M; 26; Pima; F; S; Son; 2118; Yes; Yes; AI. 1907/Id. 3107
2108; Esther T.; F; 16; Pima; F; S; Dau.; 2120; Yes; Yes; AI. 3268/Id. 3109
2109; Howard; M; 13; Pima; F; S; Son; 2121; Yes; Yes; AI. 4608/Id. 3110

LEWIS

2110; J. Roe; M; 20; Pima; F; M; Head; 2119; Yes; Yes; AI. 1914/Id. 3108
2111; Carmel, (Manuel, Carmel); F; 21; Pima; F; M; Wife; 2420; Yes; Yes; AI. 338/Id. 5241

LEWIS

2112; Juanna; F; 67; Pima; F; Wd.; Head; 2122; Yes; Yes; AI. 2071/Id. 3262

LEWIS

2113; Judea M.; M; 35; Pima; F; S; Head; 2123; Yes; Yes; AI. 654/Id. 7168

LEWIS

2114; Juliana; F; 14; Pima; F; S; alone; 2124; Yes; Yes; AI./Id. 1951

LEWIS

2115; Kenneth H.; M; 24; Pima; F; M; Head; 2125; Yes; Yes; AI. 196/Id. 5267
2116; Marvin; M; 2; Pima; F; S; Son; 2126; Yes; Yes; AI./Id. 7099

LEWIS

2117; Lahena; M; 29; Pima; F; Wd.; Head; 2127; Yes; Yes; AI. 2518/Id. 7169

Census of the **Gila River** reservation of the **Pima Agency** jurisdiction; as of **April 1** ; 1932; taken by **A. H. Kneale** ; Superintendent.

Key: Number; Surname; Given; Sex (M/F); Age at Last Birthday; Tribe; Degree of Blood (F=Full); Marital Status; Relationship to Head of Family & Last Census No; At Jurisdiction Where Enrolled (Yes/No); (If no – Where); Ward (Yes/No); Allotment Annuity and/or Identification Numbers

2118; Sylvester; M; 6; Pima; F; S; Son; 2128; Yes; Yes; AI./Id. 7170

LEWIS

2119; Lancisco; M; 31; Pima; F; M; Head; 2129; Yes; Yes; AI. 2650/Id. 6997
2120; Katie N, (Nosuch, Katie); F; 26; Pima; F; M; Wife; 2130; Yes; Yes; AI. 1593/Id. 6998

LEWIS

2121; Louisa; F; 57; Pima; F; Wd.; Head; 2131; Yes; Yes; AI. 3326/Id. 5677
2122; Evaline; F; 21; Pima; F; S; Dau.; 2132; Yes; Yes; AI. 3342/Id. 5679

LEWIS

2123; Lucas; M; 33; Pima; F; M; Head; 2133; Yes; Yes; AI. 3968/Id. 1641
2124; Frances, (Estrella, Frances); F; 32; Pima; F; M; Wife; 2134; Yes; Yes; AI. 4379/Id. 1642
2125; Adeline; F; 10; Pima; F; S; Dau.; 2135; Yes; Yes; AI./Id. 1643

LEWIS

2126; Lucy; F; 78; Pima; F; Wd.; Head; 2136; Yes; Yes; AI. 3337/Id. 5672

LEWIS

2127; Lucas; M; 22; Pima; F; M; Head; 2137; Yes; Yes; AI. 1222/Id. 6698
~~Negina Mary; F; 17; Unk.; F; M; Wife; –; Yes~~; Yes; AI./Id.

LEWIS

2128; Lucas; M; 27; Pima; F; M; Head; 2138; Yes; Yes; AI. 4252/Id. 1417
2129; Agnes, (Lappie, Agnes); F; 22; Pima; F; M; Wife; 2139; Yes; Yes; AI. 4433/Id. 1418
2130; Augustina; F; 3; Pima; F; S; Dau.; 2140; Yes; Yes; AI./Id. 1980

LEWIS

2131; Maggie; F; 47; Pima; F; Wd.; Head; 2141; Yes; Yes; AI. 3330/Id. 5673
2132; Crouse; M; 19; Pima; F; S; Son; 2142; Yes; Yes; AI. 3335/Id. 5904
2133; Cora; F; 13; Pima; F; S; Dau.; 2143; Yes; Yes; AI. 4853/Id. 5905

LEWIS

~~Manuela; F; 65; Pima; F; Wd.; Head; 2144; Died; 10-9-31.~~; Yes; AI. 1616/Id. 1884
2134; Lucy; F; 27; Pima; F; S; Orp.; 2145; Yes; Yes; AI. 1918/Id. 1885
2135; Lizzie; F; 19; Pima; F; S; Orp.; 2146; Yes; Yes; AI. 1917/Id. 1956

LEWIS

2136; Maricopa; M; 64; Maricopa; F; Wd.; Head; 2147; Yes; Yes; AI. 3301/Id. 534

LEWIS

2137; Mark; M; 72; Pima; F; M; Head; 2148; Yes; Yes; AI. 3553/Id. 1402

91

Key: Number; Surname; Given; Sex (M/F); Age at Last Birthday; Tribe; Degree of Blood (F=Full); Marital Status; Relationship to Head of Family & Last Census No; At Jurisdiction Where Enrolled (Yes/No); (If no – Where); Ward (Yes/No); Allotment Annuity and/or Identification Numbers

2138; Laura Y., (Yokan, Laura); F; 57; Pima; F; M; Wife; 2149; Yes; Yes; AI. 3568/Id. 1403

2139; George; M; 27; Pima; F; S; Son; 2150; Yes; Yes; AI. 3555/Id. 1404

2140; Matilda J.; F; 20; Pima; F; S; Dau.; 2151; Yes; Yes; AI. 3556/Id. 1363

LEWIS

2141; Morton; M; 49; Pima; F; M; Head; 2152; Yes; Yes; AI. 1136/Id. 6687

2142; Josephine; F; 47; Pima; F; M; Wife; 2153; Yes; Yes; AI. 1137/Id. 6688

2143; Moody; M; 27; Pima; F; S; Son; 2154; Yes; Yes; AI. 1138/Id. 6689

2144; Wallace; M; 17; Pima; F; S; Son; 2155; Yes; Yes; AI. 2657/Id. 6691

2145; Lester; M; 25; Pima; F; S; Son; 2156; Yes; Yes; AI. 1140/Id. 6690

LEWIS

2146; Nick (Santeo); M; 26; Maricopa; F; M; Head; 2157; Yes; Yes; AI. 3966/Id. 431

2147; Margaret, (Wellington, Margaret); F; 24; Maricopa; F; M; Wife; 2158; Yes; Yes; AI. 3775/Id. 432

2148; Alfred; M; 7; Maricopa; F; S; Son; 2159; Yes; Yes; AI./Id. 433

2149; Raymond; M; 4; Maricopa; F; S; Son; 2160; Yes; Yes; AI./Id. 434

LEWIS

2150; Paul; M; 38; Pima; F; M; Head; 2161; No; Phoenix Maricopa Ariz.; Yes; AI. 1209/Id. 4315

2151; Fannie H., (Havalina, Fannie); F; 34; Pima; F; M; Wife; 2162; No; Phoenix Maricopa Ariz.; Yes; AI. 3104/Id. 4316

2152; Dorothy; F; 13; Pima; F; S; Dau.; 2163; No; Phoenix Maricopa Ariz.; Yes; AI. 4739/Id. 4317

2153; Marian; F; 12; Pima; F; S; Dau.; 2164; No; Phoenix Maricopa Ariz.; Yes; AI./Id. 4318

2154; Lenore E.; F; 8; Pima; F; S; Dau.; 2165; No; Phoenix Maricopa Ariz.; Yes; AI./Id. 4319

2155; Clifford; M; 6; Pima; F; S; Son; 2166; No; Phoenix Maricopa Ariz.; Yes; AI./Id. 4320

LEWIS

2156; Philip; M; 57; Pima; F; Wd.; Head; 2167; Yes; Yes; AI. 154/Id. 5647

LEWIS

2157; Robert; M; 50; Pima; F; M; Head; 2168; Yes; Yes; AI. 2069/Id. 3537

LEWIS

2158; Robert; M; 30; Pima; F; M; Head; 2169; Yes; Yes; AI. 3887/Id. 1520

2159; Lucy D.; F; 30; Pima; F; M; Wife; 2170; Yes; Yes; AI./Id. 1521

2160; Johnson; Michael; M; 12; Pima; F; S; St.son; 2171; Yes; Yes; AI./Id. 1740

Census of the **Gila River** reservation of the **Pima Agency** jurisdiction; as of **April 1** ; 1932; taken by **A. H. Kneale** ; Superintendent.

Key: Number; Surname; Given; Sex (M/F); Age at Last Birthday; Tribe; Degree of Blood (F=Full); Marital Status; Relationship to Head of Family & Last Census No; At Jurisdiction Where Enrolled (Yes/No); (If no – Where); Ward (Yes/No); Allotment Annuity and/or Identification Numbers

LEWIS

2161; Roe Blain; M; 18; Pima; F; S; Alone; 2172; Yes; Yes; AI. 83/Id. 5183
2162; Richard; M; 14; Pima; F; S; Bro.; 2173; Yes; Yes; AI./Id. 5184

LEWIS

2163; Roy; M; 31; Pima; F; M; Head; 2174; Yes; Yes; AI. 3331/Id. 6486
2164; Nancy C., (Cyrus, Nancy); F; 26; Maricopa; F; M; Wife; 2175; Yes; Yes; AI. 2154/Id. 6487
2165; Sidney; M; 13; Pima; F; S; Son; 2176; Yes; Yes; AI. 4714/Id. 6488
2166; Lorrina J.; F; 12; Pima; F; S; Dau.; 2177; Yes; Yes; AI./Id. 6489
2167; Timothy D.; M; 7; Pima; F; S; Son; 2178; Yes; Yes; AI./Id. 3260
2168; Reuben; M; 1; Pima; F; S; Son; 2179; Yes; Yes; AI./Id. 7271

LEWIS

2169; Samuel; M; 33; Pima; F; S; Head; 2180; Yes; Yes; AI. 2443/Id. 3260

LEWIS

2170; Simon P.; M; 40; Pima; F; M; Head; 2181; Yes; Yes; AI. 2666/Id. 3538

LEWIS

2171; Irene A.; F; 47; Pima; F; M; Head; 2182; Yes; Yes; AI. 2667/Id. 3539
2172; Louis; M; 18; Pima; F; S; Son; 2183; Yes; Yes; AI. 4586/Id. 3540

LEWIS

2173; Simon; M; 24; Pima; F; M; Head; 2184; Yes; Yes; AI. 3341/Id. 5678
2174; Louis; M; 1; Pima; F; S; Son; 2185; Yes; Yes; AI./Id. 6105

LEWIS

2175; Smith; M; 45; Pima; F; M; Head; 2186; Yes; Yes; AI. 2521/Id. 6885
2176; Lena O.; F; 43; Pima; F; M; Wife; 2187; Yes; Yes; AI. 2522/Id. 6886
~~Elsie; F; 19; Pima; F; M; Dau.; 2188; Yes; (Married to Jasper Donohue);~~ Yes; AI. 3176/Id. 6887
2177; Ruthian; F; 12; Pima; F; S; Dau.; 2189; Yes; Yes; AI./Id. 6888
2178; Dorothy; F; 9; Pima; F; S; Dau.; 2190; Yes; Yes; AI./Id. 6889
2179; Bessie; F; 7; Pima; F; S; Dau.; 2191; Yes; Yes; AI./Id. 6890
2180; Della; F; 4; Pima; F; S; Dau.; 2192; Yes; Yes; AI./Id. 6891

LEWIS

2181; Susie M., (Miguel, Susie); F; 35; Pima; F; M; Wife; 2193; No; Phoenix Ariz. Gila; Salt River Res.; ~~Scottsdale Maricopa Ariz.;~~ Yes; AI. 653/Id. 5907

LEWIS

2182; Thomas; M; 56; Pima; F; M; Head; 2194; Yes; Yes; AI. 2288/Id. 3007
2183; Martha, (Johnson, Martha); F; 50; Pima; F; M; Wife; 2195; Yes; Yes; AI. 2274/Id. 3008

2184; Lawrence; M; 23; Pima; F; S; Son; 2196; Yes; Yes; AI. 2097/Id. 3261
2185; Evelina; F; 20; Pima; F; S; Dau.; 2197; Yes; Yes; AI. 2072/Id. 3536

LEWIS

2186; Thomas; M; 45; Pima; F; M; Head; 2198; Yes; Yes; AI. 3881/Id. 1700
2187; Mary; F; 44; Pima; F; M; Wife; 2199; Yes; Yes; AI. 3882/Id. 1701
~~Emma; F; 16; Pima; F; S; Dau.; 2200; Died 10-9-31.;~~ Yes; AI. 3890/Id. 1702
2188; Elijah; M; 14; Pima; F; S; Son; 2201; Yes; Yes; AI. 3891/Id. 1703
2189; Flora H.; F; 7; Pima; F; S; Dau.; 2202; Yes; Yes; AI./Id. 1704

LEWIS

2190; William; M; 22; Pima; F; M; Head; 2203; Yes; Yes; AI. 1244/Id. 6597
2191; Vivian J., (James, Viviana); F; 22; Pima; F; M; Wife; 2204; Yes; Yes; AI. 1240/Id. 6598
2192; Bertina; F; 1; Pima; F; S; Dau.; 2205; Yes; Yes; AI./Id. 7277

LEWIS

2193; Vincent; M; 47; Pima; F; M; Head; 2206; Yes; Yes; AI. 1241/Id. 6590
2194; Maggie; F; 47; Pima; F; M; Wife; 2207; Yes; Yes; AI. 1242/Id. 6591
2195; Francisco; M; 13; Pima; F; S; Son; 2208; Yes; Yes; AI. 4636/Id. 6592
2196; Vincent; M; 12; Pima; F; S; Son; 2209; Yes; Yes; AI./Id. 6593
2197; Bernard; M; 9; Pima; F; S; Son; 2210; Yes; Yes; AI./Id. 6594
2198; Bessie; F; 6; Pima; F; S; Dau.; 2211; Yes; Yes; AI./Id. 6595
2199; Ruthina; F; 4; Pima; F; S; Dau.; 2212; Yes; Yes; AI./Id. 6596

LIGHTS

2200; Sherman; M; 45; Pima; F; Wd.; Head; 2213; Yes; Yes; AI. 1553/Id. 1856

LIGHTS

2201; Thomas M.; M; 30; Pima; F; M; Head; 2214; Yes; Yes; AI. 1554/Id. 1766
2202; Mary Giff; F; 36; Pima; F; M; Wife; 2215; Yes; Yes; AI. 4223/Id. 1767

LISTON

2203; Alice; F; 30; Pima; F; S; Head; 2216; Yes; Yes; AI. 1471/Id. 6808

LISTON

2204; Edward; M; 52; Pima; F; Wd.; Head; 2217; Yes; Yes; AI. 1028/Id. 5908

LISTON

2205; Enoch; M; 42; Pima; F; Wd.; Head; 2218; Yes; Yes; AI. 2512/Id. 5909

LISTON

2206; Isaac; M; 65; Pima; F; M; Head; 2219; Yes; Yes; AI. 1466/Id. 6806
2207; Anna; F; 60; Pima; F; M; Wife; 2220; Yes; Yes; AI. 1467/Id. 6807
2208; Albert; M; 28; Pima; F; S; Son; 2221; Yes; Yes; AI. 1470/Id. 6809

Census of the **Gila River** reservation of the **Pima Agency** jurisdiction; as of **April 1** ; 1932; taken by **A. H. Kneale** ; Superintendent.

Key: Number; Surname; Given; Sex (M/F); Age at Last Birthday; Tribe; Degree of Blood (F=Full); Marital Status; Relationship to Head of Family & Last Census No; At Jurisdiction Where Enrolled (Yes/No); (If no – Where); Ward (Yes/No); Allotment Annuity and/or Identification Numbers

LISTON

2209; Isasiah; M; 34; Pima; F; S; Head; 2222; Yes; Yes; AI. 2525/Id. 6893

LISTON

2210; Bertha; F; 62; Pima; F; Wd.; Head; 2224; Yes; Yes; AI. 86/Id. 5603
2211; Herman; M; 24; Pima; F; S; Gr.son; 2225; Yes; Yes; AI. 638/Id. 5604

LIVES

2212; Harry; M; 32; Pima; F; M; Head; 2226; Yes; Yes; AI. 3853/Id. 1549
2213; Edith H., (Howard, Edith); F; 35; Pima; F; M; Wife; 2227; Yes; Yes; AI. 503/Id. 1957

LIVES

2214; Henry; M; 57; Pima; F; M; Head; 2228; Yes; Yes; AI. 3932/Id. 1547
2215; Mollie; F; 54; Pima; F; M; Wife; 2229; Yes; Yes; AI. 3850/Id. 1548
2216; Edison; M; 27; Pima; F; S; Son; 2230; Yes; Yes; AI. 3852/Id. 1550

LOCKWOOD

2217; Hudson; M; 32; Pima; F; M; Head; 2231; Yes; Yes; AI./Id. 5536
2218; Alice J., (Juan, Alice); F; 32; Pima; F; M; Wife; 2232; Yes; Yes; AI. 8/Id. 5537

LOMAUHIE

2219; Daisy L.; F; 29; Pima; F; Wd.; Head; 2233; Yes; Yes; AI. 699/Id. 5367
2220; Elinor; F; 6; Pima; F; S; Dau.; 2234; Yes; Yes; AI./Id. 5368
2221; Roberta; F; 4; Pima; F; S; Dau.; 2235; Yes; Yes; AI./Id. 5369

LOPEZ

2222; Alzelo; M; 32; Pima; F; M; Head; 2236; Yes; Yes; AI. 483/Id. 5334
2223; Eunice H., (Howard, Eunice); F; 32; Pima; F; M; Wife; 2237; Yes; Yes; AI. 299/Id. 5335
2224; Peter P.; M; 10; Pima; F; S; Son; 2238; Yes; Yes; AI. 3852/Id. 5336
2225; Wilma V.; F; 9; Pima; F; S; Dau.; 2239; Yes; Yes; AI./Id. 5337
2226; Elsie; F; 7; Pima; F; S; Dau.; 2240; Yes; Yes; AI./Id. 5338
2227; Selma; F; 4; Pima; F; S; Dau.; 2241; Yes; Yes; AI./Id. 5837

LOPEZ

2228; Josepha; F; 87; Pima; F; Wd.; Head; 2242; Yes; Yes; AI. 522/Id. 6448

LOPEZ

2229; Jose; M; 52; Pima; F; M; Head; 2243; Yes; Yes; AI./Id. 6725
2230; Carlmi M; F; 48; Pima; F; M; Wife; 2244; Yes; Yes; AI./Id. 6726
2231; Anton, Clara; F; 22; Pima; F; S; St.dau.; 2245; Yes; Yes; AI. 1270/Id. 6727
2232; Anton, George; M; 19; Pima; F; S; St.son; 2246; Yes; Yes; AI. 1272/Id. 6728

Census of the **Gila River** reservation of the **Pima Agency** jurisdiction; as of **April 1** ; 1932; taken by **A. H. Kneale** ; Superintendent.

Key: Number; Surname; Given; Sex (M/F); Age at Last Birthday; Tribe; Degree of Blood (F=Full); Marital Status; Relationship to Head of Family & Last Census No; At Jurisdiction Where Enrolled (Yes/No); (If no – Where); Ward (Yes/No); Allotment Annuity and/or Identification Numbers

LOPEZ

2233; Agnes; F; 42; Pima; F; Wd.; Head; 2247; Yes; Yes; AI. 555/Id. 5458
2234; Jacob; M; 28; Pima; F; S; Son; 2248; Yes; Yes; AI. 738/Id. 5440
2235; Cepriana; M; 24; Pima; F; S; Son; 2249; Yes; Yes; AI. 108/Id. 5439

LOPEZ

2236; Ramon; M; 31; Pima; F; M; Head; 2250; Yes; Yes; AI. 109/Id. 5298
2237; Juanna T., (Thomas, Juanna); F; 31; Pima; F; M; Wife; 2251; Yes; Yes; AI. 695/Id. 5299
2238; Patrick; M; 5; Pima; F; S; Son; 2252; Yes; Yes; AI./Id. 5982

LORING

2239; George; M; 27; Maricopa; F; M; Head; 2253; Yes; Yes; AI. 2852/Id. 231

LORING

2240; Mary; F; 57; Maricopa; F; Wd.; Head; 2254; Yes; Yes; AI. 2846/Id. 227
2241; Philip; M; 22; Maricopa; F; S; Son; 2255; Yes; Yes; AI. 2853/Id. 228
2242; Fannie R.; F; 17; Maricopa; F; S; Dau.; 2256; Yes; Yes; AI. 2854/Id. 229
2243; Russell; M; 13; Maricopa; F; S; Son; 2257; Yes; Yes; AI. 4747/Id. 230

LOSA

2244; Susanna, (Snyder, Susanna); F; 69; Pima; F; M; Wife; 2258; Yes; Yes; AI. 1867/Id. 4130

LOSE

2245; Albert; M; 74; Pima; F; Wd.; Head; 2259; Yes; Yes; AI. 3525/Id. 1401

LOSE

2246; Eunice; F; 27; Pima; F; S; Head; 2260; Yes; Yes; AI. 3516/Id. 1371
2247; Eula; F; 5; Pima; F; S; Dau.; 2261; Yes; Yes; AI./Id. 1372

LOSE

2248; Joseph; M; 58; Pima; F; M; Head; 2262; Yes; Yes; AI. 3513/Id. 1366
2249; Mollie; F; 47; Pima; F; M; Wife; 2263; Yes; Yes; AI. 3514/Id. 1367
2250; Hattie; F; 30; Pima; F; S; Dau.; 2264; Yes; Yes; AI. 3515/Id. 1981
2251; Mary; F; 7/12; Pima; F; S; Gr.dau.; --; Yes; Born; 8-15-31.; Yes; AI./Id. 2053
2252; Elsie; F; 23; Pima; F; S; Dau.; 2265; Yes; Yes; AI. 3517/Id. 1368
2253; Edward H.; M; 2; Pima; F; S; Gr.son; 2266; Yes; Yes; AI./Id. 1889
2254; Jerome; M; 19; Pima; F; S; Son; 2267; Yes; Yes; AI. 3518/Id. 1369
2255; Nora; F; 16; Pima; F; S; Dau.; 2268; Yes; Yes; AI. 3519/Id. 1370
2256; Rena; F; 3; Pima; F; S; Dau.; 2269; Yes; Yes; AI./Id. 1982

LOSE

2257; Pancho; M; 42; Pima; F; M; Head; 2270; Yes; Yes; AI. 3527/Id. 7171

Census of the **Gila River** reservation of the **Pima Agency** jurisdiction; as of **April 1** ; 1932; taken by **A. H. Kneale** ; Superintendent.

Key: Number; Surname; Given; Sex (M/F); Age at Last Birthday; Tribe; Degree of Blood (F=Full); Marital Status; Relationship to Head of Family & Last Census No; At Jurisdiction Where Enrolled (Yes/No); (If no – Where); Ward (Yes/No); Allotment Annuity and/or Identification Numbers

2258; Mary L., (Luna, Mary); F; 48; Pima; F; M; Wife; 2271; Yes; Yes; AI. 733/Id. 7172

2259; Listine Pablo; F; 12; Pima; F; S; Dau.; 2272; Yes; Yes; AI. 4883/Id. 7173

2260; Myra; F; 7; Pima; F; S; Dau.; 2273; Yes; Yes; AI./Id. 7174

2261; Myron H.; M; 5; Pima; F; S; Son; 2274; Yes; Yes; AI./Id. 7175

2262; Luna, Herbert; M; 19; Pima; F; S; St.son; 2275; Yes; Yes; AI. 734/Id. 5286

2263; Luna, Clyde E.; M; 18; Pima; F; S; St.son; 2276; Yes; Yes; AI. 735/Id. 5287

LOUISE

2264; Eunice; F; 77; Pima; F; Wd.; Head; 2277; Yes; Yes; AI. 1647/Id. 4233

LUCAS

2265; Jay; M; 62; Pima; F; M; Head; 2278; Yes; Yes; AI. 2235/Id. 2393

2266; Maggie; F; 42; Pima; F; M; Wife; 2279; Yes; Yes; AI. 2236/Id. 3294

~~Esther; F; 17; Pima; F; S; Dau.; 2280; Yes; Transferred to Esther Miguel.~~; Yes; AI. 2239/Id. 3295

2267; Ruth; F; 13; Pima; F; S; Dau.; 2281; Yes; Yes; AI./Id. 3296

LUCERO

~~N.E.; Victor; M; Unk.; Unk.; F; M; Head;~~ --; Yes; Yes; AI./Id.

2268; Edith P., (Pablo, Edith); F; 35; Pima; F; M; Wife; 2282; Yes; Yes; AI. 1683/Id. 4884

2269; Carolina; F; 7; Pima; F; S; Dau.; 2283; Yes; Yes; AI./Id. 4885

2270; Juanita; F; 1; Pima; F; S; Dau.; 2284; Yes; Yes; AI./Id. 6106

2271; Pablo, Gladys; F; 11; Pima; F; S; Niece; 2285; Yes; Yes; AI./Id. 4886

LUDLOW

2272; Josephine; F; 17; Pima; F; S; alone; 2286; Yes; Yes; AI. 2332/Id. 3541

2273; Frank Jr.; M; 15; Pima; F; S; alone; 2287; Yes; Yes; AI./Id. 3542

LUNA

2274; Lorenzo; M; 43; Pima; F; Wd.; Head; 2288; Yes; Yes; AI./Id. 3544

LYON

2275; Harley E.; M; 30; Pima; F; M; Head; 2289; Yes; Yes; AI. 53/Id. 5526

2276; Martina F., (Francisco, Martina); F; 30; Pima; F; M; Wife; 2290; Yes; Yes; AI. 4782/Id. 5527

2277; Harley Jr.; M; 7; Pima; F; S; Son; 2291; Yes; Yes; AI./Id. 5528

2278; Clyde; M; 4; Pima; F; S; Son; 2292; Yes; Yes; AI./Id. 5529

LYONS

2279; Jackson; M; 26; Pima; F; M; Head; 2293; Yes; Yes; AI. 1015/Id. 5911

2280; Inez J., (James, Inez); F; 28; Pima; F; M; Wife; 2294; Yes; Yes; AI. 1238/Id. 5912

2281; Essie; 7; Pima; F; S; Dau.; 2295; Yes; Yes; AI./Id. 5913

Key: Number; Surname; Given; Sex (M/F); Age at Last Birthday; Tribe; Degree of Blood (F=Full); Marital Status; Relationship to Head of Family & Last Census No; At Jurisdiction Where Enrolled (Yes/No); (If no – Where); Ward (Yes/No); Allotment Annuity and/or Identification Numbers

2282; Rose; 3; Pima; F; S; Dau.; 2296; Yes; Yes; AI./Id. 5914

LYON[sic]
2283; John; M; 66; Pima; F; M; Head; 2297; Yes; Yes; AI. 50/Id. 5915
2284; Julia; F; 59; Pima; F; M; Wife; 2298; Yes; Yes; AI. 51/Id. 5916
2285; Ida; 28; Pima; F; S; Dau.; 2299; Yes; Yes; AI. 52/Id. 5917
2286; Phillus; 3/12; Pima; F; S; Gr.dau.; --; Yes; Born; 1-4-32.; Yes; AI./Id. 6130

LYONS
2287; Willard; M; 75; Pima; F; Wd.; Head; 2300; Yes; Yes; AI. 1485/Id. 5918

LYONS
2288; Francis; M; 22; Pima; F; M; Head; 2301; Yes; Yes; AI. 1016/Id. 6951
2289; Margaret, (Nelson, Margaret); F; 27; Pima; F; M; Wife; 2302; Yes; Yes; AI. 1227/Id. 6952
2290; Eric R.; M; 6; Pima; F; S; St.son; 2303; Yes; Yes; AI./Id. 6953
2291; Frederick; M; 3; Pima; F; S; Son; 2304; Yes; Yes; AI./Id. 6954

LYON[sic]
2292; Kisto; M; 77; Pima; F; M; Head; 2305; Yes; Yes; AI. 1011/Id. 7177
2293; Mollie O., (Osife, Mollie); F; 45; Pima; F; M; Wife; 2306; Yes; Yes; AI. 1012/Id. 7178

LYON[sic]
2294; Oliver J., (Enos, Oliver Jefferson); M; 45; Pima; F; M; Head; 2307; Yes; Yes; AI. 1013/Id. 6601
2295; Lucy J.; F; 45; Pima; F; M; Wife; 2308; Yes; Yes; AI. 1014/Id. 6602
2296; George; M; 12; Pima; F; S; Son; 2309; Yes; Yes; AI./Id. 6603
2297; Clinton; M; 10; Pima; F; S; Son; 2310; Yes; Yes; AI./Id. 6604
2298; Eloise; F; 4; Pima; F; S; Dau.; 2311; Yes; Yes; AI./Id. 6605

MACHILE
2299; John; M; 45; Pima; F; M; Head; 2312; Yes; Yes; AI. 579/Id. 4876
2300; Ida (Ada); F; 50; Pima; F; M; Wife; 2313; Yes; Yes; AI. 580/Id. 4877
2301; Irene; F; 18; Pima; F; S; Dau.; 2314; Yes; Yes; AI. 2470/Id. 4878
2302; Edna; F; 14; Pima; F; S; Dau.; 2315; Yes; Yes; AI. 4575/Id. 4879
2303; Raba; F; 12; Pima; F; S; Dau.; 2316; Yes; Yes; AI./Id. 4880
2304; Lottie; F; 11; Pima; F; S; Dau.; 2317; Yes; Yes; AI./Id. 4881
2305; Juan, Runnie; M; 19; Pima; F; S; Nephew; 2318; Yes; Yes; AI./Id. 4882

MACK
2306; John; M; 48; Pima[sic]; F; Wd.; Head; 2319; Yes; Yes; AI. 4183/Id. 359

MACK
2307; Joseph; M; 72; Pima; F; M; Head; 2320; Yes; Yes; AI. 860/Id. 4321

Key: Number; Surname; Given; Sex (M/F); Age at Last Birthday; Tribe; Degree of Blood (F=Full); Marital Status; Relationship to Head of Family & Last Census No; At Jurisdiction Where Enrolled (Yes/No); (If no – Where); Ward (Yes/No); Allotment Annuity and/or Identification Numbers

2308; Lossie; F; 70; Pima; F; M; Wife; 2321; Yes; Yes; AI. 861/Id. 4322

2309; John; M; 40; Pima; F; S; Son; 2322; Yes; Yes; AI. 862/Id. 4323

MACK

2310; Josephine; F; 35; Pima; F; Wd.; Head; 2323; Yes; Yes; AI. 1114/Id. 4113

MACK

2311; Lewis; M; 35; Pima; F; M; Head; 2324; Yes; Yes; AI. 1113/Id. 4377

2312; Katherine; F; 34; Pima; F; M; Wife; 2325; Yes; Yes; AI./Id. 4378

2313; Freda; F; 8; Pima; F; S; Dau.; 2326; Yes; Yes; AI./Id. 4379

2314; Eugene; M; 6; Pima; F; S; Son; 2327; Yes; Yes; AI./Id. 4380

2315; Elizabeth Virginia; F; 5/12; Pima; F; S; Dau.; --; Yes; Born; 10-23-31.; Yes; AI./Id. 3950

MACK

2316; Peter; M; 45; Maricopa; F; M; Head; 2328; Yes; Yes; AI. 2897/Id. 30

2317; Effie; F; 43; Maricopa; F; M; Wife; 2329; Yes; Yes; AI. 2942/Id. 31

2318; Robert; M; 20; Maricopa; F; S; Son; 2330; Yes; Yes; AI. 2943/Id. 32

2319; Juan; M; 15; Maricopa; F; S; Son; 2331; Yes; Yes; AI. 4670/Id. 33

2320; Virginia; F; 15; Maricopa; F; S; Dau.; 2332; Yes; Yes; AI. 4671/Id. 34

2321; Cora; F; 6; Maricopa; F; S; Dau.; 2333; Yes; Yes; AI./Id. 35

MACKEL

2322; Martha; F; 62; Pima; F; Wd.; Head; 2334; Yes; Yes; AI. 3407/Id. 7178

MACKIL

2323; Jose; M; 54; Pima; F; M; Head; 2335; Yes; Yes; AI. 1302/Id. 7179

2324; Lucy; F; 46; Pima; F; M; Wife; 2336; Yes; Yes; AI. 1303/Id. 7180

2325; Martha; F; 19; Pima; F; S; Dau.; 2337; Yes; Yes; AI. 1304/Id. 7181

2326; Timon; M; 14; Pima; F; S; Son; 2338; Yes; Yes; AI. 4837/Id. 7182

2327; Linus; M; 5; Pima; F; S; Son; 2339; Yes; Yes; AI./Id. 7183

MACKUKEY

2328; Louis; M; 28; Pima; F; M; Head; 2340; Yes; Yes; AI./Id. 1768

2329; Lucy; F; 24; Pima; F; M; Wife; 2341; Yes; Yes; AI./Id. 1769

2330; Marie; F; 6; Pima; F; S; Dau.; 2342; Yes; Yes; AI./Id. 1770

2331; Teresa; F; 5; Pima; F; S; Dau.; 2343; Yes; Yes; AI./Id. 1771

MALYA

2332; Savia; F; 77; Pima; F; Wd.; Head; 2344; Yes; Yes; AI. 3185/Id. 1963

MANO

2333; Jose; M; 75; Pima; F; M; Head; 2345; Yes; Yes; AI./Id. 1857

2334; Martha; F; Unk.; Pima; F; M; Wife; 2346; Yes; Yes; AI./Id. 1858

2335; Schum; F; Unk.; Pima; F; S; Dau.; 2347; Yes; Yes; AI./Id. 1859

Census of the **Gila River** reservation of the **Pima Agency** jurisdiction; as of **April 1** ; 1932; taken by **A. H. Kneale** ; Superintendent.

Key: Number; Surname; Given; Sex (M/F); Age at Last Birthday; Tribe; Degree of Blood (F=Full); Marital Status; Relationship to Head of Family & Last Census No; At Jurisdiction Where Enrolled (Yes/No); (If no – Where); Ward (Yes/No); Allotment Annuity and/or Identification Numbers

MANSFIELD
2336; Ida J.; F; 35; Pima; F; Wd.; Head; 2348; Yes; Yes; AI. 4029/Id. 1959

MANUEL
No Number; ---; M; 52; Pima; F; M; Head; 2349; Yes; Yes; AI. 3455/Id. 5919
2337; Tomassa; F; 52; Pima; F; M; Wife; 2350; Yes; Yes; AI. 3456/Id. 5920
2338; Jesus; M; 24; Pima; F; S; Son; 2351; Yes; Yes; AI. 3457/Id. 5921
2339; David; M; 21; Pima; F; S; Son; 2352; Yes; Yes; AI. 3458/Id. 5922

MANUEL
2340; Anna; F; 67; Pima; F; Wd.; Head; 2353; Yes; Yes; AI. 408/Id. 5228

MANUEL
2341; Anton; M; 41; Pima; F; M; Head; 2354; Yes; Yes; AI. 5706/Id. 1405
2342; Ramona L., (Lewis, Ramona); F; 37; Pima; F; M; Wife; 2355; Yes; Yes; AI. 4293/Id. 1406
2343; Hanson; M; 14; Pima; F; S; Son; 2356; Yes; Yes; AI./Id. 1407
2344; Victor; M; 9; Pima; F; S; Son; 2357; Yes; Yes; AI./Id. 1408
2345; Dora; F; 5; Pima; F; S; Dau.; 2358; Yes; Yes; AI./Id. 1958

MANUEL
2346; Anton; M; 37; Pima; F; M; Head; 2359; Yes; Yes; AI. 4332/Id. 1961
2347; Isabella; F; 37; Pima; F; M; Wife; 2360; Yes; Yes; AI. 4333/Id. 1962

MANSFIELD
2348; Emily M., (Manuel, Emily); F; 31; Pima; F; M; Wife; 2361; Yes; Yes; AI. 4390/Id. 1960

MANUEL
2349; Bessie; F; 52; Maricopa; F; Wd.; Head; 2362; Yes; Yes; AI. 4077/Id. 435
2350; Newton; M; 24; Maricopa; F; S; Son; 2363; Yes; Yes; AI. 4393/Id. 438
2351; Essie; F; 19; Maricopa; F; S; Dau.; 2364; Yes; Yes; AI. 4394/Id. 439
2352; Mack; M; 17; Maricopa; F; S; Son; 2365; Yes; Yes; AI. 4075/Id. 440

MANUEL
2353; Ida H., (Howard, Ida); F; 31; Pima; F; M; Wife; 2366; Yes; Yes; AI. 2538/Id. 5924
2354; Bernard; M; 11; Pima; F; S; Son; 2367; Yes; Yes; AI./Id. 5925
2355; Harrington; M; 10; Pima; F; S; Son; 2368; Yes; Yes; AI./Id. 5926
2356; Olive P.; F; 9; Pima; F; S; Dau.; 2369; Yes; Yes; AI./Id. 5927

MANUEL
2357; Charles; M; 37; Pima; F; S; Head; 2370; Yes; Yes; AI. 1159/Id. 6529

Key: Number; Surname; Given; Sex (M/F); Age at Last Birthday; Tribe; Degree of Blood (F=Full); Marital Status; Relationship to Head of Family & Last Census No; At Jurisdiction Where Enrolled (Yes/No); (If no – Where); Ward (Yes/No); Allotment Annuity and/or Identification Numbers

MANUEL

2358; Chiago; M; 26; Pima; F; M; Head; 2371; Yes; Yes; AI. 371/Id. 5165

2359; Mabel Y., (Yask, Mabel); F; 25; Pima; F; M; Wife; 2372; Yes; Yes; AI. 422/Id. 5166

2360; Burnett; M; 9; Pima; F; S; Son; 2373; Yes; Yes; AI./Id. 5167

2361; Elmer; M; 6; Pima; F; S; Son; 2374; Yes; Yes; AI./Id. 5168

MANUEL

2362; Chola; M; 82; Pima; F; M; Head; 2375; Yes; Yes; AI. 398/Id. 5254

2363; Sophia E., (Edwards, Sophia); F; 77; Pima; F; M; Wife; 2376; Yes; Yes; AI. 723/Id. 5255

2364; David; M; 32; Pima; F; S; Son; 2377; Yes; Yes; AI. 4391/Id. 4306

2365; Williams, Elizabeth; F; 7/12; Pima; F; S; Gr.dau.; --; Yes; ~~Born; 8-29-31.~~; Yes; AI./Id. 3934

MANUEL

2366; Dennis; M; 23; Pima; F; M; Head; 2378; Yes; Yes; AI./Id. 1409

2367; Lienete; F; 23; Pima; F; M; Wife; 2379; Yes; Yes; AI./Id. 1410

2368; Regina; F; 3; Pima; F; S; Dau.; 2380; Yes; Yes; AI./Id. 1411

MANUEL

2369; Ethel; F; 30; Maricopa; F; M; Head; 2381; Yes; Yes; AI. 4392/Id. 437

2370; Helen; F; 1; Maricopa; F; S; Dau.; 2382; Yes; Yes; AI./Id. 600

MANUEL

2371; Jennie, (Parsons, Jennie); F; 38; Pima; F; M; Wife; 2383; No; Phoenix Sch. Ariz.; Salt River Res.; ~~Scottsdale Maricopa Ariz.~~; Yes; AI. 243/Id. 5924

2372; Edmund; M; 16; Pima; F; S; Son; 2384; No; Phoenix Sch. Ariz.; Salt River Res.; ~~Scottsdale Maricopa Ariz.~~; Yes; AI./Id. 5983

2373; Nettie; F; 11; Pima; F; S; Dau.; 2385; No; Phoenix Sch. Ariz.; Salt River Res.; ~~Scottsdale Maricopa Ariz.~~; Yes; AI./Id. 5984

MANUEL

2374; Francisco; M; 43; Pima; F; M; Head; 2386; Yes; Yes; AI. 1436/Id. 6473

2375; Anita L., (Lewis, Anita); F; 47; Pima; F; M; Wife; 2387; Yes; Yes; AI. 2517/Id. 6474

2376; Agnes; F; 21; Pima; F; S; Dau.; 2388; Yes; Yes; AI. 1438/Id. 6475

2377; Leo; M; 9; Pima; F; S; Son; 2389; Yes; Yes; AI./Id. 6476

2378; Elizabeth; F; 7; Pima; F; S; Dau.; 2390; Yes; Yes; AI. 1438/Id. 6477

2379; Dennis; M; 5; Pima; F; S; Son; 2391; Yes; Yes; AI./Id. 6478

MANUEL

2380; Frank; M; 39; Pima; F; S; Head; 2392; Yes; Yes; AI. 936/Id. 1774

Census of the **Gila River** reservation of the **Pima Agency** jurisdiction; as of **April 1** ; 1932; taken by **A. H. Kneale** ; Superintendent.

Key: Number; Surname; Given; Sex (M/F); Age at Last Birthday; Tribe; Degree of Blood (F=Full); Marital Status; Relationship to Head of Family & Last Census No; At Jurisdiction Where Enrolled (Yes/No); (If no – Where); Ward (Yes/No); Allotment Annuity and/or Identification Numbers

MANUEL
2381; Mary M.; F; 11; Pima; F; S; Alone; 2393; Yes; Yes; AI. 4891/Id. 4623
2382; Lottie; F; 7; Pima; F; S; Sister; --; Yes; Yes; AI./Id. 4624

MANUEL
2383; Martha; F; 67; Pima; F; Wd.; Head; 2394; Yes; Yes; AI. 3896/Id. 7189
2384; Sipaia; M; 31; Pima; F; S; Son; 2395; Yes; Yes; AI. 2655/Id. 7190

MANUEL
2385; Jose; M; 32; Pima; F; M; Head; 2396; Yes; Yes; AI. 2482/Id. 5206
2386; Eva T., (Terry, Eva); F; 27; Pima; F; M; Wife; 2397; Yes; Yes; AI. 669/Id. 5207

MANUEL
2387; Jose; M; 29; Pima; F; M; Head; 2398; Yes; Yes; AI. 410/Id. 5926
2388; Jose Juan; M; 93; Pima; F; Wd.; Father; 2399; Yes; Yes; AI. 1924/Id. 4625

MANUEL
2389; Jose L.; M; 39; Pima; F; M; Head; 2400; Yes; Yes; AI. 1809/Id. 4720
2390; Lena; F; 39; Pima; F; M; Wife; 2401; Yes; Yes; AI. 1810/Id. 4721
2391; George; M; 24; Pima; F; S; Son; 2402; Yes; Yes; AI. 1811/Id. 4722
2392; Kenneth L.; M; 13; Pima; F; S; Son; 2403; Yes; Yes; AI. 4488/Id. 4723
2393; Hubert; M; 7; Pima; F; S; Son; 2404; Yes; Yes; AI./Id. 4724

MANUEL
2394; John; M; 77; Pima; F; Wd.; Head; 2405; Yes; Yes; AI. 229/Id. 5925

MANUEL
2395; John; M; 52; Pima; F; M; Head; 2406; Yes; Yes; AI. 2208/Id. 3010
2396; Mollie; F; 49; Pima; F; M; Wife; 2407; Yes; Yes; AI. 2209/Id. 3011
2397; Reba; F; 13; Pima; F; S; Dau.; 2408; Yes; Yes; AI. 4825/Id. 3012
2398; Rita; F; 12; Pima; F; S; Dau.; 2409; Yes; Yes; AI. 4825/Id. 3013

MANUEL
2399; Jose; M; 77; Pima; F; M; Head; 2410; Yes; Yes; AI. 5273/Id. 5377
~~Ahliel F. (Ramon, Ahliel); F; 67; Pima; F; M; Wife; 2411; Died 6-22-31.~~; Yes; AI. 36/Id. 5378

MANUEL
2400; Jose; M; 52; Pima; F; M; Head; 2412; Yes; Yes; AI. 1863/Id. 4617
2401; Juanita; F; 43; Pima; F; M; Wife; 2413; Yes; Yes; AI. 1864/Id. 4618
2402; Lulu; F; 24; Pima; F; S; Dau.; 2414; Yes; Yes; AI. 1925/Id. 4619
2403; Nancy; F; 21; Pima; F; S; Dau.; 2415; Yes; Yes; AI. 3225/Id. 4620
2404; Virginia; F; 18; Pima; F; S; Dau.; 2416; Yes; Yes; AI. 3226/Id. 4621
2405; Paul; M; 16; Pima; F; S; Son; 2417; Yes; Yes; AI./Id. 4622

Census of the **Gila River** reservation of the **Pima Agency** jurisdiction; as of **April 1** ; 1932; taken by **A. H. Kneale** ; Superintendent.

Key: Number; Surname; Given; Sex (M/F); Age at Last Birthday; Tribe; Degree of Blood (F=Full); Marital Status; Relationship to Head of Family & Last Census No; At Jurisdiction Where Enrolled (Yes/No); (If no – Where); Ward (Yes/No); Allotment Annuity and/or Identification Numbers

MANUEL
2406; Juan; M; 67; Pima; F; M; Head; 2418; Yes; Yes; AI. 935/Id. 5239
2407; Mary M. (Lewis, Manita); F; 58; Pima; F; M; Wife; 2419; Yes; Yes; AI. 337/Id. 5240
~~Carmel; F; 22; Pima; F; S; Dau.; 2420; Yes; Married to J. Roe Lewis;~~ Yes; AI. 338/Id. 5241

MANUEL
2408; Juan; M; 50; Pima; F; Wd.; Head; 2421; Yes; Yes; AI. 3520/Id. 1358

MANUEL
2409; Juan; M; 75; Pima; F; M; Head; 2422; Yes; Yes; AI. 1871/Id. 4782
2410; Jose Mollie. (Smith, Jose Mollie); F; 57; Pima; F; M; Wife; 2423; Yes; Yes; AI. 2144/Id. 4783

MANUEL
2411; Mollie; F; 57; Pima; F; Wd.; Head; 2424; Yes; Yes; AI. 2975/Id. 3344
2412; Manwell; M; 28; Pima; F; S; Son; 2425; Yes; Yes; AI. 2976/Id. 3345

MANUEL
2413; Juan; M; 46; Pima; F; M; Head; 2426; Yes; Yes; AI. 3905/Id. 1376
2414; Mollie Anna; F; 58; Pima; F; M; Wife; 2427; Yes; Yes; AI. 3906/Id. 1377
2415; Lucy; F; 23; Pima; F; S; Dau.; 2428; Yes; Yes; AI. 3908/Id. 1378

MANUEL
2416; Juan L.; M; 57; Pima; F; M; Head; 2429; Yes; Yes; AI. 5927/Id. 3477
2417; Gualupa; F; 57; Pima; F; M; Wife; 2430; Yes; Yes; AI. 3478/Id. 5928
2418; Jose E.; M; 35; Pima; F; S; Son; 2431; Yes; Yes; AI. 3479/Id. 5929
2419; Delaine; F; 33; Pima; F; S; Dau.; 2432; Yes; Yes; AI. 3480/Id. 5930
2420; Jaun[sic] T.; M; 20; Pima; F; S; Son; 2433; Yes; Yes; AI. 3482/Id. 5932

MANUEL
2421; Juan Jr.; M; 21; Pima; F; M; Head; 2434; Yes; Yes; AI. 3481/Id. 5931
2422; Anistacia, (Osife, Anestacia[sic]); F; 20; Pima; F; M; Wife; 2435; Yes; Yes; AI. 1561/Id. 5997
2423; Leroy P.; M; 1; Pima; F; S; Son; 2436; Yes; Yes; AI./Id. 6107

MANUEL
2424; Juanna M.; F; 72; Pima; F; Wd.; Head; 2437; Yes; Yes; AI. 1599/Id. 7192

MANUEL
2425; Lanson; M; 31; Pima; F; M; Head; 2438; Yes; Yes; AI. 378/Id. 5159
2426; Paula Campia; F; 25; Papago; F; M; Wife; 2439; Yes; Yes; AI./Id. 5160
2427; Mary A.; F; 3; Pima-Papago; F; S; Dau.; 2440; Yes; Yes; AI./Id. 5161
2428; Betty Lowe; F; 1; Pima-Papago; F; S; Dau.; 2441; Yes; Yes; AI./Id. 6111

Key: Number; Surname; Given; Sex (M/F); Age at Last Birthday; Tribe; Degree of Blood (F=Full); Marital Status; Relationship to Head of Family & Last Census No; At Jurisdiction Where Enrolled (Yes/No); (If no – Where); Ward (Yes/No); Allotment Annuity and/or Identification Numbers

MANUEL
2429; Lancisco; M; 35; Pima; F; S; Head; 2442; Yes; Yes; AI. 717/Id. 5149

MANUEL
2430; Lewis E.; M; 48; Pima; F; M; Head; 2443; Yes; Yes; AI. 1767/Id. 4793
2431; Zella; F; 45; Pima; F; M; Wife; 2444; Yes; Yes; AI. 1768/Id. 4794
2432; Irene; F; 20; Pima; F; S; Dau.; 2445; Yes; Yes; AI. 2352/Id. 4795
2433; Bennett; M; 19; Pima; F; S; Son; 2446; Yes; Yes; AI. 3804/Id. 4796
2434; Allegra; F; 18; Pima; F; S; Dau.; 2447; Yes; Yes; AI. 3940/Id. 4797

MANUEL
2435; Lizzie; F; 67; Pima; F; Wd.; Head; 2448; Yes; Yes; AI. 3704/Id. 7193
2436; Nicodemus; M; 23; Pima; F; S; Son; 2449; Yes; Yes; AI. 3709/Id. 7194

MANUEL
2437; Mark L.; M; 35; Pima; F; M; Head; 2450; Yes; Yes; AI. 377/Id. 5157
2438; Antonia T., (Thomas, Antonia); F; 31; Pima; F; M; Wife; 2451; Yes; Yes; AI. 295/Id. 5158

MANUEL
2439; Martha P., (Phillips, Martha); F; 40; Pima; F; M; Wife; 2452; Yes; Yes; AI. 4291/Id. 799
2440; Leslie; M; 15; Pima; F; S; Son; 2463; Yes; Yes; AI. 4292/Id. 1964

MANUEL
2441; Matthew; M; 24; Pima; F; M; Head; 2454; Yes; Yes; AI. 1812/Id. 4666
2442; Anita, (Kisto, Anito[sic]); F; 23; Pima; F; M; Wife; 2455; Yes; Yes; AI. 1880/Id. 4667
2443; Eloise; F; 5; Pima; F; S; Dau.; 2456; Yes; Yes; AI./Id. 4668
2444; Pansy; F; 2; Pima; F; S; Dau.; 2457; Yes; Yes; AI./Id. 4668

MANUEL
2445; Martin; M; 57; Pima; F; M; Head; 2458; Yes; Yes; AI. 4045/Id. 1772
2446; Petra; F; 57; Pima; F; M; Wife; 2459; Yes; Yes; AI. 4046/Id. 1773
2447; Frank; M; 29; Pima; F; S; Son; 2460; Yes; Yes; AI. 4047/Id. 1774
2448; Lawrence; M; 14; Pima; F; S; Son; 2461; Yes; Yes; AI. 4053/Id. 1775

MANUEL
2449; Mary; F; 92; Pima; F; Wd.; Head; 2462; Yes; Yes; AI. 2227/Id. 3226

MANUEL
2450; Mollie A.; F; 62; Pima; F; Wd.; Head; 2463; Yes; Yes; AI. 2171/Id. 3018
2451; Felix; M; 31; Pima; F; S; Son; 2464; Yes; Yes; AI. 2174/Id. 3019
2452; Ruth; F; 13; Pima; F; S; Dau.; 2465; Yes; Yes; AI. 2179/Id. 3023

Key: Number; Surname; Given; Sex (M/F); Age at Last Birthday; Tribe; Degree of Blood (F=Full); Marital Status; Relationship to Head of Family & Last Census No; At Jurisdiction Where Enrolled (Yes/No); (If no – Where); Ward (Yes/No); Allotment Annuity and/or Identification Numbers

MANUEL

2453; Luke; M; 27; Pima; F; M; Head; 2466; Yes; Yes; AI. 2177/Id. 3021

2454; Catherine, (Enis, Catherine); F; 29; Pima; F; M; Wife; 2467; Yes; Yes; AI. 924/Id. 4327

2455; Eula; F; 1; Pima; F; S; Dau.; 2468; Yes; Yes; AI./Id. 3600

MANUEL

2456; Newton; M; 24; Maricopa; F; S; Head; 2469; Yes; Yes; AI. 4393/Id. 438

MANUEL

2457; Paul; M; 23; Pima; F; S; Head; 2470; Yes; Yes; AI. 2178/Id. 3022

MANUEL

2458; Paul; M; 37; Pima; F; M; Head; 2471; Yes; Yes; AI. 4048/Id. 1776

2459; Annie N., (Nelson, Annie); F; 29; Pima; F; M; Wife; 2472; Yes; Yes; AI. 3681/Id. 1768

2460; Mary; F; 5; Pima; F; S; Dau.; 2473; Yes; Yes; AI./Id. 1977

2461; Nelson; Patrick; M; 9; Pima; F; S; St.son; 2474; Yes; Yes; AI./Id. 1965

2462; Nelson; Ethel; F; 7; Pima; F; S; St.dau.; 2475; Yes; Yes; AI./Id. 1966

MANUEL

2463; Peter; M; 65; Maricopa; F; S; Head; 2476; Yes; Yes; AI. 3413/Id. 551

2464; Emma; F; 63; Maricopa; F; M; wife; 2477; Yes; Yes; AI. 3414/Id. 552

2465; Miles; M; 25; Maricopa; F; S; Son; 2478; Yes; Yes; AI. 3415/Id. 553

2466; Jason; M; 20; Maricopa; F; S; Son; 2479; Yes; AI. 3416/Id. 554

MANUEL

2467; Robert; M; 26; Pima; F; M; Head; 2480; Yes; Yes; AI. 3708/Id. 7195

2468; Leceta, (Miguel, Leecita[sic] Waluga); F; 32; Pima; F; M; Wife; 2481; Yes; Yes; AI. 3917/Id. 7196

2469; Victor; M; 5; Pima; F; S; Son; 2482; Yes; Yes; AI./Id. 7197

MANUEL

2470; Rose; F; 42; Pima; F; S; Head; 2483; Yes; Yes; AI. 934/Id. 7198

2471; Susanna; F; 92; Pima; F; Wd.; Gr.mother; 2484; Yes; Yes; AI. 789/Id. 4128

MANUEL

2472; Warren; M; 27; Pima; F; M; Head; 2485; Yes; Yes; AI. 2973/Id. 4331

2473; Ella J., (Jay, Ella); F; 29; Pima; F; M; Wife; 2486; Yes; Yes; AI. 1979/Id. 4332

2474; Herman; M; 12; Pima; F; S; Son; 2487; Yes; Yes; AI. 3705/Id. 4333

2475; Clarence; M; 10; Pima; F; S; Son; 2488; Yes; Yes; AI./Id. 4334

2476; Leo; M; 9; Pima; F; S; Son; 2489; Yes; Yes; AI./Id. 4335

2477; Leonard; M; 5; Pima; F; S; Son; 2490; Yes; Yes; AI./Id. 4337

Census of the **Gila River** reservation of the **Pima Agency** jurisdiction; as of **April 1** ; 1932; taken by **A. H. Kneale** ; Superintendent.

Key: Number; Surname; Given; Sex (M/F); Age at Last Birthday; Tribe; Degree of Blood (F=Full); Marital Status; Relationship to Head of Family & Last Census No; At Jurisdiction Where Enrolled (Yes/No); (If no – Where); Ward (Yes/No); Allotment Annuity and/or Identification Numbers

MANUEL
2478; Cyrus; M; 21; Pima; F; M; Head; 2491; Yes; Yes; AI. 1157/Id. 6531
2479; Iris; F; 1; Pima; F; S; Dau.; 2492; Yes; Yes; AI./Id. 7278

MANUELL
2480; Jose J.; M; 43; Pima; F; M; Head; 2493; Yes; Yes; AI. 1155/Id. 6530
2481; Annie S., (Scott, Anna); F; 35; Pima; F; M; Wife; 2494; Yes; Yes; AI. 592/Id. 4918
2482; Paul; M; 18; Pima; F; S; Son; 2495; Yes; Yes; AI. 1633/Id. 6532
2483; Jerry; M; 14; Pima; F; S; Son; 2496; Yes; Yes; AI. 3487/Id. 6533
2484; Daisy; F; 11; Pima; F; S; Dau.; 2497; Yes; Yes; AI./Id. 6534

MAN-YAN
2485; ---; 71; Maricopa; F; M; Head; 2498; Yes; Yes; AI. 2806/Id. 9
2486; Mutsawyae; F; 71; Maricopa; F; M; Wife; 2499; Yes; Yes; AI. 2807/Id. 10
2487; Ben; M; 39; Maricopa; F; S; Son; 2500; Yes; Yes; AI. 2861/Id. 11
2488; Lizzie; F; 27; Maricopa; F; S; Dau.; 2501; Yes; Yes; AI. 4759/Id. 12

MAN-YAN
2489; Robert; 31; Maricopa; F; M; Head; 2502; Yes; Yes; AI. 2862/Id. 47
2490; Salome C., (Collins, Salome); F; 29; Maricopa; F; M; Wife; 2503; Yes; Yes; AI. 2954/Id. 45

MARAIDO
2491; Anton; M; 61; Pima; F; M; Head; 2504; Yes; Yes; AI. 4729/Id. 4557
2492; Juanna; F; 51; Pima; F; M; Wife; 2505; Yes; Yes; AI. 4730/Id. 4558
2493; Isaac; M; 24; Pima; F; S; Son; 2506; Yes; Yes; AI. 4732/Id. 4559
2494; Mary; F; 18; Pima; F; S; Dau.; 2507; Yes; Yes; AI. 4733/Id. 4560
2495; Antonia; F; 16; Pima; F; S; Dau.; 2508; Yes; Yes; AI. 4734/Id. 4561
2496; William; M; 9; Pima; F; S; Son; 2509; Yes; Yes; AI./Id. 4562

MARAIDO
2497; David; M; 27; Pima; F; M; Head; 2510; Yes; Yes; AI. 4731/Id. 4563
2498; Mollie A.; F; 29; Pima; F; M; Wife; 2511; Yes; Yes; AI./Id. 4564
2499; Violet; F; 6; Pima; F; S; Dau.; 2512; Yes; Yes; AI./Id. 4565

MARCUS
2500; Claude; M; 25; Pima; F; S; Head; 2513; Yes; Yes; AI. 766/Id. 5933

MARCUS
2501; Elizabeth, (Cannon, Elizabeth); F; 25; Pima; F; M; Wife; 2514; Yes; Yes; AI. 1196/Id. 6660

MARIANO
2502; Edward M.; M; 42; Pima; F; M; Head; 2515; Yes; Yes; AI. 838/Id. 4127

Census of the **Gila River** reservation of the **Pima Agency** jurisdiction; as of **April 1** ; 1932; taken by **A. H. Kneale** ; Superintendent.

Key: Number; Surname; Given; Sex (M/F); Age at Last Birthday; Tribe; Degree of Blood (F=Full); Marital Status; Relationship to Head of Family & Last Census No; At Jurisdiction Where Enrolled (Yes/No); (If no – Where); Ward (Yes/No); Allotment Annuity and/or Identification Numbers

2503; Helen M., (Molino, Helen); F; 36; Pima; F; M; Wife; 2516; Yes; Yes; AI. 839/Id. 4126

2504; Elmer; M; 16; Pima; F; S; Son; 2517; Yes; Yes; AI. 4474/Id. 4125

2505; Elsie; F; 10; Pima; F; S; Dau.; 2518; Yes; Yes; AI./Id. 4124

2506; Jones; M; 7; Pima; F; S; Son; 2519; Yes; Yes; AI./Id. 4123

MARIE

2507; Jose; M; 43; Pima; F; M; Head; 2520; Yes; Yes; AI./Id. 1379

2508; Frances; F; 42; Pima; F; M; Wife; 2521; Yes; Yes; AI. 839/Id. 4110

MARIE

2509; Juan; M; 38; Pima; F; M; Head; 2522; Yes; Yes; AI. 757/Id. 5934

2510; (Eunice), Enicia; F; 37; Pima; F; M; Wife; 2523; Yes; Yes; AI. 426/Id. 5935

2511; Irene; F; 19; Pima; F; S; Dau.; 2524; Yes; Yes; AI. 427/Id. 5936

2512; Lucile; F; 18; Pima; F; S; Dau.; 2525; Yes; Yes; AI. 758/Id. 5937

2513; Pedro; M; 13; Pima; F; S; Son; 2526; Yes; Yes; AI. 3628/Id. 5938

2514; Cepriano; M; 11; Pima; F; S; Son; 2527; Yes; Yes; AI./Id. 5939

2515; Jacob; M; 10; Pima; F; S; Son; 2528; Yes; Yes; AI./Id. 5940

MARIE

2516; Lewis; M; 64; Pima; F; M; Head; 2529; Yes; Yes; AI. 318/Id. 5500

2517; Juanna L.; F; 62; Pima; F; M; Wife; 2530; Yes; Yes; AI. 319/Id. 5501

MARIE

2518; Jose; M; 33; Maricopa; F; S; Head; 2531; Yes; Yes; AI. 75/Id. 55

MARIETTA

2519; Anton; M; 29; Pima; F; M; Head; 2532; Yes; Yes; AI. 3216/Id. 5643

2520; Effie K., (Stone, Effie Kisto); F; 26; Pima; F; M; Wife; 2533; Yes; Yes; AI. 352/Id. 5644

2521; Hastings; M; 11; Pima; F; S; Son; 2534; Yes; Yes; AI./Id. 5645

2522; Timothy; M; 8; Pima; F; S; Son; 2535; Yes; Yes; AI./Id. 5646

2523; Harry; M; 2; Pima; F; S; Son; 2536; Yes; Yes; AI./Id. 5986

MARIETTA

2524; Juan F.; M; 62; Pima; F; M; Head; 2537; Yes; Yes; AI. 3213/Id. 5598

2525; Leona; F; 67; Pima; F; M; Wife; 2538; Yes; Yes; AI. 3214/Id. 5599

2526; Anton, Clara; F; 19; Pima; F; S; Gr.dau.; 2539; Yes; Yes; AI. 2426/Id. 5987

MARIETTA

2527; Lewis; M; 41; Pima; F; M; Head; 2540; Yes; Yes; AI. 1962/Id. 4767

2528; Cremacia; F; 41; Pima; F; M; Wife; 2541; Yes; Yes; AI. 1963/Id. 4768

2529; Francisco; M; 19; Pima; F; S; Son; 2542; Yes; Yes; AI. 1964/Id. 4769

2530; Joseph; M; 17; Pima; F; S; Son; 2543; Yes; Yes; AI. 3290/Id. 4770

2531; Angelita; F; 16; Pima; F; S; Dau.; 2544; Yes; Yes; AI. 3284/Id. 4771

Census of the **Gila River** reservation of the **Pima Agency** jurisdiction; as of **April 1** ; 1932; taken by **A. H. Kneale** ; Superintendent.

Key: Number; Surname; Given; Sex (M/F); Age at Last Birthday; Tribe; Degree of Blood (F=Full); Marital Status; Relationship to Head of Family & Last Census No; At Jurisdiction Where Enrolled (Yes/No); (If no – Where); Ward (Yes/No); Allotment Annuity and/or Identification Numbers

2532; Eva; F; 15; Pima; F; S; Dau.; 2545; Yes; Yes; AI. 4808/Id. 4772
2533; Nora; F; 12; Pima; F; S; Dau.; 2546; Yes; Yes; AI./Id. 4774
2534; Jessie; F; 6; Pima; F; S; Dau.; 2547; Yes; Yes; AI./Id. 4775
2535; Annie R.; F; 5; Pima; F; S; Dau.; 2548; Yes; Yes; AI./Id. 4776

MARIETTA
2536; Thomas; M; 39; Pima; F; M; Head; 2549; Yes; Yes; AI. 1965/Id. 4274
2537; Carrie J., (Johnson, Carrie); F; 31; Pima; F; M; Wife; 2550; Yes; Yes; AI. 2006/Id. 4275
2538; Fred A.; M; 14; Pima; F; S; Son; 2551; Yes; Yes; AI. 4811/Id. 4276
2539; Harrison J.; M; 11; Pima; F; S; Son; 2552; Yes; Yes; AI. 4889/Id. 4277
2540; Otis; M; 5; Pima; F; S; Son; 2553; Yes; Yes; AI./Id. 4278
2541; Arrat Tom; M; 1/12; Pima; F; S; Son; --; Yes; ~~Born 3-28-32~~.[sic] Yes; AI./Id. 3948
2542; Cornelio Tony; M; 1/12; Pima; F; S; Son; --; Yes; ~~Born 3-23-32~~.[sic] Yes; AI./Id. 3947

MARIANO
~~N.E.; Alfred;~~
2543; Dora S., (Sweet, Dora); F; 40; Pima; F; M; Wife; 2554; Yes; Yes; AI. 3768/Id. 5942

MARKS
2544; Joseph; M; 51; Maricopa; F; Wd.; Head; 2555; Yes; Yes; AI. 3740/Id. 485
2545; Aloysius; M; 22; Maricopa; F; S; Son; 2556; Yes; Yes; AI. 3742/Id. 486
2546; Andres; M; 21; Maricopa; F; S; Son; 2557; Yes; Yes; AI. 3743/Id. 487
2547; Pauline; F; 19; Maricopa; F; S; Dau.; 2558; Yes; Yes; AI. 3744/Id. 488
2548; Gerard; M; 12; Maricopa; F; S; Son; 2559; Yes; Yes; AI. 4832/Id. 489

MARTIN
2549; Jose; M; 47; Pima; F; M; Head; 2560; Yes; Yes; AI. 3151/Id. 1817
2550; Sarah V., (Valenzuala, Sarah); F; 47; Pima; F; M; Wife; 2561; Yes; Yes; AI. 3588/Id. 1818
2551; Ruth; F; 12; Pima; F; S; Dau.; 2562; Yes; Yes; AI. 4757/Id. 1819
2552; Bertha; F; 7; Pima; F; S; Dau.; 2563; Yes; Yes; AI./Id. 1820
2553; Amilda M.; F; 5; Pima; F; S; Dau.; 2564; Yes; Yes; AI./Id. 1821
2554; Valenzuala, Blanche R.; F; 20; Pima; F; S; St.dau.; 2565; Yes; Yes; AI. 3589/Id. 5176

MARTINEZ
2555; Chona; F; 67; Pima; F; Wd.; Head; 2566; Yes; Yes; AI. 3281/Id. 7199
2556; Lulya; F; 25; Pima; F; S; Dau.; 2567; Yes; Yes; AI. 3283/Id. 7200
2557; Domingo; M; 27; Pima; F; S; Son; 2568; Yes; Yes; AI. 3282/Id. 4777
2558; Billy; M; 16; Pima; F; S; Son; 2569; Yes; Yes; AI. 3796/Id. 7213
2559; Gladys; F; 13; Pima; F; S; Dau.; 2570; Yes; Yes; AI./Id. 7201

Census of the **Gila River** reservation of the **Pima Agency** jurisdiction; as of **April 1** ; 1932; taken by **A. H. Kneale** ; Superintendent.

Key: Number; Surname; Given; Sex (M/F); Age at Last Birthday; Tribe; Degree of Blood (F=Full); Marital Status; Relationship to Head of Family & Last Census No; At Jurisdiction Where Enrolled (Yes/No); (If no - Where); Ward (Yes/No); Allotment Annuity and/or Identification Numbers

MARTINEZ
2560; John; M; 41; Pima; F; Wd.; Head; 2571; Yes; Yes; AI. 2444/Id. 7202
2561; Conzuela; F; 19; Pima; F; S; Dau.; 2572; Yes; Yes; AI. 2445/Id. 4246
2562; Henry; M; 18; Pima; F; S; Son; 2573; Yes; Yes; AI. 2446/Id. 4247

MARTINEZ
2563; Manuel; M; Unk.; Pima; F; Wd.; Head; 2574; Yes; Yes; AI./Id. 3546
2564; Alice L., (Lewis, Alice); F; 35; Pima; F; M; Wife; 2575; Yes; Yes; AI. 2441/Id. 3312
2565; Wilbur; M; 20; Pima; F; S; Son; 2576; Yes; Yes; AI./Id. 3313

MATHEWS
2566; Andrew; M; 27; Pima; F; M; Head; 2577; Yes; Yes; AI. 905/Id. 4566
2567; Minnie M., (Miles, Minnie); F; 36; Pima; F; M; Wife; 2578; Yes; Yes; AI. 416/Id. 4567
2568; Rupert H.; M; 11; Pima; F; S; Son; 2579; Yes; Yes; AI./Id. 4568
2569; Andrew Jr..; M; 6/12; Pima; F; S; Son; --; Yes; ~~Born 10-13-31.~~; Yes; AI./Id. 3949

MATHEWS
2570; Charley; M; Unk.; Pima; F; Wd.; Head; 2580; Yes; Yes; AI./Id. 4483
2571; Paul; M; 24; Pima; F; S; Son; 2581; Yes; Yes; AI./Id. 4484
2572; Archie; M; 22; Pima; F; S; Son; 2582; Yes; Yes; AI./Id. 4485
2573; Lydia; F; 14; Pima; F; S; Dau.; 2583; Yes; Yes; AI./Id. 4486
2574; Clyde; M; 10; Pima; F; S; Son; 2584; Yes; Yes; AI./Id. 4487

MATHEWS
2575; Hanna; F; 53; Pima; F; Wd.; Head; 2585; Yes; Yes; AI. 903/Id. 7203

MATHEWS
2576; Joseph; M; 35; Pima; F; M; Head; 2586; Yes; Yes; AI. 1666/Id. 3219
2577; Lucile; F; 35; Pima; F; M; Wife; 2587; Yes; Yes; AI. 1667/Id. 3220
2578; Lyle; M; 15; Pima; F; S; Son; 2588; Yes; Yes; AI. 3805/Id. 3221
2579; Stella; F; 10; Pima; F; S; Dau.; 2589; Yes; Yes; AI./Id. 3222
2580; Yeldy G.; F; 4; Pima; F; S; Dau.; 2590; Yes; Yes; AI./Id. 3223
2581; Cramer; M; 2; Pima; F; S; Son; 2591; Yes; Yes; AI./Id. 3502
2582; Charles; M; 4/12; Pima; F; S; Son; --; Yes; ~~Died 11-17-31.~~; Yes; AI./Id. 3615

MATHEWS
2583; Minnie M.; F; 52; Pima; F; Wd.; Head; 2592; Yes; Yes; AI. 1756/Id. 4122

MATHIAS
2584; Frank J.; M; 43; Pima; F; M; Head; 2593; Yes; Yes; AI. 3465/Id. 1798

Census of the **Gila River** reservation of the **Pima Agency** jurisdiction; as of **April 1** ; 1932; taken by **A. H. Kneale** ; Superintendent.

Key: Number; Surname; Given; Sex (M/F); Age at Last Birthday; Tribe; Degree of Blood (F=Full); Marital Status; Relationship to Head of Family & Last Census No; At Jurisdiction Where Enrolled (Yes/No); (If no – Where); Ward (Yes/No); Allotment Annuity and/or Identification Numbers

MATLEWAH
2585; Hamecksevai; F; 71; Maricopa; F; Wd.; Head; 2594; Yes; Yes; AI. 2857/Id. 164

MATHIAS
2586; John M.; M; 65; Pima; F; Wd.; Head; 2595; Yes; Yes; AI. 3460/Id. 1653
2587; Sylvester; M; 21; Pima; F; S; Son; 2596; Yes; Yes; AI. 3463/Id. 1654
2588; Regina; F; 19; Pima; F; S; Dau.; 2597; Yes; Yes; AI. 3464/Id. 1655

MCAFEE
2589; Johnson; M; 36; Pima; F; M; Head; 2598; Yes; Yes; AI. 3685/Id. 5272
2590; Sarah P., (Patton, Sarah); F; 35; Pima; F; M; Wife; 2599; Yes; Yes; AI. 1076/Id. 5273
2591; Luella P.; F; 11; Pima; F; S; Dau.; 2600; Yes; Yes; AI./Id. 5274
2592; Johnson; M; 9; Pima; F; S; Son; 2601; Yes; Yes; AI./Id. 5275
2593; Cameron L.; M; 7; Pima; F; S; Son; 2602; Yes; Yes; AI./Id. 5276
2594; Wilmer L.; M; 6; Pima; F; S; Son; 2603; Yes; Yes; AI./Id. 5943
2595; Marcella R.; F; 3; Pima; F; S; Dau.; 2604; Yes; Yes; AI./Id. 5277

MCAFEE
2596; Mason; M; 70; Maricopa; F; Wd.; Head; 2605; Yes; Yes; AI. 3683/Id. 360

MCARTHUR
2597; Dean; M; 63; Maricopa; F; M; Head; 2606; Yes; Yes; AI. 643/Id. 397
2598; Catherine; F; 63; Maricopa; F; M; Wife; 2607; Yes; Yes; AI. 644/Id. 398
2599; Olsen; M; 21; Maricopa; F; M; Son; 2608; Yes; Yes; AI. 647/Id. 400

MCARTHUR
2600; Dean; M; 42; Maricopa; F; M; Head; 2609; Yes; Yes; AI. 4468/Id. 399

MCDONALD
2601; Joseph; M; 56; Maricopa; F; M; Head; 2610; Yes; Yes; AI. 3756/Id. 447
2602; Mary B., (Benson, Mary); F; 52; Maricopa; F; M; Wife; 2611; Yes; Yes; AI. 3993/Id. 448
2603; William S.; M; 19; Maricopa; F; M; Son; 2612; Yes; Yes; AI. 3760/Id. 449

MCCASLIN
2604; Marian; F; 46; Pima; F; S; Head; 2613; Yes; Yes; AI. 3260/Id. 5945

MCKAY
2605; Lucy; F; 42; Pima; F; Wd.; Head; 2614; Yes; Yes; AI. 3687/Id. 5946
2606; Evalina; F; 17; Pima; F; S; Dau.; 2615; Yes; Yes; AI. 3688/Id. 5947
2607; John; M; 15; Pima; F; S; Son; 2616; Yes; Yes; AI. 3689/Id. 5948
2608; Herbert; M; 13; Pima; F; S; Son; 2617; Yes; Yes; AI./Id. 5949
2609; Florence; F; 6; Pima; F; S; Dau.; 2618; Yes; Yes; AI./Id. 5950

Census of the **Gila River** reservation of the **Pima Agency** jurisdiction; as of **April 1** ; 1932; taken by **A. H. Kneale** ; Superintendent.

Key: Number; Surname; Given; Sex (M/F); Age at Last Birthday; Tribe; Degree of Blood (F=Full); Marital Status; Relationship to Head of Family & Last Census No; At Jurisdiction Where Enrolled (Yes/No); (If no – Where); Ward (Yes/No); Allotment Annuity and/or Identification Numbers

MCKAY
2610; Oscar; M; 42; Pima; F; Wd.; Head; 2619; Yes; Yes; AI. 3686/Id. 5951

MCKINLEY
2611; James; M; 58; Maricopa; F; Wd.; Head; 2620; Yes; Yes; AI. 2866/Id. 184
2612; David; M; 24; Maricopa; F; S; Son; 2621; Yes; Yes; AI. 2868/Id. 185

MCKINLEY
2613; Pearl; F; 39; Maricopa; F; Wd.; Head; 2622; Yes; Yes; AI. 2867/Id. 186
2614; Rosabelle; F; 13; Maricopa; F; S; Dau.; 2623; Yes; Yes; AI./Id. 187

MCKINLEY
2615; William; M; 48; Maricopa; F; Wd.; Head; 2624; Yes; Yes; AI. 2864/Id. 189
2616; Fannie; F; 21; Maricopa; F; S; Dau.; 2625; Yes; Yes; AI. 2915/Id. 190
2617; William Jr.; M; 19; Maricopa; F; S; Son; 2626; Yes; Yes; AI. 2916/Id. 192
2618; Carl; M; 18; Maricopa; F; S; Son; 2627; Yes; Yes; AI. 2917/Id. 191

MEGUIL
2619; Hugh; M; 57; Pima; F; M; Head; 2628; Yes; Yes; AI. 937/Id. 4120
2620; Ramona; F; 57; Pima; F; M; Wife; 2629; Yes; Yes; AI. 938/Id. 4119

MEGUIL
2621; Pancho; M; 42; Pima; F; M; Head; 2630; Yes; Yes; AI. 634/Id. 4358
2622; Mary; F; 35; Pima; F; M; Wife; 2631; Yes; Yes; AI. 635/Id. 4359
2623; Bernice; F; 18; Pima; F; S; Dau.; 2632; Yes; Yes; AI. 636/Id. 4360
2624; Daniel; M; 16; Pima; F; S; Son; 2633; Yes; Yes; AI. 1673/Id. 4361
2625; Leon; M; 8; Pima; F; S; Son; 2634; Yes; Yes; AI./Id. 4363
2626; Dorothy; F; 14; Pima; F; S; Dau.; 2635; Yes; Yes; AI. 4720/Id. 4362
2627; Ruby; F; 6; Pima; F; S; Dau.; 2636; Yes; Yes; AI./Id. 4364

MEGUIL
2628; San[sic]; M; 49; Pima; F; M; Head; 2637; Yes; Yes; AI. 1110/Id. 6746
2629; Joanna L., (Lewis, Joanna); F; 30; Pima; F; M; Wife; 2638; Yes; Yes; AI. 1478/Id. 6747
2630; Wallace; M; 10; Pima; F; S; Son; 2639; Yes; Yes; AI./Id. 6748
2631; Lydia; F; 5; Pima; F; S; Dau.; 2640; Yes; Yes; AI./Id. 6749

MEKOLAS
2632; Mary; F; 72; Pima; F; Wd.; Head; 2641; Yes; Yes; AI. 1891/Id. 4758

MENSON
2633; Nellie B., (Bread, Nellie); F; 32; Maricopa; F; M; Wife; 2642; Yes; Yes; AI. 2882/Id. 575
2634; Richard; M; 5; Maricopa; F; S; Son; 2643; Yes; Yes; AI./Id. 576

Census of the **Gila River** reservation of the **Pima Agency** jurisdiction; as of **April 1** ; 1932; taken by **A. H. Kneale** ; Superintendent.

Key: Number; Surname; Given; Sex (M/F); Age at Last Birthday; Tribe; Degree of Blood (F=Full); Marital Status; Relationship to Head of Family & Last Census No; At Jurisdiction Where Enrolled (Yes/No); (If no – Where); Ward (Yes/No); Allotment Annuity and/or Identification Numbers

MENDOZA
~~Carlos; M; 62; Papago; F; Wd.; Head; 2644; Died; 4-22-31.~~; Yes; AI. 939/Id. 5370
2635; Louisa; F; 15; Papago; F; S; Dau.; 2645; Yes; Yes; AI. 4726/Id. 5372

MENDOZA
2636; Jose; M; 82; Papago; F; Wd.; Head; 2646; Yes; Yes; AI. 3142/Id. 5952
2637; Danan; F; 27; Papago; F; S; Dau.; 2647; Yes; Yes; AI. 3147/Id. 5953
2638; Angelito; M; 29; Papago; F; S; Son; 2648; Yes; Yes; AI. 3149/Id. 5954
2639; Manuel; M; 23; Papago; F; S; Son; 2649; Yes; Yes; AI. 3148/Id. 5955
2640; Ramon; M; 21; Papago; F; S; Son; 2650; Yes; Yes; AI. 3146/Id. 5956
2641; Mary; F; 15; Papago; F; S; Dau.; 2651; Yes; Yes; AI. 4535/Id. 5957

MENDOZA
2642; Juan M.; M; Unk.; Papago; F; S; Head; 2652; Yes; Yes; AI./Id. 5426

MESKEER
2643; Thomas; M; 61; Maricopa; F; M; Head; 2653; Yes; Yes; AI. 2796/Id. 252
2644; Lena; F; 61; Maricopa; F; M; Wife; 2654; Yes; Yes; AI. 2797/Id. 281

MICHAEL
2645; John; M; 49; Pima; F; M; Head; 2655; Yes; Yes; AI. 3860/Id. 1785
2646; Mary I., (Ignace, Mary); F; 47; Pima; F; M; Wife; 2656; Yes; Yes; AI. 3861/Id. 1786
2647; Leo B.; M; 21; Pima; F; S; Son; 2657; Yes; Yes; AI. 3862/Id. 1787
2648; Clestine; M; 19; Pima; F; S; Son; 2658; Yes; Yes; AI. 3863/Id. 1788
2649; Pancratius; M; 10; Pima; F; S; Son; 2659; Yes; Yes; AI./Id. 1789
2650; Priscilla; F; 3; Pima; F; S; Dau.; 2660; Yes; Yes; AI./Id. 1981

MIGUEL
2651; Lena; F; 70; Pima; F; Wd.; Head; 2661; Yes; Yes; AI. 4262/Id. 1969

MIGUEL
2652; Albert J.; M; 32; Pima; F; M; Head; 2662; Yes; Yes; AI. 506/Id. 5582
2653; Minnie M., (Meyers, Minnie); F; 32; Pima; F; M; Wife; 2663; Yes; Yes; AI. 1756/Id. 5583
2654; Leona; F; 11; Pima; F; S; Dau.; 2664; Yes; Yes; AI. 4814/Id. 5585
2655; Melinda; F; 13; Pima; F; S; Dau.; 2665; Yes; Yes; AI. 4881/Id. 5584
2656; Esther J.; F; 7; Pima; F; S; Dau.; 2666; Yes; Yes; AI./Id. 5586
2657; Thelma; F; 6; Pima; F; S; Dau.; 2667; Yes; Yes; AI./Id. 5587
2658; Regina; F; 4; Pima; F; S; Dau.; 2668; Yes; Yes; AI./Id. 5588

MIGUEL
2659; Andreas J.; M; 52; Pima; F; M; Head; 2669; Yes; Yes; AI. 2593/Id. 7014
2660; Gualupa; F; 52; Pima; F; M; Wife; 2670; Yes; Yes; AI. 2594/Id. 7015
2661; Miguel; M; 18; Pima; F; S; Son; 2671; Yes; Yes; AI. 2597/Id. 7016

Key: Number; Surname; Given; Sex (M/F); Age at Last Birthday; Tribe; Degree of Blood (F=Full); Marital Status; Relationship to Head of Family & Last Census No; At Jurisdiction Where Enrolled (Yes/No); (If no – Where); Ward (Yes/No); Allotment Annuity and/or Identification Numbers

2662; Dennis; M; 15; Pima; F; S; Son; 2672; Yes; Yes; AI. 4527/Id. 7017
2663; Augustus; M; 12; Pima; F; S; Son; 2673; Yes; Yes; AI. 4838/Id. 7018
2664; Gerald; M; 9; Pima; F; S; Son; 2674; Yes; Yes; AI./Id. 7019

MIGUEL
2665; Cyrus; M; 30; Pima; F; S; Head; 2675; Yes; Yes; AI. 2258/Id. 3393

MIGUEL
2666; Domingo; M; 44; Pima; F; M; Head; 2676; Yes; Yes; AI. 1356/Id. 5958
2667; (Annily), Andelay; F; 45; Pima; F; M; Wife; 2677; Yes; Yes; AI. 1357/Id. 6016
2668; Julia; F; 15; Pima; F; S; Dau.; 2678; Yes; Yes; AI./Id. 5960
2669; John; M; 13; Pima; F; S; Son; 2679; Yes; Yes; AI./Id. 5961
2670; Matthew; M; 10; Pima; F; S; Son; 2680; Yes; Yes; AI./Id. 5962
2671; Irene; F; 8; Pima; F; S; Dau.; 2681; Yes; Yes; AI./Id. 5963

MIGUEL
2672; Hosea; M; 67; Pima; F; M; Head; 2682; Yes; Yes; AI. 1273/Id. 7204
2673; Juanne; F; 53; Pima; F; M; Wife; 2683; Yes; Yes; AI. 1274/Id. 7205

MIGUEL
2674; Howard J.; M; 52; Pima; F; M; Head; 2684; Yes; (Known as Howard Mathew also) Yes; AI. 477/Id. 5077
2675; Juanna F., (Cheerless, Juanna); F; 42; Pima; F; M; Wife; 2685; Yes; Yes; AI. 478/Id. 5078
2676; Irene J.; F; 21; Pima; F; S; Dau.; 2686; Yes; Yes; AI. 509/Id. 5079
2677; Freeman J.; M; 17; Pima; F; S; Son; 2687; Yes; Yes; AI. 3714/Id. 5080
2678; Willie; M; 18; Pima; F; S; Son; 2688; Yes; Yes; AI. 510/Id. 5081
2679; Mita; F; 10; Pima; F; S; Dau.; 2689; Yes; Yes; AI. 0/Id. 5082

MIGUEL
2680; Joseba; M; 89; Pima; F; Wd.; Head; 2690; Yes; Yes; AI. 4265/Id. 1970

MIGUEL
2681; Jessie; F; 27; Pima; F; S; Head; 2691; Yes; Yes; AI. 674/Id. 1971

MIGUEL
2682; John J.; M; 59; Pima; F; M; Head; 2692; Yes; Yes; AI. 745/Id. 5965
2683; Susiana; F; 64; Pima; F; M; Wife; 2693; Yes; Yes; AI./Id. 5966

MIGUEL
2684; Johnson; M; 42; Pima; F; M; Head; 2694; Yes; Yes; AI. 2257/Id. 3424
2685; Eva L., (Lucas, Eva); F; 22; Pima; F; M; Wife; 2695; Yes; Yes; AI. 2238/Id. 3425
2686; Rebecca; F; 2; Pima; F; S; Dau.; 2696; Yes; Yes; AI./Id. 3565

Census of the **Gila River** reservation of the **Pima Agency** jurisdiction; as of **April 1** ; 1932; taken by **A. H. Kneale** ; Superintendent.

Key: Number; Surname; Given; Sex (M/F); Age at Last Birthday; Tribe; Degree of Blood (F=Full); Marital Status; Relationship to Head of Family & Last Census No; At Jurisdiction Where Enrolled (Yes/No); (If no – Where); Ward (Yes/No); Allotment Annuity and/or Identification Numbers

MIGUEL

2687; Jose; M; 47; Pima; F; M; Head; 2697; Yes; Yes; AI. 548/Id. 5967
2688; Dorothy B., (Beginning, Dorothy); F; 57; Pima; F; M; Wife; 2698; Yes; Yes; AI. 2185/Id. 5968

MIGUEL

2689; Jose; M; 30; Pima; F; M; Head; 2699; Yes; Yes; AI./Id. 1882
2690; Listiana, (Lewis, Lisciana); F; 30; Pima; F; M; Wife; 2700; Yes; Yes; AI. 1618/Id. 1883
2691; Wilford; M; 2; Pima; F; S; Son; 2701; Yes; Yes; AI./Id. 1988

MIGUEL

2692; Jose; M; 53; Pima; F; Wd.; Head; 2702; Yes; Yes; AI./Id. 1360

MIGUEL

2693; Jose; M; Unk.; Pima; F; M; Head; 2703; Yes; Yes; AI. 3140/Id. 7206
2694; Laura; F; Unk.; Pima; F; M; Wife; 2704; Yes; Yes; AI. 3141/Id. 7207

MIGUEL

2695; Jose D.; M; 31; Pima; F; S; Head; 2705; Yes; Yes; AI. 2696/Id. 7208

MIGUEL

2696; Juan; M; 83; Pima; F; Wd.; Head; 2706; Yes; Yes; AI. 530/Id. 4929

MIGUEL

2697; Juen[sic]; M; 83; Pima; F; Wd.; Head; 2707; Yes; Yes; AI. 4362/Id. 7209

MIGUEL

2698; Juanecio; M; 25; Pima; F; M; Head; 2708; Yes; Yes; AI. 741/Id. 5210
2699; Marie E., (Enos, Marie); F; 26; Pima; F; M; Wife; 2709; Yes; Yes; AI. 329/Id. 5211
2700; Patricia; F; 6; Pima; F; S; Dau.; 2710; Yes; Yes; AI./Id. 5212

MIGUEL

2701; Krelin; M; 32; Pima; F; M; Head; 2711; Yes; Yes; AI. 1276/Id. 6793
2702; Lucile; F; 32; Pima; F; M; Wife; 2712; Yes; Yes; AI./Id. 6794

MIGUEL

2703; Lena; F; 71; Pima; F; Wd.; Head; 2713; Yes; Yes; AI. 1394/Id. 6485

MIGUEL

2704; Lewis; M; 42; Pima; F; S; Head; 2714; Yes; Yes; AI. 1639/Id. 4788

MIGUEL

2705; Loreta; F; 37; Pima; F; Wd.; Head; 2715; Yes; Yes; AI. 4785/Id. 5971

Key: Number; Surname; Given; Sex (M/F); Age at Last Birthday; Tribe; Degree of Blood (F=Full); Marital Status; Relationship to Head of Family & Last Census No; At Jurisdiction Where Enrolled (Yes/No); (If no - Where); Ward (Yes/No); Allotment Annuity and/or Identification Numbers

2706; Juliana; F; 12; Pima; F; S; Dau.; 2716; Yes; Yes; AI. 4786/Id. 5972

MIGUEL
2707; Michael; M; 65; Pima; F; M; Head; 2717; Yes; Yes; AI. 428/Id. 5172
2708; Mollie, (Malyea); F; 67; Pima; F; M; Wife; 2718; Yes; Yes; AI. 429/Id. 5173
2709; Miley; F; 25; Pima; F; S; Dau.; 2719; Yes; Yes; AI. 487/Id. 5174
2710; Albert; M; 32; Pima; F; S; Son; 2720; Yes; Yes; AI. 485/Id. 5175

MIGUEL
2711; Miguel; M; 57; Pima; F; Wd.; Head; 2721; Yes; Yes; AI. 3914/Id. 1346

MIGUEL
2712; Peter Wilson; M; 39; Pima; F; M; Head; 2722; Yes; Yes; AI. 2261/Id. 3388
2713; Martha P.; F; 29; Papago; F; M; Wife; 2723; Yes; Yes; AI./Id. 3389
2714; Peter W., Jr.; M; 4; Pima-Papago; F; S; Son; 2724; Yes; Yes; AI./Id. 3566

MIGUEL
2715; Roy J.; M; 26; Pima; F; M; Head; 2725; Yes; Yes; AI. 508/Id. 5973

MIGUEL
2716; Vincent; M; 42; Pima; F; Wd.; Head; 2726; Yes; Yes; AI. 693/Id. 5974

MIGUEL
2717; Clara V., (Valenzuala, Clara); F; 67; Pima; F; Wd.; Head; 2727; Yes; Yes; AI. 2295/Id. 4311
2718; Ellen; F; 27; Pima; F; S; Dau.; 2728; Yes; Yes; AI. 2264/Id. 3394

MIGUEL
2719; Albert; M; 22; Pima; F; M; Head; 2729; Yes; Yes; AI. 2265/Id. 3392
2720; Esther Lucas; F; 17; Pima; F; M; Wife; 2730; Yes; Yes; AI. 2239/Id. 3295

MILDE
2721; Jose; M; 58; Pima; F; M; Head; 2730; Yes; Yes; AI. 1249/Id. 6571
2722; Lucy; F; 49; Pima; F; M; Wife; 2731; Yes; Yes; AI. 1250/Id. 6572
2723; Ruby; F; 22; Pima; F; S; Dau.; 2732; Yes; Yes; AI. 1252/Id. 6574
2724; Jonah; M; 19; Pima; F; S; Son; 2733; Yes; Yes; AI. 1253/Id. 6575
2725; Gilbert; M; 18; Pima; F; S; Son; 2734; Yes; Yes; AI. 2591/Id. 6576
2726; David; M; 12; Pima; F; S; Son; 2735; Yes; Yes; AI. 4839/Id. 6577

MILDE
2727; Richard; M; 28; Pima; F; M; Head; 2736; Yes; Yes; AI. 1252/Id. 6573
~~Clemencia Ramon; F; 22; Papago; F; M; Wife; --; Yes; Sells Agency allottee.~~; Yes; AI./Id.
2728; Peggy Annette; F; 2/12; Pima-Papago; F; S; Dau.; --; Yes; ~~Born. 2-19-32~~; Yes; AI. 1252/Id. 6574

Census of the **Gila River** reservation of the **Pima Agency** jurisdiction; as of **April 1** ; 1932; taken by **A. H. Kneale** ; Superintendent.

Key: Number; Surname; Given; Sex (M/F); Age at Last Birthday; Tribe; Degree of Blood (F=Full); Marital Status; Relationship to Head of Family & Last Census No; At Jurisdiction Where Enrolled (Yes/No); (If no – Where); Ward (Yes/No); Allotment Annuity and/or Identification Numbers

MILES

2729; David; M; 39; Pima; F; M; Head; 2737; Yes; Yes; AI. 4791/Id. 1972
2730; Eva C., (Grant, Eva); F; 35; Pima; F; M; Wife; 2738; Yes; Yes; AI. 4019/Id. 1973
2731; Louise; F; 12; Pima; F; S; Dau.; 2739; Yes; Yes; AI. 4856/Id. 1934
2732; Marien; F; 11; Pima; F; S; Dau.; 2740; Yes; Yes; AI./Id. 1975
2733; David J.; M; 8; Pima; F; S; Son; 2741; Yes; Yes; AI./Id. 1976

MILES

2734; Ethel; F; 23; Pima; F; Wd.; Head; 2742; Yes; Yes; AI. 66/Id. 5521
2735; Leslie R.; M; 7; Pima; F; S; Son; 2743; Yes; Yes; AI./Id. 5522

MILES

2736; John; M; 55; Pima; F; M; Head; 2744; Yes; Yes; AI. 207/Id. 5514
2737; Lucy; F; 55; Pima; F; M; Wife; 2745; Yes; Yes; AI. 208/Id. 5515
2738; Helen; F; 32; Pima; F; S; Dau.; 2746; Yes; Yes; AI. 3113/Id. 5516
2739; Felix; M; 28; Pima; F; S; Son; 2747; Yes; Yes; AI. 3115/Id. 5517
2740; Susan; F; 24; Pima; F; S; Dau.; 2748; Yes; Yes; AI. 765/Id. 5518
2741; Nathaniel; M; 20; Pima; F; S; Son; 2749; Yes; Yes; AI. 3165/Id. 5519
2742; Hubert M.; M; 16; Pima; F; S; Son; 2750; Yes; Yes; AI. 4857/Id. 5520

MILES

2743; Joseph; M; 52; Pima; F; M; Head; 2751; Yes; Yes; AI. 415/Id. 5178
2744; Susie B.; F; 42; Pima; F; M; Wife; 2752; Yes; Yes; AI./Id. 5179
2745; Isadora; F; 11; Pima; F; S; Dau.; 2753; Yes; Yes; AI./Id. 5180
2746; Margery; F; 8; Pima; F; S; Dau.; 2754; Yes; Yes; AI./Id. 5181
2747; Henry; M; 4; Pima; F; S; Son; 2755; Yes; Yes; AI./Id. 5182
2748; Joseph Jr.; M; 1; Pima; F; S; Son; 2756; Yes; Yes; AI./Id. 6103

MILES

2749; Joseph; M; 33; Pima; F; M; Head; 2757; Yes; Yes; AI. 3144/Id. 5474
2750; Jennie T., (Turner, Jennie); F; 31; Pima; F; M; Wife; 2758; Yes; Yes; AI. 80/Id. 5475
2751; Donald T.; M; 13; Pima; F; S; Son; 2759; Yes; Yes; AI. 4848/Id. 5476
2752; Eddie T.; M; 10; Pima; F; S; Son; 2760; Yes; Yes; AI./Id. 5477
2753; Dennis T.; M; 8; Pima; F; S; Son; 2761; Yes; Yes; AI./Id. 5478
2754; Elsie; F; 6; Pima; F; S; Dau.; 2762; Yes; Yes; AI./Id. 5479
2755; Ella; F; 4; Pima; F; S; Dau.; 2763; Yes; Yes; AI./Id. 5480

MILES

2756; Julian; M; 34; Pima; F; M; Head; 2764; Yes; Yes; AI. 1497/Id. 6606
2757; Ethel S., (Snyder, Ethel); F; 37; Pima; F; M; Wife; 2765; Yes; Yes; AI. 1969/Id. 6607
2758; Chester; M; 11; Pima; F; S; Son; 2766; Yes; Yes; AI./Id. 6608
2759; Edna; F; 9; Pima; F; S; Dau.; 2767; Yes; Yes; AI./Id. 6609

Census of the **Gila River** reservation of the **Pima Agency** jurisdiction; as of **April 1** ; 1932; taken by **A. H. Kneale** ; Superintendent.

Key: Number; Surname; Given; Sex (M/F); Age at Last Birthday; Tribe; Degree of Blood (F=Full); Marital Status; Relationship to Head of Family & Last Census No; At Jurisdiction Where Enrolled (Yes/No); (If no – Where); Ward (Yes/No); Allotment Annuity and/or Identification Numbers

MILES

2760; Ramon; M; 33; Pima; F; M; Head; 2768; Yes; Yes; AI. 417/Id. 4975
2761; Alice Enos; F; 40; Pima; F; M; Wife; 827; Yes; Yes; AI. 2010/Id. 3070
2762; Clifford; M; 11; Pima; F; S; Son; 2769; Yes; Yes; AI. 4976/Id. 4043
2763; Geraldine; F; 5/12; Pima; F; S; Dau.; --; Yes; Born 11-10-31; Yes; AI./Id. 6125

MILLER

2764; Frank; M; 72; Pima; F; M; Head; 2770; Yes; Yes; AI. 4043/Id. 1586
2765; Eva; F; 72; Pima; F; M; Wife; 2771; Yes; Yes; AI. 4044/Id. 1587

MILLER

2766; Homer; M; 53; Pima; F; M; Head; 2772; Yes; Yes; AI. 271/Id. 5263
2767; Antonia; F; 53; Pima; F; M; Wife; 2773; Yes; Yes; AI. 272/Id. 5264
2768; Frank Quinn; M; 19; Pima; F; S; Son; 2774; Yes; Yes; AI. 714/Id. 5265
2769; Felix Quinn; M; 13; Pima; F; S; Son; 2775; Yes; Yes; AI. 4508/Id. 5266

MIX

2770; Lopez; M; 28; Pima; F; M; Head; 2776; Yes; Yes; AI. 1544/Id. 4872
2771; Esther S., (Smith, Esther); F; 29; Pima; F; M; Wife; 2777; Yes; Yes; AI. 578/Id. 4873
2772; Eugenia L.; F; 6; Pima; F; S; Dau.; 2778; Yes; Yes; AI./Id. 4874
2773; Delma F.; F; 4; Pima; F; S; Dau.; 2779; Yes; Yes; AI./Id. 4875

MIX

2774; Lorenzo; M; 24; Pima; F; S; Head; 2780; Yes; Yes; AI. 1539/Id. 7210
2775; Eliza Scott; F; 22; Pima; F; S; Sis.; 2781; Yes; Yes; AI. 1540/Id. 4726
2776; Emily; F; 14; Pima; F; S; Sis.; 2782; Yes; Yes; AI./Id. 4727
2777; Justine C.; M; 12; Pima; F; S; Nephew; 2783; Yes; Yes; AI./Id. 4728

MIX

2778; Pablo; M; 27; Pima; F; S; Head; 2784; Yes; Yes; AI. 1542/Id. 4726

MOFFIT

2779; Joseph; M; 49; Pima; F; M; Head; 2785; Yes; Yes; AI. 712/Id. 5309
2780; Margaret; F; 45; Pima; F; M; Wife; 2786; Yes; Yes; AI. 713/Id. 5310
2781; Thomas; M; 23; Pima; F; S; Son; 2787; Yes; Yes; AI. 768/Id. 5311
2782; Irene; F; 22; Pima; F; S; Dau.; 2788; Yes; Yes; AI. 770/Id. 5312
2783; Russell; M; 14; Pima; F; S; Son; 2789; Yes; Yes; AI. 4547/Id. 5313
2784; Robert; M; 13; Pima; F; S; Son; 2790; Yes; Yes; AI./Id. 5314
2785; Jonah; M; 9; Pima; F; S; Son; 2791; Yes; Yes; AI./Id. 5315
2786; Lillie; F; 7; Pima; F; S; Dau.; 2792; Yes; Yes; AI./Id. 5316

MOFFIT

2787; Samuel; M; 66; Pima; F; M; Head; 2793; Yes; Yes; AI. 1359/Id. 7047
2788; Mabel; F; 57; Pima; F; M; Wife; 2794; Yes; Yes; AI. 1360/Id. 7048

Census of the **Gila River** reservation of the **Pima Agency** jurisdiction; as of **April 1** ; 1932; taken by **A. H. Kneale** ; Superintendent.

Key: Number; Surname; Given; Sex (M/F); Age at Last Birthday; Tribe; Degree of Blood (F=Full); Marital Status; Relationship to Head of Family & Last Census No; At Jurisdiction Where Enrolled (Yes/No); (If no – Where); Ward (Yes/No); Allotment Annuity and/or Identification Numbers

MOLINO

2789; Eugene E.; M; 42; Pima; F; M; Head; 2795; Yes; Yes; AI. 3430/Id. 6627
2790; Fannie; F; 34; Pima; F; M; Wife; 2796; Yes; Yes; AI. 1363/Id. 6628
2791; Albert B.; M; 9; Pima; F; S; Son; 2797; Yes; Yes; AI./Id. 6629
2792; Francis B.; M; 7; Pima; F; S; Son; 2798; Yes; Yes; AI./Id. 6630
2793; Violet; F; 4; Pima; F; S; Dau.; 2799; Yes; Yes; AI./Id. 1631

MOLLIE

2794; Josea; M; 64; Pima; F; S; Head; 2800; No; Phoenix Sch. Ariz.; Salt River Res.; ~~Scottsdale Maricopa Ariz.~~; Yes; AI. 3372/Id. 5975

MONTANA

2795; Mollie; F; 64; Pima; F; Wd.; Head; 2801; Yes; Yes; AI. 1642/Id. 7211

MONTEZUMA

2796; Jose M.; M; 59; Pima; F; M; Head; 2802; Yes; Yes; AI. 2286/Id. 3427
2797; Louisa Marie; F; 57; Pima; F; M; Wife; 2803; Yes; Yes; AI. 2287/Id. 3428

MOORE

2798; Amy; F; 51; Pima; F; Wd.; Head; 2804; Yes; Yes; AI. 3604/Id. 6980
2799; Florence; F; 25; Pima; F; S; Dau.; 2805; Yes; Yes; AI. 3607/Id. 6981
2800; Russell; M; 20; Pima; F; S; Son; 2806; Yes; Yes; AI. 3608/Id. 6982

MOORE

2801; Clark; M; 34; Pima; F; S; Head; 2807; Yes; Yes; AI. 3605/Id. 6977

MOORE

2802; Josiah; M; 65; Pima; F; M; Head; 2808; Yes; Yes; AI. 3599/Id. 6975
2803; Rose; F; 62; Pima; F; M; Wife; 2809; Yes; Yes; AI. 3600/Id. 6976

MOORE

2804; William T.; M; 42; Pima; F; M; Head; 2810; No; Blue Island Cook Ill.; Yes; AI. 3601/Id. 6978
2805; Everett N.; M; 12; Pima; F; S; Son; 2811; No; Blue Island Cook Ill.; Yes; AI. 4770/Id. 6983

MORAGO

2806; Edith; F; 38; Pima; F; M; Wife; 2812; No; Los Angeles L.A. Cal.; Yes; AI. 1648/Id. 4118

MORAGO

2807; Ida; F; 27; Pima; F; M; Wife; 2813; Yes; Yes; AI. 2668/Id. 3547
2808; Rufus; M; 22; Pima; F; S; Bro.; 2814; Yes; Yes; AI. 1660/Id. 4415
2809; William F.; M; 19; Pima; F; S; Bro.; 2815; Yes; Yes; AI. 1650/Id. 4416
2810; Henry H.; M; 4; Pima; F; S; Son; 2816; Yes; Yes; AI./Id. 4448

Key: Number; Surname; Given; Sex (M/F); Age at Last Birthday; Tribe; Degree of Blood (F=Full); Marital Status; Relationship to Head of Family & Last Census No; At Jurisdiction Where Enrolled (Yes/No); (If no – Where); Ward (Yes/No); Allotment Annuity and/or Identification Numbers

MORAGO

2811; Kisto; M; 53; Pima; F; M; Head; 2817; Yes; Yes; AI. 1651/Id. 4475

2812; Retta O., (Osife, Retta); F; 44; Pima; F; M; Wife; 2818; Yes; Yes; AI. 1412/Id. 7069

2813; Lewis; M; 23; Pima; F; S; Son; 2819; Yes; Yes; AI. 1652/Id. 4476

2814; Otis; M; 21; Pima; F; S; Son; 2820; Yes; Yes; AI. 1653/Id. 4477

MORAGO

2815; Jay Roe; M; 36; Pima; F; M; Head; 2821; Yes; Yes; AI. 1649/Id. 4424

~~N.E.; Florence; F; Unk.; Crow; F; M; Wife; --; Yes; Crow Indian allottee.~~; Yes; AI./Id.

2816; Jay Roe; M; 14; Pima-Crow; F; S; Son; 2822; Yes; Yes; AI. 4820/Id. 4426

2817; Leslie W.; M; 13; Pima-Crow; F; S; Son; 2823; Yes; Yes; AI. 4821/Id. 4427

2818; Gwendolyn; F; 12; Pima-Crow; F; S; Dau.; 2824; Yes; Yes; AI./Id. 4428

2819; Joseph; M; 11; Pima-Crow; F; S; Son; 2825; Yes; Yes; AI./Id. 4429

2820; Edith E.; F; 9; Pima-Crow; F; S; Dau.; 2826; Yes; Yes; AI./Id. 4430

2821; Edna Mae; F; 5; Pima-Crow; F; S; Dau.; 2827; Yes; Yes; AI./Id. 4431

MORALES

2822; Hal; M; 43; Pima; F; M; Head; 2828; Yes; Yes; AI. 782/Id. 4535

2823; Ida W.; F; 35; Pima; F; M; Wife; 2829; Yes; Yes; AI. 783/Id. 4536

2824; Margaret; F; 20; Pima; F; S; Dau.; 2830; Yes; Yes; AI. 784/Id. 4537

2825; Lorena; F; 10; Pima; F; S; Dau.; 2831; Yes; Yes; AI./Id. 4538

2826; Ione; F; 7; Pima; F; S; Dau.; 2832; Yes; Yes; AI./Id. 4539

MORALES

2827; Jose A.; M; 69; Pima; F; Wd.; Head; 2833; Yes; Yes; AI. 1953/Id. 4591

MORALES

2828; Jose P.; M; 45; Pima; F; S; Head; 2834; Yes; Yes; AI. 1955/Id. 4593

MORGAN

2829; Adam T.; M; 40; Pima; F; M; Head; 2835; Yes; Yes; AI. 1721/Id. 4353

2830; Helen M., (Manuel, Helen); F; 23; Pima; F; M; Wife; 2836; Yes; Yes; AI. 1876/Id. 4354

2831; Betty Jean; F; 3; Pima; F; S; Dau.; 2837; Yes; Yes; AI./Id. 4355

MORGAN

2832; Gene; F; 47; Pima; F; S; Head; 2838; Yes; Yes; AI. 4007/Id. 301

MORGAN

~~Thomas; M; 84; Pima; F; Wd.; Head; 2839; Died 1-16-32.~~; Yes; AI. 1698/Id. 4365

119

Census of the **Gila River** reservation of the **Pima Agency** jurisdiction; as
of **April 1** ; 1932; taken by **A. H. Kneale** ; Superintendent.

Key: Number; Surname; Given; Sex (M/F); Age at Last Birthday; Tribe; Degree of Blood (F=Full);
Marital Status; Relationship to Head of Family & Last Census No; At Jurisdiction Where Enrolled
(Yes/No); (If no – Where); Ward (Yes/No); Allotment Annuity and/or Identification Numbers

MORGAN
2833; Thomas; M; 47; Maricopa; F; S; Head; 2840; Yes; Yes; AI. 4006/Id. 302

MCARTHUR
~~N.E.; Nina E.; Unk.; Unk;; Head; --; AI./Id.~~
2834; Norris; Joshua Jr.; M; 10; Pima; F; S; Son; 2841; Yes; Yes; AI./Id. 3362
2835; Norris; Eugene W.; M; 7; Pima; F; S; Son; 2842; Yes; Yes; AI./Id. 3363
2836; Norris; Sylvia; F; 6; Pima; F; S; Dau.; 2843; Yes; Yes; AI./Id. 3364

MORRIS
2837; Victor; M; 72; Pima; F; M; Head; 2844; Yes; Yes; AI. 3275/Id. 1669
2838; Antonio; F; 72; Pima; F; M; Wife; 2845; Yes; Yes; AI. 3276/Id. 1670

MORRISON
2839; Sepie; F; 72; Pima; F; Wd.; Head; 2846; Yes; Yes; AI. 367/Id. 5106

MOYAH
2840; Delain; M; 47; Pima; F; M; Head; 2847; Yes; Yes; AI. 2101/Id. 3548
2841; Nannie; F; 26; Pima; F; M; Wife; 2848; Yes; Yes; AI. 2102/Id. 3549
2842; Hazel; F; 20; Pima; F; S; Dau.; 2849; Yes; Yes; AI. 2103/Id. 3550
2843; Elmer; M; 9; Pima; F; S; Son; 2850; Yes; Yes; AI./Id. 3551
2844; Roland; M; 7; Pima; F; S; Son; 2851; Yes; Yes; AI./Id. 3552

MUMHY
2845; Philip; M; 37; Maricopa; F; M; Head; 2852; Yes; Yes; AI. 2893/Id. 5
2846; Lola, (Loring, Lola); F; 31; Maricopa; F; M; Wife; 2853; Yes; Yes;
AI. 2850/Id. 6
2847; Dottie; F; 7; Maricopa; F; S; Dau.; 2854; Yes; Yes; AI./Id. 7
2848; Bernice; F; 5; Maricopa; F; S; Dau.; 2855; Yes; Yes; AI./Id. 8
2849; Lola; F; 1; Maricopa; F; S; Dau.; 2856; Yes; Yes; AI./Id. 599

MYERS
2850; Edgar; M; 54; Pima; F; M; Head; 2857; Yes; Yes; AI. 1755/Id. 5577
2851; Hattie; F; 51; Pima; F; M; Wife; 2858; Yes; Yes; AI. 26/Id. 5578

MYERS
2852; Enis; M; 40; Pima; F; S; Head; 2859; Yes; Yes; AI. 1063/Id. 7134

MYERS
2853; Jose; M; 47; Pima; F; S; Head; 2860; Yes; Yes; AI. 2107/Id. 3385

MYERS
2854; Joseph; M; 46; Pima; F; Wd.; Head; 2861; Yes; Yes; AI. 1061/Id. 6618

Census of the **Gila River** reservation of the **Pima Agency** jurisdiction; as of **April 1** ; 1932; taken by **A. H. Kneale** ; Superintendent.

Key: Number; Surname; Given; Sex (M/F); Age at Last Birthday; Tribe; Degree of Blood (F=Full); Marital Status; Relationship to Head of Family & Last Census No; At Jurisdiction Where Enrolled (Yes/No); (If no – Where); Ward (Yes/No); Allotment Annuity and/or Identification Numbers

MYERS

2855; Nelson Miguel; M; 45; Pima; F; M; Head; 2862; Yes; Yes; AI. 1057/Id. 6514
2856; Frances W., (Wiston, Frances); F; 28; Pima; F; M; Wife; 2863; Yes; Yes; AI. 1740/Id. 4351
2857; Evaline; F; 23; Pima; F; S; Dau.; 2864; Yes; Yes; AI. 1059/Id. 6515
2858; Marion; F; 20; Pima; F; S; Dau.; 2865; Yes; Yes; AI. 1060/Id. 3815
2859; Rose; F; 14; Pima; F; S; Dau.; 2866; Yes; Yes; AI./Id. 6517
2860; Greta; F; 12; Pima; F; S; Dau.; 2867; Yes; Yes; AI. 4818/Id. 6518
2861; Elwood; M; 10; Pima; F; S; Son; 2868; Yes; Yes; AI./Id. 6519
2862; Edwardune; F; 1; Pima; F; S; Dau.; 2870; Yes; Yes; AI./Id. 7274
2863; Estella; F; 5/12; Pima; F; S; Dau.; --; Yes; ~~Born; 11-14-31.~~; Yes; AI./Id. 7294
2864; Wiston, Marjorie; F; 4; Pima; F; S; St.dau.; 2869; Yes; Yes; AI./Id. 4332

NACHO

2865; Jose; M; 57; Pima; F; Wd.; Head; 2871; Yes; Yes; AI. 4530/Id. 1442
2866; Juan; M; 18; Pima; F; S; Son; 2872; Yes; Yes; AI. 4534/Id. 1444
2867; Ambrose; M; 14; Pima; F; S; Son; 2873; Yes; Yes; AI./Id. 1445
2868; Margaret J.; F; 7; Pima; F; S; Dau.; 2874; Yes; Yes; AI. 4533/Id. 1443

NARCIA

2869; Lucile R., (Ramirez, Lucile); F; 23; Pima; F; M; Wife; 2875; Yes; Yes; AI. 2436/Id. 4109
2870; Mary Ann; F; 6; Pima; F; S; Dau.; 2876; Yes; Yes; AI./Id. 4108

NARSA

2871; Anton; M; 42; Pima; F; M; Head; 2877; Yes; Yes; AI. 3454/Id. 5740
2872; Catalina L., (Lewis, Catalina); F; 49; Pima; F; M; Wife; 2878; Yes; Yes; AI. 2649/Id. 5741
2873; Laura; F; 19; Pima; F; S; Dau.; 2879; Yes; Yes; AI. 4552/Id. 5991
2874; Clara; F; 16; Pima; F; S; Dau.; 2880; Yes; Yes; AI. 3453/Id. 5989
2875; Lewis, Stanislaus; M; 20; Pima; F; S; St.son; 2881; Yes; Yes; AI. 4551/Id. 5742

NARSA

2876; Jose Sr.; M; 71; Pima; F; Wd.; Head; 2882; Yes; Yes; AI. 4827/Id. 5990

NARSA

2877; Jose Jr.; M; 35; Pima; F; M; Head; 2883; Yes; Yes; AI. 4828/Id. 1777
2878; Agnes, (Estrella, Agnes); F; 34; Pima; F; M; Wife; 2884; Yes; Yes; AI. 4378/Id. 1778
2879; Paul; M; 7; Pima; F; S; Son; 2885; Yes; Yes; AI./Id. 1781
2880; Mary; F; 11; Pima; F; S; Dau.; 2886; Yes; Yes; AI. 4829/Id. 1779
2881; Ernest; M; 4; Pima; F; S; Son; 2887; Yes; Yes; AI./Id. 1782
2882; Peter; M; 2; Pima; F; S; Son; 2888; Yes; Yes; AI./Id. 1792
2883; Charles; M; 4/12; Pima; F; S; Son; --; Yes; ~~Born; 12-5-31.~~; Yes; AI./Id. 2054

Census of the **Gila River** reservation of the **Pima Agency** jurisdiction; as of **April 1** ; 1932; taken by **A. H. Kneale** ; Superintendent.

Key: Number; Surname; Given; Sex (M/F); Age at Last Birthday; Tribe; Degree of Blood (F=Full); Marital Status; Relationship to Head of Family & Last Census No; At Jurisdiction Where Enrolled (Yes/No); (If no – Where); Ward (Yes/No); Allotment Annuity and/or Identification Numbers

NATHAN
2884; Charles; M; 56; Pima; F; M; Head; 2889; Yes; Yes; AI. 1939/Id. 4570
2885; Mattie; F; 52; Pima; F; M; Wife; 2890; Yes; Yes; AI. 1940/Id. 4571
2886; Andrew; M; 19; Pima; F; S; Nephew; 2891; Yes; Yes; AI. 2378/Id. 4595

NATHAN
2887; Dewitt; M; 31; Pima; F; S; Head; 2892; Yes; Yes; AI. 2359/Id. 4572

NELSON
2888; Abraham; M; 40; Pima; F; M; Head; 2893; Yes; Yes; AI. 1257/Id. 6457
2889; Contra; F; 37; Pima; F; M; Wife; 2894; Yes; Yes; AI. 2382/Id. 6458
2890; Edmund; M; 11; Pima; F; S; Son; 2895; Yes; Yes; AI./Id. 6459
2891; Everett D.; M; 8; Pima; F; S; Son; 2896; Yes; Yes; AI./Id. 6460
2892; Inez D.; F; 4; Pima; F; S; Dau.; 2897; Yes; Yes; AI./Id. 7215

NELSON
2893; Dana; M; 29; Pima; F; M; Head; 2898; Yes; Yes; AI. 981/Id. 4458
2894; Herbert D.; M; 7; Pima; F; S; Son; 2899; Yes; Yes; AI./Id. 4460

NELSON
2895; David; M; 37; Pima; F; M; Head; 2900; Yes; Yes; AI. 2039/Id. 3437
2896; Lily, (Johnson, Lily);; F; 42; Pima; F; M; Wife; 2901; Yes; Yes; AI. 250/Id. 3438

NELSON
2897; Edwin V.; M; 31; Pima; F; M; Head; 2902; Yes; Yes; AI. 980/Id. 6408

NELSON
2898; Frank; M; 35; Pima; F; S; Head; 2903; Yes; Yes; AI. 2040/Id. 3435

NELSON
2899; Harry; M; 27; Pima; F; S; Head; 2904; Yes; Yes; AI. 2041/Id. 3436

NELSON
2900; Henry; M; 49; Pima; F; S; Head; 2905; Yes; Yes; AI. 1259/Id. 3466

NELSON
2901; Joanna; F; 64; Pima; F; Wd.; Head; 2906; Yes; Yes; AI. 1256/Id. 6454

NELSON
2902; Jose J.; M; 53; Pima; F; Wd.; Head; 2907; Yes; Yes; AI. 1223/Id. 6950

NELSON
2903; Jose N.; M; 33; Pima; F; M; Head; 2908; Yes; Yes; AI. 1405/Id. 7216

Census of the **Gila River** reservation of the **Pima Agency** jurisdiction; as of **April 1** ; 1932; taken by **A. H. Kneale** ; Superintendent.

Key: Number; Surname; Given; Sex (M/F); Age at Last Birthday; Tribe; Degree of Blood (F=Full); Marital Status; Relationship to Head of Family & Last Census No; At Jurisdiction Where Enrolled (Yes/No); (If no – Where); Ward (Yes/No); Allotment Annuity and/or Identification Numbers

2904; Tomassa A., (Anton, Thomassia[sic]); F; 33; Pima; F; M; Wife; 2909; Yes; Yes; AI. 1267/Id. 7217
2905; Anton, Mary G.; F; 11; Pima; F; S; St.Dau.; 2910; Yes; Yes; AI./Id. 5793
2906; Anton, Lila; F; 7; Pima; F; S; St.dau.; 2911; Yes; Yes; AI./Id. 5794

NELSON

2907; Joseph; M; 67; Pima; F; Wd.; Head; 2912; Yes; Yes; AI. 2035/Id. 3434
2908; Logie; M; 23; Pima; F; S; Son; 2913; Yes; Yes; AI. 2042/Id. 3459

NELSON

2909; Joseph M.; M; 25; Pima; F; M; Head; 2914; Yes; Yes; AI. 983/Id. 6417
2910; Angelita; F; 25; Pima; F; M; Wife; 2915; Yes; Yes; AI./Id. 6418

NELSON

2911; Juan T.; M; 41; Pima; F; S; Head; 2916; Yes; Yes; AI. 640/Id. 4987

NELSON

2912; Lewis D.; M; 59; Pima; F; M; Head; 2917; Yes; Yes; AI. 979/Id. 6401
2913; Helen; F; 52; Pima; F; M; Wife; 2918; Yes; Yes; AI. 835/Id. 6402
2914; Thomas McDougal; M; 21; Pima; F; S; Son; 2919; Yes; Yes; AI. 984/Id. 6403
2915; Eula P.; F; 17; Pima; F; S; Dau.; 2920; Yes; Yes; AI. 3169/Id. 6404
2916; Richenda; F; 12; Pima; F; S; Dau.; 2921; Yes; Yes; AI. 4803/Id. 6405
2917; Otis B.; M; 8; Pima; F; S; Son; 2922; Yes; Yes; AI./Id. 6406

NELSON

2918; Lyman; M; 26; Pima; F; M; Head; 2923; Yes; Yes; AI. 982/Id. 6413
2919; Sara E., (Enos, Sara); F; 29; Pima; F; M; Wife; 2924; Yes; Yes; AI. 2012/Id. 6414
~~Donna G.; F; 5; Pima; F; S; Dau.; 2925; Yes; Died 10-18-31.~~; Yes; AI./Id. 6415
2920; Betty; F; 4; Pima; F; S; Dau.; 2926; Yes; Yes; AI./Id. 6416
2921; Joyce; F; 2/12; Pima; F; S; Dau.; --; Yes; ~~Born; 2-16-32.~~; Yes; AI./Id. 7295

NELSON

2922; Silendo; M; 24; Pima; F; S; Head; 2927; Yes; Yes; AI. 3680/Id. 1470

NELSON

2923; Candace, (Redbird, Candace); F; 26; Maricopa; F; M; Wife; 2928; Yes; Yes; AI. 2718/Id. 218
2924; Genevieve; F; 5; Maricopa; F; S; Dau.; 2929; Yes; Yes; AI./Id. 219

NELSON

2925; Thomas M.; M; 47; Pima; F; M; Head; 2930; Yes; Yes; AI. 1634/Id. 5992
2926; Martha; F; 37; Pima; F; M; Wife; 2931; Yes; Yes; AI. 1637/Id. 5993
2927; Nina; F; 20; Pima; F; S; Dau.; 2932; Yes; Yes; AI. 5994/Id. 1635

Census of the **Gila River** reservation of the **Pima Agency** jurisdiction; as of **April 1** ; 1932; taken by **A. H. Kneale** ; Superintendent.

Key: Number; Surname; Given; Sex (M/F); Age at Last Birthday; Tribe; Degree of Blood (F=Full); Marital Status; Relationship to Head of Family & Last Census No; At Jurisdiction Where Enrolled (Yes/No); (If no – Where); Ward (Yes/No); Allotment Annuity and/or Identification Numbers

NELSON
2928; William; M; 33; Pima; F; Wd.; Head; 2933; Yes; Yes; AI. 641/Id. 4988
2929; William, Jr.; M; 6; Pima; F; S; Son; 2934; Yes; Yes; AI./Id. 4989
2930; Earl T.; M; 5; Pima; F; S; Son; 2935; Yes; Yes; AI./Id. 4990

NELSON
2931; William; M; 45; Pima; F; M; Head; 2936; Yes; Yes; AI. 2037/Id. 7218
2932; Minnie B., (Breckenridge, Minnie); F; 27; Pima; F; M; Wife; 2937; Yes; Yes; AI. 4132/Id. 7219
2933; Edna F.; F; 8; Pima; F; S; Dau.; 2938; Yes; Yes; AI./Id. 7220
2934; Patricia J.; F; 5; Pima; F; S; Dau.; 2939; Yes; Yes; AI./Id. 7221
2935; Carol R.; F; 4; Pima; F; S; Dau.; 2940; Yes; Yes; AI./Id. 7222

NEWMAN
2936; Emma; F; 38; Pima; F; S; Head; 2941; Yes; Yes; AI. 3246/Id. 3279

NEWMAN
2937; Harvey; M; 32; Pima; F; M; Head; 2942; Yes; Yes; AI. 3249/Id. 3281
2938; Bessie; F; 26; Pima; F; M; Wife; 2943; Yes; Yes; AI./Id. 3559

NEWMAN
2939; Paul; M; 35; Pima; F; S; Head; 2944; Yes; Yes; AI. 3247/Id. 3277

NEWMAN
2940; Pelion; M; 60; Pima; F; M; Head; 2945; Yes; Yes; AI. 2114/Id. 6065
2941; Anna Lewis; F; 39; Pima; F; M; Wife; 2946; Yes; Yes; AI. 710/Id. 5066
2942; Nina; F; 10; Pima; F; S; Dau.; 2947; Yes; Yes; AI./Id. 5067

NEWMAN
2943; Samuel; M; 53; Pima; F; Wd.; Head; 2948; Yes; Yes; AI. 1130/Id. 6736
2944; Hilda; F; 23; Pima; F; S; Dau.; 2949; Yes; Yes; AI. 1133/Id. 6738
2945; Matthew; M; 12; Pima; F; S; Son; 2950; Yes; Yes; AI./Id. 6739
2946; Claudine; F; 7; Pima; F; S; Dau.; 2951; Yes; Yes; AI./Id. 6740
2947; George; M; 2; Pima; F; S; Gr.son; 2952; Yes; Yes; AI./Id. 7214

NEWMAN
2948; Theresa; F; 62; Pima; F; Wd.; Head; 2953; Yes; Yes; AI. 3245/Id. 3276
2949; Peter; M; 25; Pima; F; S; Son; 2954; Yes; Yes; AI. 3251/Id. 3278

NEWMAN
2950; Thomas; M; 55; Maricopa; F; M; Head; 2955; Yes; Yes; AI. 4301/Id. 365
2951; Susie; F; 54; Maricopa; F; M; Wife; 2956; Yes; Yes; AI. 4302/Id. 366
2952; Nancy; F; 24; Maricopa; F; S; Dau.; 2957; Yes; Yes; AI. 4304/Id. 367
2953; Rita; F; 17; Maricopa; F; S; Dau.; 2958; Yes; Yes; AI. 4305/Id. 368

Key: Number; Surname; Given; Sex (M/F); Age at Last Birthday; Tribe; Degree of Blood (F=Full); Marital Status; Relationship to Head of Family & Last Census No; At Jurisdiction Where Enrolled (Yes/No); (If no – Where); Ward (Yes/No); Allotment Annuity and/or Identification Numbers

NISH

2954; Ernest; M; 26; Pima; F; M; Head; 2959; Yes; Yes; AI. 2391/Id. 4700

2955; Lohena M., (Mix, Lohena); F; 21; Pima; F; M; Wife; 2960; Yes; Yes; AI. 1541/Id. 4701

2956; Michael; M; 5; Pima; F; S; Son; 2961; Yes; Yes; AI./Id. 4702

2957; Frank; M; 53; Pima; F; S; Son; 2962; Yes; Yes; AI./Id. 4703

NISH

2958; Juan V.; M; 82; Pima; F; M; Head; 2963; Yes; Yes; AI. 1844/Id. 4736

2959; Nicholas; F; 82; Pima; F; M; Wife; 2964; Yes; Yes; AI. 2364/Id. 4737

NISH

2960; Lewis; M; 60; Pima; F; M; Head; 2965; Yes; Yes; AI. 1859/Id. 4733

2961; Lichiana, (Thomas, Kichiana[sic]); F; 57; Pima; F; M; Wife; 2966; Yes; Yes; AI. 1806/Id. 4734

2962; Irene; F; 16; Pima; F; S; Dau.; 2967; Yes; Yes; AI. 3291/Id. 4735

2963; Thomas, Joshua; M; 19; Pima; F; S; St.son; 2968; Yes; Yes; AI. 2374/Id. 4740

NISH

2964; Lizzie; F; 23; Pima; F; S; Head; 2969; Yes; Yes; AI. 2390/Id. 4738

NISH

2965; Miguel V.; M; 21; Pima; F; S; Bro.; 2970; Yes; Yes; AI. 2392/Id. 4739

NISH

2966; Osife; M; 35; Pima; F; M; Head; 2971; Yes; Yes; AI. 2365/Id. 4626

2967; Catherine, (Osife, Catherine); F; 32; Pima; F; M; Wife; 2972; Yes; Yes; AI. 2428/Id. 4627

2968; May; F; 13; Pima; F; S; Dau.; 2973; Yes; Yes; AI./Id. 4628

2969; Justine; F; 6; Pima; F; S; Dau.; 2974; Yes; Yes; AI./Id. 4629

NOBLE

2970; John; M; 67; Pima; F; Wd.; Head; 2975; Yes; Yes; AI. 1783/Id. 4744

NOBLE

2971; Vavages; M; 45; Pima; F; M; Head; 2976; Yes; Yes; AI. 1787/Id. 4741

2972; Maggie; F; 47; Pima; F; M; Wife; 2977; Yes; Yes; AI. 1788/Id. 4742

NOLAN

2973; Juan Jose; M; 42; Pima; F; S; Head; 2978; Yes; Yes; AI. 4028/Id. 1480

NONAME

2974; Antonio; M; 63; Pima; F; M; Head; 2979; Yes; Yes; AI. 4034/Id. 1718

~~Manuella; F; 60; Pima; F; M; Wife; 2980; Died; 9-12-31.~~; Yes; AI. 4035/Id. 1719

Census of the **Gila River** reservation of the **Pima Agency** jurisdiction; as of **April 1** ; 1932; taken by **A. H. Kneale** ; Superintendent.

Key: Number; Surname; Given; Sex (M/F); Age at Last Birthday; Tribe; Degree of Blood (F=Full); Marital Status; Relationship to Head of Family & Last Census No; At Jurisdiction Where Enrolled (Yes/No); (If no – Where); Ward (Yes/No); Allotment Annuity and/or Identification Numbers

NONAME
2975; Lapai; M; 37; Maricopa; F; M; Head; 2981; Yes; Yes; AI. 4036/Id. 369
2976; Minnie N., (Nobel, Minnie); F; 56; Maricopa; F; M; Wife; 2982; Yes; Yes; AI. 4295/Id. 370
2977; Adam Lee; M; 5; Maricopa; F; S; Son; 2983; Yes; Yes; AI./Id. 375
2978; Noble, Nora; F; 18; Maricopa; F; S; St.dau.; 2984; Yes; Yes; AI. 4286/Id. 372
2979; Noble, Lydia; F; 15; Maricopa; F; S; St.dau.; 2985; Yes; Yes; AI. 4297/Id. 373
2980; Noble, Lily; F; 26; Maricopa; F; S; St.dau.; 2986; Yes; Yes; AI. 4296/Id. 371
2981; Noble, Myrtle; F; 10; Maricopa; F; S; St.dau.; 2987; Yes; Yes; AI. 1022/Id. 374

NONAME
2982; Lucy G.; F; 27; Pima; F; Wd.; Head; 2988; Yes; Yes; AI. 4037/Id. 1720
2983; Leona; F; 4; Pima; F; S; Dau.; 2989; Yes; Yes; AI./Id. 1722

NORRIS
2984; Claude; M; 35; Pima; F; S; Head; 2990; Yes; Yes; AI. 4085/Id. 1982

NORRIS
2985; John; M; 49; Pima; F; M; Head; 2991; Yes; Yes; AI. 4441/Id. 1665
2986; Juanna; F; 43; Pima; F; M; Wife; 2992; Yes; Yes; AI. 4442/Id. 1666
2987; Gabriel; M; 19; Pima; F; S; Son; 2993; Yes; Yes; AI. 4443/Id. 1667
2988; Nestor; M; 15; Pima; F; S; Son; 2994; Yes; Yes; AI. 4444/Id. 1668

NORRIS
2989; Jose; M; 47; Pima; F; S; Head; 2995; Yes; Yes; AI. 1640/Id. 6910

NORRIS
2990; Irene W., (Williams, Irene); F; 23; Pima; F; M; Wife; 2996; Yes; Yes; AI. 3634/Id. 6017
2991; Juan, Edna; F; 8; Pima; F; S; Dau.; 2997; Yes; Yes; AI./Id. 1636
2992; Juan, Luke; M; 7; Pima; F; S; Son; 2998; Yes; Yes; AI./Id. 1638
2993; Juan, Brenden; M; 5; Pima; F; S; Son; 2999; Yes; Yes; AI./Id. 1637
2994; Juan, Morris; M; 3; Pima; F; S; Son; 3000; Yes; Yes; AI./Id. 1978
~~Norris; Juana; F; 1/12; Pima; F; S; Dau.; –; Born; 3-3-32.; Died; 3-4-32.;~~ Yes; AI./Id. 7296

NORRIS
2995; Jose; M; 41; Pima; F; M; Head; 3001; Yes; Yes; AI. 3015/Id. 3406
2996; Martha, (Makel, Martha); F; 37; Pima; F; M; Wife; 3002; Yes; Yes; AI. 3016/Id. 3407
2997; Clarence; M; 21; Pima; F; S; Son; 3003; Yes; Yes; AI. 3017/Id. 3408
2998; Rayma; F; 12; Pima; F; S; Dau.; 3004; Yes; Yes; AI. 4633/Id. 3409

NORRIS
2999; Juan; M; 53; Pima; F; M; Head; 3005; Yes; Yes; AI. 887/Id. 7050

Census of the **Gila River** reservation of the **Pima Agency** jurisdiction; as of **April 1** ; 1932; taken by **A. H. Kneale** ; Superintendent.

Key: Number; Surname; Given; Sex (M/F); Age at Last Birthday; Tribe; Degree of Blood (F=Full); Marital Status; Relationship to Head of Family & Last Census No; At Jurisdiction Where Enrolled (Yes/No); (If no - Where); Ward (Yes/No); Allotment Annuity and/or Identification Numbers

3000; Emma; F; 44; Pima; F; M; Wife; 3006; Yes; Yes; AI. 888/Id. 7051
3001; Blanch; F; 21; Pima; F; S; Dau.; 3007; Yes; Yes; AI. 889/Id. 7052
3002; Webster; M; 18; Pima; F; S; Son; 3008; Yes; Yes; AI. 3170/Id. 7054
3003; Theodore; M; 14; Pima; F; S; Son; 3009; Yes; Yes; AI. 4556/Id. 7055
3004; Dana; M; 6; Pima; F; S; Son; 3010; Yes; Yes; AI./Id. 7056

NORRIS
3005; Juan; M; 48; Pima; F; M; Head; 3011; Yes; Yes; AI. 2131/Id. 3090
3006; Mollie; F; 53; Pima; F; M; Wife; 3012; Yes; Yes; AI. 2132/Id. 3091
3007; Ellen; F; 21; Pima; F; S; Dau.; 3013; Yes; Yes; AI. 2133/Id. 3093
3008; Alexander; M; 19; Pima; F; S; Son; 3014; Yes; Yes; AI. 2284/Id. 3094
3009; Kemmencia; F; 16; Pima; F; S; Dau.; 3015; Yes; Yes; AI. 2285/Id. 3095
3010; Virginia; F; 14; Pima; F; S; Dau.; 3016; Yes; Yes; AI. 3803/Id. 3096
3011; Seraphina; F; 7; Pima; F; S; Dau.; 3017; Yes; Yes; AI./Id. 3097
3012; Porter, Leonard; M; 2; Pima; F; S; Gr.son; 3018; Yes; Yes; AI./Id. 3567

NORRIS
3013; Raymond; M; 26; Pima; F; M; Head; 3019; Yes; Yes; AI. 2134/Id. 3092
3014; Amelia J., (Jackson, Armelia[sic]); F; 20; Pima; F; M; Wife; 3020; Yes; Yes; AI. 3079/Id. 3244

NORTON
3015; Mary S., (Sundust, Mary); F; 27; Maricopa; F; M; Wife; 3021; Yes; Yes; AI. 2826/Id. 248
3016; Delores; F; 8; Maricopa; F; S; Dau.; 3022; Yes; Yes; AI./Id. 249

NORTON
~~N.E.; Henry; M; 22; Apache; F; M; Head; --; Sells Agency allottee~~; Yes; AI./Id.
3017; Anna L. Jones; F; 23; Pima; F; M; Wife; 1688; Yes; Yes; AI. 4232/Id. 4400
3018; Harold Cecil; M; 4/12; Pima-Apache; F; S; Son; --; Yes; Born; 12-16-31.; Yes; AI./Id. 3946

NOSUCH
3019; Anton; M; 47; Pima; F; Wd.; Head; 3023; Yes; Yes; AI. 1589/Id. 6999
~~Margaret; F; 20; Pima; F; S; Dau.; 3024; Yes; Married to Geo. Shebela.~~; Yes; AI. 1591/Id. 7000
3020; Boyd; M; 13; Pima; F; S; Son; 3025; Yes; Yes; AI. 3426/Id. 7001
3021; Dorothy; F; 11; Pima; F; S; Dau.; 3026; Yes; Yes; AI./Id. 7002

NUNAZ
~~N.E. Henry; Head;~~ AI./Id.
3022; Jessie H., (Hawthorne, Jessie); F; 33; Pima; F; M; Wife; 3027; Yes; Yes; AI. 1317/Id. 6450
3023; Urban; M; 5; Pima; F; S; Son; 3028; Yes; Yes; AI./Id. 6451
3024; Michael; M; 5; Pima; F; S; Son; 3029; Yes; Yes; AI./Id. 6452

Census of the **Gila River** reservation of the **Pima Agency** jurisdiction; as of **April 1** ; 1932; taken by **A. H. Kneale** ; Superintendent.

Key: Number; Surname; Given; Sex (M/F); Age at Last Birthday; Tribe; Degree of Blood (F=Full); Marital Status; Relationship to Head of Family & Last Census No; At Jurisdiction Where Enrolled (Yes/No); (If no – Where); Ward (Yes/No); Allotment Annuity and/or Identification Numbers

OSIFE

3025; ---; M; 61; Pima; F; M; Head; 3030; Yes; Yes; AI. 4691/Id. 5995
3026; Adeline; F; 61; Pima; F; M; Wife; 3031; Yes; Yes; AI. 4692/Id. 5996

OSIFE

3027; Caisinto; M; 43; Pima; F; M; Head; 3032; Yes; Yes; AI. 1737/Id. 5468
3028; Lena E., (Evans, Lena); F; 32; Pima; F; M; Wife; 3033; Yes; Yes; AI. 468/Id. 5469
3029; Esther; F; 15; Pima; F; S; Dau.; 3034; Yes; Yes; AI. 4543/Id. 5470
3030; Delbert; M; 12; Pima; F; S; Son; 3035; Yes; Yes; AI. 4858/Id. 5471
3031; Willard; M; 9; Pima; F; S; Son; 3036; Yes; Yes; AI./Id. 5472

OSIFE

3032; Catherine; F; 69; Pima; F; S; Head; 3037; Yes; Yes; AI. 4493/Id. 5988

OSIFE

3033; Cheerless; M; 57; Pima; F; Wd.; Head; 3038; Yes; Yes; AI. 361/Id. 5218
3034; Mary; F; 22; Pima; F; S; Dau.; 3040; Yes; Yes; AI. 365/Id. 5221
3035; David; M; 21; Pima; F; S; Son; 3041; Yes; Yes; AI. 364/Id. 5222
3036; Bertha; F; 20; Pima; F; S; Dau.; 3042; Yes; Yes; AI. 362/Id. 5223

OSIFE

3037; Jacob; M; 23; Pima; F; M; Head; 3039; Yes; Yes; AI. 705/Id. 5220
3038; Genevea A., (Ahliel, Genevive); F; 22; Pima; F; M; Wife; 3070; Yes; Yes; AI. 2393/Id. 4293
3039; Dennis; M; 1; Pima; F; S; Son; 3071; Yes; Yes; AI./Id. 3975

OSIFE

3040; Enos; M; 43; Pima; F; M; Head; 3043; Yes; Yes; AI. 1952/Id. 5068
3041; Marie M., (Lewis, Marie Meguil); F; 42; Pima; F; M; Wife; 3044; Yes; Yes; AI. 652/Id. 5069

OSIFE

3042; Eugene; M; 29; Pima; F; M; Head; 3045; Yes; Yes; AI. 871/Id. 6968
3043; Elizabeth; F; 29; Pima; F; M; Wife; 3046; Yes; Yes; AI. 662/Id. 6969
3044; Roger E.; M; 7; Pima; F; S; Son; 3047; Yes; Yes; AI./Id. 6970
3045; Boniface; M; 4; Pima; F; S; Son; 3048; Yes; Yes; AI./Id. 6971
3046; Lenora; F; 2; Pima; F; S; Dau.; 3049; Yes; Yes; AI./Id. 7235

OSIFE

3047; George; M; 30; Pima; F; S; Head; 3050; Yes; Yes; AI. 388/Id. 5219

OSIFE

3048; Harvier; M; 39; Pima; F; M; Head; 3051; Yes; Yes; AI. 385/Id. 5231

Census of the **Gila River** reservation of the **Pima Agency** jurisdiction; as of **April 1** ; 1932; taken by **A. H. Kneale** ; Superintendent.

Key: Number; Surname; Given; Sex (M/F); Age at Last Birthday; Tribe; Degree of Blood (F=Full); Marital Status; Relationship to Head of Family & Last Census No; At Jurisdiction Where Enrolled (Yes/No); (If no – Where); Ward (Yes/No); Allotment Annuity and/or Identification Numbers

3049; Juanita M., (Manuel, Juanita); F; 26; Pima; F; M; Wife; 3052; Yes; Yes; AI. 498/Id. 5232

3050; James F.; M; 19; Pima; F; S; Son; 3053; Yes; Yes; AI. 387/Id. 5233

3051; McDonald; M; 16; Pima; F; S; Son; 3054; Yes; Yes; AI. 3449/Id. 5234

3052; Osborne; M; 14; Pima; F; S; Son; 3055; Yes; Yes; AI. 4479/Id. 5235

3053; Eugene; M; 12; Pima; F; S; Son; 3056; Yes; Yes; AI./Id. 5236

3054; Dana W.; M; 8; Pima; F; S; Son; 3057; Yes; Yes; AI./Id. 5237

3055; Louise; F; 8; Pima; F; S; Dau.; 3058; Yes; Yes; AI./Id. 5238

OSIFE

3056; Gideon; M; 19; Pima; F; M; Head; 3242; Yes; Yes; AI. 2474/Id. 7062

3057; Naomi, (Pancot, Naomi White); F; 18; Pima; F; M; Wife; 4340; Yes; Yes; AI. 2622/Id. 6915

OSIFE

3058; Harvier A.; M; 53; Pima; F; Wd.; Head; 3059; Yes; Yes; AI. 873/Id. 6972

OSIFE

3059; John; M; 35; Pima; F; M; Head; 3060; Yes; Yes; AI. 1536/Id. 6894

3060; Maggie N., (Nelson, Maggie); F; 31; Pima; F; M; Wife; 3061; Yes; Yes; AI. 1406/Id. 6895

3061; Marcelina; F; 12; Pima; F; S; Dau.; 3062; Yes; Yes; AI./Id. 6896

3062; Agnes; F; 9; Pima; F; S; Dau.; 3063; Yes; Yes; AI./Id. 6897

3063; Edna; F; 5; Pima; F; S; Dau.; 3064; Yes; Yes; AI./Id. 6898

OSIFE

3064; Jose T.; M; 45; Pima; F; M; Head; 3065; Yes; Yes; AI. 1824/Id. 4732

3065; Waulupa J., (Jackson, Waulupa); F; 47; Pima; F; M; Wife; 3066; Yes; Yes; AI. 2297/Id. 4200

3066; Jose; M; 12; Pima; F; S; Son; 3067; Yes; Yes; AI./Id. 4199

OSIFE

3067; Jessie M., (Miguel, Jessie); F; 30; Pima; F; M; Wife; 3068; No; Phoenix Sch. S.R. Res. ~~Scottsdale Maricopa Ariz.~~; Yes; AI. 674/Id. 6018

OSIFE

3068; Jacob; M; 22; Pima; F; S; Head; 3069; Yes; Yes; AI. 2362/Id. 4693

OSIFE

3069; Juan; M; 47; Pima; F; M; Head; 3072; Yes; Yes; AI. 3557/Id. 7236

3070; Antonia M., (Miguel, Antonio[sic] Waluga); F; 42; Pima; F; M; Wife; 3073; Yes; Yes; AI. 3946/Id. 5998

OSIFE

3071; Juan; M; 62; Pima; F; M; Head; 3074; Yes; Yes; AI. 4446/Id. 5999

Census of the **Gila River** reservation of the **Pima Agency** jurisdiction; as of **April 1** ; 1932; taken by **A. H. Kneale** ; Superintendent.

Key: Number; Surname; Given; Sex (M/F); Age at Last Birthday; Tribe; Degree of Blood (F=Full); Marital Status; Relationship to Head of Family & Last Census No; At Jurisdiction Where Enrolled (Yes/No); (If no – Where); Ward (Yes/No); Allotment Annuity and/or Identification Numbers

3072; Cordoriu; F; 57; Pima; F; M; Wife; 3075; Yes; Yes; AI. 4447/Id. 6000

OSIFE
~~N.E. Harvey; M; Head; Yes; Yes; AI./Id.~~
3073; Julio; F; 27; Pima; F; M; Wife; 3076; Yes; Yes; AI. 702/Id. 6001
3074; Carroll; M; 14; Pima; F; S; Son; 3077; Yes; Yes; AI./Id. 6002
3075; Percy; M; 13; Pima; F; S; Son; 3078; Yes; Yes; AI./Id. 6003
3076; Irene J.; F; 11; Pima; F; S; Dau.; 3079; Yes; Yes; AI./Id. 6004
3077; Walter; M; 9; Pima; F; S; Son; 3080; Yes; Yes; AI./Id. 6005
3078; Nora; F; 7; Pima; F; S; Dau.; 3081; Yes; Yes; AI./Id. 6006
3079; Laura; F; 5; Pima; F; S; Dau.; 3082; Yes; Yes; AI./Id. 6007
3080; Norman; M; 4; Pima; F; S; Son; 3083; Yes; Yes; AI./Id. 6008

OSIFE
3081; Lagreta; M; 24; Pima; F; S; Head; 3084; Yes; Yes; AI. 663/Id. 6009

OSIFE
3082; Listine; F; 57; Pima; F; Wd.; Head; 3085; Yes; Yes; AI. 4540/Id. 6010
3083; Lewis; M; 37; Pima; F; S; Son; 3086; Yes; Yes; AI. 4541/Id. 6011

OSIFE
~~Luke; M; 69; Pima; F; Wd.; Head; 3087; Died 11-15-31.~~; Yes; AI. 2523/Id. 6892

OSIFE
3084; May R.; F; 36; Pima; F; Wd.; Head; 3088; Yes; Yes; AI. 386/Id. 6012
3085; Bennett; M; 5; Pima; F; S; Son; 3089; Yes; Yes; AI./Id. 6013

OSIFE
3086; McDonald; M; 36; Pima; F; M; Head; 3090; Yes; Yes; AI. 2429/Id. 4597
3087; Cevillia, (Pedro, Cevilla[sic]); F; 27; Pima; F; M; Wife; 3091; Yes; Yes; AI. 2356/Id. 4598
3088; Virginia; F; 18; Pima; F; S; Dau.; 3092; Yes; Yes; AI. 811/Id. 4602
3089; Margaret; F; 12; Pima; F; S; Dau.; 3093; Yes; Yes; AI. 4855/Id. 4599
3090; Joseph; M; 8; Pima; F; S; Son; 3094; Yes; Yes; AI./Id. 4600
3091; Edward; M; 6; Pima; F; S; Son; 3095; Yes; Yes; AI./Id. 4602
3092; Herman; M; 3; Pima; F; S; Son; 3096; Yes; Yes; AI./Id. 4107

OSIFE
3093; Oscar; M; 72; Pima; F; M; Head; 3097; Yes; Yes; AI. 1916/Id. 4630
3094; Savie; F; 73; Pima; F; M; Wife; 3098; Yes; Yes; AI. 1917/Id. 4631

OSIFE
3095; Pabloa; F; 35; Pima; F; S; Head; 3099; Yes; Yes; AI. 4542/Id. 6019

Census of the **Gila River** reservation of the **Pima Agency** jurisdiction; as of **April 1** ; 1932; taken by **A. H. Kneale** ; Superintendent.

Key: Number; Surname; Given; Sex (M/F); Age at Last Birthday; Tribe; Degree of Blood (F=Full); Marital Status; Relationship to Head of Family & Last Census No; At Jurisdiction Where Enrolled (Yes/No); (If no – Where); Ward (Yes/No); Allotment Annuity and/or Identification Numbers

OSIFE

3096; Pedro; M; 39; Pima; F; M; Head; 3100; Yes; Yes; AI. 1800/Id. 5224
3097; Vera; F; 34; Pima; F; M; Wife; 3101; Yes; Yes; AI. 701/Id. 5225
3098; Alfred J.; M; 19; Pima; F; S; Son; 3102; Yes; Yes; AI. 3297/Id. 5226

OSIFE

3099; Philip; M; 26; Pima; F; M; Head; 3103; Yes; Yes; AI. 1801/Id. 5227
N.E. Mary B.; F; 20; Wife; --; Yes; Yes; AI./Id.
3100; Philip Jr.; M; 2; Pima; F; S; Son; 3104; Yes; Yes; AI./Id. 6099

OWENS

3101; Elizabeth; F; 67; Pima; F; Wd.; Head; 3105; Yes; Yes; AI. 1444/Id. 6622

OXPE

3102; Houston; M; 29; Pima; F; M; Head; 3106; Yes; Yes; AI. 2584/Id. 7057
3103; Julia O., (Osife, Julia); F; 19; Pima; F; M; Wife; 3107; Yes; Yes; AI. 1413/Id. 7058
3104; George U.; M; 2; Pima; F; S; Son; 3108; Yes; Yes; AI./Id. 7238
3105; Paul; M; 1; Pima; F; S; Son; 3109; Yes; Yes; AI./Id. 7279

OXPE

3106; Kisto; M; 60; Pima; F; M; Head; 3110; Yes; Yes; AI. 2581/Id. 6874
3107; Perchilla; F; 60; Pima; F; M; Wife; 3111; Yes; Yes; AI. 2582/Id. 6875
3108; Lisciana; F; 25; Pima; F; S; Dau.; 3112; Yes; Yes; AI. 2585/Id. 6877

OXPE

3109; Louis; M; 32; Pima; F; M; Head; 3113; Yes; Yes; AI. 2583/Id. 6870
3110; Mary V., (Vavages, Mary); F; 26; Pima; F; M; Wife; 3114; Yes; Yes; AI. 1529/Id. 6871
3111; Celestine; F; 8; Pima; F; S; Dau.; 3115; Yes; Yes; AI./Id. 6872
3112; Aloysius; M; 6; Pima; F; S; Son; 3116; Yes; Yes; AI./Id. 6873
3113; Veronica; F; 4; Pima; F; S; Dau.; 3117; Yes; Yes; AI./Id. 7224

PABLO

3114; Andrew; M; 54; Pima; F; M; Head; 3118; Yes; Yes; AI. 1164/Id. 5099
3115; May; F; 40; Pima; F; M; Wife; 3119; Yes; Yes; AI. 242/Id. 5100
3116 ; Ida; F; 17; Pima; F; S; Dau.; 3120; Yes; Yes; AI. 3190/Id. 5101

PABLO

3117; Coney; M; 53; Pima; F; Wd.; Head; 3121; Yes; Yes; AI. 1643/Id. 4589
3118; Clara; F; 20; Pima; F; S; Dau.; 3122; Yes; Yes; AI. 1645/Id. 4590
3119; Nathaniel; M; 6/12; Pima; F; S; Son; --; Yes; Born; 9-21-31.; Yes; AI./Id. 3945

PABLO

3120; Daisy; F; 29; Pima; F; S; Head; 3123; Yes; Yes; AI. 4663/Id. 6014

Census of the **Gila River** reservation of the **Pima Agency** jurisdiction; as of **April 1** ; 1932; taken by **A. H. Kneale** ; Superintendent.

Key: Number; Surname; Given; Sex (M/F); Age at Last Birthday; Tribe; Degree of Blood (F=Full); Marital Status; Relationship to Head of Family & Last Census No; At Jurisdiction Where Enrolled (Yes/No); (If no – Where); Ward (Yes/No); Allotment Annuity and/or Identification Numbers

PABLO

3121; Elmer; M; 26; Pima; F; M; Head; 3124; Yes; Yes; AI. 2642/Id. 7028
3122; Messilla L., (Lewis, Messilla); F; 23; Pima; F; M; Wife; 3125; Yes; Yes; AI. 3912/Id. 7029

PABLO

3123; Felix; M; 37; Pima; F; M; Head; 3126; Yes; Yes; AI. 2481/Id. 3560
3124; Acension, (Lewis, Acension); F; 31; Pima; F; M; Wife; 3127; Yes; Yes; AI. 4251/Id. 3561
3125; Mary B.; F; 6; Pima; F; S; Dau.; 3128; Yes; Yes; AI./Id. 3562
3126; Stanislaus; M; 3; Pima; F; S; Son; 3129; Yes; Yes; AI./Id. 3563

PABLO

3127; George; M; 22; Pima; F; M; Head; 3141; Yes; Yes; AI. 2276/Id. 3053
3128; Claudina O., (Pablo, Claudina O.); F; 22; Pima; F; M; Wife; 3166; Yes; Yes; AI. 1840/Id. 4190

PABLO

3129; John; M; 62; Pima; F; Wd.; Head; 3130; Yes; Yes; AI. 1759/Id. 4766

PABLO

3130; Jose; M; 52; Pima; F; Wd.; Head; 3131; Yes; Yes; AI. 3375/Id. 5696

PABLO

3131; Jose; M; 62; Pima; F; Wd.; Head; 3132; Yes; Yes; AI. 3875/Id. 1841

PABLO

3132; Jose; M; 47; Pima; F; M; Head; 3133; Yes; Yes; AI. 1017/Id. 6700
3133; Jane; F; 37; Pima; F; M; Wife; 3134; Yes; Yes; AI. 1018/Id. 6701
3134; William; M; 21; Pima; F; S; Son; 3135; Yes; Yes; AI. 1019/Id. 6702
3135; Lily; F; 20; Pima; F; S; Dau.; 3136; Yes; Yes; AI. 1021/Id. 6703
3136; Clytie; F; 12; Pima; F; S; Dau.; 3137; Yes; Yes; AI./Id. 6704
3137; Lathan; M; 8; Pima; F; S; Son; 3138; Yes; Yes; AI./Id. 6705

PABLO

3138; Jose; M; 38; Pima; F; M; Head; 3139; Yes; Yes; AI. 2201/Id. 3083
3139; Susie; F; 37; Pima; F; M; Wife; 3140; Yes; Yes; AI. 2201/Id. 3084
3140; Philip; M; 12; Pima; F; S; Son; 3142; Yes; Yes; AI./Id. 3087
3141; Martin; M; 7; Pima; F; S; Son; 3143; Yes; Yes; AI./Id. 3088
3142; Bernard; M; 4; Pima; F; S; Son; 3144; Yes; Yes; AI./Id. 3089

PABLO

3143; Jose; M; 61; Pima; F; Wd.; Head; 3145; Yes; Yes; AI. 2673/Id. 7020
3144; Lucy G.; F; 22; Pima; F; S; Dau.; 3146; Yes; Yes; AI. 2639/Id. 7021
3145; Irene; F; 17; Pima; F; S; Dau.; 3147; Yes; Yes; AI. 4008/Id. 7022

Key: Number; Surname; Given; Sex (M/F); Age at Last Birthday; Tribe; Degree of Blood (F=Full); Marital Status; Relationship to Head of Family & Last Census No; At Jurisdiction Where Enrolled (Yes/No); (If no – Where); Ward (Yes/No); Allotment Annuity and/or Identification Numbers

PABLO

3146; Jose; M; 54; Pima; F; M; Head; 3148; Yes; Yes; AI. 3836/Id. 1604
3147; Alice; F; 43; Pima; F; M; Wife; 3149; Yes; Yes; AI. 3836/Id. 1604
3148; Rosa; F; 23; Pima; F; S; Dau.; 3150; Yes; Yes; AI./Id. 1605
3149; Richard; M; 15; Pima; F; S; Son; 3151; Yes; Yes; AI. 3839/Id. 1607
3150; Rachel; F; 15; Pima; F; S; Dau.; 3152; Yes; Yes; AI. 3840/Id. 1608
3151; Floyd; M; 8; Pima; F; S; Son; 3153; Yes; Yes; AI. 3839/Id. 1609
3152; Jose Jr.; M; 5; Pima; F; S; Son; 3154; Yes; Yes; AI./Id. 1984

PABLO

3153; Juan Jose; M; 33; Pima; F; M; Head; 3155; Yes; Yes; AI. 2640/Id. 7023
3154; Cecelia L., (Lewis, Cecelia); F; 29; Pima; F; M; Wife; 3156; Yes; Yes; AI. 1619/Id. 7024
3155; Francis; M; 14; Pima; F; S; Son; 3157; Yes; Yes; AI./Id. 7025
3156; Lillian; F; 8; Pima; F; S; Dau.; 3158; Yes; Yes; AI./Id. 7026
3157; Dennis; M; 6; Pima; F; S; Son; 3159; Yes; Yes; AI./Id. 7027
3158; Raymond; M; 1; Pima; F; S; Son; 3160; Yes; Yes; AI./Id. 7270

PABLO

3159; Lancisco; M; 42; Pima; F; S; Head; 3161; Yes; Yes; AI. 1819/Id. 4677

PABLO

3160; Mathew; M; 36; Pima; F; Wd;; Head; 3162; Yes; Yes; AI. 1166/Id. 5703

PABLO

3161; Milyca; F; 67; Pima; F; Wd;; Head; 3163; Yes; Yes; AI. 1808/Id. 4114

PABLO

3162; Mondan; M; 30; Pima; F; S; Head; 3164; Yes; Yes; AI. 942/Id. 6020

PABLO

3163; Ralph O.; M; 47; Pima; F; Wd;; Head; 3165; Yes; Yes; AI. 1837/Id. 4192
3164; Inez; F; 25; Pima; F; S; Dau.; 3167; Yes; Yes; AI. 1839/Id. 4191
3165; Naomi; F; 19; Pima; F; S; Dau.; 3168; Yes; Yes; AI./Id. 4189

PABLO

3166; Raymond; M; 39; Pima; F; M; Head; 3169; Yes; Yes; AI. 3873/Id. 1860
3167; Amelia; F; 34; Pima; F; M; Wife; 3170; Yes; Yes; AI. 3874/Id. 1861
3168; Dora; F; 13; Pima; F; S; Dau.; 3171; Yes; Yes; AI. 4009/Id. 1862

PABLO

3169; Sam; M; 72; Pima; F; Wd;; Head; 3172; Yes; Yes; AI./Id. 5271

PABLO

3170; San; M; 90; Pima; F; M; Head; 3173; Yes; Yes; AI. 2548/Id. 6776

3171; Mollie; F; 82; Pima; F; M; Wife; 3174; Yes; Yes; AI. 2549/Id. 6777

PABLO

3172; Valena; F; 67; Pima; F; Wd;; Head; 3175; Yes; Yes; AI. 1818/Id. 4676

PADDIS

3173; Joseph; M; 47; Pima; F; M; Head; 3176; Yes; Yes; AI. 191/Id. 5344

3174; Mary H. (Knox, Mary); F; 33; Pima; F; M; Wife; 3177; Yes; Yes; AI. 1009/Id. 5838

3175; Ceverino; M; 23; Pima; F; S; Son; 3178; Yes; Yes; AI. 389/Id. 5346

3176; Howard, Delina; F; 14; Pima; F; S; St.dau.; 3179; Yes; Yes; AI. 4563/Id. 5450

3177; Howard, Margaret; F; 13; Pima; F; S; St.dau.; 3180; Yes; Yes; AI. 4571/Id. 5451

3178; Paddis, Warner L.; M; 1/12; Pima; F; S; Gr.son; --; Yes; ~~Born 3-3-32.~~; Yes; AI./Id. 6136

PADDIS

3179; Josepha; F; 77; Pima; F; Wd;; Head; 3181; Yes; Yes; AI. 193/Id. 5349

PADGELY

3180; Jose; M; 45; Pima; F; M; Head; 3182; Yes; Yes; AI. 1700/Id. 4510

3181; Mary; F; 43; Pima; F; M; Wife; 3183; Yes; Yes; AI. 1701/Id. 4511

3182; Nina; F; 23; Pima; F; S; Dau.; 3184; Yes; Yes; AI. 820/Id. 4512

3183; Wilbert; M; 22; Pima; F; S; Son; 3185; Yes; Yes; AI. 821/Id. 4513

3184; Rosetta; F; 16; Pima; F; S; Dau.; 3186; Yes; Yes; AI. 3162/Id. 4514

PADGLEY

3185; Mary; F; 87; Pima; F; Wd;; Head; 3187; Yes; Yes; AI. 1738/Id. 4225

PALCISCO

3186; Laura; F; 75; Pima; F; Wd;; Head; 3188; Yes; Yes; AI. 4209/Id. 1990

PALOMA

3187; Chiago; M; 42; Pima; F; M; Head; 3189; Yes; Yes; AI. 2635/Id. 5755

3188; Maria G., (Gatai, Maria); F; 30; Pima; F; M; Wife; 3190; Yes; Yes; AI. 1558/Id. 5756

3189; Virginia; F; 8; Pima; F; S; Dau.; 3191; Yes; Yes; AI./Id. 5757

3190; Lola; F; 6; Pima; F; S; Dau.; 3192; Yes; Yes; AI./Id. 5758

3191; Julinia; F; 4; Pima; F; S; Dau.; 3193; Yes; Yes; AI./Id. 5851

PALOMA

3192; Juan; M; 70; Pima; F; Wd;; Head; 3194; Yes; Yes; AI. 2634/Id. 7239

PANCOT

3193; Anton; M; 35; Pima; F; M; Head; 3195; Yes; Yes; AI. 1748/Id. 4220

Key: Number; Surname; Given; Sex (M/F); Age at Last Birthday; Tribe; Degree of Blood (F=Full); Marital Status; Relationship to Head of Family & Last Census No; At Jurisdiction Where Enrolled (Yes/No); (If no – Where); Ward (Yes/No); Allotment Annuity and/or Identification Numbers

3194; Jessie P., (Porter, Jessie); F; 34; Pima; F; M; Wife; 3196; Yes; Yes; AI. 1848/Id. 4221

3195; Clarence; M; 12; Pima; F; S; Son; 3197; Yes; Yes; AI. 4865/Id. 4222

3196; Glen; M; 5; Pima; F; S; Son; 3198; Yes; Yes; AI./Id. 4223

3197; Priscilla; F; 1; Pima; F; S; Dau.; 3199; Yes; Yes; AI./Id. 3973

PANCOT

3198; Leonard; M; 14; Pima; F; S; Alone; 3200; Yes; Yes; AI./4724Id. 7240

PANTALON

3199; ---; M; 71; Maricopa; F; Wd;; Head; 3201; Yes; Yes; AI. 2634/Id. 7239

PABLO

3200; Lucy G., (Charles, Lucy); F; 72; Pima; F; M; Wife; 3202; Yes; Yes; AI. 2021/Id. 4374

PARKER

3201; ---; M; 57; Maricopa; F; M; Head; 3203; Yes; Yes; AI. 2832/Id. 22

3202; Chas-koo-al; F; 56; Maricopa; F; M; Wife; 3204; Yes; Yes; AI. 2833/Id. 23

3203; Charles; M; 36; Pima; F; S; Son; 3205; Yes; Yes; AI. 2835/Id. 108

PARKER

3204; Elsie S.; F; 27; Maricopa; F; Wd.; Head; 3206; Yes; Yes; AI. 2909/Id. 180

3205; Elsie M.; F; 5; Maricopa; F; S; Dau.; 3207; Yes; Yes; AI./Id. 181

PARSONS

3206; Dora L.; F; 15; Pima; F; S; Alone; 3208; Yes; Yes; AI. 4402/Id. 1991

PARSONS

3207; Juan; M; 28; Pima; F; M; Head; 3209; Yes; Yes; AI. 248/Id. 5649

3208; Ella P., (Perkins, Ella); F; 28; Pima; F; M; Wife; 3210; Yes; Yes; AI. 129/Id. 5650

3209; Virginia; F; 5; Pima; F; S; Dau.; 3211; Yes; Yes; AI./Id. 5651

PARSONS

3210; Pancho; M; 37; Pima; F; M; Head; 3212; Yes; Yes; AI. 4399/Id. 1992

3211; Lulu B., (Bending, Lulu); F; 27; Pima; F; M; Wife; 3213; Yes; Yes; AI. 3617/Id. 1993

3212; Rupert; M; 6; Pima; F; S; Son; 3214; Yes; Yes; AI./Id. 1994

3213; Chester; M; 3; Pima; F; S; Son; 3215; Yes; Yes; AI./Id. 1995

PASQUALE

3214; Andrew; M; 45; Pima; F; M; Head; 3216; Yes; Yes; AI. 1895/Id. 4548

3215; Anna L., (Lyons, Anna); F; 32; Pima; F; M; Wife; 3217; Yes; Yes; AI. 796/Id. 4549

Key: Number; Surname; Given; Sex (M/F); Age at Last Birthday; Tribe; Degree of Blood (F=Full); Marital Status; Relationship to Head of Family & Last Census No; At Jurisdiction Where Enrolled (Yes/No); (If no – Where); Ward (Yes/No); Allotment Annuity and/or Identification Numbers

3216; Leslie; M; 5; Pima; F; S; Son; 3218; Yes; Yes; AI./Id. 4550
3217; Clifford; M; 2; Pima; F; S; Son; 3219; Yes; Yes; AI./Id. 4169
3218; Webb, Jessie; M; 13; Pima; F; S; St.son; 3220; Yes; Yes; AI. 3194/Id. 5532
3219; Webb, Ulysses; M; 10; Pima; F; S; St.son; 3221; Yes; Yes; AI./Id. 5533

PASQUALE

3220; Juan; M; 69; Pima; F; M; Head; 3222; Yes; Yes; AI. 1893/Id. 4635
3221; Luso; F; 69; Pima; F; M; Wife; 3223; Yes; Yes; AI. 1894/Id. 4636
3222; Encelia; M; 27; Pima; F; S; Son; 3224; Yes; Yes; AI. 1897/Id. 4637
3223; Juan M.; M; 26; Pima; F; S; Son; 3225; Yes; Yes; AI. 1896/Id. 4638

PASQUALE

3224; Henry; M; 26; Pima; F; M; Head; 3226; Yes; Yes; AI. 1898/Id. 4632
3225; Frances, (Manuel, Frances); F; 27; Pima; F; M; Wife; 3227; Yes; Yes; AI. 1769/Id. 4633
3226; Stillman; M; 5; Pima; F; S; Son; 3228; Yes; Yes; AI./Id. 4634
3227; Elmer; M; 1; Pima; F; S; Son; 3229; Yes; Yes; AI./Id. 3980

PASQUEL

3228; Assint; M; 44; Pima; F; M; Head; 3230; Yes; Yes; AI. 1928/Id. 4639
3229; Lizzie M.; F; 35; Pima; F; M; Wife; 3231; Yes; Yes; AI./Id. 4640
3230; Dominick; M; 7; Pima; F; S; Son; 3232; Yes; Yes; AI./Id. 4641
3231; Benjamin; M; 5; Pima; F; S; Son; 3233; Yes; Yes; AI./Id. 4642

PATRICK

3232; Joseph; M; 47; Pima; F; M; Head; 3234; Yes; Yes; AI. 1407/Id. 6613
3233; Antonia; F; 47; Pima; F; M; Wife; 3235; Yes; Yes; AI. 1408/Id. 6614
3234; Philipi; F; 18; Pima; F; S; Dau.; 3236; Yes; Yes; AI. 1409/Id. 6615
3235; Delphine; F; 7; Pima; F; S; Dau.; 3237; Yes; Yes; AI./Id. 6616
3236; Anestacia; F; 6; Pima; F; S; Dau.; 3238; Yes; Yes; AI./Id. 6617
3237; Alfred; M; 1; Pima; F; S; Son; 3239; Yes; Yes; AI./Id. 7172

PATRICK

3238; Rudolph; M; 49; Pima; F; M; Head; 3240; Yes; Yes; AI. 1411/Id. 7241
3239; Osife, Francis; M; 23; Pima; F; S; St.son; 3241; Yes; Yes; AI. 1414/Id. 7061

PATTON

3240; Hugh; M; 62; Pima; F; M; Head; 3243; Yes; Yes; AI. 1072/Id. 4449
3241; Martha; F; 61; Pima; F; M; Wife; 3244; Yes; Yes; AI. 1073/Id. 4450
3242; Francis; M; 29; Pima; F; S; Son; 3245; Yes; Yes; AI. 1081/Id. 4451
3243; Bernice; F; 20; Pima; F; S; Dau.; 3246; Yes; Yes; AI. 1074/Id. 4452
~~Wilford; M; 18; Pima; F; S; Son; 3247; Died; 3-12-32.~~; Yes; AI. 1075/Id. 4453
3244; Marion; F; 15; Pima; F; S; Dau.; 3248; Yes; Yes; AI. 3821/Id. 4454
3245; Verna; F; 13; Pima; F; S; Dau.; 3249; Yes; Yes; AI. 4573/Id. 4455

Census of the **Gila River** reservation of the **Pima Agency** jurisdiction; as of **April 1** ; 1932; taken by **A. H. Kneale** ; Superintendent.

Key: Number; Surname; Given; Sex (M/F); Age at Last Birthday; Tribe; Degree of Blood (F=Full); Marital Status; Relationship to Head of Family & Last Census No; At Jurisdiction Where Enrolled (Yes/No); (If no – Where); Ward (Yes/No); Allotment Annuity and/or Identification Numbers

PAUL

3246; Enos; M; 32; Pima; F; M; Head; 3250; Yes; Yes; AI. 949/Id. 7036
3247; Ida E., (Enos, Ida); F; 26; Pima; F; M; Wife; 3251; Yes; Yes; AI. 292/Id. 5023
3248; Jasper; M; 5; Pima; F; S; Son; 3252; Yes; Yes; AI./Id. 5025
3249; Enos, Lena; F; 7; Pima; F; S; St.dau.; 3253; Yes; Yes; AI. 4573/Id. 4455
3250; Enos, Edward E.; M; 10; Pima; F; S; St.son; 3254; Yes; Yes; AI./Id. 5024

PAUL

3251; Alex; M; 30; Pima; F; S; Head; 3255; Yes; Yes; AI. 950/Id. 7041

PAUL

3252; Isaac; M; 28; Pima; F; M; Head; 3256; Yes; Yes; AI. 951/Id. 7039
3253; Mary J., (Johns, Maria); F; 28; Pima; F; M; Wife; 3257; Yes; Yes;
AI. 878/Id. 7040

PAUL

3254; Joseph; M; 57; Pima; F; M; Head; 3258; Yes; Yes; AI. 29/Id. 7245
3255; Catherine; F; 55; Pima; F; M; Wife; 3259; Yes; Yes; AI. 30/Id. 7246

PEDRO

3256; Love C.; M; 49; Maricopa; F; Wd.; Head; 3260; Yes; Yes; AI. 2949/Id. 266
3257; Arthur; M; 23; Maricopa; F; S; Son; 3261; Yes; Yes; AI. 2950/Id. 267
3258; Sexsmith; Nellie; F; 15; Pima; F; S; Dau.; 3262; Yes; Yes; AI. 4666/Id. 286

PEDRO

3259; Cancio; M; 37; Pima; F; Wd.; Head; 3263; Yes; Yes; AI. 2354/Id. 4789
3260; Lonnie; M; 13; Pima; F; S; Son; 3264; Yes; Yes; AI. 4470/Id. 4790
3261; Stanley; M; 12; Pima; F; S; Son; 3265; Yes; Yes; AI. 4644/Id. 4791
3262; Apkaw, Clifford; M; 11; Pima; F; S; St.son; 3266; Yes; Yes; AI. 4765/Id. 4792
3263; Pedro, Lawrence R.; M; 2; Pima; F; S; Son; 3267; Yes; Yes; AI./Id. 3981

PEDRO

3264; Harvier; M; 54; Pima; F; M; Head; 3268; Yes; Yes; AI. 2268/Id. 3150
3265; Minnie B., (Brown, Minnie); F; 62; Pima; F; M; Wife; 3269; Yes; Yes;
AI. 3036/Id. 3151
3266; Minnie; F; 27; Pima; F; S; Dau.; 3270; Yes; Yes; AI. 2206/Id. 3564

PEDRO

3267; Isaac; M; 23; Pima; F; M; Head; 3271; Yes; Yes; AI. 2381/Id. 5751

PEDRO

3268; Jose; M; 35; Pima; F; M; Head; 3272; Yes; Yes; AI./Id. 6946
3269; Susie Y., (Young, Susie); F; 34; Pima; F; M; Wife; 3273; Yes; Yes;
AI. 1084/Id. 6947
3270; Elizabeth; F; 12; Pima; F; S; Dau.; 3274; Yes; Yes; AI./Id. 6028

Key: Number; Surname; Given; Sex (M/F); Age at Last Birthday; Tribe; Degree of Blood (F=Full); Marital Status; Relationship to Head of Family & Last Census No; At Jurisdiction Where Enrolled (Yes/No); (If no – Where); Ward (Yes/No); Allotment Annuity and/or Identification Numbers

3271; Clinton; M; 9; Pima; F; S; Son; 3275; Yes; Yes; AI./Id. 6948
3272; Arlene; F; 3; Pima; F; S; Dau.; 3276; Yes; Yes; AI./Id. 6949

PEDRO
3273; Jose Sr;; M; 72; Pima; F; Wd.; Head; 3277; Yes; Yes; AI. 1835/Id. 4594
3274; Jose Jr;; M; 32; Pima; F; S; Son; 3278; Yes; Yes; AI. 1836/Id. 4596

PEDRO
3275; Luke; M; 30; Pima; F; S; Head; 3279; Yes; Yes; AI. 4465/Id. 5750

PEDRO
3276; Pancho; M; 33; Pima; F; M; Head; 3280; Yes; (Called Pancho Pablo); Yes; AI. 2355/Id. 4286
3277; Eunice D., (Davis, Eunice); F; 31; Pima; F; M; Wife; 3281; Yes; Yes; AI. 1120/Id. 4287
3278; Norman; M; 11; Pima; F; S; Son; 3282; Yes; Yes; AI./Id. 4288
3279; Silas; M; 9; Pima; F; S; Son; 3283; Yes; Yes; AI./Id. 4289
3280; Delphina; F; 3; Pima; F; S; Dau.; 3284; Yes; Yes; AI./Id. 4100
3281; Roselene; F; 4/12; Pima; F; S; Dau.; --; Yes; Born; 12-19-31.; Yes; AI./Id. 3944

PEDRO
3282; Rueben; M; 25; Pima; F; S; Head; 3285; Yes; Yes; AI. 2379/Id. 4103

PENA
3283; Henry; M; 43; Pima; F; M; Head; 3286; Yes; Yes; AI. 2405/Id. 4228
3284; Emily; F; 42; Pima; F; M; Wife; 3287; Yes; Yes; AI. 2406/Id. 4229
3285; Christine; F; 12; Pima; F; S; Cousin; 3288; Yes; Yes; AI. 4800/Id. 4231

PERCHERO
3286; George; M; 41; Maricopa; F; M; Head; 3289; Yes; Yes; AI. 2904/Id. 69
3287; Grace; F; 32; Maricopa; F; M; Wife; 3290; Yes; Yes; AI./Id. 70
3288; Joseph; M; 17; Maricopa; F; S; Son; 3291; Yes; Yes; AI. 2919/Id. 71

PERCHERO
3289; Luke; M; 30; Maricopa; F; M; Head; 3292; Yes; Yes; AI. 2703/Id. 135
3290; Mattie S., (Somegustava, Mattie); F; 32; Maricopa; F; M; Wife; 3293; Yes; Yes; AI. 2841/Id. 136
3291; John; M; 8; Maricopa; F; S; Son; 3294; Yes; Yes; AI./Id. 583
3292; Keaton; M; 9; Maricopa; F; S; Son; 3295; Yes; Yes; AI./Id. 137
3293; Eddie; M; 7; Maricopa; F; S; Son; 3296; Yes; Yes; AI./Id. 138
3294; Lee R.; M; 5; Maricopa; F; S; Son; 3297; Yes; Yes; AI./Id. 139
3295; Mattie; F; 2; Pima; F; S; Dau.; 3298; Yes; Yes; AI./Id. 591

PERCY
3296; Jones; M; 28; Pima; F; M; Head; 3299; Yes; Yes; AI. 400/Id. 5190

Key: Number; Surname; Given; Sex (M/F); Age at Last Birthday; Tribe; Degree of Blood (F=Full); Marital Status; Relationship to Head of Family & Last Census No; At Jurisdiction Where Enrolled (Yes/No); (If no – Where); Ward (Yes/No); Allotment Annuity and/or Identification Numbers

3297; Lucy; F; 34; Pima; F; M; Wife; 3300; Yes; Yes; AI. 4226/Id. 1733
3298; Dennis; M; 12; Pima; F; S; Son; 3301; Yes; Yes; AI./Id. 1734
3299; Julia; F; 7; Pima; F; S; Dau.; 3302; Yes; Yes; AI./Id. 6015
3300; Arnold L.; M; 12; Pima; F; S; Son; 3303; Yes; Yes; AI./Id. 6100

PERCY
3301; William; M; 68; Pima; F; M; Head; 3304; Yes; Yes; AI. 346/Id. 5188
3302; Susie M., (Anton, Susie Mollie); F; 64; Pima; F; M; Wife; 3305; Yes; Yes; AI. 2475/Id. 5189

PEREZ
3303; Assick; F; 40; Pima; F; Wd.; Head; 3306; Yes; Yes; AI. 228/Id. 6021
3304; Theresa; F; 19; Pima; F; S; Dau.; 3307; Yes; Yes; AI. 391/Id. 5435
3305; Fred J.; M; 12; Pima; F; S; Son; 3308; Yes; Yes; AI. 4787/Id. 5348

PERKINS
3306; Crouse; M; 46; Pima; F; M; Head; 3309; Yes; Yes; AI. 2335/Id. 3417
3307; Mildred; F; 45; Pima; F; M; Wife; 3310; Yes; Yes; AI./Id. 3418
3308; Allen; M; 21; Pima; F; S; Son; 3311; Yes; Yes; AI. 2340/Id. 3419
3309; Hubert; M; 19; Pima; F; S; Son; 3312; Yes; Yes; AI. 2337/Id. 3420
3310; George; M; 14; Pima; F; S; Son; 3313; Yes; Yes; AI. 4591/Id. 3421
3311; Eunice; F; 12; Pima; F; S; Dau.; 3314; Yes; Yes; AI. 4826/Id. 3422
3312; James; M; 9; Pima; F; S; Son; 3315; Yes; Yes; AI. 2340/Id. 3423

PERKINS
3313; Hattie H., (Hall, Hattie); F; 35; Pima; F; M; Wife; 3316; No; Salt River Res.; Phoenix Sch.; Scottsdale Maricopa Ariz.; Yes; AI. 540/Id. 7227
3314; Orlene; F; 14; Pima; F; S; Dau.; 3317; No; Salt River Res.; Phoenix Sch.; Scottsdale Maricopa Ariz.; Yes; AI./Id. 7228
3315; Margarita; F; 11; Pima; F; S; Dau.; 3318; No; Salt River Res.; Phoenix Sch.; Scottsdale Maricopa Ariz.; Yes; AI./Id. 7229
3316; Alfred; M; 8; Pima; F; S; Son; 3319; No; Salt River Res.; Phoenix Sch.; Scottsdale Maricopa Ariz.; Yes; AI./Id. 7230
3317; Viola; F; 5; Pima; F; S; Dau.; 3320; No; Salt River Res.; Phoenix Sch.; Scottsdale Maricopa Ariz.; Yes; AI./Id. 7231
3318; Violet; F; 5; Pima; F; S; Dau.; 3321; No; Salt River Res.; Phoenix Sch.; Scottsdale Maricopa Ariz.; Yes; AI./Id. 7232

PERKINS
3319; Joseph; M; 57; Pima; F; M; Head; 3322; Yes; Yes; AI. 182/Id. 4963
3320; Lulu; F; 57; Pima; F; M; Wife; 3323; Yes; Yes; AI. 183/Id. 4964
3321; Christine; F; 22; Pima; F; S; Dau.; 3324; Yes; Yes; AI. 184/Id. 4965
3322; Elmer; M; 19; Pima; F; S; Son; 3325; Yes; Yes; AI. 185/Id. 2339

Census of the **Gila River** reservation of the **Pima Agency** jurisdiction; as of **April 1** ; 1932; taken by **A. H. Kneale** ; Superintendent.

Key: Number; Surname; Given; Sex (M/F); Age at Last Birthday; Tribe; Degree of Blood (F=Full); Marital Status; Relationship to Head of Family & Last Census No; At Jurisdiction Where Enrolled (Yes/No); (If no – Where); Ward (Yes/No); Allotment Annuity and/or Identification Numbers

PERKINS
3323; Oscar; M; 31; Pima; F; M; Head; 3326; Yes; Yes; AI. 2339/Id. 3412
3324; Rosario; F; 34; Pima; F; M; Wife; 3327; Yes; Yes; AI. 4589/Id. 3413
3325; Marie B.; F; 12; Pima; F; S; Dau.; 3328; Yes; Yes; AI. 4590/Id. 3414
3326; Evelyn; F; 11; Pima; F; S; Dau.; 3329; Yes; Yes; AI./Id. 3415
3327; Willard; M; 10; Pima; F; S; Son; 3330; Yes; Yes; AI./Id. 3416

PESOS
3328; Daniel; M; 67; Pima; F; Wd.; Head; 3331; Yes; Yes; AI. 4071/Id. 1544
3329; Clinton; M; 19; Pima; F; S; Gr.son; 3332; Yes; Yes; AI. 4834/Id. 1541
3330; Edgar; M; 22; Pima; F; S; Gr.son; 3333; Yes; Yes; AI./Id. 1538
3331; Nathan; M; 17; Pima; F; S; Gr.son; 3334; Yes; Yes; AI. 4835/Id. 1540
3332; Percy; M; 13; Pima; F; S; Gr.son; 3335; Yes; Yes; AI./Id. 1541
3333; Elliott; M; 7; Pima; F; S; Gr.son; 3336; Yes; Yes; AI./Id. 1542

PETERS
3334; Alex P.; M; 20; Pima; F; M; Head; 3337; Yes; Yes; AI. 1834/Id. 4650
3335; Vivian J., (Johnson, Vivian); F; 19; Pima; F; M; Wife; 3338; Yes; Yes; AI. 2253/Id. 3145

PETERS
3336; David P.; M; 30; Pima; F; M; Head; 3339; Yes; Yes; AI. 3237/Id. 4356
3337; Ada M., (Morgan, Ada Thomas); F; 26; Pima; F; M; Wife; 3340; Yes; Yes; AI. 1722/Id. 4357

PETERS
3338; George; M; 30; Pima; F; M; Head; 3341; Yes; Yes; AI. 3822/Id. 5702
3339; Helen S., (Stone, Helen); F; 24; Pima; F; M; Wife; 3342; Yes; Yes; AI. 353/Id. 5703
3340; Norman; M; 5; Pima; F; S; Son; 3343; Yes; Yes; AI./Id. 5704
3341; Raymond; M; 2; Pima; F; S; Son; 3344; Yes; Yes; AI./Id. 5854
3342; Charlotte; F; 1/12; Pima; F; S; Dau.; --; Born; 3-14-32.; Yes; AI./Id. 6131

PETERS
3343; James; M; 64; Pima; F; M; Head; 3345; Yes; Yes; AI. 4436/Id. 1886
3344; Jennie K., (Kipp, Jennie); F; 64; Pima; F; M; Wife; 3346; Yes; Yes; AI. 3716/Id. 1887

PETERS
3345; Jose P.; M; 55; Pima; F; M; Head; 3347; Yes; Yes; AI. 1829/Id. 4645
3346; Milsie; F; 55; Pima; F; M; Wife; 3348; Yes; Yes; AI. 1830/Id. 4646
3347; Annie P.; F; 28; Pima; F; S; Dau.; 3349; Yes; Yes; AI. 1832/Id. 4647
3348; Iva P.; F; 19; Pima; F; S; Dau.; 3350; Yes; Yes; AI. 1833/Id. 4651
3349; Nettie P.; F; 26; Pima; F; S; Dau.; 3351; Yes; Yes; AI. 3238/Id. 4649

Census of the **Gila River** reservation of the **Pima Agency** jurisdiction; as of **April 1** ; 1932; taken by **A. H. Kneale** ; Superintendent.

Key: Number; Surname; Given; Sex (M/F); Age at Last Birthday; Tribe; Degree of Blood (F=Full); Marital Status; Relationship to Head of Family & Last Census No; At Jurisdiction Where Enrolled (Yes/No); (If no – Where); Ward (Yes/No); Allotment Annuity and/or Identification Numbers

PETERS

3350; Lewis; M; 74; Pima; F; Wd.; Head; 3352; Yes; Yes; AI. 4194/Id. 1997

PETERS

3351; Manuel; M; 37; Pima; F; M; Head; 3353; Yes; Yes; AI. 3597/Id. 1425

3352; Anestacia, (Ramon, Anestacia); F; 31; Pima; F; M; Wife; 3354; Yes; Yes; AI. 3406/Id. 1426

3353; Josephine; F; 15; Pima; F; S; Dau.; 3355; Yes; Yes; AI. 4440/Id. 1429

3354; Nicholas; M; 8; Pima; F; S; Son; 3356; Yes; Yes; AI./Id. 1427

3355; Theodore; M; 5; Pima; F; S; Son; 3357; Yes; Yes; AI./Id. 1428

3356; Emalissa; F; 2; Pima; F; S; Dau.; 3358; Yes; Yes; AI./Id. 1998

PETERS

3357; Roy C.; M; 37; Maricopa; F; M; Head; 3359; Yes; Yes; AI. 2805/Id. 265

PETERS

3358; Simon; M; 50; Pima; F; M; Head; 3360; Yes; Yes; AI. 4189/Id. 1311

3359; Vilicianna; F; 48; Pima; F; M; Wife; 3361; Yes; Yes; AI. 4190/Id. 1312

3360; Alice; F; 16; Pima; F; S; Dau.; 3362; Yes; Yes; AI. 4192/Id. 1998

3361; Michael; M; 12; Pima; F; S; Son; 3363; Yes; Yes; AI./Id. 1315

3362; Berthina; F; 7; Pima; F; S; Dau.; 3364; Yes; Yes; AI. 4192/Id. 1316

PETERS

3363; Solomon; M; 30; Pima; F; M; Head; 3365; Yes; Yes; AI. 4193/Id. 1430

3364; Joseba S., (Sahsahn, Joseba); F; 31; Pima; F; M; Wife; 3366; Yes; Yes; AI. 3665/Id. 1431

3365; Arnold; M; 7; Pima; F; S; Son; 3367; Yes; Yes; AI./Id. 1432

3366; Christine; F; 3; Pima; F; S; Dau.; 3368; Yes; Yes; AI./Id. 1433

PETERS

3367; William; M; 52; Pima; F; M; Head; 3369; Yes; Yes; AI. 3668/Id. 1211

3368; Ellen; F; 44; Pima; F; M; Wife; 3370; Yes; Yes; AI. 3669/Id. 1212

3369; Prudence; F; 21; Pima; F; S; Dau.; 3371; Yes; Yes; AI. 3671/Id. 1213

3370; Catherine; F; 20; Pima; F; S; Dau.; 3372; Yes; Yes; AI. 3672/Id. 1214

3371; Milton; M; 18; Pima; F; S; Son; 3373; Yes; Yes; AI. 3673/Id. 1215

3372; Margery; F; 14; Pima; F; S; Dau.; 3374; Yes; Yes; AI. 3834/Id. 1216

3373; Johnson; M; 12; Pima; F; S; Son; 3375; Yes; Yes; AI. 4661/Id. 1217

3374; Georgiana; F; 10; Pima; F; S; Dau.; 3376; Yes; Yes; AI./Id. 1218

3375; Pauline; F; 8; Pima; F; S; Dau.; 3377; Yes; Yes; AI./Id. 1219

3376; William E.; M; 6; Pima; F; S; Son; 3378; Yes; Yes; AI./Id. 1220

PETERSON

3377; Albert; M; 30; Pima; F; S; Head; 3379; Yes; Yes; AI. 446/Id. 6023

3378; May; F; 32; Pima; F; S; Sister; 3380; Yes; Yes; AI. 445/Id. 6024

Census of the **Gila River** reservation of the **Pima Agency** jurisdiction; as of **April 1** ; 1932; taken by **A. H. Kneale** ; Superintendent.

Key: Number; Surname; Given; Sex (M/F); Age at Last Birthday; Tribe; Degree of Blood (F=Full); Marital Status; Relationship to Head of Family & Last Census No; At Jurisdiction Where Enrolled (Yes/No); (If no – Where); Ward (Yes/No); Allotment Annuity and/or Identification Numbers

PHILIPS
3379; Martha M., (Matthews, Martha); F; 36; Pima; F; M; Wife; 3381; Yes; Yes; AI. 904/Id. 7242

PHILLIPS
3380; Anton; M; 79; Pima; F; M; Head; 3382; Yes; Yes; AI. 612/Id. 5127
3381; Manuella; F; 60; Pima; F; M; Wife; 3383; Yes; Yes; AI. 613/Id. 5128
3382; Samuel; M; 21; Pima; F; S; Sdpt.son; 3384; Yes; Yes; AI. 615/Id. 1985

PHILLIPS
3383; Chiago; M; 73; Pima; F; Wd.; Head; 3385; Yes; Yes; AI. 3865/Id. 1790

PHILLIPS
3384; Joseph; M; 32; Pima; F; M; Head; 3386; Yes; Yes; AI. 251/Id. 4312
3385; Lulu S., (Smart, Lulu); F; 27; Pima; F; M; Wife; 3387; Yes; Yes; AI. 853/Id. 4313
3386; Kenneth; M; 3; Pima; F; S; Son; 3388; Yes; Yes; AI./Id. 4500

PHILLIPSON
3387; Alice; F; 47; Pima; F; S; Head; 3389; Yes; Yes; AI. 3425/Id. 6025

PLAN
3388; Jose; M; 50; Pima; F; M; Head; 3390; Yes; Yes; AI. 4484/Id. 1617
3389; Lessa; F; 61; Pima; F; M; Wife; 3391; Yes; Yes; AI. 4485/Id. 1618

PORTER
3390; Adam; M; 25; Pima; F; M; Head; 3392; Yes; Yes; AI. 546/Id. 4577
3391; Susan K., (Nathan, Susan); F; 32; Pima; F; M; Wife; 3393; Yes; Yes; AI. 2358/Id. 4609

PORTER
3392; Andrew; M; 61; Pima; F; M; Head; 3394; Yes; Yes; AI. 2120/Id. 3290
3393; Edith; F; 37; Pima; F; M; Wife; 3395; Yes; Yes; AI. 2121/Id. 3291
3394; Ella E.; F; 11; Pima; F; S; Dau.; 3396; Yes; Yes; AI. 4877/Id. 3292

PORTER
Ben, (See Benjamin Stone)

PORTER
3395; Charles; M; 67; Pima; F; M; Head; 3397; Yes; Yes; AI. 1716/Id. 4751
3396; Flora; F; 62; Pima; F; M; Wife; 3398; Yes; Yes; AI. 1717/Id. 4752
3397; Lucy; F; 29; Pima; F; S; Dau.; 3399; Yes; Yes; AI. 1849/Id. 4753
3398; Rachel; F; 25; Pima; F; S; Dau.; 3400; Yes; Yes; AI. 1850/Id. 4754
3399; Dennis; M; 21; Pima; F; S; Son; 3401; Yes; Yes; AI. 1851/Id. 4755
3400; Patrick; M; 18; Pima; F; S; Son; 3402; Yes; Yes; AI. 1718/Id. 4756

Census of the **Gila River** reservation of the **Pima Agency** jurisdiction; as of **April 1** ; 1932; taken by **A. H. Kneale** ; Superintendent.

Key: Number; Surname; Given; Sex (M/F); Age at Last Birthday; Tribe; Degree of Blood (F=Full); Marital Status; Relationship to Head of Family & Last Census No; At Jurisdiction Where Enrolled (Yes/No); (If no – Where); Ward (Yes/No); Allotment Annuity and/or Identification Numbers

3401; Agnes; F; 13; Pima; F; S; Dau.; 3403; Yes; Yes; AI. 3927/Id. 4757

PORTER
3402; David; M; 29; Pima; F; S; Head; 3404; Yes; Yes; AI. 544/Id. 4811

PORTER
3403; Felix; M; 30; Pima; F; M; Head; 3405; Yes; Yes; AI. 544/Id. 4817
3404; Anna E., (Eschief, Anna); F; 35; Pima; F; M; Wife; 3406; Yes; Yes; AI. 2137/Id. 3230
3405; Felix Jr.; M; 7; Pima; F; S; Son; 3407; Yes; Yes; AI. 0/Id. 4819
3406; Gladys; F; 7; Pima; F; S; Dau.; 3408; Yes; Yes; AI./Id. 4820
3407; Alex Jr.; M; 3; Pima; F; S; Son; 3409; Yes; Yes; AI. 0/Id. 4822
3408; Everett W.; M; 2; Pima; F; S; Son; 3410; Yes; Yes; AI. 0/Id. 5782
3409; Glen Bernard; M; 7/12; Pima; F; S; Son; --; Yes; Born; 9-4-31.; Yes; AI./Id. 6133

PORTER
3410; Frank; M; 36; Pima; F; M; Head; 3411; Yes; Yes; AI. 1846/Id. 6692
3411; Anna L., (Lewis, Anna); F; 30; Pima; F; M; Wife; 3412; Yes; Yes; AI. 1139/Id. 6693
3412; Gladys R.; F; 7; Pima; F; S; Dau.; 3413; Yes; Yes; AI./Id. 6694
3413; Lenox H.; M; 3; Pima; F; S; Son; 3414; Yes; Yes; AI./Id. 6695

PORTER
3414; Isaac; M; 37; Pima; F; M; Head; 3415; Yes; Yes; AI. 2194/Id. 3568
3415; Ruth J., (Jackson, Ruth); F; 27; Pima; F; M; Wife; 3416; Yes; Yes; AI. 2188/Id. 3569
3416; Betty A.; F; 9; Pima; F; S; Dau.; 3417; Yes; Yes; AI./Id. 3570
3417; Beatrice; F; 7; Pima; F; S; Dau.; 3418; Yes; Yes; AI./Id. 3571
3418; Delores; F; 5; Pima; F; S; Dau.; 3419; Yes; Yes; AI./Id. 3572
3419; Claudine; F; 1; Pima; F; S; Dau.; 3420; Yes; Yes; AI./Id. 3597

PORTER
No Number. John; M; 67; Pima; F; Wd.; Head; 3421; Yes; Yes; AI. 1565/Id. 6792

PORTER
3420; Narcissus; M; 51; Pima; F; M; Head; 3422; Yes; Yes; AI. 542/Id. 4809
3421; Eliza; F; 46; Pima; F; M; Wife; 3423; Yes; Yes; AI. 543/Id. 4810
3422; Joshua; M; 21; Pima; F; S; Son; 3424; Yes; Yes; AI. 547/Id. 3812
3423; Effie E.; F; 18; Pima; F; S; Dau.; 3425; Yes; Yes; AI. 551/Id. 4813
3424; Edison; M; 16; Pima; F; S; Son; 3426; Yes; Yes; AI. 3725/Id. 4914
3425; Evelena; F; 14; Pima; F; S; Dau.; 3427; Yes; Yes; AI. 4517/Id. 4815
3426; Lawrence; M; 10; Pima; F; S; Son; 3428; Yes; Yes; AI./Id. 4816

Census of the **Gila River** reservation of the **Pima Agency** jurisdiction; as of **April 1** ; 1932; taken by **A. H. Kneale** ; Superintendent.

Key: Number; Surname; Given; Sex (M/F); Age at Last Birthday; Tribe; Degree of Blood (F=Full); Marital Status; Relationship to Head of Family & Last Census No; At Jurisdiction Where Enrolled (Yes/No); (If no - Where); Ward (Yes/No); Allotment Annuity and/or Identification Numbers

PORTER
3427; Olive; F; 77; Pima; F; Wd.; Head; 3429; Yes; Yes; AI. 550/Id. 4823

PORTER
3428; Peter; M; 36; Pima; F; M; Head; 3430; Yes; Yes; AI. 2122/Id. 4418
3429; Helen, (Padgely, Helen); F; 26; Pima; F; M; Wife; 3431; Yes; Yes; AI. 818/Id. 4419
3430; Irving R.; M; 11; Pima; F; S; Son; 3432; Yes; Yes; AI. 4876/Id. 4420
3431; Emmett; M; 10; Pima; F; S; Son; 3433; Yes; Yes; AI./Id. 4421
3432; Hazel W.; F; 7; Pima; F; S; Dau.; 3434; Yes; Yes; AI./Id. 4422
3433; Merrill J.; M; 4; Pima; F; S; Son; 3435; Yes; Yes; AI./Id. 4423
3434; Harless Clayton; M; 5/12; Pima; F; S; Son; --; Yes; Born; 10-22-31.; Yes; AI./Id. 3943

PORTER
3435; George; M; 51; Pima; F; M; Head; 3436; Yes; Yes; AI. 1727/Id. 4470
3436; Annily E.; F; 49; Pima; F; M; Wife; 3437; Yes; Yes; AI. 1728/Id. 4471
3437; Janette; F; 18; Pima; F; S; Dau.; 3438; Yes; Yes; AI. 1730/Id. 4474

PRATT
3438; John; M; 39; Pima; F; Wd.; Head; 3439; Yes; Yes; AI. 4455/Id. 1756
3439; Valentine; M; 14; Pima; F; S; Son; 3440; Yes; Yes; AI./Id. 1758
3440; Burton T.; M; 10; Pima; F; S; Son; 3441; Yes; Yes; AI./Id. 1759

PRATT
3441; Samuel; M; 24; Pima; F; M; Head; 3442; Yes; Yes; AI. 1491/Id. 1473
3442; Agnes J., (Jackson, Agnes); F; 24; Pima; F; M; Wife; 3443; Yes; Yes; AI. 1658/Id. 4206
3443; Barbara; F; 2; Pima; F; S; Dau.; 3444; Yes; Yes; AI./Id. 3983
3444; Lorene; F; 4/12; Pima; F; S; Dau.; --; Yes; Born; 12-18-31.; Yes; AI./Id. 3942

PRATT
3445; Willard; M; 27; Pima; F; M; Head; 3445; Yes; Yes; AI. 1729/Id. 4472
3446; Minnie N., (Nathan, Minnie); F; 26; Pima; F; M; Wife; 3446; Yes; Yes; AI. 1941/Id. 4573

PRESTON
3447; David; M; 44; Pima; F; S; Head; 3447; Yes; Yes; AI. 3222/Id. 8284

PRESTON
3448; Luke; M; 47; Pima; F; M; Head; 3448; Yes; Yes; AI. 3218/Id. 3283
3449; Lupa; F; 47; Pima; F; M; Wife; 3449; Yes; Yes; AI. 3219/Id. 3573
3450; Daniel; M; 14; Pima; F; S; Son; 3450; Yes; Yes; AI./Id. 3574

Census of the **Gila River** reservation of the **Pima Agency** jurisdiction; as of **April 1** ; 1932; taken by **A. H. Kneale** ; Superintendent.

Key: Number; Surname; Given; Sex (M/F); Age at Last Birthday; Tribe; Degree of Blood (F=Full); Marital Status; Relationship to Head of Family & Last Census No; At Jurisdiction Where Enrolled (Yes/No); (If no - Where); Ward (Yes/No); Allotment Annuity and/or Identification Numbers

PRESTON
3451; Maud; F; 50; Pima; F; M; Wife; 3451; Yes; Yes; AI. 3224/Id. 3575

PRESTON
3452; William; M; 72; Pima; F; Wd.; Head; 3452; Yes; Yes; AI. 3220/Id. 3585

QUARCH
3453; Luke; M; 44; Pima; F; M; Head; 3453; Yes; Yes; AI. 799/Id. 4501
3454; Beatrice E., (Anton, Petra Harvier); F; 44; Pima; F; M; Wife; 3454; Yes; Yes; AI. 1706/Id. 4502
3455; Matio; M; 11; Pima; F; S; Son; 3455; Yes; Yes; AI. 4887/Id. 4503
3456; Agatha; F; 9; Pima; F; S; Dau.; 3456; Yes; Yes; AI./Id. 4504

QUARCH
3457; John; M; 64; Maricopa; F; Wd.; Head; 3457; Yes; Yes; AI. 2801/Id. 262
3458; James; M; 25; Maricopa; F; S; Son; 3458; Yes; Yes; AI. 2804/Id. 263
3459; Nora; F; 39; Maricopa; F; S; Dau.; 3459; Yes; Yes; AI. 2847/Id. 264

RAINBOLT
~~N.E.; R.P.; Head;~~
3460; Esther A., (Azule, Esther); F; 27; Pima; F; M; Wife; 3460; Yes; Yes; AI. 65/Id. 4178
3461; Harry; M; 5; Pima; 1/4x; S; Son; 3461; Yes; Yes; AI./Id. 4177
3462; Philip; M; 3; Pima; 1/4x; S; Son; 3462; Yes; Yes; AI./Id. 4176

RAMON
3463; Donald; M; 57; Pima; F; M; Head; 3463; Yes; Yes; AI. 2180/Id. 3001
3464; Sienna; F; 46; Pima; F; M; Wife; 3464; Yes; Yes; AI. 2181/Id. 3002
3465; Joshua; M; 19; Pima; F; S; Son; 3465; Yes; Yes; AI. 2185/Id. 3005
3466; Jones, Alberta; F; 11; Pima; F; S; Niece; 1655; Yes; Yes; AI./Id. 5881
3467; Jones, Edison; M; 16; Pima; F; S; Nephew; 1656; Yes; Yes; AI. 3267/Id. 5129

RAMON
3468; Frank; M; 62; Pima; F; M; Head; 3466; Yes; Yes; AI. 3937/Id. 6026
3469; Anita, (Aneeta); F; 34; Pima; F; M; Wife; 3467; Yes; Yes; AI. 3938/Id. 6027
3470; Clara; F; 18; Pima; F; S; Dau.; 3468; Yes; Yes; AI. 3939/Id. 6028

RAMON
3471; John A.; M; 33; Pima; F; M; Head; 3469; Yes; Yes; AI. 39/Id. 5543
3472; Susanna L., (Lyons, Susanna); F; 28; Pima; F; M; Wife; 3470; Yes; Yes; AI. 1047/Id. 5544
3473; Anestacio; M; 8; Pima; F; S; Son; 3471; Yes; Yes; AI./Id. 5545
3474; Stanley; M; 5; Pima; F; S; Son; 3472; Yes; Yes; AI./Id. 5546
3475; Leonard; M; 3; Pima; F; S; Son; 3473; Yes; Yes; AI./Id. 5855
3476; Eula; F; 1; Pima; F; S; Dau.; 3474; Yes; Yes; AI. 3939/Id. 6113

Key: Number; Surname; Given; Sex (M/F); Age at Last Birthday; Tribe; Degree of Blood (F=Full); Marital Status; Relationship to Head of Family & Last Census No; At Jurisdiction Where Enrolled (Yes/No); (If no – Where); Ward (Yes/No); Allotment Annuity and/or Identification Numbers

RAMON
3477; Jose G.; M; 28; Pima; F; M; Head; 3475; Yes; Yes; AI. 57/Id. 5547
3478; Bessie O., (Osife, Bessie); F; 29; Pima; F; M; Wife; 3476; Yes; Yes; AI. 704/Id. 5548
3479; Joe H.; M; 4; Pima; F; S; Son; 3477; Yes; Yes; AI./Id. 5549

RAMON
3480; Juan; M; 42; Pima; F; S; Head; 3478; Yes; Yes; AI. 1625/Id. 7243

RAMON
3481; Laura; F; 74; Pima; F; Wd.; Head; 3479; Yes; Yes; AI. 3934/Id. 4515
3482; Chico; M; 34; Pima; F; S; Son; 3480; Yes; Yes; AI. 3935/Id. 6029

RAMON
3483; Shannon; M; 68; Pima; F; M; Head; 3482; Yes; Yes; AI. 3972/Id. 1373
3484; Juanna L., (Lancisco, Juanna); F; 64; Pima; F; M; Wife; 3483; Yes; Yes; AI. 3973/Id. 1374
3485; Lancisco; M; 22; Pima; F; S; Son; 3484; Yes; Yes; AI. 3975/Id. 1375

RANDALL
3486; Sahovey; F; 57; Pima; F; Wd.; Head; 3485; Yes; Yes; AI. 307/Id. 4979

RANDALL
3487; Samuel; M; 53; Pima; F; M; Head; 3486; Yes; Yes; AI. 304/Id. 4980
3488; Mollie L., (Lewis, Mollie); F; 33; Pima; F; M; Wife; 3487; Yes; Yes; AI. 618/Id. 4981
3489; Frederick; M; 8; Pima; F; S; Son; 3488; Yes; Yes; AI./Id. 4982
3490; Virginia; F; 7; Pima; F; S; Dau.; 3489; Yes; Yes; AI./Id. 4983
3491; Myrtle; F; 5; Pima; F; S; Dau.; 3490; Yes; Yes; AI./Id. 4984
3492; Dennis L.; M; 20; Pima; F; S; Son; 3491; Yes; Yes; AI. 619/Id. 7244

RAY
3493; Joseph; M; 60; Pima; F; M; Head; 3492; Yes; Yes; AI. 1675/Id. 4955
3494; Jessie, (Josie); F; 58; Pima; F; M; Wife; 3493; Yes; Yes; AI. 1676/Id. 4956
3495; Luke; M; 21; Pima; F; S; Son; 3494; Yes; Yes; AI. 1679/Id. 4957

RAY
3496; Joseph; M; 72; Pima; F; M; Head; 3495; Yes; Yes; AI. 2212/Id. 3375
3497; Mary; F; 72; Pima; F; M; Wife; 3496; Yes; Yes; AI. 2213/Id. 3576

REEMS
3498; Nellie; F; 54; Maricopa; F; Wd.; Head; 3497; Yes; Yes; AI. 2812/Id. 303
3499; John; M; 27; Maricopa; F; S; Son; 3498; Yes; Yes; AI. 3150/Id. 304
3500; Edna; F; 23; Maricopa; F; S; Dau.; 3499; Yes; Yes; AI. 3151/Id. 305
3501; Nina; F; 18; Maricopa; F; S; Dau.; 3500; Yes; Yes; AI. 3253/Id. 306

Census of the **Gila River** reservation of the **Pima Agency** jurisdiction; as of **April 1** ; 1932; taken by **A. H. Kneale** ; Superintendent.

Key: Number; Surname; Given; Sex (M/F); Age at Last Birthday; Tribe; Degree of Blood (F=Full); Marital Status; Relationship to Head of Family & Last Census No; At Jurisdiction Where Enrolled (Yes/No); (If no – Where); Ward (Yes/No); Allotment Annuity and/or Identification Numbers

3502; Thelma; F; 5; Maricopa; F; S; Gr.dau.; 3501; Yes; Yes; AI./Id. 307
3503; David; M; 7/12; Maricopa; F; S; Gr.Son; --; Yes; Born; 9-10-31.; Yes; AI./Id. 607

REDBIRD

3504; Charles; M; 59; Maricopa; F; M; Head; 3502; Yes; Yes; AI. 2714/Id. 220
3505; Ida; F; 39; Maricopa; F; M; Wife; 3503; Yes; Yes; AI. 2715/Id. 221
3506; Carroll; M; 16; Maricopa; F; S; Son; 3504; Yes; Yes; AI. 3792/Id. 222
3507; Wilton; M; 13; Maricopa; F; S; Son; 3505; Yes; Yes; AI. 3636/Id. 223
3508; Eva; F; 11; Maricopa; F; S; Daug.; 3506; Yes; Yes; AI./Id. 224
3509; Margaret; F; 7; Maricopa; F; S; Dau.; 3507; Yes; Yes; AI./Id. 225
3510; Melinda; F; 5; Maricopa; F; S; Dau.; 3508; Yes; Yes; AI./Id. 226
3511; Charles; M; 1; Maricopa; F; S; Son; 3509; Yes; Yes; AI./Id. 601

REDBIRD

3512; Richard; M; 30; Maricopa; F; M; Head; 3510; Yes; Yes; AI. 2716/Id. 152
3513; Lily E.; F; 33; Maricopa; F; M; Wife; 3511; Yes; Yes; AI./Id. 153

REDMORE

3514; Samuel; M; 62; Pima; F; M; Head; 3512; Yes; Yes; AI. 2660/Id. 3429
3515; (Manuel, Lahleeta); F; 42; Pima; F; M; Wife; 3513; Yes; Yes; AI. 2993/Id. 3339
3516; Labis; M; 25; Pima; F; S; Son; 3514; Yes; Yes; AI. 2662/Id. 3431
3517; Lopez; M; 21; Pima; F; S; Son; 3515; Yes; Yes; AI./Id. 3432
3518; Manuel, Juan; M; 22; Pima; F; S; St.son; 3516; Yes; Yes; AI. 1877/Id. 3545
3519; Manuel, Seanna; M; 7; Pima; F; S; St.dau.; 3517; Yes; Yes; AI./Id. 3340
3520; Manuel, Mark; M; 4; Pima; F; S; St.son; 3518; Yes; Yes; AI./Id. 3342

REED

3521; Oliver; M; 65; Pima; F; M; Head; 3519; Yes; Yes; AI. 3649/Id. 1561
3522; May; F; 55; Pima; F; M; Wife; 3520; Yes; Yes; AI. 3650/Id. 1562
3523; Levi; M; 34; Pima; F; S; Son; 3521; Yes; Yes; AI. 3651/Id. 1563
3524; Edward; M; 27; Pima; F; S; Son; 3522; Yes; Yes; AI. 3652/Id. 1564
3525; Allen H.; M; 23; Pima; F; S; Son; 3523; Yes; Yes; AI. 3653/Id. 1565

REED

3526; Sammy; M; 62; Pima; F; S; Head; 3524; Yes; Yes; AI. 4330/Id. 1996

RAYS

3527; Juan; M; 51; Pima; F; Wd.; Head; 3525; Yes; Yes; AI. 3123/Id. 3577

RHODES

3528; Charles; M; 42; Pima; F; M; Head; 3526; Yes; Yes; AI. 3762/Id. 1512
3529; Edna; F; 42; Pima; F; M; Wife; 3527; Yes; Yes; AI. 3763/Id. 1513
3530; Pearl; F; 12; Pima; F; S; Dau.; 3528; Yes; Yes; AI./Id. 1514

147

Census of the **Gila River** reservation of the **Pima Agency** jurisdiction; as of **April 1** ; 1932; taken by **A. H. Kneale** ; Superintendent.

Key: Number; Surname; Given; Sex (M/F); Age at Last Birthday; Tribe; Degree of Blood (F=Full); Marital Status; Relationship to Head of Family & Last Census No; At Jurisdiction Where Enrolled (Yes/No); (If no – Where); Ward (Yes/No); Allotment Annuity and/or Identification Numbers

3531; Thelma; F; 9; Pima; F; S; Dau.; 3529; Yes; Yes; AI./Id. 1515
3532; Harold; M; 7; Pima; F; S; Son; 3530; Yes; Yes; AI./Id. 1516

RHODES
3533; Lena S., (James, Lena Stone); F; 37; Pima; F; M; Wife; 3531; Yes; Yes; AI. 340/Id. 6030

RHODES
3534; John; M; 67; Pima; F; M; Head; 3532; Yes; Yes; AI. 3736/Id. 5143
3535; Eva C., (Carpenter, Eva); F; 62; Pima; F; M; Wife; 3533; Yes; Yes; AI. 458/Id. 5144

RHODES
3536; Mark; M; 37; Maricopa; F; M; Head; 3534; Yes; Yes; AI. 3738/Id. 429
3537; Teresa, (Andreas, Teresa); F; 37; Maricopa; F; M; Wife; 3535; Yes; Yes; AI. 376/Id. 430

RHODES
3538; Walter; M; 44; Maricopa; F; M; Head; 3536; Yes; Yes; AI. 4113/Id. 469
3539; Virginia; F; 21; Maricopa; F; S; Dau.; 3537; Yes; Yes; AI. 4114/Id. 471
3540; Harold; M; 20; Maricopa; F; S; Son; 3538; Yes; Yes; AI. 4115/Id. 472
3541; Dallas; M; 12; Maricopa; F; S; Son; 3539; Yes; Yes; AI./Id. 473
3542; Neele; F; 8; Maricopa; F; S; Dau.; 3540; Yes; Yes; AI./Id. 474
3543; Roy; M; 5; Maricopa; F; S; Son; 3541; Yes; Yes; AI./Id. 475
3544; Spencer; M; 1; Maricopa; F; S; Son; 3542; Yes; Yes; AI./Id. 596

RICHARDS
3545; Ammasa; M; 31; Pima; F; M; Head; 3543; Yes; Yes; AI. 774/Id. 6031
N.E.; Anna J.; ~~Wife~~;
3536; Felix; M; 6; Pima; F; S; Son; 3544; Yes; Yes; AI./Id. 6032

RICHARDS
3547; Lancisco; M; 17; Pima; F; S; Alone; 3545; Yes; Yes; AI. 4473/Id. 6033

RIGGS
~~John; M; 64; Pima; F; S; Head; 3546; Died; 10-31-31.~~; Yes; AI. 1791/Id. 4718

RIGGS
3548; Lewis; M; 63; Pima; F; S; Head; 3547; Yes; Yes; AI. 1797/Id. 4715

RIGGS
3549; Mark T.; M; 67; Pima; F; S; Head; 3548; Yes; Yes; AI. 1790/Id. 4717

Census of the **Gila River** reservation of the **Pima Agency** jurisdiction; as of **April 1** ; 1932; taken by **A. H. Kneale** ; Superintendent.

Key: Number; Surname; Given; Sex (M/F); Age at Last Birthday; Tribe; Degree of Blood (F=Full); Marital Status; Relationship to Head of Family & Last Census No; At Jurisdiction Where Enrolled (Yes/No); (If no – Where); Ward (Yes/No); Allotment Annuity and/or Identification Numbers

RINGLARO

3550; Lewis; M; 42; Pima; F; M; Head; 3549; No; Phoenix Maricopa Ariz.; Yes; AI. 3445/Id. 6034

3551; Marving[sic]; M; 18; Pima; F; S; Son; 3550; No; Phoenix Maricopa Ariz.; Yes; AI./Id. 6035

3552; Lewis Jr.; M; 16; Pima; F; S; Son; 3551; No; Phoenix Maricopa Ariz.; Yes; AI./Id. 6036

3553; Robert; M; 5; Pima; F; S; Son; 3552; No; Phoenix Maricopa Ariz.; Yes; AI./Id. 6037

3554; Frederick; M; 4; Pima; F; S; Son; 3553; No; Phoenix Maricopa Ariz.; Yes; AI./Id. 6038

RIVERA

N.E.; Edward; M; 24; Yaqui; F; S; Head; --; Yes; Tucson Pima Ariz.; Yes; AI./Id.

3555; Mary C., (Cook, Mary); F; 27; Pima; F; M; Wife; 3554; Yes; Tucson Pima Ariz.; Yes; AI. 2552/Id. 4285

3556; Verna; F; 7/12; Pima-Yaqui; F; S; Dau.; --; Yes; Tucson Pima Ariz.; Yes; AI./Id. 3941

RIVERA

3557 Edward; M; 57; Maricopa; F; Wd.; Head; 3555; Yes; Yes; AI. 3233/Id. 441

3558; Benjamin; M; 30; Maricopa; F; S; Son; 3556; Yes; Yes; AI. 3228/Id. 442

3559; Clarence; M; 27; Maricopa; F; S; Son; 3557; Yes; Yes; AI. 3229/Id. 443

3560; Clinton; M; 19; Maricopa; F; S; Son; 3558; Yes; Yes; AI. 3230/Id. 444

3561; Christine; F; 18; Maricopa; F; S; Dau.; 3559; Yes; Yes; AI. 5231/Id. 445

RIVOS

3562; Malesta; M; 44; Pima; F; Wd.; Head; 3560; Yes; Yes; AI. 4861/Id. 3578

3563; Dorothy; F; 12; Pima; F; S; Dau.; 3561; Yes; Yes; AI. 4863/Id. 3579

ROBERTS

3564; Annily; M; 32; Pima; F; Wd.; Head; 3562; Yes; Yes; AI. 2100/Id. 4919

ROBERTS

3565; David; M; 45; Pima; F; S; Head; 3563; Yes; Yes; AI. 1141/Id. 6945

ROBERTS

3566; George; M; 38; Pima; F; S; Head; 3564; Yes; Yes; AI. 3072/Id. 3458

ROBERTS

3567; Jacob L.; M; 50; Pima; F; Wd.; Head; 3565; Yes; Yes; AI. 2214/Id. 3439

3568; Lucretia V.; F; 21; Pima; F; S; Dau.; 3566; Yes; Yes; AI. 2216/Id. 3440

3569; Jonah; M; 23; Pima; F; S; Son; 3567; No; U.S.N.; US Navy; Yes; AI. 3070/Id. 3581

Census of the **Gila River** reservation of the **Pima Agency** jurisdiction; as of **April 1** ; 1932; taken by **A. H. Kneale** ; Superintendent.

Key: Number; Surname; Given; Sex (M/F); Age at Last Birthday; Tribe; Degree of Blood (F=Full); Marital Status; Relationship to Head of Family & Last Census No; At Jurisdiction Where Enrolled (Yes/No); (If no – Where); Ward (Yes/No); Allotment Annuity and/or Identification Numbers

3570; Josephine; F; 32; Pima; F; S; Dau.; 3568; Yes; Yes; AI. 2218/Id. 3441

ROBERTS
3571; Mathew; M; 41; Pima; F; M; Head; 3569; Yes; Yes; AI. 2679/Id. 4465
3572; Harriette; F; 47; (White); M; Wife; 3570; Yes; Yes; AI. 2680/Id. 4466
3573; Mathew Jr.; M; 20; Pima; 1/4x; S; Son; 3571; Yes; Yes; AI. 2681/Id. 4467
3574; George F.; M; 17; Pima; 1/4x; S; Son; 3572; Yes; Yes; AI. 3136/Id. 4468
3575; Barbara L.; F; 14; Pima; 1/4x; S; Dau.; 3573; Yes; Yes; AI. 4618/Id. 4469

ROBERTS
3576; May; F; 34; Pima; F; S; Head; 3574; Yes; Yes; AI. 3071/Id. 3074

ROBERTS
3577; Mollie; F; 79; Pima; F; Wd.; Head; 3575; Yes; Yes; AI. 2317/Id. 3054

ROGERS
3578; John; M; 47; Pima; F; M; Head; 3576; Yes; Yes; AI. 516/Id. 5374
3579; Ataloya; M; 47; Pima; F; M; Wife; 3577; Yes; Yes; AI. 517/Id. 5375
3580; Sarah F.; F; 19; Pima; F; S; Dau.; 3578; Yes; Yes; AI. 3298/Id. 5376

ROOTS
3581; Caleb; M; 67; Maricopa; F; M; Head; 3579; Yes; Yes; AI. 3883/Id. 546
3582; Alice; F; 67; Maricopa; F; M; Wife; 3580; Yes; Yes; AI. 3884/Id. 547

ROVALES
3583; Pedro; M; 27; Pima; F; S; Head; 3581; Yes; Yes; AI. 1884/Id. 3582

ROVALES
3584; Blain; M; 32; Pima; F; M; Head; 3582; Yes; Yes; AI. 1883/Id. 4695
3585; Lupa M., (Anton, Lupa); F; 25; Pima; F; M; Wife; 3583; Yes; Yes; AI. 1919/Id. 4696
3586; Ersula; F; 6; Pima; F; S; Dau.; 3584; Yes; Yes; AI./Id. 4697
3587; Mercia; F; 3; Pima; F; S; Dau.; 3585; Yes; Yes; AI./Id. 4698

ROVALES
3588; Zacfein; M; 28; Pima; F; M; Head; 3586; Yes; Yes; AI. 1885/Id. 4652
3589; Mary C., (Cook, Mary); F; 38; Pima; F; M; Wife; 3587; Yes; Yes; AI. 1281/Id. 4653
3590; Estella M.; F; 6; Pima; F; S; Dau.; 3588; Yes; Yes; AI./Id. 4654
3591; Edna M.; F; 3; Pima; F; S; Dau.; 3589; Yes; Yes; AI./Id. 4655

ROVIE
3592; Charles; M; 60; Pima; F; M; Head; 3590; Yes; Yes; AI. 2461/Id. 1530
3593; Annily; F; 55; Pima; F; M; Wife; 3591; Yes; Yes; AI. 2462/Id. 1531
3594; Thomas; M; 24; Pima; F; S; Son; 3592; Yes; Yes; AI. 2466/Id. 1535

Census of the **Gila River** reservation of the **Pima Agency** jurisdiction; as of **April 1** ; 1932; taken by **A. H. Kneale** ; Superintendent.

Key: Number; Surname; Given; Sex (M/F); Age at Last Birthday; Tribe; Degree of Blood (F=Full); Marital Status; Relationship to Head of Family & Last Census No; At Jurisdiction Where Enrolled (Yes/No); (If no – Where); Ward (Yes/No); Allotment Annuity and/or Identification Numbers

3595; Eva; F; 20; Pima; F; S; Dau.; 3593; Yes; Yes; AI. 2468/Id. 1533
3596; Felix; M; 14; Pima; F; S; Son; 3594; Yes; Yes; AI. 3880/Id. 1534

ROVIE
3597; Hattie; F; 29; Pima; F; M; Wife; 3595; Yes; Yes; AI. 2465/Id. 2000

ROVIE
3598; Jones; M; 30; Pima; F; S; Head; 3596; Yes; Yes; AI. 2464/Id. 2006

ROVIE
3599; Luke; M; 27; Pima; F; M; Head; 3597; Yes; Yes; AI. 2467/Id. 1517
3600; Vivian; F; 22; Pima; F; M; Wife; 3598; Yes; Yes; AI./Id. 1518
3601; Donald; M; 2; Pima; F; S; Son; 3599; Yes; Yes; AI./Id. 2007

ROVIE
3602; Stephen; M; 34; Pima; F; S; Head; 3600; Yes; Yes; AI. 2463/Id. 1532

ROY
3603; Enacio; M; 81; Pima; F; Wd.; Head; 3601; Yes; Yes; AI. 4238/Id. 2001
3604; John; M; 48; Pima; F; S; Son; 3602; Yes; Yes; AI. 4241/Id. 2002

ROY
3605; Mary; F; 62; Pima; F; Wd.; Head; 3603; Yes; Yes; AI. 1588/Id. 5754

ROY
3606; Carmelita, (Carmelia); F; 41; Pima; F; M; Wife; 3604; No; Salt River Res.; ~~Scottsdale Maricopa Ariz.~~; Yes; AI. 4655/Id. 6039
3607; Ernest; M; 13; Pima; F; M; Son; 3605; No; Salt River Res.; ~~Scottsdale Maricopa Ariz.~~; Yes; AI. 4656/Id. 6040
3608; Margaret; F; 12; Pima; F; M; Dau.; 3606; No; Salt River Res.; ~~Scottsdale Maricopa Ariz.~~; Yes; AI./Id. 6041
3609; Leonara; F; 10; Pima; F; M; Dau.; 3607; No; Salt River Res.; ~~Scottsdale Maricopa Ariz.~~; Yes; AI./Id. 6042
3610; Bernice; F; 8; Pima; F; M; Dau.; 3608; No; Salt River Res.; ~~Scottsdale Maricopa Ariz.~~; Yes; AI./Id. 6043
3611; Alice; F; 6; Pima; F; M; Dau.; 3609; No; Salt River Res.; ~~Scottsdale Maricopa Ariz.~~; Yes; AI./Id. 6044

ROY
3612; Thomas; M; 38; Pima; F; M; Head; 3610; Yes; Yes; AI. 1585/Id. 2004
3613; Daisy P., (Peters, Daisy); F; 35; Pima; F; M; Wife; 3611; Yes; Yes; AI. 3825/Id. 2005

ROY
3614; Mollie; F; 35; Pima; F; Wd.; Head; 3612; Yes; Yes; AI. 1586/Id. 7247

Census of the **Gila River** reservation of the **Pima Agency** jurisdiction; as of **April 1** ; 1932; taken by **A. H. Kneale** ; Superintendent.

Key: Number; Surname; Given; Sex (M/F); Age at Last Birthday; Tribe; Degree of Blood (F=Full); Marital Status; Relationship to Head of Family & Last Census No; At Jurisdiction Where Enrolled (Yes/No); (If no – Where); Ward (Yes/No); Allotment Annuity and/or Identification Numbers

3615; Dollie; F; 18; Pima; F; S; Dau.; 3613; Yes; Yes; AI. 1587/Id. 7248

ROY
3616; Thomas; M; 57; Pima; F; S; Head; 3614; Yes; Yes; AI. 4240/Id. 5743

RUBIN
3617; John; M; 82; Pima; F; Wd.; Head; 3615; Yes; Yes; AI. 2270/Id. 3111

RUSSELL
3618; Ada; F; 33; Pima; F; M; Wife; 3616; Yes; Yes; AI. 393/Id. 6045
3619; Apachese, Andrew; M; 17; Pima; F; S; Son; 3617; Yes; Yes; AI. 3450/Id. 5796

RUSSELL
3620; George J.; M; 33; Pima; F; M; Head; 3618; Yes; Yes; AI. 376/Id. 5151
3621; Mary W., (Williams, Mary); F; 39; Pima; F; M; Wife; 3619; Yes; Yes; AI. 1010/Id. 5152
3622; Charlotte; F; 15; Pima; F; S; Dau.; 3620; Yes; Yes; AI. 4802/Id. 5153
3623; Arthur; M; 14; Pima; F; S; Son; 3621; Yes; Yes; AI. 3587/Id. 5154

RUSSELL
3624; John; M; 77; Pima; F; Wd.; Head; 3622; Yes; Yes; AI. 392/Id. 5156
3625; Job; M; 35; Pima; F; S; Son; 3623; Yes; Yes; AI. 395/Id. 5155

RUSSELL
3626; Joshua; M; 65; Pima; F; M; Head; 3624; Yes; Yes; AI. 764/Id. 5229
3627; Josepha, (Howard, Josepha); F; 37; Pima; F; M; Wife; 3625; Yes; Yes; AI. 472/Id. 5230

RUSSELL
3628; Peter; M; 37; Pima; F; M; Head; 3626; Yes; Yes; AI. 375/Id. 7067
3629; Rahab W., (Williams, Rahap[sic]); F; 23; Pima; F; M; Wife; 3627; Yes; Yes; AI. 2589/Id. 7068

SAHSAHN
3630; Francis; F; 29; Pima; F; S; Head; 3628; Yes; Yes; AI. 3667/Id. 7249

SAKOPAR
3631; May, (Redbird, May); F; 33; Maricopa; F; M; Wife; 3629; Yes; Yes; AI. 2776/Id. 584

SAKOPAR
3632; Thomas; M; 68; Maricopa; F; M; Head; 3630; Yes; Yes; AI. 2773/Id. 150
3633; Fannie, (Redbird, Fannie); F; 59; Maricopa; F; M; Wife; 3631; Yes; Yes; AI. 2774/Id. 151

Census of the **Gila River** reservation of the **Pima Agency** jurisdiction; as of **April 1** ; 1932; taken by **A. H. Kneale** ; Superintendent.

Key: Number; Surname; Given; Sex (M/F); Age at Last Birthday; Tribe; Degree of Blood (F=Full); Marital Status; Relationship to Head of Family & Last Census No; At Jurisdiction Where Enrolled (Yes/No); (If no – Where); Ward (Yes/No); Allotment Annuity and/or Identification Numbers

SALKEY
3634; Charles F.; M; 37; Pima; F; S; Head; 3632; Yes; Yes; AI. 625/Id. 4962

SALKEY
3635; Isaac; M; 36; Pima; F; M; Head; 3633; Yes; Yes; AI. 626/Id. 4958
3636; Inez, (Lewis, Inez); F; 23; Pima; F; M; Wife; 3634; Yes; Yes; AI. 771/Id. 4559
3637; Wayne H.; F; 7; Pima; F; S; Dau.; 3635; Yes; Yes; AI./Id. 4960
3638; Walter J.; M; 4; Pima; F; S; Son; 3636; Yes; Yes; AI./Id. 4961
3639; Alberta; F; 2; Pima; F; S; Dau.; 3637; Yes; Yes; AI./Id. 6059

SAMPSON
3640; Charles; M; 82; Pima; F; Wd.; Head; 3638; Yes; Yes; AI. 2543/Id. 6757

SAMPSON
3641; James; M; 38; Pima; F; M; Head; 3639; Yes; Yes; AI. 1294/Id. 6759
3642; Nina; F; 49; Pima; F; M; Wife; 3640; Yes; Yes; AI. 1295/Id. 6760
3643; Eloise; F; 18; Pima; F; S; Dau.; 3641; Yes; Yes; AI. 1296/Id. 6758
3644; Margaret; F; 16; Pima; F; S; Dau.; 3642; Yes; Yes; AI. 3806/Id. 6762

SAMPSON
3645; Peter; M; Unk.; Pima; F; M; Head; 3643; Yes; Yes; AI. 616/Id. 6047
3646; Emma M., (Miguel, Emma); F; 24; Pima; F; M; Wife; 3644; Yes; Yes; AI. 675/Id. 6048
3647; Miguel, Kenneth; M; 12; Pima; F; S; Nephew; 3645; Yes; Yes; AI. 676/Id. 5970

SAMPSON
3648; William; M; 28; Pima; F; M; Head; 3646; Yes; Yes; AI. 2559/Id. 6772
3649; Jane T., (Terry, Jane); F; 31; Pima; F; M; Wife; 3647; Yes; Yes; AI. 317/Id. 6773
3650; Terry, Herman; M; 14; Pima; F; S; St.son; 3648; Yes; Yes; AI. 4490/Id. 5850
3651; Phillips, Hilda A.; F; 12; Pima; F; S; St.dau.; 3649; Yes; Yes; AI. 3881/Id. 1986

SANCELO
3652; Francisco; M; 35; Pima; F; S; Head; 3650; No; Ajo Yes; AI. 4218/Id. 2008

SANCELO
3653; Manuel; M; 35; Pima; F; M; Head; 3651; Yes; Yes; AI. 4218/Id. 2008
3654; Martha Ann; F; 36; Pima; F; M; Wife; 3652; Yes; Yes; AI. 4216/Id. 2010
3655; Philip; M; 22; Pima; F; S; Son; 3653; Yes; Yes; AI. 4219/Id. 2011
3656; Vivian; F; 18; Pima; F; S; Dau.; 3654; Yes; Yes; AI. 4220/Id. 2012

SAN CHIAGO
3657; Alice, (Jacobs, Alice); F; 31; Maricopa; F; S; Head; 3655; Yes; Yes; AI. 3002/Id. 283

153

Census of the **Gila River** reservation of the **Pima Agency** jurisdiction; as of **April 1** ; 1932; taken by **A. H. Kneale** ; Superintendent.

Key: Number; Surname; Given; Sex (M/F); Age at Last Birthday; Tribe; Degree of Blood (F=Full); Marital Status; Relationship to Head of Family & Last Census No; At Jurisdiction Where Enrolled (Yes/No); (If no – Where); Ward (Yes/No); Allotment Annuity and/or Identification Numbers

SANDERSON

3658; Howard; M; 53; Maricopa; F; Wd.; Head; 3656; Yes; Yes; AI. 4103/Id. 450
3659; Edith; F; 24; Maricopa; F; S; Dau.; 3657; Yes; Yes; AI. 4106/Id. 452
3660; Nathan; M; 16; Maricopa; F; S; Son; 3658; Yes; Yes; AI. 4109/Id. 453
3661; Hugh M.; M; 13; Maricopa; F; S; Son; 3659; Yes; Yes; AI. 1631/Id. 454
3662; Justin; M; 28; Maricopa; F; S; Son; 3660; Yes; Yes; AI. 4107/Id. 3992

SANDERSON

3663; Oliver; M; 73; Maricopa; F; M; Head; 3661; Yes; Yes; AI. 4110/Id. 483
3664; Maggie; F; 65; Maricopa; F; M; Wife; 3662; Yes; Yes; AI. 4111/Id. 484

SANTEO

3665; Edwin; M; 55; Papago; F; Wd.; Head; 3663; Yes; Yes; AI./Id. 4839
3666; Esther; F; 21; Papago; F; S; Dau.; 3664; Yes; Yes; AI./Id. 6060
3667; Melinda; F; 19; Pima[sic]; F; S; Dau.; 3665; Yes; Yes; AI./Id. 6061
3668; Claudine; F; 17; Pima[sic]; F; S; Dau.; 3666; Yes; Yes; AI./Id. 6062
3669; Clifford; M; 16; Pima[sic]; F; S; Son; 3667; Yes; Yes; AI./Id. 6063
3670; Eunice; F; 12; Pima[sic]; F; S; Dau.; 3668; Yes; Yes; AI./Id. 6064

SANTO

3671; Anton; M; 36; Pima; F; M; Head; 3669; Yes; Yes; AI. 4689/Id. 5656
3672; Alice T., (Thompson, Alice); F; 30; Pima; F; M; Wife; 3670; Yes; Yes; AI. 3507/Id. 5657
3673; Thurman; M; 8; Pima; F; S; Son; 3671; Yes; Yes; AI./Id. 5658
3674; Remah; F; 4; Pima; F; S; Dau.; 3672; Yes; Yes; AI./Id. 5659
3675; Anton Jr.; M; 2; Pima; F; S; Son; 3673; Yes; Yes; AI./Id. 1890

SANTO

3676; Juan; M; 49; Pima; F; M; Head; 3674; Yes; Yes; AI. 1369/Id. 6750
3677; Mary; F; 39; Pima; F; M; Wife; 3675; Yes; Yes; AI. 1370/Id. 6751
3678; Gilbert; M; 10; Pima; F; S; Son; 3676; Yes; Yes; AI. 1371/Id. 6752
3679; Molinsa; F; 14; Pima; F; S; Dau.; 3677; Yes; Yes; AI. 4564/Id. 6753
3680; Clement; M; 12; Pima; F; S; Son; 3678; Yes; Yes; AI. 4815/Id. 6754
3681; Lucas; M; 9; Pima; F; S; Son; 3679; Yes; Yes; AI./Id. 6755
3682; Margaret; F; 5; Pima; F; S; Dau.; 3680; Yes; Yes; AI./Id. 6756
3683; Florence; F; 1; Pima; F; S; Dau.; 3681; Yes; Yes; AI./Id. 6756

SAVANT

3684; Charles; M; 66; Pima; F; Wd.; Head; 3682; Yes; Yes; AI. 3710/Id. 7250

SCHURZ

3685; Charles; M; 43; Pima; F; M; Head; 3683; Yes; Yes; AI. 929/Id. 4443
3686; Elizabeth S., (Sunn, Elizabeth); F; 26; Maricopa; F; M; Wife; 3684; Yes; Yes; AI. 2722/Id. 198
3687; Herman; M; 19; Pima-Maricopa; F; S; Son; 3685; Yes; Yes; AI. 931/Id. 4444

Census of the **Gila River** reservation of the **Pima Agency** jurisdiction; as of **April 1** ; 1932; taken by **A. H. Kneale** ; Superintendent.

Key: Number; Surname; Given; Sex (M/F); Age at Last Birthday; Tribe; Degree of Blood (F=Full); Marital Status; Relationship to Head of Family & Last Census No; At Jurisdiction Where Enrolled (Yes/No); (If no – Where); Ward (Yes/No); Allotment Annuity and/or Identification Numbers

3688; Margaret; F; 5; Pima-Maricopa; F; S; Dau.; 3686; Yes; Yes; AI./Id. 4445
3689; Morgan, Janette; F; 18; Pima; F; S; St.dau.; 3687; Yes; Yes; AI. 3265/Id. 4116
3690; Morgan, Clifford; M; 13; Pima; F; S; St.son; 3688; Yes; Yes; AI. 931/Id. 4115

SCHURZ

3691; Henry; M; 38; Pima; F; M; Head; 3689; Yes; Yes; AI. 102/Id. 4488
3692; Frattie E., (Eschief, Frattie); F; 24; Pima; F; M; Wife; 3690; Yes; Yes; AI. 3646/Id. 1557
3693; Enos; Esther; F; 8; Pima; F; S; St.dau.; 3691; Yes; Yes; AI./Id. 1558
3694; Enos; Mathew; M; 7; Pima; F; S; St.son; 3692; Yes; Yes; AI./Id. 1559
3695; Enos; Gordon L.; M; 3; Pima; F; S; St.son; 3693; Yes; Yes; AI./Id. 1560
3696; Henrita; F; 7/12; Pima; F; S; Daug.; --; Yes; Born; 9-9-31.; Yes; AI./Id. 3940

SCHRUZ[sic]

3697; Herbert; M; 39; Pima; F; M; Head; 3694; Yes; Yes; AI. 140/Id. 4176
3698; Harvey; M; 14; Pima; F; S; Son; 3695; Yes; Yes; AI. 4562/Id. 4175
3699; Viola C.; F; 11; Pima; F; S; Dau.; 3696; Yes; Yes; AI./Id. 4174
3700; Glenda B.; F; 7; Pima; F; S; Dau.; 3697; Yes; Yes; AI./Id. 4173
3701; Harold; M; 5; Pima; F; S; Son; 3698; Yes; Yes; AI./Id. 4172
3702; Marlin E.; M; 2; Pima; F; S; Son; 3699; Yes; Yes; AI./Id. 4171

SCHURZ

3703; Mark; M; 39; Pima; F; M; Head; 3700; Yes; Yes; AI. 2550/Id. 4392
3704; Emma J., (Jackson, Emma); F; 29; Pima; F; M; Wife; 3701; Yes; Yes; AI. 3953/Id. 4393
3705; Eben A.; M; 11; Pima; F; S; Son; 3702; Yes; Yes; AI./Id. 4394
3706; Ella M.; F; 7; Pima; F; S; Dau.; 3703; Yes; Yes; AI./Id. 4395
3707; Elmer; M; 4; Pima; F; S; Son; 3704; Yes; Yes; AI./Id. 4396
3708; Byron; M; 1; Pima; F; S; Son; 3705; Yes; Yes; AI./Id. 3971

SCOFER

3709; Helen; F; 22; Pima; F; S; Alone; 3706; Yes; Yes; AI. 2060/Id. 3071
3710; Clara; F; 19; Pima; F; S; Alone; 3707; Yes; Yes; AI. 2282/Id. 3072
3711; Herbert; M; 18; Pima; F; S; Alone; 3708; Yes; Yes; AI. 3055/Id. 3073

SCOFER

3712; Horace; M; 38; Pima; F; M; Head; 3709; Yes; Yes; AI. 2283/Id. 3040
3713; Pauline, (Manuel, Palna); F; 30; Pima; F; M; Wife; 3710; Yes; Yes; AI. 409/Id. 3041
3714; Eva; F; 11; Pima; F; S; Dau.; 3711; Yes; Yes; AI./Id. 3042
3715; Horace Jr.; M; 9; Pima; F; S; Son; 3712; Yes; Yes; AI./Id. 3043
3716; Agnes; F; 6; Pima; F; S; Dau.; 3713; Yes; Yes; AI./Id. 3044
3717; Dana; F; 4; Pima; F; S; Dau.; 3714; Yes; Yes; AI./Id. 3045

Census of the **Gila River** reservation of the **Pima Agency** jurisdiction; as of **April 1** ; 1932; taken by **A. H. Kneale** ; Superintendent.

Key: Number; Surname; Given; Sex (M/F); Age at Last Birthday; Tribe; Degree of Blood (F=Full); Marital Status; Relationship to Head of Family & Last Census No; At Jurisdiction Where Enrolled (Yes/No); (If no – Where); Ward (Yes/No); Allotment Annuity and/or Identification Numbers

SCOTT
3718; Hanna; F; 82; Pima; F; Wd.; Head; 3715; Yes; Yes; AI. 3383/Id. 5695

SCOTT
3719; Isaac; M; 60; Pima; F; Wd.; Head; 3716; Yes; Yes; AI. 1297/Id. 6437
3720; Daisy; F; 19; Pima; F; S; Dau.; 3717; Yes; Yes; AI. 1301/Id. 6438
3721; Hiram; M; 14; Pima; F; S; Son; 3718; Yes; Yes; AI. 3172/Id. 6439

SCOTT
3722; Jackson; M; 67; Pima; F; Wd.; Head; 3719; Yes; Yes; AI. 3379/Id. 5690
3723; Jane; F; 22; Pima; F; S; Dau.; 3720; Yes; Yes; AI. 3381/Id. 5692
3724; Leta; F; 17; Pima; F; S; Dau.; 3721; Yes; Yes; AI. 3382/Id. 5693

SCOTT
3725; Juan A.; M; 47; Pima; F; M; Head; 3722; Yes; Yes; AI. 2243/Id. 3456
3726; Barbara, (Lewis, Barbara); F; 52; Pima; F; M; Wife; 3723; Yes; Yes; AI. 2289/Id. 3451

SCOTT
3727; Winfield; M; 62; Pima; F; M; Head; 3724; Yes; Yes; AI. 590/Id. 4908
3728; Maggie; F; 62; Pima; F; M; Wife; 3725; Yes; Yes; AI. 591/Id. 4909
3729; Lily; F; 31; Pima; F; S; Dau.; 3726; Yes; Yes; AI. 594/Id. 4910
3730; Lizzie; F; 26; Pima; F; S; Dau.; 3727; Yes; AI. 596/Id. 4912
3731; Roy; M; 32; Pima; F; S; Son; 3728; Yes; Yes; AI. 595/Id. 4911
3732; Jones; M; 24; Pima; F; S; Son; 3729; Yes; Yes; AI. 597/Id. 4913
3733; McDonald; M; 18; Pima; F; S; Son; 3730; Yes; Yes; AI. 598/Id. 4914

SCOTT
3734; Winfield; M; 77; Pima; F; M; Head; 3731; Yes; Yes; AI. 2982/Id. 3263
3735; Isabelle; F; 77; Pima; F; M; Wife; 3732; Yes; Yes; AI. 2983/Id. 3264

SETO
3736; Agnes; F; 22; Pima; F; S; Alone; 3733; Yes; Yes; AI. 565/Id. 6049
3737; Clara; F; 20; Pima; F; S; Alone; 3734; Yes; Yes; AI. 566/Id. 6050
3738; Wesley; M; 18; Pima; F; S; Alone; 3735; Yes; Yes; AI. 3108/Id. 6051

SETO
3739; Paul; M; 29; Pima; F; M; Head; 3736; Yes; Yes; AI. 568/Id. 4848
3740; Doris E., (Enis, Doris); F; 30; Pima; F; M; Wife; 3737; Yes; Yes; AI. 925/Id. 4849
3741; Nina; F; 8; Pima; F; S; Dau.; 3738; Yes; Yes; AI./Id. 4850
3742; Winifred; F; 5; Pima; F; S; Dau.; 3739; Yes; Yes; AI./Id. 4851

SETOYANT
3743; Campbell; M; 47; Pima; F; M; Head; 3740; Yes; Yes; AI. 1041/Id. 7251

Census of the **Gila River** reservation of the **Pima Agency** jurisdiction; as of **April 1** ; 1932; taken by **A. H. Kneale** ; Superintendent.

Key: Number; Surname; Given; Sex (M/F); Age at Last Birthday; Tribe; Degree of Blood (F=Full); Marital Status; Relationship to Head of Family & Last Census No; At Jurisdiction Where Enrolled (Yes/No); (If no – Where); Ward (Yes/No); Allotment Annuity and/or Identification Numbers

3744; Manley, (Lyon, Manly[sic]); F; 39; Pima; F; M; Wife; 3741; Yes; Yes; AI. 1488/Id. 7252

3745; Herman; M; 11; Pima; F; S; Son; 3742; Yes; Yes; AI./Id. 7253

3746; James; M; 8; Pima; F; S; Son; 3743; Yes; Yes; AI./Id. 7254

SETOYANT

3747; Henry; M; 26; Pima; F; M; Head; 3744; Yes; Yes; AI. 1043/Id. 7255

3748; Ida L., (Liston, Ida); F; 20; Pima; F; M; Wife; 3745; Yes; Yes; AI. 1469/Id. 6810

3749; Barbara J.; F; 1; Pima; F; S; Dau.; 3746; Yes; Yes; AI./Id. 7275

SEYE

3750; Sophia M.; F; 24; Pima; F; Wd.; Head; 3747; Yes; Yes; AI. 25/Id. 5579

3751; Mary; F; 6; Pima; F; S; Dau.; 3748; Yes; Yes; AI./Id. 5581

3752; Betty Jane; F; 6; Pima; F; S; Dau.; 3749; Yes; Yes; AI./Id. 5582

SHEBELA

~~George; M; Unk.; Zuni; F; M; Head; –; Zuni from New Mexico.~~; Yes; AI./Id.

3753; Margaret, (Nosuch, Margaret); F; 19; Pima; F; M; Wife; 3024; Yes; Yes; AI. 1591/Id. 7000

~~Carolina Betty; F; 1; Pima; F; S; Dau.; –; Died; 4-28-31.; (Inadvertedly[sic] left off 1931 Census.~~; Yes; AI./Id.

SHELDE

3754; John; M; 43; Maricopa; F; M; Head; 3750; Yes; Yes; AI. 3918/Id. 538

3755; Annie; F; 41; Maricopa; F; M; Wife; 3751; Yes; Yes; AI. 3919/Id. 539

3756; Leander; M; 16; Maricopa; F; S; Son; 3752; Yes; Yes; AI. 3920/Id. 540

3757; Anselm; M; 12; Maricopa; F; S; Son; 3753; Yes; Yes; AI. 4769/Id. 541

3758; Hubert; M; 4; Maricopa; F; S; Son; 3754; Yes; Yes; AI./Id. 542

SHELDE

3759; Juan V.; M; 82; Maricopa[sic]; F; Wd.; Head; 3755; Yes; Yes; AI. 4010/Id. 1278

3760; James; M; 42; Maricopa[sic]; F; S; Son; 3756; Yes; Yes; AI. 4012/Id. 1279

3761; Sheila; F; 45; Maricopa[sic]; F; S; Daughter; 3757; Yes; Yes; AI. 4011/Id. 1280

3762; Peter; M; 31; Pima; F; S; Son; 3758; Yes; Yes; AI. 3921/Id. 1281

SHIPLEY

~~N.E.; John; M; Head; –;~~

3763; Susannah F.; F; 43; Pima; F; M; Wife; Yes; Inadvertedly[sic] left off 1931 Census.; Yes; Yes; AI. 3309/Id. 4184

3764; Helen; F; 14; Pima; F; M; Dau.; Yes; Inadvertedly[sic] left off 1931 Census.; Yes; Yes; AI. 4167/Id. 4183

3765; John Leo; M; 12; Pima; F; M; Son; Yes; Inadvertedly[sic] left off 1931 Census.; Yes; Yes; AI./Id. 4182

Census of the **Gila River** reservation of the **Pima Agency** jurisdiction; as of **April 1** ; 1932; taken by **A. H. Kneale** ; Superintendent.

Key: Number; Surname; Given; Sex (M/F); Age at Last Birthday; Tribe; Degree of Blood (F=Full); Marital Status; Relationship to Head of Family & Last Census No; At Jurisdiction Where Enrolled (Yes/No); (If no – Where); Ward (Yes/No); Allotment Annuity and/or Identification Numbers

SHOAH
~~Kenneth; M; --; F; M; Head; --;~~ Mescalero Apache.; Yes; AI./Id.
3766; Fannie S., (Scott, Fannie); F; 28; Pima; F; M; Wife; 3759; Yes; Yes; AI. 2246/Id. 4482
3767; Phyllis; F; 9/12; Pima-Apache; F; S; Dau.; --; Yes; ~~Born; 6-21-31.~~; Yes; AI./Id. 3939

SMART
3768; Wilson J.; M; 18; Pima; F; S; Alone; 3760; Yes; Yes; AI. 855/Id. 4314
3769; Charles; M; 22; Pima; F; S; Alone; 3761; Yes; Yes; AI. 852/Id. 3999

SMITH
~~Alexander; M; 75; Pima; F; Wd.; Head; 3762; Died; 2-3-31.~~; Yes; AI. 985/Id. 6935

SMITH
3770; Annily; F; 31; Pima; F; Wd.; Head; 3763; Yes; Yes; AI. 4754/Id. 2013

SMITH
3771; Anton H.; M; 102; Pima; F; Wd.; Head; 3764; Yes; Yes; AI. 620/Id. 4648

SMITH
3772; Charles; M; 54; Pima; F; M; Head; 3765; Yes; Yes; AI. 1498/Id. 6663
3773; Martha; F; 59; Pima; F; M; Wife; 3766; Yes; Yes; AI. 1499/Id. 6664
3774; Esther; F; 22; Pima; F; S; Dau.; 3767; Yes; Yes; AI. 1500/Id. 6665
3775; Adolphine; F; 19; Pima; F; S; Dau.; 3768; Yes; Yes; AI. 1501/Id. 6666
3776; Julie; F; 16; Pima; F; S; Dau.; 3769; Yes; Yes; AI. 3168/Id. 6667
3777; Celso; M; 14; Pima; F; S; Son; 3770; Yes; Yes; AI. 4452/Id. 6668
3778; Ella; F; 12; Pima; F; S; Dau.; 3771; Yes; Yes; AI. 4778/Id. 6669
3779; Fernando; M; 7; Pima; F; S; Son; 3772; Yes; Yes; AI./Id. 6670

SMITH
3780; David; M; 45; Maricopa; F; M; Head; 3773; Yes; Yes; AI. 4001/Id. 294
3781; Lizzie; F; 42; Maricopa; F; M; Wife; 3774; Yes; Yes; AI. 4002/Id. 295
3782; Raima; F; 21; Maricopa; F; S; Dau.; 3775; Yes; Yes; AI. 4003/Id. 296
3783; Melinda; F; 17; Maricopa; F; S; Dau.; 3776; Yes; Yes; AI. 4004/Id. 297
3784; Clifford; M; 13; Maricopa; F; S; Son; 3777; Yes; Yes; AI. 4005/Id. 298
3785; Marvin; M; 11; Maricopa; F; S; Son; 3778; Yes; Yes; AI./Id. 299
3786; Lenora; F; 5; Maricopa; F; S; Dau.; 3779; Yes; Yes; AI./Id. 300

SMITH
3787; Edith; F; 32; Pima; F; S; Head; 3780; Yes; Yes; AI. 577/Id. 4871

SMITH
3788; Elijah; M; 35; Pima; F; M; Head; 3781; Yes; Yes; AI. 576/Id. 5279

Census of the **Gila River** reservation of the **Pima Agency** jurisdiction; as of **April 1** ; 1932; taken by **A. H. Kneale** ; Superintendent.

Key: Number; Surname; Given; Sex (M/F); Age at Last Birthday; Tribe; Degree of Blood (F=Full); Marital Status; Relationship to Head of Family & Last Census No; At Jurisdiction Where Enrolled (Yes/No); (If no – Where); Ward (Yes/No); Allotment Annuity and/or Identification Numbers

3789; Julia, (Enos, Julia Watson); F; 27; Pima; F; M; Wife; 3782; Yes; Yes; AI. 604/Id. 5280

SMITH
3790; Frances; F; 35; Pima; F; Wd.; Head; 3783; Yes; Yes; AI. 2117/Id. 3025
3791; Allen; M; 10; Pima; F; S; Son; 3784; Yes; Yes; AI./Id. 3026
3792; Wallace; M; 8; Pima; F; S; Son; 3785; Yes; Yes; AI./Id. 3027

SMITH
3793; Henry; M; 39; Maricopa; F; M; Head; 3786; Yes; Yes; AI. 2939/Id. 130
3794; Emily; F; 31; Maricopa; F; M; Wife; 3787; Yes; Yes; AI. 4667/Id. 131
3795; Verlin; M; 11; Maricopa; F; S; Son; 3788; Yes; Yes; AI./Id. 132
3796; Emily; F; 5; Maricopa; F; S; Dau.; 3789; Yes; Yes; AI./Id. 133

SMITH
3797; Francisco; M; 39; Papago; F; M; Head; 3790; Yes; Yes; AI./Id. 5269
3798; Clara P.; F; 35; Papago; F; M; Wife; 3791; Yes; Yes; AI./Id. 5270

SMITH
John; M; 56; Pima; F; M; Head; --; Yes; Salt River allottee Scottsdale Maricopa Ariz.; Yes; AI./Id.
3799; Carmine L., (Lewis, Carmine); F; 36; Pima; F; M; Wife; 3792; No; Phoenix Sch. Salt River Res.; Scottsdale Maricopa Ariz.; Yes; AI. 3327/Id. 6052
3800; Vivian; F; 18; Pima; F; S; St.dau.; 3793; No; Phoenix Sch. Salt River Res.; Scottsdale Maricopa Ariz.; Yes; AI. 3713/Id. 6053
3801; Margery; F; 12; Pima; F; S; St.dau.; 3794; No; Phoenix Sch. Salt River Res.; Scottsdale Maricopa Ariz.; Yes; AI. 4797/Id. 6054
3802; Leroy; M; 7; Pima; F; S; Son; 3795; No; Phoenix Sch. Salt River Res.; Scottsdale Maricopa Ariz.; Yes; AI./Id. 6055
3803; Roger; M; 7; Pima; F; S; Son; 3796; No; Phoenix Sch. Salt River Res.; Scottsdale Maricopa Ariz.; Yes; AI./Id. 6056
3804; Rose; F; 4; Pima; F; S; Dau.; 3797; No; Phoenix Sch. Salt River Res.; Scottsdale Maricopa Ariz.; Yes; AI./Id. 6057
3805; Kathleen Dorothy; F; 2/12; Pima; F; S; Dau.; --; No; ~~Born; 2-1-32.~~; Phoenix Sch. Salt River Res.; Scottsdale Maricopa Ariz.; Yes; AI./Id. 6134

SMITH
~~Herbert; M; 59; Pima; F; Wd.; Head; 3798; Died; 3-25-32.;~~ Yes; AI. 986/Id. 6936

SMITH
3806; James; M; 23; Pima; F; S; Head; 3799; Yes; Yes; AI. 2142/Id. 3125

SMITH
3807; James H.; M; 39; Pima; F; S; Head; 3800; Yes; Yes; AI. 622/Id. 4869

Census of the **Gila River** reservation of the **Pima Agency** jurisdiction; as of **April 1** ; 1932; taken by **A. H. Kneale** ; Superintendent.

Key: Number; Surname; Given; Sex (M/F); Age at Last Birthday; Tribe; Degree of Blood (F=Full); Marital Status; Relationship to Head of Family & Last Census No; At Jurisdiction Where Enrolled (Yes/No); (If no – Where); Ward (Yes/No); Allotment Annuity and/or Identification Numbers

SMITH
3808; Jose; M; 52; Pima; F; Wd.; Head; 3801; Yes; Yes; AI. 1888/Id. 4188
3809; Felicita; F; 18; Pima; F; S; Dau.; 3802; Yes; Yes; AI. 3117/Id. 4187
3810; Annie; F; 12; Pima; F; S; Dau.; 3803; Yes; Yes; AI. 4841/Id. 4186

SMITH
3811; Joseph; M; 60; Pima; F; Wd.; Head; 3804; Yes; Yes; AI. 575/Id. 4870

SMITH
3812; Pablo; M; 42; Pima; F; S; Head; 3805; Yes; Yes; AI. 2146/Id. 3126

SMITH
3813; Perkins; M; 28; Pima; F; M; Head; 3806; Yes; Yes; AI. 1502/Id. 6672
3814; Eliza, (Newman, Eliza); F; 22; Pima; F; M; Wife; 3807; Yes; Yes; AI. 1132/Id. 6673
3815; Florence; F; 2; Pima; F; S; Dau.; 3808; Yes; Yes; AI./Id. 5836

SNEED
~~Frank; M; 71; Pima; F; Wd.; Head; 3809; Died; 3-6-32.~~; Yes; AI. 4133/Id. 1252

SMITH
~~William; M, (See William S. Allison);~~

SNEED
3816; Joseph; M; 39; Pima; F; M; Head; 3910; Yes; Yes; AI. 4135/Id. 1247
3817; Nellie; F; 42; Pima; F; M; Wife; 3811; Yes; Yes; AI. 4141/Id. 1248
3818; Mildred; F; 11; Pima; F; S; Dau.; 3812; Yes; Yes; AI./Id. 1250
3819; Kenneth; M; 9; Pima; F; S; Son; 3813; Yes; Yes; AI./Id. 1251

SNYDER
3820; John E.; M; 34; Pima; F; S; Head; 3814; Yes; Yes; AI. 3120/Id. 3996

SNYDER
3821; Josepha; F; 57; Pima; F; Wd.; Head; 3815; Yes; Yes; AI. 460/Id. 5083

SNYDER
3822; Jose E.; M; 69; Pima; F; Wd.; Head; 3816; Yes; Yes; AI. 1966/Id. 3995

SNYDER
3823; Juan E.; M; 48; Pima; F; M; Head; 3817; Yes; Yes; AI. 1971/Id. 4799
3824; Eva C., (Charles, Eva); F; 38; Pima; F; M; Wife; 3818; Yes; Yes; AI. 2023/Id. 4800

SNYDER
3825; Mary E.; F; 26; Pima; F; S; Head; 3819; Yes; Yes; AI. 1968/Id. 3994

Census of the **Gila River** reservation of the **Pima Agency** jurisdiction; as of **April 1** ; 1932; taken by **A. H. Kneale** ; Superintendent.

Key: Number; Surname; Given; Sex (M/F); Age at Last Birthday; Tribe; Degree of Blood (F=Full); Marital Status; Relationship to Head of Family & Last Census No; At Jurisdiction Where Enrolled (Yes/No); (If no – Where); Ward (Yes/No); Allotment Annuity and/or Identification Numbers

SNYDER
3826; Pedro; M; 26; Pima; F; S; Head; 3820; Yes; Yes; AI. 961/Id. 5084

SOATIKEE
3827; Henry; M; 62; Maricopa; F; M; Head; 3821; Yes; Yes; AI. 3727/Id. 385
3828; Martha; F; 51; Maricopa; F; M; Wife; 3822; Yes; Yes; AI. 3728/Id. 386
3829; Priscilla; F; 22; Maricopa; F; S; Dau.; 3823; Yes; Yes; AI. 3732/Id. 388
3830; Leeds; M; 24; Maricopa; F; S; Son; 3824; Yes; Yes; AI. 3131/Id. 387
3831; Alvira; F; 18; Maricopa; F; S; Dau.; 3825; Yes; Yes; AI. 3733/Id. 389
3832; Iva; F; 16; Maricopa; F; S; Dau.; 3826; Yes; Yes; AI. 3734/Id. 390
3833; Rhoda; F; 14; Maricopa; F; S; Dau.; 3827; Yes; Yes; AI. 3735/Id. 391
3834; Pauline; F; 12; Maricopa; F; S; Dau.; 3828; Yes; Yes; AI./Id. 392
3835; Alma; F; 10; Maricopa; F; S; Dau.; 3829; Yes; Yes; AI./Id. 393
3836; Albert; M; 8; Maricopa; F; S; Son; 3830; Yes; Yes; AI./Id. 394
3837; Vincent; M; 6; Maricopa; F; S; Son; 3831; Yes; Yes; AI./Id. 395
3838; Leona; F; 4; Maricopa; F; S; Dau.; 3832; Yes; Yes; AI./Id. 396

SOKE
3839; Lewis; M; 44; Pima; F; M; Head; 3833; Yes; Yes; AI. 4185/Id. 1335
3840; Margaret A., (Anton, Margaret); F; 29; Pima; F; M; Wife; 3834; Yes; Yes; AI. 4429/Id. 1336
3841; Lennet; M; 21; Pima; F; S; Son; 3835; Yes; Yes; AI. 4186/Id. 1337
3842; Myrtle; F; 18; Pima; F; S; Dau.; 3836; Yes; Yes; AI. 4187/Id. 1338
3843; Sebastian; M; 12; Pima; F; S; Son; 3837; Yes; Yes; AI./Id. 1339
3844; Davison; M; 6; Pima; F; S; Son; 3838; Yes; Yes; AI./Id. 2017
3845; Dorefina; F; 8; Pima; F; S; Dau.; 3839; Yes; Yes; AI./Id. 1340
3846; Frederick; M; 2; Pima; F; S; Son; 3840; Yes; Yes; AI./Id. 2018

SOKE
3847; Mary; F; 64; Pima; F; Wd.; Head; 3841; Yes; Yes; AI. 4188/Id. 1229

SOKE
3848; Oliver; M; 39; Pima; F; S; Head; 3842; Yes; Yes; AI. 4285/Id. 1349

SOMEGUSTAVA
3849; Guy; M; 30; Maricopa; F; S; Head; 3843; Yes; Yes; AI. 2842/Id. 143

SOMEGUSTAVA
3850; Hoot; M; 57; Maricopa; F; Wd.; Head; 3844; Yes; Yes; AI. 2839/Id. 144
3851; Harry E.; M; 22; Maricopa; F; S; Son; 3845; Yes; Yes; AI. 2844/Id. 145

SOMEGUSTAVA
3852; James; M; 36; Maricopa; F; M; Head; 3846; Yes; Yes; AI. 2940/Id. 141
3853; Susie K., (Kovoca, Susie); F; 41; Maricopa; F; M; Wife; 3847; Yes; Yes; AI. 2940/Id. 141

Census of the **Gila River** reservation of the **Pima Agency** jurisdiction; as of **April 1** ; 1932; taken by **A. H. Kneale** ; Superintendent.

Key: Number; Surname; Given; Sex (M/F); Age at Last Birthday; Tribe; Degree of Blood (F=Full); Marital Status; Relationship to Head of Family & Last Census No; At Jurisdiction Where Enrolled (Yes/No); (If no – Where); Ward (Yes/No); Allotment Annuity and/or Identification Numbers

3854; Oscar; M; 11; Maricopa; F; S; Son; 3848; Yes; Yes; AI./Id. 142
3855; Pablo, Rose M.; F; 11; Pima; F; S; St.dau.; 3849; Yes; Yes; AI. 4679/Id. 1986

SUMEGUSTAVA[sic]
3856; May; F; 28; Maricopa; F; S; Head; 3850; Yes; Yes; AI. 2843/Id. 146
3857; Mavoca, Margaret; F; 20; Maricopa; F; S; Sister; 3851; Yes; Yes; AI. 2941/Id. 147

SOOS
3858; Mollie; F; 68; Pima; F; Wd.; Head; 3852; Yes; Yes; AI./Id. 1229

SOOS
3859; Thomas Jr.; M; 56; Pima; F; Wd.; Head; 3853; Yes; Yes; AI. 2609/Id. 5736
3860; Benito; M; 20; Pima; F; S; Son; 3854; Yes; Yes; AI. 2614/Id. 5738
3861; Pasco; M; 11; Pima; F; S; Son; 3855; Yes; Yes; AI./Id. 5747

SOROQUISARA
3862; Francis; M; 29; Maricopa; F; M; Head; 3856; Yes; Yes; AI. 2787/Id. 287

SOROQUISARA
3863; Frank; M; 40; Maricopa; F; S; Head; 3857; Yes; Yes; AI. 2785/Id. 280
3864; Shirley; F; 16; Maricopa; F; S; Sister; 3858; Yes; Yes; AI./Id. 288

SOROQUISARA
3865; Fred; M; 27; Maricopa; F; M; Head; 3859; Yes; Yes; AI. 2784/Id. 274
3866; Lola B., (Bird, Lola); F; 32; Maricopa; F; M; Wife; 3860; Yes; Yes; AI. 2754/Id. 275
3867; Maxwell; M; 12; Maricopa; F; S; Son; 3861; Yes; Yes; AI. 4680/Id. 276
3868; Florence; F; 11; Maricopa; F; S; Dau.; 3862; Yes; Yes; AI./Id. 277
3869; Louisa; F; 7; Maricopa; F; S; Dau.; 3863; Yes; Yes; AI./Id. 286
3870; Violet; F; 3; Maricopa; F; S; Dau.; 3864; Yes; Yes; AI./Id. 278

SOROQUISARA
3871; Cora; F; 46; Maricopa; F; Wd.; Head; 3865; Yes; Yes; AI. 2782/Id. 279

SOSOLDA
3872; Andrew Jr.; M; 37; Pima; F; S; Head; 3866; Yes; Yes; AI. 3898/Id. 1647

SOSOLDA
3873; Anton; M; 24; Pima; F; S; Head; 3867; Yes; Yes; AI. 3897/Id. 1350

SOSOLDA
3874; Lancisco; M; 20; Pima; F; S; Alone; 3868; Yes; Yes; AI. 3901/Id. 1804

Key: Number; Surname; Given; Sex (M/F); Age at Last Birthday; Tribe; Degree of Blood (F=Full); Marital Status; Relationship to Head of Family & Last Census No; At Jurisdiction Where Enrolled (Yes/No); (If no – Where); Ward (Yes/No); Allotment Annuity and/or Identification Numbers

SOSOLDA

3875; Josephine; F; 25; Pima; F; S; Head; 3869; Yes; Yes; AI. 3900/Id. 1649
3876; Raymond; M; 7; Pima; F; S; Son; 3870; Yes; Yes; AI./Id. 1650
3877; Lyman; M; 5; Pima; F; S; Son; 3871; Yes; Yes; AI./Id. 1651

SOSOLDA

3878; Lewis; M; 30; Pima; F; S; Head; 3872; Yes; Yes; AI. 4768/Id. 1648

SOY

3879; Bessie B., (James, Bessie); F; 36; Pima; F; M; Wife; 3873; Yes; Yes; AI. 3295/Id. 3993
3880; James, Pauline; F; 18; Pima; F; S; Dau.; 3874; Yes; Yes; AI. 3296/Id. 4116

STANLEY

3881; Josephine, (Jones, Josephine); F; 37; Pima; F; M; Wife; 3875; Yes; Yes; AI. 2222/Id. 3099

STEPP

3882; Anna T., (Moore, Anna); F; 33; Pima; F; M; Wife; 3876; Yes; Yes; AI. 3602/Id. 7256
3883; Roderick; M; 12; Pima; F; S; Son; 3877; Yes; Yes; AI./Id. 7257
3884; Adeline; F; 11; Pima; F; S; Dau.; 3878; Yes; Yes; AI./Id. 7258

STEVENS

3885; Jones; M; 36; Pima; F; M; Head; 3879; Yes; Yes; AI. 807/Id. 5784
3886; Laura T., (Thomas, Laura); F; 29; Pima; F; M; Wife; 3880; Yes; Yes; AI. 1036/Id. 5785
3887; Rogene L.; F; 2; Pima; F; S; Dau.; 3881; Yes; Yes; AI./Id. 5786

STEVENS

3888; William; M; 65; Pima; F; M; Head; 3882; Yes; Yes; AI. 48/Id. 5628
3889; Mollie, (Sava, Laura); F; 55; Pima; F; M; Wife; 3883; Yes; Yes; AI. 47/Id. 5629
3890; Mabel; F; 21; Pima; F; S; Dau.; 3884; Yes; Yes; AI. 809/Id. 5630

STEWART

3891; Alice; F; 73; Pima; F; Wd.; Head; 3885; Yes; Yes; AI. 1101/Id. 6484

STEWART

3892; Edward; M; 31; Pima; F; M; Head; 3886; Yes; Yes; AI. 1858/Id. 4679
3893; Jean N., (Newman, Jean); F; 34; Pima; F; M; Wife; 3887; Yes; Yes; AI. 3248/Id. 4680
3894; Allen; M; 11; Pima; F; S; Son; 3888; Yes; Yes; AI. 4859/Id. 4681
3895; Roger; M; 8; Pima; F; S; Son; 3889; Yes; Yes; AI./Id. 4682
3896; Stanley; M; 2; Pima; F; S; Son; 3890; Yes; Yes; AI./Id. 3991

Census of the **Gila River** reservation of the **Pima Agency** jurisdiction; as of **April 1** ; 1932; taken by   **A. H. Kneale** ; Superintendent.

Key: Number; Surname; Given; Sex (M/F); Age at Last Birthday; Tribe; Degree of Blood (F=Full); Marital Status; Relationship to Head of Family & Last Census No; At Jurisdiction Where Enrolled (Yes/No); (If no – Where); Ward (Yes/No); Allotment Annuity and/or Identification Numbers

STEWART
3897; Joseph; M; 47; Pima; F; M; Head; 3891; Yes; Yes; AI. 1097/Id. 6479
3898; Mollie; F; 47; Pima; F; M; Wife; 3892; Yes; Yes; AI. 1098/Id. 6480
3899; Jasper; M; 21; Pima; F; S; Son; 3893; Yes; Yes; AI. 1100/Id. 6481
3900; Melissa; F; 12; Pima; F; S; Dau.; 3894; Yes; Yes; AI. 222/Id. 6482
3901; Harrison; M; 8; Pima; F; S; Son; 3895; Yes; Yes; AI./Id. 6483

STEWART
3902; Josephine; F; 34; Pima; F; S; Head; 3896; Yes; Yes; AI. 1153/Id. 6578
3903; Roland H.; M; 6; Pima; F; S; Son; 3897; Yes; Yes; AI./Id. 7259

STEWART
3904; Tom; M; 42; Maricopa; F; M; Head; 3898; Yes; Yes; AI. 2899/Id. 24
3905; Hilda, (Yarmatte, Hilda); F; 41; Maricopa; F; M; Wife; 3899; Yes; Yes; AI. 2910/Id. 25
3906; Anita; F; 11; Maricopa; F; S; Dau.; 3900; Yes; Yes; AI./Id. 26
3907; Tom Jr.; M; 9; Maricopa; F; S; Son; 3901; Yes; Yes; AI./Id. 27
3908; Edith; F; 6; Maricopa; F; S; Dau.; 3902; Yes; Yes; AI./Id. 28
3909; Herbert; M; 4; Maricopa; F; S; Son; 3903; Yes; Yes; AI./Id. 29
3910; Hilde; F; 3/12; Maricopa; F; S; Dau.; --; Yes; Born.; ~~12-27-31.~~; Yes; AI./Id. 614

STEWART
3911; William; M; 71; Maricopa; F; M; Head; 3904; Yes; Yes; AI. 2900/Id. 178
3912; Guadalupa; F; 71; Maricopa; F; M; Wife; 3905; Yes; Yes; AI. 2907/Id. 179

STONE
3913; Benjamin P.; M; 32; Pima; F; M; Head; 3906; Yes; Yes; AI. 561/Id. 5027
3914; Clara P., (Pablo, Clara); F; 24; Pima; F; M; Wife; 3907; Yes; Yes; AI. 1170/Id. 5028
3915; Bernice; F; 12; Pima; F; S; Dau.; 3908; Yes; Yes; AI. 3286/Id. 5029
3916; Leonard; M; 4; Pima; F; S; Son; 3909; Yes; Yes; AI./Id. 5030
3917; Lillian M.; F; 2; Pima; F; S; Dau.; 3910; Yes; Yes; AI. 3286/Id. 5811
3918; Harold; M; 1; Pima; F; S; Son; 3911; Yes; Yes; AI./Id. 6110
3919; Edwin Porter; M; 2/12; Pima; F; S; Son; --; Yes; ~~Born.; 2-9-32.~~; Yes; AI./Id. 6132

STONE
3920; Joe K.; M; 60; Pima; F; M; Head; 3912; Yes; Yes; AI. 587/Id. 4829
3921; Julia; F; 60; Pima; F; M; Wife; 3913; Yes; Yes; AI. 588/Id. 4830
3922; Maud; F; 22; Pima; F; S; Dau.; 3914; Yes; Yes; AI. 355/Id. 4831
3923; Sophia J.; F; 19; Pima; F; S; Dau.; 3915; Yes; Yes; AI. 350/Id. 4834
3924; Elliott; M; 17; Pima; F; S; Son; 3916; Yes; Yes; AI. 558/Id. 4833

STONE
3925; Minnie P.; F; 48; Pima; F; Wd.; Head; 3917; Yes; Yes; AI. 560/Id. 4825

Census of the **Gila River** reservation of the **Pima Agency** jurisdiction; as of **April 1** ; 1932; taken by **A. H. Kneale** ; Superintendent.

Key: Number; Surname; Given; Sex (M/F); Age at Last Birthday; Tribe; Degree of Blood (F=Full); Marital Status; Relationship to Head of Family & Last Census No; At Jurisdiction Where Enrolled (Yes/No); (If no – Where); Ward (Yes/No); Allotment Annuity and/or Identification Numbers

STONE

3926; Paul K.; M; 34; Pima; F; S; Head; 3918; Yes; Yes; AI. 348/Id. 4835

STONE

3927; Samuel; M; 23; Pima; F; M; Head; 3919; Yes; Yes; AI. 354/Id. 4827
3928; Helen, (Setoyant, Helen); F; 20; Pima; F; M; Wife; 3920; Yes; Yes; AI. 1045/Id. 4828

SUN

3929; Cyrus; M; 57; Maricopa; F; M; Head; 3921; Yes; Yes; AI. 2730/Id. 94
3930; Cora; F; 54; Maricopa; F; M; Wife; 3922; Yes; Yes; AI. 2731/Id. 95
3931; Nicholas; M; 19; Maricopa; F; S; Son; 3923; Yes; Yes; AI. 2734/Id. 102

SUN

3932; Daisy; F; 30; Maricopa; F; S; Head; 3924; Yes; Yes; AI. 2729/Id. 123

SUN

3933; David; M; 47; Maricopa; F; Wd.; Head; 3925; Yes; Yes; AI. 2698/Id. 93

SUN

3934; Joseph; M; 60; Maricopa; F; Wd.; Head; 3926; Yes; Yes; AI. 2719/Id. 195
3935; Wallace; M; 28; Maricopa; F; S; Son; 3927; Yes; Yes; AI. 2721/Id. 196
3936; Joshua; M; 18; Maricopa; F; S; Son; 3928; Yes; Yes; AI. 2723/Id. 197

SUNDUST

3937; Harry; M; 45; Maricopa; F; M; Head; 3929; Yes; Yes; AI. 2813/Id. 59
3938; Fannie; F; 42; Maricopa; F; M; Wife; 3930; Yes; Yes; AI. 2923/Id. 60
3939; Virginia; F; 21; Maricopa; F; S; Dau.; 3931; Yes; Yes; AI. 2924/Id. 61
3940; Lucille; F; 19; Maricopa; F; S; Dau.; 3932; Yes; Yes; AI. 2925/Id. 62
3941; Luther; M; 17; Maricopa; F; S; Son; 3933; Yes; Yes; AI./Id. 63
3942; Laura; F; 16; Maricopa; F; S; Dau.; 3934; Yes; Yes; AI. 2925/Id. 64
3943; Priscilla; F; 7; Maricopa; F; S; Dau.; 3935; Yes; Yes; AI. 2925/Id. 65
3944; Lucretia; F; 5; Maricopa; F; S; Dau.; 3936; Yes; Yes; AI. 2925/Id. 66

SUNDUST

3945; Henry; M; 28; Maricopa; F; S; Head; 3937; Yes; Yes; AI. 2827/Id. 67

SUNDUST

3946; Leon; M; 29; Maricopa; F; M; Head; 3938; Yes; Yes; AI. 2830/Id. 124
3947; Felipa, (Sun, Felipi); F; 29; Maricopa; F; M; Wife; 3939; Yes; Yes; AI. 2732/Id. 125
3948; Norma; F; 10; Maricopa; F; S; Dau.; 3940; Yes; Yes; AI./Id. 126
3949; Alvard; M; 8; Maricopa; F; S; Son; 3941; Yes; Yes; AI./Id. 127
3950; Imogene; F; 7; Maricopa; F; S; Dau.; 3942; Yes; Yes; AI./Id. 128
3951; Leon; M; 1; Maricopa; F; S; Son; 3943; Yes; Yes; AI./Id. 598

Census of the **Gila River** reservation of the **Pima Agency** jurisdiction; as of **April 1** ; 1932; taken by **A. H. Kneale** ; Superintendent.

Key: Number; Surname; Given; Sex (M/F); Age at Last Birthday; Tribe; Degree of Blood (F=Full); Marital Status; Relationship to Head of Family & Last Census No; At Jurisdiction Where Enrolled (Yes/No); (If no – Where); Ward (Yes/No); Allotment Annuity and/or Identification Numbers

SUNDUST

3952; Leonard; M; 26; Maricopa; F; M; Head; 3944; Yes; ~~(Also known as Louis L.)~~; Yes; AI. 2831/Id. 68

3953; Vivian Y., (Yarmata, Vivian); F; 21; Maricopa; F; M; Wife; 3945; Yes; Yes; AI. 2912/Id. 15

3954; Leonard Jr.; M; 2; Maricopa; F; S; Son; 3946; Yes; Yes; AI./Id. 592

3955; Louis Leonard; M; 9/12; Maricopa; F; S; Son; --; Yes; ~~Born.; 6-29-31.~~; Yes; AI./Id. 615

SUNDUST

3956; Mary; F; 49; Maricopa; F; Wd.; Head; 3947; Yes; Yes; AI. 2826/Id. 248

3957; Dolores; F; 8; Maricopa; F; S; Dau.; 3948; Yes; Yes; AI./Id. 249

SUNDUST

3958; Roger; M; 36; Maricopa; F; M; Head; 3949; Yes; Yes; AI. 2828/Id. 1

3959; Lasalle S., (Smith, Lasalle); F; 32; Maricopa; F; M; Wife; 3950; Yes; Yes; AI. 2927/Id. 2

3960; Thelma; F; 9; Maricopa; F; S; Dau.; 3951; Yes; Yes; AI./Id. 3

3961; Ruby; F; 6; Maricopa; F; S; Dau.; 3952; Yes; Yes; AI./Id. 4

3962; Smith, Lily; F; 17; Maricopa; F; S; Sis-in-law; 3953; Yes; Yes; AI. 2931/Id. 81

SUNNA

3963; Elmo; M; 47; Pima; F; M; Head; 3954; Yes; Yes; AI. 2402/Id. 3585

3964; May; F; 47; Pima; F; M; Wife; 3955; Yes; Yes; AI. 2403/Id. 3586

3965; Iver E.; M; 18; Pima; F; S; Son; 3956; Yes; Yes; AI. 2404/Id. 3587

SUSANNA

3966; Charles; M; 54; Pima; F; M; Head; 3957; Yes; Yes; AI. 4320/Id. 1471

3967; Josie; F; 51; Pima; F; M; Wife; 3958; Yes; Yes; AI. 4321/Id. 1472

Nina; F; 18; Pima; F; S; Dau.; 3959; Yes; Married to Wilford Thompson; Yes; AI. 4322/Id. 1473

SUSANNA

3968; Charles; M; 77; Pima; F; M; Head; 3960; Yes; Yes; AI. 4323/Id. 1727

3969; Jesus; F; 77; Pima; F; M; Wife; 3961; Yes; Yes; AI. 4324/Id. 2019

SWEET

3970; Albert; M; 65; Pima; F; M; Head; 3962; Yes; Yes; AI. 3766/Id. 1727

3971; Alice; F; 61; Pima; F; M; Wife; 3963; Yes; Yes; AI. 3767/Id. 1728

3972; Frank; M; 33; Pima; F; S; Son; 3964; Yes; Yes; AI./Id. 1729

3973; Carl; M; 35; Pima; F; S; Son; 3965; Yes; Yes; AI. 3769/Id. 2016

SWEET

3974; Lane; M; 33; Maricopa; F; M; Head; 3966; Yes; Yes; AI. 3770/Id. 495

Census of the **Gila River** reservation of the **Pima Agency** jurisdiction; as of **April 1** ; 1932; taken by **A. H. Kneale** ; Superintendent.

Key: Number; Surname; Given; Sex (M/F); Age at Last Birthday; Tribe; Degree of Blood (F=Full); Marital Status; Relationship to Head of Family & Last Census No; At Jurisdiction Where Enrolled (Yes/No); (If no – Where); Ward (Yes/No); Allotment Annuity and/or Identification Numbers

3975; Juna C., (Case, Juna); F; 29; Maricopa; F; M; Wife; 3967; Yes; Yes; AI. 3980/Id. 496

3976; Dana; F; 7; Maricopa; F; S; Dau.; 3968; Yes; Yes; AI./Id. 497

3977; Ben; M; 4; Maricopa; F; S; Son; 3969; Yes; Yes; AI./Id. 498

TASQUINTH

3978; Alex; M; 77; Maricopa; F; M; Head; 3970; Yes; Yes; AI. 3311/Id. 527

3979; Sebea; F; 77; Maricopa; F; M; Wife; 3971; Yes; Yes; AI. 3312/Id. 528

3980; Gertrude; F; 20; Maricopa; F; S; Dau.; --; Yes; ~~Inadvertedly[sic] left off 1931 Census.~~; Yes; AI./Id. 531

TASQUINTH

3981; John; M; 37; Maricopa; F; M; Head; 3972; No; Los Angeles; Los Angeles; Cal.; Yes; AI. 3310/Id. 529

~~N.E.; Eunice; F; unk.; M; Wife; --~~; Yes; AI./Id.

3982; Eula; F; 5; Maricopa; F; S; Dau.; 3973; No; Los Angeles; Los Angeles; Cal.; Yes; AI./Id. 588

TASQUINTH

3983; Jose; M; 34; Pima; F; M; Head; 3974; Yes; Yes; AI. 3313/Id. 6065

3984; Liberia; F; Unk.; Papago; F; M; Wife; 3975; Yes; Yes; AI./Id. 6066

3985; Mabel; F; 7; Pima-Papago; F; S; Dau.; 3976; Yes; Yes; AI./Id. 6067

3986; Edward; M; 5; Pima-Papago; F; S; Son; 3977; Yes; Yes; AI./Id. 6068

TASQUINTH

3987; Nellie; F; 31; Pima; F; M; Alone; 3978; No; Canton Indian ~~Hospital~~ Asylum; ~~Canton; S.R.~~ Yes; AI. 3314/Id. 1616

TASQUINTH

3988; Raymond; M; 49; Maricopa; F; M; Head; 3979; Yes; Yes; AI. 3307/Id. 532

3989; Lawrence; M; 19; Maricopa; F; S; Son; 3980; Yes; Yes; AI. 4445/Id. 533

TAWTOPS

3990; Juanna C., (Cheerless, Juanna); F; 71; Pima; F; Wd.; Head; 3981; Yes; Yes; AI. 2618/Id. 7004

TAYLOR

3991; Edith E., (Evans, Edith); F; 27; Pima; F; M; Wife; 3982; No; Phoenix Salt River Res.; ~~Scottsdale Maricopa Ariz.~~; Yes; AI. 466/Id. 5064

TAYLOR

3992; Joseph; M; 46; Pima; F; M; Head; 3983; Yes; Yes; AI. 2572/Id. 6837

TEJANE

3993; Margaret J.; F; 24; Pima; F; Wd.; Head; 3984; Yes; Yes; AI. 2007/Id. 4384

Census of the **Gila River** reservation of the **Pima Agency** jurisdiction; as of **April 1** ; 1932; taken by **A. H. Kneale** ; Superintendent.

Key: Number; Surname; Given; Sex (M/F); Age at Last Birthday; Tribe; Degree of Blood (F=Full); Marital Status; Relationship to Head of Family & Last Census No; At Jurisdiction Where Enrolled (Yes/No); (If no – Where); Ward (Yes/No); Allotment Annuity and/or Identification Numbers

TERRY

3994; Daniel; M; 52; Pima; F; M; Head; 3985; Yes; Yes; AI. 324/Id. 5201

3995; Sava M., (Malie, Sava); F; 47; Pima; F; M; Wife; 3986; Yes; Yes; AI. 325/Id. 5202

3996; Elizabeth; F; 21; Pima; F; S; Dau.; 3988; Yes; Yes; AI. 670/Id. 5203

3997; Isabelle; F; 13; Pima; F; S; Dau.; 3989; Yes; Yes; AI. 4806/Id. 5204

TERRY

3998; Henry; M; 24; Pima; F; M; Head; 3987; Yes; Yes; AI. 667/Id. 6069

N.E.; Edith, ~~(Manuel, Edith); F; unk.; Pima; F; M; Wife; --; Salt River Allottee.~~; Yes; AI. 473/Id.

3999; Wilma; F; unk.; Pima; F; S; Dau.; --; Yes; Yes; AI./Id.

TERRY

4000; Medasta; M; 27; Pima; F; S; Head; 3990; Yes; Yes; AI. 666/Id. 5205

TERRY

4001; Hiram; M; 64; Pima; F; M; Head; 3991; Yes; Yes; AI. 313/Id. 5307

4002; Alice; F; 64; Pima; F; M; Wife; 3992; Yes; Yes; AI. 314/Id. 5308

TERRY

4003; Kisto; M; 82; Pima; F; Wd.; Head; 3993; Yes; Yes; AI. 302/Id. 5328

TERRY

4004; Manuel; M; 36; Pima; F; M; Head; 3994; Yes; Yes; AI. 754/Id. 5256

4005; Ameilia, (Miguel, Amelia Jones); F; 32; Pima; F; M; Wife; 3995; Yes; Yes; AI. 511/Id. 5257

4006; Irene; F; 15; Pima; F; S; Dau.; 3996; Yes; Yes; AI. 3624/Id. 5258

4007; May; F; 14; Pima; F; S; Dau.; 3997; Yes; Yes; AI. 3625/Id. 5259

4008; Joe; M; 12; Pima; F; S; Son; 3998; Yes; Yes; AI. 4604/Id. 5260

4009; Harry; M; 9; Pima; F; S; Son; 3999; Yes; Yes; AI./Id. 5261

4010; Kenneth; M; 5; Pima; F; S; Son; 4000; Yes; Yes; AI./Id. 5262

TERRY

4011; Mary V.; F; 33; Pima; F; Wd.; Head; 4001; Yes; Yes; AI. 4498/Id. 6070

4012; Tomasa; F; 12; Pima; F; S; Dau.; 4002; Yes; Yes; AI./Id. 6071

4013; Rown; M; 10; Pima; F; S; Son; 4003; Yes; Yes; AI./Id. 6072

TERRY

4014; Miles; M; 25; Pima; F; M; Head; 4004; Yes; Yes; AI. 315/Id. 5848

4015; Delbert; M; 3; Pima; F; S; Son; 4005; Yes; Yes; AI./Id. 5849

TERRY

4016; Katherine; F; 23; Pima; F; Wd.; Head; 4006; Yes; Yes; AI. 4532/Id. 1413

Census of the **Gila River** reservation of the **Pima Agency** jurisdiction; as of **April 1** ; 1932; taken by **A. H. Kneale** ; Superintendent.

Key: Number; Surname; Given; Sex (M/F); Age at Last Birthday; Tribe; Degree of Blood (F=Full); Marital Status; Relationship to Head of Family & Last Census No; At Jurisdiction Where Enrolled (Yes/No); (If no – Where); Ward (Yes/No); Allotment Annuity and/or Identification Numbers

TERRY

4017; William; M; 62; Pima; F; M; Head; 4007; Yes; Yes; AI. 3590/Id. 1414
4018; Nellie; F; 50; Pima; F; M; Wife; 4008; Yes; Yes; AI. 3591/Id. 1415
4019; Rufus; M; 5; Pima; F; S; Son; 4009; Yes; Yes; AI./Id. 1416

THOMAS

4020; Alice; F; 67; Pima; F; Wd.; Head; 4010; Yes; Yes; AI. 2966/Id. 3177

THOMAS

4021; Anton; M; 32; Pima; F; M; Head; 4011; Yes; Yes; AI. 529/Id. 4931
4022; Mabel, (Paul, Mabel); F; 26; Pima; F; M; Wife; 4012; Yes; Yes; AI. 952/Id. 4932
4023; Margaret; F; 13; Pima; F; S; Dau.; 4013; Yes; Yes; AI./Id. 4933
4024; Steven; M; 8; Pima; F; S; Son; 4014; Yes; Yes; AI./Id. 4934
4025; Robert; M; 5; Pima; F; S; Son; 4015; Yes; Yes; AI./Id. 4935
4026; Buck; M; 2; Pima; F; S; Son; 4016; Yes; Yes; AI./Id. 5804

THOMAS

4027; Edward; M; 77; Pima; F; M; Head; 4017; Yes; Yes; AI. 308/Id. 5288
4028; Isabelle; F; 61; Pima; F; M; Wife; 4018; Yes; Yes; AI. 309/Id. 5289

THOMAS

4029; Childis; F; 36; Pima; F; M; Wife; 4019; No; Unk.; Unk.; Unk.; Yes; AI./Id. 7260
4030; Genevieve; F; 19; Pima; F; S; Dau.; 4020; Yes; Yes; AI./Id. 7261
4031; Rema; F; 15; Pima; F; S; Dau.; 4021; Yes; Yes; AI./Id. 7262

THOMAS

4032; Henry; M; 48; Pima; F; M; Head; 4022; Yes; Yes; AI. 2539/Id. 6520
4033; May; F; 44; Pima; F; M; Wife; 4023; Yes; Yes; AI. 2540/Id. 6521
4034; Selma; F; 16; Pima; F; S; Dau.; 4024; Yes; Yes; AI. 3316/Id. 6522
4035; Arthur; M; 13; Pima; F; S; Son; 4025; Yes; Yes; AI. 4613/Id. 6523
4036; Deborah; F; 11; Pima; F; S; Dau.; 4026; Yes; Yes; AI./Id. 6524

THOMAS

4037; Henry; M; 59; Pima; F; M; Head; 4027; Yes; Yes; AI. 4181/Id. 1343

THOMAS

4038; Jackson; M; 45; Pima; F; M; Head; 4028; Yes; Yes; AI. 1027/Id. 6510
4039; Elma; F; 43; Pima; F; M; Wife; 4029; Yes; Yes; AI. 2592/Id. 6511
4040; Ruth; F; 14; Pima; F; S; Dau.; 4030; Yes; Yes; AI. 3813/Id. 6512
4041; Jackson Jr.; M; 11; Pima; F; S; Son; 4031; Yes; Yes; AI./Id. 6513

THOMAS

4042; James; M; 62; Maricopa; F; Wd.; Head; 4032; Yes; Yes; AI. 4168/Id. 410

Census of the **Gila River** reservation of the **Pima Agency** jurisdiction; as of **April 1** ; 1932; taken by **A. H. Kneale** ; Superintendent.

Key: Number; Surname; Given; Sex (M/F); Age at Last Birthday; Tribe; Degree of Blood (F=Full); Marital Status; Relationship to Head of Family & Last Census No; At Jurisdiction Where Enrolled (Yes/No); (If no – Where); Ward (Yes/No); Allotment Annuity and/or Identification Numbers

THOMAS
4043; Joe; M; 62; Pima; F; Wd.; Head; 4033; Yes; Yes; AI. 1364/Id. 4795

THOMAS
4044; John; M; 44; Pima; F; Wd.; Head; 4034; Yes; Yes; AI. 257/Id.
5035; ~~Nellie W., (Wellington, Nellie); F; 57; Pima; F; M; Wife; 4035; Died.; 11-5-31.;~~
Yes; AI. 1710/Id. 5036

THOMAS
4045; John; M; 64; Pima; F; Wd.; Head; 4036; Yes; Yes; AI. 1173/Id. 6528

THOMAS
4046; John; M; 47; Pima; F; M; Head; 4037; Yes; Yes; AI. 2153/Id. 3314
4047; Elena; F; 47; Pima; F; M; Wife; 4038; Yes; Yes; AI. 2154/Id. 3315
4048; Ramon; M; 30; Pima; F; S; Son; 4039; Yes; Yes; AI. 4279/Id. 3316
4049; Clara; F; 19; Pima; F; S; Dau.; 4040; Yes; Yes; AI. 2157/Id. 3317
4050; Luke; M; 18; Pima; F; S; Son; 4041; Yes; Yes; AI. 2158/Id. 3318
4051; Josephine; F; 16; Pima; F; S; Dau.; 4042; Yes; Yes; AI. 3234/Id. 3319
4052; Norpert; M; 14; Pima; F; S; Son; 4043; Yes; Yes; AI. 4526/Id. 3320
4053; Talestine; M; 12; Pima; F; S; Son; 4044; Yes; Yes; AI. 2890/Id. 3321
4054; Isabelle; F; 9; Pima; F; S; Dau.; 4045; Yes; Yes; AI./Id. 3322
4055; Leo; M; 7; Pima; F; S; Son; 4046; Yes; Yes; AI./Id. 3323

THOMAS
4056; James; M; 69; Maricopa; F; M; Head; 4047; Yes; Yes; AI. 2745/Id. 104
4057; Martha; F; 67; Maricopa; F; M; Wife; 4048; Yes; Yes; AI. 2746/Id. 105
4058; Wilfred; M; 14; Maricopa; F; S; Gr.son; 4049; Yes; Yes; AI. 3338/Id. 106
4059; Leslie; M; 12; Maricopa; F; S; Gr.son; 4050; Yes; Yes; AI. 3635/Id. 107

THOMAS
4060; Melissa, (Pablo, Mallissa); F; 33; Pima; F; M; Wife; 4051; Yes; Yes;
AI. 1761/Id. 3990
4061; Joseph; M; 18; Pima; F; S; Son; 4052; Yes; Yes; AI. 4381/Id. 3989
4062; Carmela; F; 12; Pima; F; S; Dau.; 4053; Yes; Yes; AI./Id. 3988

THOMAS
4063; Jose; M; 62; Pima; F; M; Head; 4054; Yes; Yes; AI. 4195/Id. 1688
4064; Manuella; F; 60; Pima; F; M; Wife; 4055; Yes; Yes; AI. 4196/Id. 1687
4065; Simon; M; 24; Pima; F; S; Son; 4056; Yes; Yes; AI. 4198/Id. 1689

THOMAS
4066; Jose Jr.; M; 38; Pima; F; M; Head; 4057; Yes; Yes; AI. 4199/Id. 1690
4067; Josephine, (Kirk, Josephine); F; 32; Pima; F; M; Wife; 4058; Yes; Yes;
AI. 4163/Id. 1691
4068; Jerome; M; 8; Pima; F; S; Son; 4059; Yes; Yes; AI./Id. 1692

Census of the **Gila River** reservation of the **Pima Agency** jurisdiction; as of **April 1** ; 1932; taken by **A. H. Kneale** ; Superintendent.

Key: Number; Surname; Given; Sex (M/F); Age at Last Birthday; Tribe; Degree of Blood (F=Full); Marital Status; Relationship to Head of Family & Last Census No; At Jurisdiction Where Enrolled (Yes/No); (If no – Where); Ward (Yes/No); Allotment Annuity and/or Identification Numbers

4069; Mary B.; F; 5; Pima; F; S; Dau.; 4060; Yes; Yes; AI./Id. 1693

THOMAS

4070; Beulah P., (Peters, Beulah); F; 30; Pima; F; M; Wife; 4061; Yes; Yes; AI. 4438/Id. 2020

4071; Betty A.; F; 6; Pima; F; S; Dau.; 4062; Yes; Yes; AI./Id. 2021

4072; Donald; M; 5; Pima; F; S; Son; 4063; Yes; Yes; AI./Id. 2022

THOMAS

4073; Juan; M; 53; Pima; F; Wd.; Head; 4064; Yes; Yes; AI. 330/Id. 4930

4074; Martina; F; 18; Pima; F; S; Dau.; 4065; Yes; Yes; AI. 334/Id. 6073

THOMAS

4075; Juan; M; 63; Pima; F; M; Head; 4066; Yes; Yes; AI. 1753/Id. 1792

4076; Laura; F; 35; Pima; F; M; Wife; 4067; Yes; Yes; AI. 1754/Id. 1793

4077; Ruth; F; 18; Pima; F; S; Dau.; 4068; Yes; Yes; AI. 2492/Id. 1794

4078; Joseph; M; 13; Pima; F; S; Son; 4069; Yes; Yes; AI. 4569/Id. 1795

4079; Petra; F; 6; Pima; F; S; Dau.; 4070; Yes; Yes; AI./Id. 1796

THOMAS

4080; Juan A.; M; 51; Pima; F; M; Head; 4071; Yes; Yes; AI. 1033/Id. 6562

4081; Louise; F; 52; Pima; F; M; Wife; 4072; Yes; Yes; AI. 1034/Id. 6563

4082; Fred; M; 24; Pima; F; S; Son; 4073; Yes; Yes; AI. 1039/Id. 6564

4083; Dewitt; M; 23; Pima; F; S; Son; 4074; Yes; Yes; AI. 1040/Id. 6565

4084; Elsie; F; 18; Pima; F; S; Dau.; 4075; Yes; Yes; AI. 2569/Id. 6566

THOMAS

4085; Jose; M; 20; Pima; F; M; Head; 4076; Yes; Yes; AI. 1344/Id. 5699

4086; Germane, (Burnette, Germane); F; 18; Pima; F; M; Wife; 4077; Yes; Yes; AI. 4698/Id. 5730

THOMAS

4087; Juanna J., (Jackson, Juanna); F; 32; Pima; F; Wd.; Head; 4078; Yes; Yes; AI. 1577/Id. 4781

THOMAS

4088; Kisto; M; 49; Pima; F; M; Head; 4079; Yes; Yes; AI. 1341/Id. 5697

4089; Maria; F; 53; Pima; F; M; Wife; 4080; Yes; Yes; AI. 1342/Id. 5698

4090; Joshua; M; 25; Pima; F; S; Son; 4081; Yes; Yes; AI. 1346/Id. 5701

THOMAS

4091; Kisto; M; 49; Pima; F; M; Head; 4082; Yes; Yes; AI. 1612/Id. 7034

4092; Elizabeth Maria; F; 47; Pima; F; M; Wife; 4083; Yes; Yes; AI. 1613/Id. 7035

Census of the **Gila River** reservation of the **Pima Agency** jurisdiction; as of **April 1** ; 1932; taken by **A. H. Kneale** ; Superintendent.

Key: Number; Surname; Given; Sex (M/F); Age at Last Birthday; Tribe; Degree of Blood (F=Full); Marital Status; Relationship to Head of Family & Last Census No; At Jurisdiction Where Enrolled (Yes/No); (If no – Where); Ward (Yes/No); Allotment Annuity and/or Identification Numbers

THOMAS
4093; Lewis; M; 25; Pima; F; M; Head; 4084; Yes; Yes; AI. 332/Id. 5617
4094; Martha D., (Davis, Martha); F; 30; Pima; F; M; Wife; 4085; Yes; Yes; AI. 199/Id. 5618
4095; Deleon; M; 6; Pima; F; S; Son; 4086; Yes; Yes; AI./Id. 5619
4096; George K.; M; 4; Pima; F; S; Son; 4087; Yes; Yes; AI./Id. 5620

THOMAS
4097; Lewis; M; 42; Pima; F; M; Head; 4088; Yes; Yes; AI. 1780/Id. 4704
4098; Mary; F; 40; Pima; F; M; Wife; 4089; Yes; Yes; AI. 1781/Id. 4705
4099; James L.; M; 19; Pima; F; S; Son; 4090; Yes; Yes; AI. 1782/Id. 4706
4100; Vincent; M; 13; Pima; F; S; Son; 4091; Yes; Yes; AI. 4561/Id. 4707
4101; Agatha; F; 11; Pima; F; S; Dau.; 4092; Yes; Yes; AI./Id. 4708
4102; Elizabeth; F; 7; Pima; F; S; Dau.; 4093; Yes; Yes; AI./Id. 4709

THOMAS
4103; Louis; M; 32; Pima; F; M; Head; 4094; Yes; Yes; AI./Id. 7042
4104; Lucia L.; F; 27; Pima; F; M; Wife; 4095; Yes; Yes; AI./Id. 7043
4105; Frederick; M; 8; Pima; F; S; Son; 4096; Yes; Yes; AI./Id. 7044
4106; Albina; F; 6; Pima; F; S; Dau.; 4097; Yes; Yes; AI./Id. 7045
4107; Rebecca; F; 3; Pima; F; S; Dau.; 4098; Yes; Yes; AI./Id. 5852

THOMAS
4108; Mary; F; 72; Pima; F; Wd.; Head; 4099; Yes; Yes; AI. 1026/Id. 6588

THOMAS
4109; Manuel; M; 33; Pima; F; M; Head; 4100; Yes; Yes; AI. 694/Id. 5290
4110; Juanna P., (Percy, Juanna); F; 30; Pima; F; M; Wife; 4101; Yes; Yes; AI. 347/Id. 5291
4111; Philip; M; 17; Pima; F; S; Son; 4102; Yes; Yes; AI. 3627/Id. 5292
4112; Paul; M; 15; Pima; F; S; Son; 4103; Yes; Yes; AI. 4651/Id. 5293
4113; Margaret; F; 12; Pima; F; S; Dau.; 4104; Yes; Yes; AI. 453/Id. 5294
4114; George; M; 9; Pima; F; S; Son; 4105; Yes; Yes; AI./Id. 5295
4115; Rita; F; 4; Pima; F; S; Dau.; 4106; Yes; Yes; AI./Id. 5297

THOMAS
4116; Pablo; M; 48; Maricopa; F; M; Head; 4107; Yes; Yes; AI. 4175/Id. 376
4117; Anna; F; 47; Maricopa; F; M; Wife; 4108; Yes; Yes; AI. 4176/Id. 377
4118; Erile; F; 24; Maricopa; F; S; Dau.; 4109; Yes; Yes; AI. 4177/Id. 378
4119; Matilda; F; 18; Maricopa; F; S; Dau.; 4110; Yes; Yes; AI. 4178/Id. 379
4120; Flora; F; 15; Maricopa; F; S; Dau.; 4111; Yes; Yes; AI. 4180/Id. 380
4121; Nellie V.; F; 14; Maricopa; F; S; Dau.; 4112; Yes; Yes; AI. 4179/Id. 381
4122; Anita; F; 13; Maricopa; F; S; Dau.; 4113; Yes; Yes; AI. 4600/Id. 382
4123; Coit; M; 10; Maricopa; F; S; Son; 4114; Yes; Yes; AI./Id. 383
4124; Eulata; F; 9; Maricopa; F; S; Dau.; 4115; Yes; Yes; AI./Id. 384

Census of the **Gila River** reservation of the **Pima Agency** jurisdiction; as of **April 1** ; 1932; taken by **A. H. Kneale** ; Superintendent.

Key: Number; Surname; Given; Sex (M/F); Age at Last Birthday; Tribe; Degree of Blood (F=Full); Marital Status; Relationship to Head of Family & Last Census No; At Jurisdiction Where Enrolled (Yes/No); (If no – Where); Ward (Yes/No); Allotment Annuity and/or Identification Numbers

4125; Daniel; M; 2; Maricopa; F; S; Son; 4116; Yes; Yes; AI./Id. 568

THOMAS
4126; Peter; M; 33; Pima; F; S; Head; 4117; Yes; Yes; AI. 737/Id. 4977

THOMAS
4127; Peter; M; 42; Pima; F; M; Head; 4118; Yes; Yes; AI. 1178/Id. 6535
4128; Elva H., (Hayes, Elva); F; 46; Pima; F; M; Wife; 4119; Yes; Yes; AI. 1446/Id. 6536
4129; Lonella; F; 8; Pima; F; S; Dau.; 4120; Yes; Yes; AI./Id. 6537
4130; Harold; M; 5; Pima; F; S; Son; 4121; Yes; Yes; AI./Id. 6538
4131; Hayes; Irene; F; 21; Pima; F; S; St.dau.; 4122; Yes; Yes; AI. 1447/Id. 6818
4132; Hayes; Florence; F; 18; Pima; F; S; St.dau.; 4123; Yes; Yes; AI. 3188/Id. 6820

THOMAS
4133; Peter; M; 25; Pima; F; M; Head; 4124; Yes; Yes; AI. 2155/Id. 3170
4134; Lucy; F; 40; Pima; F; M; Wife; 4125; Yes; Yes; AI. 2241/Id. 3171
4135; Irene; F; 20; Pima; F; S; St.dau.; 4126; Yes; Yes; AI. 2967/Id. 3172
4136; Marion; F; 18; Pima; F; S; St.dau.; 4127; Yes; Yes; AI. 2242/Id. 3173
4137; Samuel; M; 15; Pima; F; S; St.son; 4128; Yes; Yes; AI. 3324/Id. 3174
4138; Arthur; M; 12; Pima; F; S; St.son; 4129; Yes; Yes; AI. 4713/Id. 3175
4139; Roy; M; 9; Pima; F; S; Son; 4130; Yes; Yes; AI./Id. 3176
4140; Geraldine; F; 2; Pima; F; S; Dau.; 4131; Yes; Yes; AI./Id. 3588
4141; Charlotte; F; 2; Pima; F; S; Dau.; 4132; Yes; Yes; AI./Id. 3589

THOMAS
4142; Ramon; M; 43; Papago; F; M; Head; 4133; Yes; Yes; AI. 4279/Id. 1436
4143; Molly A., (Sancelo, Molly Ann); F; 36; Pima; F; M; Wife; 4134; Yes; Yes; AI. 4217/Id. 1437
4144; Mary B.; F; 14; Pima-Papago; F; S; Dau.; 4135; Yes; Yes; AI./Id. 1438
4145; Carmelita; F; 12; Pima-Papago; F; S; Dau.; 4136; Yes; Yes; AI./Id. 1439
4146; Hilda; F; 6; Pima-Papago; F; S; Dau.; 4137; Yes; Yes; AI./Id. 1440
4147; Francis J.; M; 1; Pima[sic]; F; S; Son; 4138; Yes; Yes; AI./Id. 2035

THOMAS
4148; Saline; M; 70; Pima; F; Wd.; Head; 4139; Yes; Yes; AI. 2491/Id. 5073

THOMAS
~~Thomas; M; 80; Pima; F; Wd.; Head; 4140; Yes; Died summer 1931; and heretofore not reported.~~; Yes; AI. 4154/Id. 2023

THOMAS
4149; William; M; 49; Maricopa; F; M; Head; 4141; Yes; Yes; AI. 4170/Id. 403
4150; Luella; F; 45; Maricopa; F; M; Wife; 4142; Yes; Yes; AI. 4171/Id. 404
4151; Stephen; M; 20; Maricopa; F; S; Son; 4143; Yes; Yes; AI. 4172/Id. 405

Census of the **Gila River** reservation of the **Pima Agency** jurisdiction; as of **April 1** ; 1932; taken by **A. H. Kneale** ; Superintendent.

Key: Number; Surname; Given; Sex (M/F); Age at Last Birthday; Tribe; Degree of Blood (F=Full); Marital Status; Relationship to Head of Family & Last Census No; At Jurisdiction Where Enrolled (Yes/No); (If no – Where); Ward (Yes/No); Allotment Annuity and/or Identification Numbers

4152; Daniel; M; 16; Maricopa; F; S; Son; 4144; Yes; Yes; AI. 4173/Id. 406
4153; Lena; F; 14; Maricopa; F; S; Dau.; 4145; Yes; Yes; AI. 4174/Id. 407
4154; Mary R.; F; 11; Maricopa; F; S; Dau.; 4146; Yes; Yes; AI./Id. 587
4155; Laura; F; 9; Maricopa; F; S; Dau.; 4147; Yes; Yes; AI./Id. 408
4156; Leonard; M; 4; Maricopa; F; S; Son; 4148; Yes; Yes; AI./Id. 409

THOMAS

4157; Vavages; M; 33; Pima; F; M; Head; 4149; Yes; Yes; AI. 4197/Id. 1873
4158; Lizzie, (Wade, Lizzie); F; 25; Pima; F; M; Wife; 4150; Yes; Yes; AI. 3749/Id. 1874
4159; Richard; M; 7; Pima; F; S; Son; 4151; Yes; Yes; AI./Id. 1875
4160; Tom; M; 5; Pima; F; S; Son; 4152; Yes; Yes; AI./Id. 1876

THOMPSON

4161; Benjamin; M; 83; Pima; F; M; Head; 4153; Yes; Yes; AI. 2968/Id. 3371
4162; Ella; F; 81; Pima; F; M; Wife; 4154; Yes; Yes; AI. 2969/Id. 3371

THOMPSON

4163; Nellie J., (Jones, Nellie); F; 27; Pima; F; Wd.; Head; 4155; Yes; Yes; AI. 150/Id. 5421
4164; Lawrence; M; 8; Pima; F; S; Son; 4156; Yes; Yes; AI./Id. 5422
4165; Jose; M; 6; Pima; F; S; Son; 4157; Yes; Yes; AI./Id. 6074
4166; Thomas; M; 1; Pima; F; S; Son; 4158; Yes; Yes; AI./Id. 3979

THOMPSON

4167; Francisco; M; 74; Pima; F; M; Head; 4159; Yes; Yes; AI. 4356/Id. 6075
4168; Juana R., (Rose, Juana); F; 66; Pima; F; M; Wife; 4160; Yes; Yes; AI. 4357/Id. 6076

THOMPSON

4169; James; M; 32; Pima; F; M; Head; 4161; Yes; Yes; AI. 1055/Id. 6599

THOMPSON

4170; Joseph; M; 62; Pima; F; M; Head; 4162; Yes; Yes; AI. 3505/Id. 1462
4171; Jessie; F; 57; Pima; F; M; Wife; Head; 4163; Yes; Yes; AI. 3506/Id. 1463
4172; Raymond; M; 17; Pima; F; S; Son; 4164; Yes; Yes; AI. 3511/Id. 1464
4173; Ivan; M; 10; Pima; F; S; Son; 4165; Yes; Yes; AI./Id. 1466

THOMPSON

4174; Leslie; M; 29; Pima; F; M; Head; 4166; Yes; Yes; AI. 3509/Id. 5061
4175; Flora E., (Evans, Flora); F; 29; Pima; F; M; Wife; 4167; Yes; Yes; AI. 467/Id. 5059
4176; Marian L.; F; 5; Pima; F; S; Dau.; 4168; Yes; Yes; AI./Id. 5060
4177; Eula; F; 2; Pima; F; S; Dau.; 4169; Yes; Yes; AI./Id. 1891
4178; Flora; F; 5/12; Pima; F; S; Dau.; --; Yes; ~~Born.; 1-6-32.~~; Yes; AI./Id. 6135

Census of the **Gila River** reservation of the **Pima Agency** jurisdiction; as of **April 1** ; 1932; taken by **A. H. Kneale** ; Superintendent.

Key: Number; Surname; Given; Sex (M/F); Age at Last Birthday; Tribe; Degree of Blood (F=Full); Marital Status; Relationship to Head of Family & Last Census No; At Jurisdiction Where Enrolled (Yes/No); (If no – Where); Ward (Yes/No); Allotment Annuity and/or Identification Numbers

THOMPSON
4179; Luke; M; 46; Pima; F; M; Head; 4170; Yes; Yes; AI. 87/Id. 5550
4180; Edith J., (Juan, Edith); F; 46; Pima; F; M; Wife; 4171; Yes; Yes; AI. 56/Id. 5334
4181; Boyd; M; 18; Pima; F; S; Son; 4172; Yes; Yes; AI. 1930/Id. 5551
4182; Uretta; F; 12; Pima; F; S; Dau.; 4173; Yes; Yes; AI. 4844/Id. 5552
4183; Lois; F; 10; Pima; F; S; Gr.dau.; 4174; Yes; Yes; AI./Id. 5553
4184; Rosa J.; F; 16; Pima; F; S; St.dau.; 4175; Yes; Yes; AI./Id. 5555
4185; Dorothy E.; F; 14; Pima; F; S; St.dau.; 4176; Yes; Yes; AI./Id. 5556

THOMPSON
4186; Wilbur; M; 26; Pima; F; M; Head; --; Yes; ~~Inadvertedly~~[sic] ~~left off 1930 and 1931 Census.~~; Yes; AI. 3510/Id. 1464
4187; Nina, (Susanna, Nina); F; 17; Pima; F; M; Wife; 3959; Yes; Yes; AI. 4322/Id. 1473
4188; Wilda Lovena; F; 4/12; Pima; F; S; Dau.; --; Yes; ~~Born.; 12-7-31.~~; Yes; AI./Id. 2056

THOMPSON
4189; Wilson; M; 32; Pima; F; M; Head; 4177; Yes; Yes; AI. 3508/Id. 1460
4190; Cheerless, (Manuel, Cheerless); F; 28; Pima; F; M; Wife; 4178; Yes; Yes; AI. 3987/Id. 1461

TOMASSA
4191; Fred; M; 46; Pima; F; M; Head; 4179; Yes; Yes; AI. 3830/Id. 1528
4192; Minnie; F; 45; Pima; F; M; Wife; 4180; Yes; Yes; AI. 3831/Id. 1529
4193; Raline; F; 6; Pima; F; S; Cousin; 4181; Yes; Yes; AI./Id. 2025

TOMASSA
4194; Juanna L.; F; 67; Pima; F; Wd.; Head; 4182; Yes; Yes; AI. 3679/Id. 1469

TOM
4195; Lena; F; 72; Pima; F; Wd.; Head; 4183; Yes; Yes; AI./Id. 1487

TROWELL
4196; Elizabeth, (Nolan, Elizabeth); F; 32; Pima; F; M; Wife; 4184; Yes; Yes; AI. 4032/Id. 2024

TURNER
4197; Emily; F; 57; Pima; F; Wd.; Head; 4185; Yes; Yes; AI. 93/Id. 5631
4198; Mark; M; 25; Pima; F; S; Son; 4186; Yes; Yes; AI. 94/Id. 5632
4199; Albert; M; 20; Pima; F; S; Son; 4187; Yes; Yes; AI. 519/Id. 5633
4200; Sarah; F; 14; Pima; F; S; Dau.; 4188; Yes; Yes; AI. 4728/Id. 5634

Key: Number; Surname; Given; Sex (M/F); Age at Last Birthday; Tribe; Degree of Blood (F=Full);
Marital Status; Relationship to Head of Family & Last Census No; At Jurisdiction Where Enrolled
(Yes/No); (If no – Where); Ward (Yes/No); Allotment Annuity and/or Identification Numbers

TURNER

4201; Philip; M; 29; Pima; F; S; Head; 4189; Yes; Yes; AI. 81/Id. 5448

VALENCIA

4202; Degratia; M; 24; Pima; F; S; Head; 4190; Yes; Yes; AI. 4496/Id. 6077
4203; Jesus; M; 27; Pima; F; S; Bro.; 4191; Yes; Yes; AI. 4501/Id. 6078
4204; Jaun[sic]; M; 35; Pima; F; S; Bro.; 4192; Yes; Yes; AI. 4497/Id. 6079

VALENCIA

4205; Miguel; M; 30; Pima; F; S; Head; 4193; Yes; Yes; AI. 4499/Id. 6080
4206; Pablo; M; 29; Pima; F; S; Bro.; 4194; Yes; Yes; AI. 4500/Id. 6081

VANICO

4207; James; M; 99; Maricopa; F; Wd.; Head; 4195; Yes; Yes; AI. 4112/Id. 519

VAVAGES

4208; Anton; M; 26; Pima; F; M; Head; 4196; Yes; Yes; AI. 1378/Id. 6878
4209; Lottie L., (Liston, Lottie); F; 28; Pima; F; M; Wife; 4197; Yes; Yes;
AI. 1030/Id. 6879
4210; Elma; F; 5; Pima; F; S; Dau.; 4198; Yes; Yes; AI./Id. 6880
4211; Leonard; M; 3; Pima; F; S; Son; 4199; Yes; Yes; AI./Id. 7263

VAVAGES

4212; Augustine; M; 61; Pima; F; M; Head; 4200; Yes; Yes; AI. 3876/Id. 1723
4213; Lucy Ann; F; 60; Pima; F; M; Wife; 4201; Yes; Yes; AI. 3877/Id. 1724

VAVAGES

4214; Clement; M; 31; Pima; F; S; Head; 4202; Yes; Yes; AI. 3879/Id. 1726

VAVAGES

4215; Frances; M; 25; Pima; F; M; Head; 4203; Yes; Yes; AI. 311/Id. 4198
N.E.; Lena, (Montgomery, ~~Lena); F; 22; Mojave; F; M; Wife; –; Mojave allottee~~;
Yes; AI./Id.
4216; Blanche; F; 5; Pima-Mojave; F; S; Dau.; 4204; Yes; Yes; AI./Id. 4196
4217; Lena; F; 4; Pima-Mojave; F; S; Dau.; 4205; Yes; Yes; AI./Id. 4195
4218; Marjorie Janne[sic]; F; 7/12; Pima-Mojave; F; S; Dau.; --; Yes; ~~Born.; 9-24-31.~~;
Yes; AI./Id. 3937

VAVAGES

4219; Jose; M; 57; Pima; F; M; Head; 4206; Yes; Yes; AI. 1373/Id. 6881
4220; Josepha; F; 67; Pima; F; M; Wife; 4207; Yes; Yes; AI. 1374/Id. 6882
4221; Andrew; M; 25; Pima; F; S; Son; 4208; Yes; Yes; AI. 1377/Id. 6883
4222; Laura; F; 11; Pima; F; S; St.dau.; 4209; Yes; Yes; AI. 4789/Id. 4694

Census of the **Gila River** reservation of the **Pima Agency** jurisdiction; as of **April 1** ; 1932; taken by **A. H. Kneale** ; Superintendent.

Key: Number; Surname; Given; Sex (M/F); Age at Last Birthday; Tribe; Degree of Blood (F=Full); Marital Status; Relationship to Head of Family & Last Census No; At Jurisdiction Where Enrolled (Yes/No); (If no – Where); Ward (Yes/No); Allotment Annuity and/or Identification Numbers

VAVAGES

4223; Isaac; M; 45; Pima; F; M; Head; 4210; Yes; Yes; AI. 1527/Id. 6899
4224; Letta; F; 44; Pima; F; M; Wife; 4211; Yes; Yes; AI. 1528/Id. 6900
~~Emma; F; 25; Pima; F; S; Dau.; 4212; Yes; Married to Tony Hendricks~~; Yes; AI. 1530/Id. 6907
4225; Nona; F; 21; Pima; F; S; Dau.; 4213; Yes; Yes; AI. 1531/Id. 6901
4226; Laura; F; 17; Pima; F; S; Dau.; 4214; Yes; Yes; AI. 1552/Id. 6902
4227; Elizabeth; F; 16; Pima; F; S; Dau.; 4215; Yes; Yes; AI. 3177/Id. 6903
4228; George; M; 14; Pima; F; S; Son; 4216; Yes; Yes; AI. 4794/Id. 6904
4229; Victor; M; 10; Pima; F; S; Son; 4217; Yes; Yes; AI./Id. 6905
4230; Stephen; M; 4; Pima; F; S; Son; 4218; Yes; Yes; AI./Id. 6906

VAVAGES

4231; Jose J.; M; 47; Pima; F; M; Head; 4219; Yes; Yes; AI. 1853/Id. 4691
4232; Josepha O., (Osife, Josepha); F; 46; Pima; F; M; Wife; 4220; Yes; Yes; AI. 2361/Id. 4692

VAVAGES

4233; Jose P.; M; 31; Pima; F; S; Head; 4221; Yes; Yes; AI. 1856/Id. 4729

VAVAGES

4234; Juan; M; 67; Pima; F; M; Head; 4222; Yes; Yes; AI. 269/Id. 4784
4235; Milea; F; 67; Pima; F; M; Wife; 4223; Yes; Yes; AI. 270/Id. 4785
4236; Juan Jr.; M; 30; Pima; F; S; Son; 4224; Yes; Yes; AI. 744/Id. 4197

VAVAGES

4237; Juan; M; 57; Pima; F; M; Head; 4225; Yes; Yes; AI. 2384/Id. 5379
4238; Mary E., (Enos, Mary); F; 63; Pima; F; M; Wife; 4226; Yes; Yes; AI. 2480/Id. 5380
4239; Juan; M; 32; Pima; F; S; Son; 4227; Yes; Yes; AI./Id. 5381

VAVAGES

4240; Juan; M; 77; Pima; F; Wd.; Head; 4228; Yes; Yes; AI. 4339/Id. 6082

VAVAGES

4241; Juan; M; 51; Pima; F; M; Head; 4229; Yes; Yes; AI. 4687/Id. 5645
4242; Mollie E., (Enos, Mollie); F; 66; Pima; F; M; Wife; 4230; Yes; Yes; AI. 4688/Id. 3866

VAVAGES

4243; Lancisco; M; 35; Pima; F; M; Head; 4231; Yes; Yes; AI. 1855/Id. 4579
4244; Manuella, (Dixon, Manuella); F; 29; Pima; F; M; Wife; 4232; Yes; Yes; AI. 1998/Id. 4580
4245; Eleanor; F; 5; Pima; F; S; Dau.; 4233; Yes; Yes; AI./Id. 4581
4246; Dolores; F; 4; Pima; F; S; Dau.; 4234; Yes; Yes; AI./Id. 4582

177

Census of the **Gila River** reservation of the **Pima Agency** jurisdiction; as of **April 1** ; 1932; taken by **A. H. Kneale** ; Superintendent.

Key: Number; Surname; Given; Sex (M/F); Age at Last Birthday; Tribe; Degree of Blood (F=Full); Marital Status; Relationship to Head of Family & Last Census No; At Jurisdiction Where Enrolled (Yes/No); (If no – Where); Ward (Yes/No); Allotment Annuity and/or Identification Numbers

4247; Lancisco Jr.; M; 5/12; Pima; F; S; Son; --; Yes; Born.; 11-1-31.; Yes; AI./Id. 3938

VAVAGES
4248; Leo; M; 40; Papago; F; M; Head; 4235; Yes; Yes; AI. 200/Id. 5428

4249; Juanna R., (Ramirez, Juanna); F; 38; Papago; F; M; Wife; 4236; Yes; Yes; AI. 2435/Id. 5429

4250; Ambrose; M; 22; Papago; F; S; Son; 4237; Yes; Yes; AI. 219/Id. 5430

4251; Philllipi; F; 18; Papago; F; S; Dau.; 4238; Yes; Yes; AI. 4476/Id. 5431

4252; Andrew; M; 8; Pima[sic]; F; S; Son; 4239; Yes; Yes; AI./Id. 5432

4253; Susie; F; 6; Pima[sic]; F; S; Dau.; 4240; Yes; Yes; AI./Id. 5433

VAVAGES
4254; Liscia; F; 78; Pima; F; Wd.; Head; 4241; Yes; Yes; AI. 1085/Id. 6083

VAVAGES
4255; Martina; F; 54; Pima; F; Wd.; Head; 4242; Yes; Yes; AI. 3532/Id. 1705

4256; Anores; F; 15; Pima; F; S; Dau.; 4243; Yes; Yes; AI. 3535/Id. 1707

4257; Nelson; M; 20; Pima; F; S; Son; 4244; Yes; Yes; AI. 3533/Id. 1706

VAVAGES
4258; Samuel; M; 42; Pima; F; M; Head; 4245; Yes; Yes; AI.1854/Id. 4713

4259; Mary R., (Riggs, Mary); F; 34; Pima; F; M; Wife; 4246; Yes; Yes; AI. 1794/Id. 4714

VEST
N.E.; Fred; Maricopa; Head;

4260; Dora C., (Cyrus, Dora); F; 37; Pima; F; M; Wife; 4247; Yes; Yes; AI. 1205/Id. 6470

4261; Joan; F; 6; Pima-Maricopa; F; S; Dau.; 4248; Yes; Yes; AI./Id. 6471

4262; Ernest; M; 4; Pima-Maricopa; F; S; Son; 4249; Yes; Yes; AI./Id. 6472

4263; Carlton; M; 2; Pima-Maricopa; F; S; Son; 4250; Yes; Yes; AI./Id. 7171

VEST
4264; Annily Isk., (Isk, Annily Isabel Dora); F; 28; Maricopa; F; M; Wife; 4251; Yes; Yes; AI. 2751/Id. 589

VICTOR
4265; Cruz; M; 30; Pima; F; S; Head; 4252; Yes; Yes; AI. 3496/Id. 3591

VICTORIAN
~~Haven; M; 67; Pima; F; Wd.; Head; 4253; Died June 15; 1930; but heretofore not reported.~~; Yes; AI. 4155/Id. 1863

4266; Juan; M; 39; Pima; F; S; Son; 4254; Yes; Yes; AI. 4157/Id. 1864

Census of the **Gila River** reservation of the **Pima Agency** jurisdiction; as of **April 1** ; 1932; taken by **A. H. Kneale** ; Superintendent.

Key: Number; Surname; Given; Sex (M/F); Age at Last Birthday; Tribe; Degree of Blood (F=Full); Marital Status; Relationship to Head of Family & Last Census No; At Jurisdiction Where Enrolled (Yes/No); (If no – Where); Ward (Yes/No); Allotment Annuity and/or Identification Numbers

VICTORIAN

4267; Ramon; M; 49; Pima; F; M; Head; 4255; Yes; Yes; AI./Id. 1865
4268; Annie; F; 31; Pima; F; M; Wife; 4256; Yes; Yes; AI./Id. 1866
4269; Vincent; M; 14; Pima; F; S; Son; 4257; Yes; Yes; AI./Id. 1867
4270; Sebastian; M; 12; Pima; F; S; Son; 4258; Yes; Yes; AI./Id. 1868
4271; Julia; F; 9; Pima; F; S; Dau.; 4259; Yes; Yes; AI./Id. 1869
4272; Michael; M; 8; Pima; F; S; Son; 4260; Yes; Yes; AI./Id. 1870
4273; Edna; F; 7; Pima; F; S; Dau.; 4261; Yes; Yes; AI./Id. 1871
4274; Mathias; F; 4; Pima; F; S; Dau.; 4262; Yes; Yes; AI./Id. 1872

VICTORIAN

4275; Rosa R., (Radmoore, Rosa); F; 32; Pima; F; M; Wife; 4263; Yes; Yes; AI. 2663/Id. 3433

VILLA

4276; Juanna; F; 38; Pima; F; Wd.; Head; 4264; Yes; Yes; AI. 2085/Id. 3051
4277; Theresa; F; 19; Pima; 1/4x; S; Dau.; 4265; Yes; Yes; AI. 2086/Id. 3052
4278; John; M; 18; Pima; 1/4x; S; Son; 4266; Yes; Yes; AI. 2084/Id. 3053

VINCENT

4279; Ramon; M; 26; Pima; F; M; Head; 4267; Yes; Yes; AI. 1994/Id. 5074
4280; Annie J., (Justine, Annie); F; 25; Pima; F; M; Wife; 4268; Yes; Yes; AI. 4149/Id. 5075
4281; Clarence; M; 4; Pima; F; S; Son; 4269; Yes; Yes; AI./Id. 5076

VINCENT

4282; Chiago; M; 24; Pima; F; M; Head; 4270; Yes; Yes; AI. 995/Id. 6853
4283; Edith P., (Pratt, Edith); F; 23; Pima; F; M; Wife; 4271; Yes; Yes; AI. 4228/Id. 6854
4284; Lorene; F; 2; Pima; F; S; Dau.; 4272; Yes; Yes; AI./Id. 7070
4285; Pratt, Lucilla; F; 20; Pima; F; S; Sis-in-law.; 4273; Yes; Yes; AI. 4229/Id. 1783

VINCENT

4286; Sophia K., (Kipp, Sophia); F; 68; Pima; F; Wd.; Head; 4274; Yes; Yes; AI. 3976/Id. 2027

VINCENT

4287; Juanna; F; 54; Pima; F; Wd.; Head; 4275; Yes; Yes; AI. 3563/Id. 1361
4288; Joaquin, Lloyd; M; 17; Pima; F; S; Adpt.son; 4276; Yes; Yes; AI. 3561/Id. 1364
4289; Joaquin; Rosita; F; 12; Pima; F; S; Adpt.dau; 4277; Yes; Yes; AI./Id. 1365

VINCENT

4290; Encela; F; 36; Pima; F; S; Head; 4278; Yes; Yes; AI. 3564/Id. 1362

Census of the **Gila River** reservation of the **Pima Agency** jurisdiction; as of **April 1** ; 1932; taken by **A. H. Kneale** ; Superintendent.

Key: Number; Surname; Given; Sex (M/F); Age at Last Birthday; Tribe; Degree of Blood (F=Full); Marital Status; Relationship to Head of Family & Last Census No; At Jurisdiction Where Enrolled (Yes/No); (If no – Where); Ward (Yes/No); Allotment Annuity and/or Identification Numbers

WADE

4291; Anna; F; 31; Maricopa; F; S; Head; 4279; Yes; Yes; AI. 3802/Id. 308
4292; Luella N.; F; 1; Maricopa; F; S; Dau.; 4280; Yes; Yes; AI./Id. 595
4293; Jane; F; 77; Maricopa; F; Wd.; Mother; 4281; Yes; Yes; AI./Id. 309

WADE

4294; Mark; M; 58; Pima; F; M; Head; 4282; Yes; Yes; AI. 3745/Id. 1812
4295; Lottie; F; 50; Pima; F; M; Wife; 4283; Yes; Yes; AI. 3746/Id. 1813
4296; Stephen; M; 28; Pima; F; S; Son; 4284; Yes; Yes; AI. 3752/Id. 1814
4297; Stephen; M; 30; Pima; F; S; Son; 4285; Yes; Yes; AI. 3747/Id. 1815
4298; Zachrist; M; 21; Pima; F; S; Son; 4286; Yes; Yes; AI. 3750/Id. 1816

WAHAPTA

4299; Eschief; M; 52; Pima; F; M; Head; 4287; Yes; Yes; AI. 682/Id. 5503
4300; Anna; F; 47; Pima; F; M; Wife; 4288; Yes; Yes; AI. 683/Id. 5504
4301; Mateo; M; 27; Pima; F; S; Son; 4289; Yes; Yes; AI. 684/Id. 5505
4302; Elipa; M; 21; Pima; F; S; Son; 4290; Yes; Yes; AI. 685/Id. 5506
4303; Richenda; F; 19; Pima; F; S; Dau.; 4291; Yes; Yes; AI. 686/Id. 5507
4304; Marie; F; 18; Pima; F; S; Dau.; 4292; Yes; Yes; AI. 3154/Id. 5508

WALKER

4305; Mary; F; 71; Maricopa; F; Wd.; Head; 4293; Yes; Yes; AI. 4354/Id. 314

WALKER

4306; Millard; M; 59; Maricopa; F; M; Head; 4294; Yes; Yes; AI. 3779/Id. 354
4307; Luby; F; 59; Maricopa; F; M; Wife; 4295; Yes; Yes; AI. 3780/Id. 355
4308; Reuben; M; 19; Maricopa; F; S; Son; 4296; Yes; Yes; AI. 3783/Id. 356
4309; Lena; F; 17; Maricopa; F; S; Dau.; 4297; Yes; Yes; AI. 3784/Id. 357
4310; Rosa[sic]; M; 25; Maricopa; F; S; Son; 4298; Yes; Yes; AI. 3782/Id. 358

WALKER

4311; William; M; 41; Maricopa; F; M; Head; 4299; Yes; Yes; AI. 4353/Id. 310
4112; Evelyn B., (Barehand, Evelyne[sic]); F; 24; Maricopa; F; M; Wife; 4300; Yes; Yes; AI. 3129/Id. 311
4113; Welden; M; 8; Maricopa; F; S; Son; 4301; Yes; Yes; AI./Id. 312
4314; Yvonne; F; 5; Maricopa; F; S; Dau.; 4302; Yes; Yes; AI./Id. 313
4315; Amelia; F; 2; Maricopa; F; S; Dau.; 4303; Yes; Yes; AI./Id. 590
4316; Charles; M; 1/12; Maricopa; F; S; Son; --; Yes; Born.; 5-6-32.; Yes; AI./Id. 616

WALKER

4317; Wilson; M; 45; Pima; F; Wd.; Head; 4304; Yes; Yes; AI. 1521/Id. 6634
4318; William; M; 23; Pima; F; S; Son; 4305; Yes; Yes; AI. 1524/Id. 6635
4319; Rowland; M; 20; Pima; F; S; Son; 4306; Yes; Yes; AI. 1525/Id. 6636
4320; Freeman; M; 18; Pima; F; S; Son; 4307; Yes; Yes; AI. 1526/Id. 6637
4321; Burke; M; 16; Pima; F; S; Son; 4308; Yes; Yes; AI. 3394/Id. 6638

Key: Number; Surname; Given; Sex (M/F); Age at Last Birthday; Tribe; Degree of Blood (F=Full); Marital Status; Relationship to Head of Family & Last Census No; At Jurisdiction Where Enrolled (Yes/No); (If no - Where); Ward (Yes/No); Allotment Annuity and/or Identification Numbers

4322; Raymond; M; 12; Pima; F; S; Son; 4309; Yes; Yes; AI. 4878/Id. 6639

4323; Dorothy; F; 9; Pima; F; S; Dau.; 4310; Yes; Yes; AI./Id. 6640

WANDA

4324; Juan; M; 67; Pima; F; Wd.; Head; 4311; Yes; Yes; AI. 1372/Id. 7264

WARREN

4325; Mathew; M; 47; Pima; F; Wd.; Head; 4312; Yes; Yes; AI. 1022/Id. 6567

4326; Marguerite; F; 18; Pima; F; S; Dau.; 4313; Yes; Yes; AI. 1025/Id. 6569

4327; Eleanor; F; 11; Pima; F; S; Dau.; 4314; Yes; Yes; AI./Id. 6570

WEBB

4328; George; M; 41; Pima; F; M; Head; 4315; Yes; Yes; AI. 4088/Id. 1253

4329; Mattie, (McDonald , Mattie); F; 34; Pima; F; M; Wife; 4316; Yes; Yes; AI. 3758/Id. 1254

4330; George Jr.; M; 12; Pima; F; S; Son; 4317; Yes; Yes; AI. 4605/Id. 1255

4331; Winifred; F; 11; Pima; F; S; Dau.; 4318; Yes; Yes; AI./Id. 1256

4332; Paul L.; M; 8; Pima; F; S; Son; 4319; Yes; Yes; AI./Id. 1257

4333; Lionel; M; 6; Pima; F; S; Son; 4320; Yes; Yes; AI./Id. 1258

4334; Alfred E.; M; 4; Pima; F; S; Son; 4321; Yes; Yes; AI./Id. 1259

WEBB

4335; Simon; M; 92; Pima; F; M; Head; 4322; Yes; Yes; AI. 4086/Id. 1266

4336; Sarah; F; 91; Pima; F; M; Wife; 4323; Yes; Yes; AI. 4087/Id. 1267

WELLINGTON

4337; Oliver; M; 57; Pima; F; Wd.; Head; 4324; Yes; Yes; AI. 209/Id. 4224

4338; Aurelia; F; 20; Pima; F; S; Dau.; 4325; Yes; Yes; AI. 842/Id. 4227

WELLINGTON

4339; Lyman; M; 22; Pima; F; M; Head; 4326; Yes; Yes; AI. 841/Id. 4226

4340; Juanita S., (Sampson, Juanita); F; 29; Pima; F; M; Wife; 4327; Yes; Yes; AI. 2558/Id. 6738

WELLINGTON

4341; Sidney; M; 24; Pima; F; S; Head; 4328; Yes; Yes; AI. 3776/Id. 6096

4342; Ede; F; 22; Pima; F; S; Sister; 4329; Yes; Yes; AI. 3777/Id. 6097

4343; Naomi; F; 15; Pima; F; S; Sister; 4330; Yes; Yes; AI. 3778/Id. 6098

WELLS

4344; Alice; F; 82; Pima; F; Wd.; Head; 4331; Yes; Yes; AI. 211/Id. 5301

WESLEY

4345; Louise; F; 82; Pima; F; Wd.; Head; 4332; Yes; Yes; AI. 2409/Id. 3119

Census of the **Gila River** reservation of the **Pima Agency** jurisdiction; as of **April 1** ; 1932; taken by **A. H. Kneale** ; Superintendent.

Key: Number; Surname; Given; Sex (M/F); Age at Last Birthday; Tribe; Degree of Blood (F=Full); Marital Status; Relationship to Head of Family & Last Census No; At Jurisdiction Where Enrolled (Yes/No); (If no – Where); Ward (Yes/No); Allotment Annuity and/or Identification Numbers

WESLEY
4346; Nole; M; 35; Pima; F; S; Head; 4333; Yes; Yes; AI. 2106/Id. 3592

WHITE
4347; Andreas; M; 29; Pima; F; S; Head; 4334; Yes; Yes; AI. 2537/Id. 5282

WHITE
4348; Anton; M; 42; Pima; F; M; Head; 4335; Yes; Yes; AI. 300/Id. 5302
4349; Louise M.; F; 61; Pima; F; M; Wife; 4336; Yes; Yes; AI./Id. 5303

WHITE
4350; Eugene E.; M; 29; Pima; F; M; Head; 4337; Yes; Yes; AI. 1183/Id. 6552
4351; Lucille, (Miguel, Lucille); F; 47; Pima; F; M; Wife; 4338; Yes; Yes; AI. 549/Id. 6553

WHITE
~~Anyonda, (Amanda Pancet); F; 20; Pima; F; S; Alone; 4339; Died.; 3-28-32.~~; Yes; AI. 1388/Id. 6914
~~Naomi; F; 16; Pima; F; M; Wife; 4340; Yes; Married to Gibson Osife.~~; Yes; AI. 2622/Id. 6915

WHITE
4352; Harvey; M; 30; Pima; F; S; Head; 4341; Yes; Yes; AI. 1201/Id. 6561

WHITE
4353; Annie T.; F; 24; Pima; F; Wd.; Head; 4342; Yes; Yes; AI. 1003/Id. 7265

WHITE
4354; Edith N.; F; 48; Pima; F; S; Head; 4343; Yes; Yes; AI. 1131/Id. 7266

WHITE
4355; Jacob; M; 28; Pima; F; M; Head; 4344; Yes; Yes; AI. 4412/Id. 1323
4356; Ella; F; 22; Pima; F; M; Wife; 4345; Yes; Yes; AI./Id. 1324

WHITE
4357; James; M; 35; Pima; F; M; Head; 4346; Yes; Yes; AI. 1386/Id. 6733
4358; Clara A., (Juan, Clara); F; 38; Pima; F; M; Wife; 4347; Yes; Yes; AI. 3855/Id. 6734
4359; Raymond; M; 4; Pima; F; S; Son; 4348; Yes; Yes; AI./Id. 6735
4360; Leonard; M; 2; Pima; F; S; Son; 4349; Yes; Yes; AI./Id. 7269

WHITE
4361; Joe; M; 60; Pima; F; M; Head; 4350; Yes; Yes; AI. 4408/Id. 1306
4362; Josepha; F; 46; Pima; F; M; Wife; 4351; Yes; Yes; AI. 4409/Id. 1307
4363; Amelia; F; 22; Pima; F; S; Dau.; 4352; Yes; Yes; AI. 4413/Id. 1308

Census of the **Gila River** reservation of the **Pima Agency** jurisdiction; as of **April 1** ; 1932; taken by **A. H. Kneale** ; Superintendent.

Key: Number; Surname; Given; Sex (M/F); Age at Last Birthday; Tribe; Degree of Blood (F=Full); Marital Status; Relationship to Head of Family & Last Census No; At Jurisdiction Where Enrolled (Yes/No); (If no – Where); Ward (Yes/No); Allotment Annuity and/or Identification Numbers

4364; Irene; F; 20; Pima; F; S; Dau.; 4353; Yes; Yes; AI. 4414/Id. 1309
4365; Mary; F; 16; Pima; F; S; Dau.; 4354; Yes; Yes; AI. 4415/Id. 1310

WHITE

4366; John; M; 47; Pima; F; M; Head; 4355; Yes; Yes; AI. 1385/Id. 6729
4367; Vivian, (Francisco, Vivian); F; 45; Pima; F; M; Wife; 4356; Yes; Yes;
AI. 3398/Id. 6730
4368; Nellie; F; 14; Pima; F; S; Dau.; 4357; Yes; Yes; AI. 4494/Id. 6731
4369; Francisco, Adam; M; 18; Pima; F; S; St.son; 4358; Yes; Yes; AI. 3400/Id. 6732

WHITE

4370; Jose; M; 54; Pima; F; Wd.; Head; 4359; Yes; Yes; AI. 1179/Id. 6548
4371; Snyder; M; 24; Pima; F; S; Son; 4360; Yes; Yes; AI. 1181/Id. 6551
4372; San T.; M; 26; Pima; F; S; Son; 4361; Yes; Yes; AI. 1182/Id. 6550

WHITE

4373; Manuel; M; 30; Pima; F; M; Head; 4362; Yes; Yes; AI. 1184/Id. 6549
4374; Lena; F; 38; Pima; F; M; Wife; 4363; Yes; Yes; AI./Id. 3721

WHITE

4375; Juan; M; 46; Pima; F; M; Head; 4364; Yes; Yes; AI. 1398/Id. 6912
4376; Josepha; F; 38; Pima; F; M; Wife; 4365; Yes; Yes; AI. 1399/Id. 6913

WHITE

Jula; M; 87; Pima; F; Wd.; Head; 4366; Died.; 3-23-32.; Yes; AI. 1387/Id. 6633

WHITE

4377; Justin; M; 31; Pima; F; M; Head; 4367; Yes; Yes; AI. 4411/Id. 1304
4378; Lizzie, (Jose, Lizzie); F; 22; Pima; F; M; Wife; 4368; Yes; Yes;
AI. 3582/Id. 1305

WHITE

4379; Mark; M; 35; Pima; F; M; Head; 4369; Yes; Yes; AI. 1200/Id. 6556
4380; Delphine C., (Chico, Delphine); F; 37; Pima; F; M; Wife; 4370; Yes; Yes;
AI. 3207/Id. 6557
4381; Donald; M; 17; Pima; F; S; Son; 4371; Yes; Yes; AI. 3208/Id. 6558
4382; Bernard; M; 11; Pima; F; S; Son; 4372; Yes; Yes; AI./Id. 6559
4383; Jeanette P.; F; 5; Pima; F; S; Dau.; 4373; Yes; Yes; AI./Id. 6560

WHITE

4384; Victor; M; 33; Pima; F; M; Head; 4374; Yes; Yes; AI. 716/Id. 5354
4385; Lulu, (Jones, Lulu); F; 31; Pima; F; M; Wife; 4375; Yes; Yes; AI. 149/Id. 5355
4386; Lemon; M; 8; Pima; F; S; Son; 4376; Yes; Yes; AI./Id. 5356
4387; Elmon; M; 4; Pima; F; S; Son; 4377; Yes; Yes; AI./Id. 5357
4388; Lucille; F; 1; Pima; F; S; Dau.; 4378; Yes; Yes; AI./Id. 6101

Census of the **Gila River** reservation of the **Pima Agency** jurisdiction; as of **April 1** ; 1932; taken by **A. H. Kneale** ; Superintendent.

Key: Number; Surname; Given; Sex (M/F); Age at Last Birthday; Tribe; Degree of Blood (F=Full); Marital Status; Relationship to Head of Family & Last Census No; At Jurisdiction Where Enrolled (Yes/No); (If no – Where); Ward (Yes/No); Allotment Annuity and/or Identification Numbers

WHITE
4389; Walter; M; 53; Pima; F; M; Head; 4379; Yes; Yes; AI. 1198/Id. 6554
4390; Susie; F; 50; Pima; F; M; Wife; 4380; Yes; Yes; AI. 1199/Id. 6555

WHITMAN
4391; Charles; M; 60; Pima; F; M; Head; 4381; Yes; Yes; AI. 432/Id. 5154
4392; Catherine, (Thomas, Catherine); F; 67; Pima; F; M; Wife; 4382; Yes; Yes; AI. 402/Id. 5146
4393; Lenora; F; 22; Pima; F; S; Dau.; 4383; Yes; Yes; AI. 438/Id. 5147
4394; Rose; F; 18; Pima; F; S; Dau.; 4384; Yes; Yes; AI. 439/Id. 5148

WHITMAN
4395; Leonard; M; 24; Pima; F; M; Head; 4385; Yes; Yes; AI. 357/Id. 3147
4396; Ina J., (Johnson, Ina); F; 26; Pima; F; M; Wife; 4386; Yes; Yes; AI. 2250/Id. 3148
4397; Sharon; F; 1; Pima; F; S; Dau.; 4387; Yes; Yes; AI./Id. 3599
4398; Dayton; M; 1/12; Pima; F; S; Son; --; Yes; Born.; 5-13-32.; Yes; AI./Id. 3616

WHITMAN
4399; Donald; M; 29; Pima; F; M; Head; 4388; Yes; Yes; AI. 435/Id. 5640
4400; Julie P., (Paddis, Celestine); F; 27; Pima; F; M; Wife; 4389; Yes; Yes; AI. 197/Id. 5641

WHITMAN
4401; Earl; M; 56; Pima; F; M; Head; 4390; Yes; Yes; AI. 829/Id. 4528
4402; Catherine; F; 47; Pima; F; M; Wife; 4391; Yes; Yes; AI. 830/Id. 4529
4403; Irene; F; 23; Pima; F; S; Dau.; 4392; Yes; Yes; AI. 833/Id. 4531
4404; Belford; M; 18; Pima; F; S; Son; 4393; Yes; Yes; AI. 1657/Id. 4530
4405; Earl M.; M; 12; Pima; F; S; Son; 4394; Yes; Yes; AI. 4609/Id. 4533
4406; Jennie F.; F; 11; Pima; F; S; Dau.; 4395; Yes; Yes; AI. 4886/Id. 4534
4407; Oriena R.; F; 1; Pima; F; S; Gr.dau.; 4396; Yes; Yes; AI. 4886/Id. 4534
4408; Marcus; M; 29; Pima; F; S; Son; 4397; Yes; Yes; AI. 831/Id. 4531

WHITMAN
4409; Eddie M.; M; 32; Pima; F; M; Head; 4398; Yes; Yes; AI. 434/Id. 5185
4410; Christina, (Reed, Christina); F; 42; Pima; F; M; Wife; 4399; Yes; Yes; AI. 356/Id. 5844
4411; Reed, Frank; M; 18; Pima; F; S; St.son; 4400; Yes; Yes; AI. 345/Id. 5187
4412; Reed, Hazel; F; 3; Pima; F; S; Dau.; 4401; Yes; Yes; AI./Id. 5845

WHITMAN
4413; Mark; M; 27; Pima; F; M; Head; 4402; Yes; Yes; AI. 832/Id. 4516
4414; Gladys, (Miguel, Gladys); F; 25; Pima; F; M; Wife; 4403; Yes; Yes; AI. 1674/Id. 4517
4415; Cornelius; M; 7; Pima; F; S; Son; 4404; Yes; Yes; AI./Id. 4518

Census of the **Gila River** reservation of the **Pima Agency** jurisdiction; as of **April 1** ; 1932; taken by **A. H. Kneale** ; Superintendent.

Key: Number; Surname; Given; Sex (M/F); Age at Last Birthday; Tribe; Degree of Blood (F=Full); Marital Status; Relationship to Head of Family & Last Census No; At Jurisdiction Where Enrolled (Yes/No); (If no – Where); Ward (Yes/No); Allotment Annuity and/or Identification Numbers

4416; Elvey H.; M; 5; Pima; F; S; Son; 4405; Yes; Yes; AI./Id. 4519
4417; Delamer; F; 3; Pima; F; S; Dau.; 4406; Yes; Yes; AI./Id. 3986

WHITMAN
4418; William; M; 38; Pima; F; Wd.; Head; 4407; Yes; Yes; AI. 356/Id. 5177

WHITTAKER
4419; George; M; 29; Pima; F; M; Head; 4408; Yes; Yes; AI. 420/Id. 5214
4420; Flora A., (Azule, Flora Morago); F; 44; Pima; F; M; Wife; 4409; Yes; Yes; AI. 2248/Id. 4414

WHITTAKER
4421; William; M; 67; Pima; F; Wd.; Head; 4410; Yes; Yes; AI. 2043/Id. 3379
4422; Clinton; M; 28; Pima; F; S; Son; 4411; Yes; Yes; AI. 2418/Id. 3381
4423; Lewis; M; 41; Pima; F; S; Son; 4412; Yes; Yes; AI. 2117/Id. 3380

WHITTAKER
4424; Horace; M; 38; Pima; F; M; Head; 4413; Yes; Yes; AI. 2046/Id. 4215
4425; Susie J., (Jackson, Susie); F; 32; Pima; F; M; Wife; 4414; Yes; Yes; AI. 857/Id. 4216
4426; Gladys; F; 12; Pima; F; S; Dau.; 4415; Yes; Yes; AI. 4606/Id. 4217
4427; Evelyn M.; F; 11; Pima; F; S; Dau.; 4416; Yes; Yes; AI./Id. 4218
4428; Eugenia A.; F; 6; Pima; F; S; Dau.; 4417; Yes; Yes; AI./Id. 4219
4429; Omar Bruce; M; 5/12; Pima; F; S; Son; --; Yes; Born.; 11-8-32.; Yes; AI./Id. 3936

WHITTAKER
4430; John D.; M; 44; Pima; F; M; Head; 4418; Yes; Yes; AI. 2191/Id. 3382
4431; Ida, (Miguel, Flora); F; 31; Pima; F; M; Wife; 4419; Yes; Yes; AI. 2263/Id. 3383
4432; Edmund; M; 23; Pima; F; S; Son; 4420; Yes; Yes; AI. 2192/Id. 3384

WHITTAKER
4433; Jose M.; M; 62; Pima; F; M; Head; 4421; Yes; Yes; AI. 283/Id. 5304
4434; Mabel Marie; F; 62; Pima; F; M; Wife; 4422; Yes; Yes; AI. 284/Id. 5305

WHITTAKER
4435; Juan; M; 39; Pima; F; M; Head; 4423; Yes; Yes; AI. 520/Id. 5092
4436; Elizabeth, (Meguil, Elizabeth); F; 29; Pima; F; M; Wife; 4424; Yes; Yes; AI. 486/Id. 5093
4437; Josephine; F; 11; Pima; F; S; Dau.; 4425; Yes; Yes; AI./Id. 5094
4438; Elizabeth; F; 1; Pima; F; S; Dau.; 4426; Yes; Yes; AI./Id. 6112

WHITTAKER
4439; Juan C.; M; 48; Pima; F; M; Head; 4427; Yes; Yes; AI. 1950/Id. 3132

Census of the **Gila River** reservation of the **Pima Agency** jurisdiction; as of **April 1** ; 1932; taken by **A. H. Kneale** ; Superintendent.

Key: Number; Surname; Given; Sex (M/F); Age at Last Birthday; Tribe; Degree of Blood (F=Full); Marital Status; Relationship to Head of Family & Last Census No; At Jurisdiction Where Enrolled (Yes/No); (If no - Where); Ward (Yes/No); Allotment Annuity and/or Identification Numbers

4440; Mildred, (May); F; 36; Pima; F; M; Wife; 4428; Yes; Yes; AI. 1951/Id. 3133
4441; Amos Noble; M; 17; Pima; F; S; Son; 4429; Yes; Yes; AI. 3262/Id. 3590

WHITTIER
4442; John G.; M; 63; Pima; F; M; Head; 4430; Yes; Yes; AI. 1423/Id. 5095
4443; Katie; F; 29; Pima; F; M; Wife; 4431; Yes; Yes; AI./Id. 5097
4444; Bernie; M; 30; Pima; F; S; Son; 4432; Yes; Yes; AI. 1427/Id. 5098
4445; Ella; F; 23; Pima; F; S; Dau.; 4433; Yes; Yes; AI. 1426/Id. 5096

WICKEY
4446; Paul; M; 51; Maricopa; F; Wd.; Head; 4434; Yes; Yes; AI. 2670/Id. 422
4447; Mary A.; F; 20; Maricopa; F; S; Dau.; 4435; Yes; Yes; AI. 2672/Id. 424
4448; Josiah F.; M; 19; Maricopa; F; S; Son; 4436; Yes; Yes; AI. 2673/Id. 425
4449; Ethel V.; F; 13; Maricopa; F; S; Dau.; 4437; Yes; Yes; AI. 3930/Id. 426
4450; Helen; F; 14; Maricopa; F; S; Dau.; 4438; Yes; Yes; AI. 4682/Id. 427
4451; Thelma; F; 12; Maricopa; F; S; Dau.; 4439; Yes; Yes; AI./Id. 428
4452; Sepia; F; 6; Maricopa; F; S; Dau.; 4440; Yes; Yes; AI./Id. 591

WILLA
4453; Lizzie, (Ferguson, Lizzie); F; 28; Pima; F; M; Wife; 4441; Yes; Yes; AI. 2166/Id. 3593
4454; Reuben; M; 12; Pima; F; S; Son; 4442; Yes; Yes; AI. 4777/Id. 3594
4455; Ruda; F; 11; Pima; F; S; Dau.; 4443; Yes; Yes; AI./Id. 3595

WILLIAMS
~~N.E. Bernard; M; Unk.; Unk.; M; Head;~~
4456; Ina Brown; F; 20; Pima; F; M; Wife; 398; Yes; Yes; AI. 4601/Id. 330
4457; Frieda Louise; F; 4/12; Pima; F; S; Dau.; --; Yes; Born.; 12-13-31.; Yes; AI./Id. 617

WILLIAMS
4458; Rose A., (Aw aw katch, Susanna); F; 36; Pima; F; M; Wife; 4444; Yes; Yes; AI. 4645/Id. 6084
4459; Leland; M; 9; Pima; F; S; Son; 4445; Yes; Yes; AI./Id. 6085
4460; Naomi; F; 6; Pima; F; S; Dau.; 4446; Yes; Yes; AI./Id. 6086
4461; Francis; M; 4; Pima; F; S; Son; 4447; Yes; Yes; AI./Id. 6087

WILLIAMS
4462; Horace; M; 63; Pima; F; M; Head; 4448; Yes; Yes; AI. 2586/Id. 7065
4463; Nellie; F; 62; Pima; F; M; Wife; 4449; Yes; Yes; AI. 2587/Id. 7066

WILLIAMS
4464; James; M; 72; Pima; F; S; Head; 4450; Yes; Yes; AI. 661/Id. 6088

Census of the **Gila River** reservation of the **Pima Agency** jurisdiction; as of **April 1** ; 1932; taken by **A. H. Kneale** ; Superintendent.

Key: Number; Surname; Given; Sex (M/F); Age at Last Birthday; Tribe; Degree of Blood (F=Full); Marital Status; Relationship to Head of Family & Last Census No; At Jurisdiction Where Enrolled (Yes/No); (If no – Where); Ward (Yes/No); Allotment Annuity and/or Identification Numbers

WILLIAMS

4465; James; M; 36; Pima; F; M; Head; 4451; Yes; Yes; AI. 865/Id. 6963
4466; Juanna E., (Enis, Juanna); F; 51; Pima; F; M; Wife; 4452; Yes; Yes; AI. 800/Id. 6964

WILLIAMS

4467; Jeff; M; 33; Pima; F; S; Head; 4453; Yes; Yes; AI. 868/Id. 6967

WILLIAMS

4468; Jones; M; 41; Pima; F; M; Head; 4454; Yes; Yes; AI. 2032/Id. 3046
4469; Emma J., (Nish, Emma Jackson); F; 48; Pima; F; M; Wife; 4455; Yes; Yes; AI. 1903/Id. 3047
4470; Frances I.; F; 18; Pima; F; S; Dau.; 4456; Yes; Yes; AI. 2034/Id. 3050
4471; Marjorie; F; 13; Pima; F; S; Dau.; 4457; Yes; Yes; AI./Id. 3048
4472; Jones Jr.; M; 11; Pima; F; S; Son; 4458; Yes; Yes; AI./Id. 3049

WILLIAMS

4473; Jose M.; M; 29; Pima; F; M; Head; 4459; Yes; Yes; AI. 2486/Id. 1290
4474; Agatha J., (Jose, Emma Agatha); F; 24; Pima; F; M; Wife; 4460; Yes; Yes; AI. 3581/Id. 1291
4475; Panoratius; M; 8; Pima; F; S; Son; 4461; Yes; Yes; AI./Id. 1292
4476; Victor B.; M; 7; Pima; F; S; Son; 4462; Yes; Yes; AI./Id. 1293
4477; Tobias; M; 2; Pima; F; S; Son; 4463; Yes; Yes; AI./Id. 2026

WILLIAMS

4478; Marcus; M; 34; Pima; F; S; Head; 4464; Yes; Yes; AI. 4182/Id. 7281

WILLIAMS

4479; San Chiago; M; 55; Pima; F; M; Head; 4465; Yes; Yes; AI. 2486/Id. 1260
4480; Juanna Rose; F; 49; Pima; F; M; Wife; 4466; Yes; Yes; AI. 2485/Id. 1261
4481; Elenia R.; F; 21; Pima; F; S; Dau.; 4467; Yes; Yes; AI. 2489/Id. 1262
4482; Matilda; F; 19; Pima; F; S; Dau.; 4468; Yes; Yes; AI. 2490/Id. 1263
4483; Angelo R.; F; 13; Pima; F; S; Dau.; 4469; Yes; Yes; AI. 3928/Id. 1264
4484; Pascal Z.; M; 6; Pima; F; S; Son; 4470; Yes; Yes; AI./Id. 1265
4485; Herman; M; 2; Pima; F; S; Son; 4471; Yes; Yes; AI./Id. 2830

WILSON

4486; Adolph; M; 40; Pima; F; M; Head; 4472; Yes; Yes; AI. 488/Id. 4902
4487; Fannie; F; 39; Pima; F; M; Wife; 4473; Yes; Yes; AI. 489/Id. 4903
4488; Flora; F; 21; Pima; F; S; Dau.; 4474; Yes; Yes; AI. 490/Id. 4904
4489; Ruth; F; 18; Pima; F; S; Dau.; 4475; Yes; Yes; AI. 491/Id. 4905
4490; Leonard; M; 14; Pima; F; S; Son; 4476; Yes; Yes; AI. 3242/Id. 4906
4491; Opet; M; 13; Pima; F; S; Son; 4477; Yes; Yes; AI. 4695/Id. 4907

WILSON

4492; Albert; M; 32; Pima; F; S; Head; 4478; Yes; Yes; AI. 1421/Id. 5803

WILSON

4493; Alex; M; 67; Pima; F; M; Head; 4479; Yes; Yes; AI. 4144/Id. 1684
4494; Johanna; F; 70; Pima; F; M; Wife; 4480; Yes; Yes; AI. 4145/Id. 1865

WILSON

4495; Barney; M; 23; Pima; F; S; Head; 4481; Yes; Yes; AI. 3378/Id. 6089

WISON[sic]

4496; Earl; M; 32; Pima; F; S; Head; 4482; Yes; Yes; AI. 4118/Id. 2028

WILSON

4497; Petra; F; 56; Pima; F; Wd.; Head; 4483; Yes; Yes; AI. 125/Id. 5465
4498; Slida; F; 20; Pima; F; S; Dau.; 4484; Yes; Yes; AI. 493/Id. 5466
4499; Woodrow; M; 13; Pima; F; S; Son; 4485; Yes; Yes; AI. 4657/Id. 5467

WILSON

4500; Herbert; M; 28; Pima; F; M; Head; 4486; Yes; Yes; AI. 1422/Id. 6955
4501; Isabelle N., (Nelson, Isabelle); F; 34; Pima; F; M; Wife; 4487; Yes; Yes; AI. 1229/Id. 6956
4502; Herbert Jr.; M; 11; Pima; F; S; Son; 4488; Yes; Yes; AI./Id. 6857
4503; Barbara A.; F; 4; Pima; F; S; Dau.; 4489; Yes; Yes; AI./Id. 6958

WILSON

4504; James; M; 67; Maricopa; F; M; Head; 4490; Yes; Yes; AI. 4116/Id. 479
4505; Lucy; F; 66; Maricopa; F; M; Wife; 4491; Yes; Yes; AI. 4117/Id. 480
4506; Markray; M; 29; Maricopa; F; S; Son; 4492; Yes; Yes; AI. 4120/Id. 481

WILSON

4507; John; M; 75; Pima; F; Wd.; Head; 4493; Yes; Yes; AI. 1118/Id. 7267

WILSON

4508; Robert; M; 60; Pima; F; M; Head; 4494; Yes; Yes; AI. 1417/Id. 6801
4509; Hattie; F; 60; Pima; F; M; Wife; 4495; Yes; Yes; AI. 1418/Id. 6802
4510; Harry; M; 22; Pima; F; S; Son; 4496; Yes; Yes; AI. 1420/Id. 6805
4511; Luke; M; 28; Pima; F; S; Son; 4497; Yes; Yes; AI. 1419/Id. 6804

WILSON

4512; Robert M.; M; 3; Pima; F; S; Alone; 4498; Yes; Yes; AI./Id. 3985

WIND

4513; ---. M; 67; Maricopa; F; Wd.; Head; 4499; Yes; Yes; AI. 2863/Id. 53

Census of the **Gila River** reservation of the **Pima Agency** jurisdiction; as of **April 1** ; 1932; taken by **A. H. Kneale** ; Superintendent.

Key: Number; Surname; Given; Sex (M/F); Age at Last Birthday; Tribe; Degree of Blood (F=Full); Marital Status; Relationship to Head of Family & Last Census No; At Jurisdiction Where Enrolled (Yes/No); (If no – Where); Ward (Yes/No); Allotment Annuity and/or Identification Numbers

WIND

4514; Gualupa; F; 77; Maricopa; F; Wd.; Head; 4500; Yes; Yes; AI. 2922/Id. 54

WIND

4515; Henry W.; M; 35; Maricopa; F; M; Head; 4501; Yes; Yes; AI. 2921/Id. 55

4516; Alma K., (Komcess, Allna[sic]); F; 33; Maricopa; F; M; Wife; 4502; Yes; Yes; AI. 2389/Id. 56

4517; Ruby; F; 9; Maricopa; F; S; Dau.; 4503; Yes; Yes; AI./Id. 57

4518; Norma; F; 4; Maricopa; F; S; Dau.; 4504; Yes; Yes; AI./Id. 58

WINN

4519; Andrew; M; 29; Pima; F; M; Head; 4505; Yes; Yes; AI. 4125/Id. 3112

4516; Emma, (Lewis, Emma); F; 24; Pima; F; M; Wife; 4506; Yes; Yes; AI. 2130/Id. 3113

4521; Alfred; M; 3; Pima; F; S; Son; 4507; Yes; Yes; AI. 1419/Id. 3596

WINN

4522; John; M; 52; Pima; F; M; Head; 4508; Yes; Yes; AI. 3227/Id. 5748

4523; Emily; F; 47; Pima; F; M; Wife; 4509; Yes; Yes; AI. 4464/Id. 5749

WINN

4524; Mark; M; 49; Maricopa; F; M; Head; 4510; Yes; Yes; AI. 4122/Id. 499

4525; Molly; F; 47; Maricopa; F; M; Wife; 4511; Yes; Yes; AI. 4123/Id. 500

4526; Allen; M; 18; Maricopa; F; S; Son; 4512; Yes; Yes; AI. 4126/Id. 501

4527; Mathew A.; M; 15; Maricopa; F; S; Son; 4513; Yes; Yes; AI./Id. 502

WINN

4528; Savia; F; 62; Pima; F; Wd.; Head; 4514; Yes; Yes; AI. 3461/Id. 7268

WISTON

4529; David; M; 44; Pima; F; M; Head; 4515; Yes; Yes; AI. 916/Id. 4368

4530; Molly; F; 44; Pima; F; M; Wife; 4516; Yes; Yes; AI. 917/Id. 4369

4531; Wallace; M; 18; Pima; F; S; Son; 4517; Yes; Yes; AI./Id. 4370

WISTON

4532; John; M; 57; Pima; F; M; Head; 4518; Yes; Yes; AI. 908/Id. 4338

4533; Lena; F; 43; Pima; F; M; Wife; 4519; Yes; Yes; AI. 909/Id. 4339

4534; Albert; M; 18; Pima; F; S; Son; 4520; Yes; Yes; AI. 1741/Id. 4341

4535; Edison; M; 15; Pima; F; S; Son; 4521; Yes; Yes; AI. 3808/Id. 4342

4536; Charles A.; M; 10; Pima; F; S; Son; 4522; Yes; Yes; AI./Id. 4343

WISTON

4537; Joseph; M; 77; Pima; F; M; Head; 4523; Yes; Yes; AI. 912/Id. 6924

4538; Josephine; F; 77; Pima; F; M; Wife; 4524; Yes; Yes; AI. 913/Id. 6925

Census of the **Gila River** reservation of the **Pima Agency** jurisdiction; as of **April 1** ; 1932; taken by **A. H. Kneale** ; Superintendent.

Key: Number; Surname; Given; Sex (M/F); Age at Last Birthday; Tribe; Degree of Blood (F=Full); Marital Status; Relationship to Head of Family & Last Census No; At Jurisdiction Where Enrolled (Yes/No); (If no – Where); Ward (Yes/No); Allotment Annuity and/or Identification Numbers

WISTON
4539; Lester; M; 26; Pima; F; M; Head; 4525; Yes; Yes; AI. 918/Id. 4371
4540; Olive N., (Newman, Olive); F; 25; Pima; F; M; Wife; 4526; Yes; Yes; AI. 2113/Id. 4372
~~4541; Unnamed; M; 9/12; Pima; F; S; Son; –; Born and Died;. 9-21-31.; (N.B. Should have been Omitted).;~~ Yes; AI./Id.

WOOD
4542; Edward H.; M; 62; Pima; F; M; Head; 4527; Yes; Yes; AI. 776/Id. 4520
4543; Stella McI., (McLean, Stella); F; 42; Pima; F; M; Wife; 4528; Yes; Yes; AI. 1087/Id. 4521
4544; Edgar H.; M; 19; Pima; F; S; Son; 4529; Yes; Yes; AI. 781/Id. 4522
4545; Delia; F; 17; Pima; F; S; Dau.; 4530; Yes; Yes; AI. 3158/Id. 4523
4546; Wilbur; M; 13; Pima; F; S; Son; 4531; Yes; Yes; AI. 3820/Id. 4524
4547; McLean, Levina H.; F; 21; Pima; F; S; St.dau.; 4532; Yes; Yes; AI. 1088/Id. 3984

WOOD
4548; Paul; M; 24; Pima; F; M; Head; 4533; Yes; Yes; AI. 779/Id. 4232
4549; Helen, (Pena, Helen); F; 18; Pima; F; M; Wife; 4534; Yes; Yes; AI. 2407/Id. 4230

WOOD
4550; Irene; F; 25; Pima; F; M; Head; 4535; Yes; Yes; AI. 780/Id. 4569

WOOD
4551; Jane; F; 46; Maricopa; F; Wd.; Head; 4536; Yes; Yes; AI. 1094/Id. 545

YARMATA
4552; Harry; M; 45; Maricopa; F; M; Head; 4537; Yes; Yes; AI. 2889/Id. 13
4553; Joanna; F; 40; Maricopa; F; M; Wife; 4538; Yes; Yes; AI. 2911/Id. 14
4554; August; M; 18; Maricopa; F; S; Son; 4539; Yes; Yes; AI. 2913/Id. 16
4555; Stanley R.; M; 14; Maricopa; F; S; Son; 4540; Yes; Yes; AI. 4668/Id. 17
4556; Forrest; M; 13; Maricopa; F; S; Son; 4541; Yes; Yes; AI. 4669/Id. 18
4557; Oliver; M; 7; Maricopa; F; S; Son; 4542; Yes; Yes; AI./Id. 19
4558; Carolina; F; 5; Maricopa; F; S; Dau.; 4543; Yes; Yes; AI./Id. 20
4559; Lena; F; 3; Maricopa; F; S; Dau.; 4544; Yes; Yes; AI./Id. 22

YARMATA
4560; James; M; 66; Maricopa; F; M; Head; 4545; Yes; Yes; AI. 2871/Id. 211
4561; Sequapai; F; 61; Maricopa; F; M; Wife; 4546; Yes; Yes; AI. 2872/Id. 212
4562; Gladys; F; 24; Maricopa; F; S; Dau.; 4547; Yes; Yes; AI. 2874/Id. 213
4563; Vera; F; 20; Maricopa; F; S; Dau.; 4548; Yes; Yes; AI. 2875/Id. 214
4564; Vesta; F; 20; Maricopa; F; S; Dau.; 4549; Yes; Yes; AI. 2876/Id. 215
4565; Arthur; M; 18; Maricopa; F; S; Son; 4550; Yes; Yes; AI. 2890/Id. 216

Census of the **Gila River** reservation of the **Pima Agency** jurisdiction; as of **April 1** ; 1932; taken by **A. H. Kneale** ; Superintendent.

Key: Number; Surname; Given; Sex (M/F); Age at Last Birthday; Tribe; Degree of Blood (F=Full); Marital Status; Relationship to Head of Family & Last Census No; At Jurisdiction Where Enrolled (Yes/No); (If no – Where); Ward (Yes/No); Allotment Annuity and/or Identification Numbers

4566; Wilford; M; 15; Maricopa; F; S; Son; 4551; Yes; Yes; AI./Id. 217

YARMATA
4567; Thomas; M; 32; Maricopa; F; M; Head; 4552; Yes; Yes; AI. 2873/Id. 207
4568; Mabelle P., (Cameron, Mabel); F; 36; Maricopa; F; M; Wife; 4553; Yes; Yes; AI. 2803/Id. 208
4569; Floyd; M; 12; Maricopa; F; S; Son; 4554; Yes; Yes; AI. 4756/Id. 209
4570; Barbara; F; 9; Maricopa; F; S; Dau.; 4555; Yes; Yes; AI./Id. 210

YASK
4571; Jose H.; M; 39; Pima; F; S; Head; 4556; Yes; Yes; AI. 413/Id. 6090

YASK
4572; Morgan; M; 36; Pima; F; Wd.; Head; 4557; Yes; Yes; AI. 421/Id. 5133
4573; Hattie; F; 9; Pima; F; S; Dau.; 4558; Yes; Yes; AI./Id. 5134

YIACK
4574; Henry; M; 62; Pima; F; S; Head; 4559; Yes; Yes; AI. 4351/Id. 1737

YO-HO-LATCH
4575; Tus-no-nol; F; 71; Pima; F; Wd.; Head; 4560; Yes; Yes; AI. 4648/Id. 6091
4576; Julianne; F; 46; Pima; F; S; Dau.; 4561; Yes; Yes; AI. 4649/Id. 6092
4577; Thomas; M; 51; Pima; F; S; Son; 4562; Yes; Yes; AI. 4650/Id. 6093

YONAL
4578; Philip; M; 57; Pima; F; M; Head; 4563; Yes; Yes; AI. 4281/Id. 1347
4579; Margaret; F; 57; Pima; F; M; Wife; 4564; Yes; Yes; AI. 4282/Id. 1348

YOUNG
4580; David; M; 69; Pima; F; Wd.; Head; 4565; Yes; Yes; AI. 1082/Id. 7049

ZACHERY
4581; Anestacia; F; 26; Pima; F; S; Head; 4566; Yes; Yes; AI. 3367/Id. 5688

ZACHERY
4582; Anton; M; 37; Pima; F; M; Head; 4567; Yes; Yes; AI. 3370/Id. 6094
4583; Isabelle; F; 37; Pima; F; M; Wife; 4568; Yes; Yes; AI. 3371/Id. 4095[sic]

ZACHERY
4584; Anton; M; 39; Pima; F; M; Head; 4569; Yes; Yes; AI. 3366/Id. 5687

ZACHERY
4585; Lewis; M; 24; Pima; F; S; Head; 4570; Yes; Yes; AI. 3368/Id. 5689

Census of the **Gila River** reservation of the **Pima Agency** jurisdiction; as of **April 1** ; 1932; taken by **A. H. Kneale** ; Superintendent.

Key: Number; Surname; Given; Sex (M/F); Age at Last Birthday; Tribe; Degree of Blood (F=Full); Marital Status; Relationship to Head of Family & Last Census No; At Jurisdiction Where Enrolled (Yes/No); (If no – Where); Ward (Yes/No); Allotment Annuity and/or Identification Numbers

ZIPP
4586; Sophia K.; M; 86; Pima; F; Wd.; Head; 4571; Yes; Yes; AI. 3976/Id. 2029

ZUNI
N.E.; Max T.; M; Head

4587; Agnes B., (Bird, Agnes); F; 23; Maricopa; F; M; Wife; 4572; Yes; Yes; AI. 2881/Id. 43

4588; Victoria; F; 3; Maricopa; F; S; Dau.; 4573; Yes; Yes; AI./Id. 44

Ak Chin Reservation

of the **Pima Agency**

as of **April 1**, 1932

[Papago]

Census of the **Ak Chin** reservation of the **Pima Agency** jurisdiction, as of
April 1 , 1932, taken by **A. H. Kneale**, Superintendent.

Key: Number; Surname, Given; Sex (M/F); Age at Last Birthday; Tribe; Degree of Blood (F=Full); Marital Status; Relationship to Head of Family & Last Census No; At Jurisdiction Where Enrolled (Yes/No); (If no – Where); Ward (Yes/No); Identification Numbers

ANTONE
4589; ---; M; 69; Papago; F; Wd.; Head; 4574; Yes; Yes; Id. 8937

ANTONE
4590; Albert; M; 31; Papago; F; M; Head; 4575; Yes; Yes; Id. 8935
4591; Juanita; F; 29; Papago; F; M; Wife; 4576; Yes; Yes; Id. 8936

ANTONE
4592; Andrew; M; 48; Papago; F; M; Head; 4577; Yes; Yes; Id. 9076
4593; Listo; F; 10; Papago; F; M; Wife; 4578; Yes; Yes; Id. 9077
4594; Roy; M; 24; Papago; F; S; Son; 4579; Yes; Yes; Id. 9079
4595; Louis; M; 26; Papago; F; S; Son; 4580; Yes; Yes; Id. 9078
4596; Conde; M; 19; Papago; F; S; Son; 4581; Yes; Yes; Id. 9080
4597; Mark; M; 8; Papago; F; S; Son; 4582; Yes; Yes; Id. 9081

ANTONE
4598; Ascenseion; M; 26; Papago; F; M; Head; 4583; Yes; Yes; Id. 9111
4599; Narcia; F; 20; Papago; F; M; Wife; 4584; Yes; Yes; Id. 9112

ANTONE
4600; George; M; 65; Papago; F; M; Head; 4585; Yes; Yes; Id. 9102
4601; Anestasia; F; 62; Papago; F; M; Wife; 4586; Yes; Yes; Id. 9103
4602; Mary; F; 22; Papago; F; S; Dau.; 4587; Yes; Yes; Id. 9104
4603; Rose; F; 18; Papago; F; S; Dau.; 4588; Yes; Yes; Id. 9105
4604; Benedict; M; 15; Papago; F; S; Son; 4589; Yes; Yes; Id. 9106

ANTONE
4605; John; M; 38; Papago; F; M; Head; 4590; Yes; Yes; Id. 9108
4606; Delphine; F; 41; Papago; F; M; Wife; 4591; Yes; Yes; Id. 9109
4607; Juan L.; M; 21; Papago; F; S; Son; 4592; Yes; Yes; Id. 9110
4608; Herbert; M; 19; Papago; F; S; Son; 4593; Yes; Yes; Id. 9111
4609; Sam; M; 17; Papago; F; S; Son; 4594; Yes; Yes; Id. 9112
4610; Elizabeth; F; 16; Papago; F; S; Dau.; 4595; Yes; Yes; Id. 9113
4611; Agatha; F; 11; Papago; F; S; Dau.; 4596; Yes; Yes; Id. 9114
4612; Clarence; M; 7; Papago; F; S; Son; 4597; Yes; Yes; Id. 9115

ANTONE
4613; Jose; M; 29; Papago; F; M; Head; 4598; Yes; Yes; Id. 8857
4614; Lanasia; F; 27; Papago; F; M; Wife; 4599; Yes; Yes; Id. 8858
4615; Lucy; F; 13; Papago; F; S; Son[sic]; 4600; Yes; Yes; Id. 8859
4616; Willie; M; 11; Papago; F; S; Son; 4601; Yes; Yes; Id. 8860
4617; Francis; M; 9; Papago; F; S; Son; 4602; Yes; Yes; Id. 8861
4618; Matilda; F; 6; Papago; F; S; Son[sic]; 4603; Yes; Yes; Id. 8862
4619; Pauline; F; 4; Papago; F; S; Dau.; 4604; Yes; Yes; Id. 8863
4620; Juan; M; 11; Papago; F; S; St.son; 4605; Yes; Yes; Id. 8903

Census of the **Ak Chin** reservation of the **Pima Agency** jurisdiction, as of **April 1** , 1932, taken by **A. H. Kneale** , Superintendent.

Key: Number; Surname, Given; Sex (M/F); Age at Last Birthday; Tribe; Degree of Blood (F=Full); Marital Status; Relationship to Head of Family & Last Census No; At Jurisdiction Where Enrolled (Yes/No); (If no – Where); Ward (Yes/No); Identification Numbers

4621; Felix; M; 1; Papago; F; S; Son; 4606; Yes; Yes; Id. 9156

ANTONE
4622; ---; M; 64; Papago; F; M; Head; 4607; Yes; Yes; Id. 9016
4623; Juanna; F; 60; Papago; F; M; Wife; 4608; Yes; Yes; Id. 9017

ANTONE
4624; Lawrence; M; 24; Papago; F; M; Head; 4609; Yes; Yes; Id. 8943
4625; Seraphina; F; 22; Papago; F; M; Wife; 4610; Yes; Yes; Id. 8944
4626; Mardard; M; 3; Papago; F; S; Son; 4611; Yes; Yes; Id. 8945

ANTONE
4627; Lupa; F; 53; Papago; F; Wd.; Head; 4612; Yes; Yes; Id. 8948

ANTONE
4628; Mathias; M; 34; Papago; F; M; Head; 4613; Yes; Yes; Id. 9018
4629; Julia; F; 32; Papago; F; M; Wife; 4614; Yes; Yes; Id. 9019
4630; Mathias Jr.; M; 1; Papago; F; S; Son; 4615; Yes; Yes; Id. 9160

ANTONE
4631; Quincy; M; 34; Papago; F; S; Head; 4616; Yes; Yes; Id. 8938

ANTONE
4632; Thomas; M; 43; Papago; F; M; Head; 4617; Yes; Yes; Id. 9064
4633; Victoria; F; 36; Papago; F; M; Wife; 4618; Yes; Yes; Id. 9065

ANTONE
4634; Thomas; M; 45; Papago; F; M; Head; 4619; Yes; Yes; Id. 9004
4635; Listine; F; 40; Papago; F; M; Wife; 4620; Yes; Yes; Id. 9005
4636; Mollie; F; 20; Papago; F; S; Dau.; 4621; Yes; Yes; Id. 9006
4637; Clara; F; 18; Papago; F; S; Dau.; 4622; Yes; Yes; Id. 9007

ANTONE
4638; Tom; M; 34; Papago; F; S; Head; 4623; Yes; Yes; Id. 9155

ANTONE
4639; Willie; M; 42; Papago; F; M; Head; 4624; Yes; Yes; Id. 9128
4640; Savalla; F; 37; Papago; F; M; Wife; 4625; Yes; Yes; Id. 9129
4641; Lancito; F; 19; Papago; F; S; Dau.; 4626; Yes; Yes; Id. 9130
4642; Joselinso; M; 12; Papago; F; S; Son; 4627; Yes; Yes; Id. 9131
4643; Helomaine; M; 11; Papago; F; S; Son; 4628; Yes; Yes; Id. 9132
4644; Nonita; F; 7; Papago; F; S; Dau.; 4629; Yes; Yes; Id. 9133
4645; Savilla; F; 4; Papago; F; S; Dau.; 4630; Yes; Yes; Id. 9134

Census of the **Ak Chin** reservation of the **Pima Agency** jurisdiction, as of
April 1 , 1932, taken by **A. H. Kneale** , Superintendent.

Key: Number; Surname, Given; Sex (M/F); Age at Last Birthday; Tribe; Degree of Blood (F=Full); Marital
Status; Relationship to Head of Family & Last Census No; At Jurisdiction Where Enrolled (Yes/No); (If no
– Where); Ward (Yes/No); Identification Numbers

BAAKJ
4646; Juan; M; 65; Papago; F; S; Head; 4631; Yes; Yes; Id. 9030

CARLYLE
4647; Jose J.; M; 42; Papago; F; M; Head; 4632; Yes; Yes; Id. 8913
4648; Nancy; F; 42; Papago; F; M; Wife; 4633; Yes; Yes; Id. 8914
4649; Hiram; M; 21; Papago; F; S; Son; 4634; Yes; Yes; Id. 8915

CARLYLE
4650; Susanna; F; 63; Papago; F; Wd.; Head; 4635; Yes; Yes; Id. 8908

CHARLIE
4651; Palsick; M; 33; Papago; F; S; Head; 4636; Yes; Yes; Id. 9003

CHOLLIES
4652; Juanna; F; 58; Papago; F; Wd.; Head; 4637; Yes; Yes; Id. 9002

CHOOCHI
4653; Juan; M; 68; Papago; F; Wd.; Head; 4638; Yes; Yes; Id. 9113

CHIAGO
4654; Juan; M; 56; Papago; F; S; Head; 4639; Yes; Yes; Id. 9075

DAVIS
4655; Miles; M; 29; Papago; F; M; Head; 4640; Yes; Yes; Id. 8941
4656; Elizabeth; F; 26; Papago; F; M; Wife; 4641; Yes; Yes; Id. 8942

ELLIA
4657; Juan; M; 24; Papago; F; M; Head; 4642; Yes; Yes; Id. 9000
4658; Rose; F; 25; Papago; F; M; Wife; 4643; Yes; Yes; Id. 9001

ENOS
4659; George; M; 23; Papago; F; S; Head; 4644; Yes; Yes; Id. 9040

ENOS
4660; Jose; M; 56; Papago; F; M; Head; 4645; Yes; Yes; Id. 8939
4661; Lasia; F; 45; Papago; F; M; Wife; 4646; Yes; Yes; Id. 8940

ENOS
4662; Jose; M; 61; Papago; F; Wd.; Head; 4647; Yes; Yes; Id. 9142
4663; Willie; M; 22; Papago; F; S; Son; 4648; Yes; Yes; Id. 9143
4664; Hilomain; M; 19; Papago; F; S; Son; 4649; Yes; Yes; Id. 9144
~~Anita; F; 17; Papago; F; S; Dau.; 4650; Yes; Married to Liko Miguel.~~; Yes; Id. 9145
4665; Lazzeri; F; 13; Papago; F; S; Dau.; 4651; Yes; Yes; Id. 9146

Census of the **Ak Chin** reservation of the **Pima Agency** jurisdiction, as of **April 1** , 1932, taken by **A. H. Kneale** , Superintendent.

Key: Number; Surname, Given; Sex (M/F); Age at Last Birthday; Tribe; Degree of Blood (F=Full); Marital Status; Relationship to Head of Family & Last Census No; At Jurisdiction Where Enrolled (Yes/No); (If no – Where); Ward (Yes/No); Identification Numbers

ENOS

4666; Juan; M; 41; Papago; F; M; Head; 4652; Yes; Yes; Id. 8954
4667; Hilomina; F; 39; Papago; F; M; Wife; 4653; Yes; Yes; Id. 8955
4668; Magdalena; F; 21; Papago; F; S; Dau.; 4654; Yes; Yes; Id. 8956
4669; Agnes; F; 17; Papago; F; S; Dau.; 4655; Yes; Yes; Id. 8957
4670; Lucy; F; 15; Papago; F; S; Dau.; 4656; Yes; Yes; Id. 8958
4671; Minnie; F; 10; Papago; F; S; Dau.; 4657; Yes; Yes; Id. 8959
4672; Isabelle; F; 6; Papago; F; S; Dau.; 4658; Yes; Yes; Id. 8960
4673; Jessie; F; 4; Papago; F; S; Dau.; 4659; Yes; Yes; Id. 8961

ENOS

4674; Johnnie; M; 26; Papago; F; S; Head; 4660; Yes; Yes; Id. 8962

ENOS

4675; Logis; M; 27; Papago; F; S; Head; 4661; Yes; Yes; Id. 8918

ENOS

4676; Martin; M; 29; Papago; F; M; Head; 4662; Yes; Yes; Id. 9140
4677; Helen; F; 28; Papago; F; M; Wife; 4663; Yes; Yes; Id. 9141

FRANK

4678; Juan; M; 59; Papago; F; S; Head; 4664; Yes; Yes; Id. 9029

GARCIA

4679; Pablo; M; 24; Papago; F; S; Head; 4665; Yes; Yes; Id. 8933

HARVIER

4680; Stephen; M; 39; Papago; F; M; Head; 4666; Yes; Yes; Id. 8922
4681; Helen; F; 34; Papago; F; M; Wife; 4667; Yes; Yes; Id. 8923
4682; Amelia; F; 9; Papago; F; S; Dau.; 4668; Yes; Yes; Id. 8925
4683; Constantia; F; 7; Papago; F; S; Dau.; 4669; Yes; Yes; Id. 8926
4684; Joseph; M; 3; Papago; F; S; Son; 4670; Yes; Yes; Id. 8927
4685; Bernard; M; 19; Papago; F; S; Son; 4671; Yes; Yes; Id. 8928

JOHNSON

4686; Ben; M; 53; Papago; F; M; Head; 4672; Yes; Yes; Id. 8887
4687; Savill; F; 53; Papago; F; M; Wife; 4673; Yes; Yes; Id. 8888

JOAQUIN

4688; John; M; 28; Papago; F; M; Head; 4674; Yes; Yes; Id. 9047
4689; Mollie T.; F; 17; Papago; F; M; Wife; 4675; Yes; Yes; Id. 8995

JOHNSON

4690; Chino; M; 60; Papago; F; Wd.; Head; 4676; Yes; Yes; Id. 8885
4691; Velindlo; M; 31; Papago; F; S; Son; 4677; Yes; Yes; Id. 8886

Census of the **Ak Chin** reservation of the **Pima Agency** jurisdiction, as of
April 1 , 1932, taken by   **A. H. Kneale** , Superintendent.

Key: Number; Surname, Given; Sex (M/F); Age at Last Birthday; Tribe; Degree of Blood (F=Full); Marital
Status; Relationship to Head of Family & Last Census No; At Jurisdiction Where Enrolled (Yes/No); (If no
– Where); Ward (Yes/No); Identification Numbers

JONES
4692; Jose; M; 36; Papago; F; M; Head; 4678; Yes; Yes; Id. 9031
4693; Vanita; F; 45; Papago; F; M; Wife; 4679; Yes; Yes; Id. 9032
4694; Vanita; F; 3; Papago; F; S; Dau.; 4680; Yes; Yes; Id. 8938

JONES
4695; Juan; M; 52; Papago; F; M; Head; 4681; Yes; Yes; Id. 8812
4696; Lola; F; 57; Papago; F; M; Wife; 4682; Yes; Yes; Id. 8813

JOSE
4697; Julia; F; 66; Papago; F; Wd.; Head; 4683; Yes; Yes; Id. 8934

JUAN
4698; Enos; M; 43; Papago; F; M; Head; 4684; Yes; Yes; Id. 9044
4699; Josito; F; 45; Papago; F; M; Wife; 4685; Yes; Yes; Id. 9045
4700; Adam; M; 20; Papago; F; S; Son; 4686; Yes; Yes; Id. 9046

JOAQUIN
4701; Boniface; M; 26; Papago; F; S; Head; 4687; Yes; Yes; Id. 9048
4702; Agnes; F; 24; Papago; F; S; Sister; 4688; Yes; Yes; Id. 9049
4703; Frank; M; 21; Papago; F; S; Bro.; 4689; Yes; Yes; Id. 9050
4704; Joshua; M; 20; Papago; F; S; Bro.; 4690; Yes; Yes; Id. 9051

KISTO
4705; Jose; M; 55; Papago; F; M; Head; 4691; Yes; Yes; Id. 9135
4706; Josea M.; F; 54; Papago; F; M; Wife; 4692; Yes; Yes; Id. 9136
4707; Pauline; F; 26; Papago; F; S; Dau.; 4693; Yes; Yes; Id. 9137
4708; Aulilh; F; 24; Papago; F; S; Dau.; 4694; Yes; Yes; Id. 9138
4709; Clara; F; 22; Papago; F; S; Dau.; 4695; Yes; Yes; Id. 9139

KISTO
4710; Juan; M; 53; Papago; F; M; Head; 4696; Yes; Yes; Id. 8946
4711; Mollie C.; F; 63; Papago; F; M; Wife; 4697; Yes; Yes; Id. 8947

KISTO
4712; Milsie; M; 32; Papago; F; Wd.; Head; 4698; Yes; Yes; Id. 9124
4713; Armento; M; 14; Papago; F; S; Son; 4699; Yes; Yes; Id. 9125

KISTO
4714; Severin; M; 30; Papago; F; M; Head; 4700; Yes; Yes; Id. 8984
4715; Cecelia; F; 25; Papago; F; M; Wife; 4701; Yes; Yes; Id. 8985
4716; Lucilda; F; 5; Papago; F; S; Dau.; 4702; Yes; Yes; Id. 8986
4717; Jacob; M; 3; Papago; F; S; Son; 4703; Yes; Yes; Id. 8987

Census of the **Ak Chin** reservation of the **Pima Agency** jurisdiction, as of **April 1** , 1932, taken by **A. H. Kneale** , Superintendent.

Key: Number; Surname, Given; Sex (M/F); Age at Last Birthday; Tribe; Degree of Blood (F=Full); Marital Status; Relationship to Head of Family & Last Census No; At Jurisdiction Where Enrolled (Yes/No); (If no – Where); Ward (Yes/No); Identification Numbers

LEWIS
4718; Joe; M; 33; Papago; F; M; Head; 4704; Yes; Yes; Id. 9126
4719; Maria; F; 23; Papago; F; M; Wife; 4705; Yes; Yes; Id. 9127

LEWIS
4720; Serbaco; M; 56; Papago; F; M; Head; 4706; Yes; Yes; Id. 9023
4721; Juanna M.; F; 58; Papago; F; M; Wife; 4707; Yes; Yes; Id. 9024

LISTIA
4722; ---; F; 63; Papago; F; Wd.; Head; 4708; Yes; Yes; Id. 8929

LOOS
4723; Loughi; M; 53; Papago; F; M; Head; 4709; Yes; Yes; Id. 8842
4724; Susie; F; 46; Papago; F; M; Wife; 4710; Yes; Yes; Id. 8843

LOOS
4725; Jesus; M; 73; Papago; F; Wd.; Head; 4711; Yes; Yes; Id. 8912

LOUIS
4726; Tom; M; 51; Papago; F; M; Head; 4712; Yes; Yes; Id. 8930
4727; Elaria; F; 39; Papago; F; M; Wife; 4713; Yes; Yes; Id. 8931
4728; John; M; 16; Papago; F; S; Son; 4714; Yes; Yes; Id. 9099
4729; Anselmo; M; 13; Papago; F; S; Son; 4715; Yes; Yes; Id. 8932

LOUIS
4730; Juan; M; 30; Papago; F; M; Head; 4716; Yes; Yes; Id. 8853
4731; Asiana; F; 22; Papago; F; M; Wife; 4717; Yes; Yes; Id. 8854
4732; Catherine; F; 5; Papago; F; S; Dau.; 4718; Yes; Yes; Id. 8855
4733; Agnes; F; 4; Papago; F; S; Dau.; 4719; Yes; Yes; Id. 8856

LOPEZ
4734; Gonzalo; M; 23; Papago; F; M; Head; 4720; Yes; Yes; Id. 8826
4735; Rosina; F; 22; Papago; F; M; Wife; 4721; Yes; Yes; Id. 8827

LOPEZ
4736; Jose; M; 41; Papago; F; M; Head; 4722; Yes; Yes; Id. 8828
4737; Juliana; F; 51; Papago; F; M; Wife; 4723; Yes; Yes; Id. 8829
4738; Ross; M; 18; Papago; F; S; Son; 4724; Yes; Yes; Id. 8830
4739; Alice; F; 14; Papago; F; S; Dau.; 4725; Yes; Yes; Id. 8831

LOPEZ
4740; Juan; M; 78; Papago; F; Wd.; Head; 4726; Yes; Yes; Id. 8916

LOPEZ
4741; Raphael; M; 38; Papago; F; M; Head; 4727; Yes; Yes; Id. 8815

Key: Number; Surname, Given; Sex (M/F); Age at Last Birthday; Tribe; Degree of Blood (F=Full); Marital Status; Relationship to Head of Family & Last Census No; At Jurisdiction Where Enrolled (Yes/No); (If no – Where); Ward (Yes/No); Identification Numbers

4742; Licentia; F; 38; Papago; F; M; Wife; 4728; Yes; Yes; Id. 8816
4743; Dora; F; 19; Papago; F; S; Dau.; 4729; Yes; Yes; Id. 8817
4744; Annie; F; 16; Papago; F; S; Dau.; 4730; Yes; Yes; Id. 8818
4745; James; M; 15; Papago; F; S; Son; 4731; Yes; Yes; Id. 8819
4746; David; M; 13; Papago; F; S; Son; 4732; Yes; Yes; Id. 8820
4747; George; M; 9; Papago; F; S; Son; 4733; Yes; Yes; Id. 8821

MANUEL
4748; Henry; M; 23; Papago; F; M; Head; 4734; Yes; Yes; Id. 9020
4749; Martha, (Thomas, Martha); F; 18; Papago; F; M; Wife; 4735; Yes; Yes; Id. 8982
4750; George; M; 19; Papago; F; S; Bro.; 4736; Yes; Yes; Id. 9021
4751; Harry; M; 1; Papago; F; S; Son; 4737; Yes; Yes; Id. 9157
4752; Elmer Thomas; M; 1/12; Papago; F; S; Son; --; Yes; Born 3-13-32.; Yes; Id. 9163

MANUEL
4753; Jose; M; 51; Papago; F; M; Head; 4738; Yes; Yes; Id. 8833
4754; Elaria; F; 51; Papago; F; M; Wife; 4739; Yes; Yes; Id. 8834
4755; Miguel, Ralph; M; 19; Papago; F; S; Adpt.son; 4740; Yes; Yes; Id. 8835
4756; Miguel, Malinda; F; 16; Papago; F; S; Adpt.dau.; 4741; Yes; Yes; Id. 8836

MANUEL
4757; Vincent; M; 17; Papago; F; S; alone; 4742; Yes; Yes; Id. 9022

MANUEL
4758; Juan; M; 60; Papago; F; S; Head; 4743; Yes; Yes; Id. 8846

MANUEL
4759; Mark; M; 28; Papago; F; M; Head; 4744; Yes; Yes; Id. 9147
4760; Josepha; F; 27; Papago; F; M; Wife; 4745; Yes; Yes; Id. 9148
4761; Bernard; M; 8; Papago; F; S; Son; 4746; Yes; Yes; Id. 8838
4762; Rema; F; 5; Papago; F; S; Dau.; 4747; Yes; Yes; Id. 8839

MANUEL
4763; Vincent; M; 40; Papago; F; M; Head; 4748; Yes; Yes; Id. 9085
4764; Rosario; F; 42; Papago; F; M; Wife; 4749; Yes; Yes; Id. 9086
4765; Carrie; F; 23; Papago; F; S; Dau.; 4750; Yes; Yes; Id. 9087
4766; Dennis; M; 17; Papago; F; S; Son; 4751; Yes; Yes; Id. 9088
4767; Regina; F; 14; Papago; F; S; Dau.; 4752; Yes; Yes; Id. 9089
4768; Ernest; M; 13; Papago; F; S; Son; 4753; Yes; Yes; Id. 9090
4769; Lincoln; M; 11; Papago; F; S; Son; 4754; Yes; Yes; Id. 9091
4770; Sarah; F; 9; Papago; F; S; Dau.; 4755; Yes; Yes; Id. 9092
4771; Lita; F; 6; Papago; F; S; Dau.; 4756; Yes; Yes; Id. 9093

Census of the **Ak Chin** reservation of the **Pima Agency** jurisdiction, as of **April 1** , 1932, taken by **A. H. Kneale** , Superintendent.

Key: Number; Surname, Given; Sex (M/F); Age at Last Birthday; Tribe; Degree of Blood (F=Full); Marital Status; Relationship to Head of Family & Last Census No; At Jurisdiction Where Enrolled (Yes/No); (If no – Where); Ward (Yes/No); Identification Numbers

MANUEL

4772; Enos; M; 67; Papago; F; M; Head; 4757; Yes; Yes; Id. 8951
4773; Lucy; F; 62; Papago; F; M; Wife; 4758; Yes; Yes; Id. 9952
4774; Lola; F; 20; Papago; F; S; Dau.; 4759; Yes; Yes; Id. 8953

MIGUEL

4775; Lasia; F; 73; Papago; F; Wd.; Head; 4760; Yes; Yes; Id. 8845

MIGUEL

4776; Lika; M; 24; Papago; F; M; Head; 4763; Yes; Yes; Id. 9042
4777; Anita Enos; F; 18; Papago; F; M; Wife; 4651[sic]; Yes; Yes; Id. 9145
4778; Marie; F; 2/12; Papago; F; S; Dau.; --; Yes; Yes; Id. 9162

MIGUEL

4779; Mathis; M; 54; Papago; F; M; Head; 4761; Yes; Yes; Id. 9041
4780; Likano; F; 54; Papago; F; M; Wife; 4762; Yes; Yes; Id. 9043

MIGUEL

4781; Philip; M; 43; Papago; F; M; Head; 4764; Yes; Yes; Id. 8840
4782; Anastasia; F; 48; Papago; F; M; Wife; 4765; Yes; Yes; Id. 8841

MIGUEL

4783; Pevelo; M; 42; Papago; F; M; Head; 4766; Yes; Yes; Id. 8971
4784; Susie; F; 36; Papago; F; M; Wife; 4767; Yes; Yes; Id. 8972
4785; Annie; F; 19; Papago; F; S; Dau.; 4768; Yes; Yes; Id. 8973
4786; Ripa; F; 16; Papago; F; S; Dau.; 4769; Yes; Yes; Id. 8974
4787; Anastasia; F; 12; Papago; F; S; Dau.; 4770; Yes; Yes; Id. 8975
4788; Samuel; M; 11; Papago; F; S; Son; 4771; Yes; Yes; Id. 8976
4789; Majooi; M; 9; Papago; F; S; Son; 4772; Yes; Yes; Id. 8977

MOOCHOO

4790; Jose; M; 54; Papago; F; Wd.; Head; 4773; Yes; Yes; Id. 9119
4791; Lita; F; 36; Papago; F; S; Dau.; 4774; Yes; Yes; Id. 9120

NARCIA

4792; Jose; M; 61; Papago; F; M; Head; 4775; Yes; Yes; Id. 8909
4793; Susie; F; 64; Papago; F; M; Wife; 4776; Yes; Yes; Id. 8910
4794; Augustine; M; 19; Papago; F; S; Son; 4777; Yes; Yes; Id. 8911

NARCIA

4795; Roy; M; 32; Papago; F; M; Head; 4778; Yes; Yes; Id. 8904
4796; Mary; F; 24; Papago; F; M; Wife; 4779; Yes; Yes; Id. 8905
4797; Dennis; M; 6; Papago; F; S; Son; 4780; Yes; Yes; Id. 8906
4798; Leonard; M; 5; Papago; F; S; Son; 4781; Yes; Yes; Id. 8907

Census of the **Ak Chin** reservation of the **Pima Agency** jurisdiction, as of April 1 , 1932, taken by **A. H. Kneale**, Superintendent.

Key: Number; Surname, Given; Sex (M/F); Age at Last Birthday; Tribe; Degree of Blood (F=Full); Marital Status; Relationship to Head of Family & Last Census No; At Jurisdiction Where Enrolled (Yes/No); (If no – Where); Ward (Yes/No); Identification Numbers

NAWLIS
4799; Jose; M; 29; Papago; F; M; Head; 4782; Yes; Yes; Id. 9097
4800; Irene W.; F; 27; Papago; F; M; Wife; 4783; Yes; Yes; Id. 9098

NORRIS
4801; Josepha; F; 63; Papago; F; Wd.; Head; 4784; Yes; Yes; Id. 9028

NORRIS
4802; Juan; M; 50; Papago; F; M; Head; 4785; Yes; Yes; Id. 8873
4803; Ramona; F; 39; Papago; F; M; Wife; 4786; Yes; Yes; Id. 8874
4804; Juan A.; M; 24; Papago; F; S; Son; 4787; Yes; Yes; Id. 8875
4805; Carmelita; F; 20; Papago; F; S; Dau.; 4788; Yes; Yes; Id. 8877
4806; Mary; F; 16; Papago; F; S; Dau.; 4789; Yes; Yes; Id. 8878
4807; Agnes; F; 12; Papago; F; S; Dau.; 4790; Yes; Yes; Id. 8879

NORRIS
4808; Jose M.; M; 22; Papago; F; M; Head; 4791; Yes; Yes; Id. 8876
4809; Tilianna; F; 20; Papago; F; M; Wife; 4792; Yes; Yes; Id. 8850

NORRIS
4810; Ventura; M; 35; Papago; F; M; Head; 4793; Yes; Yes; Id. 9115
4811; Kalisto; F; 33; Papago; F; M; Wife; 4794; Yes; Yes; Id. 9116
4812; Isabel; F; 7; Papago; F; S; Dau.; 4795; Yes; Yes; Id. 9117
4813; Nancy; F; 5; Papago; F; S; Dau.; 4796; Yes; Yes; Id. 9118

OSIF
4814; Juan; M; 70; Papago; F; M; Head; 4797; Yes; Yes; Id. 9082
4815; Candelario; F; 53; Papago; F; M; Wife; 4798; Yes; Yes; Id. 9083
4816; Miguel, Alice; F; 9; Papago; F; S; Gr.dau.; 4799; Yes; Yes; Id. 9084

PABLO
4817; Yonall; M; 24; Papago; F; M; Head; 4800; Yes; Yes; Id. 8823
4818; Eliza; F; 22; Papago; F; M; Wife; 4801; Yes; Yes; Id. 8824
4819; Regina; F; 5; Papago; F; S; Dau.; 4802; Yes; Yes; Id. 8825

PABLO
4820; Yasilo; M; 43; Papago; F; M; Head; 4803; Yes; Yes; Id. 8880
4821; Tonia; F; 25; Papago; F; M; Wife; 4804; Yes; Yes; Id. 8881
4822; Verena; F; 9; Papago; F; S; Dau.; 4805; Yes; Yes; Id. 8882
4823; Philipa; F; 6; Papago; F; S; Dau.; 4806; Yes; Yes; Id. 8883
4824; Angelita; F; 3; Papago; F; S; Dau.; 4807; Yes; Yes; Id. 8884

PALONE
4825; Juan; M; 49; Papago; F; M; Head; 4808; Yes; Yes; Id. 8847
4826; Jesus; F; 47; Papago; F; M; Wife; 4809; Yes; Yes; Id. 8848

Census of the **Ak Chin** reservation of the **Pima Agency** jurisdiction, as of **April 1** , 1932, taken by **A. H. Kneale** , Superintendent.

Key: Number; Surname, Given; Sex (M/F); Age at Last Birthday; Tribe; Degree of Blood (F=Full); Marital Status; Relationship to Head of Family & Last Census No; At Jurisdiction Where Enrolled (Yes/No); (If no – Where); Ward (Yes/No); Identification Numbers

4827; Ahill J.; M; 23; Papago; F; S; Son; 4810; Yes; Yes; Id. 8849
4828; Raphael; M; 17; Papago; F; S; Son; 4811; Yes; Yes; Id. 8851
4829; Elist; F; 9; Papago; F; S; Dau.; 4812; Yes; Yes; Id. 8852

PATOPISA
4830; Fannie; F; 41; Papago; F; M; Wife; 4813; Yes; Yes; Id. 8811

PATRICIO
4831; Andres; M; 45; Papago; F; M; Head; 4814; Yes; Yes; Id. 8919
4832; Lola; F; 39; Papago; F; M; Wife; 4815; Yes; Yes; Id. 8920
4833; Andrew, Amelia; F; 8; Papago; F; S; St.dau.; 4816; Yes; Yes; Id. 8921

PAVILO
~~Frank; M; 63; Papago; F; M; Head; 4817; Died; 6-17-31.~~; Yes; Id. 8864
4834; Maria; F; 54; Papago; F; Wd.; Head; 4818; Yes; Yes; Id. 8865
4835; Frank; M; 23; Papago; F; S; Son; 4819; Yes; Yes; Id. 8866
4836; Vavages; M; 21; Papago; F; S; Son; 4820; Yes; Yes; Id. 8867

QUISKO
4837; Xavier; M; 40; Papago; F; M; Head; 4821; Yes; Yes; Id. 9149
4838; Mollie T.; F; 39; Papago; F; M; Wife; 4822; Yes; Yes; Id. 9150
4839; Vincent; M; 17; Papago; F; S; Son; 4823; Yes; Yes; Id. 9151
4840; Jose; M; 14; Papago; F; S; Son; 4824; Yes; Yes; Id. 9152
4841; Claviana; F; 6; Papago; F; S; Dau.; 4825; Yes; Yes; Id. 9153
4842; Sarah; F; 4; Papago; F; S; Dau.; 4826; Yes; Yes; Id. 9154

RAMON
4843; Jose; M; 58; Papago; F; S; Head; 4827; Yes; Yes; Id. 8844

RAMON
4844; Spraad; M; 61; Papago; F; M; Head; 4828; Yes; Yes; Id. 9121
4845; Paula; F; 60; Papago; F; M; Wife; 4829; Yes; Yes; Id. 9122
4846; Vilihina; F; 29; Papago; F; S; Dau.; 4830; Yes; Yes; Id. 9123

RAPHAEL
4847; Juan; M; 31; Papago; F; M; Head; 4831; Yes; Yes; Id. 8868
4848; Maria; F; 39; Papago; F; M; Wife; 4832; Yes; Yes; Id. 8869
4849; Lena; F; 17; Papago; F; S; Dau.; 4833; Yes; Yes; Id. 8870
4850; Annie; F; 11; Papago; F; S; Dau.; 4834; Yes; Yes; Id. 8871
4851; Xavier; M; 10; Papago; F; S; Son; 4835; Yes; Yes; Id. 8872

SMITH
4852; Charlie; M; 26; Papago; F; S; Head; 4836; Yes; Yes; Id. 8832

Census of the **Ak Chin** reservation of the **Pima Agency** jurisdiction, as of **April 1**, 1932, taken by **A. H. Kneale**, Superintendent.

Key: Number; Surname, Given; Sex (M/F); Age at Last Birthday; Tribe; Degree of Blood (F=Full); Marital Status; Relationship to Head of Family & Last Census No; At Jurisdiction Where Enrolled (Yes/No); (If no - Where); Ward (Yes/No); Identification Numbers

SMITH
4853; Charlie; M; 57; Papago; F; M; Head; 4837; Yes; Yes; Id. 8899
4854; Juanna; F; 45; Papago; F; M; Wife; 4838; Yes; Yes; Id. 8900
4855; Mathew; M; 11; Papago; F; S; Son; 4839; Yes; Yes; Id. 8901
4856; Amos; M; 8; Papago; F; S; Son; 4840; Yes; Yes; Id. 8902

STEEN
4857; Lucas; M; 58; Papago; F; Wd.; Head; 4841; Yes; Yes; Id. 9039

TASHQUINTH
4858; Joe; M; 27; Papago; F; M; Head; 4842; Yes; Yes; Id. 9107
4859; Liboria; F; 27; Papago; F; M; Wife; 4843; Yes; Yes; Id. 9108
4860; Mable; F; 7; Papago; F; S; Dau.; 4844; Yes; Yes; Id. 9109
4861; Edward; M; 5; Papago; F; S; Son; 4845; Yes; Yes; Id. 9110

THOMAS
4862; Ferdinand; M; 41; Papago; F; Wd.; Head; 4846; Yes; Yes; Id. 8814
4863; Helen; F; 16; Papago; F; S; Dau.; 4847; Yes; Yes; Id. 8967
4864; Celestine; F; 11; Papago; F; S; Dau.; 4848; Yes; Yes; Id. 8968
4865; Catherine; F; 7; Papago; F; S; Dau.; 4849; Yes; Yes; Id. 8969
4866; Martha; F; 12; Papago; F; S; Dau.; 4850; Yes; Yes; Id. 8970

THOMAS
4867; Joseph; M; 62; Papago; F; M; Head; 4851; Yes; Yes; Id. 8980
4868; Maria; F; 51; Papago; F; M; Wife; 4852; Yes; Yes; Id. 8981
4869; Ventura; M; 16; Papago; F; S; Son; 4853; Yes; Yes; Id. 8983

THOMAS
4870; Joseph; M; 46; Papago; F; M; Head; 4854; Yes; Yes; Id. 8890
4871; Josepha; F; 40; Papago; F; M; Wife; 4855; Yes; Yes; Id. 8891
4872; Lena; F; 14; Papago; F; S; Dau.; 4856; Yes; Yes; Id. 8893
4873; Anthony; M; 12; Papago; F; S; Son; 4857; Yes; Yes; Id. 8894
4874; Harry; M; 11; Papago; F; S; Son; 4858; Yes; Yes; Id. 8895
4875; Herbert; M; 10; Papago; F; S; Son; 4859; Yes; Yes; Id. 8896
4876; Bernice; F; 6; Papago; F; S; Dau.; 4860; Yes; Yes; Id. 8897
4877; Mathias; M; 4; Papago; F; S; Son; 4861; Yes; Yes; Id. 8898
4878; Edmund; M; 1; Papago; F; S; Son; 4862; Yes; Yes; Id. 9159

THOMAS
4879; Pete; M; 45; Papago; F; Wd.; Head; 4863; Yes; Yes; Id. 9052
4880; Regina; F; 8; Papago; F; S; Dau.; 4864; Yes; Yes; Id. 9053
4881; Josephine; F; 17; Papago; F; S; Dau.; 4865; Yes; Yes; Id. 9054

THOMAS
4882; Juan; M; 50; Papago; F; M; Head; 4866; Yes; Yes; Id. 9060

Census of the **Ak Chin** reservation of the **Pima Agency** jurisdiction, as of **April 1**, 1932, taken by **A. H. Kneale**, Superintendent.

Key: Number; Surname, Given; Sex (M/F); Age at Last Birthday; Tribe; Degree of Blood (F=Full); Marital Status; Relationship to Head of Family & Last Census No; At Jurisdiction Where Enrolled (Yes/No); (If no – Where); Ward (Yes/No); Identification Numbers

4883; Josepha; F; 47; Papago; F; M; Wife; 4867; Yes; Yes; Id. 9061
4884; Mary; F; 21; Papago; F; S; Dau.; 4868; Yes; Yes; Id. 9062
4885; Ignacio; F; 18; Papago; F; S; Dau.; 4869; Yes; Yes; Id. 9063

THOMAS
4886; Marcus; M; 59; Papago; F; M; Head; 4870; Yes; Yes; Id. 8988
4887; Ciana; F; 55; Papago; F; M; Wife; 4871; Yes; Yes; Id. 8989
4888; Miguel; M; 30; Papago; F; S; Son; 4872; Yes; Yes; Id. 8990
4889; Sanatoriata; M; 27; Papago; F; S; Son; 4873; Yes; Yes; Id. 8991
4890; Justin; M; 25; Papago; F; S; Son; 4874; Yes; Yes; Id. 8992
4891; Jack; M; 21; Papago; F; S; Son; 4875; Yes; Yes; Id. 8993
4892; Cisko; M; 19; Papago; F; S; Son; 4876; Yes; Yes; Id. 8994
4893; Alonzo; M; 15; Papago; F; S; Son; 4877; Yes; Yes; Id. 8996
4894; Sarah; M; 11; Papago; F; S; Dau.; 4878; Yes; Yes; Id. 8997
4895; Lucas; M; 7; Papago; F; S; Son; 4879; Yes; Yes; Id. 8998
4896; Enick; M; 4; Papago; F; S; Son; 4880; Yes; Yes; Id. 8999

THOMAS
4897; Nestor; M; 31; Papago; F; M; Head; 4881; Yes; Yes; Id. 9055
4898; Listiana; F; 28; Papago; F; M; Wife; 4882; Yes; Yes; Id. 9056
4899; Dorothy; M; 10; Papago; F; S; Dau.; 4883; Yes; Yes; Id. 9057
4900; Edith; M; 8; Papago; F; S; Dau.; 4884; Yes; Yes; Id. 9058
4901; Everett; M; 6; Papago; F; S; Son; 4885; Yes; Yes; Id. 9059

THOMAS
4902; Norris; M; 53; Papago; F; M; Head; 4886; Yes; Yes; Id. 8963
4903; Lita; F; 88; Papago; F; M; Wife; 4887; Yes; Yes; Id. 8964
4904; Jose A.; M; 32; Papago; F; S; Son; 4888; Yes; Yes; Id. 8965
4905; Ambrose; M; 25; Papago; F; S; Son; 4889; Yes; Yes; Id. 8966

VASILO
4906; Jose; M; 29; Papago; F; S; Head; 4890; Yes; Yes; Id. 8889

VAVAGES
4907; Jose; M; 51; Papago; F; M; Head; 4891; Yes; Yes; Id. 8801
4908; Helen; F; 51; Papago; F; M; Wife; 4892; Yes; Yes; Id. 8802
4909; Narcis, Davidson; M; 18; Papago; F; S; St.son; 4893; Yes; Yes; Id. 8803
4910; Narcis, Francis; M; 15; Papago; F; S; St.son; 4894; Yes; Yes; Id. 8804
4911; Narcis, Edward; M; 13; Papago; F; S; St.son; 4895; Yes; Yes; Id. 8805

VAVAGES
4912; Juan; M; 53; Papago; F; M; Head; 4896; Yes; Yes; Id. 9066
4913; Viliana; F; 51; Papago; F; M; Wife; 4897; Yes; Yes; Id. 9067

Census of the **Ak Chin** reservation of the **Pima Agency** jurisdiction, as of **April 1** , 1932, taken by **A. H. Kneale** , Superintendent.

Key: Number; Surname, Given; Sex (M/F); Age at Last Birthday; Tribe; Degree of Blood (F=Full); Marital Status; Relationship to Head of Family & Last Census No; At Jurisdiction Where Enrolled (Yes/No); (If no – Where); Ward (Yes/No); Identification Numbers

VAVAGES
4914; Juan; M; 63; Papago; F; Wd.; Head; 4898; Yes; Yes; Id. 9025
4915; Stanley; M; 21; Papago; F; S; Son; 4899; Yes; Yes; Id. 9026

VINCENT
4916; Gaulupe; F; 74; Papago; F; Wd.; Head; 4900; Yes; Yes; Id. 9101

VINCENT
4917; James; M; 32; Papago; F; M; Head; 4901; Yes; Yes; Id. 8806
4918; Listiana; F; 26; Papago; F; M; Wife; 4902; Yes; Yes; Id. 8807

VINCENT
4919; Jose; M; 34; Papago; F; M; Head; 4903; Yes; Yes; Id. 8808
4920; Margarita; F; 24; Papago; F; M; Wife; 4904; Yes; Yes; Id. 8809
4921; Lester B.; M; 4; Papago; F; S; Son; 4905; Yes; Yes; Id. 8810
4922; Loraine G.; F; 1; Papago; F; S; Dau.; 4906; Yes; Yes; Id. 9158

YAYAPO
4923; ---; M; 72; Papago; F; Wd.; Head; 4907; Yes; Yes; Id. 8917

YONALL
4924; Alvaretta; M; 26; Papago; F; S; Head; 4908; Yes; Yes; Id. 9069
4925; Ellesa; F; 22; Papago; F; S; Sister; 4909; Yes; Yes; Id. 9070
4926; Lobis; M; 15; Papago; F; S; Brother; 4910; Yes; Yes; Id. 9071
4927; Venalso; M; 12; Papago; F; S; Brother; 4911; Yes; Yes; Id. 9072
4928; Ango; M; 8; Papago; F; S; Brother; 4912; Yes; Yes; Id. 9074
4929; Kooga; M; 10; Papago; F; S; Brother; 4913; Yes; Yes; Id. 9073

YONALL
4930; Yonalso; M; 31; Papago; F; S; Head; 4914; Yes; Yes; Id. 9068

YOUNG
4931; Augustine; M; 30; Papago; F; M; Head; 4915; Yes; Yes; Id. 9033
4932; Mary; F; 26; Papago; F; M; Wife; 4916; Yes; Yes; Id. 9034
4933; Felix; M; 10; Papago; F; S; Son; 4917; Yes; Yes; Id. 9035
4934; Viltma; F; 8; Papago; F; S; Dau.; 4918; Yes; Yes; Id. 9036

YOUNG
4935; Louis; M; 71; Papago; F; M; Head; 4919; Yes; Yes; Id. 9094
4936; Annie; F; 32; Papago; F; M; Wife; 4920; Yes; Yes; Id. 9095
4937; Jonas; M; 27; Papago; F; S; Son; 4921; Yes; Yes; Id. 9096

Gila Bend Reservation
of the **Pima Agency**
as of **April 1**, 1932
[Papago]

Census of the **Gila Bend** reservation of the **Pima Agency** jurisdiction; as of **April 1** ; 1932; taken by **A. H. Kneale** ; Superintendent.

Key: Number; Surname; Given; Sex (M/F); Age at Last Birthday; Tribe; Degree of Blood (F=Full); Marital Status; Relationship to Head of Family & Last Census No; At Jurisdiction Where Enrolled (Yes/No); (If no – Where); Ward (Yes/No); Identification Numbers

AGNICIO
4938; Juan; M; 38; Papago; F; M; Head; 4922; Yes; Yes; Id. 10696
4939; Rose; F; 34; Papago; F; M; Wife; 4923; Yes; Yes; Id. 10697

ANDREW
4940; James; M; 28; Papago; F; M; Head; 4924; Yes; Yes; Id. 10676
4941; Licita; F; 25; Papago; F; M; Wife; 4925; Yes; Yes; Id. 10677
4942; Josepha; F; 9; Papago; F; S; Dau.; 4926; Yes; Yes; Id. 10678
4943; Andreas; M; 7; Papago; F; S; Son; 4927; Yes; Yes; Id. 10679
4944; Henry; M; 6; Papago; F; S; Son; 4928; Yes; Yes; Id. 10680

BAJOS
4945; Juan; M; 28; Papago; F; M; Head; 4929; Yes; Yes; Id. 10547
4946; Susanna; F; 23; Papago; F; M; Wife; 4930; Yes; Yes; Id. 10548
4947; Jose; M; 6; Papago; F; S; Son; 4931; Yes; Yes; Id. 10549

BURRULL
4948; Cecelia; F; 48; Papago; F; Wd.; Wife; 4932; Yes; Yes; Id. 10644
4949; Valdez; M; 22; Papago; F; S; Son; 4933; Yes; Yes; Id. 10645

CALINA
4950; Jose; M; 27; Papago; F; M; Head; 4934; Yes; Yes; Id. 10673
4951; Lola; F; 22; Papago; F; M; Wife; 4935; Yes; Yes; Id. 10674
4952; Felix; M; 6; Papago; F; S; Son; 4936; Yes; Yes; Id. 10675

CIPRIANO
4953; Carlos; M; 30; Papago; F; M; Head; 4937; Yes; Yes; Id. 10716
4954; Valiciana; F; 26; Papago; F; M; Wife; 4938; Yes; Yes; Id. 10717
4955; Ramon; M; 8; Papago; F; S; Son; 4939; Yes; Yes; Id. 10718
4956; Antonia; F; 6; Papago; F; S; Dau.; 4940; Yes; Yes; Id. 10719

CIPRIANA
4957; Charley; M; 33; Papago; F; M; Head; 4941; Yes; Yes; Id. 10520
4958; Threna S; F; 23; Papago; F; M; Wife; 4942; Yes; Yes; Id. 10521
4959; Lee; M; 6; Papago; F; S; Son; 4943; Yes; Yes; Id. 10522

CIPRIANA
4960; Louis; M; 29; Papago; F; S; Head; 4944; Yes; Yes; Id. 10720

CURLEY
4961; George; M; 33; Papago; F; M; Head; 4945; Yes; Yes; Id. 10569
4962; Vejila; F; 25; Papago; F; M; Wife; 4946; Yes; Yes; Id. 10570
4963; Delphina; F; 9; Papago; F; S; Head[sic]; 4947; Yes; Yes; Id. 10571
4964; Johnny; M; 6; Papago; F; S; Son; 4948; Yes; Yes; Id. 10572
4965; Jenny; F; 4; Papago; F; S; Dau.; 4949; Yes; Yes; Id. 10573

211

Census of the **Gila Bend** reservation of the **Pima Agency** jurisdiction; as of **April 1** ; 1932; taken by **A. H. Kneale** ; Superintendent.

Key: Number; Surname; Given; Sex (M/F); Age at Last Birthday; Tribe; Degree of Blood (F=Full); Marital Status; Relationship to Head of Family & Last Census No; At Jurisdiction Where Enrolled (Yes/No); (If no – Where); Ward (Yes/No); Identification Numbers

DOLPHITO
4966; Jose; M; 31; Papago; F; S; Head; 4950; Yes; Yes; Id. 10688

DOMINGO
4967; Joe; M; 43; Papago; F; M; Head; 4951; Yes; Yes; Id. 10649
4968; Mollie; F; 43; Papago; F; M; Wife; 4952; Yes; Yes; Id. 10650
4969; Alverito; M; 22; Papago; F; S; Son; 4953; Yes; Yes; Id. 10651
4970; Talos; M; 19; Papago; F; S; Son; 4954; Yes; Yes; Id. 10652
4971; Jesus; M; 12; Papago; F; S; Son; 4955; Yes; Yes; Id. 10653
4972; Anton; M; 7; Papago; F; S; Son; 4956; Yes; Yes; Id. 10654

ENIS
4973; Dora; F; 52; Papago; F; Wd.; Head; 4957; Yes; Yes; Id. 10721
4974; John; M; 22; Papago; F; S; Son; 4958; Yes; Yes; Id. 10722

FLORES
4975; Alovencia; M; 48; Papago; F; M; Head; 4959; Yes; Yes; Id. 10624
4976; Andrea; F; 43; Papago; F; M; Wife; 4960; Yes; Yes; Id. 10623
4977; Charlie; M; 17; Papago; F; S; Son; 4961; Yes; Yes; Id. 10625
4978; Levine; M; 13; Papago; F; S; Son; 4962; Yes; Yes; Id. 10626
4979; Miguel J.; M; 16; Papago; F; S; Son; 4963; Yes; Yes; Id. 10627
4980; Jose L.; M; 19; Papago; F; S; Son; 4964; Yes; Yes; Id. 10628

HELIPA
4981; Pete; M; 63; Papago; F; M; Head; 4965; Yes; Yes; Id. 10509
4982; Matiano S.; F; 48; Papago; F; M; Wife; 4966; Yes; Yes; Id. 10510
4983; Alina; F; 20; Papago; F; S; Dau.; 4967; Yes; Yes; Id. 10511
4984; Lorenzo; M; 17; Papago; F; S; Son; 4968; Yes; Yes; Id. 10512

JACK
4985; Romo; M; 55; Papago; F; M; Head; 4969; Yes; Yes; Id. 10506
4986; Jesus; F; 43; Papago; F; M; Wife; 4970; Yes; Yes; Id. 10507
4987; Telejo; F; 20; Papago; F; S; Dau.; 4971; Yes; Yes; Id. 10508

JESUS
4988; Chappo; M; 28; Papago; F; M; Head; 4972; Yes; Yes; Id. 10550
4989; Saviano; F; 28; Papago; F; M; Wife; 4973; Yes; Yes; Id. 10551
4990; Enylora; F; 9; Papago; F; S; Dau.; 4974; Yes; Yes; Id. 10552
4991; Alvase; M; 7; Papago; F; S; Son; 4975; Yes; Yes; Id. 10553
4992; Margaret; F; 5; Papago; F; S; Dau.; 4976; Yes; Yes; Id. 10554

JOAQUIN
4993; Swasta; M; 28; Papago; F; M; Head; 4977; Yes; Yes; Id. 10527
4994; Sarah; F; 28; Papago; F; M; Wife; 4978; Yes; Yes; Id. 10528
4995; Lancisco; M; 7; Papago; F; S; Son; 4979; Yes; Yes; Id. 10529

Census of the **Gila Bend** reservation of the **Pima Agency** jurisdiction; as of **April 1** ; 1932; taken by **A. H. Kneale** ; Superintendent.

Key: Number; Surname; Given; Sex (M/F); Age at Last Birthday; Tribe; Degree of Blood (F=Full); Marital Status; Relationship to Head of Family & Last Census No; At Jurisdiction Where Enrolled (Yes/No); (If no – Where); Ward (Yes/No); Identification Numbers

4996; Jose; M; 6; Papago; F; S; Son; 4980; Yes; Yes; Id. 10530
4997; Enecia L.; F; 12; Papago; F; S; Dau.; 4981; Yes; Yes; Id. 10531

JONES
4998; Alcilina; M; 32; Papago; F; M; Head; 4982; Yes; Yes; Id. 10703
4999; Lois; F; 22; Papago; F; M; Wife; 4983; Yes; Yes; Id. 10704

JOSE
5000; Moore; M; 33; Papago; F; M; Head; 4984; Yes; Yes; Id. 10681
5001; Philipa; F; 33; Papago; F; M; Wife; 4985; Yes; Yes; Id. 10682
5002; Helen; F; 7; Papago; F; S; Dau.; 4986; Yes; Yes; Id. 10683

JOSE
5003; Pancho; M; 48; Papago; F; M; Head; 4987; Yes; Yes; Id. 10574
5004; Marie; F; 43; Papago; F; M; Wife; 4988; Yes; Yes; Id. 10575
5005; Juan; M; 24; Papago; F; S; Son; 4989; Yes; Yes; Id. 10576
5006; Maria; F; 8; Papago; F; S; Dau.; 4990; Yes; Yes; Id. 10577
5007; Jesus; F; 6; Papago; F; S; Dau.; 4991; Yes; Yes; Id. 10578

JUAN
5008; Jose; M; 43; Papago; F; Wd.; Head; 4992; Yes; Yes; Id. 10612
5009; Lavonine; F; 23; Papago; F; S; Dau.; 4993; Yes; Yes; Id. 10613
5010; Logan; M; 19; Papago; F; S; Son; 4994; Yes; Yes; Id. 10614
5011; Tagler; F; 18; Papago; F; S; Dau.; 4995; Yes; Yes; Id. 10615
5012; Tulla; F; 17; Papago; F; S; Dau.; 4996; Yes; Yes; Id. 10616

LEWIS
5013; Jose; M; 38; Papago; F; M; Head; 4997; Yes; Yes; Id. 10610
5014; Tellecito; F; 33; Papago; F; M; Wife; 4998; Yes; Yes; Id. 10611

LEWIS
5015; Juan; M; 47; Papago; F; M; Head; 4999; Yes; Yes; Id. 10560
5016; Juanna; F; 43; Papago; F; M; Wife; 5000; Yes; Yes; Id. 10561
5017; Tomassa; F; 8; Papago; F; S; Dau.; 5001; Yes; Yes; Id. 10562
5018; Peter; M; 19; Papago; F; S; St.son; 5002; Yes; Yes; Id. 10563
5019; Elizabeth; F; 9; Papago; F; S; Dau.; 5003; Yes; Yes; Id. 10564

LEWIS
5020; Juan; M; 27; Papago; F; M; Head; 5004; Yes; Yes; Id. 10583
5021; Mollie A.; F; 25; Papago; F; M; Wife; 5005; Yes; Yes; Id. 10584

LEWIS
5022; Juan; M; 58; Papago; F; M; Head; 5006; Yes; Yes; Id. 10501
5023; Melly J.; F; 53; Papago; F; M; Wife; 5007; Yes; Yes; Id. 10502
5024; Vincent; M; 12; Papago; F; S; Son; 5008; Yes; Yes; Id. 10503

Census of the **Gila Bend** reservation of the **Pima Agency** jurisdiction; as of **April 1** ; 1932; taken by **A. H. Kneale** ; Superintendent.

Key: Number; Surname; Given; Sex (M/F); Age at Last Birthday; Tribe; Degree of Blood (F=Full); Marital Status; Relationship to Head of Family & Last Census No; At Jurisdiction Where Enrolled (Yes/No); (If no – Where); Ward (Yes/No); Identification Numbers

5025; Miguel; M; 10; Papago; F; S; Son; 5009; Yes; Yes; Id. 10504
5026; Abel; M; 8; Papago; F; S; Son; 5010; Yes; Yes; Id. 10505

LORA
5027; Jose; M; 38; Papago; F; M; Head; 5011; Yes; Yes; Id. 10590
5028; Melcia; F; 38; Papago; F; M; Wife; 5012; Yes; Yes; Id. 10591
5029; Avianita; F; 19; Papago; F; S; Dau.; 5013; Yes; Yes; Id. 10592
5030; Josianna; F; 18; Papago; F; S; Dau.; 5014; Yes; Yes; Id. 10593
5031; Pauline; F; 9; Papago; F; S; Dau.; 5015; Yes; Yes; Id. 10594
5032; Viotisch; M; 7; Papago; F; S; Son; 5016; Yes; Yes; Id. 10595
5033; Mary M.; F; 4; Papago; F; S; Dau.; 5017; Yes; Yes; Id. 10596

LINSO
5034; Jose; M; 28; Papago; F; M; Head; 5018; Yes; Yes; Id. 10660
5035; Evelena; F; 25; Papago; F; M; Wife; 5019; Yes; Yes; Id. 10661
5036; Magdalene; F; 7; Papago; F; S; Dau.; 5020; Yes; Yes; Id. 10662
5037; Elihu; M; 5; Papago; F; S; Son; 5021; Yes; Yes; Id. 10663

LOPEZ
5038; Juan; M; 48; Papago; F; Wd.; Head; 5022; Yes; Yes; Id. 10691
5039; Mike; M; 29; Papago; F; S; Son; 5023; Yes; Yes; Id. 10692

LORENZO
5040; ---; M; 52; Papago; F; M; Head; 5024; Yes; Yes; Id. 10513
5041; Josepha; F; 48; Papago; F; M; Wife; 5025; Yes; Yes; Id. 10514
5042; Carlos; M; 22; Papago; F; S; Son; 5026; Yes; Yes; Id. 10515
5043; Juan; M;20; Papago; F; S; Son; 5027; Yes; Yes; Id. 10516
5044; Miguel; M; 15; Papago; F; S; Son; 5028; Yes; Yes; Id. 10517
5045; Mario L.; F; 17; Papago; F; S; Dau.; 5029; Yes; Yes; Id. 10518
5046; Pauline; F; 13; Papago; F; S; Dau.; 5030; Yes; Yes; Id. 10519
5047; Valcia; F; 10; Papago; F; S; Dau.; 5031; Yes; Yes; Id. 10520

LUCA
5048; Juan; M; 38; Papago; F; M; Head; 5032; Yes; Yes; Id. 10707
5049; Josalia; F; 31; Papago; F; M; Wife; 5033; Yes; Yes; Id. 10708
5050; Raviana; M; 16; Papago; F; S; Son; 5034; Yes; Yes; Id. 10709
5051; Rosila; F; 15; Papago; F; S; Dau.; 5035; Yes; Yes; Id. 10710
5052; Chiquita; F; 11; Papago; F; S; Dau.; 5036; Yes; Yes; Id. 10711
5053; Louis; M; 10; Papago; F; S; Son; 5037; Yes; Yes; Id. 10712

MANUEL
5054; John; M; 29; Papago; F; M; Head; 5038; Yes; Yes; Id. 10523
5055; Mildred A; F; 22; Papago; F; M; Wife; 5039; Yes; Yes; Id. 10524
5056; Jose M.; M; 4; Papago; F; S; Son; 5040; Yes; Yes; Id. 10525
5057; Salphin; F; 7; Papago; F; S; St.Dau.; 5041; Yes; Yes; Id. 10526

Census of the **Gila Bend** reservation of the **Pima Agency** jurisdiction; as of **April 1** ; 1932; taken by **A. H. Kneale** ; Superintendent.

Key: Number; Surname; Given; Sex (M/F); Age at Last Birthday; Tribe; Degree of Blood (F=Full); Marital Status; Relationship to Head of Family & Last Census No; At Jurisdiction Where Enrolled (Yes/No); (If no – Where); Ward (Yes/No); Identification Numbers

MANUEL

5058; Miguel; M; 30; Papago; F; M; Head; 5042; Yes; Yes; Id. 10555
5059; Espelieto; F; 26; Papago; F; M; Wife; 5043; Yes; Yes; Id. 10556
5060; Juan M.; M; 12; Papago; F; S; Son; 5044; Yes; Yes; Id. 10557
5061; Lossa M.; F; 9; Papago; F; S; Dau.; 5045; Yes; Yes; Id. 10559
5062; Francisco; M; 7; Papago; F; S; Son; 5046; Yes; Yes; Id. 10558

MANUEL

5063; Susie; F; 49; Papago; F; Wd.; Head; 5047; Yes; Yes; Id. 10699
5064; Paul; M; 28; Papago; F; S; Son; 5048; Yes; Yes; Id. 10700
5065; Oulina M.; F; 20; Papago; F; S; Dau.; 5049; Yes; Yes; Id. 10706

MIGUEL

5066; Juan; M; 43; Papago; F; M; Head; 5050; Yes; Yes; Id. 10639
5067; Helena; F; 32; Papago; F; M; Wife; 5051; Yes; Yes; Id. 10640
5068; Essau; M; 9; Papago; F; S; Son; 5052; Yes; Yes; Id. 10641
5069; John; M; 8; Papago; F; S; Son; 5053; Yes; Yes; Id. 10642
5070; Ramona; F; 7; Papago; F; S; Dau.; 5054; Yes; Yes; Id. 10643

MIKE

5071; Johnny; M; 43; Papago; F; M; Head; 5055; Yes; Yes; Id. 10602
5072; Selaphina; F; 38; Papago; F; M; Wife; 5056; Yes; Yes; Id. 10603
5073; Onor; M; 18; Papago; F; S; Son; 5057; Yes; Yes; Id. 10604
5074; Jocinta; M; 17; Papago; F; S; Son; 5058; Yes; Yes; Id. 10605
5075; Joe; M; 16; Papago; F; S; Son; 5059; Yes; Yes; Id. 10606

MOLISTA

5076; Juan; M; 41; Papago; F; S; Head; 5060; Yes; Yes; Id. 10693
5077; Guadulupa; F; 61; Papago; F; Wd.; Mother; 5061; Yes; Yes; Id. 10694
5078; Anastasia; F; 23; Papago; F; S; Sister; 5062; Yes; Yes; Id. 10695

MOORE

5079; Jose; M; 48; Papago; F; M; Head; 5063; Yes; Yes; Id. 10597
5080; Lucianna; F; 43; Papago; F; M; Wife; 5064; Yes; Yes; Id. 10598
5081; Lose; F; 17; Papago; F; S; Dau.; 5065; Yes; Yes; Id. 10599
5082; Anistacio; F; 16; Papago; F; S; Dau.; 5066; Yes; Yes; Id. 10600
5083; Edward; M; 24; Papago; F; S; Son; 5067; Yes; Yes; Id. 10601

MULLA

5084; Juan; M; 43; Papago; F; M; Head; 5068; Yes; Yes; Id. 10684
5085; Ignacio; F; 45; Papago; F; M; Wife; 5069; Yes; Yes; Id. 10685

OIGUIN

5086; Cecelia; F; 53; Papago; F; M; Head; 5070; Yes; Yes; Id. 10607
5087; Isabelle; F; 23; Papago; 1/4x; S; Dau.; 5071; Yes; Yes; Id. 10723

Census of the **Gila Bend** reservation of the **Pima Agency** jurisdiction; as of **April 1** ; 1932; taken by **A. H. Kneale** ; Superintendent.

Key: Number; Surname; Given; Sex (M/F); Age at Last Birthday; Tribe; Degree of Blood (F=Full); Marital Status; Relationship to Head of Family & Last Census No; At Jurisdiction Where Enrolled (Yes/No); (If no – Where); Ward (Yes/No); Identification Numbers

5088; Alora; F; 22; Papago; 1/4x; S; Dau.; 5072; Yes; Yes; Id. 10608
5089; Louis; M; 19; Papago; 1/4x; S; Son; 5073; Yes; Yes; Id. 10609

OLOSO

5090; Paulo; M; 31; Papago; F; M; Head; 5074; Yes; Yes; Id. 10622
5091; Eyleen; F; 28; Papago; F; M; Wife; 5075; Yes; Yes; Id. 10713

ORTEGA

5092; Manuel; M; 35; Papago; F; M; Head; 5076; Yes; Yes; Id. 10714
5093; Theresa; F; 33; Papago; F; M; Wife; 5077; Yes; Yes; Id. 10715

PABLO

5094; Alejo; M; 31; Papago; F; M; Head; 5078; Yes; Yes; Id. 10655
5095; Eyleena; F; 31; Papago; F; M; Wife; 5079; Yes; Yes; Id. 10656
5096; Thomas; M; 9; Papago; F; S; Son; 5080; Yes; Yes; Id. 10657
5097; Alunia; M; 7; Papago; F; S; Son; 5081; Yes; Yes; Id. 10658
5098; Amelia; F; 6; Papago; F; S; Dau.; 5082; Yes; Yes; Id. 10659

PABLO

5099; Jose; M; 48; Papago; F; M; Head; 5083; Yes; Yes; Id. 10686
5100; Marie; F; 46; Papago; F; M; Wife; 5084; Yes; Yes; Id. 10687

PABLO

5101; Jose; M; 39; Papago; F; M; Head; 5085; Yes; Yes; Id. 10579
5102; Josepha; F; 36; Papago; F; M; Wife; 5086; Yes; Yes; Id. 10580
5103; Vincensen; M; 17; Papago; F; S; Son; 5087; Yes; Yes; Id. 10581
5104; Metinta; M; 15; Papago; F; S; Son; 5088; Yes; Yes; Id. 10582

PABLO

5105; Stephen; M; 31; Papago; F; M; Head; 5089; Yes; Yes; Id. 10689
5106; Cecelia; F; 23; Papago; F; M; Wife; 5090; Yes; Yes; Id. 10690

PELONE

5107; Victor; M; 43; Papago; F; M; Head; 5091; Yes; Yes; Id. 10646
5108; Salela; F; 43; Papago; F; M; Wife; 5092; Yes; Yes; Id. 10647
5109; Susie; F; 18; Papago; F; S; Dau.; 5093; Yes; Yes; Id. 10648

RICARDO

5110; Pilone; M; 22; Papago; F; M; Head; 5094; Yes; Yes; Id. 10664
5111; Antonia; F; 22; Papago; F; M; Wife; 5095; Yes; Yes; Id. 10665
5112; George; M; 5; Papago; F; S; Son; 5096; Yes; Yes; Id. 10666

SANDIEGO

5113; Lewis; M; 42; Papago; F; M; Head; 5097; Yes; Yes; Id. 10542
5114; Listianna; F; 35; Papago; F; M; Wife; 5098; Yes; Yes; Id. 10543

Census of the **Gila Bend** reservation of the **Pima Agency** jurisdiction; as of **April 1** ; 1932; taken by **A. H. Kneale** ; Superintendent.

Key: Number; Surname; Given; Sex (M/F); Age at Last Birthday; Tribe; Degree of Blood (F=Full); Marital Status; Relationship to Head of Family & Last Census No; At Jurisdiction Where Enrolled (Yes/No); (If no – Where); Ward (Yes/No); Identification Numbers

5115; Alex L.; M; 18; Papago; F; S; Son; 5099; Yes; Yes; Id. 10544
5116; Consuela; F; 16; Papago; F; S; Dau.; 5100; Yes; Yes; Id. 10545
5117; Celius L.; M; 15; Papago; F; S; Son; 5101; Yes; Yes; Id. 10546

SANDIEGO
5118; Valestio; M; 37; Papago; F; M; Head; 5102; Yes; Yes; Id. 10585
5119; Martha; F; 33; Papago; F; M; Wife; 5103; Yes; Yes; Id. 10586
5120; John; M; 13; Papago; F; S; Son; 5104; Yes; Yes; Id. 10587
5121; Viltova; M; 11; Papago; F; S; Son; 5105; Yes; Yes; Id. 10588
5122; Lloyd; M; 9; Papago; F; S; Son; 5106; Yes; Yes; Id. 10589

SANTO
5123; Augustine; M; 48; Papago; F; M; Head; 5107; Yes; Yes; Id. 10532
5124; Marcelino; F; 48; Papago; F; M; Wife; 5108; Yes; Yes; Id. 10533
5125; Samone; M; 23; Papago; F; S; Son; 5109; Yes; Yes; Id. 10534
5126; Jose; M; 20; Papago; F; S; Son; 5110; Yes; Yes; Id. 10535
5127; Subelthu; M; 18; Papago; F; S; Son; 5111; Yes; Yes; Id. 10536
5128; Sebano; M; 12; Papago; F; S; Son; 5112; Yes; Yes; Id. 10537
5129; Lacito; F; 8; Papago; F; S; Dau.; 5113; Yes; Yes; Id. 10538
5130; Nocinda; M; 7; Papago; F; S; Son; 5114; Yes; Yes; Id. 10539
5131; Mary; F; 6; Papago; F; S; Dau.; 5115; Yes; Yes; Id. 10540
5132; Magalita; F; 5; Papago; F; S; Dau.; 5116; Yes; Yes; Id. 10541

SWASTAK
5133; Clvis; M; 30; Papago; F; M; Head; 5117; Yes; Yes; Id. 10701
5134; Matilda; F; 29; Papago; F; M; Wife; 5118; Yes; Yes; Id. 10702

SWASTAK
5135; Ramon; M; 27; Papago; F; S; Head; 5119; Yes; Yes; Id. 10703

THOMAS
5136; Cecalde; M; 28; Papago; 1/4x; M; Head; 5120; Yes; Yes; Id. 10656
5137; Dora; F; 27; Papago; 1/4x; M; Wife; 5121; Yes; Yes; Id. 10566
5138; Charlie; M; 10; Papago; 1/4x; S; Son; 5122; Yes; Yes; Id. 10567
5139; Mark; M; 9; Papago; 1/4x; S; Son; 5123; Yes; Yes; Id. 10568

THOMAS
5140; Joe; M; 57; Papago; F; M; Head; 5124; Yes; Yes; Id. 10617
5141; Maglaria; F; 55; Papago; F; M; Wife; 5125; Yes; Yes; Id. 10618
5142; Edna; F; 18; Papago; F; S; Dau.; 5126; Yes; Yes; Id. 10619
5143; Albert; M; 16; Papago; F; S; Son; 5127; Yes; Yes; Id. 10620
5144; John; M; 5; Papago; F; S; Son; 5128; Yes; Yes; Id. 10621

VALDEN[sic]
5145; Louis; M; 43; Papago; F; M; Head; 5129; Yes; Yes; Id. 10634

Census of the **Gila Bend** reservation of the **Pima Agency** jurisdiction; as of **April 1** ; 1932; taken by **A. H. Kneale** ; Superintendent.

Key: Number; Surname; Given; Sex (M/F); Age at Last Birthday; Tribe; Degree of Blood (F=Full); Marital Status; Relationship to Head of Family & Last Census No; At Jurisdiction Where Enrolled (Yes/No); (If no – Where); Ward (Yes/No); Identification Numbers

5146; Margaret; F; 43; Papago; F; M; Wife; 5130; Yes; Yes; Id. 10635
5147; Clara; F; 20; Papago; F; S; Dau.; 5131; Yes; Yes; Id. 10636
5148; Callolena; F; 14; Papago; F; S; Dau.; 5132; Yes; Yes; Id. 10637
5149; Leandro; M; 10; Papago; F; S; Son; 5133; Yes; Yes; Id. 10638

VALITO
5150; Jose; M; 36; Papago; F; M; Head; 5134; Yes; Yes; Id. 10667
5151; Julina M.; F; 39; Papago; F; M; Wife; 5135; Yes; Yes; Id. 10668
5152; Juan; M; 21; Papago; F; S; Son; 5136; Yes; Yes; Id. 10669
5153; Lacita; F; 18; Papago; F; S; Dau.; 5137; Yes; Yes; Id. 10670
5154; Havier; M; 9; Papago; F; S; Son; 5138; Yes; Yes; Id. 10671
5155; Jose C.; M; 7; Papago; F; S; Son; 5139; Yes; Yes; Id. 10672

VOGA[sic]
5156; Antonio; M; 48; Papago; F; M; Head; 5140; Yes; Yes; Id. 10698
5157; Antonia; F; 38; Papago; F; M; Wife; 5141; Yes; Yes; Id. 10629
5158; Chico B.; M; 22; Papago; F; S; Son; 5142; Yes; Yes; Id. 10630
5159; Stephen; M; 21; Papago; F; S; Son; 5143; Yes; Yes; Id. 10631
5160; Alocia; F; 15; Papago; F; S; Dau.; 5144; Yes; Yes; Id. 10632
5161; Pedro; M; 11; Papago; F; S; Son; 5145; Yes; Yes; Id. 10633

Gila River Reservation

Pima Agency

April 1, 1932

Additions to the 1932 Census Roll

[Maricopa-Pima]

Key: Number; Surname; Given; Sex (M/F); Age at Last Birthday; Tribe; Degree of Blood (F=Full); Marital Status; Relationship to Head of Family & Last Census No; Census Year/ Last Census Number; Comment. Allotment Annuity and/or Identification Numbers

Additions to the 1932 Census Roll

DONOHUE
692; Beulah; F; ; Maricopa; 1/4x; S; Dau.; 1929/707; Inadvertedly[sic] omitted on 1930 and 1931 Census Roll; AI. 3741/Id. 238

ELLIS
713; Minnie; F; 88; Pima; F; Wd.; Head; 1930/748; Inadvertedly omitted on 1931 Census; AI. 3034/Id. 3289

SHEBELA
Caroline Betty; F; 1; Pima; F; S; Dau.; none; Born 2-12-30; but omitted on Census roll.

SHIPLEY
3763; Susannah F.; F; 43; Pima; F; M; Wife; 1930/3774; Inadvertedly omitted on 1931 Census; AI. 3309/Id. 4184

3764; Helen; F; 12; Pima; F; S; Dau.; 1930/3775; Inadvertedly omitted on 1931 Census; AI. 4167/Id. 4183

3765; John Leon; M; 10; Pima; F; S; Son; 1930/3776; Inadvertedly omitted on 1931 Census; Id. 4182

TASQUINTH
3980; Gertrude; F; 20; Maricopa; F; S; Dau.; 1929/3972; Inadvertedly omitted on 1930 and 1931 Census; Id. 531

TERRY
Wilma; F; Unk.; Pima; F; M; Head; ---; Never reported heretofore.

THOMPSON
4186; Wilbur; M; 26; Pima; F; S; Son; 1929/4172; Inadvertedly omitted on 1930 and 1931 Census; AI. 2510/Id. 1464

THOMAS
Thomas; M; 80; Pima; F; Wd.; Head; 1930/4140; Inadvertedly omitted on 1931 Census; AI. 4154/Id. 2023

221

Gila River Reservation

Pima Agency

April 1, 1931

Additions to the 1931 Census Roll

[Pima]

Census of the **Gila River** reservation of the **Pima Agency** jurisdiction; as of **April 1** ; 1931; taken by **A. H. Kne[sic]**; Superintendent.

Key: Number; Surname; Given; Sex (M/F); Age at Last Birthday; Tribe; Degree of Blood (F=Full); Marital Status; Relationship to Head of Family & Last Census No; Census Year/ Last Census Number; Comment.
Allotment Annuity and/or Identification Numbers

Additions to the 1931 Census Roll

ARTHUR
1; William; M; 40; Pima; F; S; Head; Omitted; error.; AI. 1595/Id.

BROOKS
2; Lawrence; M; 80; Pima; F; S; Head; Omitted; error.; AI. 1203/Id. 6638

JACKSON
3; Ambrose; M; 36; Pima; F; Wd.; Head; Omitted; error.; AI./Id. 4142

LEWIS
4; Juan; M; 50; Pima; F; S; Head; Reported dead in error.; AI. 4614/Id. 3604

LEWIS
5; Juan; M; Unk.; Pima; F; S; Head; Reported dead in error.; AI. 616/Id. 6114

MANUEL
6; Frank; M; 27; Pima; F; S; Head; Omitted; error.; AI. 4047/Id. 1774

WILLIAMS
7; Marcus; M; 33; Pima; F; S; Head; Omitted; error.; AI. 4182/Id. 7281

GAUDALUPA
8; --; M; Unk.; Pima; F; S; Head; Omitted; error.; AI. 4674/Id. 2041

VAVAGES
9; Mollie E; F; 62; Pima; F; M; Wife; Omitted; error.; AI. 4688/Id. 3866

Gila River Reservation

Pima Agency

April 1, 1932

Subtractions to the 1932 Census Roll

[Pima]

Census of the **Gila River** reservation of the **Pima Agency** jurisdiction; as of **April 1** ; 1932; taken by **A. H. Kneale** ; Superintendent.

Key: Number; Surname; Given; Sex (M/F); Age at Last Birthday; Tribe; Degree of Blood (F=Full); Marital Status; Relationship to Head of Family & Last Census No; Census Year/ Last Census Number; Comment; Allotment Annuity and/or Identification Numbers

Subtractions to the 1932 Census Roll

HOWARD

1286; George; M; 36; Pima; F; M; Head; 1931/1295-1292; Duplication on 1931 Census Roll.; AI. 2626/Id. 6984

1287; Clara O.; F; 32; Pima; F; M; Wife; 1931/1296-1293; Duplication on 1931 Census Roll.; AI. 6985/Id. 1563

1288; Mildred; F; 9; Pima; F; M; Dau.; 1931/1297-1294; Duplication on 1931 Census Roll.; AI./Id. 6986

229

Ak Chin Reservation

Pima Agency

April 1, 1931

Additions to the 1931 Census Roll

and

Subtractions to the 1931 Census Roll

[Papago]

Census of the **Ak Chin** reservation of the **Pima Agency** jurisdiction; as of **April 1** ; 1931; taken by **A. H. [Kneale]**; Superintendent.

Key: Number; Surname; Given; Sex (M/F); Age at Last Birthday; Tribe; Degree of Blood (F=Full); Marital Status; Relationship to Head of Family & Last Census No; Census Year/ Last Census Number; Comment; Identification Numbers

Additions to 1931 Census Roll

THOMAS

1; Martha; F; 11; Papago; F; S; Dau.; Omitted from previous roll.; Id. 8970

Subtractions to 1931 Census Roll

MIGUEL

1; Ralph; M; 18; Papago; F; S; Son; Duplicate; also under Jose Manuel; Id. 8835

2; Malinda; F; 15; Papago; F; S; Dau.; Duplicate; also under Jose Manuel; Id. 8836

THOMAS

3; Helen; F; 15; Papago; F; S; Dau.; Duplicate; also under Ferdinand Thomas.; Id. 8967

4; Martha; F; 10; Papago; F; S; Dau.; Duplicate; also under Ferdinand Thomas.; Id. 8968

5; Celestine; F; 9; Papago; F; S; Dau.; Duplicate; also under Ferdinand Thomas.; Id. 8969

6; Catherine; F; 6; Papago; F; S; Dau.; Duplicate; also under Ferdinand Thomas.; Id. 8970

CHOOHI

7; Maliatoola; F; 64; Papago; F; S; Wife; Dead; unreported heretofore.; Id. 9114

233

Gila River Reservation

Pima Agency

April 1, 1931

Subtractions to the 1931 Census Roll

[Pima, Apache, Pawnee, Oneida

Shawnee, Crow, Maricopa]

Census of the **Gila River** reservation of the **Pima Agency** jurisdiction; as of **April 1** ; 1931; taken by **A. H. Kn[eale]** ; Superintendent.

Key: Number; Surname; Given; Sex (M/F); Age at Last Birthday; Tribe; Degree of Blood (F=Full); Marital Status; Relationship to Head of Family & Last Census No; Census Year/ Last Census Number; Comment; Allotment Annuity and/or Identification Numbers

Subtractions to 1931 Census Roll

ADAMS
1; Harvier; M; 37; Pima; F; M; Head; Enrolled on Salt River Reservation.; AI. SR/Id.

ANTON
2; Cheerless; F; 49; Pima; F; M; Wife; Enrolled on Salt River Reservation.; AI. SR/Id. 7075

ANTON
3; Clara; F; 18; Pima; F; S; Dau.; Duplicate also under Juan F. Marietta.; AI. 2426/Id. 7080

ANTON
4; Robert; M; 28; Pima; F; M; Head; Enrolled on Salt River Reservation.; AI. SR/Id. 6716

BIRD
5; Eddie; M; Unk.; Apache; F; M; Head; Enrolled on Apache Roll.; AI./Id.

BRECKENRIDGE
6; Alice; F; 41; Pawnee; F; M; Wife; Enrolled on the Pawnee Roll.; AI./Id. 346

CARLYLE
7; John; M; Unk.; Pima; F; M; Head; Enrolled on Salt River Reservation.; AI. SR/Id. 1596

HOUSTON
8; Ada; F; 71; Pima; F; Wd.; Head; Duplicate; same as Ellie Houston.; AI. 1050/Id. 6587

JACKSON
9; Florence; F; 38; Oneida; F; M; Wife; Enrolled on Oneida Roll.; AI./Id. 4211

KNOX
10; Gertrude; F; 46; Oneida; 1/4x; M; Wife; Enrolled on Shawnee Roll.; AI./Id. 6775

LAWS
11; Gladys; F; 16; Pima; F; M; Wife; Duplicate; also under C. Barehand.; AI. 3662/Id. 1497

MORAGO
12; Florence; F; 36; Crow; 1/4x; M; Wife; Enrolled on Crow Agency Roll of Montana.; AI. 345/Id. 5187[sic]

237

Census of the **Gila River** reservation of the **Pima Agency** jurisdiction; as of **April 1** ; 1931; taken by **A. H. Kn[eale]**; Superintendent.

Key: Number; Surname; Given; Sex (M/F); Age at Last Birthday; Tribe; Degree of Blood (F=Full); Marital Status; Relationship to Head of Family & Last Census No; Census Year/ Last Census Number; Comment; Allotment Annuity and/or Identification Numbers

REED

13; Nelson F.; M; 17; Maricopa[sic]; F; S; Son; Duplicate; also under Whitman.; AI. 345/Id. 5187

Live Births
Occurring Between
July 1, 1924 and June 30, 1925
Pima Indian Agency

Live-Births Occurring Between the Dates of July 1, 1924 and June 30, 1925 to Parents Enrolled at Jurisdiction

Key: 1925 Census Roll Number; Surname; Given; Date of Birth (Year-Month-Day); Live Birth (Yes/No); Still-birth (Yes/No); Sex; Tribe; Ward (Yes/No); Degree of Blood (Father-Mother-Child); At Jurisdiction Where Enrolled (Yes/No); (If no – Where – Jurisdiction; State; Post Office; State)

25; Allen, Walter; 1924-Sept-3; Yes; No; M; Pima; Yes; F; F; F; Yes

123; Anton, Ernest; 1924-July-23; Yes; No; M; Pima; Yes; F; F; F; Yes

122; Anton, Louis; 1924-July-23; Yes; No; M; Pima; Yes; F; F; F; Yes

167; Antone, Simon; 1924-Oct-10; Yes; M; Pima; Yes; F; F; F; Yes

260; Azule, Clyde Elmer; 1925-March-29; Yes; M; Pima; Yes; F; F; F; Yes

369; Breckenridge, Hazel; 1924-Nov-5; Yes; F; Pima; Yes; F; F; F; Yes

433; Card, Elmer; 1924-July-9; Yes; M; Pima; Yes; F; F; F; Yes

633; Domingo, Carmain; 1924-July-22; Yes; M; Pima & Papago; Yes; Pima; Pap; 1/2-1/2; Yes

Unrecorded; Duron, Winfred George; 1925-Jan-16; Yes; M; Pima; Yes; Sp; Pima; 1/2; Yes

1931-753; Enas[sic], Marcus; 1925-Jan-2; Yes; M; Pima; Yes; F; F; F; Yes

Unrecorded; Enos, Appolionia; 1925-Feb-1; Yes; M; Papago; Yes; F; F; F; Yes

1926-835; Enos, Dorlie Pablo; 1925-May-25; Yes; F; Pima; Yes; F; F; F; Yes

1926-747; Enas, Hilda; 1925-Feb-7; Yes; F; Pima; Yes; F; F; F; Yes

1023; Hall, Burgess; 1925-May-24; Yes; M; Pima; Yes; F; F; F; Yes

1115; Houston, Irene; 1925-Jan-22; Yes; F; Pima; Yes; F; F; F; Yes

1173; Howard, Gertrude; 1925-April-24; Yes; F; Pima; Yes; F; F; F; Yes

1226; Hugo, Milenda Hazel; 1925-May-15; Yes; F; Pima; Yes; F; F; F; Yes

1351; Jackson, Matilda Evelyn; 1924-Nov-5; Yes; F; Pima; Yes; F; F; F; Yes

Unrecorded; James, Veronica; 1925-Jan-16; Yes; F; Pima; Yes; F; F; F; Yes

1329; (John) Jackson, Wilford (Willard); 1925-Jan-16; Yes; M; Pima; Yes; [?]; F; F; Yes

1529; Johnson, Alfred; 1924-Sept-3; Yes; M; Pima; Yes; F; F; F; Yes

Unrecorded; Johnson, Henry; 1925-Jan-14; Yes; M; Pima; Yes; F; F; F; Yes

1473; Johnson, Luke Hillis; 1925-May-10; Yes; No; M; Pima; Yes; F; F; F; Yes

1534; Johnson, Viola; 1924-Oct-7; Yes; F; Pima; Yes; F; F; F; Yes

1568; Jones, Robert Jr; 1924-July-26; Yes; M; Choctaw & Pima; Yes; F; F; 1/2-1/2; Yes

Unrecorded; Juan, Clara; 1924-July-12; Yes; F; Pima; Yes; F; F; F; Yes

Unrecorded; Juan, Harriet; 1925-(Unknown); Yes; F; Pima; Yes; F; F; F; Yes

1900; Lesso, Luella May; 1925-April-28; Yes; F; Hopi & Pima; Yes; F; F; 1/2 & 1/2; Yes

1929-929; Lewis, Enos, Lester Joseph; 1925-Jan-2; Yes; M; Pima; Yes; F; F; F; Yes

2113; Luceroiu, Victor Euret; 1924-Aug-27; Yes; M; Pueblo & Pima; Yes; F; F; F[sic]; Yes

2127; Lych, Harley Enos; 1925-April-14; Yes; M; Pima; Yes; F; F; F; Yes

2153; Mack, Freda; 1924-July-20; Yes; F; Pima; Yes; F; F; F; Yes

2280; Manuel, Leo; 1924-July-3; Yes; M; Pima; Yes; F; F; F; Yes

2458; Michael, Fernando; 1924-Dec-3; Yes; M; Pima; Yes; F; F; F; Yes

1926-2509; Miguel, Elizabeth; 1924-July-13; Yes; F; Pima; Yes; F; F; F; Yes

2542; Miles, Lesley R; 1925-June-9; Yes; M; Pima; Yes; F; F; F; Yes

2634; Morris, Eugene Wallace; 1925-Jan-22; Yes; M; Pima; Yes; F; F; F; Yes

State **Arizona** Reservation **Gila River Indian Reservation** Agency or jurisdiction **Pima Indian Agency**; Office of Indian Affairs

Live-Births Occurring Between the Dates of July 1, 1924 and June 30, 1925 to Parents Enrolled at Jurisdiction

Key: 1925 Census Roll Number; Surname; Given; Date of Birth (Year-Month-Day); Live Birth (Yes/No); Still-birth (Yes/No); Sex; Tribe; Ward (Yes/No); Degree of Blood (Father-Mother-Child); At Jurisdiction Where Enrolled (Yes/No); (If no – Where – Jurisdiction; State; Post Office; State)

Unrecorded; Napolee, ---; 1924-Aug-25; Yes; M; Pueblo & Pima; Yes; F; F; 1/2-1/2; Yes

Unrecorded; Nelson, Dennis; 1925-May-28; Yes; M; Papago; Yes; F; F; F; Yes

2612; Nelson, Everett Milton; 1924-Oct-16; Yes; M; Pima; Yes; F; F; F; Yes

1926-2770; Nelson, Herbert; 1925-April-23; Yes; M; Pima & Pueblo; Yes; F; F; F; 1/2-1/2; Yes

2637; Newman, Claudina Rosline; 1925-Jan-2; Yes; F; Pima; Yes; F; F; F; Yes

Unrecorded; Norris, Mary A; 1925; Yes; F; Pima; Yes; F; F; F; Yes

2732; Osif, Dana Wilbur; 1924-Sept-14; Yes; M; Pima; Yes; F; F; F; Yes

1926-2895; Osife, Louise Lowe; 1924-Sept-14; Yes; No; F; Pima; Yes; F; F; F; Yes

1926-2997; Pablo, Lillian Jane; 1925-Feb 15; Yes; F; Pima; Yes; F; F; F; Yes

2502; Parker, Matilda; 1925-Jan-24; Yes; M; Maricopa; Yes; F; F; F; Yes

1926-3066; Pasquel, Dominick; 1925-Feb-12; Yes; M; Pima; Yes; F; F; F; Yes

1926-3061; Pasquell, Slayton; 1925-May-5; Yes; M; Pima; Yes; F; F; F; Yes

1926-3233; Porter, Gladys; R; 1925-May-11; Yes; F; Pima; Yes; F; F; F; Yes

2695; Pratt, Laura May; 1925-May-21; Yes; F; Pima; Yes; F; F; F; Yes

2801; Rhodes, Neele Mae; 1924-Dec-26; Yes; F; Pima & Cheyenne; Yes; F; F; 1/2-1/2; Yes

2987; Seto, Nina; 1924-July-15; Yes; F; Pima; Yes; F; F; F; Yes

2996; Seye, Bobby; 1924-Oct-3; Yes; M; Pima; Yes; F; F; F; No; Phoenix, Ariz

1929-3975; Tasquinth, Mabel; 1925-Feb-19; Yes; F; Pima; Yes; F; F; F; No; Casa Grande, Ariz

Unrecorded; Terry, Jonas; 1925-Feb-3; Yes; M; Pima; Yes; F; F; F; Yes

3242; Thomas, Aloysius; 1925-June-5; Yes; M; Pima & Papago; Yes; F; F; 1/2-1/2; Yes

Unrecorded; Thomas, Daniel; 1925-Jan-5; Yes; M; Papago; Yes; F; F; F; Yes

3284; Thomas, Leo; 1924-Dec-25; Yes; M; Pima; Yes; F; F; F; Yes

Unrecorded; Thompson, Mabel; 1925-Jan-1; Yes; F; Papago; Yes; F; F; F; Yes

1926-4119; Thompson, Jose; 1924-Feb-12; Yes; M; Pima; Yes; F; F; F; Yes

3488; Walker, Weldon; 1924-Sept-14; Yes; M; Pima; Yes; F; F; F; Yes

1927-4119; Whitman, Cornelius; 1925-June-25; Yes; M; Pima; Yes; F; F; F; Yes

3531; Yarmata, Oliver; 1924-Sept-17; Yes; M; Maricopa; Yes; F; F; F; Yes

Live Births
Occurring Between
July 1, 1925 and June 30, 1926
Pima Indian Agency

State **Arizona** Reservation **Gila River Indian Reservation** Agency or
jurisdiction **Pima Indian Agency**; Office of Indian Affairs

Live-Births Occurring Between the Dates of July 1, 1925 and June 30, 1926 to Parents Enrolled at Jurisdiction

Key: 1926 Census Roll Number; Surname; Given; Date of Birth (Year-Month-Day); Live Birth
(Yes/No); Still-birth (Yes/No); Sex; Tribe; Ward (Yes/No); Degree of Blood (Father-Mother-Child);
At Jurisdiction Where Enrolled (Yes/No); (If no – Where – Jurisdiction; State; Post Office; State)

36; Allen, Lambert; 1926-Mar-26; Yes; No; M; Pima; Yes; F; F; F; Yes
58; Allison, Geraldine; 1926-Mar-3; Yes; F; Pima; Yes; F; F; F; Yes
46; Allison, Robert Eugene; 1926-May-28; Yes; M; Pima; Yes; F; F; F; Yes
176; Antone, Della; 1925-Nov-26; Yes; F; Pima; Yes; F; F; F; Yes
Unnumbered; Antone, Irene; 1925-July-11; Yes; F; Papago; Yes; F; F; F; Yes
1927-122; Antone, McKenney; 1926-Feb-5; Yes; M; Pima; Yes; F; F; F; Yes
1929-24; Antone, Matilda; 1926-Jan-28; Yes; F; Papago; Yes; F; F; F; Yes
255; Apkaw, Louisa Melinda; 1925-Sept-21; Yes; F; Pima; Yes; F; F; F; Yes
304; Barehand, Cymo; 1926-Mar-3; Yes; M; Pima; Yes; F; F; F; Yes
348; Blackwater, Elmer; 1925-Sept-10; Yes; M; Pima; Yes; F; F; F; Yes
1927-430; Cannon, Constance; 1926-June-16; Yes; F; Pima; Yes; F; F; F; Yes
462; Card, Howard; 1925-Dec-1; Yes; M; Pima; Yes; F; F; F; Yes
465; Carmen, Edward; 1925-Sept-14; Yes; M; Pima; Yes; F; F; F; Yes
628; Davis, Flora; 1926-Mar-26; Yes; F; Pima; Yes; F; F; F; Yes
668; Donohue, Dorine; 1926-Feb-17; Yes; F; Pima; Yes; F; F; F; Yes
Unrecorded; Enos, Alfronica; 1926-May-14; Yes; F; Papago; Yes; F; F; F; Yes
Unrecorded; Enos, Blanche; 1926-Feb-26; Yes; F; Papago; Yes; F; F; F; Yes
1927-818; Enos, Jessie; 1926-Feb-7; Yes; F; Pima; Yes; F; F; F; Yes
884; Enos, Leo; 1926-Mar-26; Yes; M; Pima; Yes; F; F; F; Yes
760; Enis[sic], March; 1926-Mar-2; Yes; M; Pima; Yes; F; F; F; Yes
795; Enos, Margaret; 1926-April-10; Yes; F; Pima; Yes; F; F; F; Yes
Unrecorded; Enos, Raymond; 1925-Dec-26; Yes; M; Papago; Yes; F; F; F; Yes
1927-922; Evans, Mardella; 1926-Mar-5; Yes; No; F; Pima; Yes; F; F; F; Yes
965; French, Albert; 1925-Aug-26; Yes; M; Pima; Yes; F; F; F; Yes
981; Garcia, Louisa; 1926-May-7; Yes; F; Pima; Yes; F; F; F; Yes
991; Gatia, (Paul) Leona ??; 1925-July-3; Yes; F; Pima; Yes; F; F; F; Yes
1019; Hall, Hilda; 1925-July-25; Yes; F; Pima; Yes; F; F; F; Yes
1233; Howard, Marie M; 1926-March; 15; Yes; F; Pima; Yes; F; F; F; Yes
1324; Jackson, Alice; 1925-July-29; Yes; F; Pima; Yes; F; F; F; Yes
1928-1273; Jackson, Daniel Jr; 1926-June-4; Yes; M; Pima; Yes; F; F; F; Yes
1927-1291; Jackson, Marion S; 1926-Feb-3; Yes; F; Pima; Yes; F; F; F; Yes
Unnumbered; Jackson, Grace; 1925-Aug-3; Yes; F; Pima; Yes; F; F; F; Yes
Unrecorded; Jackson, Marion S; 1925-Dec-18; Yes; F; Pima; Yes; -; F; F; Yes
1927-1327; Jackson, Patrick; 1926-June-9; Yes; M; Pima; Yes; F; F; F; Yes
Unrecorded; Jarvis, Edison; 1925-Nov-26; Yes; M; Pima; Yes; F; F; F; Yes
1432; James (John), Bernard; 1926-April-23; Yes; M; Pima; Yes; F; F; F; Yes
1495; Johns, Georgiana; 1925-Aug-24; Yes; F; Pima; Yes; F; F; F; Yes
1533; Johnson, Juana; 1926-April-25; Yes; F; Pima; Yes; F; F; F; Yes
Unrecorded; Johnson, Mark Jr; 1926-May-9; Yes; F; Maricopa; Yes; F; F; F; Yes
1509; Johnson, Simon; 1926-April-9; Yes; M; Pima; Yes; F; F; F; Yes
1566; Johnson, Wigene; 1926-June-5; Yes; M; Pima; Yes; F; F; F; Yes
1927-1587; Jones, Evanele; 1926-May-20; Yes; F; Pima; Yes; F; F; F; Yes
1600; Jones, May Fern; 1926-May-19; Yes; F; Choctaw & Pima; Yes; F; F; 1/2-1/2;
Yes

245

State **Arizona** Reservation **Gila River Indian Reservation** Agency or
jurisdiction **Pima Indian Agency**; Office of Indian Affairs
Live-Births Occurring Between the Dates of July 1, 1925 and June 30, 1926 to Parents Enrolled at Jurisdiction

Key: 1926 Census Roll Number; Surname; Given; Date of Birth (Year-Month-Day); Live Birth
(Yes/No); Still-birth (Yes/No); Sex; Tribe; Ward (Yes/No); Degree of Blood (Father-Mother-Child);
At Jurisdiction Where Enrolled (Yes/No); (If no – Where – Jurisdiction; State; Post Office; State)

1638; Jose, Gladys; 1925-July-10; Yes; F; Pima; Yes; F; F; F; No; Phoenix, Ariz
1929-1928; Kisto, Bernard A; 1925-Oct-4; Yes; No; M; Pima; Yes; F; F; F; Yes
1927-1817; Kisto, Gerard; 1926-April-27; Yes; M; Pima; Yes; F; F; F; Yes
1886; Kyyitan, Gertrude; 1926-April-8; Yes; F; Pima; Yes; F; F; F; Yes
1927-1869; Lappie, Margaret J; 1926-May-1; Yes; F; Pima; Yes; F; F; F; Yes
1908; Laws, Evan Joseph; 1925-July-2; Yes; M; Pima; Yes; F; F; F; No; Phoenix,
Ariz
1929-2026; Leonard, Luella; 1925-Aug-11; Yes; F; Papago; Yes; F; F; F; No; Salt
River Res, Ariz
1961; Lewis, Bessie; 1926-April-5; Yes; F; Pima; Yes; F; F; F; Yes
2069; Lewis, Clifford S; 1926-April-10; Yes; M; Pima; Yes; F; F; F; Yes
1929; Lewis, Edward T; 1925-Oct-17; Yes; M; Pima; Yes; F; F; F; Yes
1998; Lewis, Enoch Rath Jr; 1926-Jan-31; Yes; M; Pima; Yes; F; F; F; Yes
2091; Lewis, Flora Hilda; 1925-Oct-12; Yes; F; Pima; Yes; F; F; F; Yes
1927-1919; Lewis, Norman Henry; 1926-Feb-24; Yes; M; Maricopa; Yes; F; F; F;
Yes
~~Unrecorded; Leho, Salvadore; 1926-May-18; Yes; M; Pima; Yes; F; F; F; Yes~~
2145; Lomanhee, Elinor Lewis; 1926-Jan-26; Yes; F; Pima; Yes; F; F; F; Yes
2158; Lopez, Elsie; 1925-Aug-24; Yes; F; Pima; Yes; F; F; F; Yes
Unrecorded; Louis, Annie Ruth; 1925-Dec-5; Yes; F; Pima; Yes; F; F; F; Yes
2187; Lucero, Carolina; 1925-Nov-29; Yes; F; Pueblo & Pima; Yes; F; F; 1/2-1/2;
Yes
2270; Manuel, Elizabeth; 1925-Dec-29; Yes; F; Pima; Yes; F; F; F; Yes
2355; Manuel, Gabriel; 1926-Feb-12; Yes; M; Pima; Yes; F; F; F; Yes
2306; Manuel, Lottie; 1925-Aug-2; Yes; F; Pima; Yes; F; F; F; Yes
2347; Manuel, Nathan; 1925-Oct-9; Yes; M; Pima; Yes; F; F; F; Yes
4447; Manuel, Nellie Jr; 1926-May-26; Yes; F; Papago; Yes; F; F; F; Yes
2408; Marietta, Jessie; 1926-May-4; Yes; No; F; Pima; Yes; F; F; F; Yes
2229; Mack, Effie Jr; 1926-April-14; Yes; F; Maricopa; Yes; F; F; F; Yes
2491; McKay, Florence; 1926-Jan-5; Yes; F; Mexican & Pima; Yes; -; F; 1/2; No;
Phoenix, Ariz
Unrecorded; Miguel, Clementia; 1925-Aug---; Yes; F; Papago; Yes; F; F; F; Yes
2503; Miguel, Patricia; 1926-April-7; Yes; F; Pima; Yes; F; F; F; Yes
4463; Miguel, Susie Jr; 1925-Sept-7; Yes; F; Papago; Yes; F; F; F; Yes
2682; Morales, Ione; 1925-July-5; Yes; F; Pima; Yes; F; F; F; Yes
Unrecorded; Narcia, Lizzie Jr; 1926-Feb-5; Yes; F; Pima; Yes; F; F; F; Yes
1927-2733; Narcia, Mary Ann; 1926-May-28; Yes; F; Pima; Yes; F; F; F; Yes
2831; Nish, Leonard; 1926-April-2; Yes; M; Pima; Yes; F; F; F; Yes
2774; Nelson, Eric Robert; 1926-March; 5; Yes; M; Pima; Yes; F; F; F; Yes
1927-2938; Osif, Edward; 1926-June-26; Yes; M; Pima; Yes; F; F; F; Yes
Unnumbered; Pablo, Enos; 1925-July-14; Yes; M; Pima; Yes; F; F; F; Yes
1927-2996; Pablo, Floyd; 1926-May-24; Yes; M; Pima; Yes; F; F; F; Yes
Unrecorded; Pablo, John Evans; 1925-Aug-15; Yes; M; Pima; Yes; F; F; F; Yes
3010; Pablo, Jose Jr; 1926-May-24; Yes; M; Pima; Yes; F; F; F; Yes

State **Arizona** Reservation **Gila River Indian Reservation** Agency or jurisdiction **Pima Indian Agency**; Office of Indian Affairs

<u>Live-Births Occurring Between the Dates of July 1, 1925 and June 30, 1926 to Parents Enrolled at Jurisdiction</u>

Key: 1926 Census Roll Number; Surname; Given; Date of Birth (Year-Month-Day); Live Birth (Yes/No); Still-birth (Yes/No); Sex; Tribe; Ward (Yes/No); Degree of Blood (Father-Mother-Child); At Jurisdiction Where Enrolled (Yes/No); (If no – Where – Jurisdiction; State; Post Office; State)

1930-237; Pablo, Philipa; 1925-Dec---; Yes; F; Papago; Yes; F; F; F; Yes

1927-2985; Pablo, Martin; 1925-Oct-17; Yes; M; Pima; Yes; F; F; F; Yes

3039; Pancot, Fredrick; 1925-Oct-6; Yes; M; Pima; Yes; F; F; F; Yes

3218; Porter, Felix Jr; 1925-Nov-27; Yes; M; Pima; Yes; F; F; F; Yes

3241; Porter, Hazel Wilma; 1925-Nov-28; Yes; F; Pima; Yes; F; F; F; Yes

Unnumbered; Porter, Jerome Wilbert; 1926-June-20; Yes; M; Pima; Yes; F; F; F; Yes

Unnumbered; Ramon, Simon R; 1925-July-19; Yes; No; M; Pima; Yes; F; F; F; Yes

3342; Rhodes, Harold; 1926-May-24; Yes; M; Pima; Yes; F; F; F; Yes

1927-3384; Roveless, Estalla Maria; 1926-June-29; Yes; F; Pima; Yes; F; F; F; Yes

1927-3483; Scofer, Agnes; 1926-April-28; Yes; F; Pima; Yes; F; F; F; Yes

1927-3533; Shelde, Anna Jr; 1926-June-12; Yes; F; Pima; Yes; F; F; F; Yes

1927-3218; Stewart, Roland Hilman; 1926-April-23; Yes; M; Pima; Yes; F; F; F; No; Phoenix, Ariz

3722; Sweet, Dana; 1925-Oct-13; Yes; M; Pima; Yes; F; F; F; Yes

1927-1526; Tejano, Everett Carlos; 1926-April-30; Yes; M; Papago & Pima; Yes; F; F; F 1/2-1/2; Yes

1927-3828; Thomas, Betty Arlene; 1926-May-6; Yes; F; Papago; Yes; F; F; 1/2-1/2; No; Salt River Res, Ariz

3821; Thomas, Elizabeth; 1925-Dec-5; Yes; F; Pima; Yes; F; F; F; Yes

3850; Thomas, Jane Margery; 1926-Jan-1; Yes; F; Pima; Yes; F; F; F; Yes

1927-4540; Thomas, Bernice; 1925-Dec-3; Yes; F; Papago; Yes; F; F; F; Yes

3933; Vasquez, Laurita; 1925-Nov-14; Yes; F; Pima; Yes; F; F; F; Yes

3940; Vavages, Susie; 1926-May-21; Yes; F; Pima; Yes; F; F; F; Yes

4041; Webb, Lionel; 1926-April-24; Yes; M; Pima; Yes; F; F; F; Yes

4136; Whittaker, Eugenia Ann; 1926-May-24; Yes; F; Pima; Yes; F; F; F; Yes

5154; Wickey, Sepia Jr; 1926-May-15; Yes; F; Hopi & Pima; Yes; F; F; 1/2-1/2; Yes

Unnumbered; Wilson,, May; 1926-Mar-30; Yes; F; Pima; Yes; F; F; F; Yes

4229; Winn, Lucy; 1925-Aug-25; Yes; F; Pima; Yes; F; F; F; Yes

Live Births
Occurring Between
July 1, 1926 and June 30, 1927
Pima Indian Agency

State **Arizona** Reservation **Gila River Indian Reservation** Agency or
jurisdiction **Pima Indian Agency**; Office of Indian Affairs
Live-Births Occurring Between the Dates of July 1, 1926 and June 30, 1927 to Parents Enrolled at Jurisdiction
Key: 1927 Census Roll Number; Surname; Given; Date of Birth (Year-Month-Day); Live Birth
(Yes/No); Still-birth (Yes/No); Sex; Tribe; Ward (Yes/No); Degree of Blood (Father-Mother-Child);
At Jurisdiction Where Enrolled (Yes/No); (If no – Where – Jurisdiction; State; Post Office; State)

159; Antone, Isabel Maria; 1926-July-27; Yes; F; Pima; Yes; F; F; F; Yes

Unrecorded; Antone, Mary; 1927-Jan-16; Yes; F; Pima; Yes; F; F; F; Yes

252; Apkaw, Thelma; 1927-June-19; Yes; F; Pima; Yes; F; F; F; Yes

378; Breckenridge, Verna Clara; 1926-Sept-7; Yes; F; Pima; Yes; F; F; F; Yes

1928-449; Cannon, Benton Francis; 1926-Dec-27; Yes; M; Pima; Yes; F; F; F; Yes

1928-532; Cook, Delma Hester; 1927-June-14; Yes; F; Pima; Yes; F; F; F; Yes

635; Domingo, Mary Charlotte; 1926-Oct-16; Yes; F; Pima; Yes; F; F; F; Yes

664; Elias, Raymond R.; 1927-Feb-4; Yes; M; Pima; Yes; F; F; F; Yes

684; Elsmere, Aselda Mary; 1926-Aug-30; Yes; F; Pima; Yes; F; F; F; Yes

1929-859; Enos, Daniel Jr.; 1926-Mar-6; Yes; M; Pima; Yes; F; F; F; Yes

1928-839; Enos, Euphrasia; 1927-June-6; Yes; F; Pima; Yes; F; F; F; Yes

Unrecorded; Enos, Justin; 1926-Oct-9; Yes; M; Papago; Yes; F; F; F; Yes

730; Enos, Lester; 1927-April-19; Yes; M; Pima; Yes; F; F; F; Yes

810; Enos, Lucy Jr.; 1927-June-27; Yes; F; Pima; Yes; F; F; F; Yes

805; Enos, Rhoda; 1926-Nov-7; Yes; F; Pima; Yes; F; F; F; Yes

1037; Harris, Adeline; 1926-Oct-24; Yes; F; Pima; Yes; F; F; F; Yes

1158; Honwesima, Barbara Louise; 1927-May-3; Yes; F; Hopi & Pima; Yes; F; F;
1/2-1/2; No; Phoenix, Ariz.

1926-1232; Howard, Catherine L.; 1927-Sept-30; Yes; F; Pima; Yes; F; F; F; Yes

1240; Hugo, Burns Jr.; 1927-April-23; Yes; M; Pima; Yes; F; F; F; Yes

1319; Jackson, John Jr.; 1927-April-19; Yes; M; Pima; Yes; F; F; F; Yes

1265; Jackson, Julia; 1927-May-18; Yes; F; Pima; Yes; F; F; F; Yes

1352; Jackson, Leta; 1926-Sept-10; Yes; M[sic]; Pima; Yes; F; F; F; Yes

1411; James, Henry; 1926-Sept-23; Yes; No; M; Pima; Yes; F; F; F; Yes

1928-1489; Johnson, Clara; 1927-June-16; Yes; F; Pima; Yes; F; F; F; Yes

1509; Johnson, Ella; 1926-Oct-18; Yes; F; Pima; Yes; F; F; F; Yes

1928-1523; Johnson, Elsie; 1927-Feb-3; Yes; F; Pima; Yes; F; F; F; Yes

1518; Johnson, John Jr.; 1927-May-30; Yes; M; Pima; Yes; F; F; F; Yes

1532; Johnson, Len; 1927-June-17; Yes; M; Pima; Yes; F; F; F; No; Palo Verde, Ariz.

1562; Jones, Parmela; 1926-Oct-25; Yes; F; Pima; Yes; F; F; F; Yes

1569; Jones, Thomas; 1926-Dec-25; Yes; M; Pima; Yes; F; F; F; Yes

1651; Joseph, Eddie; 1926-July-1; Yes; M; Pima; Yes; F; F; F; Yes

Unrecorded; Juan, Catherine; 1927-April---; Yes; F; Papago; Yes; F; F; F; Yes

Unrecorded; Juan, Katherine; 1927-Feb-1; Yes; F; Papago; Yes; F; F; F; Yes

Unrecorded; Juan, Severa Jr.; 1926-Sept-7; Yes; F; Papago; Yes; F; F; F; Yes

1792; Kirk, Mildred; 1927-Sept-3; Yes; M[sic]; Pima; Yes; F; F; F; Yes

4387; Kisto, Simon; 1927-April-18; Yes; M; Papago; Yes; F; F; F; Yes

Unnumbered; Knox, Christiana; 1927-Jan-10; Yes; F; Pima; Yes; F; F; F; Yes

1894; Lesso, Eloise Marlyn; 1926-Oct-23; Yes; F; Pima; Yes; F; F; F; Yes

1914; Lewis, Avery; 1927-Jan-7; Yes; M; Pima; Yes; F; F; F; Yes

1929-430; Lewis, Enos, Daniel; 1926-Dec-11; Yes; M; Papago; Yes; F; F; F; Yes

1992; Lewis, Juan E. Jr.; 1927-Mar-21; Yes; M; Pima; Yes; F; F; F; Yes

2016; Lewis, Richard; 1927-May-1; Yes; M; Pima; Yes; F; F; F; Yes

251

State **Arizona** Reservation **Gila River Indian Reservation** Agency or jurisdiction **Pima Indian Agency**; Office of Indian Affairs

Live-Births Occurring Between the Dates of July 1, 1926 and June 30, 1927 to Parents Enrolled at Jurisdiction

Key: 1927 Census Roll Number; Surname; Given; Date of Birth (Year-Month-Day); Live Birth (Yes/No); Still-birth (Yes/No); Sex; Tribe; Ward (Yes/No); Degree of Blood (Father-Mother-Child); At Jurisdiction Where Enrolled (Yes/No); (If no – Where – Jurisdiction; State; Post Office; State)

1980; Lewis, Sylvester; 1926-Sept-20; Yes; M; Papago & Pima; Yes; F; F; 1/2-1/2; Yes

2176; Lose, Myron Henry; 1927-April-18; Yes; M; Pima; Yes; F; F; F; Yes

Unnumbered; Lyons, Joseph; 1927-May-20; Yes; No; M; Pima; Yes; F; F; F; Yes

2220; Mack, Eugene; 1926-Sept-17; Yes; M; Pima; Yes; F; F; F; Yes

1928-2212; Makil, Linus; 1927-Mar-24; Yes; M; Pima; Yes; F; F; F; Yes

2259; Manuel, Elmer; 1926-Nov-25; Yes; M; Pima; Yes; F; F; F; Yes

2344; Manuel, Elsie; 1927-June-9; Yes; F; Pima; Yes; F; F; F; Yes

Unrecorded; Manuel, Gustive; 1927-June-26; Yes; F; Maricopa; Yes; F; F; F; Yes

2312; Manuel, Jose Jr.; 1927-Mar-24; Yes; M; Pima; Yes; F; F; F; Yes

Unrecorded; Marcus, David Daniel; 1927-April-3; Yes; M; Papago; Yes; F; F; F; No; Chandler, Ariz.

~~Unrecorded; Miguel, Flora Marie; 1927-April-26; Yes; F; Papago; Yes; F; F; F; Yes;~~

2505; Miguel, Ruby; 1926-Oct-10; Yes; F; Pima; Yes; F; F; F; Yes

2621; Miles, Elsie; 1926-Aug-12; Yes; F; Pima; Yes; F; F; F; Yes

2637; Mix, Eugenia Lillian; 1926-July-7; Yes; F; Pima; Yes; F; F; F; Yes

2704; Morris, Sylvia; 1926-Dec-5; Yes; F; Pima; Yes; F; F; F; Yes

2737; Nelson, Donna Gloria; 1927-Feb-17; Yes; F; Pima; Yes; F; F; F; Yes

Unrecorded; Nelson, Leonard; 1926-Sept-21; Yes; M; Papago; Yes; F; F; F; Yes

Unnumbered; Nelson, Mary Jane; 1927-Feb-25; Yes; F; Cherokee & Pueblo; Yes; F; F; 1/2-1/2; Yes

Unnumbered; Newman, Leola Rachel; 1926-Aug-3; Yes; F; Pima; Yes; F; F; F; Yes

2833; Nish, Justina; 1926-Oct-4; Yes; F; Pima; Yes; F; F; F; Yes

2820; Nish, Michael; 1927-Mar-10; Yes; M; Pima; Yes; F; F; F; Yes

2863; Norris, Dana; 1926-Sept---; Yes; M; Pima; Yes; F; F; F; Yes

2914; Osif, Lawrence Larry; 1926-Sept-3; Yes; M; Pima; Yes; F; F; F; Yes

1928-2903; Osife, Bennet Russell; 1927-Feb-8; Yes; M; Navajo & Pima; Yes; F; F; 1/2-1/2; F; No; Phoenix, Ariz.

2955; Oxpe, Aloysius; 1926-July-2; Yes; M; Pima; Yes; F; F; F; Yes

Unnumbered; Oxpe, Julia; 1927-Feb-28; Yes; F; Pima; Yes; F; F; F; Yes

3002; Pablo, Dennis; 1926-Dec-6; Yes; M; Pima; Yes; F; F; F; Yes

2969; Pablo, Mary Barbara; 1926-Sept-3; Yes; F; Pima; Yes; F; F; F; Yes

3014; Parker, Ella Jr.; 1927-April-10; Yes; F; Maricopa; Yes; F; F; F; Yes

3055; Parsons, Floyd; 1926-Nov-29; Yes; M; Pima; Yes; F; F; F; Yes

1928-3036; Pasquel, Leslie; 1927-May-7; Yes; M; Pima; Yes; F; F; F; Yes

3074; Patrick, Anastacia; 1926-Sept-1; Yes; F; Pima; Yes; F; F; F; Yes

3107; Pedro, Silas; 1926-Sept-29; Yes; M; Pima; Yes; F; F; F; Yes

Unnumbered; Peters, Theodore; 1926-Oct-16; Yes; M; Pima; Yes; F; F; F; Yes

3226; Porter, Dolores; 1927-April-28; Yes; F; Pima; Yes; F; F; F; No; Phoenix, Ariz.

1925-3247; Ramon, Stanley; 1927-Mar-2; Yes; M; Pima; Yes; F; F; F; Yes

3381; Roveless, Ersula; 1926-Sept-13; Yes; F; Pima; Yes; F; F; F; Yes

1928-3423; Santo, Margaret; 1927-Mar-29; Yes; F; Pima; Yes; F; F; F; Yes

3449; Santo, Remah; 1927-May-14; Yes; F; Pima; Yes; F; F; F; Yes

3475; Schurz, Henry; 1927-Feb-4; Yes; M; Pima; Yes; F; F; F; Yes

State **Arizona** Reservation **Gila River Indian Reservation** Agency or jurisdiction **Pima Indian Agency**; Office of Indian Affairs

Key: 1927 Census Roll Number; Surname; Given; Date of Birth (Year-Month-Day); Live Birth (Yes/No); Still-birth (Yes/No); Sex; Tribe; Ward (Yes/No); Degree of Blood (Father-Mother-Child); At Jurisdiction Where Enrolled (Yes/No); (If no – Where – Jurisdiction; State; Post Office; State)

3462; Schurz, Margarett Jr.; 1927-June-22; Yes; F; Pima; Yes; F; F; F; Yes

1928-3483; Seoto, Winifred; 1927-Mar-6; Yes; F; Pima; Yes; F; F; F; Yes

3424; Seye, Bettie; 1926-July-27; Yes; F; Pima; Yes; F; F; F; Yes

3523; Seye, Mary Alice; 1926-July-27; Yes; F; Pima; Yes; F; F; F; Yes

3610; Soatikee, Vincent; 1926-Oct-11; Yes; M; Pima; Yes; F; F; F; Yes

1929-3976; Tasquinth, Edward; 1927-Feb-7; Yes; No; M; Pima; Yes; F; F; F; No; Casa Grande, Ariz.

Unnumbered; Terry, Felix; 1926-Aug-5; Yes; M; Pima; Yes; F; F; F; Yes

1929-3101; Thomas, Albina; 1926-Nov-2; Yes; F; Pima; Yes; F; F; F; Yes

3852; Thomas, Darrell Leo; 1926-July-8; Yes; M; Pima; Yes; F; F; F; Yes

3881; Thomas, Harold; 1927-Jan-2; Yes; M; Pima; Yes; F; F; F; Yes

3885; Thomas, Hilda; 1926-Aug-18; Yes; F; Pima; Yes; F; F; F; Yes

1929-238; Thomas, Pevlit P.; 1927-Jan-1; Yes; F; Papago; Yes; F; F; F; No; Casa Grande, Ariz.

3915; Thompson, Marian Louise; 1927-June-2; Yes; F; Pima; Yes; F; F; F; No; Phoenix, Ariz.

1929-4231; Vavages, L. Nora; 1926-Aug-20; Yes; F; Pima; Yes; F; F; F; Yes

4039; Warren, Winona; 1927-Feb-3; Yes; F; Pima; Yes; F; F; F; Yes

4091; White, Jeanette; 1927-Jan-3; Yes; F; Papago; Yes; F; F; F; Yes

4120; Whitman, Elvery Homer; 1927-June-6; Yes; M; Pima; Yes; F; F; F; Yes

4185; Williams, Pascal; 1926-Nov-7; Yes; M; Pima; Yes; F; F; F; Yes

Unrecorded; Wilson, Jessie; 1927-April-8; Yes; F; Papago; Yes; F; F; F; Yes

Live Births

Occurring Between

July 1, 1927 and June 30, 1928

Pima Indian Agency

Key: 1928 Census Roll Number; Surname; Given; Date of Birth (Year-Month-Day); Live Birth (Yes/No); Still-birth (Yes/No); Sex; Tribe; Ward (Yes/No); Degree of Blood (Father- Mother- Child); At Jurisdiction Where Enrolled (Yes/No); (If no – Where – Jurisdiction; State; Post Office; State)

1929-31; Albert, Enoch; 1928-May-16; Yes; No; M; Maricopa & Pima; Yes; F; F; 1/2-1/2; Yes
1929-51; Allen, Ralston; 1928-June-6; Yes; M; Papago; Yes; F; F; F; Yes
1929-40; Allen, Rosalie; 1927-July-5; Yes; F; Pima; Yes; F; F; F; Yes
1929-80; Allison, Beulah; 1928-May-14; Yes; F; Pima; Yes; F; F; F; Yes
19290[sic]-102; Allison, Clifford; 1928-June-25; Yes; M; Maricopa; Yes; F; F; F; Yes
1930-127; Anton, Annie; 1927-Nov-17; Yes; F; Pima; Yes; F; F; F; Yes
1929-129; Anton, Bill Harris; 1928-June-20; Yes; M; Pima; Yes; F; F; F; Yes
1928-173; Anton, Rose; 1927-Sept-16; Yes; F; Pima; Yes; F; F; F; Yes
Unrecorded; Antone, Roy Pancho Jr.; 1928-May-8; Yes; M; Papago; Yes; F; F; F; No; Tucson, Ariz.
1928-283; Azule, Theodore D.; 1927-Aug-12; Yes; M; Pima; Yes; F; F; F; Yes
Unnumbered; Blackwater, Domingo; 1927-Nov-19; Yes; M; Pima; Yes; F; F; F; Yes
425; Campbell, Elizabeth; 1927-Nov-16; Yes; F; Pima; Yes; F; F; F; Yes
1929-493; Carlyle, Lillian; 1928-April-18; Yes; F; Pima; Yes; F; F; F; Yes
608; Daymond, Marie Jr.; 1927-Dec-5; Yes; F; Ottawa & Pima; Yes; F; F; 1/2-1/2; No; Phoenix, Ariz.
630; Domingo, Bernice Louise; 1928-Feb-15; Yes; F; Maricopa; Yes; F; F; F; Yes
636; Donohue, Felice; 1927-July-28; Yes; F; Maricopa & Papago; Yes; F; F; 1/2-1/2; Yes
Unnumbered; Enas[sic], Helen; 1927-July-28; Yes; F; Pima; Yes; F; F; F; Yes
862; Enos, Henry; 1927-Aug-17; Yes; M; Pima; Yes; F; F; F; Yes
774; Enos, Benedict; 1927-July-9; Yes; M; Pima; Yes; F; F; F; Yes
867; Eschief, Alexander; 1927-Aug-5; Yes; M; Pima; Yes; F; F; F; Yes
1929-995; Evans, Jasper; 1928-May-28; Yes; M; Pima; Yes; F; F; F; Yes
1025; Hall, Margaret Jr.; 1927-July-18; Yes; F; Pima; Yes; F; F; F; Yes
1041; Harrison, Clayton; 1928-Jan-7; Yes; No; M; Pima; Yes; F; F; F; Yes
1929-1141; Harrison, Bennett; 1928-April-25; Yes; M; Pima; Yes; F; F; F; Yes
1929-1074; Harvier, Agatha; 1927-Nov-13; Yes; F; Maricopa & Pima; Yes; F; F; 1/2-1/2; Yes
1207; Howard, Frances; 1928-Jan-25; Yes; F; Pima; Yes; F; F; F; Yes
1280; Jackson, ---; 1927-Dec-5; Yes; M; Pima; Yes; F; F; F; Yes
1296; Jackson, Bettie; 1927-July-3; Yes; F; Pima; Yes; F; F; F; Yes
1356; Jackson, Fernando; 1927-Nov-11; Yes; M; Mexican & Pima; Yes; -; F; 1/2; Yes
1456; John, Mary Jr.; 1927-Dec-18; Yes; F; Pima; Yes; F; F; F; Yes
1498; Johnson, May; 1928-May-14; Yes; F; Pima; Yes; F; F; F; Yes
1747; Justin, Christine; 1928-Jan-18; Yes; F; Pima; Yes; F; F; F; Yes
1272; Juan, Germaine; 1928-Feb-1; Yes; F; Pima; Yes; F; F; F; Yes
1776; Kelly, Bridget; 1927-Oct-19; Yes; F; Walapai & Pima; Yes; F; F; 1/2-1/2; Yes
Unrecorded; Kisto, ---; 1928-April-28; Yes; F; Pima; Yes; F; F; F; Yes
1823; Kisto, Jose Jr.; 1927-Nov-1; Yes; M; Papago; Yes; F; F; F; Yes
1929-2057; Lewis, Edmund R.; 1928-May-26; Yes; M; Pima; Yes; F; F; F; Yes
1994; Lewis, Juan N. Jr.; 1927-Oct-7; Yes; M; Pima; Yes; F; F; F; Yes
2089; Lewis, Maggie Jr.; 1928-May-7; Yes; F; Pima; Yes; F; F; F; Yes

257

State **Arizona** Reservation **Gila River Indian Reservation** Agency or
jurisdiction **Pima Indian Agency**; Office of Indian Affairs
Live-Births Occurring Between the Dates of July 1, 1927 and June 30, 1928 to Parents Enrolled at Jurisdiction

Key: 1928 Census Roll Number; Surname; Given; Date of Birth (Year-Month-Day); Live Birth
(Yes/No); Still-birth (Yes/No); Sex; Tribe; Ward (Yes/No); Degree of Blood (Father- Mother- Child);
At Jurisdiction Where Enrolled (Yes/No); (If no – Where – Jurisdiction; State; Post Office; State)

1929-2260; Lopez, Selma; 1928-April-26; Yes; F; Pima; Yes; F; F; F; Yes

2137; Losey, ---; 1927-July-24; Yes; F; Maricopa; Yes; -; F; 1/2; Yes

2166; Lyon, Clyde; 1928-June-10; Yes; M; Pima; Yes; F; F; F; Yes

1930-2368; Macukay, Theresa; 1927-Dec-22; Yes; F; Pima; Yes; F; F; F; Yes

Unnumbered; Manuel, Barbara; 1927-Sept-29; Yes; F; Papago; Yes; F; F; F; Yes

2257; Manuel, Dennis; 1927-Sept-21; Yes; No; M; Pima; Yes; F; F; F; Yes

2225; Manuel, Dora; 1927-Oct-20; Yes; F; Pima; Yes; F; F; F; Yes

Unrecorded; (Miguel) Marie, ---; 1928-Jan-22; Yes; No; M; Papago & Pima; Yes; F; F; 1/2-1/2; No; Chandler, Ariz.

2394; Marietta, Annie R.; 1927-Aug-11; Yes; F; Papago & Pima; Yes; F; F; 1/2-1/2; Yes

2427; Matthews, Minnie Jr.; 1927-Sept-2; Yes; F; Pima; Yes; F; F; F; Yes

2655; Morago, Edna Mae; 1927-Sept-13; Yes; F; Pima & Crow; Yes; F; 1/2; 1/2; Yes

2648; Morago (Nasewytewa), Henry H.; 1928-Feb-1; Yes; M; Hopi & Pima; Yes; F; F; 1/2-1/2; No; Phoenix, Ariz.

2717; Narsa, Ernest; 1928-Feb-24; Yes; M; Maricopa; Yes; F; F; F; Yes

2769; Nelson, Patricia J.; 1927-Aug-16; Yes; F; Pima; Yes; F; F; F; No; Phoenix, Ariz.

1929-3005; Noname, Leona A.; 1928-May-16; Yes; F; Pima; Yes; -; F; F; Yes

2849; Nunez, Michael; 1927-Oct-27; Yes; M; Pima; Yes; F; F; F; No; Tucson, Ariz.

2848; Nunez, Urban; 1927-Oct-27; Yes; M; Pima; Yes; F; F; F; No; Tucson, Ariz.

3168; Pablo, Edwina; 1928-June-21; Yes; F; Pima; Yes; F; F; F; Yes

1929-201; Pablo, Regina; 1927-Aug-14; Yes; F; Papago; Yes; F; F; F; Yes

3007; Pancot, Glen; 1927-Nov-30; Yes; M; Pima; Yes; F; F; F; Yes

3018; Parsons, Virginia; 1927-Oct-12; Yes; F; Pima; Yes; F; F; F; Yes

3033; Pasquel, Henry Jr.; 1927-Aug-17; Yes; M; Pima; Yes; F; F; F; Yes

3119; Peters, Norman; 1927-Aug-14; Yes; M; Pima; Yes; F; F; F; Yes

Unrecorded; Peter, Delphina; 1927-Oct---; Yes; F; Papago; Yes; F; F; F; Yes

3208; Porter, Merrill Joe; 1928-Feb-9; Yes; M; Pima; Yes; F; F; F; Yes

3316; Ringlaro, Robert; 1927-Nov-25; Yes; M; Pima & Papago; Yes; F; F; 1/2-1/2; No; Phoenix, Ariz.

1929-3596; Rovie, Betty Jane; 1928-April-27; Yes; F; Pima; Yes; F; F; F; Yes

3426; Santo, Bettie E.; 1928-Feb-25; Yes; No; F; Pima; Yes; F; F; F; Yes

1929-3707; Schaeffer, Dana; 1928-Jan-9; Yes; M; Pima; Yes; F; F; F; Yes

3535; Smith, Emily; 1927-Aug-27; Yes; F; Maricopa; Yes; F; F; F; Yes

Unnumbered; Smith, Harry P.; 1928-June-13; Yes; M; Pima; Yes; F; F; F; No; Phoenix, Ariz.

1929-3836; Soatikee, Leona; 1928-April-14; Yes; M; Pima; Yes; F; F; F; Yes

3642; Stone, Leonard; 1928-June-3; Yes; M; Pima; Yes; F; F; F; Yes

Unnumbered; Terry, Mary; 1927-Aug-1; Yes; F; Pima; Yes; F; F; F; Yes

3918; Vavages, Elma; 1927-July-18; Yes; F; Pima; Yes; F; F; F; Yes

1929-249; Vincent, Lester; 1927-Nov-25; Yes; M; Maricopa; Yes; F; F; F; Yes

Live Births
Occurring Between
July 1, 1928 and June 30, 1929
Pima Indian Agency

State **Arizona** Reservation **Gila River Indian Reservation** Agency or jurisdiction **Pima Indian Agency**; Office of Indian Affairs

<u>Live-Births Occurring Between the Dates of July 1, 1928 and June 30, 1929 to Parents Enrolled at Jurisdiction</u>

Key: 1929 Census Roll Number; Surname; Given; Date of Birth (Year-Month-Day); Live Birth (Yes/No); Still-birth (Yes/No); Sex; Tribe; Ward (Yes/No); Degree of Blood (Father- Mother- Child); At Jurisdiction Where Enrolled (Yes/No); (If no – Where – Jurisdiction; State; Post Office; State)

24; Ahliel, Sarah Jane; 1928-July-2; Yes; No; F; Pima; Yes; F; F; F; Yes

Unnumbered; Allison, Herbert Jr.; 1928-Sept-12; Yes; M; Pima; Yes; F; F; F; Yes

217; Anton, Anna; 1929-Feb-11; Yes; F; Pima & Navajo; Yes; F; F; 1/2-1/2; No; Zuni, N. Mex.

196; Antone, Clayton; 1929-Mar-12; Yes; M; Pima; Yes; F; F; F; Yes

50; Antone, Mardard; 1928-July-30; Yes; F; Pima; Yes; F; F; F; Yes

272; Apkaw, Josephine; 1929-June-21; Yes; F; Pima; Yes; F; F; F; Yes

354; Blackwater, Cora May; 1929-Mar-13; Yes; F; Pima; Yes; F; F; F; Yes

359; Blackwater, Earling M.; 1928-Aug-18; Yes; M; Pima; Yes; F; F; F; Yes

Unrecorded; Blaine, Leonard; 1928-Dec-6; Yes; M; Papago; Yes; F; F; F; No; Phoenix, Ariz.

431; Brown, Irma Mae; 1929-Apr-3; Yes; F; Pima; Yes; F; F; F; No; Glendale, Ariz.

443; Burke, Eleanor; 1928-Nov-22; Yes; F; Pima; Yes; F; F; F; Yes

482; Cannon, Gabriel; 1928-Sept-27; Yes; M; Pima; Yes; F; F; F; Yes

559; Chopin, Lester; 1928-Sept-1; Yes; M; Pima; Yes; F; F; F; Yes

Unnumbered; Cook, Luke Jr.; 1928-Feb-1; Yes; M; Pima & Choctaw; Yes; F; F; 1/2-1/2; No; Phoenix, Ariz.

665; Davis, Leonard Mae; 1928-Oct-19; Yes; F; Pima; Yes; F; F; F; Yes

705; Donohue, Byron; 1928-Sept-25; Yes; M; Maricopa-Pima-White; Yes; 1/2; F; 1/2; No; Levine[sic], Ariz.

715; Donohue, Lila; 1928-Nov-29; Yes; F; Maricopa; Yes; F; F; F; Yes

802; Enis, Barbara; 1928-Oct-26; Yes; F; Pima & Navajo; Yes; F; F; 1/2-1/2; Yes

945; Enos, Russell J.; 1929-April-8; Yes; M; Pima; Yes; F; F; F; No; Lavine[sic], Ariz.

894; Enos, Walter; 1929-Feb-20; Yes; M; Pima; Yes; F; F; F; No; Laveen, Ariz.

955; Eschief, Gerald E.; 1929-Feb-7; Yes; M; Papago & Pima; Yes; F; F; 1/2-1/2; Yes

984; Evans, Millie; 1929-May- 12; Yes; F; Pima; Yes; F; F; F; Yes

1024; Francisco, ---; 1929-April-26; Yes; No; F; Pima; Yes; F; F; F; Yes

1930-1050; Gage, Lorena; 1929-April-16; Yes; F; Pima; Yes; F; F; F; Yes

1174; Havier, Joe; 1929-Jan-14; Yes; M; Papago & Pima; Yes; F; F; F[sic]; 1/2-1/2; Yes

1270; Hoover, Irene; 1928-July-7; Yes; F; Pima; Yes; -; F; F; Yes

1283; Houston, Ola; 1928-May- 18; Yes; F; Pima; Yes; F; F; F; Yes

1394; Jackson, ---; 1929-June-22; Yes; M; Pima; Yes; F; F; F; Yes

Unnumbered; Jackson, Allen Jr.; 1929-Jan-30; Yes; M; Pima; Yes; F; F; F; Yes

1429; Jackson, Arnold G.; 1928-Dec-7; Yes; M; Pima; Yes; F; F; F; Yes

Unrecorded; Jackson, Betty; 1929-April-24; Yes; F; Pima; Yes; F; F; F; No; Salt River Res., Ariz.

1930-1468; Jackson, Blanche; 1928-Nov-26; Yes; F; Pima; Yes; F; F; F; Yes

1438; Jackson, Elmyra; 1929-June-10; Yes; F; Pima; Yes; F; F; F; Yes

1481; Jackson, Fern; 1929-April-29; Yes; F; Pima; Yes; F; F; F; Yes

1366; Jackson, Milton; 1928-Nov-27; Yes; M; Pima & Onida[sic]; Yes; F; F; 1/2-1/2; Yes

1448; Jackson, Ross; 1928-Aug-11; Yes; M; Pima & Mission; Yes; F; F; 1/2-1/2; Yes

1563; John, Delsie Ione; 1928-Dec-6; Yes; F; Pima; Yes; F; F; F; Yes

State **Arizona** Reservation **Gila River Indian Reservation** Agency or
jurisdiction **Pima Indian Agency**; Office of Indian Affairs
Live-Births Occurring Between the Dates of July 1, 1928 and June 30, 1929 to Parents Enrolled at Jurisdiction

Key: 1929 Census Roll Number; Surname; Given; Date of Birth (Year-Month-Day); Live Birth
(Yes/No); Still-birth (Yes/No); Sex; Tribe; Ward (Yes/No); Degree of Blood (Father- Mother- Child);
At Jurisdiction Where Enrolled (Yes/No); (If no – Where – Jurisdiction; State; Post Office; State)

1602; Johnson, Thurman; 1928-July-25; Yes; M; Pima; Yes; F; F; F; Yes
1656; Johnson, Wayne; 1929-May- 14; Yes; M; Pima; Yes; F; F; F; No; Palo Verde, Ariz.
1720; Jones, Sylvester; 1928-Oct-10; Yes; M; Choctaw & Pima; Yes; F; F; 1/2-1/2; Yes
1736; Jose, Byron; 1929-Feb-22; Yes; M; Pima; Yes; F; F; F; Yes
Unnumbered; Joseph, Margaret Jr.; 1929-April-1; Yes; F; Pima & Papago; Yes; F; F; 1/2-1/2; Yes
1817; Juan, Hazel Frances; 1928-Nov-13; Yes; F; Pima; Yes; F; F; F; Yes
1853; Juan, Lauretta; 1928-Sept-1; Yes; F; Pima; Yes; F; F; F; Yes
1991; Kyyitan, Camelia; 1928-Oct-10; Yes; F; Pima; Yes; F; F; F; Yes
Unrecorded; Lewis, Caroline; 1928-Dec-24; Yes; No; F; Pueblo & Pima; Yes; F; F; 1/2-1/2; Yes
2124; Lewis, Dennis; 1928-Dec-7; Yes; M; Pima; Yes; F; F; F; Yes
2039; Lewis, Elmira; 1928-July-20; Yes; F; Pima; Yes; F; F; F; Yes
2070; Lewis, Lena Jr.; 1929-Jan-18; Yes; F; Pima & Papago; Yes; F; F; 1/2-1/2; Yes
2254; Lomauhie, Roberta; 1928-Nov-1; Yes; F; Pima; Yes; -; F; F; Yes
2296; Lowe, Mary Ann; 1929-Jan-13; Yes; F; Pima & papago[sic]; Yes; F; F; 1/2-1/2; No; Calif.
2328; Lyons, Eloise; 1928-July-6; Yes; F; Pima; Yes; F; F; F; Yes
2321; Lyons, Frederick; 1928-Sept-21; Yes; M; Pima; Yes; F; F; F; Yes
2401; Manuel, Isabel; 1928-Aug-16; Yes; F; Pima; Yes; F; F; F; Yes
2400; Manuel, Mark Miles; 1928-Aug-16; Yes; M; Pima; Yes; F; F; F; Yes
2514; Manyahn, Roberta; 1928-July-18; Yes; F; Maricopa; Yes; F; F; F; Yes
1930-2559; Marietta, Harry; 1929-June-23; Yes; M; Pima; Yes; F; F; F; Yes
2564; Marietta, Sila LaVerne; 1929-April-13; Yes; F; Papago & Pima; Yes; F; F; 1/2-1/2; Yes
2764; Miles, ---; 1928-July-9; Yes; M; Pima; Yes; F; F; F; Yes
2943; Nelson, Betty; 1928-July-7; Yes; F; Pima; Yes; F; F; F; Yes
2957; Nelson, Carol; 1928-Dec-20; Yes; F; Pima; Yes; F; F; F; No; Phoenix, Ariz.
Unnumbered; Nelson, Mona; 1928-Aug-23; Yes; F; Pima; Yes; F; F; F; Yes
Unnumbered; Nish, Austin; 1928-Oct-16; Yes; M; Pima; Yes; F; F; F; Yes
3080; Osife, Byron; 1928-Aug-25; Yes; M; Pima; Yes; F; F; F; Yes
3280; Pedro, Arlene; 1929-Jan-2; Yes; F; Papago & Pima; Yes; F; F; F; No; Los Angeles, Calif.
1930-3312; Pedro, Pablo, Delphena; 1929-June-25; Yes; F; Pima; Yes; F; F; F; Yes
3390; Philips, Kenneth; 1929-Mar-6; Yes; M; Pima; Yes; F; F; F; Yes
Unnumbered; Porter, Benard W.; 1929-Jan-30; Yes; M; Pima; Yes; F; F; F; No; Phoenix, Ariz.
3479; Ramon, Joe Henry; 1928-Aug-12; Yes; No; M; Pima; Yes; F; F; F; Yes
3476; Ramon, Leonard; 1929-June-2; Yes; M; Pima; Yes; F; F; F; Yes
3550; Ringlere, Frederick; 1928-Dec-5; Yes; M; Mission & Pima; Yes; F; F; 1/2-1/2; No; Phoenix, Ariz.

262

State **Arizona** Reservation **Gila River Indian Reservation** Agency or jurisdiction **Pima Indian Agency**; Office of Indian Affairs

Live-Births Occurring Between the Dates of July 1, 1928 and June 30, 1929 to Parents Enrolled at Jurisdiction

Key: 1929 Census Roll Number; Surname; Given; Date of Birth (Year-Month-Day); Live Birth (Yes/No); Still-birth (Yes/No); Sex; Tribe; Ward (Yes/No); Degree of Blood (Father- Mother- Child); At Jurisdiction Where Enrolled (Yes/No); (If no – Where – Jurisdiction; State; Post Office; State)

Unnumbered; Rivera, Ernestine; 1929-June-23; Yes; F; Mex. & Pima; Yes; [-]; F; 1/2; No; Tucson, Ariz.

3682; Santos, Lordina; 1929-May- 8; Yes; F; Pima; Yes; F; F; F; Yes

3698; Schurz, Guy Elmer; 1928-Nov-27; Yes; M; Pima; Yes; F; F; F; Yes

3903; Stewart, Herbert; 1928-Nov-7; Yes; M; Maricopa; Yes; F; F; F; Yes

3945; Sundust, Carmen; 1928-Sept-18; Yes; F; Maricopa; Yes; F; F; F; Yes

4232; Vavages, Dolores; 1928-Sept-5; Yes; F; Pima; Yes; F; F; F; Yes

4196; Vavages, Leonard; 1929-April-16; Yes; M; Pima; Yes; F; F; F; Yes

4264; Vincent, Clarence; 1929-Nov-2; Yes; M; Pima; Yes; F; F; F; Yes

4312; Webb, Alford; 1928-July-12; Yes; M; Pima; Yes; F; F; F; Yes

4401; Whittaker, Vivian Fay; 1929-Mar-26; Yes; F; Pima; Yes; F; F; F; Yes

4473; Wilson, Barbara; 1928-July-28; Yes; F; Pima; Yes; F; F; F; Yes

Unnumbered; Wilson, Joe Ann; 1928-July-28; Yes; F; Pima; Yes; F; F; F; Yes

4483; Wilson, Robert Morgan; 1929-Feb-15; Yes; M; Apache & Pima; Yes; F; F; 1/2-1/2; No; Phoenix, Ariz.

4493; Winn, Alfred; 1929-Feb-13; Yes; M; Pima; Yes; F; F; F; Yes

4502; Yaramata, Lena; 1929-Jan-18; Yes; F; Maricopa; Yes; F; F; F; Yes

Live Births
Occurring Between
July 1, 1929 and June 30, 1930
Pima Indian Agency

State **Arizona** Reservation **Gila River Indian Reservation** Agency or
jurisdiction **Pima Indian Agency**; Office of Indian Affairs

Live-Births Occurring Between the Dates of July 1, 1929 and June 30, 1930 to Parents Enrolled at Jurisdiction

Key: 1930 Census Roll Number; Surname; Given; Date of Birth (Year-Month-Day); Live Birth
(Yes/No); Still-birth (Yes/No); Sex; Tribe; Ward (Yes/No); Degree of Blood (Father- Mother- Child);
At Jurisdiction Where Enrolled (Yes/No); (If no – Where – Jurisdiction; State; Post Office; State)

70; Allison, Delbert; 1930-Feb-9; Yes; No; M; Pima; Yes; Yes; F; F; F; Yes
153; Anton, Priscilla; 1929-Nov-5; Yes; F; Pima; Yes; F; F; F; Yes
Unnumbered; Anton, Ernest; 1930-May-23; Yes; M; Pima; Yes; F; F; F; Yes
Unnumbered; Anton, Ernestine; 1930-May-23; Yes; F; Pima; Yes; F; F; F; Yes
139; Antone, Charles; 1929-Nov-1; Yes; M; Pima; Yes; F; F; F; Yes
1931-203; Antone, Clara; 1930-May-12; Yes; F; Pima & Navajo; Yes; F; F; 1/2-1/2;
No; Zuni Reservation, N. Mex.
1931-4606; Antone, Felix; 1930-Mar-12; Yes; M; Papago; Yes; F; F; F; Yes
Unnumbered; Antone, Harriet; 1930-June-28; Yes; F; Pima; Yes; F; F; F; Yes
Unrecorded; Antone, Joseph; 1930-Mar-29; Yes; M; Papago; Yes; F; F; F; Yes
1870; Antone, Juan; 1929-Oct-18; Yes; M; Pima; Yes; F; F; F; Yes
1931-302; Barehand, ---; 1930-April-11; Yes; F; Pima; Yes; F; F; F; Yes
375; Blackwater, Oren Sibyl; 1930-Mar-5; Yes; F; Pima; Yes; F; F; F; Yes
410; Breckenridge, Harriet; 1930-April-7; Yes; F; Pima; Yes; F; F; F; Yes
489; Cannon, Herold; 1930-Jan-26; Yes; M; Pima; Yes; F; F; F; Yes
471; Canner, Percy; 1929-July- 3; Yes; M; Maricopa & Pima; Yes; F; F; 1/2-1/2; Yes
510; Carmen, Raymond; 1930-Mar-7; Yes; M; Papago & Pima; Yes; F; F; 1/2-1/2;
Yes
1931-661; Daymond, Lucile; 1930-Jan-27; Yes; F; Pima & Mohawk; Yes; F; F; 1/2-
1/2; Yes
1931-695; Donohue, Bruce Derwin; 1930-May-20; Yes; M; Klamath & Maricopa &
Pima; Yes; F; F; F; No; Laveen, Ariz.
1931-722; Ellis, Alice; 1930-May-7; Yes; F; Pima & white; Yes; -; F; 1/2; Yes
794; Enas, Priscilla; 1929-Oct-30; Yes; F; Pima & Maricopa; Yes; F; F; 1/2-1/2; Yes
Unnumbered; Eschief, ---; 1929-Aug-6; Yes; M; Pima; Yes; F; F; F; Yes
978; Eschief, Ruth Ann; 1929-Oct-7; Yes; F; Pima; Yes; F; F; F; Yes
990; Eschief, George; 1929-July- 8; Yes; M; Pima; Yes; F; F; F; No; Paston, Ariz.
1931-992; Fohrenkam, Milton; 1930-Jan-1; Yes; No; M; Maricopa & white; Yes; -; F;
1/2; No; Minneapolis; Minn.
1075; ~~Gazula~~ Kasuri, Iva; 1929-Nov-19; Yes; F; Pima; Yes; F; F; F; Yes
1931-1200; Hayes, Lillian; 1930-Mar-12; Yes; F; Pima; Yes; F; F; F; No; Salt River
Res., Ariz.
1931-1256; Homa, Patricia; 1930-Mae- 18; Yes; F; Pima; Yes; -; F; F; Yes
1334; Howard, Harvier; 1929-Nov-21; Yes; M; Pima; Yes; F; F; F; Yes
Unrecorded; Jackson, Carleton; 1930-Mar-26; Yes; M; Pima; Yes; F; F; F; No;
Glendale, Ariz.
Unnumbered; Jackson, Lucy; 1930-June-29; Yes; F; Pima; Yes; F; F; F; Yes
1421; Jackson, Verton; 1930-March; 20; Yes; M; Papago & Pima; Yes; F; F; F; Yes
1686; Johnson, Delbert R.; 1929-Dec-15; Yes; M; Pima; Yes; F; F; F; Yes
1617; Johnson, Evelyn C.; 1930-Jan-1; Yes; F; Pima; Yes; F; F; F; Yes
1674; Johnson, Grace Viola; 1929-Oct-13; Yes; F; Pima; Yes; F; F; F; Yes
Unrecorded; Jones, ---; 1930-June-29; Yes; M; Pima; Yes; F; F; F; Yes
1931-1666; Jones, Isadora; 1930-June-30; Yes; F; Pima; Yes; F; F; F; Yes
1783; Jose, Elizabeth; 1930-March; 31; Yes; F; Pima; Yes; -; F; F; Yes

267

State **Arizona** Reservation **Gila River Indian Reservation** Agency or
jurisdiction **Pima Indian Agency**; Office of Indian Affairs

Live-Births Occurring Between the Dates of July 1, 1929 and June 30, 1930 to Parents Enrolled at Jurisdiction

Key: 1930 Census Roll Number; Surname; Given; Date of Birth (Year-Month-Day); Live Birth
(Yes/No); Still-birth (Yes/No); Sex; Tribe; Ward (Yes/No); Degree of Blood (Father- Mother- Child);
At Jurisdiction Where Enrolled (Yes/No); (If no – Where – Jurisdiction; State; Post Office; State)

1950; Kisto, Everett (Frank); 1929-July- 2; Yes; M; Pima; Yes; F; F; F; Yes

Unnumbered; Kisto, (Felix Jr. Coops) Felix; 1930-Jan-22; Yes; M; Pima; Yes; F; F; F;
No; Sweetwater, Ariz.

2010; Lamore, Gladys; 1929-Oct-14; Yes; F; Mex. & White & Maricopa; Yes; -; F;
1/2; No; Los Angeles, Calif.

1931-1987; Lappie, Henry Jr.; 1930-June-15; Yes; M; Pima; Yes; F; F; F; Yes

2028; Laws, Joan Charoline[sic]; 1929-Nov-17; Yes; F; Pima; Yes; F; F; F; No;
Phoenix, Ariz.

2171; Lewis, Augustina; 1929-Aug-28; Yes; F; Pima; Yes; F; F; F; Yes

1931-2206; Lewis, Bertina; 1930-May-10; Yes; F; Pima; Yes; F; F; F; Yes

Unrecorded; Lewis, Connie Jr.; 1929-July- 1; Yes; F; Pima; Yes; F; F; F; No; Tucson,
Ariz.

2052; Lewis, Idella Peggy; 1920[sic]; Jan-18; Yes; F; Pima; Yes; F; F; F; Yes

1931-2180; Lewis, Reuben; 1930-May-1; Yes; M; Pima; Yes; F; F; F; Yes

Unrecorded; Lilo, Angelica; 1930-May-7; Yes; F; Hope & Pima; Yes; F; F; F; No;
Salt River Res., Ariz.

2293; Lose, Edward H.; 1929-Dec-28; Yes; M; Pima; Yes; F; F; F; Yes

1931-3303 ~~Unrecorded~~; Lowe, Percy; Arnold; 1930-May-30; Yes; M; Pima; Yes; F;
F; F; No; Phoenix, Ariz.

1931-4737; Manuel, Harry; 1930-June-26; Yes; M; Papago; Yes; F; F; F; Yes

2614; Mathews, Cramer; 1930-Jan-10; Yes; M; Pima; Yes; F; F; F; Yes

2915; Narsa, Peter; 1930-Jan-12; Yes; M; Pima & Papago; Yes; F; F; F; Yes

2983; Newman, George; 1930-Mar-15; Yes; M; Pima & Papago; Yes; F; F; F; Yes

3049; Norris, Leonard; 1929-July- 3; Yes; M; Pima; Yes; F; F; F; Yes

1931-3105; Osife, Philip; L930[sic]; April-22; Yes; M; Pima; Yes; F; F; F; Yes

3139; Oxpe, George Kisto; 1929-Aug-18; Yes; M; Pima & Papago; Yes; F; F; F; Yes

1931-3161; Pablo, Raymond; 1929-Nov-27; Yes; M; Pima; Yes; F; F; F; Yes

3254; Pasquale, Cliford[sic]; 1929-Oct-23; Yes; M; Pima; Yes; F; F; F; Yes

3246; Parsons, Delbert Leroy; 1930-Jan-4; Yes; M; Pima; Yes; F; F; F; Yes

1931-3268; Pedro, Lawrence Roger; 1930-May-2; Yes; M; Pima; Yes; F; F; F; No;
Phoenix, Ariz.

1931-3299; Perchero, Mattie; 1930-April-26; Yes; F; Maricopa; Yes; F; F; F; Yes

3390; Peter, Pauline; 1929-Aug-20; Yes; F; Pima; Yes; F; F; F; Yes

3382; Peters, Emalais; 1929-July- 28; Yes; F; Pima; Yes; F; F; F; Yes

3365; Peters, Raymond; 1930-March; 11; Yes; M; Pima; Yes; F; F; F; Yes

1931-3421; Porter, Claudine; 1930-May-12; Yes; F; Pima; Yes; F; F; F; No; Phoenix,
Ariz.

3459; Porter, Everett W.; 1930-March; 5; Yes; M; Pima & Papago; Yes; F; 1/2;
3/4[sic]; No; Phoenix, Ariz.

1931-3445; Pratt, Barbara; 1930-April-7; Yes; F; Pima; Yes; F; F; F; Yes

1931-3542; Rhodes, Spencer; 1930-May-31; Yes; M; Pima & Cheyenne; Yes; F; F; F;
No; Laveen, Ariz.

3693; Santo, Anton Jr.; 1929-Dec-29; Yes; No; M; Pima; Yes; F; F; F; Yes

State **Arizona** Reservation **Gila River Indian Reservation** Agency or jurisdiction **Pima Indian Agency**; Office of Indian Affairs

<u>Live-Births Occurring Between the Dates of July 1, 1929 and June 30, 1930 to Parents Enrolled at Jurisdiction</u>

Key: 1930 Census Roll Number; Surname; Given; Date of Birth (Year-Month-Day); Live Birth (Yes/No); Still-birth (Yes/No); Sex; Tribe; Ward (Yes/No); Degree of Blood (Father- Mother- Child); At Jurisdiction Where Enrolled (Yes/No); (If no – Where – Jurisdiction; State; Post Office; State)

1931-3711; Schurz, Merlin; 1930-Feb-19; Yes; M; Pima; Yes; F; F; F; No; Mesa, Ariz.

3808; Smith, Florence; 1929-July- 28; Yes; F; Pima; Yes; F; F; F; Yes

3863; Soke, Frederick; 1929-Sept-8; Yes; M; Pima; Yes; F; F; F; Yes

3901; Stevens, Hogene Louise; 1930-Mar-14; Yes; F; Pima; Yes; F; F; F; No; Los Angeles, Ariz[sic]

3930; Stone, Lillian May; 1929-July- 6; Yes; F; Pima; Yes; F; F; F; Yes

1931-3946; Sundust, Leonard Jr.; 1930-April-28; Yes; M; Maricopa; Yes; F; F; F; Yes

4155; Thomas, Charlotte; 1929-Aug-5; Yes; F; Pima; Yes; F; F; F; Yes

1931-4862; Thomas, Edmund; 1930-April-8; Yes; M; Papago; Yes; F; F; F; Yes

4154; Thomas, Geraldine; 1929-Aug-5; Yes; F; Pima; Yes; F; F; F; Yes

4190; Thompson, Eula; 1929-Nov-27; Yes; F; Pima; Yes; F; F; F; Yes

1931-4906; Vincent, Loraine G.; 1930-April-8; Yes; F; Papago; Yes; F; F; F; Yes

4293; Vincent, Lorene M.; 1930-Jan-19; Yes; F; Pima; Yes; F; F; F; Yes

1931-4280; Wade, Luella May; 1930-May-13; Yes; F; Pima & Maricopa; Yes; F; F; F; Yes

4417; Whitman, Hazel; 1929-July- 15; Yes; F; Pima; Yes; F; F; F; Yes

4480; Williams, Tobias; 1929-July- 17; Yes; M; Pima; Yes; F; F; F; Yes

269

Live Births

Occurring Between

April 1, 1930 and March 31, 1931

Pima Indian Agency

State **Arizona** Reservation **Gila River Indian Reservation** Agency or jurisdiction **Pima Indian Agency**; Office of Indian Affairs

Live-Births Occurring Between the Dates of April 1, 1930 and March 31, 1931 to Parents Enrolled at Jurisdiction

Key: 1931 Census Roll Number; Surname; Given; Date of Birth (Year-Month-Day); Live Birth (Yes/No); Still-birth (Yes/No); Sex; Tribe; Ward (Yes/No); Degree of Blood (Father- Mother- Child); At Jurisdiction Where Enrolled (Yes/No); (If no – Where – Jurisdiction; State; Post Office; State)

Unnumbered; Anton, Ernest; 1930-May-23; Yes; No; M; Pima; Yes; F; F; F; Yes

Unnumbered; Anton, Ernestine; 1930-May-23; Yes; F; Pima; Yes; F; F; F; Yes

203; Antone, Clara V.; 1930-May-12; Yes; F; Pima & Navajo; Yes; F; F; F; No; Zuni, N. Mex.

Unnumbered; Antone, Harriet; 1930-June-28; Yes; F; Pima; Yes; F; F; F; Yes

4615; Anton, Mathias Jr.; 1930-Sept-17; Yes; M; Papago; Yes; F; F; F; Yes

294; Baptisto, ---; 1930-Sept-2; Yes; F; Pima; Yes; -; F; F; Yes

302; Barehand, ---; 1930-April-11; Yes; F; Maricopa; Yes; F; F; F; Yes

358; Blackwater, Lewis; 1931-Feb-22; Yes; M; Pima; Yes; F; F; F; Yes

1930-410; Breckenridge, Harriet; 1930-April-7; Yes; F; Pima; Yes; F; F; F; Yes

Unnumbered; Campbell, ---; 1930-Dec-17; Yes; F; Pima; Yes; F; F; F; Yes

487; Carlyle, Richard; 1930-Aug-29; Yes; M; Maricopa & Pima; Yes; F; F; F; Yes

666; Delowe, ---; 1931-Feb-2; Yes; F; Maricopa; Yes; F; F; F; Yes

695; Donohue, Bruce; 1930-May-20; Yes; F; Klamath & Maricopa & Pima; Yes; F; F; F; No; Laveen, Ariz.

722; Ellis, Alice; 1930-May-7; Yes; F; Pima; Yes; -; F; 1/2; Yes

874; Enos, ---; 1931-Jan-19; Yes; F; Maricopa; Yes; F; F; F; Yes

966; Evans, Erma; 1930-Dec-13; Yes; F; Pima; Yes; F; F; F; Yes

1029; Gage, Maurrine; 1930-Dec-6; Yes; F; Pima; Yes; F; F; F; Yes

Unnumbered; Harrison, Stella; 1930-Oct-2; Yes; F; Pima; Yes; F; F; F; Yes

1161; Harvier, Eileen; 1930-Oct-12; Yes; F; Pima & Walapai; Yes; F; F; F; Yes

Unnumbered; Howard, Rufus; 1931-Mar-17; Yes; M; Pima; Yes; F; F; F; No; Salt River Res., Ariz.

1454; Jackson, Lorraine; 1930-Oct-15; Yes; F; Pima; Yes; F; F; F; Yes

Unnumbered; Jackson, Lucy; 1930-June-29; Yes; F; Pima; Yes; F; F; F; Yes

Unnumbered; Jackson, Vilma; 1930-Aug-10; Yes; F; Pima; Yes; F; F; F; Yes

1506; James, Mary Ann; 1930-July-30; Yes; No; F; Pima; Yes; F; F; F; Yes

1572; Johns, Pearl; 1930-Aug-6; Yes; F; Pima; Yes; -; F; F; Yes

Unnumbered; James (Johns), Marcella; 1931-Feb-26; Yes; F; Pima; Yes; F; F; F; Yes

Unnumbered; Johnson, Caroline; 1931-Jan-3; Yes; F; Pima & Papago; Yes; F; F; F; Yes

Unrecorded; Jones, ---; 1930-June-29; Yes; M; Pima; Yes; F; F; F; Yes

1666; Jones, Isadora; 1930-June-30; Yes; F; Pima; Yes; F; F; F; Yes

1720; Jose, Doris; 1930-Dec-5; Yes; F; Pima; Yes; F; F; F; Yes

1767; Joseph, Theora; 1930-Oct-30; Yes; F; Pima & Papago; Yes; F; F; F; Yes

1987; Lappie, Henry Jr.; 1930-June-15; Yes; M; Pima; Yes; F; F; F; Yes

2186; Lewis, Avery; 1930-Sept-9; Yes; M; Pima & Papago; Yes; F; 1/2; 1/2-3/4; Yes

2206; Lewis, Bertina; 1930-May-10; Yes; F; Pima; Yes; F; F; F; Yes

Unnumbered; Lewis, Jose; 1931-Feb-8; Yes; M; Papago; Yes; F; F; F; Yes

2180; Lewis, Reuben; 1930-May-1; Yes; M; Pima; Yes; F; F; F; Yes

~~Unrecorded; Lilo, Angelica; 1930-May-7; Yes~~; F; Hope & Pima; Yes; F; F; F; Yes

Unnumbered; Lopez, Leppe; 1930-Dec-24; Yes; F; Pima; Yes; F; F; F; Yes

Unrecorded; Lowe, Arnold; 1930-May-30; Yes; M; Pima; Yes; F; F; F; Yes;

2284; Lucero, Juanita; 1930-Sept-30; Yes; F; Pima & Pueblo; Yes; F; F; F; Yes

State **Arizona** Reservation **Gila River Indian Reservation** Agency or jurisdiction **Pima Indian Agency**; Office of Indian Affairs

Live-Births Occurring Between the Dates of April 1, 1930 and March 31, 1931 to Parents Enrolled at Jurisdiction

Key: 1931 Census Roll Number; Surname; Given; Date of Birth (Year-Month-Day); Live Birth (Yes/No); Still-birth (Yes/No); Sex; Tribe; Ward (Yes/No); Degree of Blood (Father- Mother- Child); At Jurisdiction Where Enrolled (Yes/No); (If no – Where – Jurisdiction; State; Post Office; State)

Unnumbered; Manuel, Austin; 1930-Nov-9; Yes; M; Pima; Yes; F; F; F; Yes

2442; Manuel, Betty; 1931-Mar-21; Yes; F; Pima & Papago; Yes; F; F; F; Yes

2469; Manuel, Eula; 1930-Aug-21; Yes; F; Pima; Yes; F; F; F; Yes

4737; Manuel, Harry; 1930-June-26; Yes; M; Papago; Yes; F; F; F; Yes

2382; Manuel, Helen; 1930-Nov-9; Yes; F; Maricopa; Yes; F; F; F; Yes

2493; Manuel, Iris; 1931-Mar-27; Yes; F; Maricopa & Pima; Yes; F; F; F; No; Lehigh, Ariz.

2437; Manuel, Leroy; 1930-Sept-14; Yes; No; M; Pima; Yes; F; F; F; Yes

Unnumbered; Marcus, Esther; 1930-Aug-31; Yes; F; Papago; Yes; F; F; F; No; Coolidge, Ariz.

2871; Myers (Meyers), Edwardyn; 1930-Sept-11; Yes; F; Pima; Yes; F; F; F; Yes

2757; Miles, Joseph Jr.; 1930-July-29; Yes; M; Pima; Yes; F; F; F; Yes

2857; Mumhy, ---; 1930-Oct-6; Yes; M; Maricopa; Yes; F; F; F; Yes

Unrecorded; Napalee, Mary; 1930-Aug-25; Yes; F; Zuni & Pima; Yes; F; F; F; No; Phoenix, Ariz.

Unrecorded; Narcia, Edmond; 1930-Dec-7; Yes; M; Papago; Yes; F; F; F; Yes

Unnumbered; Nelson, Virgil; 1930-Aug-25; Yes; M; Pima; Yes; F; F; F; No; Phoenix, Ariz.

Unnumbered; Nish, Elizabeth; 1931-Mar-30; Yes; F; Pima; Yes; F; F; F; Yes

3072; Osif, Dennis; 1930-Aug-13; Yes; M; Pima & Papago; Yes; F; F; F; Yes

Unnumbered; Osife, Pansy Mary; 1930-Nov-22; Yes; F; Pima; Yes; F; F; F; Yes

3105; Osife, Philip; 1930-April-22; Yes; M; Pima; Yes; F; F; F; Yes

Unrecorded; Oxpe, Donald; 1930-July-4; Yes; M; Pima; Yes; F; F; F; Yes

3110; Oxpe, Paul; 1931-Mar-13; Yes; M; Pima; Yes; F; F; F; Yes

3200; Pancotte, Priscilla; 1930-Dec-15; Yes; F; Pima; Yes; F; F; F; Yes

3230; Pasqual, Elmer; 1930-July-26; Yes; M; Pima; Yes; F; F; F; Yes

3240; Patrick, Alfred; 1930-Aug-14; Yes; M; Pima; Yes; F; F; F; Yes

3268; Pedro, Lawrence; 1930-May-2; Yes; M; Pima; Yes; F; F; F; No; Phoenix, Ariz.

3299; Perchero, Mattie; 1930-April-26; Yes; F; Maricopa; Yes; F; F; F; Yes

3421; Porter, Claudine; 1930-May-12; Yes; F; Pima; Yes; F; F; F; No; Phoenix, Ariz.

3445; Pratt, Barbara; 1930-April-7; Yes; F; Pima; Yes; F; F; F; Yes

3475; Ramon, Eula; 1931-Mar-19; Yes; F; Pima; Yes; F; F; F; Yes

3509; Redbird, Charles; 1931-Jan-11; Yes; M; Maricopa; Yes; F; F; F; No; Laveen, Ariz.

3542; Rhodes, Spencer; 1930-May-31; Yes; No; M; Pima & Cheyenne; Yes; F; F; F; No; Laveen, Ariz.

Unnumbered; Santos, Florence; 1930-Dec-19; Yes; F; Pima; Yes; F; F; F; No; Salt River Res., Ariz.

3705; Schurz, Byron; 1931-Feb-20; Yes; M; Pima; Yes; F; F; F; Yes

3746; Setoyant, Barbara; 1930-Sept-3; Yes; F; Pima; Yes; F; F; F; Yes

3911; Stone, Harold; 1930-Dec-5; Yes; M; Pima; Yes; F; F; F; Yes

3943; Sundust, Leon; 1930-Sept-15; Yes; M; Maricopa; Yes; F; F; F; Yes

3946; Sundust, Leonard Jr.; 1930-April-20[sic]; Yes; M; Maricopa; Yes; F; F; F; Yes

4862; Thomas, Edmund; 1930-April-8; Yes; M; Papago; Yes; F; F; F; Yes

State **Arizona** Reservation **Gila River Indian Reservation** Agency or jurisdiction **Pima Indian Agency**; Office of Indian Affairs

Live-Births Occurring Between the Dates of April 1, 1930 and March 31, 1931 to Parents Enrolled at Jurisdiction

Key: 1931 Census Roll Number; Surname; Given; Date of Birth (Year-Month-Day); Live Birth (Yes/No); Still-birth (Yes/No); Sex; Tribe; Ward (Yes/No); Degree of Blood (Father- Mother- Child); At Jurisdiction Where Enrolled (Yes/No); (If no – Where – Jurisdiction; State; Post Office; State)

Unnumbered; Thomas, Beulah; 1930-Sept-26; Yes; F; Pima; Yes; F; F; F; Yes
4138; Thomas, Francis; 1930-Aug-27; Yes; M; Pima & Papago; Yes; F; F; F; Yes
4906; Vincent, Loraine; 1930-April-8; Yes; F; Papago; Yes; F; F; F; Yes
4280; Wade, Luella; 1930-May-13; Yes; F; Pima & Maricopa; Yes; F; F; F; Yes
Unnumbered; White, Mary; 1930-Nov-13; Yes; F; Pima; Yes; F; F; F; Yes
4396; Whitman, Oriana; 1930-Dec-19; Yes; F; Pima; Yes; F; F; F; Yes
4387; Whitman, Sheron; 1930-July-8; Yes; F; Pima; Yes; F; F; F; Yes
4426; Whittier, Elizabeth; 1931-Mar-26; Yes; F; Pima; Yes; F; F; F; Yes
Unrecorded; Wiston, ---; 1930-Oct-5; Yes; F; Pima; Yes; F; F; F; Yes

275

Live Births
Occurring Between
April 1, 1931 and March 31, 1932
Pima Indian Agency

State **Arizona** Reservation **Gila River Indian Reservation** Agency or jurisdiction **Pima Indian Agency**; Office of Indian Affairs

Live-Births Occurring Between the Dates of April 1, 1931 and March 31, 1932 to Parents Enrolled at Jurisdiction

Key: 1932 Census Roll Number; Surname; Given; Date of Birth (Year-Month-Day); Live Birth (Yes/No); Still-birth (Yes/No); Sex; Tribe; Ward (Yes/No); Degree of Blood (Father- Mother- Child); At Jurisdiction Where Enrolled (Yes/No); (If no – Where – Jurisdiction; State; Post Office; State)

Unnumbered; Ahliel, Marjorie; 1931-June-10; Yes; No; F; Pima; Yes; F; F; F; Yes

98; Allison, Louella May; 1932-Febr; 7; Yes; F; Pima; Yes; F; F; F; Yes

98; Anton, Nelle; 1931-Sept-17; Yes; F; Pima; Yes; F; F; F; Yes

338; Blackwater, Marvin; 1932-Jan-25; Yes; M; Pima; Yes; F; F; F; Yes

415; Brown, Roderick B.; 1931-Oct-10; Yes; M; Maricopa; Yes; F; F; F; Yes

542; Chiago, Stanley, Jr.; 1932-Jan-7; Yes; M; Pima; Yes; F; F; F; Yes

588; Cooper, Margaret Mary; 1931-Nov-26; Yes; F; Pima; Yes; F; F; F; Yes

621; Cumhayia, John; 1931-Nov-23; Yes; M; Maricopa; Yes; F; F; F; Yes

390; Donohue, Clarice Fidella; 1932-Febr; 21; Yes; F; Maricopa; Yes; 1/4x; F; 1/4x; Yes

779; Enos, Lawrence; 1931-Dec-22; Yes; M; Pima; Yes; F; F; F; Yes

968; Evans, John; 1931-Nov-16; Yes; M; Pima; Yes; F; F; F; Yes

1066; Giff, Joseph, Jr.; 1932-Jan-28; Yes; M; Pima; Yes; F; F; F; Yes

1234; Hill, Mary; 1932-Jan-30; Yes; F; Pima; Yes; F; F; F; Yes

1252; Honwasima, Nadine; 1931-Dec-9; Yes; F; Maricopa; Yes; F; F; F; Yes

1303; Howard, Caroline Doris; 1932-Mar-18; Yes; F; Maricopa; Yes; F; F; F; Yes

1340; Jack, Mitchell Harris; 1931-Oct-24; Yes; M; Pima; Yes; F; F; F; Yes

1377; Jackson, Audrey Geraldine; 1931-Aug-2; Yes; F; Pima; Yes; F; F; F; Yes

1399; Jackson, Leonard; 1932-Mar-4; Yes; M; Pima; Yes; F; F; F; Yes

1462; Jackson, Corrine Doris; 1932-Jan-8; Yes; F; Pima; Yes; F; F; F; Yes

1540; Johns, Robert; 1931-Nov-21; Yes; M; Pima; Yes; F; F; F; Yes

1632; Johnson, Marcella; 1931-Dec-5; Yes; F; Pima; Yes; F; F; F; Yes

1377; Jones, Marie; 1932-Jan-10; Yes; F; Pima; Yes; F; F; F; Yes

1863; Kalka, Marjory Dorothy; 1932-Febr; 21; Yes; No; F; Pima; Yes; F; F; F; Yes

1903; Kisto, Sylvester; 1932-Mar-17; Yes; M; Pima; Yes; F; F; F; Yes

1926; Kisto, Helen; 1932-Febr; 2; Yes; F; Pima; Yes; F; F; F; Yes

1970; Lamore, Arthur; 1932-Nov-4; Yes; M; Pima; Yes; F; F; F; Yes

2251; Lose, Mary; 1931-Aug-15; Yes; F; Pima; Yes; F; F; F; Yes

2286; Lyon, Phillus; 1932-Jan-4; Yes; F; Pima; Yes; F; F; F; Yes

2315; Mack, Elizabeth Virginia; 1931-Oct-23; Yes; F; Pima; Yes; F; F; F; Yes

2541; Marietta, Arrat Tom; 1932-Mar-28; Yes; M; Pima; Yes; F; F; F; Yes

2542; Marietta, Cornelio Tony; 1932-Mar-28; Yes; M; Pima; Yes; F; F; F; Yes

2569; Matthews, Jr., Albert; 1931-Oct-13; Yes; M; Pima; Yes; F; F; F; Yes

2582; Matthews, Charles; 1931-Nov-17; Yes; M; Pima; Yes; F; F; F; Yes

2728; Milda, Peggy Annette; 1932-Febr; 19; Yes; F; Pima; Yes; F; F; F; Yes

2763; Miles, Geraldine; 1931-Nov-18; Yes; F; Pima; Yes; F; F; F; Yes

2863; Myers, Estella; 1931-Nov-16; Yes; F; Pima; Yes; F; F; F; Yes

2883; Narsa, Charles; 1931-Dec-5; Yes; M; Pima; Yes; F; F; F; Yes

2921; Nelson, Joyce; 1932-Feb-16; Yes; F; Pima; Yes; F; F; F; Yes

Unnumbered; Norris, Joanna; 1932-Mar-3; Yes; F; Pima; Yes; F; F; F; Yes

3018; Norton, Harold Cecil; 1931-Dec-16; Yes; M; Pima; Yes; F; F; F; Yes

3119; Pablo, Nathaniel; 1931-Sept-21; Yes; M; Pima; Yes; F; F; F; Yes

3178; Paddis, Warner L.; 1932-Mar-3; Yes; M; Pima; Yes; F; F; F; Yes

3281; Pedro, Roselene; 1931-Dec-19; Yes; F; Pima; Yes; F; F; F; Yes

Live-Births Occurring Between the Dates of **April 1, 1931** and **March 31, 1932** to Parents Enrolled at Jurisdiction

Key: 1932 Census Roll Number; Surname; Given; Date of Birth (Year-Month-Day); Live Birth (Yes/No); Still-birth (Yes/No); Sex; Tribe; Ward (Yes/No); Degree of Blood (Father- Mother- Child); At Jurisdiction Where Enrolled (Yes/No); (If no – Where – Jurisdiction; State; Post Office; State)

3342; Peters, Charlotte; 1932-Mar-14; Yes; F; Pima; Yes; F; F; F; Yes

3409; Porter, Glenn Bernard; 1931-Sept-4; Yes; No; M; Pima; Yes; F; F; F; Yes

3434; Porter, Harless Clayton; 1931-Sept-4; Yes; M; Pima; Yes; F; F; F; Yes

3444; Pratt, Lorene; 1931-Dec-18; Yes; F; Pima; Yes; F; F; F; Yes

3503; Reams, David; 1931-Sept-10; Yes; M; Pima; Yes; F; F; F; Yes

3556; Rivera, Verna; 1931-Sept-14; Yes; F; Pima; Yes; F; F; F; No; Tucson, Arizona.

3696; Schurz, Henry; 1931-Sept-9; Yes; M F[sic]; Pima; Yes; F; F; F; Yes

3767; Shosh, Phyllis; 1931-July-21; Yes; F; Pima; Yes; F; F; F; Yes

3805; Smith, Kathleen Dorothy; 1932-Febr; 21; Yes; F; Pima; Yes; F; F; F; No; Salt River Res., Ariz.

3910; Stewart, Hilda; 1931-Dec-27; Yes; F; Maricopa; Yes; F; F; F; Yes

3919; Stone, Edwin Porter; 1932-Febr; 9; Yes; M; Pima; Yes; F; F; F; Yes

3955; Sundust, Lewis Leonard; 1931-July-29; Yes; M; Maricopa; Yes; F; F; F; Yes

4178; Thompson, Flora; 1932-Jan-6; Yes; F; Pima; Yes; F; F; F; Yes

4188; Thompson, Wilda Lovena; 1931-Dec-7; Yes; F; Pima; Yes; F; F; F; Yes

4818; Vavages, Marjorie Janne; 1931-Sept-24; Yes; F; Pima; Yes; F; F; F; Yes

4247; Vavages, Lancisco, Jr.; 1931-Nov-1; Yes; M; Pima; Yes; F; F; F; Yes

4316; Walker, Charles; 1932-Mar-6; Yes; M; Pima; Yes; F; F; F; Yes

4398; Whitman, Dayton; 1932-Mar-13; Yes; M; Pima; Yes; F; F; F; Yes

4429; Whittaker, Omer Bruce; 1931-Nov-8; Yes; M; Pima; Yes; F; F; F; Yes

2365; Williams, Elizabeth Manuel; 1931-Aug-29; Yes; F; Pima; Yes; F; F; F; Yes

4456; Williams, Frieda Louise; 1932-Dec-13; Yes; F; Pima; Yes; F; F; F; Yes

4541; Wiston, Unnamed; 1931-Sept-21; Yes; F; Pima; Yes; F; F; F; Yes

Live Births

Occurring Between

April 1, 1931 and March 31, 1932

Ak Chin Agency

State **Arizona** Reservation **Ak Chin** Agency or jurisdiction **Pima Indian Agency**; Office of Indian Affairs

Live-Births Occurring Between the Dates of **April 1, 1931** and **March 31, 1932** to Parents Enrolled at Jurisdiction

Key: 1932 Census Roll Number; Surname; Given; Date of Birth (Year-Month-Day); Live Birth (Yes/No); Still-birth (Yes/No); Sex; Tribe; Ward (Yes/No); Degree of Blood (Father- Mother- Child); At Jurisdiction Where Enrolled (Yes/No); (If no – Where – Jurisdiction; State; Post Office; State)

4752; Manuel, Elmer Thomas; 1932-Mar-13; Yes; No; M; Papago; Yes; F; F; F; Yes
4778; Miguel, Marie; 1932-Febr-24; Yes; F; Papago; Yes; F; F; F; Yes

Deaths

Occurring Between

July 1, 1924 and June 30, 1925

Pima Indian Agency

State **Arizona** Reservation **Gila River Reservation** Agency or
jurisdiction **Pima Indian Agency**; Office of Indian Affairs
Deaths Occurring Between the Dates of July 1, 1924 and June 30, 1925 to Indians Enrolled at Jurisdiction

Key: Year and Number on Last Census Roll; Surname; Given; Date of Death (Year-Month-Day); Age
at Death; Sex; Tribe; Ward (Yes/No); Degree of Blood); Cause of Death;
At Jurisdiction Where Enrolled (Yes/No); (If no – Where – Jurisdiction; State; Post Office; State)

1925-41; Allis, Francis; 1925-June-22; 5; M; Pima; Yes; Full; Snakebite; Yes
Unrecorded; Antone, Anna; 1925-June-3; 15; F; Papago; Yes; Full; Unknown; Yes
1925-246; Apkaw, Eliza; 1924-July-11; 60; F; Pima; Yes; Full; Acute Indigestion;
Yes
1925-362; Blackwater, Lewis T.; 1925-May-2; 60; M; Pima; Yes; Full; Nephritis
Chronic; Yes
1925-398; Brooks, Edith; 1925-April-24; 88; F; Pima; Yes; Full; Unknown; Yes
1922[sic];---; Cook, Luke H.; 1924-July-13; 5; M; Pima; Yes; Full; Unknown; Yes
1922[sic];---; Cook, Thelma B.; 1925-April-11; 2; F; Pima; Yes; Full; Diarrhea; Yes
1925-586; Coops, Lancisco; 1925-Jan-14; 79; M; Pima; Yes; Full; Burned to Death;
Yes
1925-600; Crouse, Inez; 1924-Aug-14; 95; F; Pima; Yes; Full; Burned to Death; Yes
1925-695; Emerson, Fred; 1925-May-30; 56?; M; Pima; Yes; Full; Chronic Nephritis;
Yes
Unrecorded; Enos, Appolonia; 1925-May-27; 3 mo.; F; Papago; Yes; Full; Unknown;
Yes
Unrecorded; Enos, Elizabeth; 1925-June-18; 24; F; Pima; Yes; Full; Pulmonary TB;
Yes
Unrecorded; Enos, Leslie; 1925-April-25; 9 mo.; M; Pima; Yes; Full; Influenza; Yes
1925-901; Evans, Gertrude; M.; 1924-Dec-4; 2; F; Pima; Yes; Full; Pneumonia; Yes
Unrecorded; Flores, Edna F.; 1925-May-31; 1; F; Papago; Yes; Full; Pneumonia; Yes
Unrecorded; Gage, Henry; 1925-Feb-20; 70; M; Pima; Yes; Full; Unknown; Yes
Unrecorded; Hall, Bernard; 1925-May-2; 2; M; Pima; Yes; Full; Diarrhea Enteritis;
Yes
1925-1174; Hawthorne, Minnie; 1924-July-8; 19; F; Pima; Yes; Full; Tuberculosis;
Yes
1925-1243; Holden, James; 1924-July-26; 74; M; Pima; Yes; Full; General Debility;
Yes
1925-1226; Hugo, Burns Jr.; 1924-Dec-20; --; M; Pima; Yes; Full; Pneumonia; Yes
1925-1294; Jackson, Elmer; 1924-Sept-27; 15 mo.; F[sic]; Pima; Yes; Full; Unknown;
Yes
1925-1408; James, Frederick; 1925-June-21; 7 mo.; F[sic]; Pima; Yes; Full; Enters
Colitis; Yes
1925-1507; James, Joseph F.; 1924-Oct-25; 60; M; Pima; Yes; Full; Injury from fall;
Yes
Unrecorded; James, Veronica J.; 1925-Jan-29; 13 d.; F; Pima; Yes; Full; Unknown;
Yes
1925-1575; Johns, Mary Agnes; 1924-Nov-26; --; F; Pima; Yes; Full; Unknown; Yes
1925-1529; Johnson, Alfred; 1924-Nov-29; 2 mo.; M; Pima; Yes; Full; Unknown;
Yes
1925-1660; Johnson, Chester B.; 1924-Dec-20; 11 mo.; M; Pima; Yes; Full;
Pneumonia; Yes
1925-1676; Johnson, Owen J.; 1924-Nov-15; 3; M; Pima; Yes; Full; Unknown; Yes
1925-1725; Jones, Rebecka; 1924-Nov-3; 14; F; Pima; Yes; Full; Unknown; Yes

State **Arizona** Reservation **Gila River Reservation** Agency or jurisdiction **Pima Indian Agency**; Office of Indian Affairs

Deaths Occurring Between the Dates of July 1, 1924 and June 30, 1925 to Indians Enrolled at Jurisdiction

Key: Year and Number on Last Census Roll; Surname; Given; Date of Death (Year-Month-Day); Age at Death; Sex; Tribe; Ward (Yes/No); Degree of Blood); Cause of Death; At Jurisdiction Where Enrolled (Yes/No); (If no – Where – Jurisdiction; State; Post Office; State)

1925-1827; Joseph, Charles; 1925-March-4; 18; M; Pima; Yes; Full; Unknown; Yes

Unrecorded; Kietta, Benedict C.; 1925-June-11; 11 mo.; M; Pima; Yes; Full; Unknown; Yes

1925-1976; Kipp, Lewis; 1924-Sept-20; 76; M; Pima; Yes; Full; Automobile Accident; Yes

1925-1997; Kisto, Martha; 1924-July-14; 25; F; Pima; Yes; Full; Unknown; Yes

1925-1914; Lewis, Elenor; 1924-Aug-25; 18 mo.; F; Pima; Yes; Full; Unknown; Yes

1925-2519; Manuel, Esther; 1925-April-15; 14; F; Pima; Yes; Full; Pulmonary TB; Yes

1925-2559; Manuel, Jose; 1925-March-16; 51; M; Pima; Yes; Full; Unknown; Yes

1925-2214; Manuel, Leonard; 1924-July-24; 1; M; Pima; Yes; Full; Unknown; Yes

1925-2444; Manuel, Lula; 1925-Feb-1; 42; F; Pima; Yes; Full; Unknown; Yes

Unrecorded; Margarita, ---; 1925-Jan-24; 1; F; Pima; Yes; Full; Unknown; Yes

1924----; Martinez, Myrtle S.; 1924-Dec-18; 3; F; Pima; Yes; Full; Pneumonia; Yes

1925-2630; Mathews, Steven; 1925-April-19; 52; M; Pima; Yes; Full; Unknown; Yes

1925-2880; Morago, Marie; 1925-April-17; 40; F; Pima; Yes; Full; Pulmonary TB; Yes

1923[sic]; ---; Narsa, Electina; 1925-April-25; 45; F; Pima; Yes; Full; Pneumonia; Yes

1925-2584; Nathan, Benjamin; 1925-April-26; 32; M; Pima; Yes; Full; Pulmonary TB; Yes

1925-2971; Nathan, Elmer; 1925-Feb-15; 10; M; Pima; Yes; Full; Unknown; Yes

Unrecorded; Napolee, ---; 1924-Aug-27; 2 days; M; Papago; Yes; Full; Unknown; Yes

1925-3083; Noble, Robert; 1925-Feb-25; 40; M; Pima; Yes; Full; Pulmonary TB; Yes

1925-2723; Nosuch, Ethel; 1925-May-2; 39; F; Pima; Yes; Full; Unknown; Yes

1925-2750; Osife, Juan; 1925-June-30; 75; M; Pima; Yes; Full; TB; Yes

1925-3226; Pablo, Anestacia; 1925-March-14; 65; F; Pima; Yes; Full; TB; Yes

1925-3275; Pablo, Claudina; 1925-May-22; 1; F; Pima; Yes; Full; Influenza; Yes

Unrecorded; Pablo, Edward; 1925-May-19; 4; M; Pima; Yes; Full; Acute Dysentery; Yes

Unrecorded; Pablo, Jose; 1925-March-13; 67; M; Pima; Yes; Full; Pneumonia; Yes

1925-2817; Pablo, Louisa; 1925-June-7; 60; F; Pima; Yes; Full; Liver Trouble; Yes

1925-3224; Pablo, Solomon; 1925-March-24; 23; M; Pima; Yes; Full; Unknown; Yes

1925-2492; Pancho, Elizabeth (Isabelle); 1924-July-5; 18; F; Pima; Yes; Full; Pulmonary TB; Yes

Unrecorded; Pancotte, Katherine I.; 1925-June-15; 3; F; Pima; Yes; Full; Automobile Accident; Yes

Unrecorded; Parker, Matilda; 1925-Feb-2; 12 d.; F; Maricopa; Yes; Full; Unknown; Yes

1925-2519; Pasquell, Emery; 1925-April-26; 2; M; Pima; Yes; Full; Influenza; Yes

1925-3362; Paul, John; 1925-June-24; 54; M; Pima; Yes; Full; Influenza; Yes

Unrecorded; Pedro, Chester; 1925-May-20; 1; M; Pima; Yes; Full; Unknown; Yes

1925-3669; Roberts, Lucy; 1925-May-4; 40; F; Pima; Yes; Full; Tabes Mesenteric; Yes

Deaths Occurring Between the Dates of July 1, 1924 and June 30, 1925 to Indians Enrolled at Jurisdiction

Key: Year and Number on Last Census Roll; Surname; Given; Date of Death (Year-Month-Day); Age
at Death; Sex; Tribe; Ward (Yes/No); Degree of Blood); Cause of Death;
At Jurisdiction Where Enrolled (Yes/No); (If no – Where – Jurisdiction; State; Post Office; State)

1925-3788; Schurz, Mark Jr.; 1924-Dec-6; 1; M; Pima; Yes; Full; Unknown; Yes

1925-3789; Scoffer, Rose; 1925-April-6; 60; F; Pima; Yes; Full; Pulmonary TB; Yes

1925-2996; Seye, Bobby; 1924-Dec-12; 2 mo.; M; Pima; Yes; Full; Pneumonia; Yes

Unrecorded; Stanley, Carolina Mae; 1925-June-13; 2; F; Pima; Yes; Full; Accident; Yes

1925-3116; Stein, Louis; 1925-May-2; 77; M; Pima; Yes; Full; Old Age; Yes

1925-3927; Snyder, Arthur; 1924-Oct-8; 13; M; Pima; Yes; Full; Unknown; Yes

1925-3277; Thomas, Clement; 1925-Jan-10; 7 mo.; M; Pima; Yes; Full; Unknown; Yes

Unrecorded; Thomas, Daniel; 1925-June-2; 4 mo.; M; Papago; Yes; Full; Unknown; Yes

1925-3364; Thompson, Frank Louis; 1925-June-29; 29; M; Pima; Yes; Full; Pulmonary TB; Yes

Unrecorded; Thompson, Mabel; 1925-Jan-19; 18 d.; M; Papago; Yes; Full; Unknown; Yes

Deaths

Occurring Between

July 1, 1925 and June 30, 1926

Pima Indian Agency

State **Arizona** Reservation **Gila River Reservation** Agency or
jurisdiction **Pima Indian Agency**; Office of Indian Affairs
Deaths Occurring Between the Dates of July 1, 1925 and June 30, 1926 to Indians Enrolled at Jurisdiction

Key: Year and Number on Last Census Roll; Surname; Given; Date of Death (Year-Month-Day); Age
at Death; Sex; Tribe; Ward (Yes/No); Degree of Blood); Cause of Death;
At Jurisdiction Where Enrolled (Yes/No); (If no – Where – Jurisdiction; State; Post Office; State)

1926-147; Antone, Barbara; 1926-May-26; 16; F; Pima; Yes; Full; TB; Yes
1926----; Antone, Candleria; 1925-Oct-30; 65; F; Pima; Yes; Full; Pulmonary TB;
Yes
1926-123; Anton, Ernest; 1926-April-5; 1; M; Pima; Yes; Full; Broncho Pneumonia;
Yes
1926-181; Anton, Miguel; 1926-June-26; 59; M; Pima; Yes; Full; Chronic Nephritis;
Yes
Unrecorded; Antone, Irene; 1925-Oct-29; 3 mo.; F; Pima; Yes; Full; Unknown; Yes
1926-122; Antone, Louis; 1926-April-10; 1; M; Pima; Yes; Full; Broncho Pneumonia;
Yes
Unrecorded; Chiago, Joseph; 1926-Mar-7; 3 40; M; Pima; Yes; Full; Heart Disease;
No; Salt River Res., Ariz.
Unnumbered; Cook, Victoria; 1926-June-1; 8 mo.; F; Pima; Yes; Full; Entrocolitis;
Yes
1926-544; Crawford, Edgar; 1926-Feb-27; 3; M; Pima; Yes; Full; Pulmonary TB; Yes
1926-544[sic]; Cruz, Titus; 1925-Aug-3; 60; M; Pima; Yes; Full; Pulmonary TB; Yes
1926-635; Delow, Perry; 1926-May-15; 6; M; Pima; Yes; Full; Diarrhea; Yes
1926-621; Dodge, Louis; 1926-April-27;38; M; Pima; Yes; Full; Pulmonary TB; Yes
Unrecorded; Ellison, Marie; 1926-May-23; 45; F; Maricopa; Yes; Full; TB; Yes
Unrecorded; Ennis, Chester; 1925-Sept-16; 8; M; Maricopa; Yes; Full; Spinal
Meningitis; Yes
1926-708; Enos, Albert; 1925-July-25; 20; M; Pima; Yes; Full; Nephritis Chronic;
Yes
1926-723; Enos, John; 1925-Aug-7; 38; M; Pima; Yes; Full; Chronic Appendicitis;
Yes
1926-703; Enos, Joshua; 1925-July-2; 18; M; Pima; Yes; Full; Pulmonary TB; Yes
1926-1017; Hall, Burgess; 1925-May-20; 11 mo.; M; Pima; Yes; Full; Influenza; Yes
1926-1022; Ha-Moo-Ki, Gertrude; 1926-Feb-20; 100; F; Pima; Yes; Full; Influenza;
Yes
Unrecorded; Havier, Steven; 1925-April-15; 2; M; Pima; Yes; Full; Broncho
Pneumonia; Yes
1926-1344; Jackson, Alexander; 1925-Dec-5; 25; M; Pima; Yes; Full; Pulmonary TB;
Yes
Unnumbered; Jackson, Grace; 1926-Mar-3; 7 mo.; F; Pima; Yes; Full; Influenza; Yes
1926-1350; Jackson, Jones; 1926-Mar-25; 30; M; Pima; Yes; Full; Pneumonia Lobar;
Yes
Unnumbered; Jackson, Lawrence; 1926-Feb-17; 2; M; Pima; Yes; Full; Influenza; Yes
Unrecorded; James, Habelina; 1925-Sept-28; 20; F; Pima; Yes; Full; Typhoid; Yes
1926-1368; James, Hazel; 1925-July-8; 4; F; Pima; Yes; Full; Broncho Pneumonia;
Yes
1926-1364; James, Juan; 1926-Feb-7; 37; M; Pima; Yes; Full; Pulmonary TB; Yes
1926-1542; Johnson, Jennie; 1926-April-16; 67; F; Pima; Yes; Full; Nephritis; Yes
1926-1571; Jones, Cantia; 1926-May-25; 40; F; Pima; Yes; Full; Pulmonary TB; Yes
1926-1586; Jones, Cyrus; 1925-Aug-20; 60; M; Pima; Yes; Full; Found Dead; Yes

State **Arizona** Reservation **Gila River Reservation** Agency or
jurisdiction **Pima Indian Agency**; Office of Indian Affairs
<u>Deaths Occurring Between the Dates of July 1, 1925 and June 30, 1926 to Indians Enrolled at Jurisdiction</u>

Key: Year and Number on Last Census Roll; Surname; Given; Date of Death (Year-Month-Day); Age
at Death; Sex; Tribe; Ward (Yes/No); Degree of Blood); Cause of Death;
At Jurisdiction Where Enrolled (Yes/No); (If no – Where – Jurisdiction; State; Post Office; State)

1926-1592; Jones, Paul; 1926-May-23; 81; M; Pima; Yes; Full; Pulmonary TB; Yes
Unnumbered; Jones, Pete Jr.; 1926-April-30; 9 mos.; M; Pima; Yes; Full; Colitis; Yes
Unnumbered; Jones, Ruth Mary; 1926-April-9; 5; F; Pima; Yes; Full; Influenza; Yes
Unrecorded; Jose, Juan; 1925-July-1; 50; M; Pima; Yes; Full; Unknown; Yes
Unrecorded; Jose, Mary; 1926-Feb-25; 70; F; Pima; Yes; Full; Senility; Yes
1926-1617; Jose, Mary; 1926-Mar-30; 51; F; Papago; Yes; Full; Cancer of breast; Yes
Unrecorded; Juan, Henry; 1925-Nov-29; 14; M; Papago; Yes; Full; Pulmonary TB; Yes
1926-1702; Juan, Josia; 1926-Jan-15; 45; F; Pima; Yes; Full; Lobar Pneumonia; Yes
1926-1824; Kisto, Cepriano; 1926-April-14; 30; M; Pima; Yes; Full; Crushed Accident; Yes
1926-1837; Kisto, Dora; 1926-Mar-14; 51; F; Pima; Yes; Full; Pulmonary TB; Yes
1926-1872; Knox, Lewis; 1925-Sept-24; 68; M; Pima; Yes; Full; TB; Yes
1926-1927; Lewis, Dorothy; 1926-May-2; 6; F; Pima; Yes; Full; Automobile Accident; Yes
1926-1924; Lewis, Wilma; 1926-Jan-5; 2; F; Pima; Yes; Full; Measles; Yes
1926-2459; Matthews, Elinore; 1926-Jan-23; 1; F; Pima; Yes; Full; Measles; Yes
1926-2461; Matthews, Irene; 1926-Mar-30; 9; F; Pima; Yes; Full; Pulmonary TB; Yes
1926-2523; Mendoza, Emporia; 1926-June-19; 41; F; Pima; Yes; Full; A—tic Insufficiency; Yes
1926-2509; Miguel, Elizabeth; 1925-Oct-14; 1; F; Pima; Yes; Full; Entero Colitis; Yes
1926-4463; Miguel, Susie; 1926-Mar-20; 7 mo; F; Papago; Yes; Full; Influenza; Yes
Unrecorded; Narcisco, ---; 1926-May-22; 80; M; Papago; Yes; Full; Unknown; Yes
1926-2859; Nolan, Ada; 1926-Mar-24; 16; F; Pima; Yes; Full; Pulmonary TB; Yes
1926-2858; Nolan, Sianna; 1926-Jan-27; 66; F; Pima; Yes; Full; Influenza; Yes
Unrecorded; Norris, Mary A.; 1925-Oct-19; 2 mo; F; Pima; Yes; Full; Unknown; Yes
1926-2738; Osife, Calme; 1925-Aug-28; 73; F; Pima; Yes; Full; Unknown; Yes
1926-2961; Osif, Josepha; 1926-June-21; 61; F; Pima; Yes; Full; Pulmonary TB; Yes
1926-2979; Osife, Seba; 1926-Mar-3; 60; F; Pima; Yes; Full; Influenza; Yes
1926-3053; Pablo, Juan; 1925-Nov-27; 60; M; Pima; Yes; Full; Vertral Regurgitation; Yes
1926-3003; Pablo, Mariana; 1925-Nov-30; 32; F; Pima; Yes; Full; Carcinoma; Yes
1926-2985; Pablo, Patrick; 1926-May-25; 3; M; Pima; Yes; Full; EntroColitis; Yes
Unrecorded; Panelo's, ---; 1926-May-6; 100; F; Papago; Yes; Full; Senility; Yes
1926-3346; Patrick, Paul; 1925-July-1; 7; M; Pima; Yes; Full; Chronic Nephritis; Yes
Unnumbered; Pedro, Enos; 1925-July-19; 5 days; M; Pima; Yes; Full; Enteritis; Yes
1926-3183; Pesos, Betty; 1926-May-19; 60; F; Pima; Yes; Full; Cancer of breast; Yes
1926-3233; Phillips, Willie; 1926-Feb-18; 30; M; Pima; Yes; Full; Pulmonary TB; Yes
Unrecorded; Porter, Harold Lee; 1925-Dec-1; 4 d.; M; Pima; Yes; Full; Heart Disease; No; Phoenix; Ariz.
1925-2701; Preston, Malenda; 1925-Nov-11; 5; F; Pima; Yes; Full; Acute Urenia[sic]; Yes

Deaths Occurring Between the Dates of July 1, 1925 and June 30, 1926 to Indians Enrolled at Jurisdiction

**Key: Year and Number on Last Census Roll; Surname; Given; Date of Death (Year-Month-Day); Age
at Death; Sex; Tribe; Ward (Yes/No); Degree of Blood); Cause of Death;
At Jurisdiction Where Enrolled (Yes/No); (If no – Where – Jurisdiction; State; Post Office; State)**

Unnumbered; Ramon, Simon R.; 1926-May-14; 10 mo; M; Pima; Yes; Full; Colitis;
Yes

1926-3433; Roberts, Laura; 1926-May-23; 65; F; Pima; Yes; Full; Lober Pnermonia;
Yes

Unrecorded; Sagar, Juan; 1926-Mar-1; 70; M; Pima; Yes; Full; Influenza; Yes

1926-3578; Seto, James; 1926-April-16; 61; M; Pima; Yes; Full; Influenza; Yes

Unnumbered; Terry, Jones; 1925-Aug-25; 7 mo; M; Pima; Yes; Full; Broncho
Pneumonia; Yes

Unrecorded; Thomas, Blases; 1925-July-12; 1 mo; M; Papago; Yes; Full; Unknown;
Yes

1926-3886; Thomas, Elizabeth; 1926-Jan-17; 17; F; Pima; Yes; Full; Pulmonary TB;
Yes

1926-3835; Thomas, Lupa; 1925-July-16; 23; F; Papago; Yes; Full; Pulmonary TB;
Yes

1926-3900; Thomas, Pheobie; 1925-Sept-13; 12; F; Pima; Yes; Full; TB; Yes

1926-3935; Thompson, Isabelle; 1926-April-5; 37; F; Pima; Yes; Full; Chronic
Nephritis; Yes

1926-3391; Valenzuela, Sarah; 1926-Feb-24; 68; F; Pima; Yes; Full; Influenza; Yes

Unnumbered; Vavages, James; 1925-July-10; 1; M; Pima; Yes; Full; Entero Colitis;
Yes

Unnumbered; Vavages, Stephen; 1926-Jan-11; 4; M; Pima; Yes; Full; Measles; Yes

1926-4110; Wesley, Edward; 1926-May-30; 64; M; Pima; Yes; Full; Chronic
Nephritis; Yes

Unnumbered; Wilson, Mary; 1926-May-6; 1 mo; F; Pima; Yes; Full; Mal Nutrition;
Yes

Deaths

Occurring Between

July 1, 1926 and June 30, 1927

Pima Indian Agency

State **Arizona** Reservation **Gila River Reservation** Agency or
jurisdiction **Pima Indian Agency**; Office of Indian Affairs
<u>Deaths Occurring Between the Dates of July 1, 1926 and June 30, 1927 to Indians Enrolled at Jurisdiction</u>
Key: Year and Number on Last Census Roll; Surname; Given; Date of Death (Year-Month-Day); Age
at Death; Sex; Tribe; Ward (Yes/No); Degree of Blood); Cause of Death;
At Jurisdiction Where Enrolled (Yes/No); (If no – Where – Jurisdiction; State; Post Office; State)

Unrecorded; Albert, Joseph; 1926-Nov-18; 65; M; Pima; Yes; Full; Pulmonary TB;
Yes
1927-90; Andreas, Juan; 1926-Aug-16; 60; M; Pima; Yes; Full; Drowned; Yes
1927-183; Anton, Ralphi M.; 1927-Mar-15; 17; M; Pima; Yes; Full; Pulmonary TB;
Yes
1927-105; Antone, Manilla; 1927-June-27; 15; F; Pima; Yes; Full; Pulmonary TB;
Yes
Unrecorded; Antone, Mary; 1927-Jan-19; 3 d; F; Pima; Yes; Full; Unknown; Yes
Unrecorded; Carlisle, Melvin; 1927-Jan-15; 1; M; Papago & Pima; Yes; Full; Broncho
Pneumonia; No; Salt River Res., Ariz.
1927-471; Case, Charles; 1927-May-26; 82; M; Pima; Yes; Full; Lobar Pneumonia;
Yes
1927-503; Cheewat, Juan; 1927-Jan-27; 63; M; Pima; Yes; Full; Unknown; Yes
1927-499; Chiago, Juan; 1927-May-13; 46; M; Pima; Yes; Full; Unknown; Yes
1927-640; Dixon, Josepha; 1926-Sept-27; 61; F; Pima; Yes; Full; Brights Disease;
Yes
Unrecorded; Domingo, Clara; 1926-Oct-5; 16; F; Papago; Yes; Full; Typhoid; Yes
1927-655; Domingo, Germain; 1926-Nov-24; 2; M; Pima; Yes; Full; Unknown; Yes
Unrecorded; Domingo, Juanna; 1927-Feb-6; 65; F; Papago; Yes; Full; Unknown; Yes
1927-658; Ellis, Ella; 1926-Dec-8; 40; F; Pima; Yes; Full; Endocarditis; Yes
1927-874; Enas, Joanna; 1927-Mar-24; 18; F; Maricopa; Yes; Full; Phthisis; Yes
1927-805; Ennis, Juanna; 1926-Dec-22; 81; F; Mexican & Pima; Yes; 1/2-1/2;
Unknown; Yes
Unrecorded; Enos, ---; 1926-Sept-12; 55; M; Pima; Yes; Full; Pulmonary TB; Yes
Unrecorded; Enos, Alfronica; 1926-July-2; 1 mo; F; Papago; Yes; Full; Enter Colitis;
Yes
Unrecorded; Enos, Havier; 1927-May-28; 69; M; Pima; Yes; Full; Unknown; Yes
Unnumbered; Enos, Ina; 1927-June-22; 14 mo; F; Papago; Yes; Full; Enter Colitis;
Yes
Unrecorded; Enos, Jose; 1927-March-1; 47; M; Papago; Yes; Full; Ptomaine
Poisoning; Yes
1927-984; Enos, Leo; 1927-May-11; 1; M; Pima; Yes; Full; Colitis; No; Laveen, Ariz.
1927-853; Enos, Pearl; 1927-April-23; 21 mo; F; Pima; Yes; Full; Colitis; Yes
1927-738; Enos, Ruth; 1926-July-13; 3; F; Pima; Yes; Full; Broncho Pneumonia; Yes
Unrecorded; French, Anna; 1926-July-10; 90; F; Pima; Yes; Full; Senility; Yes
Unrecorded; Gemes, Lewis; 1927-Jan-27; 60; M; Pima; Yes; Full; Unknown; Yes
1927-1092; Havelina, Lily; 1927-Feb-26; 16; F; Pima; Yes; Full; Influenza; Yes
Unrecorded; Hice, Lily; 1926-July-6; 80; F; Pima; Yes; Full; Influenza; Yes
1927-1221; Howard, Samuel; 1926-Dec-15; 65; M; Pima; Yes; Full; Acute Nephritis;
Yes
1927-1341; Jackson, Calma Iva; 1926-July-27; 10; F; Pima; Yes; Full; Scorpion Sting;
Yes
1927-2699; Jackson, Hazel May; 1927-March-6; 5; F; Pima; Yes; Full; Tubercular
Meningitis; No; Phoenix, Ariz.

State **Arizona** Reservation **Gila River Reservation** Agency or
jurisdiction **Pima Indian Agency**; Office of Indian Affairs
Deaths Occurring Between the Dates of July 1, 1926 and June 30, 1927 to Indians Enrolled at Jurisdiction

Key: Year and Number on Last Census Roll; Surname; Given; Date of Death (Year-Month-Day); Age
at Death; Sex; Tribe; Ward (Yes/No); Degree of Blood); Cause of Death;
At Jurisdiction Where Enrolled (Yes/No); (If no – Where – Jurisdiction; State; Post Office; State)

1927-2016; Jackson, Lewis (Lenox; 1927-June-27; 17; M; Pima; Yes; Full;
Pulmonary TB; Yes
1927-1499; Johnson, Josephine; 1927-Jan-30; 52; F; Pima; Yes; Full; Unknown; Yes
1927-1542; Johnson, Louise; 1927-May-19; 66; F; Pima; Yes; Full; Pulmonary TB;
Yes
1927-1607; Jones, Sam; 1926-Dec-1; 39; M; Pima; Yes; Full; Pulmonary TB; Yes
1927-1708; Juan, Mary; 1927-Jan-30; 72; F; Pima; Yes; Full; Unknown; Yes
1927-1783; Kalka, Josephine; 1927-June-8; 2; F; Pima; Yes; Full; Tubercular
Meningitis; Yes
1927-1858; Kisto, Kisto; 1927-Jan-15; 76; M; Pima; Yes; Full; Unknown; Yes
1927-Unnumbered; Knox, Christiana; 1927-Jan-14; 4 d; F; Pima & Papago; Yes; 1/2-
1/2; Unknown; Yes
1926-2031; Lewis, Alice; 1926-Nov-2; 21; F; Pima; Yes; Full; Pulmonary TB; Yes
1926-2120; Lights, Sava; 1926-Aug-1; 39; F; Pima; Yes; Abscess of Liver; Yes
1927-Unnumbered; Lyons, Joseph; 1927-May-20; 2 hrs; M; Pima; Yes; Full;
Unknown; Yes
1927-2347; Manuel, Nathan; 1927-Jan-9; 1; M; Pima; Yes; Full; Unknown; Yes
1927-2633; Mix, Mina; 1927-Mar-25; 47; F; Pima; Yes; Full; Unknown; Yes
1927-2787; Nelson, Florence; 1927-June-5; 13; F; Pima; Yes; Full; Pulmonary TB;
Yes
Unnumbered; Nelson, Mary; 1927-May-9; 2 mo; F; Cherokee & Pueblo; Yes; 1/2-1/2;
Cholera Infantum; Yes
Unnumbered; Newman, Leola; 1927-May-3; 9 mo; F; Pima; Yes; Full; Unknown; Yes
Unrecorded; Osif, Isabelle; 1926-Dec-15; 70; F; Pima; Yes; Full; Senility; Yes
Unrecorded; Oxpe, Lillian; 1927-April-22; 1 mo; F; Pima; Yes; Full; Unknown; Yes
Unrecorded; Pablo, Cipriano; 1926-July-18; 25; M; Papago; Yes; Full; Pulmonary
TB; Yes
Unrecorded; Pablo, Juan; 1927-May-23; 65; M; Pima; Yes; Full; Pneumonia; Yes
1927-2984; Pablo, Mary; 1927-June-15; 14; F; Pima; Yes; Full; Nephritis; Yes
Unrecorded; Pablo, Peter; 1927-March-13; 20; M; Pima; Yes; Full; Acute
Alcoholism; Yes
1927-3061; Pasquel, Slayton; 1927-June-7; 2; M; Pima; Yes; Full; EnteroColitis; Yes
Unnumbered; Peters, Theodore; 1927-Jan-11; 2 mo; M; Pima; Yes; Full; Colitis; Yes
Unnumbered; Philips, Joseph Jr.; 1926-Sept-3; 3days; M; Pima; Yes; Full; Premature
Birth; Yes
Unnumbered; Porter, Jerome.; 1927-June-22; 1; M; Pima; Yes; Full; Broken Neck;
Yes
1927-5270; Quaroh, Cheerless; 1927-April-21; 37; F; Pima; Yes; Full; Pulmonary TB;
Yes
Unrecorded; Rogers, Eunice; 1926-Aug-18; 85; F; Pima; Yes; Full; Old Age; Yes
1927-3462; Schurz, Maggie; 1927-April-22; 75; F; Pima; Yes; Full; Pneumonia; Yes
1927-1526; Tejano, Everett; 1926-Dec-15; 7 mo; M; Papago; Yes; Full; Colitis; Yes
Unnumbered; Terry, Felix.; 1927-May-13; 9 mo; M; Pima; Yes; Full; Unknown; Yes
1927-3759; Terry, Lucile; 1927-Jan-13; 16; F; Pima; Yes; Full; Tuberculosis; Yes

State **Arizona** Reservation **Gila River Reservation** Agency or jurisdiction **Pima Indian Agency**; Office of Indian Affairs

Deaths Occurring Between the Dates of July 1, 1926 and June 30, 1927 to Indians Enrolled at Jurisdiction

Key: Year and Number on Last Census Roll; Surname; Given; Date of Death (Year-Month-Day); Age at Death; Sex; Tribe; Ward (Yes/No); Degree of Blood); Cause of Death; At Jurisdiction Where Enrolled (Yes/No); (If no – Where – Jurisdiction; State; Post Office; State)

1927-3834; Thomas, Cyrus; 1927-June-15; 39; M; Pima; Yes; Full; Pulmonary TB; Yes

1927-3842; Thomas, Cyrus M.; 1927-May-16; 1; M; Pima; Yes; Full; Pulmonary TB; Yes

1927-3850; Thomas, Jane M.; 1927-Feb-18; 1; F; Pima; Yes; Full; Broncho Pneumonia; Yes

Unrecorded; Thomas, Michael; 1926-July-2; 21; M; Papago; Yes; Full; Unknown; Yes

Unrecorded; Thompson, Jennie; 1926-Nov-28; 70; F; Pima; Yes; Full; Unknown; Yes

Unrecorded; Valenzuela, Charles; 1927-Jan-19; 15; M; Papago; Yes; Full; Pulmonary TB; Yes

1927-3979; Vavages, Juan; 1926-July-31; 45; M; Pima; Yes; Full; Pulmonary TB; Yes

1927-3992; Vincent, Mise; 1927-March-17; 92; M; Mexican & Pima; Yes; 1/2; Unknown; Yes

Unrecorded; Voltares, Fernando; 1927-June-25; 5; M; Papago; Yes; Full; Pneumonia; Yes

1927-3997; Wade, Eva; 1927-April-23; 18; F; Pima; Yes; Full; Unknown; Yes

1927-4031; Warren, Willard; 1926-Sept-9; 16; M; Pima; Yes; Full; Pulmonary TB; Yes

1927-4074; White, Lillian; 1927-Feb-26; 8; F; Papago; Yes; Full; Broncho Pneumonia; Yes

1927-4070; White, Sarah; 1927-June-22; 65; F; Pima; Yes; Full; Chronic Nephritis; Yes

1927-4143; Whittier, Emma; 1926-Sept-25; 60; F; Pima; Yes; Full; Cirrhosis of Liver; Yes

Deaths

Occurring Between

July 1, 1927 and June 30, 1928

Pima Indian Agency

State **Arizona** Reservation **Gila River Reservation** Agency or
jurisdiction **Pima Indian Agency**; Office of Indian Affairs
<u>Deaths Occurring Between the Dates of July 1, 1927 and June 30, 1928 to Indians Enrolled at Jurisdiction</u>

Key: Year and Number on Last Census Roll; Surname; Given; Date of Death (Year-Month-Day); Age
at Death; Sex; Tribe; Ward (Yes/No); Degree of Blood); Cause of Death;
At Jurisdiction Where Enrolled (Yes/No); (If no – Where – Jurisdiction; State; Post Office; State)

1928-80; Allison, Sarah; 1927-July-14; 62; F; Pima; Yes; Full; Chronic Nephritis; Yes
1928-121; Anton, Jose M.; 1928-June-11; 2; M; Pima; Yes; Full; Measles; Yes
Unnumbered; Blackwater, Domingo; 1927-Nov; --; M; Pima; Yes; Full; Unknown;
Yes
1928-386; Brown, Benjamin; 1928-April-28; 70; M; Pima; Yes; Full; Old Age; Yes
1928-520; Colt, Josiah; 1927-Sept-512; 17; M; Pima; Yes; Full; Pulmonary TB; Yes
1928-554; Coops, Lila W.; 1927-Nov-10; 23; F; Pima; Yes; Full; Cancer of Stomach;
Yes
Salt River; 1928-193; Emerson, Hoffman; 1928-Feb-3; 24; M; Papago; Yes; Full;
Ulcers; Yes
Unnumbered; 1928-Enas, Helen Jr.; 1927-Aug-4; 7 d; F; Pima; Yes; Full; Unknown;
Yes
1928-749; Enis, Emily P.; 1927-Sept-522; 30; F; Pima; Yes; Full; Umbilical Hernia;
Yes
1928-793; Enos, Harry; 1927-Aug-13; 54; M; Pima; Yes; Full; TB of Throat; No;
Laveen, Ariz.
Unnumbered; Gazula, Wallace; 1928-April-23; 2 mo; F; Pima; Yes; Full; Colitis; Yes
1928-1221; Howard, Perrett; 1928-May-30; 35; M; Pima; Yes; Full; Burns; Yes
1928-1240; Hugo, Burn Jr.; 1927-Sept-520; 5 mo; M; Pima & Walapai; Yes; Full;
Colitis; Yes
1928-1241; Innis, Catherine; 1928-June-12; 44; F; Pima; Yes; Full; Sepais-
Childbirth; No; Laveen, Ariz.
1928-1362; Jackson, Victor; 1927-Dec-29; 72; M; Pima; Yes; Full; Pulmonary TB;
Yes
1928-1420; Joaquin, Bah-i; 1927-Sept-514; 65; M; Pima; Yes; Full; Nephritis; Yes
1928-1489; Johnson, Clara; 1928-June-23; 1; F; Maricopa; Yes; Full; Injury---Head;
Yes
1928-1535; Johnson, Sarah; 1928-Jan-20; 82; F; Pima; Yes; Full; Chronic Nephritis;
Yes
1928-1675; Juan, Margarett; 1927-July-17; 13; F; Pima; Yes; Full; Acute Nephritis;
Yes
1928-1731; Juan, Sibley; 1928-Jan-25; 40; F; Pima; Yes; Full; Automobile Accident;
Yes
1928-4387; Kisto, Simon; 1928-Feb-13; 9 mo; M; Papago; Yes; Full; Pulmonary TB;
Yes
1928-2029; Lewis, Manuela P.; 1927-Oct-10; 60; F; Pima; Yes; Full; Pulmonary TB;
Yes
1928-1913; Lewis, Michael J.; 1927-Sept-510; 3; M; Pima; Yes; Full; Unknown; Yes
1928-2124; Liston, Luther; 1927-Oct-25; 13; M; Pima; Yes; Full; Typhoid; Yes
1928-4416; Loos, Juan; 1927-Nov-22; 75; M; Papago; Yes; Full; Unknown; Yes
1928-2152; Lopez, Aloysius; 1927-Dec-5; 1; M; Pima; Yes; Full; Unknown; Yes
1928-2146; Lopez, Pancho; 1927-Oct-16; 45; M; Pima; Yes; Full; Nephritis Chronic;
Yes

State **Arizona** Reservation **Gila River Reservation** Agency or
jurisdiction **Pima Indian Agency**; Office of Indian Affairs
Deaths Occurring Between the Dates of July 1, 1927 and June 30, 1928 to Indians Enrolled at Jurisdiction

Key: Year and Number on Last Census Roll; Surname; Given; Date of Death (Year-Month-Day); Age
at Death; Sex; Tribe; Ward (Yes/No); Degree of Blood); Cause of Death;
At Jurisdiction Where Enrolled (Yes/No); (If no – Where – Jurisdiction; State; Post Office; State)

Unnumbered; Manuel, Barbara; 1927-Dec-28; 2 mo; F; Papago; Yes; Full; Pulmonary
TB; Yes

1928-2312; Manuel, Jose Jr.; 1927-Oct-6; 6 mo; M; Pima; Yes; Full; Colitis; Yes

1928-4445; Manuel, Veronica; 1927-Dec-29; 19; F; Papago; Yes; Full; Pulmonary
TB; Yes

Salt River; 1928-191; Morris, Joshua; 1927-Oct-16; 37; M; Pima; Yes; Full;
Pulmonary TB; Yes

1928-2819; Nish, Leonard; 1927-Nov-22; 1; M; Pima; Yes; Full; Colitis; Yes

1928-2881; Osif, John; 1927-Oct-4; 30; M; Pima; Yes; Full; Typhoid Fever; Yes

1928-2916; Osife, Lena; 1927-July-19; 26; F; Pima; Yes; Full; Pneumonia Lobar; Yes

1928-3040; Pancot, Frederick; 1927-Nov-22; 2; M; Pima; Yes; Full; Colitis; Yes

Unnumbered; Parsons, Floyd; 1928-June-13; 3; M; Pima; Yes; Full; Pneumonia
Bronchial; Yes

1928-3084; Paul, Mary; 1927-July-1; 82; F; Pima; Yes; Full; Senility; Yes

1928-4522; Ramon, Eugene; 1928-Jan-2; 28; M; Papago; Yes; Full; Pulmonary TB;
Yes

1928-3341; Richards, Antonio; 1928-Jan-26; 67; M; Pima; Yes; Full; Unknown; Yes

1928-3359; Robert, Elizabeth; 1928-April-21; 35; F; Pima; Yes; Full; Lobar
Pneumonia; No; Phoenix, Ariz.

1928-3540; Smart, Carl; 1928-Jan-31; 50; M; Pima; Yes; Full; Pulmonary TB; Yes

1928-3594; Snyder, Jose; 1927-Aug-22; 60; M; Pima; Yes; Full; Wound Infection;
Yes

Unnumbered; Terry, Mary; 1927-Oct-23; 2 mo; F; Pima; Yes; Full; Accident; Yes

1928-4029; Walker, Sebi; 1928-June-6; 37; F; Pima; Yes; Full; Septicimia; No; Salt
River Res., Ariz

1928-4039; Warren, Winona; 1927-Oct-13; 7 mo; F; Pima; Yes; Full; Pulmonary TB;
Yes

1928-4095; White, Thomas; 1927-Dec-27; 72; M; Pima; Yes; Full; Unknown; Yes

1928-4115; Whitman, Maggie; 1927-Nov-6; 20; F; Pima; Yes; Full; Pneumonia
Lobar; Yes

Deaths

Occurring Between

July 1, 1928 and June 30, 1929

Pima Indian Agency

State **Arizona** Reservation **Gila River Reservation** Agency or jurisdiction **Pima Indian Agency**; Office of Indian Affairs

<u>Deaths Occurring Between the Dates of July 1, 1928 and June 30, 1929 to Indians Enrolled at Jurisdiction</u>

Key: Year and Number on Last Census Roll; Surname; Given; Date of Death (Year-Month-Day); Age at Death; Sex; Tribe; Ward (Yes/No); Degree of Blood); Cause of Death; At Jurisdiction Where Enrolled (Yes/No); (If no – Where – Jurisdiction; State; Post Office; State)

1929-73; Allison, Herbert; 1928-Sept-15; 3 d; M; Pima; Yes; Full; Bronchial Pneumonia; Yes

1929-90; Ambrose, Juan; 1928-Dec-6; 77; M; Pima; Yes; Full; Pulmonary TB; Yes

1929-96; Andrew, Isaac; 1928-Oct-20; 25; M; Pima; Yes; Full; Struck by Lightning; Yes

1928-97; Andrew, Lucy; 1928-Nov-2; 38; F; Pima; Yes; Full; Unknown; Yes

1928-219; Anton, Manuella; 1928-April-3; 53; F; Pima; Yes; Full; Tuberculosis; Yes

1929-30; Anton, Visande; 1929-March-10; 15; F; Papago; Yes; Full; Pulmonary TB; Yes

1929-275; Azule, Harry; 1928-Dec-9; 57; M; Pima; Yes; Full; Automobile Accident; Yes

1929-319; Benson, Myda; 1928-Aug-20; 14; F; Pima; Yes; Full; Typhoid Fever; Yes

1929-327; Blackwater; May; 1929-Mar-28; 40; F; Pima; Yes; Full; Parturition; Yes

1929-354; Boss, Santa; 1928-Oct-1; 43; F; Pima; Yes; Full; Tuberculosis; Yes

1929-442; Cannon, Kisto; 1929-March-7; 57; M; Pima; Yes; Full; Nephritis; Yes

1929-503; Chopin, John; 1928-Oct-17; 33; M; Pima; Yes; Full; Automobile Accident; Yes

Unnumbered; Cook, Luke Jr.; 1929-Feb-2; 1 d; M; Pima & Choctaw; Yes; 1/2-1/2; Congenital Weakness; No; Phoenix, Ariz.

1929-603; Davis, Mary; 1929-May-7; 84; F; Papago; Yes; Full; Stomach Trouble; Yes

Unnumbered; Eldridge, Lawrence; 1929-April-23; 2; M; Pima; Yes; Full; Acute Colitis; Yes

Unnumbered; Enas, Lester; 1928-Oct-16; 8 mo; M; Pima & Mojave; Yes; 1/2-1/2; Cardiac Paralysis; Yes

1929-746; Enis, John B.; 1928-Aug-20; 45; M; Pima; Yes; Full; Septicemia; Yes

Unrecorded; Enos, John; 1929-Apr-20; 1; M; Pima; Yes; Full; Pneumonia; Yes

1929-853; Enos, Philip; 1928-July-16; 98; M; Pima; Yes; Full; Unknown; Yes

Unnumbered; Enos, Ruth; 1928-Sept-1; 2 mo; F; Pima; Yes; Full; Unknown; Yes

1929-857; Enos, Simon; 1929-April-27; 23; M; Pima; Yes; Full; Tuberculosis; Yes

1929-909; Evans, Luke; 1928-Nov-11; 62; M; Pima; Yes; Full; Nephritis; Yes

1929-896; Evans, Olive; 1928-Nov-8; 19; F; Pima; Yes; Full; Tuberculosis; Yes

1929-968; Gatai, Juana; 1929-Mar-24; 64; F; Pima; Yes; Full; Stomach Trouble; Yes

1929-1042; Harrison, Ned; 1929-Mar-3; 18; M; Pima; Yes; Full; Tuberculosis; Yes

Unrecorded; Harvey, Juanita; 1929-Jan-30; 5; F; Papago; Yes; Full; Burns; Yes

1929-1156; Honwesima, Elaine; 1928-July-7; 23; F; Pima; Yes; Full; Tuberculosis; Yes

1929-1200; Howard, Aurelia; 1929-May-2; 9; F; Pima; Yes; Full; Unknown; Yes

1929-1199; Howard, Josepha; 1929-April-30; 39; F; Pima; Yes; Full; Unknown; Yes

1929-1218; Howard, Judah; 1928-Sept-9; 73; M; Pima; Yes; Full; Blood Poison; Yes

1929-1244; Innis, Alfred; 1928-Sept-5; 11; M; Maricopa; Yes; Full; Gun shot wound; Yes

Unnumbered; Jackson, Allen; 1929-Feb-1; 2 d; M; Pima; Yes; Full; Congenital Weakness; Yes

1929-1265; Jackson, Anton; 1928-Dec-22; 68; M; Pima; Yes; Full; Nephritis; Yes

309

Deaths Occurring Between the Dates of July 1, 1928 and June 30, 1929 to Indians Enrolled at Jurisdiction

Key: Year and Number on Last Census Roll; Surname; Given; Date of Death (Year-Month-Day); Age at Death; Sex; Tribe; Ward (Yes/No); Degree of Blood); Cause of Death; At Jurisdiction Where Enrolled (Yes/No); (If no – Where – Jurisdiction; State; Post Office; State)

1929-1266; Jackson, Josepha; 1928-Sept-15; 68; F; Pima; Yes; Full; Unknown; Yes

1929-1312; Jackson, Job; 1929-Jan-26; 23; M; Papago; Yes; Full; Pulmonary TB; Yes

1929-1295; Jackson, Mollie; 1928-Aug-8; 23; F; Pima; Yes; Full; Tuberculosis; Yes

1929-1398; James, Peter; 1928-Oct-8; 68; M; Pima; Yes; Full; Myocarditis; Yes

1929-1442; John, J. Roe; 1929-Mar-3; 22; M; Pima; Yes; Full; Pulmonary TB; Yes

1929-1423; John, Willie; 1929-June-1; 20; M; Pima; Yes; Full; Pulmonary TB; Yes

Unrecorded; Johnson, Jonah; L929[sic]; Mar-11; 3; M; Pima; Yes; Full; Influenza; Yes

Unnumbered; Joseph, Margaret Jr.; 1929-April-1; 2 d; F; Pima; Yes; Full; Congenital Weakness; Yes

1929-1695; Juan, Jose; 1929-April-21; 46; M; Pima; Yes; Full; Pulmonary TB; Yes

Unrecorded; Juan, Jose; 1929-April-22; --; M; Pima; Yes; Full; Pertonitis[sic]; Yes

1928-1772; Keen, Mary; 1928-Aug-28; 77; F; Pima; Yes; Full; Unknown; Yes

1929-1837; Knox, John; 1928-Nov-5; 78; M; Pima; Yes; Full; Old Age; Yes

1929-1846; Komcess, ---; 1928-Dec-29; 70; M; Maricopa; Yes; Full; Influenza; Yes

Unrecorded; Lewis, Juan; 1929-June-29; 48; M; Pima; Yes; Full; Pulmonary TB; Yes

1929-2008; Lewis, Lancisco; 1929-Jan-23; 42; M; Pima; Yes; Full; Unknown; Yes

Unnumbered; Lewis, Lena; 1929-Jan-18; 23; F; Papago; Yes; Full; Pneumonia; Yes

1929-2158; Ludlow, Lizzie; 1929-Feb-4; 35; F; Pima; Yes; Full; Tuberculosis; Yes

1929-2174; Lyon, Margaret; 1929-Jan-14; 72; F; Pima; Yes; Full; Unknown; Yes

Unnumbered; Mack, Effie; 1928-Oct-10; 70; F; Pima; Yes; Full; Old Age; Yes

1929-2244; Manuel, Enos; 1928-Nov-6; 46; M; Pima; Yes; Full; Pneumonia; Yes

1929-2293; Manuel, Juan; 1929-June-2; 69; M; Pima; Yes; Full; Nephritis; Yes

Unnumbered; Marie, Jose; 1928-Dec-26; 50; M; Papago; Yes; Full; Peritonitis; No; Chandler, Ariz.

1929-2428; Mathews, Eloise; 1929-Jan-14; 15; F; Pima; Yes; Full; Tuberculosis; Yes

1929-2484; Mekolas, Jack; 1928-Aug-31; 78; M; Pima; Yes; Full; Tuberculosis; Yes

1929-2535; Miguel, Jennie; 1929-Jan-6; 37; F; Pima; Yes; Full; Nephritis; Yes

Unnumbered; Miguel, Juan; 1929-Feb-4; 70; M; Pima; Yes; Full; Unknown; Yes

1929-2503; Mikah, McGill; 1928-Nov-23; 60; M; Pima; Yes; Full; Gastritis Chronic; Yes

Unnumbered; Nelson, John; 1928-Oct-1; 73; M; Pima; Yes; Full; Unknown; Yes

1929-2926; Nelson, Laura; 1928-Aug-18; 60; F; Pima; Yes; Full; Unknown; Yes

1929-2754; Nelson, Lloyd; 1928-Aug-8; 14; M; Pima; Yes; Full; Meningitis; Yes

Unnumbered; Nelson, Mona Lee; 1929-June-25; 10 mo; F; Pima; Yes; Full; Colitis; Yes

1929-2272; Newman, Henry; 1928-Oct-26; 23; M; Papago; Yes; Full; Tuberculosis; Yes

Unnumbered; N/ash[sic], Austin; 1928-Nov-17; 1 mo; M; Pima; Yes; Full; Paralysis; Yes

1929-2931; Pablo, Narcia; 1929-Nov-4; 49; F; Pima; Yes; Full; Abscess; Yes

1929-2977; Pablo, Ruth; 1928-July-21; 16; F; Pima; Yes; Full; Tuberculosis; Yes

1929-2990; Paddis, Flora; 1929-June-3; 15; F; Pima; Yes; Full; Tuberculosis; Yes

1929-3187; Porter, Frank; 1928-Aug-15; 93; M; Pima; Yes; Full; Nephritis; Yes

1929-3220; Pratt, Selina; 1929-Mar-27; 24; M[sic]; Pima; Yes; Full; Rheumatism; Yes

Deaths Occurring Between the Dates of July 1, 1928 and June 30, 1929 to Indians Enrolled at Jurisdiction

Key: Year and Number on Last Census Roll; Surname; Given; Date of Death (Year-Month-Day); Age at Death; Sex; Tribe; Ward (Yes/No); Degree of Blood); Cause of Death; At Jurisdiction Where Enrolled (Yes/No); (If no – Where – Jurisdiction; State; Post Office; State)

1929-3312; Riggs, Enacia; 1929-Apr-8; 16; F; Pima; Yes; Full; Tuberculosis; Yes
Unnumbered; Rivera, Ernestine; 1929-June-28; 5 d; F; Papago-Pima; Yes; Full; Mitral Insufficiency; No; Tucson, Ariz.
1929-3394; Sampson, Lucy; 1929-April-13; 64; F; Pima; Yes; Full; Carcenoma[sic] of Cervis[sic]; Yes
1929-3403; San Chiago, Jacob; 1929-Mar-21; 40; M; Pima; Yes; Full; Tuberculosis; Yes
1929-3445; Schurz, Henry; 1928-Dec-20; 1; M; Pima; Yes; Full; Influenza; Yes
1929-3431; Schurz, Margaret; 1928-Aug-4; 34; F; Pima; Yes; Full; Nephritis; Yes
1929-3519; Smith, Clifford; 1928-Oct-24; 6; M; Pima; Yes; Full; Tuberculosis; Yes
Unnumbered; Smith, Harry; 1929-Jan-20; 58 mo; M; Pima; Yes; Full; Influenza; No; Phoenix, Ariz.
Unnumbered; Soroquisara (Young), ---; 1928-Oct-28; 1; F; Maricopa; Yes; Full; Enteritis; Yes
1929-3662; Sundust, ---; 1928-Dec-19; 70; M; Maricopa; Yes; Full; Tuberculosis; Yes
1929-3870; Thompson, Elliott; 1928-Nov-8; 26; M; Pima; Yes; Full; Tuberculosis; Yes
1929-3895; Tomaso, Geo.; 1928-Dec-23; 68; M; Pima; Yes; Full; Pneumonia; Yes
1929-4063; White, Annie; 1929-Jan-1; 80; F; Maricopa; Yes; Full; Influenza; Yes
1929-4031; White (Juan), Fannie; 1929-Jan-3; 36; F; Pima; Yes; Full; Tuberculosis; Yes
1929-4049; White, Lucy; 1928-Dec-27; 49; F; Pima; Yes; Full; Pneumonia; Yes
1929-4391; Whittaker, Anton Marie; 1929-June-29; 31; M; Pima; Yes; Full; Tuberculosis; Yes
1929-4113; Whittier, Bertha; 1928-Nov-25; 65; F; Pima; Yes; Full; Intersupeption[sic]; Yes
1929-4150; Williams, Alice; 1929-Feb-22; 79; F; Pima; Yes; Full; Unknown; Yes
Unnumbered; Wilson, Joe Ann; 1928-July-29; 1 d; F; Pima; Yes; Full; Asphyxiz[sic]; Yes
1929-1286; Wilson, May; 1929-Feb-16; 30; F; Pima; Yes; Full; Toxemia of Pregnancy; Yes
1928-4202; Wiston, Willet; 1928-Aug-16; 7; M; Pima; Yes; Full; Tuberculosis; Yes
1929-4234; Yask, Jose M.; 1929-Mar-11; 64; M; Pima; Yes; Full; Cirrhosis of Liver; Yes

Deaths
Occurring Between
July 1, 1929 and June 30, 1930
Pima Indian Agency

State **Arizona** Reservation **Gila River Reservation** Agency or jurisdiction **Pima Indian Agency**; Office of Indian Affairs

Deaths Occurring Between the Dates of July 1; 1929 and June 30; 1930 to Indians Enrolled at Jurisdiction

Key: Year and Number on Last Census Roll Number; Surname; Given; Date of Death (Year-Month-Day); Age at Death; Sex; Tribe; Ward (Yes/No); Degree of Blood); Cause of Death; At Jurisdiction Where Enrolled (Yes/No); (If no – Where – Jurisdiction; State; Post Office; State)

1929-211; Anton, Miguel; 1930-March-22; 47; M; Pima; Yes; Full; Tuberculosis; Yes
Unrecorded; Antone, Joseph; 1930-March-30; 1 hr; M; Papago; Yes; Full; Premature Birth; Yes
1929-612; Coops, Betty; 1930-April-17; 2; F; Pima; Yes; Full; Pneumonia; Yes
1929-686; Dixon, Gertrude; 1930-Feb-8; 49; F; Pima; Yes; Full; Uremic Poisoning; Yes
1929-732; Elias, Raymond; 1929-Sept-7; 2; M; Pima; Yes; Full; Acute Dysentery; Yes
1929-675; Edwards (Ellis), Violet; 1929-Nov-25; 21; F; Pima; Yes; Full; Pulmonary TB; Yes
1929-952; Eschief, Sarah; 1929-Aug-6; 24; F; Pima; Yes; Full; Dilation of Heart; Yes
1929-981; Evans, Delia; 1930-Feb-7; 80; F; Pima; Yes; Full; Cholecystitis; Yes
1929-1048; Gage, Jerome; 1929-Sept-19; 1; M; Pima; Yes; Full; Gastro-enteritis; Yes
Unrecorded; Garcia, Andrew; 1930-June-7; 6 mo; M; Pima; Yes; Full; Unknown; Yes
1929-1190; Havalina, Nellie; 1929-Oct-30; 20; F; Pima; Yes; Full; Child Birth; Yes
1929-1245; Hice, John; 1930-June-16; 71; M; Pima; Yes; Full; Gastric Ulcer; Yes
1929-1341; Hughes, Lucy; 1929-Nov-22; 79; F; Pima; Yes; Full; Influenza; Yes
Unnumbered; Jackson, ---; 1929-Oct-1; 3 d; M; Pima; Yes; Full; Accidental death; Yes
Unnumbered; John, Robert; 1929-Nov-15; 1; M; Pima; Yes; Full; Pneumonia; Yes
1929-1659; Johnson, Lillian; 1929-Oct-13; 21; F; Pima; Yes; Full; Cardiac Failure; Yes
1929-1602; Johnson, Thurman; 1930-June-20; 23 mo; M; Pima; Yes; Full; Acute Meningitis; Yes
1929-1698; Jones, Lewis; 1929-Dec-7; 62; M; Pima; Yes; Full; Tuberculosis; Yes
1929-1796; Josepha, Mollie; 1929-Oct-26; 90; F; Pima; Yes; Full; Pneumonia; Yes
1929-1860; Juan, Ramon; 1930-April-29; 24; M; Pima; Yes; Full; Stomach Traouble[sic]; Yes
Unnumbered; Lewis, Alfred; 1930-June-12; 1; M; Pima; Yes; Full; Enteritis; Yes
Unnumbered; Lewis, Delphine; 1930-May-13; 10 mo; F; Pima; Yes; Full; Cholera; Yes
1929-2030; Lewis, Elmira; 1929-Dec-19; 1; F; Pima; Yes; Full; Convulsions; Yes
Unnumbered; Lewis, Jean; 1929-July-2; 1 d; F; Pima; Yes; Full; Cardiac Insufficiency; Yes
1929-2152; Lewis, Leon; 1930-June-23; 5; M; Pima; Yes; Full; Pneumonia; Yes
1929-2153; Lewis, Richard; 1930-May-27; 3; M; Pima; Yes; Full; Pneumonia; Yes
Unrecorded; Lopez, Pablo; 1930-April-13; 17; M; Papago; Yes; Full; Meningitis; Yes
1929-2501; Manuel, Gabriel; 1930-May-23; 4; M; Pima; Yes; Full; Measles; Yes
1929-2401; Manuel, Isabel; 1929-Oct-13; 1; F; Pima; Yes; Full; Unknown; Yes
Unrecorded; Manuel, Nellie; 1929-Aug-3; 29; F; Papago; Yes; Full; Pulmonary TB; Yes
1929-2514; Manyahn, Roberta; 1929-Oct-3; 1; F; Maricopa; Yes; Full; Paralysis; Yes
1929-2555; Marrietta[sic], Panitik; 1929-Nov-7; 10; M; Papago; Yes; Full; Tuberculosis; Yes

State **Arizona** Reservation **Gila River Reservation** Agency or
jurisdiction **Pima Indian Agency**; Office of Indian Affairs
Deaths Occurring Between the Dates of July 1; 1929 and June 30; 1930 to Indians Enrolled at Jurisdiction

Key: Year and Number on Last Census Roll Number; Surname; Given; Date of Death (Year-Month-
Day); Age at Death; Sex; Tribe; Ward (Yes/No); Degree of Blood); Cause of Death;
At Jurisdiction Where Enrolled (Yes/No); (If no – Where – Jurisdiction; State; Post Office; State)

Unnumbered; Martin, Virginia; 1930-June-26; 1; F; Pima; Yes; Full; Gastro Enteritis;
Yes
1929-2717; Miguel, Francis; 1929-Oct-16; 1; M; Pima; Yes; Full; Acute Indigestion;
Yes
1929-2738; Mikateez, xxx; 1929-Dec-15; 88; F; Maricopa; Yes; Full; Influenza; Yes
Unnumbered; Miles, Myers; Rosalinda; 1930-May-6; 7 mo; F; Pima; Yes; Full;
Scorpion Sting; Yes
Unnumbered; Morago, ---; 1929-Oct-5; 15 d; F; Hopi & Pima; Yes; Full; Premature
Birth; Yes
1929-2923; Nelson, John; 1930-April-1; 74; M; Pima; Yes; Full; Unknown; Yes
1929-3000; Noname, Edward; 1929-Dec-11; 41; M; Pima; Yes; Full; Pulmonary TB;
Yes
1929-3120; Oxpe, Bernardin; 1930-June-12; 2; M; Pima; Yes; Full; Measles; Yes
1929-3163; Pablo, Edna; 1930-May-12; 16; F; Pima; Yes; Full; Pulmonary TB; Yes
1929-3168; Pablo, Edwina; 1930-May-2; 1; F; Pima; Yes; Full; Pneumonia; Yes
Unnumbered; Patrick, Gladys; 1929-Oct-23; 9 mo; F; Hopi & Pima; Yes; Full;
Unknown; Yes
1929-3361; Peters, Bertha; 1930-June-3; 12; F; Pima; Yes; Full; Pulmonary TB; Yes
1929-3386; Phillips, Isabelle; 1930-Jan-11; 88; F; Pima; Yes; Full; Unknown; Yes
1929-3576; Rovie, Betty J.; 1929-Dec-23; 1; F; Pima; Yes; Full; Pneumonia; Yes
1929-3682; Santo, Lorrina; 1929-Nov-24; 6 mo; F; Pima; Yes; Full; Whooping
Cough; No; Salt River Res., Ariz.
1929-3695; Scherez, Josephine; 1930-May-31; 13; F; Pima; Yes; Full; Pulmonary TB;
Yes
1929-3713; Scott, Carrie; 1930-May-1; 53; F; Pima; Yes; Full; Pneumonia; Yes
Unrecorded; Sequiera (Siquiera), Joaquina; 1930-June-9; 32; F; Papago; Yes; Full;
Childbirth; Yes
1929-3812; Sneed, Erwin; 1930-May-9; 15; M; Pima; Yes; Full; Pulmonary TB; Yes
1929-3916; Stone, Lewis; 1930-June-13; 50; M; Pima; Yes; Full; Peritonitis; Yes
1929-3945; Sundust, Carmen; 1930-May-29; 1; F; Pima; Yes; Full; Gastro Ebteritis;
Yes
1929-4007; Taylor (Terry), Roy; 1929-Aug-7; 23; M; Pima; Yes; Full; Pulmonary TB;
Yes
1929-3721; Terry, Anastacia; 1929-Dec-3; 53; F; Pima; Yes; Full; Pneumonia; Yes
1929-4084; Thomas, Logan; 1930-April-18; 17; M; Pima; Yes; Full; T.B.; Yes
1929-4199; Vavages, Brown; 1930-March-24; 82; M; Pima; Yes; Full; Old Age; Yes
1929-4222; Vavages, Juan; 1930-June-15; 75; M; Pima; Yes; Full; Pneumonia; Yes
1929-4223; Vavages, Lupa; 1929-Sept-15; 79; F; Pima; Yes; Full; Hernia; Yes
Unnumbered; Vavages, Sepherina; 1929-Sept-6; 5 mo; F; Pima; Yes; Full; Colitis;
Yes
1929-4303; Warren, Lena; 1929-Oct-19; 35; F; Pima; Yes; Full; Pulmonary TB; Yes
1929-4401; Whittaker, Vivian; 1930-June-10; 1; F; Pima; Yes; Full; Hernia; Yes
1929-4454; Williams, Thomas; 1930-May-1; 78; M; Pima; Yes; Full; Old Age; Yes

State **Arizona** Reservation **Gila River Reservation** Agency or jurisdiction **Pima Indian Agency**; Office of Indian Affairs

Deaths Occurring Between the Dates of July 1; 1929 and June 30; 1930 to Indians Enrolled at Jurisdiction

Key: Year and Number on Last Census Roll Number; Surname; Given; Date of Death (Year-Month-Day); Age at Death; Sex; Tribe; Ward (Yes/No); Degree of Blood); Cause of Death; At Jurisdiction Where Enrolled (Yes/No); (If no – Where – Jurisdiction; State; Post Office; State)

1929-4477; Wilson, Nancy; 1930-April-24; 18; F; Pima; Yes; Full; Pulmonary TB; Yes

1929-4530; Zachery, Elizabeth; 1930-Jan-6; 14; F; Pima; Yes; Full; Pulmonary TB; Yes

Unrecorded; Zuni, Victoria; 1929-Aug-12; 2; F; Zuni & Maricopa; Yes; Full; Typhoid Fever; Yes

Deaths
Occurring Between
April 1, 1930 and March 31, 1931
Pima Indian Agency

State **Arizona** Reservation **Gila River Reservation** Agency or
jurisdiction **Pima Indian Agency**; Office of Indian Affairs

Deaths Occurring Between the Dates of April 1, 1930 and March 31, 1931 to Indians Enrolled at Jurisdiction

Key: Year and Number on Last Census Roll Number; Surname; Given; Date of Death (Year-Month-
Day); Age at Death; Sex; Tribe; Ward (Yes/No); Degree of Blood); Cause of Death;
At Jurisdiction Where Enrolled (Yes/No); (If no – Where – Jurisdiction; State; Post Office; State)

Unrecorded; Anton, ---; 1930-July-7; 10 d; F; Pima; Yes; Full; Unknown; Yes

1929-186; Anton, Martha; 1930-July-13; 5; F; Pima; Yes; Full; Burns; Yes

1930-245; Anton, Mollie; 1930-Aug-25; 70; F; Pima; Yes; Full; Old Age; Yes

1930-39; Antone, Albert; 1930-Sept-2; 16; M; Papago; Yes; Full; Suicide; Yes

Unnumbered; Antone, Ernestine; 1930-Dec-20; 6 mo; F; Maricopa; Yes; Full;
Malnutrition; Yes

1930-57; Antone, Mollie; 1930-Sept-19; 60 [70]; F; Papago; Yes; Full; Influenza; Yes

1930-153; Antone, Priscilla; 1930-Aug-3; 1; F; Pima; Yes; Full; Pneumonia; Yes

1930-188; Antone, Ruth; 1930-Dec-5; 1; F; Pima; Yes; Full; Meningitis; Yes

Unnumbered; Brown, Lloyd; 1931-Jan-5; 1; M; Pima; Yes; Full; Pneumonia; Yes

Unnumbered; Campbell, ---; 1930-Dec-18; 1 d; F; Pima; Yes; Full; Lymphaticua[sic];
Yes

1930-461; Campbell, Robert; 1930-Dec-31; 36; M; Pima; Yes; Full; Pulmonary TB;
Yes

1930-519; Catha, Raymond; 1930-Oct-9; 60; M; Pima; Yes; Full; Tuberculosis; Yes

Unnumbered; Cooper, Sylvia; 1930-Dec-20; 10 mo; F; Pima; Yes; Full; Unknown;
Yes

1930-3426; Coops, Betty; 1930-April-17; 2; F; Pima; Yes; Full; Pneumonia; Yes

1929-619; Coops, Cheerless; 1931-Jan-31;81; F; Pima; Yes; Full; Pneumonia; Yes

1930-699; Dixon, Kisto; 1930-Nov-21; 75; M; Pima; Yes; Full; Accidental Fall; Yes

1930-732; Elies, Juan; 1930-Dec-28; 41; M; Pima; Yes; Full; Pneumonia; No;
Phoenix, Ariz.

1930-922; Enos, Juan; 1930-Sept-30; 73; M; Maricopa; Yes; Full; Tuberculosis; Yes

1929-1018; Francisco, Katherine; 1930-Nov-3;57; F; Pima; Yes; Full; Stomach
Trouble; Yes

Unrecorded; Garcia, Andrew; 1930-June-7; 6 mo; M; Pima; Yes; Full; Unknown; Yes

1930-1204; Hawthorne, Nathanial; 1930-July-16; 65; M; Maricopa; Yes; Full;
Nephritis; Yes

Unnumbered; Hayes, Cecil; 1930-Aug-19; 1; M; Pima; Yes; Full; Meningitis; No;
Phoenix, Ariz.

1929-1245; Hice, John; 1930-June-16; 71; M; Pima; Yes; Full; Ulcer; Yes

1930-1314; Howard, Norman; 1930-Aug-11; 2; M; Pima; Yes; Full; Syphilis; No; Salt
River Res., Ariz.

1930-1306; Howard, Lyman; 1930-Sept-11; 57; M; Maricopa; Yes; Full; Peritonitis;
Yes

Unnumbered; Jackson, Lucy; 1930-July-3; 5 d; F; Pima; Yes; Full; Lymphaticus[sic];
Yes

1930-1472; Jackson, McDonald; 1931-Feb-5; 21; M; Pima; Yes; Full; Tuberculosis;
Yes

1930-1504; James, Hattie; 1930-July-23; 64; F; Pima; Yes; Full; Tuberculosis; Yes

Unnumbered; Johns, Marcella; 1931-Mar-12; 14 d; F; Pima; Yes; Full;
Lymphaticus[sic]; Yes

1929-1602; Johnson, Thurman; 1930-June-20; 23 mo; M; Pima; Yes; Full;
Meningitis; Yes

State **Arizona** Reservation **Gila River Reservation** Agency or
jurisdiction **Pima Indian Agency**; Office of Indian Affairs
Deaths Occurring Between the Dates of April 1, 1930 and March 31, 1931 to Indians Enrolled at Jurisdiction

Key: Year and Number on Last Census Roll Number; Surname; Given; Date of Death (Year-Month-
Day); Age at Death; Sex; Tribe; Ward (Yes/No); Degree of Blood); Cause of Death;
At Jurisdiction Where Enrolled (Yes/No); (If no – Where – Jurisdiction; State; Post Office; State)

1929-1860; Juan, Ramone; 1930-April-29; 24; M; Pima; Yes; Full; Stomach Trouble;
Yes
Unnumbered; Lewis, Alfred; 1930-June-12; 1; M; Pima; Yes; Full; Enteritis; Yes
Unnumbered; Lewis, Delphine; 1930-May-13; 10 mo; F; Pima; Yes; Full; Cholera;
Yes
1929-2152; Lewis, Leon; 1930-June-20; 5; M; Pima; Yes; Full; Pneumonia; Yes
1929-2153; Lewis, Richard; 1930-May-27; 3; M; Pima; Yes; Full; Pneumonia; Yes
1930-2252; Liston, Joseph; 1930-Dec-10; 62; M; Pima; Yes; Full; Nephritis; Yes
Unnumbered; Lopez, Leppe; 1931-Jan-4; 11 d; F; Pima; Yes; Full; Heart Disease; Yes
Unrecorded; Lopez, Pablo; 1930-April-13; 17; M; Papago; Yes; Full; Meningitis; Yes
1929-2501; Manuel, Gabriel; 1930-May-23; 4; M; Pima; Yes; Full; Measles; Yes
1930-2422; Manuel, Jose; 1930-July-20; 69; M; Pima; Yes; Full; Tuberculosis; Yes
Unnumbered; Marietta, Jobe; 1930-Dec-4; 2 mo; M; Pima & Papago; Yes; Full;
Pneumonia; Yes
Unnumbered; Martin, Virginia; 1930-May-25; 1; F; Pima; Yes; Full; Enteritis; Yes
Unnumbered; Miles, Rosalinda; 1930-May-8; 7 mo; F; Pima; Yes; Full; Scorpion
Sting; Yes
1930-2859; Morales, Enacia; 1930-Sept-23; 62; F; Pima; Yes; Full; Senility; Yes
1929-2923; Nelson, John; 1930-April-1; 74; M; Pima; Yes; Full; Unknown; Yes
Unnumbered; Nelson, Virgil; 1930-Aug-30; 5 d; M; Pima; Yes; Full; Heart Failure;
No; Phoenix, Ariz.
1930-3040; Morris, Juan; 1931-March-13; 95; M; Pima; Yes; Full; Senility; Yes
1929-3120; Oxpe, Bernardin; 1930-June-12; 2; M; Pima; Yes; Full; Measles; Yes
Unnumbered; Oxpe, Donald; 1930-July-29; 25 d; M; Pima; Yes; Full; Unknown; Yes
1929-3163; Pablo, Edna; 1930-May-12; 16; F; Pima; Yes; Full; Pulmonary TB; Yes
1929-3168; Pablo, Edwina; 1930-May-2; 1; F; Pima; Yes; Full; Pneumonia; Yes
1930-3246; Parsons, Delbert; 1930-Sept-25; 8 mo; M; Pima; Yes; Full; Dysentery;
Yes
1929-3361; Peters, Bertha; 1930-May-3; 12; F; Pima; Yes; Full; Pulmonary TB; Yes
1930-3373; Peters, Juanna; 1930-Aug-2; 25; F; Pima; Yes; Full; Tuberculosis; Yes
1930-3376; Peters, Mrs. Manley; 1931-Jan-15; 82; F; Pima; Yes; Full; Nephritis; Yes
1929-3373; Phillips, Isabelle; 1930-Nov-11; 68; F; Pima; Yes; Full; Unknown; Yes
1930-3437; Porter, Donald; 1931-Mar-5; 4; M; Pima; Yes; Full; Pneumonia; No;
Phoenix, Ariz.
1930-3511; Randall, Harvier; 1931-Feb-4; 55; M; Pima; Yes; Full; Nephritis; Yes
1930-3675; Sanderson, Josie; 1931-Jan-16; 57; F; Maricopa; Yes; Full;
Cholelithiesis[sic]; Yes
1929-3695; Scherez, Josephine; 1930-May-31; 13; F; Pima; Yes; Full; Tuberculosis;
Yes
1929-3713; Scott, Carrie; 1930-May-1; 53; F; Pima; Yes; Full; Pneumonia; Yes
1930-3746; See-Yal, ---; 1930-Sept-24; 75; M; Pima; Yes; Full; Old Age; Yes
Unrecorded; Siquieros, Joaquina; 1930-June-9; 32; F; Papago; Yes; Full; Child Birth;
Yes
1930-3791; Smith, Wilhelmina; 1931-Mar-21; 2; F; Pima; Yes; Full; Peritonitis; Yes

State **Arizona** Reservation **Gila River Reservation** Agency or
jurisdiction **Pima Indian Agency**; Office of Indian Affairs
Deaths Occurring Between the Dates of April 1, 1930 and March 31, 1931 to Indians Enrolled at Jurisdiction

Key: Year and Number on Last Census Roll Number; Surname; Given; Date of Death (Year-Month-
Day); Age at Death; Sex; Tribe; Ward (Yes/No); Degree of Blood); Cause of Death;
At Jurisdiction Where Enrolled (Yes/No); (If no – Where – Jurisdiction; State; Post Office; State)

1929-3812; Sneed, Erwin; 1930-May-2; 15; M; Pima; Yes; Full; Tuberculosis; Yes
1929-3916; Stone, Lewis; 1930-June-13; 50; M; Pima; Yes; Full; Peritonitis; Yes
1929-3945; Sundust, Carmen; 1930-May-29; 1; F; Pima; Yes; Full; Enteritis; Yes
1929-4084; Thomas, Logan; 1930-April-18; 17; M; Pima; Yes; Full; Tuberculosis;
Yes
1930-4056; Thomas, Mollie; 1931-Feb-17; 59; F; Pima; Yes; Full; Tuberculosis; Yes
1929-4222; Vavages, Juan; 1930-June-15; 75; M; Pima; Yes; Full; Pneumonia; Yes
1930-4392; White, Ramon; 1930-Sept-3; 72; M; Maricopa; Yes; Full; Old Age; Yes
1929-4401; Whittaker, Vivian; 1930-June-10; 1; F; Pima; Yes; Full; Pneumonia; Yes
1929-4454; Williams, Thomas; 1930-May-1; 70; M; Pima; Yes; Full; Old Age; Yes
1930-4500; Wilson, Francisco; 1930-Nov-29; 57; M; Pima; Yes; Full; Pneumonia;
Yes
1929-4477; Wilson, Nancy; 1930-April-24; 18; M; Pima; Yes; Full; Pulmonary TB;
Yes
Unnumbered; Wiston, ---; 1930-Oct-5; 13 hrs; F; Pima; Yes; Full; Status
Lymphatus[sic]; Yes
1930-4539; Wiston, Violet; 1930-July-16; 19; F; Pima; Yes; Full; Tuberculosis; Yes

Deaths

Occurring Between

April 1, 1931 and March 31, 1932

Pima Indian Agency

State **Arizona** Reservation **Gila River Reservation** Agency or
jurisdiction **Pima Indian Agency**; Office of Indian Affairs
Deaths Occurring Between the Dates of April 1, 1931 and March 31, 1932 to Indians Enrolled at Jurisdiction

Key: Year and Number on Last Census Roll Number; Surname; Given; Date of Death (Year-Month-
Day); Age at Death; Sex; Tribe; Ward (Yes/No); Degree of Blood); Cause of Death;
At Jurisdiction Where Enrolled (Yes/No); (If no – Where – Jurisdiction; State; Post Office; State)

1931-10; Adams, Martha; 1931-Dec-3; 86; F; Pima; Yes; Full; Pneumonia-lobar; Yes
1931-87; Allison, Herman; 1931-Oct-13; 18; M; Pima; Yes; Full; T.B. Cerebral; Yes
1931-89; Allison, Ramon; 1931-Oct-23; 50; M; Pima; Yes; Full; Gangrene of Feet; Yes
1931-91; Allison, Rachel; 1931-Oct-2; 19; F; Pima; Yes; Full; Pneumonia-Lobar; Yes
1931-102; Allison, Colleen; 1931-May-21; 1; F; Pima; Yes; Full; Dysentery-Cacillary[sic]; Yes
1932-313; Beginning, Chester; 1932-Feb-3; 56; M; Pima; Yes; Full; Fractured[sic] of Skull Auto Accident; Yes
1931-327; Bird, Agnes; 1931-Oct-22; 24; F; Maricopa; Yes; Full; Cholecystitis; Yes
1931-495; Case, Agnes; 1931-Nov-1; 56; F; Maricopa; Yes; Full; T.B. Pulmonary; Yes
1931-705; Eaton, Adam; 1932-Jan-6; 78; M; Pima; Yes; Full; T.B. Pulmonary; Yes
1930-748; Ellis, Minnie; 1932-Feb-27; 97; F; Pima; Yes; Full; Pneumonia-Lobar; Yes
1931-744; Emmerson, Hazel; 1931-Sept-13; 24; F; Pima; Yes; Full; Salpingitis[sic]; Yes
1931-939; Eschief, Lauren; 1931-Dec-29; 9; M; Papago; Yes; Full; T.B. Pulmonary; Yes
1931-961; Evans, Emily; 1931-Oct-9; 56; F; Pima; Yes; Full; Nephritis; Yes
1931-1020; Fulton, Nina; 1932-Mar-11; 17; F; Pima; Yes; Full; Septicemia; Yes
1931-1037; Gatai, James P.; 1931-May-6; 41; M; Pima; Yes; Full; T.B. Pulmonary; Yes
1931-1189; Hayes, Eugene; 1931-Sept-27; 60; M; Maricopa; Yes; Full; Cancer of Stomach; Yes
1931-1221; Hendricks, Angelita; 1932-Mar-20; 21; F; Pima; Yes; Full; Pneumonia-Lobar; Yes
1931-1281; Howard, Agnes; 1931-Apr-24; 61; F; Pima; Yes; Full; Nephritis; Yes
1931-1347; Isk, Maude; 1931-Sept-13; 68; F; Pima; Yes; Full; Asthma; Yes
1931-1437; Jackson, Annie; 1932-Feb-25; 70; F; Pima; Yes; Full; Pneumonia-Lobar; Yes
1931-1507; James, Peter; 1932-Jan-31; 58; F[sic]; Pima; Yes; Full; Pneumonia-Lobar; Yes
1931-1514; James, Inez; 1931-Oct-25; 17; F; Pima; Yes; Full; T.B. Pulmonary; Yes
1931-1548; Chapin, Clara T.; 1931-Nov-21; 20; F; Pima; Yes; Full; Septicemia; Yes
1931-1564; Johns, Fannie; 1932-Jan-23; 37; F; Pima; Yes; Full; T.B. Pulmonary; Yes
1931-1645; Johnson, William; 1931-Oct-21; 60; M; Pima; Yes; Full; Cardiac Failure; Yes
1931-1666; Jones, Isadora; 1931-Sept-10; 1; F; Pima; Yes; Full; Pyelo[sic]-Nephritis; Yes
1931-1725; Jose, Juan; 1932-Jan-19; 55; M; Pima; Yes; Full; T.B. Pulmonary; Yes
1931-1792; Juan, Isabelle; 1932-Jan-4; 18; F; Pima; Yes; Full; T.B. Pulmonary; Yes
1931-1817; Juan, Luhena; 1932-Feb-15; 100; F; Pima; Yes; Full; Cardiac Failure; Yes
1931-1852; Justine, Nathan; 1931-May-9; 75; M; Maricopa; Yes; Full; T.B. Pulmonary; Yes

State **Arizona** Reservation **Gila River Reservation** Agency or
jurisdiction **Pima Indian Agency**; Office of Indian Affairs
Deaths Occurring Between the Dates of April 1, 1931 and March 31, 1932 to Indians Enrolled at Jurisdiction

Key: **Year and Number on Last Census Roll Number; Surname; Given; Date of Death (Year-Month-Day); Age at Death; Sex; Tribe; Ward (Yes/No); Degree of Blood); Cause of Death; At Jurisdiction Where Enrolled (Yes/No); (If no – Where – Jurisdiction; State; Post Office; State)**

1931-1894; Kip, John; 1931-Dec-19; 86; M; Pima; Yes; Full; Nephritis; Yes

1931-1936; Kisto, Juan Jose; 1931-May-7; 27; M; Pima; Yes; Full; T.B. Pulmonary; Yes

1931-2108; Lewis, Robert S.; 1932-Jan-3; 5; M; Pima; Yes; Full; Pneumonia-Lobar; Yes

1931-2144; Lewis, Manuela; 1931-Oct-9; 65; F; Pima; Yes; Full; Mitral Stenosis; Yes

1931-2200; Lewis, Emma; 1931-Oct-2; 16; F; Pima; Yes; Full; T.B. Pulmonary; Yes

1931-2349; Manuel, ---; 1931-Nov-17; 65; M; Pima; Yes; Full; Pneumonia-Lobar; Yes

1931-2644; Mendoza, Carlos; 1931-Apr-22; 61; M; Papago; Yes; Full; Cardiac Failure; Yes

1931-2839; Morgan, Thomas; 1932-Jan-18; 72; M; Pima; Yes; Full; Pneumonia-Lobar; Yes

1931-2925; Nelson, Donna Gloria; 1931-Oct-18; 4; F; Pima; Yes; Full; Unk; Yes

1931-2980; Noname, Manuella; 1931-Sept-12; 59; F; Pima; Yes; Full; T.B. Intestinal; Yes

1931-None; Norris, Joanna; 1932-Mar-4; 1 da; F; Pima; Yes; Full; Axphixia; Yes

1931-3087; Osif, Luke; 1931-Nov-15; 75; F[sic]; Pima; Yes; Full; Nephritis; Yes

1931-3247; Patton, Wilford; 1932-Mar-12; 17; M; Pima; Yes; Full; Typhoid Fever; Yes

1931-3421; Porter, John; 1931-Oct-1; 70; M; Pima; Yes; Full; Gangrene; Yes

1931-3546; Riggs, John; 1931-Oct-31; 74; M; Pima; Yes; Full; Nephritis; Yes

1931-None; Shebela, Caroline B.; 1931-Apr-28; 2 mo; F; Pima; Yes; Full; Pneumonia; Yes

1931-3762; Smith, Alexander; 1931-Dec-3; 73; M; Pima; Yes; Full; Pneumonia; Yes

1931-3798; Smith, Herbert; 1932-Mar-25; 60; M; Pima; Yes; Full; Diabetis; Yes

1931-3809; Snead, Frank; 1932-Mar-6; 65; M; Maricopa; Yes; Full; Arterio Sclerosis; Yes

1931-4033; Thomas, Nellie; 1931-Nov-5; 45; F; Pima; Yes; Full; Pneumonia; Yes

1931-4339; Pancotte, Amanda; 1932-Mar-28; 20; F; Pima; Yes; X1/4; T.B. Pulmonary; Yes

1931-4366; White, Juda; 1932-Mar-23; ~~100~~ 86; F; Pima; Yes; Full; Senility; Yes

1931-4817; Pavilo, Frank; 1931-June-17; 26; M; Papago; Yes; Full; Skull Fracture; Yes

1931-None; Antone, Unnamed; 1931-Dec-7; 2 da; M; Papago; Yes; Full; Premature Birth; Yes

1931-None; Bread, Unnamed; 1931-Sept-9; da 4; F; Maricopa; Yes; Full; Pneumonia; Yes

1931-3606; Jackson, Antonio Jr.; 1931-June-16; 2 da; M; Pima; Yes; Full; Status Lymphaticus[sic]; Yes

1931-None; McArthur, UnNamed; 1931-Oct-19; 1 da; M; Pima; Yes; Full; Hemorrhage Cere; Yes

1931-None; Thomas, Clifford L.; 1931-Sept-3; 3 da; M; Pima; Yes; Full; Status Lymphaticus; Yes

State **Arizona** Reservation **Gila River Reservation** Agency or
jurisdiction **Pima Indian Agency**; Office of Indian Affairs

Deaths Occurring Between the Dates of April 1, 1931 and March 31, 1932 to Indians Enrolled at Jurisdiction

Key: Year and Number on Last Census Roll Number; Surname; Given; Date of Death (Year-Month-Day); Age at Death; Sex; Tribe; Ward (Yes/No); Degree of Blood); Cause of Death; At Jurisdiction Where Enrolled (Yes/No); (If no – Where – Jurisdiction; State; Post Office; State)

1931-None; Thompson, Marjorie; 1931-Sept-16; 3 mo; F; Pima; Yes; Full; Diarrhea; Yes

1931-None; Wapati, Unnamed; 1932-Feb-14; 1 da; F; Pima; Yes; Full; Asphyxiation; Yes

Birth Certificates Not Located on Birth Rolls
and Births
Occurring Between 1928 and 1932
Pima Indian Agency

State **Arizona** Reservation __**Pima Agency**__ Agency or jurisdiction

_____ Office of Indian Affairs

~~Deaths Occurring Between the Dates of July 1, 1929 and June 30, 1930 to Indians Enrolled at Jurisdiction~~

Key: Year and Number on Last Census Roll; Surname; Given; Date of ~~Death~~ Birth (Year-Month-Day); ~~Age at Death~~; Sex; Tribe; ~~Ward (Yes/No); Degree of Blood~~ Mother; ~~Cause of Death~~ Father; At Jurisdiction Where Enrolled (Yes/No); ~~(If no — Where — Jurisdiction; State; Post Office; State)~~ Residence or Place of Birth (County; Post Office, State)

1928

Yes; ~~Anton, Ramon, Joe H; 1928-Aug-12~~; M; Pima; Bessie Osif; Jose Anton (Ramon); Yes; Pinal; Sacaton, Ariz

Illig[sic] Yes; ~~Anton, Noname, Leona; 1928-May-15; F~~; Pima; Lucy Anton (Noname); Unknown; Yes; Maricopa; Gila Crossing, Ariz

Yes; ~~Davis, Lyons, Frederick; 1928-Sept-21; M~~; Pima; Marg Nelson; Francis Davis (Lyons); Yes; Pinal; Sacaton, Ariz

Yes; ~~Jefferson, Lyons, Eloise; 1928-July-6~~; F; Pima; Lucy Josia; Olliver Jefferson (Lyons); Yes; Pinal; Sacaton, Ariz

Yes; ~~Thomas, Osife, Byron; 1928-Aug-25~~; M; Pima; Lupa Jose; Jose Thomas; Yes; Pinal; Sacaton, Ariz

Yes; ~~Thompson, Ahiel, Sarah J; 1928-July-2~~; F; Pima; Dorothy Kisto; Nathan Thompson (Ahiel); Yes; Pinal; Sacaton, Ariz

1929

Yes; ~~Juan, Jose, Fernando Bryan; 1929-Feb-22~~; M; Pima; Hazel Thomas; Jose Juan [Illegible] Jose; Yes; Pinal; Sacaton, Ariz

Yes; ~~Kisto, Oxpe, George; 1929-Aug-18~~; M; Pima; Julia Miquel; Justin Kisto Houston Oxpe; Yes; Pinal; Casa Blanca, Ariz

No; ~~Momy, J Louis Anton; 1929-Mar-20; M; Pima; Eva Reed; Louis A Momy~~; Yes; Pinal; Sacaton, Ariz

Yes; ~~Porter, Stone, [Illegible] 1929-July-6; F~~; Pima; Clara Pablo; Ben Porter Stone; Yes; Pinal; Sacaton, Ariz

Yes; ~~Sanchiago, Williams, Tobias; 1929-July-17; M~~; Pinal; Agatha Jose; Jose Maria Sanchiago; Yes; Maricopa; Santa Cruz, Ariz

1930

add Yes; Milda, Richard R; 1920-Nov-19; M; Pima; Clemenca Ramon; Richard Milda; Yes; Pinal; Sacaton, Ariz

add Yes; Pasqual, Michael; 1930-July-24; M; Pima; Lizzie Kisto; Ascint Pasqual; Yes; Pinal; Sacaton Flats, Ariz

add to roll; Yes; Smith, Helen; 1930-Mar-9; F; Pima; Etta Manuel; Allan Smith; Yes; Maricopa; Gila Crossing, Ariz

add to roll; Yes; White, Lucile D; 1930-June-27; F; Pima; Lucile Jones; Victor White; Yes; Pinal; Sacaton, Ariz

1931

Yes; Allison, Lona; 1931-Aug-20; F; Pima; Ione Chiago; Harry Allison; Yes; Pinal; Sacaton, Ariz

Yes; Antone, No Name; 1931-Dec-7; M; Eliz Jones; Ceveriand Antone; Yes; Pinal; Blackwater, Ariz

Birth Certificates not located on Birth Rolls
State **Arizona** Reservation ___**Pima Agency**___ Agency or jurisdiction
_____ Office of Indian Affairs

Key: ~~Year and Number on Last Census Roll~~; Surname; Given; Date of ~~Death~~ Birth (Year-Month-Day); ~~Age at Death~~; Sex; Tribe; ~~Ward (Yes/No); Degree of Blood~~ Mother; ~~Cause of Death~~ Father; At Jurisdiction Where Enrolled (Yes/No); ~~(If no — Where — Jurisdiction; State; Post Office; State)~~ Residence or Place of Birth (County; Post Office, State)

[1931]

Yes; Avery, Maurice; 1931-May-31; M; Pima; Lusehiana; John Avery; Yes; Pinal; Santa Cruz, Ariz

Yes; Azule, No Name; 1931-June-19; M; Pima; Edna Weston; Wm Azule; Yes; Pinal; Sacaton, Ariz

Yes; Blackwater, Charlene; 1931-June-21; F; Pima; Amelia Wellington; David Blackwater; Yes; Pinal; Sacaton, Ariz

Yes; Bred, No Name; 1931-Sept-5; F; Maricopa; Pauline George; Hiram Bred; Yes; Maricopa; Maricopa, Ariz

Yes; Brown, Wilford; 1931-July-4; M; Pima; Irene John; Fernando Brown; Yes; Pinal; Babechin[sic], Ariz

Illeg-Yes; Cook, Donald C; 1931-May-1; M; Papago; Josephine Cook; Unknown; Yes; Pinal; Sacaton Flats, Ariz

Yes; Cook, Herbert F; 1931-Apr-27; M; Pima; Annie Johnson; Luke Cook; Yes; Pinal; Sacaton Flats, Ariz

Yes; Davis, Miles, Jr; 1931-July-26; M; Pima; Eliza Vavages; Miles R Davis; Yes; Pinal; Sacaton Flats, Ariz

Yes; Domingo, Leonard, Jr; 1931-June-14; M; Pima; Maryann Cort; Leonard Domingo; Yes; Maricopa; Gila Crossing, Ariz

Yes; Jackson, Antonio, Jr; 1931-June-14; M; Pima; Marie Juan; Antonio Jackson; Yes; Pinal; Blackwater, Ariz

Yes; Jackson, Francis B; 1931-Aug-6; M; Pima; Marie Antone; Francis Jackson; Yes; Pinal; Sacaton, Ariz

Yes; Juan (Enos), Dean A; 1931-Sept-2; M; Pima; Eliz Canner; Steven Enos Juan; Yes; Pinal; Sacaton, Ariz

Yes; John, Peter, Jr; 1931-July-31; M; Pima; Isabelle Norris; Peter John; Yes; Pinal; Sweetwater, Ariz

Yes; Johnson, Emma; 1931-Aug-4; F; Maricopa; Lee Davidson; Geo Johnson; Yes; Maricopa; Maricopa, Ariz

Yes; Johnson, Henry, Jr; 1931-June-10; M; Pima; Jessie Jose; Henry Johnson; Yes; Pinal; Sacaton, Ariz

Yes; Johnson, Milton F; 1931-June-26; M; Pima; Marie Vavages; Wilbur Johnson; Yes; Pinal; Sacaton, Ariz

Yes; Jose, Dennis; 1931-June-12; M; Pima; Katherine Nelson; George Jose; Yes; Pinal; Sacaton, Ariz

Yes; Juan, Thelma D; 1931-July-9; F; Pima; Viola Juan; Peter Jones; Yes; Pinal; Sacaton, Ariz

Illig[sic]-Yes; Johnson, Alice; 1931-July-29; F; Pima-Papago; Mary Johnson; Tom Marrietta; Yes; Pinal; Sacaton Flats, Ariz

Yes; Lewis, Mary; 1931-July-25; F; Pima; Regina Enis; Luke Lewis; Yes; Maricopa; Komatke, Ariz

334

State **Arizona** Reservation __**Pima Agency**__ Agency or jurisdiction
_____ Office of Indian Affairs
~~Deaths Occurring Between the Dates of July 1, 1929 and June 30, 1930 to Indians Enrolled at Jurisdiction~~

Key: ~~Year and Number on Last Census Roll~~; Surname; Given; Date of ~~Death~~ Birth (Year-Month-Day);
~~Age at Death~~; Sex; Tribe; ~~Ward (Yes/No); Degree of Blood~~ Mother; ~~Cause of Death~~ Father; At
Jurisdiction Where Enrolled (Yes/No); ~~(If no—Where—Jurisdiction; State; Post Office; State)~~
Residence or Place of Birth (County; Post Office, State)

[1931]
Yes; Makukey, Anthony; 1931-Aug-30; M; Apache; Martha Miller; Louis Makukey;
Yes; Pinal; Sacaton, Ariz
Yes; MᶜArthur, No Name; 1931-Oct-19; M; Pima; Nina MᶜArthur; James MᶜArthur;
Yes; Maricopa; Phoenix, Ariz
Yes; Nelson, Stacey, Jr; 1931-Aug-8; M; Maricopa; Daisy Redbird; Stacey Nelson;
Yes; Maricopa; Maricopa, Ariz
Yes; Nish, Ethel; 1931-April-6; F; Pima; Lohena Scott; Ernest Nish; Yes; Pinal;
Sacaton, Ariz
Yes; Norris, Marian; 1931-July-25; F; Pima; Amelia Jackson; Raymond Norris; Yes;
Pinal; Blackwater, Ariz
Yes; Pablo, Vernon F; 1931-Apr-23; M; Pima; Sersie James; Jose Pablo; Yes; Pinal;
Blackwater, Ariz
Yes; Parsons, Wᵐ; 1931-July-6; M; Pima; Ella Perkins; Juan Parsons; Yes; Pinal;
Santan, Ariz
Yes; Scoffer, Mary R; 1931-July-15; F; Pima; Pauline Manuel; Horace Scoffer; Yes;
Pinal; Sacaton, Ariz (Hosp)
Died 9-25-31- Yes; Thomas, Clifford L; 1931-Sept-25; M; Pima; Martha Davis; Louis
Thomas; Yes; Pinal; Santan, Ariz
Yes; Thompson, Letta; 1931-Aug-26; F; Pima; Nettie Laws; Thomas Thompson; Yes;
Maricopa; Komatke, Ariz
~~No; Illeg; Valdez, No Name; 1931-Sept-12; M; Papago; Matilda~~ Valdez; Unknown;
Yes; Pima; Tucson, Ariz
Died 5/5/31; Yes; Vavages, Mary A; 1931-May-2; F; Pima; Carlotta Ramon; Clement
Vavages; Yes; Pinal; Sacaton, Ariz
Yes; Vincent, David G; 1931-July-25; M; Pima; Edith Pratt; Chiaco Vincent; Yes;
Pinal; Sacaton, Ariz
Yes; Whittaker, Blanch; 1931-June-22; F; Pima; Ida Miguel; John Whittaker; Yes;
Pinal; Sacaton, Ariz
Yes; Williams, Roy; 1931-July-1; M; Pima; Ettie Perkins; Andrew Williams; Yes;
Pinal; Blackwater, Ariz
Yes; Woods, Hilda; 1931-Aug-6; F; Pima; Helen Pina; Paul Woods; Yes; Pinal;
Sacaton, Ariz
Yes; Wellington, Wilfred; 1931-Apr-14; M; Pima; Anita Sampson; Lyman
Wellington; Yes; Pinal; Sacaton, Ariz

- 1932 -
Yes; Allison, Louella M; 1932-Feb-7; F; Pima-Papago; Marg Jose; Wᵐ S Allison;
Yes; Pinal; Snaketown, Ariz

335

State **Arizona** Reservation ___**Pima Agency**___ Agency or jurisdiction
_____ Office of Indian Affairs

~~Deaths Occurring Between the Dates of July 1, 1929 and June 30, 1930 to Indians Enrolled at Jurisdiction~~

Key: ~~Year and Number on Last Census Roll~~; Surname; Given; Date of ~~Death~~ Birth (Year-Month-Day);
~~Age at Death~~; Sex; Tribe; ~~Ward (Yes/No); Degree of Blood~~ Mother; ~~Cause of Death~~ Father; At
Jurisdiction Where Enrolled (Yes/No); ~~(If no — Where — Jurisdiction; State; Post Office; State)~~
Residence or Place of Birth (County; Post Office, State)

[The following 2 entries] Not reported until after April 1st-1932-entered on 1933 roll

Blackwater, Everett T; 1932-Feb-16; M; Pima; Josephine Evans; Vincent Blackwater;
Yes; Pinal; Blackwater, Ariz
Carlyle, Richard; 1932-Mar-18; M; Pima-Papago; Tillie Romo; Hiram Carlyle; Yes;
Pinal; Sacaton, Ariz

Yes; Manuel, Elmer T; 1932-Mar-13; M; Pima; Martha Thomas; Henry T. Manuel;
Yes; Pinal; Chen Chin[sic], Ariz

Not reported until after April 1st 1932- entered on 1933 roll
Pasquale, Tyndell A; 1932-Feb-20; M; Pima; Annie Lyons; Andrus Pasquale; Yes;
Pinal; Sacaton, Ariz

Yes; Stone, Edwin P; 1932-Feb-9; M; Pima; Clara Pablo; Benj P. Stone; Yes; Pinal;
Sacaton, Ariz
Died Same Day- Yes; Wapath, No Name; 1932-Feb-14; F; Pima; Daisy Beans; Mateo
Wapath; Yes; Pinal; Sacaton, Ariz
Yes; Whitman, Dayton; 1932-Mar-13; M; Pima; Ina Johnson; Leonard Whitman; Yes;
Pinal; Sacaton, Ariz

Death Certificates Not Located on Death Rolls

and Deaths

Occurring Between 1928 and 1932

Pima Indian Agency

Death Certificates not located on Death Rolls
State **Arizona** Reservation ___**Pima Agency**___ Agency or jurisdiction
Office of Indian Affairs
Deaths Occurring Between the Dates of July 1, 1929 and June 30, 1930 to Indians Enrolled at Jurisdiction

Key: ~~Year and Number on Last Census Roll~~; Surname; Given; Date of Death (Year-Month-Day); Age at Death; Sex; Tribe; Ward (Yes/No); Degree of Blood; Cause of Death; At Jurisdiction Where Enrolled (Yes/No); ~~(If no — Where — Jurisdiction; State; Post Office; State)~~ Residence or Place of Death (County; Post Office, State)

- 1928 -

Yes; Allison, Albert; 1928-May-16; 22; M; Pima; -; F; Tuberculosis; No; Lincoln; Canton Insane, S.D.

Yes; Anton, McKiney; 1928-June-12; 1; M; Pima; -; F; Measles; Yes; Maricopa; Gila Crossing, Ariz

Yes; Ellis, Jerry; 1928-Feb-12; 15; M; Navajo; -; F; Pneumonia; Yes; Maricopa; Phoenix-[Illegible], Ariz

Yes; (son of Paul Harvey); Harvey, Lloyd F; 1928-Feb-24; 18; M; Pima; -; F; Shock from fracture leg & ankle; No; Riverside; Sherman Institute, Calif

Yes; (dau of West Lesso); Lesso, Eloise; 1928-Aug-17; 1; F; Pima-Hopi; -; F; ?; Yes; Maricopa; Phoenix-1134 E Monroe St

Birth not reported; Patrick, Gladys; 1928-Oct-23; 9 mo; F; Pima; -; F; Unknown; Yes; Pima; Pima, Ariz

Yes; Walker, Seba Lewis; 1928-June-6; 37; F; Pima; -; F; Pima; -; F; Septocemia[sic]; Yes; Maricopa; Salt River Res, Ariz

- 1929 -

Yes; Blackwater, Charlene; 1932-July-6; 11 days; F; Pima; -; F; Status Lymphaticus[sic]; Yes; Pinal; Sacaton, Ariz

Yes=never recorded will leave off 1933; Blackwater, Emily; 1931-Aug-1; 72; F; Pima; -; F; Tuberculosis; Yes; Pinal; Sacaton, Ariz

Yes; Eschief, Juan; 1931-Apr-11; 57; M; Pima; -; F; Nephritis; Yes; Pinal; Blackwater, Ariz

~~No; Carlston, Calvin; 1931-Nov-22; 1; M; Pima~~; -; F; Pneumonia; Yes; Pinal; Sacaton, Ariz Hosp.

~~No; Davis, Juanita; 1931-July-3; 5 mo; F; Pima~~; -; F; Unknown; Yes; Pinal; Sacaton Flats, Ariz

Yes; Glieck, Louise; 1931- May-5; 80; F; Pima; -; F; Nephritis; Yes; Pinal; Sweetwater, Ariz

Yes; not recorded Heretofore; Howard, Jasper; 1931-July-3; 17; M; Pima-Papago; -; F; Tuberculosis; Yes; Pinal; Sacaton, Ariz

Birth not reported; Howard, Rufus; 1931-April-26; 1 mo; M; Pima; -; F; Diarrhea; Yes; Maricopa; Phoenix, Ariz

Yes; not recorded Heretofore; Johns, Edison; 1931-June-7; 19; M; Pima; -; F; Tuberculosis; Yes; Pinal; Blackwater, Ariz

Yes; not recorded Heretofore; Johnson, Allen; 1931-Apr-7; 3; M; Pima; -; F; Cardiac Dilatation; Yes; Pinal; Sacaton, Ariz Hosp

Yes; not recorded heretofore; Jones, O'Brian; 1931-May-1; 22 M; Pima; -; F; Tuberculosis; Yes; Pinal; Santan, Ariz

Birth not reported; Knox, Malenda; 1931-Sept-28; 1; F; Pima; -; F; Pneumonia; Yes; Pinal; Bahe Chin, Ariz

Death Certificates not located on Death Rolls

State **Arizona** Reservation ___**Pima Agency**___ Agency or jurisdiction

Office of Indian Affairs

Deaths Occurring Between the Dates of ~~July 1,~~ 1929 and ~~June 30,~~ 1930 to Indians Enrolled at Jurisdiction

Key: ~~Year and Number on Last Census Roll~~; Surname; Given; Date of Death (Year-Month-Day); Age at Death; Sex; Tribe; Ward (Yes/No); Degree of Blood; Cause of Death; At Jurisdiction Where Enrolled (Yes/No); ~~(If no—Where—Jurisdiction; State; Post Office; State)~~ Residence or Place of Death (County; Post Office, State)

1931

Yes; Williams, Juana; 1931-July-2; 40; F; Pima; -; F; Peritonitis; [?]; Pinal; Sweetwater, Ariz

Yes; Lewis, Mary; 1931-May-2; 53; F; Papago; -; F; Nephritis; yes; Pinal; Sacaton, Ariz

Birth not recorded; Lopez, Joseph; 1931-May-3; 28 days; M; Papago; -; F; Unknown; Yes; Pinal; Casa Blanca, Ariz

Yes; Lopez, Josepha; 1931-May-18; 85; F; Pima; -; F; Senility; Yes; Pinal; Casa Blanca, Ariz

Yes; Lyons, John; 1931-Aug-20; 64; M; Pima; -; F; Tuberculosis; Yes; Pinal; Santan, Ariz

Yes; Manuel;, Ahiel; 1931-June-22; 65; F; Pima; -; F; Nephritis; Yes; Nephritis; Yes; Pinal; Santan, Ariz

Yes; Miguel, Cyrus; 1931-Aug-22; 29; M; Pima; -; F; Lightning; Yes; Pinal; Blackwater, Ariz

Yes; Miguel, Juan; 1931-June-18; 81; M; Pima; -; F; Nephritis; Yes; Pinal; Sweetwater, Ariz

Yes; Morales, Ione; 1931-May-15; 6; F; Pima; -; F; Burns; Yes; Pinal; Sacaton, Ariz

Yes; Morgan (Peters), Manley; 1931-Jan-15; 82; F; Pima; -; F; Nephritis; Yes; Pinal; Sacaton, Ariz

~~Error-No; Nelson, Lizzie; 1931-June; 27; 73; F; Pima; -; Nephritis; Yes~~; Pinal; Vahki[sic], Ariz

Yes; Nish, Lichiana; 1931-June-20; 55; F; Pima; -; F; Tuberculosis; Yes; Pinal; Sacaton Flats, Ariz

Yes; Pablo (Lewis), Melissa L; 1931-July-20; 21; F; Pima; -; F; Tuberculosis; Yes; Pinal; Santa Cruz, Ariz

Yes; Pablo, Milyea; 1931-July-13; 65; F; Pima; -; F; Tuberculosis; Yes; Pinal; Sacaton Flats, Ariz

Yes; Padgely, Mary; 1931-Sept-4; 78; V; Pima; -; F; Nephritis; Yes; Pinal; Sacaton, Ariz (Hosp)

Yes; Pasquale, Lusa; 1931-Apr-2; 67; F; Pima; Dilitation[sic] of heart; Yes; Pinal; Sacaton, Ariz

Yes; Peters (Johnson), Vivian; 1931-Apr-1; 18; F; Pima; -; F; Convulsions (pregnancy); Yes; Pinal; Sacaton, Ariz (Hosp)

Yes; Smith, Marvin; 1931-July-22; 10; M; Pima; -; F; Heat Prostration; Yes; Maricopa; Phoenix Ind Sch Hosp

Yes; Smith, Joela; 1931-June-2; 14; F; Pima; -; Tuberculosis; Yes; Pinal; Casa Blanca, Ariz

Yes; Terry, Manuel; 1931-June-21; 34; M; Pima; -; Tuberculosis; Yes; Pinal; Lower Santan, Ariz

No; Valle, [Illegible]; 1931-May-30; 1 M; Pima; -; Tuberculosis (Menigitis[sic])); Yes; Pima; Tuscon[sic], Ariz

340

Death Certificates not located on Death Rolls

State **Arizona** Reservation __**Pima Agency**__ Agency or jurisdiction

Office of Indian Affairs

Deaths Occurring Between the Dates of ~~July 1, 1929~~ 1928 and ~~June 30, 1930~~ March 2, 193? to Indians Enrolled at Jurisdiction

Key: ~~Year and Number on Last Census Roll~~; Surname; Given; Date of Death (Year-Month-Day); Age at Death; Sex; Tribe; Ward (Yes/No); Degree of Blood; Cause of Death; At Jurisdiction Where Enrolled (Yes/No); ~~(If no — Where — Jurisdiction; State; Post Office; State)~~ Residence or Place of Death (County; Post Office, State)

Yes; Wade, Jane; 1931-June-3; 75; F; Pima; -; F; Nephritis; Yes; Pinal; Co-op Village, Ariz

Deaths

~~No; Chiago, Sarah; 1929-Jan-6; 64; F; Pima; -~~; F; Tuberculosis; Yes; Maricopa; Lehi, Ariz

~~Error- No; Jak, Jose M; 1929-Mar-11; 64; M; -; F~~; Cirrhosis of liver; Yes; Pinal; Santan, Ariz

~~No; Miles, Wilfred; 1928-Nov-20; 4 mo; M; -; F~~; Pneumonia; Yes; Maricopa; Phoenix Ind. Sch

Yes; Perez, Flora; 1929-June-3; 15; F; -; Tuberculosis; Yes; Pinal; Santan, Ariz

Yes; Hanier, Burnett; 1932-Mar-23; 6; M; -; F; Septic Sore Throat; Yes; Maricopa; Komatke, Ariz

Yes; Chiago, Mrs Stanley; 1932-Feb-15; 21; F; -; F; Tuberculosis; Yes; Maricopa; Maricopa, Ariz

341

Index

www.ingramcontent.com/pod-product-compliance
Lightning Source LLC
Chambersburg PA
CBHW030346050426
42336CB00049B/527